WESTERN WILDS,

AND

THE MEN WHO REDEEM THEM

AN

AUTHENTIC NARRATIVE,

EMBRACING

AN ACCOUNT OF SEVEN YEARS TRAVEL AND ADVENTURE IN THE FAR WEST;
WILD LIFE IN ARIZONA; PERILS OF THE PLAINS; LIFE IN THE CAÑON AND
DEATH ON THE DESERT; THRILLING SCENES AND ROMANTIC INCI-
DENTS IN THE LIVES OF WESTERN PIONEERS; ADVENTURES
AMONG THE RED AND WHITE SAVAGES OF THE WEST;
A FULL ACCOUNT OF THE MOUNTAIN MEADOW
MASSACRE; THE CUSTER DEFEAT; LIFE AND
DEATH OF BRIGHAM YOUNG, ETC.

INCLUDING, ALSO,

AN ELABORATE HISTORY AND DESCRIPTION OF THE MINING DISTRICTS; AN EXPERT
DISCUSSION OF THE SUBJECT OF MODERN MINING; A FULL RESUME
OF MINING MATTERS AT THE OPENING OF 1882.

By J. H. BEADLE,

Author of Life in Utah; Western Correspondent Cincinnati Commercial, etc.

ILLUSTRATED

J. C. CHILTON PUBLISHING CO.

DETROIT, MICH.

Windham Press is committed to bringing the lost cultural heritage of ages past into the 21st century through high-quality reproductions of original, classic printed works at affordable prices.

This book has been carefully crafted to utilize the original images of antique books rather than error-prone OCR text. This also preserves the work of the original typesetters of these classics, unknown craftsmen who laid out the text, often by hand, of each and every page you will read. Their subtle art involving judgment and interaction with the text is in many ways superior and more human than the mechanical methods utilized today, and gave each book a unique, hand-crafted feel in its text that connected the reader organically to the art of bindery and book-making.

We think these benefits are worth the occasional imperfection resulting from the age of these books at the time of scanning, and their vintage feel provides a connection to the past that goes beyond the mere words of the text.

As bibliophiles, we are always seeking perfection in our work, so please notify us of any errors in this book by emailing us at corrections@windhampress.com. Our team is motivated to correct errors quickly so future customers are better served. Our mission is to raise the bar of quality for reprinted works by a focus on detail and quality over mass production. To peruse our catalog of carefully curated classic works, please visit our online store at www.windhampress.com.

PREFACE

IN writing this work the author had two objects in view: to interest the reader; and to tell the exact truth about the country west of the Mississippi. As to the first, there is neither argument nor assertion; the reader can only judge for himself after perusal. But, as to the second, the author firmly believes he has accomplished it. The Far West is an immense region, and no one man ever visited all sections of it. The most to be expected is that each traveler shall seize upon the salient features of certain portions, and describe them in popular style. I have labored earnestly to give facts in regard to the lands still open to settlement; and I have been especially careful to correct certain errors as to soil and climate which I find very common in the East. We often hear it confidently asserted, and by those who ought to know, that "the American Desert is a myth—there is no desert in the West." I am sorry this statement is not true; but if there are not at least 300,000 square miles of utterly barren land, then "mine eyes are made the fools o' the other senses," for I have lived and traveled many a week where not one acre in a hundred is fertile. I have aimed to avoid personalities, but I can not altogether refrain from harsh expressions as to the misstatements made in many land circulars; or the colored falsehoods of many maps, made "to invite immigration."

Some critics will object that the work contains rather more about Utah and the Mormons than the subject warrants; and it is, perhaps, but natural that one should write at length on that which most interests him. But I apprehend this Utah question is one on which Americans generally *need* information; it is liable to call for prompt action by government at any time, and the people should be prepared to sustain their Representatives in all constitutional means to relieve the Nation of this disgrace. The author has been accused of undue prejudice against Brigham Young and other Mormon leaders; more space is therefore given to the legal evidence of their crimes than is usual in a popular work. Eight years ago I hunted up, from a score of sources, the facts of the Mountain Meadow Massacre; and, when published, there was a loud outcry that I had overdrawn the picture—"made it a newspaper sensation." I here present the testimony of witnesses in court, sworn and cross-examined, to show that my narrative of eight years ago was by far too mild; that in every charge then made against the Mormon Church I was within the truth. Nor do I admit that all the black details are yet known. Evidence is yet to be developed which will convince the most skeptical that Brigham Young was the accomplice and shield of murderers. This is a hard saying, but rest assured it will be proved.

If I have assumed too much in making myself an advocate for the political and civil rights of the Gentile minority in Utah, that minority can easily signify the same to their friends in the East who care to inquire. The Americans in Utah went there from the States, and did not change their natures when they changed their residence; they love liberty, and desire a share in the local government for the same reasons they did in the East. They have fought a good fight; they have accomplished much, and will do more. If my criticisms upon Gen. Thomas L. Kane and other apologists for Brigham appear severe, the record is presented to show their errors. The record condemns them—not I. Of course there has been a great deal of twaddle and romance on the part of the opponents of Mormonism—there always is in matters of popular discussion; but the nearer we keep to admitted facts, the more clearly we see that, on the main question, they are radically right, and Brigham's apologists radically wrong. Polygamy and incest are admitted and defended in Utah; and it is a fair assumption that men who violate law in two such important particulars, will violate it in others, if their interest seems to require it. But, as mere inference is not enough in such matters, I have, as aforesaid, given more evidence than the aim and style of the work would have made desirable.

Five million Americans expect to go West. There should be a new work on that section, written by some careful observer, at least once a year; for the changes there are many and rapid. Doubtless so plain a presentation of the discouraging features, as is here given, will have a depressing effect upon the ardent; but it is best to know the truth. There is not as much room for us to grow in that direction as is popularly supposed, and Americans can not find it out too soon. So much for the main object of this work—truth. As to the interest in the narrative—kind reader, excuse me; I touch your hand, and without further apology introduce you to MY BOOK.

J. H. B.

COLUMBUS, OHIO, October 1, 1877.

CHAPTER I.

THE HAWKEYES.

I make a start.—Fair Iowa.—Yankee, Hoosier, Buckeye, and Scandinavian.—The Aryan wave.—Hoosier grammar.—Sorrows of the non-resident land-owner.—"The walled lakes."—Greatness of the Border States.—"Hoss high, bull strong, and pig tight."—The 'hoppers.—"Omahawgs" and "Omahens."—"Milkville" and "Bilkville."—Rural Nebraska.—Agricultural wealth.—Pawnees, Otoes, Omahaws.—The Bedouin instinct.—"Go West." 17-24

CHAPTER II.

A WESTERN CHARACTER.

Unsung heroes.—Scenes in Southern Kansas.—"Shuck up."—"Fevernager."—My host's story.—He leaves Tennessee for New Orleans.—"Chawin' rags for a paper-mill."—Up into the Cherokee country.—Another run to New Orleans.—Walk home through the "Injun" country.—Murder of McIntosh and others.—War between the Rossites and Ridgeites.—Exposure and fever.—Delirium.—Rescued by the "little Cherokee girl."—Home again.—Joe and Myra.—More trouble with the Cherokees.—Journey to Iowa.—In danger from the "Danites."—Mrs. Joe's "tantrums."—Captured by the Hawkeyes.—Interview with Judge Lynch.—Horrible murder of Miller and Liecy.—Hanging of the Hodges.—Terrible times on the Half-breed Tract.—The California excitement.—Start from Independence.—Troubles on the way.—Danger and death on the great desert.—Among the gold hunters.—More murders.—Return to Tennessee.—The great war.—Death of the boys.—Removal to Indian Territory.—"Won't there be peace while I live?"—Rest at last. 25-44

CHAPTER III.

THE JOURNEY TO UTAH.

Flush times in Omaha.—Some characters.—Will Wylie's escape.—"Seen the Elephant."—"A neck-tie sociable."—"Coppered on the jack."—Apostate Mormons' caravan.—Up the slope to Cheyenne.—"Dirty Jule's."—The Plains.—"Magic City."—Passage of the Black Hills.—Virginia Dale.—Laramie Plains.—Benton.—Alkali Desert.—Evanescent "cities."—Bear River City.—Battle with the roughs.—More Mormons.—"Catfish with legs."—Horrors of Bitter Creek.—Green River.—Bridger Plains.—The author a mule-whacker.—Grandeur of Echo Cañon.—Weber Valley.—Up to Parley's Park.—Down Parley's Cañon.—First view of the Salt Lake.—"City of the Saints."—I become a Gentile sinner. 45-55

CONTENTS.

CHAPTER IV.

GEFFROY'S TRIALS.

On Griffith Mountain, Colorado.—"Are we the authors of our own destiny?"—Geffroy's narrative answers.—Beautiful Geneva.—Frenchy fancies vs. German phlegm.—A young enthusiast.—Hunting the Brotherhood of Man.—At New Harmony, Indiana.—Failure of Communism.—At Nauvoo.—At Communia.—On the plains.—Enlist with the Texan patriots of '43.—Bright pictures.—Stern realities.—"The River of Souls."—The *tierras templadas.*—In the Wild Cañon.—Posted on the Taos Trail.—Another frightful march.—Down to the Cimarron.—Another trial of the desert.—Night attack on the Mexican camp.—Victory, followed in turn by flight.—Loss of the horses.—Geffroy and friend go after them.—Surrounded by Mexicans.—A dash for life.—Headlong leap into the chasm.—Oblivion, or death? 56–71

CHAPTER V.

DOLORES.

Return to consciousness.—Laid up in the cabin.—Love and convalescence.—The captured Americans.—Dolores' plan.—The parting.—Gomez and the Pueblos.—Halt at Jemez.—Meeting the Navajoes.—A land of wonders.—Among the Moquis.—A simple, civil, and unwarlike race.—A race without envy or covetousness.—Joyful meeting with Dolores.—*Los Diabolos Gringos.*—Flight for the north.—Lost on the desert.—The horrors of thirst.—Another day of anguish.—Life in the rock.—"With our lips pressed to the rock we drew new life."—Hope revived.—Pursuit by the Mexicans.—Wounding and death of Dolores.—Agony of Geffroy.—Enlists as a soldier.—The war in Mexico.—Revisits Switzerland.—1848: the year of Revolutions.—In the army of Baden.—Capture and long imprisonment.—Liberty, when hope was dead.—Return to the Far West.—"The Brotherhood of Man comes not by spasmodic struggles, but by steady toil." 72–89

CHAPTER VI.

POLYGAMIA.

I meet Brigham & Co.—Topography of his kingdom.—I reside there a year.—And become a hated Gentile.—Mormon notabilities: Brigham, Orson Pratt, Hooper, Geo. A. Smith.—"The One-eyed Pirate of the Wasatch."—Polygamy, Bigamy, Brighamy, Monogamy, and other *gamies.*—Utah politics.—Noted Gentiles.—Liberal Mormons.—Credulous skeptics.—"No trade with non-Mormons."—Consequent troubles.—Persecution of dissenters.—Journey to Sevier.—Beauties of Pine Gulch.—Return to "Zion."—"There's a better day coming."—Religious lying.—Perjury "for Christ's sake." . . . 90–102

CHAPTER VII.

THE PACIFIC SLOPE.

Westward again.—Corinne.—Promontory.—Dead Fall, Murder Gulch, Last Chance, and Painted Post.—"Do me a favor: shoot me through the head!"—Fine morality of the gamblers.—The Great Nevada Desert.—"Sinks,"—Up the Truckee.—State Line.—Down the Sierras.—Wonders of Cape Horn.—Sacramento.—"San Joeykwinn."—Or San Wahkeen?—In Yolo County.—Davisville.—Chinese and silk culture.—*Tules.*—Fruits and wine.—Does it supersede whisky?—The California seasons.—"Frisco."—Chinese Theater.—The tragedy of Rip Sah.—Buddhist ceremonies.—A gloomy sort of religion.—"Top-side Josh."—The devil-drive.—"Chinaman like Melica man." . . 103–116

CHAPTER VIII.

TWO YEARS OF CHANGE.

Utah and trouble.—"Mormon hospitality."—The author mobbed and badly hurt, but recovers rapidly.—Healing air of the mountains.—Rich mineral discoveries in Utah.—The Gentiles take heart.—The Emma Mine.—I go to Washington as a lobbyist.—And don't like it.—Further travels in Utah.—Polygamy again.—Rev. J. P. Newman shows that there are but thirteen polygamists mentioned in the Bible.—And hundreds of good monogamists.—Orson Pratt comes back at him.—High times in the Tabernacle.—Some of the nasty features of polygamy.—Such as incest and indecency.—A village composed of Taylors.—And one made up of Winns.—General view of the Territory.—And of the Far West. 117–128

CHAPTER IX.

THE MISSOURI VALLEY.

Kansas City: a modern Rome.—We look at it, but do not invest.—The "Land of Zion."—Lawrence.—"The Wakarusa War."—The Massacre of 1863.—The Athens of the West.—Our journey southward: The Leavenworth, Lawrence, and Galveston Road.—Ottawa.—Western Yankees.—"Brother K——'s blooded mare."—"Buffalo stamps."—A progressive country.—Fertility of Allen and Neosho counties.—An incorrigible old man.—Cherryvale.—The beautiful mounds.—The social Kansian.—"Sna-a-a-kes!"—Northward to Leavenworth.—*Quindaro Chindowan.*—"A second Babylon."—Wyandotte.—Atchison.—Troy.—St. Joe.—Up the Missouri Valley.—Council Bluffs.—Omaha.—On northward.—Sioux City.—Onawa.—Woodbury.—Staging to Yankton.—Dakotians: French, Scandinavians, and Bohemians.—"Woman's Rights:" to do as much work as she can.—The gentle savage.—*Iapi Oahye!*—"Portable talk."—Northern Dakota.—Western Dakota.—We leave suddenly for California. 129–139

CHAPTER X.

THE WONDERS OF CALIFORNIA.

All aboard for Yosemite!—From chilly "Frisco" to melting Stockton.—By rail to Milton.—Hot drive among the foot-hills.—Copperopolis.—The broiling stage; air dead calm; thermometer 100°.—In the cool grove at last.—The vegetable wonders of the world.—A tree thirty-two feet thick.—"Father and Mother."—"Husband and Wife," 250 feet high.—"Uncle Tom's Cabin."—How came they here?—California names.—Over Table Mountain.—"Truthful James."—Old mining towns.—Sonora.—Chinese Camp.—Garrote.—The Tuolumne Grove.—Tamarack Flat.—Reminiscences of the "strong-minded."—First view of Yosemite.—Prospect Peak.—The terrible descent.—A fall of 2,667 feet.—El Capitan: *Tu-toch-ah-nu-la.*—A reverie on Cosmos.—Mirror Lake.—Reflected glories.—The climb to Nevada Falls.—Down by Vernal Falls.—The sublime and beautiful.—J. M. Hutchings, the pioneer.—"Spirit of the Evil Wind."—"Great Chief of the Valley."—Down hill to San Francisco.—Climate of the Coast.—A day at the Cliff House.—*Poluphloisboio Thalasses.*—Regretful good-bye to the Pacific Coast. 140–163

CONTENTS.

CHAPTER XI.

UTAH ARGENTIFERA.

Gentiles after silver; Mormons after the Gentiles.—"Revelations" and prospecting.—Up Little Cottonwood.—The silver lodes—Snow-slides.—12,000 feet above the sea.—Bald Peak, and a view of 20,000 square miles.—Big Cottonwood Cañon.—The great fire.—American Fork Cañon; the Yosemite of Utah.—Mormon farmers *vs.* Gentile mountaineers.—"The Republic of Tooele."—East Cañon and horn silver.—Chloride Cave.—Dry Cañon.—Wild times in the West Mountains.—A Goshoot feast.—I start to Dugway.—And get lost on the desert.—A lonesome night.—Danger and weariness.—Ninety miles travel in twenty-seven hours.—Independence Day on Great Salt Lake.—"No *gulls* in Utah before the Mormons came."—Sailing on the Lake.—Mines in southern Utah.—Beaver City.—Mineral wealth of the Territory.—Shall we annex Utah to Nevada? 164–181

CHAPTER XII.

A CHAPTER OF BETWEENS.

Joe Allkire talks.—Valley tan whisky calls up reminiscences.—"A bad streak o' luck."—"Sod-corn barefooted."—Millerites.—"Misses Chew splits the choir."—The grand dog-fight.—Which broke up a town.—"That yaller and spotted dog."—Abraham and the preacher clinch.—"No Morgan-killers need apply."—"The head abolishinists."—Si Duvall's luck.—Union Flats becomes very flat.—Other reminiscences.—Men who had tried many fields.—Story of the mountaineer.—Will and Bob McAfee.—Camp in Arkansas Cañon.—The storm, and falling timber.—Dreadful alternative of the unwounded brother.—He "relieves" the other's torture.—And dies of grief and remorse. 182–193

CHAPTER XIII.

OKLAHOMA.

A new route to the Pacific.—I enter the Indian Territory.—Vinita.—"White Cherokees."—Cabin Creek.—Mixed bloods.—"It comes back on 'em."—Christian Indians.—Muscogee.—Also Muskokee.—The Creeks at home.—*Ala-bah-ma:* "Here we rest."—Natchees and Hitchitees.—An Aboriginal Democracy.—House of Kings and House of Warriors.—*Puhly hohkohlen.*—Tallahassee Mission.—The Muskokee in love.—"Beautiful River."—Brad Collins and his gang.—Oklahoma *vs.* Okmulkee.—Red hot on temperance.—In the Choctaw country.—Tandy Walker.—Among the Cherokees.—The Big Rattling Gourd and other politicians.—Cherokee history.—Civilized Indians of the Territory.—What shall we do with them? 194–211

CHAPTER XIV.

JOURNEY TO THE RIO GRANDE.

Northward again.—Out on the Kansas Pacific.—A beautiful country.—Ellsworth.—Carnival of crime in 1867.—"Wild Bill."—J. H. Runkle.—"Rake Jake."—"Dad Smith."—"Shall we have a man for breakfast?"—Heroic, but murderous.—Bisons and business.—Arrival at Denver.—Rest and enjoyment.—Southward by the narrow-guage railway.—The Divide.—Timbered region.—Colorado City.—Take stage-coach.—Pueblo.—Night in the stage.—Cocharas.—The *señoritas.*—Another day of staging.—Trinidad.—The Raton Mountains.—Down upon the New Mexican side.—Wild scenes.—Maxwell's Ranche.—Passage of the Rocky Ridge.—A snow storm and a grizzly.—Down to Santa

Fe.—Disappointed with the city.—A queer old town.—High-sounding names.—Indian troubles.—Starting for Fort Wingate.—La Bajada.—*Quién Sabe?*—Pueblos Indians.—Valley of the Rio Grande.—Albuquerque—The *gente fina*.—The "Greasers."—Will they ever amount to any thing? 212-229

CHAPTER XV.

TOLTECCAN.

The oldest inhabitant.—Alvar Nunez, etc., traverses New Mexico.—What he saw and how he lied about it.—"The Seven Cities of Cibola."—Conquest of New Mexico.—Revolt of the Pueblos.—Second Conquest.—High-toned grandees.—Caste.—Sad (?) occurrence.—Should the Territory be made a State?—Citizen Indians.—Queer old customs.—Parental authority.—Enterprise.—The universal *burro*.—We cross the Rio Grande.—And enter on the desert.—The awful, the unutterable desert.—Sufferings from thirst.—Reach "Hog River."—Dead Man's Cañon.—Another desert.—Oasis of El Rito.—Degenerate Spaniards.—Pueblo de Laguna.—An Aztec relic.—El Cubero.—"Women's Rights."—*Mala Pais*.—*Agua Azul*.—The extinct volcano.—Drive to Fort Wingate.—My companion comes to grief.—Ojo del oso.—Zuni.—Stinking Springs.—The Puerco of the West.—Down to Fort Defiance. 230-248

CHAPTER XVI.

WILD LIFE IN ARIZONA.

The gathering.—Cañon Benito.—Handsome Indian girls.—Navajo patience.—A mixed tongue.—"Slim-man-with-a-white-eye."—*El-soo-see En-now-lo-kyh*.—"Big Quill."—Murder of Agent Miller.—Sorrow of the Navajoes.—Their kindness and courtesy.—Off for a trip.—My Navajo guide.—"*Tohh klohh no mos.*"—Descent into Cañon de Chelley.—Wonders on wonders.—The "cliff cities."—Moonlight in the cañon.—Out again on the desert.—An awful passage.—The hot alkali plains.—Thirst and suffering.—"*Hah-koh, Melicano!*"—Approach to the Moqui towns.—Amazement of the inhabitants.—The city set on a rock.—The strangest people in the world.—Chino and Misiamtewah.—The Moquis welcome me gladly. 249-267

CHAPTER XVII.

AMONG THE AZTECS.

Topography of Arizona.—A region of hot sands and barren mountains, of fierce savages and gentle Indians, of rich mines and wild, forbidding wastes.—The Mesa Calabasa.—Zunis, Teguas, Moquis, Oraybes, Papagoes, Pimos, and Coco-Maricopas.—Rapid decay of the wild tribes.—Noble Navajoes.—Their native shrewdness, industry and bravery.—Who are they?—Aztecs?—Barboncito.—Ganado Mucho.—Their handiwork.—Their temperance and endurance.—Life at Moqui.—"*Ho, Melicano, messay vo!*"—Jesus Papa.—Moqui theology.—The "white Indians" of Arizona.—Ruins.—Aztec or Toltec?—Comparison with mound-builders' remains.—And South American Ruins.—Only a theory.—Which no one is bound to accept. 268-286

CHAPTER XVIII.

FROM MOQUI TO THE COLORADO.

Two hundred miles of desert.—Aboriginal mail service.—A new guide.—His *nelsouss*.—Good-bye, Chino!—Journey to the new Navajo camp.—"Damn Español, shtenl mooch."—On the sandstone *mesa*.—A pleasant party of four.—"*Todos muertos, pero mas*

Apaches!"—Another sandstone waste.—First view of the river, 5,000 feet below us.—Getting down the cliff.—Water and salts.—At the river at last.—No boats.—Perilous passage.—The white woman: "My God, stranger, did you risk your life to swim that river?"—The Mormon convert's story.—Three days at the ferry.—Parting from my Navajo friends. 287–300

CHAPTER XIX.

A STARTLING INTERVIEW.

I meet with a surprise.—"Major Doyle" proves to be John D. Lee.—And tells me the story of his crime.—He describes the events leading to the Mountain Meadow Massacre.—Character of the murdered emigrants.—They are charged with being enemies of the Mormon people.—The latter incensed.—And determined on revenge.—Did they poison the spring?—Or murder friendly Indians?—Outrage on Mrs. Evans.—The Mormon Council.—Death of the emigrants determined upon.—The closing tragedy.—Lee's excuses and subterfuges.—His further history.—A story horrible enough for the most inveterate sensationalist.—I bid the Lees good-bye.—And with no regrets.—Grand cañon of the Colorado.—Ride to Jacob's Pool.—Thence to Spring-in-Rock.—Lonely camping out.—My solitary journey to Kanab.—The Pi-Ede band of savages.—"*Toh, agua,* water!"—Rest at Kanab.—Jacob Hamlin.—The Powell party.—On the desert again.—Pipe Springs.—Our bishop landlord.—Another ride over rock and sand.—Gould's Ranche.—Virgin City.—Toquerville.—"Mormon Dixie."—At Isaac Haight's.—Kanarra.—Another misfortune.—Ride to Parowan.—Little Salt Lake.—Arrive at Beaver.—Staging thence to Salt Lake City. 301–316

CHAPTER XX.

THE FAIR APOSTATE.

English homes.—Radical and Conservative; Chartist and Monarchist.—Coming of the Mormon missionary.—Simple lives changed.—Voyage to America.—The hand-cart emigration.—Frightful sufferings on the plains.—Death on all sides.—Starved, frozen, torn by the wolves.—The Old Radical finds the Brotherhood of Man.—A young hero.—Willie Manson concludes to go West.—Journeys thro' Illinois and Iowa.—Meets a queer party.—The year 1857.—His sufferings.—At Camp Floyd.—Goes to the city.—Sickness and fever.—A familiar face by his pillow. 317–331

CHAPTER XXI.

THE FAIR APOSTATE—CONTINUED.

Hot times in "Zion."—"The Reformation."—Arrival of the hand-cart emigrants.—An epidemic madness.—Horrible reign of lust and fanaticism.—United States officials driven out.—Mormon war begun.—Skill and daring of Mormon guerrillas.—But the Gentile army enters the Valley.—30,000 Mormons move south.—But return and submit peaceably.—Willie Manson's new friends.—More apostates.—John Banks and Thomas James.—Little Marian becomes Miss Marian.—And Manson does not understand the change.—In his perplexity he hears doctrine.—And reproof.—But hardens his heart.—A new prophet.—Joseph Morris.—Morrisite Camp on the Weber.—Attacked and broken up by the Brighamites.—Murder of the women.—Barbarous killing of Morris and Banks.—Flight of Thomas James.—Exhausted, he lies down to die.—Beatty and Manson off for Montana.—Relieve James.—War with the Bannocks.—Desperate encounters.—Four years amid the gold fields.—Manson becomes a *man!*—The friends hear that all is peace in Utah.—And together return to "Zion." 332–347

CHAPTER XXII.

THROUGH GREAT TRIBULATION.

Bright days in Cache Valley.—A brother and a sister restored to fellowship—Thomas James is again happy with Christina.—But he is a bishop's rival, and that means danger.—"Blood atonement."—A nameless horror.—The man becomes a creature.—Manson perplexed.—"Keep your eye peeled; this is a queer country."—Red-hot discussion of polygamy.—News from James; which is no news.—Anti-Gentile Philippics.—Manson meets Marian.—A good outcome at last.—Astonishing conduct of Elder Briarly.—Mystery added to mystery.—Another Gentile panic.—Murder of Brassfield.—Outrages on Gentile settlers.—Murder of Dr. Robinson.—Flight of the Gentile pre-emptors.—Sad fate of Thomas James.—Bishop Warren has his reward.—But heaven is kinder to Christina than her own people.—She finds release in death.—Briarly flies from the Territory.—Marian and Manson.—Their Iowa home.—But Utah is the home of the soul.—And President Grant has given us hope.—Hank Beatty's crime.—Death of his wife.—The Mansons return to Utah.—As their troubles ended with a marriage, their future state is left to faith. 348–370

CHAPTER XXIII.

SWINGING 'ROUND THE CIRCLE.

Off for Soda Springs.—A land of wonders.—A chemical laboratory ten miles square.—Soda by the ton; to be had for the taking.—The "Morrisites" again.—A little run eastward.—Denver.—Lawrence.—St. Louis.—A day in Nauvoo: "Destined capital of a religious empire."—To the new North-west.—Yankton.—Assassination of Secretary McCook.—Steamboating on the Missouri.—Sioux City again.—Enterprising, but sensational.—Off for Minnesota.—We enter the Garden State. . . 371–378

CHAPTER XXIV.

MINNESOTA.

Reminiscences of 1859.—The Bois Brules.—Full-blood Chippeways.—Minnesota pineries.—The Red Napoleon of the North-west.—"Hard times" in 1859.—I live on corn-bread, hoe corn, and cultivate muscle.—Better times.—Sioux war of 1862.—Blue-earth County.—Mankato.—Journey to St. Paul.—Topography.—St. Anthony's Falls.—Minnehaha.—Journey to Sauk Rapids.—Staging thence northward.—Belle Prairie.—Catholic outposts.—Crow Wing.—Black Pine Forest.—Brainard.—Breaking up the Sabbath.—A Chippeway dance.—Out on the North Pacific R. R.—The barren region.—Down to Red River.—Moorehead.—Navigation to British America.—Fargo.—Westward by construction train.—Dakota's Salt Lake.—Jimtown.—Eastward again.—The lake region.—Scenery on the St. Louis River.—Among the Scandinavians.—"Postoff."—Jay Cooke's Banana Zone. 379–389

CHAPTER XXV.

THE WAY TO OREGON.

"Let us try the web-feet."—Through Iowa.—Westward from Omaha.—Changes of four years.—My fourteenth trip over the Union Pacific.—More trouble in Utah.—Across the Sierras again.—Up the Sacramento.—Gen. John Bidwell's ranche.—Grapes, figs, apples, and lemons in November.—Reading.—Walk-in Miller's squaw.—His life in jail.—Great forests of the upper Sacramento.—*Six Cailloux*.—"Sleeping Dictionary."—Yreka.—Over the mountains.—Klamath River.—Cow Creek.—South Umpqua.—Roseburgh.—Oregon and California Railroad.—Down the Willamette.—"Beaver Lands."—In Portland.—"Such a fog!"—"John Chinaman."—First-class funerals needed.—"Webfeet" maidens.—Shall we go home by sea?—Down the Columbia by steamer.—"High s-a running."—"Oh, my head, my stomach! O-o-o!"—The boat goes on end.—The land-lubbers fall on all sides.—Better weather.—"On an even keel."—Beauties of the Pacific.—Cape Mendocino.—The Golden Gate.—Once more on *terra firma*. 390–405

CHAPTER XXVI.

LAS TEXAS Y LOS TEJANOS.

"G. T. T."—Bad reputation.—"You may go to hell, and I'll go to Texas."—The author finds things improved.—Through the Indian Territory.—Red River.—Denison.—"Nobih Fohk."—Healthy region.—"The spiral maginnis" or "De meninjeesus."—At Sherman.—Down Main Trinity.—Travels in Collin County.—The Cotton Belt.—In Ellis County.—Navarro and Corsicana.—Insects and other sects.—"A thousand and forty-four legs."—Through Central Texas to Houston.—Buffalo Bayou.—Delightful ride to Galveston.—Celebration of San Jacinto.—"Brave Texan: bravest man in the South, sah!"—Delights of the Galveston beach.—Beauties of the island.—Up country.—The land of border romance.—Bob Rock and his brown *mestiza*.—Hon. "Shack" Roberts.—Some political notes.—A tolerant and liberal State. 406–418

CHAPTER XXVII.

HISTORY AND DESCRIPTION OF TEXAS.

La Salle.—First Settlement on the coast.—Origin of the border question.—Murder of La Salle.—The murderers murdered.—The missions.—*Indios reducidos*.—"Reduced" by prayer and fasting.—The "men of reason."—War between the French and Spanish.—Massacre of San Saba.—Decline of the Missions.—Louisiana ceded to Spain.—Better times in Texas.—Louisiana ceded back to France.—The border question again.—The United States takes a hand.—Fearful murders and robberies.—Magee's expedition.—Desperate battle.—Magee kills himself.—Surrender of his army.—They are barbarously massacred by the Spaniards.—Revolution in Mexico.—More trouble in Texas.—Moses and Stephen Austin.—Oppression of the Texans.—Revolution.—Heroic defense of the Alamo.—Fannin's command butchered.—Glorious victory of San Jacinto.—Independence and subsequent events.—Descriptive sketch of the State. 419–431

CHAPTER XXVIII.

KANSAS REVISITED.

Through the new counties.—"Hard times."—The Grangers' War.—Woman suffrage.—Allen County.—Neosho.—Labette.—The Bender murderers.—Their real fate.—Coffeyville.—Ten square miles of cattle!—"Not a good year for stock, either."—The cattle trails.—Montgomery County.—Kansas politics.—The Osage diminished Reserve.—Independence City.—Elk River.—Wilson County.—Neodesha.—Kansas cotton.—Into the mound region.—Westward, ho!—Among the flint hills.—South-western Kansas.—General view of the State. 432–446

CHAPTER XXIX.

COLORADO.

Westward again.—1874.—Disappearance of the buffalo.—Reach Denver.—A long rest.—Narrow-guage for Georgetown.—The sublime and beautiful in Clear Creek

CONTENTS.   xiii

Cañon.—Floyd Hill.—Stage to Idaho Springs.—To Georgetown.—2,000 miners.—But where are the women?—High climbs.—Cool retreats.—Independence Day on the summit of the Rocky Mountains.—Snow banks and iced brooks.—Beauties of the upper parks.—Drive to Gray's Peak.—The September storm.—Climb through snow and ice.—14,400 feet above the sea.—And a fearful snow-storm in summer.—Down to Denver.—Up to Caribou.—Wild beauty of Boulder Cañon and Falls.—The rich silver lodes.—On the plains again.—Ride to Greeley and Evans.   447-469

CHAPTER XXX.

THE CENTENNIAL STATE.

Coronado.—Mythologic age of Colorado.—Pike sees his Peak.—The hunters and trappers.—Bloody encounters.—Love, treachery, and retribution.—Gold!—The great rush.—"Pike's Peak."—Society takes shape.—Miners' laws.—People's courts.—Attempts at a Territory.—Successful at last: the 38th State.—Our life in Georgetown.—Griffith Mountain.—"The Holy Cross."—Rich silver mines.—The Dives-Pelican Lode.—Curiosities of mining.—"Sam Wann," or Juan.—Silver by millions.—Southern Colorado.—The White Desert.—Possibilities of the new State.   470-489

CHAPTER XXXI.

THE MORMON MURDERERS.

Another year in Utah.—Capture of John D. Lee.—His awful crime.—Mormon madness in 1857.—Assassination of Parley P. Pratt.—The doomed emigrants pass Salt Lake City.—Are harassed as they go south.—Attacked and besieged.—Surrender to Lee and others.—A plot hatched in hell.—The demon Higby gives the signal.—Fearful scenes of blood.—One hundred and thirty-one Americans fall victims to Mormon malice!—And the Governor of Utah "never heard of it!"—Brigham certifies to a falsehood.—And swears to another.—Strange chain of events leading to discovery.—Lee brought to trial.—Shameful farce of selecting jurymen.—A black case made out.—Brigham's remarkable deposition.   490-511

CHAPTER XXXII.

GUILTY OR NOT GUILTY?

Astonishing conduct of Mormon jurymen.—They refuse to convict.—But the Mormon Church can not afford to sustain Lee any longer.—They decide to give him up.—Another trial in 1876.—And a Mormon jury convict Lee.—Sentence pronounced by Judge Boreman.—Appeal.—Date of execution postponed to March, 1877.—Executed upon the very spot of his crime.—Lee's final and complete confession.—His last words.—His peaceful and heroic death.—Was Brigham Young guilty?—Brigham's apologists.—Captain John Codman, Geo. Q. Cannon, Gen. Thomas L. Kane.   512-530

CHAPTER XXXIII.

THE NOBLE RED MAN.

The tragedy of June 25th, 1876.—Sketch of Custer's life.—Hancock's campaign.—Custer's first Indian fight.—Massacre of Lieutenant Kidder and party.—Sully's campaign.—Custer's Washita campaign.—Yellowstone expedition.—Murder of Honzinger and Baliran.—Arrest and escape of Rain-in-the-Face.—Black Hills expedition.—Gold.—Events of 1875.—Campaign of 1876 against Sitting Bull and Crazy Horse.—Custer in disgrace at headquarters.—Descent on the hostile camp.—The bloody ending.—Sitting Bull goes to Canada, and Crazy Horse to the happy hunting grounds—perhaps.   531-557

CONTENTS.

CHAPTER XXXIV.

PROSPECTING AND MINING.

"Hoodoo" mines.—Where not to look.—Geological formation of Mississippi Valley.—Into the mountains.—Looking for "float."—The amusing "pilgrim."—We find a "blossom."—And post a notice.—Searching for "indications."—Proportion of metal found in ore.—We have found a mine.—Taking out a United States Patent.—Counter claimants.—Summary of mining laws. 558–567

CHAPTER XXXV.

MINING FORTUNES AND MISFORTUNES.

Leadville, the Magic City.—From Hoosierdom to Denver.—Greenhorn Range.—The Royal Gorge.—Railroad enterprise.—Good spelling and bad pronunciation.—Grand scenery.—An artificial thaw.—Geological formation of Arkansas Valley.—Haphazard prospecting.—Yield of Leadville mines in 1880.—Future possibilities.—The romance of Leadville.—Early discoveries.—The big strikes.—Sudden wealth and fast life.—A business of $18,000,000 a year.—The Grand Smelter.—An expert examination of ores.—The *ides*, the *ets*, and the *ates*.—Influence of mines on a locality. . . 568–585

CHAPTER XXXVI.

MINING IN 1882.

The trans-continental railways.—The Wild West abolished.—Railway development in New Mexico.—The Desert.—The Casas Grandas ruins.—The great Silver King mine.—Globe City.—Rough roads and alkali dust.—Tombstone.—The mining interests.—Future prospects.—A view of Arizona.—New Mexico and Colorado.—Silver Cliff and Rosita.—Peculiar geological formation.—Increase in population of Colorado.—Denver.—The Black Hills.—Annual metal product of Colorado.—Natural wealth of the West. 586–596

CHAPTER XXXVII.

THE DEAD PROPHET.

Brigham dies.—His history.—"Hard working Brigham Young."—The Kirtland folly.—Brigham carries a level head.—Building up Nauvoo.—Martha Brotherton "blabs."—Hot water.—"Spiritual wifery" introduced.—"Persecution."—Death of Joe Smith.—Head of the Twelve Apostles.—Journey to Salt Lake Valley.—Trouble with the United States.—As a marrying man.—His wives: Mary Ann, Lucy, Clara, Emmeline, Amelia, and others.—An extensive parent.—Division of his estate.—John Taylor comes into an easy succession.—Collapse of Brigham's great plans.—A discussion of the problem of Mormonism.—Declining.—Moral storm approaching.—Then comes a better day. 597–610

CHAPTER XXXVIII.

WHERE SHALL WE SETTLE?

Go West!—Southern Minnesota.—Iowa.—Southern Dakota.—Nebraska.—Kansas.—The Indian Territory.—No!—Texas.—Don't believe all you hear!—The Indian border.—California: Land monopoly.—Oregon.—Climate and soil.—"The Great American Desert."—Probable population in 1900.—Where is the surplus population to go?—Good land pretty well occupied.—What will be the result?—Western Wilds will continue wild for a century to come. 611–628

LIST OF ILLUSTRATIONS.

	PAGE
MAP OF ABORIGINAL AMERICA	FRONTISPIECE
The non-resident tax-payer	19
"Our liberties, sir"	21
"Civilized"	24
"Thoroughly acclimated"	26
"I hunted the pipe-works"	29
Mrs. Joe's "tantrums"	35
"Made music all day"	40
His last chance	45
"Laying on of hands"	47
"The good old time"	49
"Only a memory"	51
Pulpit Rock: Echo Cañon	54
The Great Salt Lake	55
On the slope of Griffith Mountain	56
To the rendezvous	62
Cañon de las Aulmas	65
Getting down to the Cimarron	67
For life or death	71
"Some one came forward holding a cup"	73
"The Mexicans saw no way"	74
"Dolores fainted in my arms"	81
"The balls whistled around us"	85
Brigham Young	90
Orson Pratt	91
George A. Smith	92
Brigham's Residences	95
Humboldt Palisades	105
Seven thousand feet above the sea	107
Cape Horn	108
California Agricultural Report	112
Barbary Coast: San Francisco	115
"Bodaciously chawed up"	118
Mormon wives for summer and winter	121
Great expectations	135
Dakotas torturing a Pawnee	138
The two guardsmen	141
The Fallen Monarch	142
Something of a stump	143
A monster	145
Yosemite Falls	147
El Capitan	149
Bridal Veil Fall	152
Sentinel Rock	155
North Dome and Royal Arches	157
Nevada Falls	159
Vernal Falls	160
Mirror Lake	161
Mormon Militia	165
Chloride Cave, Lion Hill	171
Goshoot Love-feast	173
Lost on the Desert	176
Deacon Chew	183
"They broke loose and lit out down the street"	184
"And they clinched"	185
"Half the town took a shy at him"	186
The Seat of War	187
"Where warring tribes met in peace"	189
Fine field for the ethnologist	195
"Slem-lem-an-dah-mouch-wah-ger"	201

ILLUSTRATIONS.

	PAGE
"Go West"	211
Wild Bill	213
"Scattering leaden death on all sides"	214
"Divide Hotel and Ranche"	216
"Suggested wild beasts and banditti"	220
The ambush and running fight	225
Pueblo Maiden	230
Kit Carson	234
Pueblo Cacique	235
"Woman's Rights"	242
Coming to the "count"	249
On the Mesa Calabasa	269
"Converted on the spot"	271
Navajo Loom	273
Aztec Priest and Warrior	284
Down the Cliff	291
Climbing for water	295
Mouth of Pahreah Creek	301
Head of the Grand Cañon	304
"Three little Injuns"	312
A Pi-Ede Ceres	313
Winter camp of Goshoots	325
Scenes on the Colorado Plateau	330
"Dashed across the burning plain"	335
Thomas James kills the Bannock	346
"Behold our Lamanite Brother"	356
"Let me look toward old England before I die"	367
"Willie has struck chloride"	369
Shoshonees with annuity goods	372
Burning of the Mormon Temple	375
Killing of Secretary McCook	377
Pembina people and ox-carts	379
Winter in Minnesota pineries	380
Minnehaha in winter	385
Dalles of St. Louis River	389
Blue Cañon, Sierra Nevada	391
Cotillion on the stump of the mammoth tree	394
View in the Modoc country	396
Rapids, Upper Columbia	402
Cape Mendocino	404
Comanche warrior	410
"I spiled his aim"	416
Un Indio Bravo	421
Texas and Coahuila in 1830	426
General Sam Houston	428
"Droughty Kansas"	433
"Good Osage—Heap good Injun"	440
Affluent of Clear Creek	449
South-west from Gray's Peak	461
Deadly combat of Vaughn and La Bonté	474
Toiling up Griffith Mountain	480
Capture of John D. Lee	491
Mountain Meadow Massacre	498
Salt Lake City, 1857	513
Execution of John D. Lee	525
The Noble Red Man	531
Scene of Sioux War of 1876	533
"Busted"	534
Custer's first Indian Fight	536
Rude Surgery of the Plains	541
Night Scene in the Cañon	571
A new Mining Town	578
Cape Horn and Rail-road, Sierra Nevada	588
"Giantess," Big Geyser of the Yellowstone	594
The Mormon Tabernacle	605
Fort Massachusetts, New Mexico, 1855	620
The Prospector's Peril	624

WESTERN WILDS,

AND

THE MEN WHO REDEEM THEM.

CHAPTER I.

THE HAWKEYES.

THE rolling prairies of Iowa were taking on their richest summer hues when I crossed from Prairie du Chien to McGregor, the first of June, 1868, and entered upon a three hundred mile walk across the State. The "Land of the Sleepy," as the aboriginal name implies, was just then the land of men particularly wide awake to their own interests. I was but one of a grand army ever pushing westward—active, aggressive, and defiant of space and time. Iowa combined the advantages of both East and West, and men of all North-European races were crowding to possess it.

There was the Yankee, moving on with that resistless energy which distinguishes the emigrant from our "Dorian Hive." More rarely appeared the "Buckeye" and "Hoosier;" their route was a little farther south, for emigration pays some attention to isothermal lines, and as a rule older States settle the new States directly west of them. There was the blonde Swede, tall and sinewy, his blue eye lighting cheerfully at sight of such landed wealth, in a clime a little milder than his own. Dane and Norwegian were also hurrying into north-western Iowa and southern Dakota. All these Scandinavian races are rarely seen south of latitude 40°, but fill whole townships in our new North-west. Dutch, Irish, Swiss, and North Germans contributed each a small quota. One might have fancied himself borne forward on the crest of that great Aryan wave which rolled westward and northward from Babel's plains. Four years after I found many of these emigrants in Dakota; already at home upon well-improved farms, and surrounded with most of the comforts of life.

Iowa and Minnesota were doubtless settled by the best class of immigrants that ever left the East. Their laws are favorable, their institutions progressive. Born republicans, these new-comers fell, by natural law, into free and progressive commonwealths. At first view one would say that our mother English was in danger of being lost, and that a new language would, ere long, rise in these mixed communities. But English is the language of progress, and that tongue in which laws are written and courts conducted will in time become the vernacular of any new country. In no part of America is a purer English spoken. The native of Indiana finds, when settled beside the Yankee, that he must drop some of his "Hoosierisms;" while the accent and idiom brought from "Down East" are insensibly modified, till the children of both compromise on the written language. Two hundred years ago when a man spoke in the British Parliament it was known on the instant what shire he represented; travel and civilization have since made the cultured Northumbrian and East Angle to be of one speech.

No grammar of the "Hoosier" language has ever been published. Before it becomes extinct, as have so many dialects, it may be well for one who spoke it in his childhood to fix a few of its idioms. It abounds in negatives. Unlike English and Latin, an abundance of negatives is held to strengthen the sentence. "Don't know nothing" is common. "See here," says the native, looking for work, to the farmer, "you don't know o' nobody what don't want to hire nobody to do nothin' nowhere around here, don't you?" "No," is the reply, "I don't." "I reckon" is a fair offset for the Yankee "I guess"—the one, as commonly used, about as reasonable as the other. But it is on the verb *to do* that the "Hoosier" tongue is most effective. Here is the ordinary conjugation:

Present Tense.—Regular, as in English.

Imperfect Tense.—I done it, you done it, he done it. *Plural*—We 'uns done it, you 'uns done it, they 'uns done it.

Perfect Tense.—I gone done it, you gone done it, he gone done it. *Plural*—We 'uns gone done it, you 'uns gone done it, they 'uns gone done it.

Pluperfect.—I bin gone done it, you bin gone done it, etc.

First Future.—I gwine to do it, you gwine to do it, etc.

Second Future.—I gwine to gone done it, etc. *Plural*—We 'uns gwine to gone done it, you 'uns gwine to gone done it, they 'uns gwine to gone done it.

Philologically this language is the result of a union between the rude translations of "Pennsylvania Dutch," the negroisms of Kentucky and Virginia, and certain phrases native to the Ohio Valley; and in my boyhood I often heard it *verbatim* as here given.

The Iowa pioneers had developed a marked faculty for taking care of themselves, and making the non-resident owner of real estate help develop the country. Three-fourths of the taxation was laid upon land, chattels being almost exempt; and, in the valuation, no distinction was made between slough and upland, vacant and improved. Villages, where there was much non-resident property, were generally well improved; and the side-walks were always best before the non-resident's lots, direct taxation being in the same ratio. If he did not come out and enjoy the promenade he had paid for, it was his own fault. The school laws of Iowa are surprisingly liberal in this respect, allowing a school in every township or district where there are six children. The citizens have the right to organize a school district as they will, regardless of their number. One worthy in Wright County, finding himself, wife and seven children to be the only inhabitants of the township, forthwith called a school meeting, notices being posted according to law, elected himself director, fitted up one room in his dwelling for a school, and employed his oldest daughter to teach the other six children. Thus

THE NON-RESIDENT TAX-PAYER.

he gave character to the settlement, and raised the money to improve his farm by simple compliance with the law. And do such a people require Congressional protection from the bond-holders and grasping monopolists of the East?

At the end of a week's leisurely travel, I was eighty miles from the Mississippi, and the appearance of the country had greatly changed. There were vast tracts of unsettled prairie; timber had grown scarcer; cultivated farms were rare, and just as the space between them increased the people grew warmer in their welcome. I was now away from the main line of emigration; and families in out-of-the-way places are nearly always hospitable. The chance traveler is as good as a newspaper, and is apt to be put to press on arrival. I soon learned to dread the wooded vales along the larger streams on account of the heat. To leave the high prairie for the "bottom" was like going from balmy May to sultry July. Regions where there is much wind are generally healthful; but when the wind falls one is liable to fall with it. There are no hotter districts in the Union than Iowa and Minnesota during those very brief periods in summer when a dead calm prevails. Though I had started an invalid, every day's walk made it easy to walk a little farther the next; and at the end of the second week I easily made twenty miles a day. If a man would be cured by nature, he must trust her—be taken to her bosom, as it were. Many an invalid goes West for health, and imagines the climate has cured him, when, in truth, he has only forgotten his physic, and been charmed out of his cares, and taken to open air and abundant exercise.

Iowa Falls, where the Iowa River leaves the "summit divide" prairies and plunges down a series of beautiful cascades to the level of the lower valley, was the location of the prettiest city on my route, and then the terminus of the Dubuque and Sioux City road. Thence I journeyed up Coon River and out to Wall Lake. To visit this place had been a dream of my boyhood. Twenty-five years ago it was represented as a marvelous work of the "mound builders." I found the "walls" there not so wonderful as described, but well worthy a visit; not the work of any prehistoric race, but due entirely to the expansive force of ice. In the vicinity are at least a dozen lakes with the same formation—some even more curious than the one most noted. They are on the "divide," between the waters which flow northward into the Minnesota and those which drain southward; and in all countries such a region abounds in lakes. The Iowa winters freeze the lakes almost solid, and the ice gathers up stones, pebbles and mud, and year after year pushes them toward the shore; then when the lake is full and frozen, it drives them with resistless energy into the "wall," till the latter looks like the most compact of man-made masonry. In some instances the water has cut a new outlet and drained the lake, and within a few years nature has begun the formation of a new wall inside the old one. Swans and wild geese abound in this region, which warmly invites the tourist, the scientist and the sportsman.

Westward again, and nothing but prairie to be seen; an average of two or three families to the township, and half a day's travel at a time without sight of a house. The swiftly running streams, with hard bottoms and pebbly banks, disappear, and sluggish sloughs take their place. Down a long slope for six or eight miles, the road brings one at last to a slough, sometimes with current enough to be called a creek, along which is found a scattering growth of timber, and sometimes a few enclosed farms. Thence one rises by slow degrees to another divide, and again down a slope to the next creek and settlement, from ten to thirty miles from the last. But the wave of immigration was rolling in; the railroad had been located on this route, and now the line I traversed presents a constant succession of cultivated fields and tasty homes; a region rich with orchards, white and red with clover-tops, or yellow with heavy-headed grain. *Then* there was but one railroad across the State; *now* there are four from the Mississippi to the Missouri—all stimulated by the completion of the Union Pacific. *Then* Iowa had one acre in seventeen under cultivation; *now* she has one in ten, and a population of nearly two millions. With less waste land than any other State, except possibly Illinois, Iowa could sustain a population of fifteen millions, not merely in comfort, but in affluence. What American realizes the prospective greatness of that tier of States just west of the Mississippi? Minnesota has 30,000 square miles of wheat-producing soil; Iowa has more arable land than England; Missouri has more iron, coal, timber and water-power than Prussia; Arkansas in extent and richness fairly rivals the Kingdom of Italy; and Louisiana, besides her sugar and cotton, runs two State governments, decides the presidential election, and has a heavy crop of statesmen to spare.

The scarcity of timber through this section had stimulated the invention of substitutes. The chief novelty was wire fence, usually made by fastening three wires on a row of posts with slip cleats. This was only to turn cattle; but a fancy article was made with six strands, which rendered it in local parlance "horse-high, bull-strong and pig-tight." Most of the counties thought it cheaper to forbid pigs running at large. In

"OUR LIBERTIES, SIR!"

Missouri and the timbered portions of the border States, I heard this statute denounced in much the same terms as the prohibitory liquor law—"an invasion of our liberties, sir!" Further north popular sentiment was expressed in the pithy saying: "A man's a hog that 'll let a hog run." Iowa, by an overwhelming majority, had equally prohibited errant hogs and free whisky. Minnesota, when I resided there in 1859, still held many of the traditions of Maine, whence most of the pioneers had come, and had equally condemned the sale of intoxicants. But western manners proved too strong for both States, for in the larger towns at least the traffic was, and is, open and unrestricted.

Drawing near the Missouri I found the country rising into long ridges and abrupt swells of land, the sloughs disappearing for the most part, and clear streams again taking their place. The grasshoppers had come in to desolate the few settlements, and for two days' travel I heard little but complaints and forebodings. Their method that season was peculiar. They traveled along a defined track, generally not more than a mile wide; but over that area they covered the ground, while the air seemed full of white specks, the creatures flying as high as one could see. Before them were green prairies, fields rich in clover, corn and wheat; behind them blackness, desolation and mourning. But while I studied them a strong wind sprang up from the east, and in a few hours they disappeared and were seen no more; not, however, until they had destroyed about half the crops in three counties. Whence come they, and whither do they go? Science and unlearned conjecture seem equally at fault. It is certain that they can only breed on high and dry ridges and plains, and a wet season is fatal to them. An old and abandoned road is their favorite hatching ground. For the most part they confine their ravages to the border, but occasionally they sweep in destructive columns far down toward the Mississippi. A few years later I was destined to have an unprofitable experience with them in Kansas, after the State had been free from them seven years, and the least hopeful believed that their day had passed forever.

From this region I turned south-west, and the last of June crossed the Missouri to the metropolis of Nebraska. Omaha was then the city of promise. Whether that promise has been fulfilled is a matter of doubt with many who were then sanguine. The rivalry with Council Bluffs, on the Iowa side, was intense and amusing. On the west bank, one heard contemptuous allusions to "the Bluffs," "East Omaha," and "Milkville." On the other side there were withering sarcasms about "Bilkville," "Traintown," "Omahawgs," "Omahens," and "The U. P. Station across the river." The editors on one side, according to their statements, made their "libelous contemporaries" on the other "squirm" almost daily. To the stranger, who had no possessions in either place, it was a free comedy. The "Omahawgs," with cheerful disregard of grammar, spoke of their city as the "initial terminus" (in English, "beginning-end") of the Union Pacific Railroad, and future *entrepôt* of the California, China and Australia trade. It did look reasonable that they should build up a great city, and cheering prophecies were abundant. Somehow they have been slow of fulfillment. A careful census by the city authorities made the population 19,000. The next year they modestly estimated it in round numbers at 25,000; and the next came a great epidemic (of United States officials) and swept off half the number, for the United States census of 1870 credits Omaha with less than 13,000 inhabitants. The city is cosmopolitan. First Street is located in the river (at high water), and the first seven streets are supposed to be on the sandbar. The city begins at Eighth Street, and the location of the fashionables is from Eighteenth to Twenty-fifth Streets, on Capitol Hill. Such are the pleasing self-delusions of the expanding mind in the glorious free and boundless West.

It was the notable hot season in Nebraska, and a week in the metropolis satisfied me. Thence I sought the country by way of the old California trail, and traveled a month in rural Nebraska—first in the valley of the Papilion (which the people persist in calling Pappeo), and thence to Fontanelle and up the Elkhorn through what is considered the garden spot of Northern Nebraska. It is a region rich in natural wealth, and was even then so handsomely improved that travel through it was a constant delight. There were miles of corn-fields, with heavy crops, and tracts of wheat just ready for harvesting, farm products of all kinds in abundance, and plenty blessing the industrious farmer. Planted timber of nearly all kinds grows rapidly, cottonwood and locust especially; nearly every settler has an artificial grove, and these are abundant enough to greatly beautify the landscape. The soil is deep and rich, the country gently rolling, high, dry and healthful. The wheat through that region averaged twenty-five bushels per acre that year. For the width of the State north and south, and a hundred and fifty miles back from the Missouri, almost every acre is adapted for the production of grain. Thirty thousand square miles of land give abundant room for an agricultural population of a million. West of the area I have thus bounded, the land rises more into the barren ridges; only the valleys are very fertile, and most of the country is valuable only for grazing. Society is well organized; churches and schools have been handsomely provided for; vacant land in the fertile section is still abundant and cheap, and if one is native to any latitude north of 36°, Nebraska offers him first-class inducements.

The Indian still lingered. The Pawnees were the local aborigines, but Omahas (properly Mahaws) and Otoes were common, all three being among the most unprepossessing of the race. Long observation has convinced me that those tribes which fringe the white settlements, hanging between civilization and barbarism, always include the meanest looking specimens. Of course, I except the civilized residents of the Indian Territory. Cooper's Indians are extinct, but the "noble red man," in a certain sense, does exist, and I have seen him. But not near the settlements. One must go far into the interior, where they are the style and he the oddity, to see really interesting Indians. How inferior are the Pawnees to the Sioux, the Kaws to the Utes, the Osages and Otoes to the Navajoes! A few tribes may pass successfully across the awful gulf between savage life and civilized, but there is a fearful waste of raw material in the process.

"CIVILIZED."

My travels in Nebraska drew near a close, and I stood at evening of a beautiful summer day, upon a lofty hill that overlooked the fertile Platte Valley. Southward the scene was bounded by the heavy timber lining that stream; eastward I looked over a landscape rich in natural and artificial beauty to the forests on the Missouri; northward the winding Elkhorn could be traced many a mile by the tasteful groves which adorn its bluffs, while westward the view was free to the meeting of earth and sky. That way lay adventure and novel scenes; that way I was mightily drawn. The haze of evening softened the outlines of a beautiful landscape; from the eastward came the rumble and smoke of a Union Pacific train dashing out for Cheyenne, while westward up the valley a vagrant party of Pawnees were fast pressing out of sight. The scene was an emblem of progress. I breathed the spirit of borderland poetry. The Bedouin instinct stirred within me, and I burned to hasten my departure to that newer West, which already made this region seem old. But before I enter on the long detail of my Western wanderings, let me briefly sketch the labors and perils of a '49-er, who passed that way nineteen years before me.

CHAPTER II.

A WESTERN CHARACTER.

UNCONSCIOUS greatness is a Western product. There many a man, in pursuance of the humblest duties, becomes a hero without knowing it. One such let me celebrate. A most modest hero, he had seen the world without intending it; had lived a romance in the mere earning of a livelihood, and grown great in simple-hearted obedience to family affection.

In the autumn of 1873 I made a leisurely journey through the new counties of southern Kansas. The Osage Ceded Lands, which only five years before had been a game preserve for vagrant aborigines, were now dotted with neat villages flanked by well cultivated farms. From the summit of a lofty mound in Montgomery County one could look over 500 square miles of rolling prairie and fertile valley, the home of 20,000 Americans. Westward the land rose more into barren ridges, beyond which were the fertile slopes of Cowley County and the new country on the Arkansas. Between was a region almost unsettled; the rocky ridges were fit only for pasturage, and the narrow valleys were neglected till better places should be filled. There one might ride for hours without sight of a dwelling, fortunate at night if a settler's cabin furnished him shelter in a room common to all the family. At the close of a September day I had ridden ten miles without sight of a house, and eagerly scanned the horizon. A horseman from the opposite direction hailed me with equal eagerness to learn the distance to Elk Falls, his first chance for the night. On learning that it was ten miles, he indulged in a prolonged whistle, and in turn informed me he knew of no house on this road for fifteen miles. "But," he added, reflectively, "ther's old Darnells, only a mile off the road, down Grouse Creek. They'll keep you if you're a mind to stop there. They've got plenty, too, such as it is, and the old woman's a prime cook, and 'll set it 'fore you warm and clean. The old man's the wust shuck up settler on the creek, what with rheumatiz and ager and the swamps and one thing an' another; but git him stirred up and he's a powerful talker. Heap o' life in him yet."

So I went to Darnells.

The first show was not inviting. A rambling, double-log house of the South-western pattern—practically two cabins under one roof, with a broad covered passage between. But many a pleasant night have I passed, and eaten many savory meal, in those same double-log cabins; and in the long hot days of summer, south of latitude 40°, I know of no better place to loll away the delightful after-dinner hour than in the open passage aforesaid.

My host was indeed "shuck up," "doubled up," too, I should say. "Fevernager," Arkansas swamps, and prairie sloughs had done their appointed work on him, and he was that perfect wreck, a "thoroughly acclimated man." He was, in local phrase, "yaller behind the gills;" his face was of a pale orange tint, his cheeks a dirty saffron, while along the neck his skin resembled a ripe pumpkin speckled with coffee grounds. He received me with dignified welcome—in these wilds no question is made as to lodging the belated traveler—and referred the matter of supper to "the old woman."

"THOROUGHLY ACCLIMATED."

One glance at her revealed the Cherokee lineage. The deep, dark eye with slightly melancholy cast, the straight black hair, and nose just aquiline enough to give piquancy to the countenance, indicated the quarter-blood; while her air and bearing gave a hint of Ross or Boudinot stock—the aristocracy of that most aristocratic of all our aboriginal races. The supper was a surprise. She had evidently learned cooking in better schools than south-western cabins supply. Like him, she seemed preternaturally quiet, as if absorbed in thought; they lived in the past, and to them Kansas was not the home of the soul. New countries should be settled only by the young, for the tree of deepest root bears transplanting but poorly.

The broad, red sun was just dipping into the prairie horizon, when a gray haze overspread the landscape, creeping up from the sluggish stream. The old man waved his hand toward it with the brief but expressive phrase, "break-bone fever," and we retired to the cabin and evening fire. As we filled and lighted the inevitable cob pipe, common in the South-west, I spoke of Andrew Jackson's love of the same, and his Tennessee habits, whereat my host broke out with sudden animation:

"Ah, you're from Tennessee, a'nt you?"

"Not exactly," was my reply, "but I know and like the State."

"Well, I was raised there, right on the banks of the Tennessee, but I was born just over the line in Alabama. Yes, sir, sixty-four years ago, in Glen Cove, I tuck my first view of life. Nicest climate in this world, sir, and bad as I've seen it tore up since, I don't want no better country."

"But how came you to leave, if it was so good a country?"

"Well, a good many things happened; sort o' riled the current and spiled me for a steady life, though I'm pretty well anchored now, for a fact;" and glancing at his distorted limbs, he relapsed into speechlessness, puffing at his cob pipe, and waiting, Indian fashion, for the talk to break out naturally. Hot youth was more impatient of time, and I asked:

"If no offense, what caused you to leave that country for this?"

"Well, I did'nt leave there for here; that would be too big a change. They was many haps and mishaps between. It happened along o' family matters and the war. You see they was five brothers of us and one sister, me the oldest; and mammy sort o' give the rest in my charge. Poor mammy, she never seed any of us old enough to be sure of."

"But how about your father?"

"Well, daddy was a little onsettled; along o' trips down into the Cherokee country and tradin with the Injins—in fact he let his little finger ride his thumb too often, and his eyesight weakened on it."

This was a delicate allusion to his father's intemperance, given in the figurative language of the South-west.

"Fact, he took me down among the Injins in Geawjay and North Alabama one trip—fine country that, too; altogether too fine for the Injins to keep if the whites wanted it—but daddy went off at last, and that was the how of my first trip. He went off on a broad-horn. You don't know what a broad-horn is. No? Well, it's a flat-boat of the old rig; and the men come back without him. Them days they commonly walked back from Noo Orleens thro' the Injin country. All they said was he had lost all his money, and swore he'd never come back till he could come full-handed. Mammy was ailin' then, and after that she never seemed to pick up any; and the day I was sixteen she called me close to the bed and she said: 'Willy, you go find him, and bring him back, for when he dies he'll never be easy 'cept beside me,' and then she laid on me the charge of all the other five—and, stranger, I can't somehow talk about that time, but just a week after they was only me and Myra and the four little boys left. I tell you it was a sad time. I've only seen one worse and that was in the war.

"I hadn't time to cry much, for I had a family on my hands and mighty little to go on except the place. We all worked and made a crop, and then I fixed things up a little, and got a neighbor to take the place—mighty nice people they was then in old Tennessee—and I started to find dad."

"What! went to find your father at that age?"

"Yes," said the old man simply, "mammy had said so, and of course it had to be done. Daddy had been gone a year, when I took a broad-horn to Noo Orleens, and when I was paid off on the levee, I was the worst lost man you ever did see. In the middle of the thickest woods in the world wasn't a circumstance to it. Such crowds and crowds of people, and ships and boats and stores, and men all rushing here and yander, enough to distract you. Why, they wan't more'n one man in four understood a word I said. In all my life I'd never heard of any language but white-man and Injin, and there was Portagee, Mexican, Gumbo, French and Coaster, talkin' every thing, and all mixed up. My head was a swimmin—just off the boat, you know—and sometimes I half reckoned I'd walked right out o' the Ark and into the brick-yard at the Tower o' Babel; for I'd read o' that anyhow, and might a' known how things would be in Noo Orleens if I'd a thought. But says I to myself, no time to cry now; I'm here. So I went about asking every man that understood me if he'd seed a man named Hiram Darnell. Well, some of 'em cussed me, and most paid no attention to me; but bimeby one chap says: 'Oh, yes, I know Mr. Darnell; he's up on Chapitooley Street a chawin' rags for a paper mill.' And another said: 'He was at the pipe-works, and they was trainin' him to go through a drain-pipe,' and all such stuff.

"Well, I was that green I hunted the pipe-works, and there they sent me to a leather store to buy 'strap-oil,' and told me a lot more stuff. Then I walked all over the city, miles an' miles an' miles, lookin' close at every body I seed, an' it seemed to me I seed every body *but* dad. In less'n a month all my money was gone, an' I felt awful streaked. But I lit on another feller who told me the right track, and we did find out where dad had worked a while; but he was gone, and finally the police said he wan't in Noo Orleens now. So I went to work on the levee a while haulin' and pitchin', but it was awful hot then. A feller's shadder at noon was right 'tween his feet, and 'fore long I struck an ole pard o' dads, and found he'd gone away up Red River, in the new country. So I went deck-hand on a boat up Red River, and they was nothing like so many folks up there, an' people more civil; an' I traced him all through Arkansaw toward the Injin country. But it took a might of time. Sometimes I worked and sometimes I walked, and at last got where there was no houses hardly, and many a time I was alone all day in the woods, and more'n once nearly lost in the big swamps. At last I got into a more open country and some new settlements about Fort Smith, and then I fell in with some Cherokees, and sure enough they knowed dad.

"I HUNTED THE PIPE-WORKS."

"You see, a lot o' Cherokees moved out there away back before Jackson come in first time, and dad had his old liking for the tribe, and had fell in with them, and away up in the timber I found him at last. But, law, how he was changed! He come out of a cabin and looked at me as if I was a stranger. What with hot weather and whisky and the trouble and yaller fever, he wasn't just clear in his mind, and what to do I didn't know. But I'd learnt something by that time, so I watched around and got him fixed up a little, and with a good family, an' I went to work again. The Cherokees was fixin' up considerably, an' I made a pretty good job at rough carpentering; and there I worked a whole year."

"You must have been rather home-sick by that time."

"Well, I was a little anxious about the boys. Myra was nearly fifteen when I left; then come Joe, thirteen; him I played with, an' had more to do with than any of the boys. Many's the hour we've fished an' hunted along the Tennessee. Poor Joe! I've seen the time since when I wished he was a boy agin, but," with a sudden burst of triumph, "I stuck by him to the last, as I'd promised mammy."

Here the old man fell into such a protracted reverie, that I ventured to recall him to the Arkansas and his father.

"Oh, yes, I clean forgot. Well, in a year dad was so much better that we started home, takin' a job on another boat to Noo Orleens to shorten up the walk a little."

The calm way in which he spoke of shortening the walk from Fort Gibson to East Tennessee, was wonderfully suggestive. If it had been around the world, he would have entered on it with the same resolution, as something that was not to be talked about, but done.

"When we got to Noo Orleens and got paid off, we fixed up with some clean clothes, lookin' real human again, and started home. But it seemed like every thing was agin us. The trail then led away from the river, and sort o' north and east, nearly straight toward the bend o' the Tennessee. We worried along with heat, for it was late, till we struck the edge of the Injun country, where we found every thing all tore up. I never got the hang of it exactly; but the States was a pressin' the Injins to go, an' some wanted to an' some didn't; and the Choctaws they was a fussin' with their agents, an' the Cherokees a fightin' with one another, an' there was murder an' robbery an' horse-stealin' all over the country, an' their light-horse companies out arrestin' every body that passed on the roads. How I got along I don't know. Every time I laid down in an Injun cabin it seemed to me I'd have my throat cut 'fore mornin'; but dad talked the lingo like a born Injin, so they couldn't come no tricks in our hearin', an' every night I dreamed I saw mammy, an' she looked kind o' glad, an' though she said nothin', her looks meant plain enough: 'Don't cry, Willy, you'll get home all right.'

"But when we got to the Cherokee country it was worst of all. They was two parties in the tribe, Rossites and Ridgites, and just then the Rossites got up an' murdered a chief named McIntosh an' a lot of other Ridgites, an' swore that every Injun that said 'go' should be served the same way. They stopped us, an' wouldn't let us go through at all. They pow-wowed around with us for two months; then come along some that knowed Daddy, an' they said he should go or they'd have blood. So it was settled that I was to stay an' him go on, an' if it proved we was all right, I was to be let go in so long a time. When the time come they turned me loose, an' I started north on the first road I struck. But I was powerfully out o' conceit with the redskins, an' the first two nights I slept out.

"It was then September, an' the next day, when I thought I was near the Tennessee, all at once I took so cold I seemed like I'd chill to death, an' pretty soon so hot that I stopped at a spring an' drunk an' drunk till I staggered 'round like I had a load of whisky on. An' when night come on, I kept gettin' up an' layin' down first one place an' then another, an' then huntin' water an' tryin' to get into a house that was right afore me, an' yet I couldn't somehow locate it. All at once I come on Joe, an' I cried like a child, an' begged him to take me in an' give me a drink. It 'peared like Joe was scared of me, an' run, an' I run an' called to him all night thro' the woods. Then it come on to rain, an' I got down by a tree, an' it seemed like Joe was jist t'other side of the tree, an' wouldn't come an' help me. So I got up an' staggered on, an' all at once I was at myself, settin' at the foot of another tree, an' somebody was callin' thro' the woods for milk cows. And when the voice come near me I set down an' cried, for it made me think o' Mammy and Myra—it was so soft an' sweet. Then a girl come up, and I tried to speak, but shivered an' shook that bad I couldn't say a word. But how pretty that little white Cherokee looked! Stranger, you have no idee. No woman you ever see could ekal her."

I was about to demur to this, when the fire blazed up brightly, and I glanced across the hearth at the "old woman;" and—was it fancy? or did the lines in the poor, worn old face seem to fade away, and a tremulous softness steal into the dark eyes? I suspended criticism, and after a brief reverie my host continued:

"Well, I sunk down agin, an' the next I recollect I was in a cabin, an' an old conjurer was pow-wowing over me. She was the blackest, grizzliest old Cherokee I ever seed; an' as she muttered some heathen stuff, an' rattled a little bell, she sometimes went to the door and stroked her face and kissed her hand to the sun, an' somehow I got the idee she was the same as the pretty little girl that found me, an' the notion of the change made me cry agin. The next ten days I don't know much about, only they had a regular doctor once or twice; an' all at once I woke one clear morning, an' there set the pretty little Cherokee, an' my head was all right agin.

"But law, stranger, I was *that* weak! They was white Cherokees that picked me up—the man a Scotchman, married to a half-blood woman, and some of the best folks I ever struck. It was weeks before I could walk a quarter; then I got strong pretty fast, and bimeby along came dad huntin' for me. An' that girl—well, I reckon she spared nothin' that cabin could afford to help me get well. She used to sing the Cherokee songs, and her mother would tell all about the travels and troubles of the tribe from the time they left the Yemassee, in Carolina, till now. And when I was able to go it seemed like a dream—as if I hadn't been there a week. It was over two years I'd been gone, but every thing was right at home. After that I had business every two or three months down in the Cherokee Nation, an' all at once the troubles started up again. The rights of it I no more understood than I did the other trouble, only that Jackson had come in President, and took the part of Geawgey and Alabama agin the Injins, an' swore they'd got to go anyhow, an' then they quarreled among themselves agin. Then her father died—the little white Cherokee I mean—and her mother was all put out about the troubles, but finally said she must go with her people, and claim her headrights on the land where they was to settle. Then I spoke to the little girl—well, to make a long story short, I've tried for thirty years to pay up, but I'm still in her debt, an' to me she's just as pretty as she was the mornin' she found me in the woods."

And now I was sure it was no fancy, for the "old woman" had crossed the hearth and taken the gray head in her hands; the sad, dark eye was again lighted with the gleam of youthful love, the wrinkles gave place to smiles, and the worn face was transformed into something far beyond the beautiful. It was divine.

"So your troubles ended in joy at last," said I.

"Yes, I reckon you may say so;" then, with his pipe relighted, he puffed away in silence. He had acquired one habit of his stolid Indian friends—the habit of having fits of silence, waiting on the stimulus of smoke. Two lads of sixteen or seventeen years came in with the proceeds of a day's hunt.

"Our grandsons," said the hostess, in a half-apologetic tone, "and about all the dependence we've got now."

This was her first and last observation, and we seemed in a fair way to smoke the evening away in silence, when one of the young men threw a fresh knot on the fire. It blazed up brightly, and, with Indian suddenness, the old man broke out again:

"It was a bad thing, a bad, mean thing, the way them people was rooted out. Just think of a whole people, sixteen or eighteen thousand, lots of 'em with good farms, an' houses, an' shops, an' startin' schools an' newspapers, havin' to pull up whether or no, with soldiers to prod them along with bayonets, an' go away off to a country they didn't like, an' where lots an' lots of 'em died! Well, that's what they done."

"You mean the Cherokees."

"Yes, my wife's folks all went with 'em. So we bought a place of a Cherokee that was leaving, an' worked it five years, an' got every thing fixed beautiful, with lots of stock and grain. But it seemed like they was no luck in that cussed country; anyhow, I was turned out bag an' baggage."

"Turned out! How? Did you lose your land?"

"Well, yes; it amounted to that finally."

He seemed desirous of giving the story, and yet was reluctant to begin.

"But how did it happen?" I persisted.

"Well, stranger, I never just got the right of it, an' for a long time I never liked to think of it, for I always got mad an' swore under my breath, an' it worried the old woman, an' made me lose sleep, an' so I've pretty much quit thinkin' about it. You see when the Injins left, there was a deal of swindlin'. Most of 'em was ignorant, an' some signed away their land when drunk, an' a few rascally Injins traveled 'round with the speculators, signin' away others' rights, an' swearin' they was the ones. A man just come up one day with a deed to my land, an' the court pow-wowed awhile about it and said it was his'n, an' I just had to clear."

"But you had your stock."

"Well, no, not exactly. You see I lawed him awhile, an' the court made me pay for that, an' my lawyer cost something; an' the height of it was, when the thing was done I just put my wife on the only hoss we had left, with a little one behind her, an' the baby in her arms, an' me an' the oldest boy walked, an' we went back to Tennessee."

"And began again without a cent!"

"Well, not that exactly. I raised some money in a year or two. But somehow it didn't seem the old thing to me there, an' so we come over west of the mountains, an' got a little piece of land in Coffee County, an' that was our home till we come out here. After all we've got along, an' I've never been in jail but once."

"In jail! Why you never committed any crime?"

"No, but come mighty nigh it once—near enough to be took up an' mighty nigh hung for it. But that was out in Iowa."

"So you did take another trip, after all."

"Yes; it was along o' the boys, specially brother Joe—him that I always sot most store by. Joe married young—married an Irish girl in the neighborhood, though all of us opposed it. I could see she had temper; but every feller's got to take his chances on that, anyhow. You know how that is."

"No, I can't say as I do. But how did he get along?"

"Well, there was trouble. An' bimeby I persuaded Joe if they'd get away from both their folks it would be better; so he went to Injeanny, and then to Illinoy. Well, it seems like when folks get started that way they keep goin' and goin'. One place is too hot and another too cold, an' here its sickly an' there they's bad neighbors, and so on. Leastways it was that way with Joe, and finally he landed in the Half-breed Tract in Iowa. At first he could not say enough in praise of the country. Joe was a great scholar; he could write like a schoolmaster, an' cipher as fast as he could make the figures; but my wife had to read the letters an' answer for me. All at once we got no more letters for two or three years, and then come one with just a few lines, an' it wound up: 'I've writ so often an' got no answer, I'm discouraged, but I'll try once more. Come an' see old Joe before he dies!'

"Nothin' could a' stopped me after that. I fixed up every thing snug about home, an' got Ben, my youngest brother, to stay while I was gone, an' run down the Tennessee an' up the Mississip to St. Louis. Then I conceited I might need all my money, so I took a job on another boat to Nauvoo, where I landed all right, but soon found I'd run right into the trouble.

"It was the year after the Mormon prophet was killed, an' the whole country was up a boomin'. I only knowed Joe lived back in the country somewhere on the other side, an' when I asked about roads they looked at me like I was a pirate. I had to give account of myself half a dozen times 'fore I got out of town, an' then like enough when I'd step off I'd overhear some feller say, 'D—n him, he's one of 'em, and a spy at that.' Over the river it was jist as bad. Every body was afraid of every body else they didn't know. If I went nigh a house when the men was out, liker'n not the woman 'd bolt the door an' set a dog on me, or run out toward the fields and holler for the men. Every body carried a gun, or a club, or a knife, an' I never seed so many big an' savage dogs—one or two at every house; an' they looked jist as snappy an' suspicious as the people, an' watched round close an' stuck by the women whenever a stranger come along. One man I asked a civil question about the road, an' he only grinned an' said, '*Your* safest road's back towards Nauvoo; they hang horse thieves over here.' An' that night where I stopped they stood with the door open about an inch, an' made me answer a hundred questions 'fore they'd let me in. Lord, such a catekismen I was put through!—an' didn't half want to let me in then. It was jist the Cherokee country over agin, an' they might as well a been at war for any comfort they took.

"But next day I found Joe's, and it was the poorest, meanest house on the Tract. I walked in, an' what do you think I seed? Thar was my dear Joe sittin' all bent up, an' poor an' thin, an' lookin', though not over forty, like a man o' sixty. He'd rastled with ager an' roomatiz time about till nothin' was left for any sickness to tack on to, an' all the while that Irish wife o' his tormentin' him to death. When I saw him I never said a word—I couldn't—but I jist took him in my arms, an' for the first time in all my troubles I broke down an' cried! It done Joe no end o' good to see me, but it wa'nt for long. She soon spilt our comfort. She was a spitfire when he married her, an' you understand age an' bad luck hadn't improved her any—what with bein' out among such rough people, losin' her children, an' livin' in a cabin with a sick man, an' mighty little to go on, for they was poor as the low-wines o' pond-water."

Only the western traveler who has been compelled to suck up moisture from a prairie slough, or lie down and drink out of a wagon track, can appreciate the force of this simile. It is scarcely possible to conceive of a more unsatisfactory drink.

"She could swear like an ox-driver, an' when she took a tantrum every thing was ammunition that come to her hand—the poker or an old skillet-handle, it was all one to her. But I stood her off, and was gettin' Joe cheered up right smart, when one mornin' I was everlastingly took back by seein' a crowd of men with guns comin' up to the gate. 'What *does* them men want?' sez I. '*You*, like enough,' sez she, snappin'-turtle style. An', sure enough, it was me. They snatched me right out of the house, without a word o' why, an' I thought my time had come. They was all sorts o' talk about an awful murder, an' two or three o' the lot was hot to hang me up. But the captain said, 'No; every fellar should have a fair trial—Mormon or old settler, it was all the same.' They took me down to a camp in the woods, where they was more'n a hundred men, some comin' and goin' all the time, an' nearly all drinkin', and the drunker they got the more dangered I felt. One chap stuck his face nearly agin mine, an' sez he, 'Didn't you help kill Miller and Liecy?' 'No,' sez I. 'Didn't you come

MRS. JOE'S "TANTRUMS."

sneakin' along the brush road from Nauvoo t'other day, then?' says he. 'No,' sez I, and was goin' on to explain, when he yells out, 'You're a d—d lying Mormon, an' I've a mind to shoot the guts out o' you,' 'an the captain stopped him. I noticed the captain didn't touch the whisky, an' that hoped me a good deal.

"They took me an' five others to a big house, an' kept us all day an' night, an' then I heard what it was all about. An' no wonder the people was excited. It skeered me jist to hear it. It was at the only house I'd stopped at on the way where the folks was easy an' civil like. They was a Dutchman named Miller and his son-in-law Licey lived there; an' they was jist from some old civil country place in Pennsylvany, or some'rs back there, where nobody's afraid or locks their doors at night; an' these men had come on the Tract to buy land. It was talked round that the old man had five thousand dollars in a trunk, an' a job was put up by some fellers in Nauvoo. They spied 'round a day or two, an' one night three men busted in the door an' fell to shootin' an' cuttin' every thing they come to. The whole house was dashed with blood. The old man fit like a tiger. He was a Dunkard preacher, an' as stout as an ox, an' I mind well it was told 'round for a fact that he nearly killed one o' the men jist with his naked fists; an' when they run a long butcher-knife into his breast, he was so big it didn't go half way through, an' he whipped 'em off an' fell dead in the yard! What with the old man's fightin', and the women screamin', an' the dogs a barkin', the fellers was skeered off an' never got a cent o' the money. Then a neighbor galloped to Montrose, a town nigh there, an' raised the yell, an' in a little while the Hawkeyes, as they called theirselves, was out, an' that day they sarched every corner in the county. It was the roughest time for strangers you ever read of. If you ever seed a lot o' cattle bellerin' 'round where one had been shot, you've an idee.

"They was some that even proposed to hang all of us to be sure an catch the right one; an' what made it worse we was as much skeered of each other as we was of the Hawkeyes. But they was one man named Bird in our lot who cheered us up a good deal; an' pretty soon they got on the right trail, an' it led straight to Nauvoo; but the Mormons wouldn't give the fellers up. Then the sheriff took a whole boat load of men to Nauvoo, an' they had a big meetin', an' threatened war, but finally he got the men he had writs for, an' got 'em in jail; but the sheriff had his doubts, an' set up a game on 'em. They was two brothers named Hodges, an' he took four men of about their build, an' set 'em altogether, an' had Licey, who lived some days, carried in to look at 'em. The Hawkeyes had us along, for they was bound to catch somebody; an' it was the solemnest time I ever seed. The two Hodges was as cool as cowcumbers, but the other four men was skeered nearly to death. Liccy took a long look, an' then pinted his finger at the Hodges, an' says he: 'There's the man that shot me, an' there's the man that knifed me!'

"And that settled their hash. So we was all turned loose, an' Bird an' me made tracks for Joe's. When we got nigh the house, we heard an awful racket, an' run in, an' she had Joe down beatin' him with his own crutch. They'd had another row, an' she'd sort o' got the best of it. I snatched the weepin' outen her hand; then she swore at us, an' lit out on the road with a partin' blessin', an' that's the last we ever seed o' her."

"Bolted, did she?"

"Rather that way, stranger. But what do you think that woman done? Went straight to Montrose, an' swore to my havin' bogus money, an' the very next day they put me in jail—socked me right in with them two Hodges—an' I never felt so mean an' streaked in all my life. I had no learnin' 'cept to read a little, an' that was the first I ever felt bad about it. One of the sheriff's men, Hawkins Taylor, was real kind, an' got me some things an' a lot o' copies set. I put my whole head to it, an' in jest three weeks, sir, I wrote a nice letter to the old woman—didn't tell her where I boarded, though—an' then I felt easier. If it hadn't been for that, I'd 'agone crazy, shut up so with them Hodges. I've seen 'em more'n once since, in my sleep. They swore an' sung an' joked an' held up pretty stiff—they had an idee their friends in Nauvoo would take 'em out—but bimeby their brother there was found one morning with his throat cut, jist after he'd seen the head Mormons an' raised a row with 'em about givin' up these two; an' then they sort o' lost hope. It was no go. Iowa was up then, an' the Mormons might as well a'tried to take 'em from Gineral Jackson's army. I was turned loose finally, the day before they was hung.

"They was people come a hundred miles to see it, an' camped out in wagons. They had so little fun on the Tract, it was a great treat to see somebody hung. Joe an' me was there, an' that's the first an' last sight of that kind I ever took. I've seen plenty killed, but not that way. We sold Joe's place, an' got him home, an' he picked up mightily in old Tennessee. For an East Tennessee man no other place is as good as the mountains. Only place I've seed to compare with it was in Californy."

"What! Have you been to California, too?"

"Took a little trip out there."

"Little trip! It is considered a pretty big one. Did you go for gold?"

"Some'at, but more on account o' the boys."

"Your brothers again?"

"No, my own boys. You might say I went to keep them from goin', for I suspicioned it was all foolishness, from the start. I reckon you don't remember the big excitement. No? Well, it swept all Tennessee like a fire in prairie grass. I first heard it one day at Manchester, when the Whigs had a pole-raisin' along o' the election o' old Zach Taylor, an' a man jist from Noo York spoke, an' said old Zach had conquered for us a country with more gold in it than any nation on earth had. Pretty soon the news come thick. They said men just dug gold out o' the rocks—thousands in a day. You ought to heard the stories that was told for solemn facts. One man said a feller dug out one lump worth eight hundred thousand dollars, an' as he set on it, a feller come by with a plate o' pork an' beans, an' he offered him fifty thousand for it, an' the feller stood him off for seventy-five thousand. It was in the Nashville paper, an' so every body in our parts believed it.

"Then every loose-footed man wanted to go. Some jist throwed down their tools an' started; an' some men that was tied with families, actually set down an' cried 'cause they couldn't go. My boys was as crazy as the rest. But they was only sixteen an' eighteen, an' I seed it wouldn't do. So I said: 'Boys, let me go, an' I'll let you know in time,' an' then I bound 'em to take care o' their mother till I sent for 'em. It would a' been ruination for them young innocent boys to go off with such a lot o' men. Jest as soon as the Tennessee was up so boats could run over Muscle Shoals, a company of forty of us shipped teams an' started, an' landed at Independence, Missouri, the last o' March. The whole country was under water, but our fellers was crazy to git on; so they hitched up and started right across the Kaw an' into the Delawares' country. But it was all foolishness to start so early. Accident after accident we had. The mud was thicker an' stickier every day, an' all the creeks was up; but the men kept up a hoopin' an' swearin', an' often had to double teams, an' sometimes we'd stick an' pull out two or three wagon tongues 'fore we'd get through. I never seed men so crazy to git on. They whipped an' yelled, an' wouldn't listen to reason. They was plenty started three weeks after us, an' passed us on the road. An' what was strange, the trains that laid by an' kept Sunday, got to Californy first. You wouldn't believe it, but I've heard hundreds say the same thing.

"Bimeby we got righted up an' on dryer ground, an' went on after killin' two or three hosses an' leavin' one wagon. The trains got strung out all along the trail, so we had grass an' game plenty along up the Blue River an' over to the Platte. There we struck the Mormon emigration an' all the Californy trains that went that way. The whole country was et out, an' the Injins threatened, an' the men got to quarrelin'. I tell you it takes a mighty good set o' men to travel together three thousand miles an' not fuss. Sometimes it was Whig and Democrat, an' then it was Tennessee agin Geawgey. I tell you when men are tired an' dirty they'll quarrel about any thing. About half a dozen swore Californy was all humbug, an' turned back, an' at Laramie Forks the company split into two. At South Pass our half split agin, an' ten of us went off with a company to go the new route, south of the Salt Lake. We got to the Mormon City all beat out, an' more'n half a mind not to go a mile further. Plenty got there in worse humor than us. Some had split up till it was each man for himself, an' some actually divided wagons, an' made two carts out o' one, or finished the trip on hosses. We took a rest, an' traded every thing with the Mormons, givin' two of our hosses for one fresh one, an' finally got off in pretty good shape agin.

"But all we'd seed was nothin' to the country from there on. Rocks an' mountains an' sand; an' sand, an' rocks an' mountains—miles on miles of it. Sometimes the water was white as soapsuds with alkali, an' sometimes as red as brick-dust, not one time in five sweet an' clean. I reckon I swore a thousand times if I ever got home agin nothin' stronger 'n cold water should pass my lips. I've drove all day 'thout seein' a spear o' green, or a speck of any thing but sand; an' if we got grass once a day, we was in luck. Every day the men swore nothin' could beat this, an' the next day it was always worse. I reckon God knows what he made that country for—he haint told any body, though.

"At last we got into a region that was the hind end o' creation— seventy miles 'thout a drop o' water or a spear o' grass! Nothin' but hot sand an' beds of alkali as white as your shirt. The trains used to start in one afternoon an' drive two nights an' a day, an' get to water the second mornin'. The whole way was lined with boxes an' beds an' clothes, an' pieces of wagons, one thing an' another the trains ahead had left, an' the last ten miles you might a' stepped from one carcass to another on the dead hosses an' mules an' oxen. Two o' our men got crazy as loons—you can see such strange things on them deserts. My head was clear as a bell, an' yet half the time I could see off to one side of us a train jest like our'n, only the men an' hosses ten times as big, an' jist as like as not they'd raise in the air an' move off upside down. It was sort o' skeery, an' no mistake. We left four or five dead hosses on that tract, but when we got to Carson River, it was too pretty a sight to tell about. There was sweet, clean water an' grass an' trees an' trains strung along for miles a restin' their stock. Some of our men run right into the water an' swallowed an' swallowed till they staggered like drunk men. All the rest of the way was in the mountains, but grass and water was plenty, an' the trees—how I did admire to see 'em! Hundreds o' miles I hadn't seen a bush as thick as my thumb.

"MADE MUSIC ALL DAY."

"Well, we was into Californy at last, an' it looked like heaven to me. There was big trees, an' the wind blowin' soft away up in their tops; an' the pretty clear streams down the mountain side an' through the gulches made music all day. In some places the air was jist sweet that blowed out o' the pine woods, an' week after week the sky was so blue, an' the air so soft, it seemed like a man could stand any thing. An' no matter how hard you worked in the day, or how hot it was, it was always so cool an' nice at night; you could sleep anywheres—on the ground or on a pile o' limbs, in the house or out o' doors, an' never catch cold.

"But if the country was like heaven, the folks was like the other place, I reckon. Such sights—such doins'! I'd never 'a believed men would carry on so. I went to minin' in the Amador, an' first they wasn't a woman in a hundred miles. And when one did come in one day on a wagon, the men all run to look at her as if she was a show. Better she'd a' stayed away, an' twenty more like her that come in when the diggins begun to pan out rich. I believe every woman was the cause o' fifty fights an' one or two deaths. It made me mad to see men fight about 'em, when they knowed jest what they was—men that had mothers an' sisters back in the States, an' some on 'em sweethearts an' wives. They was mostly Mexican women, an' some Chilaynos an' South Spainers; an' somehow it was a sort o' comfort to me that there was hardly ever an American woman among the lot.

"Bimeby these diggins sort o' worked out, an' I went down on Tuolumne, an' then mined about Angells an' Murphy's Camp, an' finally to Sonora. Then all sorts o' new ways o' minin' come in, but they took capital, an' I let 'em alone. Men was all the time runnin' about from camp to camp—so many new excitements—no matter how rich the ground where we was, some feller would come in with a big story about a new gulch, an' away they'd go. I've seen a thousand men at work along one creek, an' a big excitement break out, an' before night they wouldn't be twenty left. Sometimes a man would get title to big ground, an' hold it at a thousand dollars, an' when the rush come you could buy him out with two mules an' a pair o' blankets. Many an' many a time I've seen a man go off that way with a little money an' never be seen alive. Like enough his body was found away down the river, an' like enough it was never found. It got so they was men there that would cut a throat for ten dollars. It wasn't all one way, though. More'n once the robbers would tackle some gritty man that was handy with his 'barkers,' an' he'd get away with two or three of 'em. Every body carried the irons with him, ready to pop at a minute's notice, an' if a man traveled alone, he took his life in his hand.

"It wa'nt long though till we got some kind o' government. Californy was made a State the year after I got there, but that didn't signify in the mountains; an' at Angell's Camp we chipped in together and hired regular guards to look after every suspicious man. The worst thing was to get down from the mines to Frisco; for if it was known that a man was a goin' to leave, it was 'sposed he'd made his pile, an' had it with him. At last I made a little raise—that was in the spring of '52—an' concluded to come home. Me an' my partner jest laid down our tools one night right where we worked, an' packed up, an' when the camp was asleep lit out over the hills 'thout sayin' a word to any human bein.' Got home 'round by Panama all right, an' found every thing chipper, an' when I figured up I was just three hundred a head on the three year's trip. Better stayed at home *for gold*—but it saved the boys."

"Then you stayed at home and took comfort for the rest of your life, I suppose."

There was dead silence. The "old woman" rose and retired to the other cabin; the youths had long before ascended the ladder which led to their bed in the garret, and my host seemed to have finished. But it was evident there was something more, and it was the most painful part of his story. The old wall-sweep clock struck nine in a loud, aggressive tone, which roused the old man, and he resumed in a different manner—a mingling of regret and indignation:

"It was a bad thing, a mighty bad thing, for old Tennessee, when the Whig party died. I felt in my bones no good could come of it. But I didn't think it would touch me so close as it did. I knowed trouble would come, but couldn't see jist how. You know all about that. Our folks was all agin the war from the start. I was down at Manchester the day they hauled down the stars an' stripes, an' sez I, 'Men, you've bit off more'n you can chaw;' an' they laughed at me. But I knowed them Northern men—seed 'em in Californy. Slow, mighty slow, to start a fight, but awful to hold on.

"But I sha'n't dwell on this. In less'n three months, sir, both my boys was in it. I held up a year or more; then come both armies sweepin' South, an' what our folks left the Federals took. I thought to make a crop yet, an' fixed up a good deal; then come both armies back north'rd agin an' swep' me clean. But my old woman an' the girls turned out an' helped, an' in '63 we 'scaped a long time. Then they come South agin, an' we give it up. I really believed they'd drive each other back an' for'rd there for years. Next year I got up one mornin', an' there was a letter stuck under the door by some gew-rillers, an' it said both my boys was bad shot, an' in the hospital at Atlanta. I felt death in my bosom right then. But I sha'n't dwell on this. An hour after sundown I was off on the only hoss we had left, an' by daylight I was in the sand-hills along the Tennessee. The country was full o' soldiers, but I got round all of 'em an' to Atlanta. It was no good—no good. Men was dyin' all round, an' families broke up an' scattered, an' women an' children naked an' starvin'! What was my troubles to them? The boys was fur gone, an' no medicines an' nothin' to help 'em could be got It was a might o' comfort, though, to see 'em 'fore they died, an' take back some keepsakes to their mother. Oh, stranger, that war was a powerful sight o' trouble to us all!

"They was buried, along with hundreds of others, an' I was gettin' ready to start back, when up steps a chap, an' sez he, 'Old man, we want *you*—can't spare a man now that can shoot.' An' I jist had a chance to send word home, an' then took the place my oldest boy had; an' nigh a year after, when that regiment give in to old Sherman, I was one of the thirty-six—all that was left of a big regiment.

"* * * I found my folks at a neighbors, but on my place they wasn't a stick nor a rail. I hadn't the heart to try it there agin. We got word that my wife's mother had died in the Cherokee Nation, an' left a good claim; so I turned over the Tennessee land to my son-in-law (he married my only girl), an' had him take the other grand-children, too, an' he outfitted us for the Nation.

"My wife proved up on her Cherokee blood, an' I was let in under their law as bein' married to a Cherokee that had head-rights, an' we took her mother's place. Nice fixed up, too, it was, on Grand River, jist across from Fort Gibson, an' there my grandsons that come with us made two crops, an' then all at once the troubles about the Cherokees started up again. I turned cold 'round the heart when I heard it—I did want rest so bad. Then I looked back only forty years, to the time when all the country, from Tennessee here, was wild, an' President, Congress, an' all said if the Cherokees would only come out here they wouldn't be bothered for ages an' ages, an' now this country's older 'n Tennessee was then. Neither did any man own his land in the Cherokee Nation; it was common, an' we owned jist the improvements. So I took a good long look at the matter, an' sez I, 'Once more, Natie, dear (that's my wife), we've got to go once more; this is too good a country for Injins to keep if white men want it, an' you can swear they will long 'fore we die.'

"So I traded that claim for this piece up here, an' my grandsons stuck, an' I guess we'll get along. What I dread more'n any thing is another war."

"Why, what reason have you to dread it?"

"'Burnt child,' you know. All my life I've been a man of peace, an' yet every fuss that come up hurt me. Three times I've been broke up an' ruined by wars an' troubles I had no hand in bringin' on. *Don't you think they'll keep peace while I live?*"

There was for a brief moment a new look in his eye—the eager, pleading look of a hunted animal. I reassured him, and his face resumed its usual air of placid humor and homely philosophy.

"The story's about done. Hope I hav'nt bored you. It's a sorter queer world, aint it? Sometimes I think it jist *was to be so*, an' no help, an' sometimes I conceit I ought to done better; but anyhow, all I git outen the whole of my experience is that a man must keep peggin' away. But you're noddin'. Better you go to sleep early." And directing me to the ladder, this uncomplaining heir of adverse fortune sought his bed in the other cabin.

Here was a man who had traveled over half the continent, been farmer, boatman, miner, soldier, and Indian trader, and never imagined that he had done more than his duty. Perhaps there is no moral to be extracted from his story; yet it somehow seems to me one on which discontented respectability, cushioned in an easy chair, might profitably ponder.

CHAPTER III.

THE JOURNEY TO UTAH.

It was an era of change and fierce excitement. Omaha was in her speculative period. Daily hundreds of adventurous fortune-seekers set out for the mountains, and daily the refluent tide landed half as many of the returning—a very few fortunate beyond their hopes, many about as well off as when they started, and quite as many utterly bankrupt. Such a country could not but develop strange characters; a man either failed, lost hope, and sank into a "floater," or developed an amazing capacity for lighting on his feet at every fall.

There, for instance, was my friend Will Wylie, who had seen the elephant in its entirety, from trunk to tail. He went out in 1862, and "struck it rich" on his first venture in the mines of Montana; started with teams and wagons to California, and on the way was robbed of every ounce of his "dust" by the then swarming "road agents." They kindly left him his stock, with which he got through to California, and thence made a highly successful trip to Arizona. There he turned his means into a freighting company, and beguiled the lonesome hours

HIS LAST CHANCE.

of his long drives over mountains and deserts by calculating his certain wealth and early return to the States. When near Fort Whipple, and not three hours ride from a well-manned United States post, the Apaches attacked his train, stampeded all his stock but the mule he rode, and burnt all his property they could not carry off. By the light of his blazing wagons he fled, with an arrow sticking in his cheek; his frightened animal ran till it dropped dead, but fortunately not till it had carried him into the quadrangle of the fort. He was picked up insensible, and in six weeks was out again with the loss of one eye. Returning to Montana, he joined the Vigilantes, and had the pleasure of presiding at a "neck-tie sociable" where two of the men who had robbed him were hanged. Some more "dust" was obtained out of the old claim in which he still held an interest, and in 1867 he came down on the Union Pacific as a trader. He had what he called a "big biz" at each successive terminus town, and was now in Omaha to buy a "little bill" of ten thousand dollars' worth of provisions, tobacco and "bitters" for the new metropolis beyond Cheyenne. Three years after I found him away up in the mountains of Utah, where he had put all his available means in a new and half-developed mine, and was sinking on the vein with tireless energy, in the daily hope of striking a *bonanza*. These hopeful ones rarely make the most money, but without them when would the Great West ever have been developed?

There, too, was Jim Garraway (who, however, will never recognize himself by this name), born and reared a gambler—never knew much else from boyhood. His father, companions, friends, all were gamblers; as a baby he played with faro checks, and learned English in the atmosphere of pool rooms. At twenty gaming was his infatuation. Now he had thoroughly reformed, never touched a card, and was in a responsible position in Wells, Fargo & Co.'s employ. Two years after he surprised me by a call at my office in Corinne, Utah. He was freighting thence to Montana, the owner of mules and wagons worth five thousand dollars. One evening, when idle time hung heavy on his hands, he strayed into one of our "sporting rooms." The smooth-spoken proprietor who so styled it, might have added, "What is sport to us is death to you," for Jim's old infatuation returned. He staked a pile of "chips" and won; then made and lost, and made and lost alternately, selling his stock when "broke," and scarcely ate or slept till the tail of his last mule was "coppered on the jack."

Repentant and returning Mormons were numerous, but seldom noisy. One I met who had been back and forth, in and out of the Church, three times. Now he declared with profane emphasis that this was the last time; he had seen enough. One little party of a hundred recusant Saints, of all ages from six months to seventy years, had made the journey in primitive style with slow and patient ox-teams, all the adults walking. They had left Salt Lake Valley as soon as the cañons were clear of snow, and been three months on the road. Their condition was wretched; for in those days, under the iron-clad laws of Utah, no apostate ever got out of the Territory with any thing worth leaving. The Mormon priesthood taught the apostolic doctrine of "laying on of hands," and, the dissenters added, what they laid hands on they generally got away with. These people were destined to a "Josephite" settlement in Iowa, and at Council Bluffs they met three hundred new converts on their way to Utah, in charge of a bishop and platoon of elders. But there was very little intercourse between the two. The latter were fresh, hopeful, cheery, singing the "songs of Zion," and rejoicing in their speedy escape from "Babylon;" the recusants sad, weary, half mad and wholly heartsick. Quick to curse Brigham, they were yet but half cured of their folly, and prepared to surrender mind and conscience to another phase of the same delusion. The elders watched their new recruits without appearing to do so, and at sight of the others were full of warnings and allusions to Demas and those who kept not the faith, and

"LAYING ON OF HANDS."

were given over to be damned. In those days most of the dissenting Saints left Utah; now they remain, and with the skeptical young Mormons are building up a party which is very troublesome to Brigham.

Council Bluffs was once almost a Mormon town, and many places in the vicinity were settled entirely by that sect. Apostates by thousands are scattered through Iowa, in faith "half Mormon and half nothing," but in practice good and industrious citizens. Mormonism does not make a man a fanatic, unless he goes where the Church has the majority and rules the country. Florence, six miles above Omaha, with as pretty a site as I saw in Nebraska, was the original winter quarters of the main body in their great exodus; and according to the sanguine belief of the Gentiles who succeeded them, was to have been the great city instead of Omaha. It had the start, and no man can say why it should not have held it. But there is a mysterious law which governs the location of great cities, and Florence is now only a pretty suburb to the metropolis of Nebraska.

The last of July, 1868, I took the evening train for Laramie, then the terminus of the Union Pacific Railroad. For a hundred and fifty miles from Omaha the Platte Valley, which the road follows, is one of the richest in the world. Then a change begins, and the country is higher, dryer, and more barren with every hour's travel toward the mountains. It is all the way up-hill. Omaha is 912 feet above sea-level; Cheyenne

5,600; and through all that long incline of 525 miles, the road-bed maintains a nearly uniform up-grade of ten feet to the mile. At a few places it sinks to a level, and for two short stages there is a down grade westward: from the Omaha level to the Platte Valley, and from the "divide" down to Crow Creek, on which Cheyenne is situated. Nature evidently designed this valley for a railroad route. The Indian had used it from time immemorial; the *voyageur* and trapper trailed it for a hundred years before California was known in the East; then the gold-hunters, Oregon settlers and Mormons turned the trail into a broad wagon road, and lastly came the railroad, obedient to the same necessities for water and a smooth route. West of Loup Fork we found the soil a little more sandy, and the grass shorter, with a dry and withered look; and this change went on till at last we saw the heavy verdure of the Missouri Valley no more, and were introduced to the bunched and seeded grasses of the high plains and Rocky Mountains. North Platte, where we took breakfast, was once a roaring terminus "city;" now a way station, with hotel and saloon attachment. Julesburg, 377 miles out, had been a busy city of 5,000 inhabitants; now it was a wilderness of blackened chimneys and falling *adobe* walls, the debris of a dead metropolis. In the old days of the overland stage, one Julia, a Cherokee exile, kept the station hotel there; and in the cheerful frankness of Western life the place was known as "Dirty Jule's Ranche." Thence "Jule's," and finally Julesburg. Similarly "Robber's Roost" has been softened to Roosaville, and "Black Bills" to Blackville. For three hundred miles we follow the course of the Platte, a broad but dirty and uninviting stream, differing only from a slough in having a swift current. Often a mile wide, but with no more water than would fill an average canal, three inches of fluid running on top of several feet of moving quicksand; too thin to walk on, too thick to drink, too shallow for navigation, too deep for safe fording, too yellow to wash in, and too pale to paint with, it is the most disappointing and useless river in America. Nevertheless, many attempts have been made to navigate it, all ending in disaster. Notable among these was the venture of a party of hunters from New England, who started from Laramie in the spring of 1843 to run two flats loaded with furs to St. Louis. After two months arduous toil, often unloading and dragging their boats over sand-bars, they at last abandoned them, *cached* the property, and walked to Council Bluffs, where they arrived in July, nearly dead from fatigue and starvation.

Three hundred miles out, and the plains in all their vastness are around us. The land rises into long ridges, stretching away swell on swell as far as the eye can reach, as if the heaving ocean had suddenly become firm fixed earth; and immense pampas spread away alternating flint and gravel with strips of wiry, curly grass, or at rare intervals a protected growth of stunted shrubs. Only the lowest vales contain any cultivable land, and that, to be productive, requires irrigation; the bright flowers of the Missouri Valley are seen no more, the lark-spur alone retaining its hues; the wild sunflower and yellow saffron become dust-hued and dwarfish, while milk-weed and resin-weed sustain a sort of dying life, and cling with sickly hold to the harsh and forbid-

"THE GOOD OLD TIME."

ding soil. Now appear depressed basins, with saline matter dried upon the soil, and long flats white with alkali, as if they had been sowed with lime. This is the "Great American Desert" of early geographers, a region practically worthless to the agriculturist, though half its surface is of some value for grazing. Antelope and prairie dog show themselves in considerable numbers, but it is too late for the buffalo; the main line of their northward migration passed two months before, nor are they to be seen as in the good old time the hunters tell about. I shall not inflict upon the reader the standard description of these animals, much less the account of dog, owl and rattlesnake as a happy family in one burrow; for this is meant to be a veracious chronicle, and though I have since spent many hours in "dog-towns," I do not *know* such association to be a fact.

Passing the last and worst stage of the barren plains, we run down into the little oasis on Crow Creek, and to the "Magic City" of Cheyenne. Its rapid rise and mad career had given it a national fame. On the 3d of July, 1867, the first house was erected; on the 1st of November there was a population of 7,000, with a city government, a municipal debt, and three daily papers. When spring dissolved the snow banks and ice-packs from Sherman summit, the railroad pushed on; Laramie became the metropolis, and Cheyenne sank to a quiet town of perhaps 1,200 people. Its further decay was arrested by the development of sheep-ranching, and its location as the junction of the Denver Pacific; and now as the capital of Wyoming and most convenient outfitting point for the Black Hills, it looks forward to another era of prosperity.

While I rested a few days at Cheyenne, the railroad was rapidly pushing westward, and soon another "metropolis" was laid off beyond Laramie. From Cheyenne the road bed is nearly level to Hazard Station, officially pronounced the eastern base of the Rocky Mountains; and thence the grade rises eighty feet per mile to Sherman, 8,342 feet above sea-level, and highest point on the Union Pacific. Beyond that we have the magnificent scenery of Granite Cañon and Virginia Dale, the last now seeming peaceful as an Arcadian dell, but with as bloody a history as any spot in the Rocky Mountains. In the olden time it was the favorite abode of land pirates, and every ravine in the vicinity was the scene of a murder. Thence the road makes a sharp bend to the north, and we run rapidly downward for forty miles to the new city of Laramie, already past its greatness, and many of its inhabitants leaving for the next "metropolis." Laramie Plains, though 7,000 feet above sea-level, abound in rich pastures; but westward the grassy slopes yield rapidly to barrenness, and at Medicine Bow we enter fairly on the three-hundred-mile desert. In the worst part of this waste we found Benton, the great terminus town, six hundred and ninety-eight miles from Omaha. Far as eye could see around the town, there was not a green tree, shrub, or spear of grass. The red hills, scorched and bare as if blasted by the lightnings of an angry God, bounded the white basin on the north and east, while to the south and west spread the gray desert till it was interrupted by another range of red and yellow hills. The whole basin looked as if it might originally have been filled with lye and sand, then dried to the consistency of hard soap, with glistening surface, tormenting alike to eye and sense.

Yet here had sprung up in two weeks—as if by the touch of Aladdin's Lamp—a city of three thousand people; there were regular squares arranged into five wards, a city government of mayor and aldermen, a daily paper, and a volume of municipal ordinances. It was the end of the freight and passenger, and beginning of the construction division; twice every day immense trains arrived and departed, and stages left for Utah, Montana and Idaho. All the goods formerly hauled across the plains came here by rail, and were reshipped, and for ten hours daily the streets were thronged with motley crowds of railroad men, Mexicans and Indians, gamblers, "cappers," and saloon-keepers, merchants, miners, and mule-whackers. The streets were eight inches deep in white dust as I entered the city of canvas tents and pole-houses; the suburbs appeared as banks of dirty white lime, and a new arrival with black clothes looked like nothing so much as a cockroach struggling through a flour barrel.

"ONLY A MEMORY."

Benton is only a memory now. A section house by the road-side, a few piles of adobes, tin cans and other debris mark the site where sales to the amount of millions were made in two months. The genesis and evolution of these evanescent railroad cities was from the overland trade. Two hundred thousand people in Colorado, Utah, Montana and Idaho had to be supplied from the States, and every ounce of freight sent them was formerly hauled from six to sixteen hundred miles. This trade successively built up Independence, Westport, Kansas City, Atchison, Leavenworth and Omaha; but as soon as the Union Pacific was started it took that route. Hence those "roaring towns" at the successive termini, which sprang up like Jonah's gourd, and in most cases withered away as suddenly when the road passed on. First on the list was Columbus, Nebraska, and then Fort Kearney, where George Francis Train confidently located the geographical center of the United States, and future capital, and invested his money and his hopes. Kearney is now a prosperous country village and Train a harmless lunatic. North Platte suddenly rose from a bare sand bank to a city of 4,000 people, with banks, insurance offices and city government, an aristocracy and common people, old settlers and first families. Three months after it consisted, in the sarcastic language of the Julesburgers, of a hotel, two saloons, a bakery, section-house and another saloon. Then came Julesburg, the wickedest city on the list. For sixty-three days there was a homicide every day; ten dance houses ran all night, and thirty saloons paid license to the evanescent corporation.

The rise culminated at Cheyenne; thenceforward Laramie, Benton, Green River City and Bryan grew successively smaller, and Bear River City closed the chapter with a carnival of crime ending in a pitched battle between citizens and roughs, in which twelve men were killed and twenty wounded. But the history would be incomplete without the annals of Wahsatch, built upon the summit of Wasatch Mountains, 7,000 feet above the sea, in ten days of January, 1869, while the mercury ranged from zero to ten degrees below. Despite the intense cold, the sound of hammer and saw was heard day and night, and restaurants were fitted up in such haste that meals were served while the carpenters were putting on the second thickness of weatherboarding. I ate my first breakfast there in one where the mercury stood at five degrees below zero! A drop of the hottest coffee spilled upon the cloth froze in a minute, while gravy and butter solidified in spite of the swiftest eater.

It was a "wicked city." During its lively existence of three months it established a graveyard with forty-three occupants, of whom not one died of disease. Some were killed by accident; a few got drunk and were frozen; three were hanged, and several killed in a fight or murdered; one "girl" stifled herself with charcoal fumes, and another inhaled sweet death from subtle chloroform.

Transactions in real estate in all these towns were, of course, most uncertain; and every thing that looked solid was a sham. Red brick fronts, brown stone fronts, and stuccoed walls, were found to have been made to order in Chicago, and shipped in (pine) sections. Ready-made houses were finally sent out in lots, boxed, marked and numbered; half a dozen men could erect a block in a day, and two boys with screw-drivers put up a "habitable dwelling" in three hours. A very good gray-stone stucco front, with plain sides, twenty by forty tent, could be had for three hundred dollars; and if one's business happened to desert him, or the town moved on, he only had to take his store to pieces, ship it on a platform car to the next city, and set up again. There was a pleasing versatility of talent in the population of such towns.

To return to Benton. The Mormon converts were going forward

in large parties; 4,000 left Europe for Utah in 1868, that being the largest emigration of any year since the Church was founded. The number of arrivals now scarcely equals that of the apostates. Freighting to Salt Lake was also active, and teamsters being in demand, I took a position as engineer of a six-mule team, at a salary of forty dollars per month. Our "outfit" numbered ten wagons, sixty-one mules and sixteen men, including a night-herder, wagon-boss and four passengers. The four hundred miles to Salt Lake occupied four weeks, two-thirds of the way being through deserts of sand, soda and alkali, where we thought ourselves fortunate in finding a patch of bunch-grass once every twenty-four hours. The first night we formed *corral* at Rawlins Springs, and the next in a walled basin on the old stage road, at what is called "Dug Springs." In the center of the basin was an alkaline lake which, moved by the evening breeze, looked like foaming soapsuds; but on its margin was a spring of pure water. Thence we moved on to the "Divide of the Continent," a plateau of sand and rock, dotted with alkaline lakes in which "cat-fish with legs," as plainsmen style them, are abundant. I afterward saw the same species at Cañon Bonito, Arizona, where the Navajo boys shot their arrows through them to secure me a few specimens. Science classes them as *siredons*, a species of lizards.

Leaving this unpleasant country by way of Bridger's Pass, we were soon upon the westward slope, and for three days toiled down Bitter Creek—the horror of overland teamsters—where all possible ills of western travel are united. At daybreak we rose, stiff with cold, to catch the only temperate hour for driving. By nine A. M. the heat was most exhausting. The road was worked up into a bed of blinding white dust by the laborers on the railroad grade, and a gray mist of ash and earthy powder hung over the valley, which obscured the sun, but did not lessen its heat. At intervals the "Twenty-mile Desert," the "Red Sand Desert," and the "White Desert" crossed our way, presenting beds of sand and soda, through which the half-choked men and animals toiled and struggled, in a dry air and under a scorching sky. In vain the yells and curses of the teamsters doubled and redoubled, blasphemies that one might expect to inspire a mule with diabolical strength; in vain the fearful "black-snake" curled and popped over the animals' backs, sometimes gashing the skin, and sometimes raising welts the size of one's finger. For a few rods they would struggle on, dragging the heavy load through the clogging banks, and then stop exhausted, sinking to their knees in the hot and ashy heaps. Then two of us would unite our teams and drag through to the next solid piece of ground, where, for a few hundred yards, the wind had removed the loose heaps, and left bare the flinty and gravelly subsoil. Thus, by most exhausting labor, we accomplished ten or twelve miles a day. Half an hour or more of temperate coolness then gave us respite till soon after sundown, when the cold wind came down, as if in heavy volumes, from the snowy range, and tropic heat was succeeded by arctic cold with amazing suddenness. On the 27th of August my mules were exhausted with heat; that night ice formed in our buckets as thick as a pane of glass.

Thence across Green River we found Bridger Plains and the valley of Bear River delightful by comparison, and at noon of September 4th passed the summit of the Wasatch and entered Echo Cañon. Two days we traveled down this great ravine, enjoying a succession of romantic views—sometimes down in the very bed of the stream, and sometimes far up the rocky sides of the cliff, where the "dug-way" wound in and out along the projecting "benches." Emerging thence into Weber Valley, we came upon the first gardens and cultivated fields I had seen for a thousand miles. The Mormon dwellings would have appeared poor and mean indeed in the States, but to one just from the barren plains the valley was pretty enough. The railroad now runs down Weber Cañon, but we followed the old stage and wagon road southward up the Weber and over the divide into Parley's Park.

PULPIT ROCK: ECHO CAÑON.

Thence down the wild gorge known as Parleys Cañon, where every turn brings to view a fresh delight in the sublime and beautiful; and out upon the "bench," on the evening of September 9th, we saw the great valley of Jordan, and the Salt Lake spreading far to the north and west. Twenty miles westward the Oquirrh Range glowed in the clear air, a shining mass of blue and white. Great Salt Lake extended beyond our sight to the northward, its surface glistening in the light of the declining sun, while to our right the "City of the Saints" as yet appeared but a white spot on the landscape. To our left the cañon of the Jordan seemed to close, giving the impression that that stream poured from the hills, while down the center of the valley the river shone like a glimmering band of silver. A little farther and I marked the great dome of the Tabernacle, and then the smaller buildings of Salt Lake City, rise out of the evening mirage, with only the interest of a traveler, and little thinking of the years in which that was to be my home, or in what mysterious ways I was to be identified with its social and political combats.

THE GREAT SALT LAKE, UTAH.

But before I enter on the hackneyed themes of Utah and Mormonism, allow me, indulgent reader, to relieve the tedium of a merely personal narrative by giving the story of one who sought the Western Wilds from more heroic motives than mine.

CHAPTER IV.

GEFFROY'S TRIALS.

WE sat, my partner Robert Geffroy and I, upon the rocky slope of Griffith Mountain, that looks down upon Georgetown, Colorado. Two thousand feet below us the city seemed sunk in a great cleft in the earth; around it rose on all sides precipitous mountains, their summits still covered with snow, though the June sun shone warm upon them, and the little pools fed by rivulets from the snow banks were bordered by bright flowers. At our feet the brawling brook formed a clear pool, the usual resting place of those who walked to the summit; a little below it plunged by a series of musical cascades into a granite cañon, and was lost among the foot hills. While our side of the mountain was still in shadow, beyond the town the line of shade and morning sunlight crept slowly down the face of Republican Mountain. My companion gazed long and earnestly upon the sublime scenery with that gentle melancholy which habitually shaded his fine countenance. At length his dark eye, beautiful with the clear depth peculiar to the Swiss mountaineer, moistened a little, and he fell into one of his rare poetical moods. I had shared with him the vicissitudes of a miner's life, and had found the usually taciturn man of some fifty years a most pleasing companion. Never intemperate, as were so many of the older miners, never garrulous or boastful, there were yet times when some undercurrent of intense thought bubbled to the surface; then, in free converse in our cabin, he was the most fascinating of men. His language, with just enough of foreign accent,

"WE SAT UPON THE ROCKY SLOPE OF GRIFFITH MOUNTAIN."

was that of one who had learned it from books rather than men; his musical voice gave utterance to sentences loaded with poetic thoughts, and his lightest remark would have borne the test of severest criticism. To me he seemed a man of naturally ardent temperament and high aims, but thwarted and long repressed, with mind turned perhaps to unhealthful introspection. But to-day he was in an unusual mood; he had just passed through one of his seasons of deep sadness, and, as it were, unconsciously, sought relief in friendly confidences. A light remark from me on the many uncertainties and disappointments of a miner's life led us on to a free discussion of the vexed questions of free will and destiny.

"Are we," he asked, "indeed the authors of our course? do we succeed by our own endeavors or fail by our own errors? or is there a chain of circumstances running concurrent with our daily lives, and ever shaping them to alien issues?"

I defended with vehemence my views that we all make or mar our own fortunes. He listened calmly, and replied:

"Hear, then, my story, and learn how often the great movements of war and politics crush the humblest lives, and that not his own acts merely, but the acts of all his contemporaries, determine one's destiny."

Thus began a series of confidences, which, continued some evenings in our cabin, gave me the incidents of an eventful though humble life.

*　　*　　*　　*　　*　　*　　*

"I am, as you know, a native of beautiful Geneva, and my first recollections are of grand mountains, mirror-like lakes, and old monuments. Mine was a childhood of rare happiness. My Swiss mother united to the earnest vigor of her race that wondrous insight into the nature and feelings of childhood, which seems a special gift of God to the German people. My French father, while he had none of that levity or cynic indifference to all religions which so many of that race affect, was yet happily free from superstition, jealous of priestcraft, and, for one in his position, quite a devotee of learning. From our English visitors and customers I early acquired a smattering of their language, and some vague ideas of that liberty which I then, in childish ignorance, supposed they enjoyed.

"Our family life is now present to my memory as a happy union of social love and intellect. My father recited the poems of Racine and Corneille, my mother rehearsed the fairy legends of her people; both delighted in the heroic annals of the Genevese, and loved to dwell on the better days of that people. Around us was the sublime scenery of Switzerland; our associations were largely with cultivated travelers, and poetry was inwrought with my childish nature. But my father was still Frenchman enough to be given to the contemplation of vast systems of social philosophy—that peculiarly French philosophy which takes great and comprehensive principles on trust, and believes that man, once they are taught him, charmed by their beauty and symmetry, will gladly embrace them. The federation of the world, the equalization of conditions, the abolition of poverty—these were the themes that charmed his leisure hours, when not employed in the struggle to further increase the inequality that was already great between him and his poorer neighbors. How pleasing is that philosophy by which great principles are first to be established, upon which society and government are to be constructed like geometrical figures, and people modeled to fit and adopt them; but how much more practical and sensible that cautious progress of your people and the English, which is taught by events, and is sometimes willing to learn humbly at the tribunal of facts.

"On such a nature as mine the daily hearing of these things had momentous influence. Had I been bred to trade, it might have gone well. Commerce would have corrected the errors of an overheated imagination, and contact with men as they are, proved a healthful corrective to too much contemplation of them as they might be. But my ambitious parents, who were vastly improved in circumstances by the prosperous years that succeeded the general peace, and the return tide of English travel, determined to bestow upon their only son a classical education, at that day in Geneva thought to be the key to all preferments in church or state. Even now I feel a pang at what must have been the keenness of their disappointment. Once entered upon my classical studies, a new world was opened to my impressible mind. Mythology I found but dull—how *could* so grand a people have believed in such filthy deities?—but the heroes of classic annals set my very soul on fire. Could it be that such men had lived—men that died by battalions for the honor of their country, or ran upon their swords rather than survive her liberty? I panted as I read, I breathed the very spirit of Livy; I shed tears over what other school-boys called the dull pages of Tacitus. In moments of such enthusiasm, I had but to close my eyes and recite the sonorous lines, and at once before me rushed the awful pageant of the returning conqueror: his triumphal car, the captured enemies of his country walking behind it, the blare of trumpets, the tramp of victorious legions, while the welkin rang with the shouts of Roman thousands. I struggled with the patriots of Thermopylæ, I defended the bridge with Horatius, with Dentalus

I bared my breast to traitors, I ran upon my sword in the despair of Brutus.

"But when I read the bright annals of Geneva's better days, it was as though I had breathed an intoxicating incense; and in the Reformation I found a vein of antique heroism. Calvin, Pascal, the Waldense, the Albigense, I wept over their sorrows and trials, was warmed with their struggles, and glad in their triumphs. Not their religion, but the exaltation of their patriotism excited me. How dull, then, seemed the common-place life of our trading town, how mean its petty economies; and how unworthy the destiny my parents had so fondly imagined for me. The beautiful land and city which patriot reformers had early saved from papal Rome, now seemed given up to the gods of materialism and sold wholly to the commercial Satan. I was blinded to the heroism of common life—the true greatness of the many who daily toil and suffer for those they love.

"Before reaching my eighteenth year I fully determined to seek a land where political systems were yet to be developed, and might be modeled upon abstract equity. I would be a citizen of the Republic of Humanity. But where was such a land to be found? The revolution of 1830 had only resulted in giving France another king; and their so-called moderate monarchy I looked upon with abhorrence. Like my classic models, I believed the very name of king incompatible with freedom. England was still less tolerable. I associated it with all that was hateful in titles and hereditary privileges. The New World was the place to look for the Brotherhood of Man; for the very air of Europe was poisoned with priestcraft, and its soil barren of high resolve. The South American States were struggling toward an autonomy, but, with the subtle instinct of the Teutonic blood, I distrusted the lofty professions of a Latin race. Their short-lived liberty demonstrated an inherent incapacity to respect the individual right, and their young republic was only old despotism under new names and forms. Republics, I was persuaded, could not coexist with priests; for with their politics I had nearly rejected my people's religion.

"With the little sum I could gain by long pleading with my parents, I sought this republic, persuaded that here, when one met a man, he met a brother.

"Need I say that I was cruelly disappointed. Without nobility, there was almost equal caste; and without old families, there was equal tyranny in the new. Wealth and color made classes as widely divergent as rank and birth, and in the boasted land of liberty, one-tenth of the whole population were bondsmen. The republic was ruled by an oligarchy of slaveholders, and along the same paths trod by Washington, black men were chased by republicans, or torn by blood-hounds, for the crime of seeking freedom, in sight of the very school-houses where boys declaimed in praise of William Tell. I visited the various communes, where a few enthusiastic spirits had sought to establish the Human Brotherhood on a basis of perfect equality. At New Harmony I found the short-lived experiment already a failure. Communia was even less satisfactory. The religious communes I found intolerable from their plentiful lack of common sense; and in the others observed a grossness of conception that raised in my mind a wonder, not that they failed, but that they should ever have been established. I turned my steps toward Nauvoo, then rising into prominence as the last and greatest attempt to establish a religious brotherhood. But there I found all the evils of the old systems, with few of their corresponding benefits: priestcraft without its paternal care, greed without a thought of future reckoning insuring the defeat of its own aims, and a fanaticism which scorned the commonest suggestions of prudence. That such a community would soon or late come into conflict with the neighboring Americans, was certain.

"From Nauvoo, in the early months of 1842, I visited St. Louis, meeting there an agent of the American Fur Company, with whom I took employment. I was nearly cured of my early dreams, but still hoped that a land might be found where humanity would have a fairer chance, and rank and wealth confer no greater power than morals and intellect. I sought the Western Wilds to commune with nature in her unbroken solitudes, convinced that there, at least, the few residents were as brothers. But humanity's weakness is common alike to the city and the desert. On the vast plains, and amid the majestic mountains, wherever man meets man, the struggle goes on even more fiercely, though not more earnestly, than beneath the smooth surface of urban society. Every-where the strong and ambitious are struggling to the front, the weak and unskillful falling to the rear. Under the pressure of common danger or common want, the pioneers do indeed become as brothers, for the safety of each is the good of all; but the danger passed or the want supplied, egotism asserts itself even more fiercely for its temporary repression. Even as you have seen the unhurt buffaloes gore a wounded mate to death, lest its struggles and bellowings attract the beast of prey, so the rushing crowd can not pause, lest he who is up to-day go down to-morrow.

"February, 1843, found me at Fort Lancaster on the Platte, without any particular aim. There I met Colonel Warfield, in the service of the young republic of Texas, bearing a commission adorned with the bold signature of Sam Houston, President. I was then twenty-two years of age, and seriously debating with myself whether I should not gladden the hearts of my parents by a return to the sober life of Geneva. A few years had done wonders for me. Practical life had taught me to dream no more of the Brotherhood of Man; that liberty and progress are to be secured by no cunningly devised schemes, but earned by slow and toilsome steps of the individual, and that priestcraft and despotism can not be argued out, but must be suffered out. But I saw more clearly that a free republic, with all its faults, is still the best attainable government, and a brief acquaintance with Colonel Warfield revived much of my old enthusiasm. The Texans had freed themselves from the tyrannous domination of another race, and were struggling toward a more perfect liberty, and instinctively I sympathized with them. With heightened color and eye glowing with patriotic ardor, Colonel Warfield recounted the undying glories of the Alamo, where Crockett, Travis and their brave companions died fighting to the last; of Goliad, Corpus Christi and San Jacinto. It was to me the classic age restored. Heroes walked the earth again. There were giants in that land and in those days. But when he unfolded the bullet-riddled flag that had waved over Corpus Christi, and told of the brave men who there died beneath its folds, I was filled with zeal to emulate their heroism.

"When he called for volunteers, a start only was needed, and, following my example, a dozen men promptly enrolled their names. We were to be part of a volunteer company of riflemen, the remainder to join us at the rendezvous just beyond the Arkansas, on the Rio de las Animas, in what was then Mexican territory. We were to act as a corps of observation to assist the main army, then on its way from Texas, and were enlisted for nine months, each man to furnish his own horse, gun, and accoutrements. The others accompanied Colonel Warfield at once, but settlement with the company detained me ten days, and I set out alone on the 9th of March. A snow-storm had raged for a week, and, with a great deal of suffering, I made my way alone to the mouth of the Fontaine Que Bouille, and thence, with a single companion, to the rendezvous. Disappointment awaited me. The expected detachment from the States had not arrived, and our whole force numbered but twenty-four men—adventurers, apparently, from every clime under heaven, and well supplied as to arms and horses. They were uniformed in dazzling variety, but in one respect harmoniously—a uniform of furs, blankets, and rags!

62   WESTERN WILDS.

"If I was amazed at the appearance of these patriots, how much more was I confounded by their language! Can I record their conversation, their absurd views of political morality, their desires, their hopes! A few were, I trust, like myself, acting from pure love of liberty, a few for the good of the republic, more from a hope of gain, and most from the pure abandon of Western character. But from the eyes of all gleamed a good nature that gave hope of social comfort and safety among them, while the cheerful frankness with which they spoke of their past indicated too plainly that a few of them felt more comfortable

TO THE RENDEZVOUS.

beyond the reach of legal process. One young man, whose conversation showed some culture, evinced great anxiety to form a junction with the main army, and penetrate at once into the Mexican settlements—and no wonder. I afterwards learned that he had left St. Louis impromptu, somewhat in arrears in his accounts with a bank in which he had been employed. His most intimate companion was equally eager for an early advance. The friends of a lady in Ohio, he frankly stated, had given him a great deal of trouble—all uncalled for, he insisted; but the laws of that Puritanic commonwealth were odious and tyrannical upon social subjects. He was an ardent advocate of individual liberty. Another avowed himself weary of a life of hardships on the mountains and plains; he was going down into Mexico for a little rest. His right-hand neighbor had left the States because he was tired of a humdrum life; he wanted a change. One went for variety, another to find a location; all seemed to think the expedition a brief holiday, which was to end in victory and abundance. They had our future course fully settled: we should travel leisurely across prairies rich in grass, thread cañons alive with game, and effect a junction with the Texan Invincibles, a thousand strong; then march on the settlements, encounter perhaps some thousands of Mexican soldiers, scatter them like the wind, dictate terms to Old Armijo, in Santa Fe, make an advantageous peace, and settle down in the mild climate and on the fertile soil of the Rio Grande to a life of dreamful ease. There was much talk of dark-eyed *senoritas*, dowered with vast ranches, where the contented owner would ride amid his thousands of sheep and cattle, pluck the luscious grape, and drink from great casks of red wine. This was their romance; the reality is to come.

"After brief consultation, a division of forces was agreed upon. Fourteen men, including the Colonel, were to go down to the 'Crossing' (where the Santa Fe trail crossed the Arkansas), and await the main body of riflemen from the States, or obey any orders from the Texan force, while the remainder, among them myself, were to proceed to the point where the Taos trail crossed the Las Animas, and act as a scouting party until further orders. We set out on the 21st of March, under command of a lieutenant, a gallant and graceful polyglot, who gave command in three languages, and joked and swore in a dozen more with inspiring fluency. That day we marched up the Timpas, then turned south south-west, toward the Las Animas. Having started with but one day's supply of provisions, and that of dried buffalo meat, we soon suffered for food. Our dependence was upon game, but at that season there is little grass, and animals are poor and shy. Two days and three nights did we toil over the high and barren lands without food, and only supplied with water from the pools filled by melting snow. Our horses were so exhausted that we walked most of the time, chewing only the cud of bitter fancies. Already the bright visions with which we set out were dissipated, and an awful sense of impending calamity seemed to weigh down the spirits of every one. The third day we killed a straggling wolf, which furnished us a miserable meal—just enough to excite a ravenous desire for something better.

Three days more we fasted, and came, completely exhausted, upon an old Indian camp, where we found some green buffalo hides, which the wolves had abandoned. These we scraped and boiled till we had a pasty mixture resembling glue thickened with scraps of leather, upon which we made a hearty meal. Again we fasted two days, and at last, faint from starvation, descended into the valley of Las Animas.

"The green growth here and there greatly restored our horses, and, despite the warning of the more experienced, some of the men ventured to eat the cactus bulb, insisting that its rank properties might be eradicated by roasting it in hot sand and ashes, in the same manner as the California Indians neutralize the virus of various roots. The first who partook felt no immediate effects, and praised it highly, upon which we all ate greedily, drinking freely at the same time of the slightly mineralized water of the Las Animas. But two hours' time showed that the inherent properties of the cactus were but slightly neutralized, if at all. Strange tremblings shook our frames, succeeded by dizziness and a desire to vomit. These were followed soon by agonizing pains, in which the sufferers rolled upon the ground in fearful contortions, and uttering heart-rending cries. It was a night of unmitigated misery. All recovered, but so weak that only three of the party were able to move about. It was simply impossible to proceed, or even hunt for game. Accordingly lots were cast between the horses, and the one thus condemned was slaughtered for food. On this we made a most delicious meal, alternately resting and eating at frequent intervals all day. Late at night we were so far restored that we feasted with glad hearts, and again the camp resounded with jokes, songs, and laughter. All were clamorous to advance at once on the Mexican settlements. Daily I saw more and more that mountaineers are much like children—unduly confident when all goes well, and correspondingly gloomy under the pressure of distress. The equal mind, preserved in arduous toils and fortune's sunshine, product of a higher mental cultivation, is not often theirs; they are elated by good omens, and cast down by auguries of ill; their plans are often disturbed by the suggestion of night-mare dreams, and gloomy apprehensions seize them from the unseasonable flights of birds or other strange outgivings of animal instinct.

"With restored strength, and some few days' supply of food, we traveled up stream, and were soon in the grand cañon of the Rio de las Animas, as it is called by the Catholic Spaniards. This strange river, with such extremes of delightful valley, barren waste, or gloomy and forbidding cañon, has received corresponding names from all races. The Indians call it the Wild River, the French christened it *Piquer*

L'Eau, or water of suffering, but the pious Spaniards name it River of Souls, which your unpoetic but practical race have shortened to Purgatory. We soon entered the grand cañon where the stream cuts its way through a high and barren table-land, running in a deep gorge, with almost perpendicular sides. Sometimes these crowd in upon the stream, and fallen rocks choke up its bed, producing a series of beautiful cascades; again, the cliffs recede, and leave a little oval valley, inclosed by red and yellow walls, rich in grass and timber, and often abounding in game. At length we reached a gorge too narrow and difficult for passage, and were compelled to turn into a side gulch and climb the almost perpendicular cliff, at least six hundred feet in height. All day we toiled along a series of rocky offsets, again and again lifting our horses over the rocks by means of ropes attached to their bodies, and at night-fall camped upon the high *mesa*. Thence we followed only the general course of the Las Animas until we arrived at our destined post, which was in a large grove of cottonwoods just below where the Taos trail crosses the stream. North and east were the sandy deserts, southward the *tierras templadas* that skirt the heads of the Cimarron and the Colorado tributary to the Canadian; but westward a more fertile plat rose even to the foot of the Huaquetories, which your people now call the Spanish Peaks. There we kept close guard upon the trail, expecting to capture some of the enemy's scouts, but beyond that and herding our stock, were free from care. Grass, game and pure water were abundant, and in a few days every man felt equal to a hundred Mexicans. Again songs were heard, and merriment reigned around the camp-fire; again did we hear of that glorious future in Mexico. All the omens were propitious; the restored mountaineers had good dreams, and the birds again flew in unison with their brightest hopes.

CAÑON DE LAS ANIMAS.

"Doubts of my companions, which had slumbered in time of toil and trouble, returned amid abundance, but were happily set at rest by a circumstance that soon occurred. One day our guards hailed a small party, who fled northward, but were captured after a sharp chase of several miles. They proved to be two Americans and an Englishman, with two Mexican guides and servants, on their way from Santa Fe to Fort Lancaster, and thence to the States. Having been successful traders, they were well equipped, and had with them a large quantity of gold and silver; but, after hearing their account, our party released them. It was evident then, that whatever our men might be, and however unworthy the motives of some, they were not marauders.

"From these travelers we received news that greatly disheartened us. A European Spaniard, who had been in the Texan army of invasion in 1842, and was then suspected of being a spy, had reported himself for reënlistment, and been assigned to Colonel Warfield's command. This action caused unusual confidence to be reposed in him, and after gleaning all the information possible, he proceeded by the shortest route to Santa Fe, and laid the whole case before the Mexican Governor, Armijo. But that worthy had received still more circumstantial accounts of us from some resident American traders, who had agents out upon the plains, and who were base enough to betray the cause of liberty for such favors in the remission of tariff duties, and other commercial advantages, as a Mexican Governor at that time could extend.

"Soon after came a messenger from Colonel Warfield with orders to join him at Rabbit Ears, a noted landmark midway between the Cimarron and Arkansas. We had enough of the Las Animas, and our lieutenant mapped out a new route, thus: south two and a half days to the Cimarron, thence down it five days to the Santa Fe trail, and thence north-west to Rabbit Ears. We entered at once upon the sandy plain, which continued all the way to the Cimarron. Sometimes cacti covered the sand so close that every step was dangerous, or thick clusters of greasewood excluded all useful growth; and again naked sterility denied footing to vegetable life. As we neared the Cimarron, the region grew still more forbidding. Behind us was the desolate table-land, before us the gloomy mountains; the few water holes were poisonous with alkali or other mineral salts, and the men, half crazed with thirst, declared with profane emphasis that such a country was little worth fighting for. We descended through a side gorge into the cañon of the Cimarron, winding along a buffalo trail, and upon a rocky bench barely wide enough for our animals. The walls of this fissure were at least eight hundred feet high, and facing each other at a distance not exceeding twenty-five yards. A large stone, loosened at the beginning of our descent, shot downward with the velocity of a cannon-ball, while the echoes sounded from side to side in gloomy reverberations. Once down to the bottom of the cañon, our route was easy enough along the course of the stream; at times in an oval vale, adorned by heavy groves and vocal with the songs of birds, again in a narrow cañon, and again out upon bare plats of burning sand.

But whether the few green plats were the beginning of mother nature's mighty reform, to redeem the whole desert, or the last survivals in the long struggle against increasing barrenness, we could not know. The stream is large, and the water pure through this part of its course, but as soon as we emerged upon the great plain, the Cimarron shrunk to a mere rivulet, and in a little while vanished entirely. Thence for hundreds of miles, it is said, scarcely a shrub or spear of grass adorns its banks. The high plains between the Cimarron and Arkansas we found even more desolate. There only the transient showers and melting snows of spring produce, in the most favored spots, a faint tinge of green. Then a few pearly drops spatter crag and peak, or linger on the plain as though desolation half relented the work she had to do, or mother nature sorrowed for her short-lived offspring; but soon all this is passed, and summer with scorching days and dewless nights hastens to ravish the evanescent beauties of spring and turn her green to stubble.

GETTING DOWN TO THE CIMARRON.

"Reaching the Santa Fe trail, we met a friendly party of Arapahoes, who told us that four hundred Mexican cavalry had gone north in search of us only two days before. As this was confirmed by evidences on the trail, we strained every nerve to get across the desert and effect a junction with the rest of the force. The season was already well advanced, and, to avoid heat and thirst, we traveled as far as possible that night. During the entire distance of some forty miles we found no water, and till late the next afternoon men and horses suffered the agonies of thirst. The animals finally became almost unmanageable, and our principal pack-horse stampeded, carrying off considerable ammunition, and could not be recovered. Coming up to the rendezvous, what was our disappointment to find, not the expected detachment from the States, but the handful we had left a few weeks before on the Arkansas. Discouragement and discontent now threatened open mutiny. The season was late, and the hottest weather approaching; the water-holes were fast drying up, the Mexicans fully apprised of our plans, and the whole country on our line of advance scoured by their cavalry. Colonel Warfield hurriedly set forth the situation; then, with one of his nervous magnetic appeals, urged us to strike at least one blow before retiring. By unanimous vote a new plan was agreed upon. It would never do for us to return the way we had come, as every water-hole was guarded, and an ambush set in every mountain pass. We must strike one blow, and then, if the Texan army never came, reach the Arkansas by a less frequented course.

"It was decided to go westward up the *arroyo* we were on, and then straight south to the Cimarron again. The two days we followed the *arroyo*, grass was abundant, and water enough found in the limestone "pockets," which appear occasionally along these cañons. Thence southward we pressed with all possible speed day and night over the barren *mesa*, and when men and horses were frantic with thirst, again arrived at the Cimarron. There we *cached* our surplus baggage, and thence made another forced march across the rocky table-lands, and over a spur of the Taos Mountains, toward the nearest Mexican settlements. Halting in a green depression of the divide between the waters flowing east and those of the Rio Grande, our scouts reported a body of sixty Mexican cavalry in a fortified camp just ahead, and commanding the only pass to the settlements. Further scouting discovered a point from which our whole force might overlook their camp. This point we gained by a circuitous route next day, and camped in a dense thicket of cedars and pines. Below was a considerable valley, through which ran a small stream bordered by cottonwood and willow; in a dense grove of the former, and on the farther bank of the stream, was the Mexican camp, beyond it a narrow pass leading to a small town. It was agreed that we should effect a surprise just beyond daylight next morning, capture the force if possible, then make a dash into the town and retreat before they could raise a force sufficient to oppose us.

"Soon after midnight we cautiously descended by a detour of some five miles, which brought us down into the cottonwood thicket nearest the enemy's camp. Thence we moved on slowly to the bank of the stream, but were disconcerted to find it three times as large as it had appeared from the hill. After a whispered consultation, it was decided that the enemy's guards were upon the opposite bank and might be surprised and disarmed. With this view we waded the almost ice-cold stream so noiselessly that we were ascending the opposite bank when the first sentinel hailed:

"'*Quienes veniren?*' (Who comes?)

"'*Que dijo?*' (What do you say?)

"'*Quienes veniren! Caraho!*' was his response, as he discharged his piece at the nearest man, and fled into camp. We followed close, and were upon the soldiers as they rose from sleep.

"'*Munchos Tejanos!*' (Many Texans!) yelled the other sentinels, as our men rushed upon and disarmed them.

"'*Si, si, munchos Tejanos—quieron los scoupetas!*' was the cry, as we sprang to prevent them. The five men named for that duty had secured most of the arms, but a short, sharp struggle ensued, in which five of the Mexicans were killed and as many wounded. But the surprise was so complete that most of them fled precipitately toward the pass. It was impossible to secure our prisoners and the captured arms, and collect our horses in time to make the intended attack upon the village before they could have been fully aroused and prepared. We therefore hastily collected the arms and horses of the fugitives, paroled the prisoners, destroyed every thing we could not carry off, and pushed with all speed for the spur by which we might reach the table-lands to the eastward. Reaching, late in the afternoon, a high point in the eastward pass, we thought ourselves beyond pursuit, and halted for a rest. In the general gayety, discipline was relaxed, and the guards stationed with the horses ventured to leave their posts for a few moments and enter camp. In the midst of our meal the shout was heard: 'There go our horses!' and all hands sprang up only to witness our noble *cavallard* under full headway before a body of Mexican horsemen, while at the same instant a brisk fire was opened upon us from flank and rear. For an instant we were paralyzed; then seized our arms, and, at the word of command, charged upon the enemy on the hill in front. The panic-stricken Mexicans rushed down the opposite slope, leaving three dead upon the ground; we followed, and soon cleared the field in all directions, till not an enemy was in sight. One of the Mexicans had been holding two mustangs in the rear of the attacking party, and though shot dead, still held the halters tight gripped in his hands. Hurriedly cutting them loose, the St. Louis man and I sprang upon the animals, and, despite the warning cry from Colonel Warfield, dashed after the *cavallard*, now on the brow of the plateau, two or three miles away, and going at full speed.

" It was madness, but we had little time to think. It was death, we considered, to lose our horses in such a place, and to die in an attempt to regain them could not be worse. A gallop of a few miles, without gaining on the *cavallard*, gave us time to reconsider, and we turned regretfully toward the camp. But as we did so, a party of at least fifty Mexican horsemen appeared on the way we had come. A wild yell of triumph rose upon the air, followed by a shower of scoupeta balls, one of which laid my companion's horse dead, leaving its rider senseless upon the ground. One instant I thought of surrender as a prisoner of war. But quickly came the thought that, in the heated condition of the enemy, certain death awaited me; or, if not that, a lingering death in a Spanish dungeon. I was nerved by desperation, and dashed down a long slope to the right.

"From every hollow, from behind every sandy hillock, horsemen seemed to rise, and still I cleared them all. The mustang was comparatively fresh, and, by frequent doubling and turning, I gained the advance on a long slope, which led westward to the plain. A hundred Mexican cavalry were strung out behind me, the nearest just out of range. Slowly I gained upon them, plying the spur savagely, and was just beginning to breathe more freely, when suddenly there yawned before me an *arroyo* with perpendicular sides, not more than twenty feet wide, but of unknown depth. I reined my mustang back upon his haunches at the very edge of the chasm, then turned to look my last upon the earth. How fair then seemed the desert, but a little while ago so wild and waste—how bright the sun—how majestic the snowy mountains, glowing far to the north through the calm air!

"A yell of triumph from the enemy came with sudden jar upon my ears, and close after it a shower of scoupeta balls; one cut my coat-sleeve, while another plowed a furrow along my cheek. The sharp sting of pain, the flow of warm blood, the insulting yell, maddened me. I would not die—would not consent to their triumph; or, if die I must, I would sell my life dearly. I turned and galloped fiercely towards the foe, discharging my pistol as I advanced. In sheer astonishment at my desperation, they drew up. Again animal fear reasserted itself—the mad instinct for one moment more of life—and I turned towards the chasm. Again the fierce, insulting yell of the mongrel cut-throats—again a shower of scoupeta balls. And now the enemy were near enough for me to hear their insulting laugh—their discussion in bastard Spanish of the best method to finish me without danger. They came on more and more slowly. Again a few scoupeta balls whistled around me, and I felt the sting of another slight wound.

"Could my mustang leap the chasm? These mountain-trained beasts were active; he was young and strong; at the worst it was but death—death sudden and bravely dared. Thus swifter than lightning ran my thoughts in the awful presence of the unknown.

"Putting him at full speed, I spurred him to the very edge, then, rising in my stirrups, loosed the reins as he bravely took the leap. I hear, as if it were but yesterday, the loud yell from the astonished Mexicans; I see again the frightful gorge—in awful dreams again I urge him to the fearful leap.

"With a tremendous bound he cleared the chasm, landing with his fore feet on the opposite side. For one brief instant the life of horse and man trembled in the balance. Hope, despair, joy, resignation—how rapidly I felt them all, but only for an instant. With deadly rebound, I felt myself thrown violently downward, and against the opposite side. Pure sunlight changed to fiery red, and again to dazzling

FOR LIFE OR DEATH.

gray; my mother's sad, sweet face looked down an instant from the narrowed sky; streams of fire darted from the firmament, and after them came darkness blacker than tongue can tell. Blow after blow was rained upon my head; my flesh was cut as with sharp knives. I was an age in falling, and yet all was over in an instant. Consciousness yielded, and I sank down, down, down into darkness, oblivion! Was it death?

CHAPTER V.

DOLORES.

"Was I in the land of spirits? Had the awful River of Souls indeed swallowed me up? Dense darkness, blackness that could be felt, was around me. Every faculty was suspended, except simple consciousness; of past or future I had no conception—I only knew that I *was*. It must be that I had passed from earth, and this was the region into which philosophy had never penetrated.

"There was a slight rustle near me, and, exerting all my force of will, I attempted to move; there shot through me such a pang of agony that I screamed aloud.

"'*Ah, povritta!*' said a soft, musical voice, and delicate fingers touched my forehead, and then were pressed upon my lips. I dimly comprehended that I was to remain silent and still; but my pain was too great, and I groaned again and again. I now perceived that my left arm and leg were tightly bandaged, and held in rude wooden frames; my head also was covered with some tenacious strips. I was helpless as a mummy. The gloom seemed to soften; a ray of light appeared here and there, and a distant tinkling was heard, like the sound of sheep bells. A cup was pressed to my lips; I drank of a bitter decoction, and soon sank into a profound sleep.

"When I awoke, comparatively free from pain, there was light enough to show that I was lying on a couch in a small room, in which some one was moving about. The blanket which served for a door was put aside, admitting the bright rays of the morning sun, and the same soft voice spoke in Spanish.

"'Are they out of sight, Gomez?'

"'Beyond El Sentinel, *senorita*,' was the reply.

"'And gone?'

"'To join the main body, *maestra mia*; they will never look here.'

"I understood barely enough of the language to know that this implied safety. The curtain was slowly drawn aside, and the speakers departed. For hours I sought in vain to take up the tangled thread of my existence. Geneva was clear in my mind, and I fancied myself in some cave in the hills of Switzerland. I thought, and thought, and thought again, 'Much wondering what I was, whence hither brought, and how.' Beyond my school days I could not get the clew. Again I slept, and awaking memory brought back my journey to the States, the Texan expedition, and—all at once I was again at the rendezvous; again I rushed madly on the chasm, again I dared the awful leap, and, with a shriek, relapsed into insensibility.

"I was dimly conscious of two persons about my bed, both men; but men of a garb and color I had seen only in dreams. The one who seemed to have most authority again pressed the bitter draught to my lips, and I sank into a long refreshing sleep. When I awoke it was midday, and I saw that I was in a room half cave, half cabin, such as the Mexican herdsmen build far up the mountains. On the wall were pictures of the Virgin and some saints, at the foot of the bed a crucifix, while a few adornments of some elegance were scattered about. It was evidently the abode of rude herdsmen, hastily refitted by a woman. All this I saw in a few seconds of half-waking consciousness. But only for an instant. As I moved, some one came forward holding a cup, and at sight of her, the red blood rushed over my enfeebled frame. She spoke. Away flew all my dreams of Texan independence, away my heroic plans for the Brotherhood of Man, away my cultivated hatred of all the Spanish race; any life was worthless that did not include *her*. In this there was no cold reasoning; there was no thought that it was best, or why it was best; it came as the hot winds come from the desert, upon the green oasis.

"SOME ONE CAME FORWARD HOLDING A CUP."

"'The Virgin be praised, he speaks and lives!'

"'But where am I?'

"'Safe.'

"'But my friends, my companions in arms?'

"'They are gone to their own country; but never mind. Rest and sleep.'

"I need not recount the progress of our attachment. Her home was at a hacienda, some miles down the valley—one of the outposts. Her parents were rich only in flocks and herds; their servants, *peons* and Pueblo Indians. As the custom of these herders is to move higher up the mountains with the advance of the season, they were in this hut at the time of our approach. It appeared that the rebound of my horse from the opposite bank had hurled me back into the bushes growing out from the side of the gorge some twenty feet down; and thence by a succession of falls among the shrubby growth, I had reached the bottom sixty feet below, fearfully bruised and broken, but not mortally hurt. The Mexicans saw no way of descending except by making a long circuit, and seeing my horse crushed to jelly at the bottom, they concluded I was dead under him. Fortunately I was found by the Pueblo Gomez, and brought to the cabin. Had a Mexican found me ——.

"THE MEXICANS SAW NO WAY OF DESCENDING."

"Had word gone to the hacienda, the command would have been prompt: 'Give him up!'" But *she* saw me first, and womanly pity subordinated all other thoughts to that of saving me. In secret the medicine man of the nearest pueblo was brought to dress my wounds and bandage my broken limbs, and at the end of ten days I slowly struggled back to life and consciousness. Still the Mexican authorities were ignorant of my existence. Should they learn it, what would be my fate? Perhaps to be honorably treated as a prisoner of war, perhaps to be murdered at sight. It would depend entirely on the first officer who took charge of me. So many are the castes among these people, and so great the difference between different clans, that with one the prisoner is treated as a guest, while by another he is butchered like a wild beast. But I was for the present safe, and in time took up the clew of my past life, and followed it down to the last moment of consciousness—slowly, painfully, as the wounded hunter drags his bleeding limbs towards home, with many halts and stumblings. The old life was gone; the new life had grown up with Dolores, for such, she told me, was her name. I seemed to have nothing I did not owe to her, and for the present it was enough to live and love. She taught me her language more perfectly, though we scarcely needed it; and the days of convalescence passed as a brief dream.

"At length I was able to leave the cabin, and, leaning upon the arm of Dolores, walked to a projecting rock, which commanded a view of the Mora pass. Then my past life seemed renewed, as familiar thoughts were excited by the scenery. But Dolores was now my arbiter. Of her people I knew little; for her religion I cared nothing. It was hers, therefore it could not be bad. Doubtless it was true as any other. I smiled at the Protestant prejudices of my youth; I gazed into the radiant eyes of Dolores, and thought the old world mad that all its religious differences had not yielded to the potent solvent of love. Our love came unbidden. We thought not of the morrow; we made no declarations; we simply understood each other. But as we sat upon the rocky point, sometimes exchanging a word, but oftener in silent bliss, we saw a moving cloud of dust rise from the pass far below, and had just time to gain a point secluded from observation when a cavalcade came into full view. Imagine my horror when I saw my old companions, and with them fifty more Americans, toiling wearily through the dust and heat, bound elbow to elbow, and urged on by the mounted Mexicans, who laughed and jeered at the captives. I was mad with rage, but what could one do against so many? With tearful eyes I watched them out of sight beyond the rock El Sentinel, then turned with a fierce determination to hasten northward and bring relief. Dolores met me with a smile, tinged with a shade of sadness. It was enough. I easily found excuse for inaction. Again was the republic forgotten, again the eternal rights of man seemed of minor importance. I was happy here. What need of dwelling on the past? Why take such heavy thoughts for the future? Love is a radically selfish passion. Waking, I counted the moments till she should return; sleeping, her image glided through my dreams. By day she smiled upon me in the landscape; by night she beamed upon me from the starry skies.

"The summer was now far advanced; hot days were followed by dewless nights, and the grass was dried upon the ground. A new danger confronted us. Dolores only made her daily visit from the hacienda to the cabin at constant risk of attracting attention to my hiding-place; she now announced with sobs that the season had come when the Pueblos must remove the herds. Her father would return from the capital; if I remained at the cabin, it must be at daily and hourly risk. Her father was a *caballero*, she said, brave and generous; but he was above all a Mexican. Duty and inclination alike would lead him to surrender me. His servants were doubtful. The few Pueblos she could trust; the *peons* never.

"It was a rude awakening. All that calm afternoon we discussed our situation, at one moment mingling our tears, the next elate with firm determination. A score of plans I proposed were in turn rejected. To regain American territory was simply impossible. The irregular war with the Texans continued, and the country between us and the Arkansas was swarming with scouts. Every point was guarded. Starvation was possible, capture certain, death probable. My late companions were now languishing in Mexican dungeons; those who lived to return home would probably do so with broken health. Death would certainly overtake many of them in prison. From such a fate she prayed the Virgin to deliver me. Hour after hour passed; I would do or dare aught for her; but to fly now was to lose her forever. At last she spoke:

"'Gomez is our hope. He is not a *peon*, but a free Pueblo. Many years absent from his town, he is bound to no *cacique*. Far to the west are other Pueblos who owe no duty to the Mexican Republic; but between them and ours there is a friendship. Once they had a common ruler, and long kept the sacred fires burning for him. Gomez will guide you to that people. In any of those pueblos you are safe. Stay till there is peace with the Tejanos; then return, and ——.' Her light smile changed to a deep blush.

"'May the Virgin bless and protect you! Every night I shall look upon the star that rises earliest above the peak where I first saw your face. In one year I feel that you will return—one year. Oh, Santa Maria, is it eternity?'

"'No, to the young and ardent it is long; but it will pass at last.'

"'Now, go to rest; and as soon as Gomez can supply his place among the *racqueros*, enter upon the journey. To him can I intrust my chief treasure.'

"Three nights after, as I lay asleep, Gomez touched me, and said in Spanish: 'The *senorita* waits; we start in an hour.' Down the sharp cañon, and out upon the western plain we found the animals tied ready for us, and in a little grove of algodones beyond the hacienda I met Dolores. Need I recount our parting. It was a short, delicious agony. I held her to my heart as we exchanged vows of eternal constancy; then, pressing kiss after kiss upon her lips, I hurried away—for I knew not what—in my ear her parting words, 'May all the saints watch over my love.'

"Hastily crossing the narrow valley and ascending the slope west of it, at daylight we reached the first pueblo, the nominal home of Gomez, who maintained semi-allegiance to its *cacique* and *fiscal*;

and in its shaded recesses we remained for the day. The chief men conversed readily in Spanish; but, among themselves, they spoke a language of which I could not catch a syllable. Nor is it known to the Mexicans, even to the interpreters who speak the tongues of all the wild tribes. They conduct all their trades in Spanish, and exclude Mexicans as much as possible from their towns. There is evidence that these people were once far more numerous than now, as the country was far more fertile. Conquered by the Spaniards nearly three centuries since, they revolted and with desperate bravery expelled or exterminated their conquerors. But, in 1690, a new and more powerful Spanish army reconquered the province; the Quiros, Tagnos, and kindred tribes submitted sullenly to the Spanish yoke, but the more warlike retreated to the defensible valleys and walled basins of the Sierra Madre Range, and maintained a fierce independence. It was to those we were bound. Those near the Rio Grande, compelled to give up their Montezumas religion and become nominal Catholics, still held to many features of their ancient faith, and long cherished plans of revolution and vengeance. But time, which reconciles us to all things, had now led them to acquiesce in the political control of the Spanish race, though they tenaciously resisted all social intercourse, and maintained their own line of priesthood and a distinct language.

"By the advice of Gomez, I here stained my face, hands, and arms with a pigment, which gave them color like that of the Pueblos; and the next night we crossed the Rio Grande, as it was well for us to avoid observation till we left that neighborhood. After another halt at Jemez, near the wonderful Hot Springs, we hastened on to Dead Man's Cañon and crossed into the land of the Navajoes. These Indians hung upon the slopes of the Sierra Madre, a living threat to the Mexican settlements. They waged a war, never intermitted for two hundred years after their fierce ancestors were driven from the fertile valleys and forced to find subsistence and refuge amid the secluded cañons and on the storm-swept *mesas* of the mountains. Ingenious, brave, and haughty, they called the Mexicans 'their herders,' and robbing without quite ruining the dwellers in the valley, they took tribute alternately from different settlements, leaving time between raids for the sufferers to renew their stock and gather wealth for future forays. But now a precarious peace existed, and each Mexican hamlet secured protection by purchasing the friendship of some Navajo chieftain.

"For the first two days of travel, I hung upon the neck of my little *burro*, weak in body and sad at recent parting; but soon fresh air and exercise, with change of scene, brought new life, and I felt a strange interest in the people we encountered. We passed hot deserts, glistening with sand and alkali; broad plateaus of bare sandstone, and occasionally green dells or wooded coves, where the natural beauty, by contrast with surrounding barrenness, awakened emotions of keen delight. Sometimes we jogged on for hours over a bare flat, then from the rocky rim walling an ancient basin descended to the beds of lakes long since dry, to find in the center and lowest depressions rich natural meadows or sullen pools, bordered by a few sickly cottonwoods. We traversed wild gorges, where from every side red precipices frowned upon yellow sands; we crossed sandy wastes where glittered quartz-crystals, garnets, and flakes of mica, and saw upon the scarred peaks the awful evidences of a thousand cosmic convulsions. We passed amid bands of savage men, who grew gentle at our approach, after a few words or signs from Gomez; and traveled for days along a valley strewn with the ruins of abandoned towns. Again we turned to the hills, crossed the lowest divide of the Sierra Madre, and traveled on over sterile flats and treeless, grassless *mesas*. It seemed a land accursed of God and forgotten of civilized men, where only hunters and herdsmen could wring a scant subsistence from unwilling nature; a land which even the all-grasping Spaniard did not covet, but left as a refuge for those who could not give him gold for blood, and would not yield the sweat of unpaid toil for his religion.

"Beyond the last range of the Sierra Madre we descended to the cañon of the Colorado Chiquito, rose again to the Mesa Calabasa, and again cautiously threaded a defile down to an oval basin some thirty miles in width, dotted with little oases rich in native grasses. In the center of this vale Gomez pointed out the goal of our hopes. A sharp *mesa* rose abruptly from the plain, and on its summit were the Moqui towns. A few friendly Navajoes had accompanied us, for there was a temporary peace between them and their fierce neighbors, the Apaches. Rushing down the rocky paths with wild cries, the Moquis came to the foot of the *mesa* in disorder and apparent anger at our approach; but a few words from Gomez reassured them, and I was conducted up the winding way by which alone the place is accessible, and led into the presence of their chief. He received me with civil dignity, assigned me a house, for many were vacant, and in a few days I was as much at home with these strange people as if I had been there for years. The

Capitan, as their chief man was called, sought to cheer the hours, as far as his simple pleasures and uneventful life could interest me, and as I grew to understand the people, they were a strange study to me. The government, if government it might be called, was a pure paternalism; but repression was unnecessary, because crime could scarcely be said to exist.

"At last, said I, the Brotherhood of Man is found. Here is no scheming of man to supplant his fellow; here all are equal, and obedience to natural law, with mutual toleration, takes the place of courts and statutes. But I soon saw that in parting with most of the faults of a progressive race, they had parted with many of its virtues and all of its advantages. There was no envy, for there was no emulation; the weak were not trodden down by the strong in a struggle for place, for there was no struggle. There was no caste, for there was neither rank nor wealth; a dead level of social mediocrity took the place of our many distinctions in birth or condition. They had not the petty vices of a trading people, as they had little intercourse with the rest of mankind; nor the faults of a manufacturing town, for every family was its own manufacturer. Political strife never disturbed them, for there was no choice as to the form of government, and no energy to change the ruler. The Capitan did not rob his people, for they had nothing worth his taking; the people did not envy their king, for he was poor as themselves. Luxury and its attendant vices they knew not—their land sufficed but for a bare existence; and unchastity was so rare as to be looked upon as a monstrous phenomenon. But their chastity resulted from a lack of aggressive energy, and a sexual coldness with which kind nature ever blesses an illy nourished and decaying race. No military ambition disturbed the placid current of their lives; they scarcely knew how to defend themselves against their savage neighbors, and retiring to these rock-defended fastnesses, had left the open country to their foes.

"Then I saw that energy is evolved only in conflict; that a vigorous combat with evil develops the individual, and that a state from which ambition should be banished to leave the citizen free from conflict, would be a state in which moral vigor would in turn decay, and social stagnation, as a living tomb, swallow up the proudest products of the march of mind. With these people one day passed as another. Whether they had a belief in immortality I could never learn; but they might well ignore it, since even in this world they were dead already. Beyond the narrow horizon of their hills, they saw nothing; this basin was to them the world. Ambition had no place in their dull emotions, and though central to a dozen warring tribes, they were simple, civil and unwarlike.

"One year I abode with these people. It was rest; but for a lifetime—ah, that would be consignment to a living tomb! But Gomez returned, and with a message from Dolores. There was peace at last; the captive Tejanos had been released, and I might safely return. The journey was a long reverie of delightful anticipation. The meeting I leave you to imagine. But all was not well; Colonel Warfield and his brave companions had been released, and many Americans were coming into Santa Fe; but the Mexican authorities felt that peace was temporary, and armed parties still hovered along the frontier. We scarcely seemed nearer the fruition of our hopes, and months of weary waiting were yet before us. Her father—but I need not tell you of Castilian pride. He was of the *gente fina* of New Mexico, and, boasting of his *sangre azul*, an alliance with an unknown foreigner would have seemed to him worse than her death. I urged immediate flight; that we would seek the States, and there remain till permanent peace should allow us to return and settle in Mexico, as I hoped—after the manner of sanguine youth—we might soon do with the wealth that I should earn. I abode at the adjacent pueblo, and as often as possible saw and conferred with Dolores, never failing to urge immediate flight. I need not recount the progress I made, if you know aught of the female heart. She yielded, and in the midst of all my distractions and uncertainties, I thought myself the happiest of men. We were to set out the first opportunity. The distance was great, and no guide to be had. In vain I sought for one in the pueblo; the honest fellows shook their heads. In their own country, among their own people, they were at my service, but not among *los Americanos, los diabolos Gringos!* We could not retreat from our project. Before a Pueblo priest we plighted our faith, and thus united in life and death, set out upon our northward route. One Pueblo accompanied us the first night and till noon the next day; then pointing out our safest route—along the higher part of the plateau to avoid Mexican scouts—bade us farewell, and we were alone upon the *tierra templada*.

"The route led to a water-hole, where we paused exhausted, and remained till midnight. Thence we rose to a dim trail higher up the rocky slope, and toiled on till late next afternoon, when fatigue and fear for our animals again compelled us to stop. A long rest, and then on to the next pool, which we reached late at night, and soon sank into a profound sleep. When we awoke late next morning, the scene had changed. A dense mist, rare at that season, hung upon the mountains, and heavy clouds drifted eastward over the plain. Nevertheless, I marked what I thought the right course, and we traveled on. Before noon we were bewildered among the projecting ridges, where the trail was obscured upon the rocky flats, and ere long were completely lost.

"Should we descend to the lower plain for a shorter route, or turn toward the mountains to be sure of grass and water? I determined to continue a due north course as far as possible, trusting either to come again upon the trail, or find water in some of the limestone 'pockets,' which occur here and there even in the red sand hills. By noon the water in the canteens I had provided was nauseating, having been almost stagnant when taken from the pool; before the next morning it was all gone, while our animals gave unmistakable signs of approaching exhaustion. Still we pressed on. It was now mid August, and the hot, dry season was at its worst. The bunch-grass was dried to a coppery hue, and though it nourished our animals, they must have water also. The stinging plants and thorny cactus constantly impeded our way, and we soon came to regard the broad flats of bare rock as a glad relief. But water, water we must have. I was then too ignorant of wood-craft to know that in the Rocky Mountains one hunts up-hill for water instead of down upon the plain; and felt keenly my need of that sixth sense wherewith the Indian and plainsman can discern the locality of a brook or pool by the appearance of surrounding hills or vegetation.

"DOLORES FAINTED IN MY ARMS."

"Night drew on. There was a dead calm and oppressive air. The animals at length refused to move a step further, and I had barely time to spring from my saddle and receive her, when Dolores fainted in my arms. For a moment my agony was terrible—the agony at once of fear and indecision. But in a moment fierce energy returned; I raised her, recalled her to consciousness, and now leading, now carrying her, toiled up and over the rocks to the mouth of a gorge that opened upon the side of a precipice a thousand feet above. Why, I scarcely knew, but had a vague hope of protection and rest in the defile. Night came on suddenly, and its coolness greatly revived us. We had as yet suffered little with actual thirst, and when

6

our first trouble was passed, sank to sleep upon a sand-heap at the base of an immense rock. Soon after midnight we awoke stiff with cold, and now beginning to feel the sharper promptings of thirst, I proposed to search for water down the cañon, but on turning we saw our animals, like us revived by the night air, slowly making their way up the dry *arroyo*, as if they would seek relief near its head. Something in this manifestation of instinct decided me. The *arroyo* showed plainly that at some seasons it contained a large stream; might there not remain a little near its source?

"For hours we toiled on up the dry channel, soon leaving the animals far behind; now stumbling over the immense stones which choked the dry bed, and now searching every clump of grass that showed the faintest tinge of green. The sun rose red and fiery, the air was filled with light haze, and another sultry day began. But with every hour's advance new signs encouraged us: there were clumps of dwarfish pines, and occasionally a shrub of other timber; the grass in places had an unmistakably green tinge, and occasional tracks showed that various small animals habitually made this passage. But every moment our thirst increased. I glanced at Dolores; her eyes gleamed with that unwholesome fire which is the precursor of delirium. I felt my own head grow giddy; my eyes were so dry it seemed I could feel the balls grate as they turned in their sockets; my tongue was swollen, my lips cracked, and I spoke with difficulty. Hastily seeking the shade of an immense rock, I broke some splinters from a mountain pine; these, rolled about in the mouth, soon created a moisture, which sensibly relieved our sufferings, and again we toiled on.

"It was now noon. The hot sun glared upon the white sand and red rocks, and our sufferings rapidly increased. Almost exhausted, I happened to turn my gaze down the cañon, and saw our animals far below, still feebly struggling up the ascent. The sight gave me renewed hope, and, with fierce energy, I rushed from side to side of the gorge, searching every spot that bore signs of the presence of moisture; but in vain. An hour longer we toiled on, then Dolores suddenly reeled, and sank, apparently lifeless, in my arms. With loud cries, I bore her hastily to the shade of a projecting rock; I chafed her hands, and implored her to look up and live. She revived, only to relapse into a half-dead condition, scarcely sensible of my presence, but babbling in Spanish of green fields and the cool brooks about her home. I pressed her to my heart, and prayed that death might come at once and end our intolerable sufferings. An hour passed thus, then suddenly we seemed to revive again—Dolores with alternate sobs and hysterical laughter, and I with renewed determination to push on. Soon we sank into half-unconsciousness, and again revived as suddenly, but with all the pangs of thirst and fatigue greater than before. Slowly this anguish receded, and we sank into a condition of almost complete exemption from suffering, to again revive as suddenly to fiercer pangs.

"But this time my vision seemed strangely cleared. The agony yielded to a dull pain, that left me power to think. I saw all the beauties of the landscape in a new light, and gazed on them with actual interest, while I pitied and blamed myself for such a feeling. I saw a mountain bluebird flit rapidly over the gorge, and wondered where he was flying and what for; then laughed loud and long at myself for such untimely curiosity. I noticed a hillock of the desert ants near me, from which the red nation was pouring by hundreds, and a sand-toad near them; then I remembered that these creatures avoid damp spots, where water is liable to percolate, and again the wild gorge rang with my fierce laughter at their strange habits. I saw a lean *coyote* steal across the cañon below us, and wondered what he was doing so far up in the hills, and why he had not remained on the plains, as usual, and whether he was lost and hunting for water; then the absurdity of this conceit struck me, and I made what I thought a very witty jest at his leanness, and laughed at my own wit till the cañon rang again. Suddenly I came to myself, and stared around me; then my gaze fell on Dolores, lying full length upon the sand, and breathing heavily, and all my fierce energy returned. I raised her with unnatural strength, fairly bounded up the cañon several rods, and laid her at the foot of another rock. Again and again I repeated this, one moment kissing her lips and vowing to save her, the next laughing at my temporary fits of strength. At last I laid her in a cool depression at the foot of a cliff, which seemed to have been split by some convulsion, and, for a space, relapsed into insensibility.

"When I revived, the cool night had come again, and Dolores was sitting by me, clasping my hand. Such was the reviving effect of the night air, now sweeping down the cañon with a strong breeze, that we were greatly refreshed, and, after a sad, sweet interchange of thought, sank into a troubled sleep. Again we waked suddenly, almost at the same moment, and again the pangs of thirst were upon us in all their fury. Nature has still some mercy, even at her worst, and though a man die in torture, for want of food or drink, she secures him intervals of perfect rest from pain. But now our sufferings were at their worst. Mere abstinence from water for two days would not have produced such effects, but for our continued exertions. The cold night air prevented delirium. I put out my hand to assure Dolores of my presence, when—was it possible? Did I feel an actual moisture at the base of the cliff, or was it only the cold, dry sand? Fiercely I scratched away the first few inches of the loose surface—eagerly I thrust my fingers into the packed dirt and gravel, and tore my nails digging beside the rock. Yes, it was unmistakable; there *was* moisture there, and somewhere above it there was water!

"New life animated me. I followed the line of moisture along the base of the rock; it suddenly ceased, and my heart stood still. An instant more, and I perceived that I had passed the immense fissure which split the cliff; in it I again found the moist trace. I followed it a few rods, and perceived that the formation had changed to limestone. Joy overcame me. I screamed aloud, and burst into tears. Every yard that I advanced up the fissure the earth grew more moist. Presently I could squeeze a few dirty drops from a handful into my mouth. Great Jupiter! Was Olympian nectar ever so sweet? A few rods more and there was dank green grass, its matted roots sodden with mud and water. Eagerly I sucked the divine fluid, then tore up a few handfuls and hastened with it to Dolores. Squeezing the scant drops into her mouth, and spreading the grass roots upon her brow, I soon had the exquisite joy of seeing her raise her head and smile. I took her in my arms and bore her to the damp grass-plat; then, foot by foot, on our knees, we searched the narrow ravine. Soon we came to where a few tiny drops trickled over a mossy stone. With our lips pressed to the rock, we drew new life from it. For an hour we alternately sucked at this source, and cheered each other—she calling upon the Virgin, and blessing all the saints by turns, I rejoicing at the happy operations of nature which gave us water in this strange place.

"Our worst tortures past, fatigue again conquered us. We sank into a sound sleep, and did not wake till the morning light fell upon our faces. I then saw that the line of green grass continued up the narrow gorge, and, following it for two hours, we came upon a pool of cold, clear water. Did you ever, after hours of toil across the desert, come upon one of those lime-rock springs, which alone make life possible in the far South-west? If so, you know their wonderful beauty; you can imagine our joy. Around were the yellow and striped mountains, seamed and scarred as if by a million years of storm and lightning; below, the cliff-walled cañon, now filled with the hot and stagnant air of mid-day, and beyond it the dry sands and treeless desert. Here was a cool spring, central to a little oasis, where the bright fluid bubbled forth from the earth, and dripped o'er the rocks in tiny, cool rivulets—where rank, green grass hung over the brim of the pool, and strange, bright flowers spoke of life, and love, and hope.

"A day's rest was imperative, and as soon as possible I filled my canteens and hastened back to find our horses. They had toiled on till morning; then one had fallen exhausted, while the other had halted in the shadow of a cliff, barely able to stand. A canteen full of water, which he drank from my Mexican sombrero, greatly revived him, but the other was past hope. I succeeded in getting the one to the mouth of the gorge, and after a dozen trips for water, he was so far restored as to graze upon the bunch-grass. Next morning we set out again, now with but one horse, and late the next night, having found the trail, reached the water-hole, which was to have been our stopping place the day we were lost. There we again rested a day, which so far restored the animal that he was able to carry Dolores and our little stock of provisions, as fast as I could walk beside him. Again we journeyed on, turning aside at night into a cañon, and keeping near the base of the mountains by day. Once past the divide of the *tierra templada* and upon the slopes leading down to the Arkansas, water-holes could be found three or four times every day. Our progress was now encouragingly rapid, and in due time we turned the last point on the mountain trail, and with a glad shout hailed the yellow Arkansas. Another day, and we should be on American soil; the land would be better watered, my gun would supply us with game, and we might travel more leisurely.

"We turned eastward and down to the plain, to reach the main cross-

"THE BALLS WHISTLED AROUND US."

ing on the Santa Fe trail, and late the next day, while our hearts beat high with satisfaction, descended to the sandy border of the Arkansas. A shout was borne to our ears from the heights behind, and turning, we saw a party of mounted Mexicans rapidly nearing us. For an instant our hearts stood still with fear; the next I bounded on the horse in front of Dolores, and urged him fiercely forward. I remembered with agony that I had no traders' permit from the Spanish authorities, and could give no plausible explanation of my condition; capture might mean death, it would certainly mean loss of Dolores. Soon we were in the middle of the stream, at that season not too deep for fording; but our pursuers gained fast upon us. As we neared the American shore they reached the opposite bank, and with a yell of rage at being foiled, discharged a volley from their scoupetas. The balls whistled around us; I only noted that the animal did not fall, then spurred him on, and in another moment he scrambled up to the northern bank, and we were safe upon American soil.

"Safe! Oh, merciful powers, why had we not an hour more in the start? Why had we come safely through such perils only to part when our haven was won? Dolores' arm tightened about my waist—she did not speak. I turned with a glad smile, a word of love and cheer upon my lips. She was deadly pale, and I had barely time to dismount, when she fainted in my arms. A shot had entered her side. * * * * * *

"But anguish was unavailing. There was no time for regrets. Cold water, rest and shade were imperative. Clasping her in my arms, I bounded up the rocks, and laid her by a little pool at the foot of the cliff. I dashed the water upon her face and loosed her clothing. She revived:

"'Holy Virgin, spare him, guide and protect him.'

"There was no word for herself. Then starting up fiercely:

"'The padre! The padre! Bring the padre!' she exclaimed. Then recollecting: 'No, it is too late! too late!'

"My agony was terrible. I wrung her hands, and implored her to live. My wife, my dear wife, with whom I had shared so many perils, who had saved my life; must she lose her own by following me? must she die here when we were beyond danger?

"She soon revived and gave me hope. For a few moments we conversed, and a thrill of delight shook my frame when she spoke and smiled. But it was brief. She felt no pain; her hurt was unto death. Soon her eye grew dim. She drew a small crucifix from her bosom, and held it before her face, while she clasped my hand. Her glazing eye was fixed upon the emblem:

"'Oh, Sancta Maria! O—ra—pro—no—bis——!'

"I took her in my arms. She glanced at me—speechless, with an ineffable smile—pointed upward, and was gone. * * It was night, but I still held her in my arms. I could not consent. I would not have it so; she was mine; I would not yield her to death. * * * Then, laying her on the grass, I raved, prayed and cursed by turns.

"Morning found me still there, but exhausted. The first fierce agony of grief had yielded to a dull pain, which seemed unending.

Farther up in the foot-hills I found a secluded cove, walled in by precipitous rocks and beautiful with bright-hued mountain flowers; and there, with my hunting-knife, I dug her grave. Taking one tress from her dark hair, I laid her to rest, then wandered away in the mountains, careless what became of me. The buds of the mountain rose, with a few raspberries, were my only food for days; often I pondered whether I should not abandon exertion, and yield a life which was worth so little. But life is sweet, and youth does not easily surrender it.

"The fifth day, I was found by a party of hunters, who took me to Fort Lancaster, where I was received as one risen from the dead. The mountain fever, natural result of my toils and sufferings, now prostrated me, and for weeks I hovered between life and death. The late autumn saw me again abroad, and with returning strength came a desire for vengeance. I sought the capital of Texas to take arms against the Mexicans, but a sort of peace had been made. Dissatisfied, restless, but with my yearning for revenge not quite gone, I drifted eastward and through the State of Louisiana. In the spring of 1846 I descended Red River to New Orleans. Retiring late the night of my arrival, and utterly ignorant of what had occurred among nations for many months, in the morning I was wakened by the noise of fife and drum, by the yells of a multitude in the streets, and the long resonant cry of a recruiting agent:

"'Turn out! Turn out! all you who are willing to fight for your country! General Taylor is surrounded, and in all probability cut to pieces, but come on and take revenge out of the d—d Mexicans!'

"I was mad with joy. Without breakfast, and scarcely more than half dressed, I ran into the street, and was soon in the ranks of the recruits. The old cannon of 1812 were brought out and thundered through the city; thousands, tens of thousands thronged the streets, with loud cries for country and vengeance, and before the next night a full regiment was ready to embark. The incoming boat from Matamoras brought news that, instead of being 'cut to pieces,' your general had really been victorious at Palo Alto and Resaca de la Palma; but there was no cessation in the excitement and the volunteering. In a wonderfully short time our little command was on the Rio Grande. But there was a long period of inaction, and before it ended, I, with many others, was transferred to the army near Vera Cruz. Then there was action enough.

"At Cerro Gordo, Cherubusco, Chepultepec, in a dozen fierce encounters, I sought death where others fell, but found it not. I stood amid smoke and carnage, and saw my companions fall on all sides; I marched where shells plowed the earth and swords gleamed in the air, but passed them all and lived. But the storm which brought death to others, brought a strange quiet to me. I saw so much death that it reconciled me to life; I saw such suffering among the poor people we had come to fight, that pity took the place of hate, and I grew ashamed of my thoughts of vengeance. The regiment to which I belonged was the first to be discharged. Then a longing grew upon me to revisit my native land, and early in 1848 I took passage for Havre. But I reached Geneva only to find all Europe rocking with revolution. Storms and tumult were to be my element; I might change my sky, I could not change my destiny.

"It was the year of revolution. France ejected Louis Philippe; Berlin followed in a few days with the students' insurrection, and the capture of the palace; the Viennese were soon in arms; Hungary struggled bravely against perfidious Austria; even the long enslaved Italians rose against Carlo Alberto, and little Baden dared the anger of Prussia. In vain the tears and prayers of my mother, in vain the caresses of my sisters and nieces, or the calm arguments of my father; they had found me only to lose me at once. I hurried to join the Badenischen insurgents, then hastily organizing against the Prussian regulars. For awhile all went well. It seemed that man was at last to be free. But our triumphing was short. France took another Napoleon; the troops fired on the Berlin patriots; Wündischgratz bombarded Vienna; Görgey surrendered without a battle, and the little band under Kossuth, driven to the inhospitable plains of inner Hungary, succumbed to the mongrel hordes of Cossack, Selav, and Carpathian, poured upon them by the Russian Czar. The Badenischen army, too, retreated, and the revolutionists mostly sought the New World. The best blood of the fatherland was expelled, and Germany's loss became America's gain.

"With many others I was captured; but, unlike them, I was a citizen of no country, and could claim no protection or ask no clemency. Four long years I languished in a German prison. Need I recall the lonesome hours? The days of unavailing struggle with myself; the nights of restless tossing, or sleep haunted by dreams of the dead. Daily I watched the gleam of yellow light breaking in through the little grating above my head, slowly moving around the walls of my dungeon, and dying away at last on the opposite side. The daily passage of that ray was my only relic of a bright past, my all of life, of light, of liberty. Nightly I sought relief by thoughts that reached beyond the tomb; the dim rays of natural religion barely gave a gleam of hope that Dolores still lived in another sphere—they might feebly cheer, they could not guide me. And even as I recalled that nightly hope, or watched that daily ray, I ultimately resigned myself to look for happiness only beyond the grave, or nursed the hope of liberty and revenge. Ah! could I escape, I would raise a band of dead hearts like mine and wage inexpiable war on kings.

"At last all hope died out. Even the desire for vengeance died. I was conscious only of a dull pain. The memory of the dead seemed as a dream of long forgotten years; and when I spoke, as sometimes I did, aloud, my own voice jarred on my ear. For two years the jailer who brought my food was all I saw; then for awhile I had a companion in captivity. But we said little; confinement had deadened the social instincts. We talked neither of the struggles of the past, nor of hope for the future; our hearts had died in the awful solitude. Without passing through death, we were inmates of the tomb.

"Why I was released finally I never knew. But I was, with all the others, probably because all danger of insurrection was past, and the government regarded us with contempt. But I came into the world as not of it. My father had died late in '48; my mother, worn with grief, had soon followed him; my sisters had married even before my return from America, and other cares and other loves filled their hearts. Worse than all, liberty was dead. France, Germany, Italy, Hungary, had yielded again to despots; I saw no hope for the rights of man. Again I sought the Rocky Mountains, whose majestic scenery brought balm to my wounded heart. I have learned that he who yields to fierce impulses or excessive feeling, does so but to lay bare his soul to a thousand strokes; that he who would move faster than his age, will soon be alone with sorrow, and that the Brotherhood of Man comes not by spasmodic struggles, but by steady toil.

"Here, where my misery began, in communion with mighty nature I find peace. The memory of Dolores has become a mild joy; her image is ever present to cheer me. The thought of our affection has become a sort of religion. Near where I found and lost her, I best love to dwell, and every returning autumn finds me a pilgrim to the little mountain glen that contains her grave."

CHAPTER VI.

POLYGAMIA.

TURN back the wheels of time, imaginative reader, from 1874 to the autumn of 1868, and allow the author to resume his personal narrative.

The first storm of the season had just tipped the summits of the Wasatch with light snow, while summer still smiled upon the valleys, when our train wound slowly through Parley's Cañon, and emerged upon the eastern "bench," from which I obtained my first view of the Mormon Capital. The city stands at the north-east corner of a valley shaped like a horse-shoe—the Wasatch the eastern boundary, the Oquirrah the western, and the lake lying to the north-west across the open end. A small spur puts out westwardly from the Wasatch, and breaks down in successive "benches" to the upper part of the city; out of it flow City Creek and several smaller streams, and along its base bubble up hot chemical springs and fountains of pure brine.

BRIGHAM YOUNG.

The topography is Palestine reproduced. We have Lake Utah, a fresh water mountain tarn, discharging through the Jordan into another Dead Sea—the Great Salt Lake. Along the Jordan extends a fertile but narrow valley, its widest section near the city; all around are mountains, and beyond those mountains long desert wastes, with only here and there a fertile spot. North of Salt Lake City numerous coves indent the mountains; in each is a small fertile tract and a Mormon settlement, while southward, for four hundred miles, is a series of narrow, fan-shaped valleys settled in like manner.

I found the city a nice place to rest in, especially in September; and after a journey of eight hundred miles over barren plains, like all visitors, I exaggerated its beauty. There was first the morning walk in the dry, bracing air, then a plunge in the warm-spring bath, and an indulgence in the luscious Salt Lake peaches, after which the day was devoted to investigating Mormonism. I called upon all the Mormon worthies. First upon Orson Pratt, solitary as the only man of learning in the Church, and that learning singularly one-sided. At once a fanatic and a mathematician (unique combination), he has devoted a lifetime of labor and sacrifice to perverting the Scripture, in the vain attempt to bring back the modern world to the social system of the Asiatics, and a worse than Jewish theocracy.

At once the poorest, proudest, most learned, and most devoted of the elders, he is also the worst snubbed by Brigham Young, who has often taken a vulgar delight in humbling the man whose culture and scholarship he can not forgive. While he is systematically ignored in the government of the Church, yet when the Tabernacle has an array of Eastern visitors, he is invariably put up to defend the doctrines of Joe Smith and Brigham; and so, while best known to the world of any man in Brigham's kingdom, he is constantly in trouble, and sometimes on the ragged edge of starvation. In early life he was a man of action—a traveling missionary, eloquent in the cause and full of zeal, a successful preacher, and voluminous writer; now he is a dreaming astronomer, whose head is among the stars.

ORSON PRATT.

Later I met W. H. Hooper, monogamous delegate in Congress from this polygamous territory, a man for whom I at first entertained some respect, but learned to distrust by reason of his action in regard to the Mountain Meadow murderers. A Marylander of the old type, native of the "eastern shore," first a merchant's clerk and then captain of a Mississippi steamer, he started across the plains in 1850 on a business venture; but on arriving in Utah found a Mormon wife and an appropriate mission, as the plausible go-between to do Brigham's work among Gentile law-makers. It is not possible that a man of his mental make-up ever *believed* Mormonism; the more reasonable supposition is that he, like many other leaders of this people, holds all religions in equal indifference, but finds his account in this one, and is willing the Church should run along as comfortably as may be, while he accumulates wealth and takes physical comfort. The husband of but one wife, he has never held ecclesiastical position in the Church, but has been remarkably useful during many years service at Washington. In 1872, Brigham concluded that a polygamous people ought to be represented by a polygamist, and accordingly sent George Q. Cannon, the four-wived apostle, to Washington. Congress, which expelled Bowen for having two wives, admitted Cannon with four, and Hooper returned to his store and bank. As all things spiritual are in doubt, any man is excusable for believing any religion; but we can barely excuse one who, in mere indifference, professes belief in the worst imposture of the age.

GEORGE A. SMITH.

My best interview was with George A. Smith, full cousin to the original Joe, and then an apostle, but a little later chosen in full conference to the place of Heber C. Kimball, deceased, as First Councilor to Brigham Young. This man was long known among Gentiles as the most gorgeous liar in the Rocky Mountains. He had four sermons, usually selecting the one most fitting to the occasion; and recited the history of the Church with such an ingenious mixture of fact and fiction, that his dazed hearers accepted the whole as gospel. In his narrative, Mormonism had a roll of martyrs longer than that of the primitive church, and an array of miracles which quite put the Mosaic record in the background. Of sanguine temperament, easily believing every thing that made for the glory of Mormonism, and throwing off with equal ease whatever might have suggested doubt to an earnest thinker, fully persuaded of the Mormon doctrine, that it was right to deceive for the good of the Church, and with a brilliant imagination, that made him believe any thing he had told three times, he was by nature well fitted for the place he had occupied from the first—that of Church Historian.

To him all doubtful points in Mormon annals were referred as to an infallible oracle. When Gentile visitors to the tabernacle were to be impressed, he stood next to Orson Pratt, and when doubtful questions were to be settled in favor of Brigham's pet designs, he found a precedent or made one with equal readiness. He consistently believed and taught that it was the duty of the Mormon laity "to be as a tallowed rag in the hands of the priesthood;" of each order of the priesthood to yield implicit obedience to their superiors next in rank; and of all orders, to be subject to the lightest command of their divinely appointed leader, Brigham Young. To the last of his life he obeyed Brigham's lightest request, and died in the confident faith that he could only enter heaven on Brigham's voucher, properly indorsed by Joseph Smith. To such depths of abasement may the heaven-born intellect sink. He was succeeded as First Councilor by Brigham's son, "Johnnie" Young; for it is one of the "first principles of the gospel" as known in Utah, that all power is to be kept concentrated in the hands of the Smiths and Youngs.

Daniel H. Wells was then, and is now, Brigham's Second Councilor, these three constituting the First Presidency of the Church, and having the right of final decision on all appeals from the lower priesthood, of whatever branch. Wells is, by popular election and "Divine appointment," a Prophet and a Squire, a Mayor and a President, a Lieutenant-General and the husband of five wives. He is a tall, angular and most ungainly Saint, whose face and head bear involuntary witness to the truth of Darwinism. Borrowing a term from dime-novel literature, the Gentiles style him "The one-eyed pirate of the Wasatch." Long acquaintance with his career has only confirmed my first impression of him: he is the most dangerous man in the priesthood. The others are mostly impostors; he *believes* it, bloody doctrines and all. Had he held the reins from 1870 till 1873, he would have precipitated a savage conflict, and the end would have been—Mormonism drowned in blood, as was the Anabaptist schism, or a new development and fresh lease of life on the cry of "persecution." It is well that he has small chance of succeeding Brigham; so much more dangerous is a fanatic than an impostor.

Brigham Young I did not see or converse with till some time after, but was for many years familiar with his appearance in the pulpit. Physically, the man is as near perfect as is ever allowed to one of our wretchedly developed race. Six feet high and uncommonly well muscled, he is yet so compactly built that strangers invariably pronounce him smaller than he is; and one who first sees him step out of his carriage on Main Street, clad in his short, gray business coat, is apt to speak of him as "dumpy." He measures forty-four inches around the chest, and weighs at least two hundred pounds; his hands and feet are rather large, his head extremely so, and very broad across the base, sloping thence before and behind toward the crown. With very light or golden hair, a cold, glittering blue eye and a massive under-jaw that shuts like a vice, he has the firmness and vigor that usually consist with such an organization, and that happy mixture of the sanguine and bilious temperaments which makes one easily believe himself a man of destiny. Of the hardiest Vermont stock, he was put up by nature to last a hundred and twenty years, but hardships and the worry of governing have shortened his life from twenty to forty years, and he may die anywhere between eighty and a hundred, retaining possession of his faculties and growing more tyrannical and avaricious to the last.

Not at all a talented man in the common sense of the word, his power is largely the result of his immense physical potency. His physique is one that makes a man do and dare, and then take the results of that doing and daring as marks of divine favor. Even sneering unbelievers who shake hands with him feel the impress of his magnetic potentiality, nor is it pleasant to face him with the consciousness that one is his enemy. Many an apostate can bear witness that long after being convinced that Mormonism was a hollow fraud, which he ought to abandon, and could abandon without danger, he still felt a grievous dread of standing up in the "School of the Prophets" to face the wrath of Brigham Young. To women of the uncultured and impressible sort, such a man is often as fascinating as a gentle and purring lion: one with all power in reserve to be exercised only for them and upon their enemies. Even a few non-Mormon women have confessed a mild admiration for this mass of power, and at least two Gentile ladies have so far forgotten themselves as to write in fulsome praise of a man whose very existence is a standing insult to womanhood. Such respect hath great native power and virile force.

Before an audience in sympathy with him he is an effective speaker; he can, by a series of strong, nervous appeals, carry them along to almost any pitch of excitement, and commit them, by voice and vote, to almost any absurdity. Add a ready command of language, albeit the vernacular of an uneducated Vermonter, and rare powers as a mimic, and we have the secret of Brigham's strength as an orator. Of eloquence he has none whatever; before a cultured or critical audience he would be a hopeless failure. Whatever greatness he has, finds its source in his splendid physical organization. Thence is his energy, his invincible will, his iron disregard of the sufferings of others—the qualities that have made him. His was also the rare good fortune to fall just at the right time into just the right place for his peculiar talents; for it is scarcely possible that in the ordinary pursuits of life he would have made more than ordinary success. The accident of one man's death and the apostasy of two others, made him President of the Twelve Apostles just before Joe Smith's death; after that event, there was none to oppose him save the flighty and unreliable Sidney Rigdon, whom the Mormons had never trusted, and so Brigham necessarily became head of the Church.

BRIGHAM'S RESIDENCES.

It is a noteworthy fact that in almost every scheme Brigham has undertaken, *except* managing the Mormons, he has completely failed. His Colorado warehouses, beet-sugar factories, Cottonwood Canal, B. Y. Express, and hand-cart emigration scheme, one and all, proved disastrous failures, the last resulting in three hundred deaths, and the most frightful suffering. Similarly every colony Brigham has sent to the surrounding territories has finally been abandoned as a failure, from Lemhi, on the north, to San Bernardino, on the south. Not a few look forward to his death as a great aid to the disintegration of Mormondom; his continued life will do far more in that direction. When he took command of the Mormons they had, according to their own accounts, over 200,000 members in all the world; now they number less than half as many. They submitted all to him, and he has spent thirty years in teaching them the terrors of a religious despotism. Thousands have learned that it is easy to surrender rights, but hard to regain them. At first he only robbed his devotees, now he insults them. A few more years of power and he will, to quote the language of a Mormon, " hitch them up and plow the ground with them."

Many intelligent men have concluded that Brigham was honest in his religious professions. I can not agree with them. I might reject all other evidence of his hypocrisy, but I can not reject his own. Again and again he has virtually admitted that his religion was a mere convenience. To a young Mormon friend of the writer, whom he was urging to return to the fold, Brigham said: "It makes no difference whether you believe in it or not; we need you; just come along and be baptized, and pay up a little on your tithing, and it will be all right." To another he said: "It's no great concern what you believe; I've got as good a right to start a new religion as Christ or Mohammed, or any other man." And yet again, when speaking of the vote of each semi-annual conference indorsing him as a prophet, he said; "I am neither a prophet nor the son of a prophet, but I have been profitable to this people." Since then the Gentiles have usually designated him "The Profit." There was a time, I think, when he believed his religion and worked hard for it; but as he rose in the Church he learned more, and became what he practically describes himself, a philosophic infidel. A man whose convictions depend largely on his interests, with a happy power of self-deception, a great deal of cunning, some executive ability, and behind it all an immense physical potency, with little mercy or conscience to temper it—such, in brief, is Brigham Young.

Late in September, I took a walk to Bear River Cañon, some eighty miles north of the city, stopping often with the rural Saints and noting their ways. This trip was through the most enlightened part of Utah, almost the only part the Eastern tourist ever sees. The villages are neat and quiet, and the little farms well watered and cultivated. But even here the great lack is apparent. The Saints have adopted the bee as their emblem, and have stopped with the blind instincts of the bee—content with food and shelter, with but little regard for the higher man. Near Ogden was an old Dane, living with a mother and two daughters as wives; in Brigham City lived a bishop, married to two of his own nieces, and near Bear River was another Dane, living with three wives in a cabin not large enough to make one comfortable. Such cases were my first select specimens of the practical operations of the "Celestial Law." As this was but one of many journeys I made in Utah, a few general notes on the topography will be in order.

The Wasatch Mountains on the east, and Sierra Nevada on the west, like the two sides of a ( ), inclose a region known as the Great Basin, in which nature appears to have worked on a different plan from that pursued in the rest of the country. All the streams run towards the center, none towards the sea; a river is larger at the head than at the mouth—when it has a mouth—very few of the lakes have any outlet, and, with rare exceptions, both pools and lakes are bitter with salt, iron, lime, or alkali. From the mountains which form the rim of the Great Basin, sub-ranges successively fall off towards the center, and the whole interior plain is an almost unbroken desert. But from the Wasatch and Sierras many streams put out towards the center, and, at the points where they leave the mountains, are bordered by little fan-shaped valleys. These constitute all the cultivable land in the Basin; the rest is fit only for timber or grazing, or is totally barren. Throughout the Basin all the detached mountains run north and south; on them is the only timber, and about their base the only grass to be found. If the mountain is high enough to supply melting snow throughout the summer, there may be a settlement at its base; otherwise all the streams that issue from it will be dry in early spring, and cultivation, that is to say, irrigation, be impossible.

Southward, the country grows steadily dryer and more barren; the valleys smaller, the deserts larger, the streams more unreliable. In Arizona and Southern Utah, I found it difficult, indeed, to get water twice in a day's ride. In the north the most rugged mountains are relieved by graceful adjuncts; there is a gradual ascent from plain to bench, from bench to foot-hill and lower sub-range, and over all is a faint green tinge from brush or bunch-grass, or a dreamy haze that softens the rudest outlines. But in the south there is a grandeur that is awfully suggestive—suggestive of death and worn-out lands, of cosmic convulsions and volcanic catastrophes that swept away whole races of pre-Adamites. There the broad plateaus are cut abruptly by deep cañons with perpendicular sides, sometimes 2000 feet in height; there is a less gradual approach to the highest ranges, and the peaks stand out sharply defined against a hard blue sky. The air is noticeably dryer; there is no haze to soften the view, and the severe outlines of the cliffs seem to frown menacingly upon one who threads the cañons. Needle rocks project hundreds of feet above the general level, while hard volcanic dykes rise above the softer lime or sandstone—mighty battlements, abrupt and unpassable—Pelion upon Ossa piled, as in Titanic war.

The western half of the great Basin is Nevada, the eastern, Mormon Utah. All that part of the Territory east of the Wasatch is still the range of the Mountain Ute, and, for the most part, unfit for white settlements. As nine-tenths of the cultivable land lies along the western base of the Wasatch, in the little detached valleys mentioned, it results that Mormon Utah consists of a narrow line of settlements down the center of the Territory: an attenuated commonwealth rarely more than ten miles wide, but nearly seven hundred miles long—from Oneida, in Idaho, to the Rio Virgen, in Arizona. Geographically, it nearly fills the definition of a line—extension without breadth or thickness. Such communities would naturally develop a different system of law and social organization from that of a continuously fertile and habitable state like Illinois. Manifestly something like the Cantonal system would spring up, with the Commune as a subdivision of the Canton. But in Utah theocracy came in to warp and distort the natural growth of government, and subordinate every thing to the strengthening of priestly power. Against this the Gentiles and Liberal Mormons have unceasingly contended, and hence that interminable struggle—theocracy vs. republicanism—which has so long made up the history of Utah, and in which for many years I was an active participant.

Through all my wanderings in the West I came back to Utah as my home, and to this contest as to my chosen field of action. Even now a glow comes over me at thought of blows given and taken, and the little circle of choice spirits, half philosophers, half politicians, that helped make my life in Utah so pleasant. There was O. J. Hollister, half enthusiast, half business man, and wholly a student and man of literary tastes, who had had, perhaps, a more varied experience than any of the number. Reared in Columbia County, New York, he early felt the "cramp" of farm life there, and sought his fortune first in Pennsylvania, and then in New Jersey and Maryland. The westward wave carried him to Kansas, and when the contest was over there, on to the gold fields of Pike's Peak; and before his frame had hardened into manhood, he was busy among the pioneers of a new State. Mining, lumbering, freighting, and ranching gave vigor to his body and mind till the war broke out, when he joined Gilpin's Colorado regiment. With them he marched a thousand miles, and helped drive Sibley out of New Mexico, then returned, and again engaged in mining, and finally graduated as an editor, in which capacity he came to Utah. Our first year there saw him enthusiastic, eager for reform, confident that wonders could be done by union and energy. A little later, he married the sister of Vice-president Colfax, took a good office, grew rich and conservative, and concluded that the Utah question was to be slowly worked out rather than quickly fought out.

There, too, was Colonel J. H. Wickizer, who for six years regulated the mails of Utah, Montana, and Idaho, and provided his Gentile friends with an unfailing store of anecdote and apt illustration. He was long a colleague and intimate friend of Abraham Lincoln, rode the circuit with him in Illinois, and contended often with him at the bar. A man of nice and discriminating taste in letters, he was a walking encyclopedia of Western wit, humor, and historic incident. His point of attack was the utter nonsense of Mormonism and its theocratic government; for it is to be noted that all of us thought little and cared less about the *religion*—it was the civil (or rather uncivil) government we objected to.

Other active participants in our political and social plans were Governor George L. Woods and Secretary Geo. A. Black. But the central figure in Utah, during our period of greatest excitement, was Chief Justice James B. McKean. Descended on one side from the Machians of Scotland, and on the other from the French Huguenots that settled on Long Island, he seemed to unite the fearless conscientiousness of the one race with the tireless energy of the other. A case has been made out against him on the charge that he was rather fanatical in his dislike of polygamy and theocracy; but it was a kind of fanaticism we were sorely in need of in Utah. He and his colleagues, Justices Hawley and Strickland, were the first Federal judges who boldly faced the difficulty presented by the anomalous organization of the district courts. For twenty years the United States judges had for the most part yielded the point, and this yielding, threw all the power into the hands of the Mormon bishops, who acted as territorial judges. Judge McKean decided that this ought not to be so; made the United States marshal the ministerial officer of his court; got a grand jury over which the Church had no control, and entered on an inquiry into the many murders committed between 1855 and 1863. The Supreme Court of the United States overruled his decision after his court had been in operation twenty months; but it was too late to save the Church from complete exposure. The good had been accomplished, the evidence had been brought out, and the guilt traced home; and though the final decision resulted in turning a hundred and twenty-eight murderers and other criminals loose, it could not suppress the evidence already published. From that time forward the Mormon Church was on the defensive, and its speakers ceased to apologize for murder. This great work these judges accomplished; and if their law was wrong, their action was right, and its results in every way good for Utah.

In time, there came to our aid many independent Mormons, men of active talents, but too much given to verbal hair-splitting. They were, one and all, infidels of the toughest stock; for the man who has been a Mormon for many years rarely takes a firm hold on any other faith. Having been so badly fooled once, he inclines to regard all religion as either fraud or delusion. I smile at thought of one such who was one of my political co-laborers. He talked long and loud of liberty, equality, and fraternity, but cursed the administration, and despaired of republican government; he quoted Tom Paine and Herbert Spencer by the hour; was eloquent on first principles and universal law, and argued on the Supreme Good, the control of passion, and the unknowable, till he was black in the face with anger. To him, the New Testament was a myth, the *Banner of Light* a gospel; he put his faith in Spiritual Philosophy, and believed nearly every thing but the Bible.

The warring factions were at peace when I entered Utah; but the October conference of the Mormons renewed the fight, by issuing a decree against all Gentile merchants. It was made cause of excommunication for any Saint to patronize them in any way whatever. In eight months ten Gentile firms had left the city, and in August, 1869, Salt Lake contained no more than two hundred Gentiles. The Union Pacific Railroad was completed in May of that year, and let a little light into the Territory; soon the interest in mining revived, and we turned our eyes towards the mountains as the last hope for non-Mormons. Had this resource failed, I am positive there would not be a hundred Gentiles in Utah to-day. The social despotism of the Church was so great they could not have remained.

In September, 1869, I made a pleasant journey to the Sevier Mines, two hundred miles south of Salt Lake, in company with some miners. My memory does not recall a more pleasant journey. All day we rolled along through grassy meads or over rocky flats, with a blue sky overhead, and fanned by the soft airs of autumn in that most delightful climate. The coves opening back into the mountains were rich in bunch-grass, in which jack-rabbits were abundant; sage hens and other small fowl were numerous on the plain, and large flocks of ducks were found along the stream. The Sevier Valley has an average elevation of five thousand feet above the sea; the summers are mild, and in winter snow rarely falls to any depth; cattle live on the range nine months in the year, and yet the region is free from the scorching heat of Arizona. Very little of the valley is cultivable, however; stock-ranching is the principal occupation. We passed through seven walled towns, which had been abandoned by the Mormons on account of hostile Indians, and were still uninhabited. At Marysvale, last town on the Sevier, we found the Mormons returning to their homes, peace having been made with the Indians. There we turned into the mountains, and toiled for six hours in advancing six miles up Pine Gulch. One moment we were on the edge of a narrow track where an overturn would have sent us a hundred feet into the bed of the stream, and the next struggling through a narrow chasm at the bottom of the gulch, with walls of granite rising on both sides of us, and above them the sloping sides of the cañon half a mile in height, and covered with timber to the very summit. The roaring brook, now beside us, now far below us, and again dashing against our wagon wheels, seemed to be singing of the snowy heights whence it came; and at every point where a depression or obstructing rock formed a pool, the shining mountain trout were to be seen in numbers through the clear fluid, though its temperature was but little above that of ice-water.

After a week in this new mining region, I returned to Salt Lake City, and to the normal condition of a polemic editor. The tide had turned. The Gentiles were coming in again, mostly to engage in mining, and in a year from that date the Territory contained several thousand non-Mormons. By the autumn of 1871, all the mountains of central Utah were dotted with miners' cabins and traversed by prospectors. By 1875, there was a non-Mormon population in Utah of fifteen or twenty thousand, with a political organization, churches, schools, and daily papers of their own, having political control of one county and half a dozen towns. But the old conflict goes on just the same. A theocracy never yields power till compelled to. The young Mormons welcome the change; the older ones, and especially the priesthood, only regret that they were not more severe and exclusive when they had the power. But Mormonism in a family never outlasts one generation. Old Mormons die, young ones grow up infidels; so in due time the system must expire by natural limitation, especially since the foreign supply has ceased. The original force of fanaticism wears itself out. So it was with the Irvingites, Muggletonians, etc., and so it will doubtless be with Mormonism. Such a delusion is like one of Utah's mountain streams, which plunges from a rocky gulch as though it would tear up all the country below; five miles down the plain it has become a gentle rivulet or sluggish slough, five miles further, and there is a channel of dry sand, with here and there a brackish pool. Such seems to be the course of all religious delusions which do not end in blood.

But the death of Mormonism will not end Utah's troubles. Instead of 75,000 fanatics, there will be 150,000 infidels—all those of Mormon parentage, having no philosophy to take the place of religion. The debris of Mormonism will encumber the land for a generation. The original Mormon converts were from the most hardy and virtuous peasantry in Europe; they came over as a rule in middle life, and Mormonism could not entirely spoil them. Their children will suffer all the evil results of polygamy and superstitious folly, with none of the restraint imposed by a theocracy—all the evil and none of the good. There will be a laxity of conduct and a general flabbiness of the moral fiber, which will not be cured till they learn by dire experience that the way of the transgressor is hard. The Mormon doctrine that "it is right to lie for the good of the Church," has made deceit an institution. It can scarcely be said that any disgrace attaches to perjury. Jews and Gentiles who live long among this people too often become addicted to the same practices; for, say they, "if we do n't, they get the advantage." There is in Utah more downright lying to the square mile than in any other region on this continent; and the religious lying is the worst of all. Thus stands the Utah situation: the Jews lie for gain, the Gentiles from association, and the Mormons "for Christ's sake."

CHAPTER VII.

THE PACIFIC SLOPE.

A YEAR in Utah had brought renewed health and strength; but the love of Western travel was aroused. I would see Nevada and California; I would enjoy the sublime scenery of the Sierras, and breathe the soft airs of the Pacific.

The Union and Central Pacific Railroads had joined in laying the last rail at Promontory, on the 10th of May, 1869, and thousands were taking this, the first, opportunity to visit the Far West in restful comfort. Corinne, my starting point, had grown with railroad suddenness to a "city" of 1,500 people; then fallen away to a rather dull village of 500. Along the track west of it had sprung up five tent-towns, whose equals were never seen: Promontory, Deadfall, Murder Gulch, Last Chance, and Painted Post. At one of these, in its brief existence of two weeks, there were five homicides. The railroad laborers, then being paid off by hundreds, were the natural prey of the harpies who occupied these towns.

Among the first families of Deadfall were two plainsmen, known as Arkansaw and Curly ——, the former a "fly shot," the latter noted for nothing more than a strange, reckless humor, and immense capacity for whisky. Crazed by intemperance and the loss of his money at gambling, he finally took on a huge disgust at life, and one day said to Arkansaw:

"Would you do me a favor?"

"With pleasure, old pard. What is it?"

"Just to shoot me through the head."

"Certainly, if you wish it—do any little thing of that sort for an old friend. But let's step down to the sand-bar; it wouldn't do to bother the folks."

The whole population turned out to witness the shooting. A line having been formed, Curly knelt in front of the crowd, and Arkansaw took position and fired, the ball just cutting the hair from the crown of Curly's head.

"D—n you, don't mangle me," was his comment; "you must do better than that."

Calling for whisky, Arkansaw swallowed an immense draught; then raised his pistol slowly and with evident deliberation. There was a sharp report, and Curly fell forward on his face, but in an instant sprang to his feet. Arkansaw's shot had cut his left ear clean from his head! The sharp sting and flow of warm blood suddenly changed his mind, and bounding into the ravine, he took to his heels, followed by the yells and laughter of the crowd. When Arkansaw told me this story in Corinne (where I then edited a paper), he laughed till the tears stood in his eyes; he considered it the champion joke of his career.

Promontory was for that season the transfer point between the Union and Central Pacific; and was composed about equally of hotels, saloons and gambling tents, with a few stores and shops. There flourished every form of "cut-throat" gambling known: three-card monte, ten-die, the strap game, chuckaluck, and the patent lock game. Occasionally "legitimate" gambling, like faro or keno, was established; but "cut-throat" games were the rule. "Cappers" boarded the cars at Corinne or Kelton, formed acquaintance with their victims by the time the train reached Promontory, and led them straight into the dens. Strange that so many men are yet deceived when these tricks have been exposed so often; strange that even old travelers can be caught by devices explained a hundred years ago in the "Rogue's Lexicon." But no less strange than true, that almost every day these fellows robbed somebody. No less a personage than Don Pico, formerly Mexican Governor of California, left $600 in gold with the "Promontory boys."

What I particularly admire in the "sports" is the fine morality they display in always having the loser in the wrong. The latter is certain he is going to cheat the gambler, otherwise he would never venture. He thinks the gambler ignorant of the fact that the card is marked, or the lock "hampered," or the trap changed, as the case may be, by the "capper;" and goes in on what he considers a "dead sure thing." Hence there should be no legal action to recover money lost in gambling. Between the gambler and the loser the moralities are equal; both are rogues at heart, only the former is the more expert.

From Promontory to the foot of the Sierra Nevadas, there seemed scarcely a break in the awful barrenness and desolation. The air was bracing and the sky beautifully clear, flecked only by light silvery clouds; but there the list of beauties ends. There are mountains red and yellow, plains dazzling white, dull gray or dirty brown, and alternate vistas of sand, flint, salt and alkali. Here and there are large tracts of bunch-grass, but that, brown as broom-sedge, does not to an Eastern eye relieve the landscape. Occasionally the mountain scenery rises to the sublime, but for the most part the view is strangely wearisome. On some people these scenes produce a deep and peculiar melancholy. It is as though all hope had died out of mother earth, leaving the dead embers of a burnt-out land as witnesses to the awful despair of nature.

HUMBOLDT PALISADES.

For hundreds of miles after leaving the fertile valley of Bear River there is scarcely place for a garden. There is first the Promontory Range and then Indian Creek Desert; then Red Dome and Red Desert; then the Goose Creek Range and the Goose Creek Desert; then the Humboldt Range and the Humbolt Desert, and finally a few detached buttes and sun-scorched sand-hills through which we pass to the Great Nevada Desert, last, longest and worst of all. Into it flow Carson, Truckee, Reese, and Humboldt rivers and a hundred smaller streams; out of it comes nothing. Salt lakes, alkaline "sinks" and mud flats alone relieve the dreary monotony; the phenomena are hot winds, blinding dust, the mirage, and the shadow of death. The only view of any grandeur is at Humboldt Cañon, now better known as the Palisades, a wild gorge through which the river has forced its way in some far distant geologic age, and where the railroad track lies along the base of a perpendicular rock many hundred feet in height. Far below the excavated track the waters of the Humboldt foam over the uneven bottom of a narrow channel, obstructed in many places by the immense rocks, which have fallen from the cliff. The lack of colors prevents that singular variety which is the charm of Echo and Weber Cañons, but the cold, unchanging gray imparts a wild and gloomy beauty instead. On the south side of the cañon the Devil's Peak rises fifteen hundred feet directly above the river.

The needs of miners and stock-ranchers in the adjacent mountains have built up a few trading towns along this route; and taking the road by sections, I spent some days at each. First, over Sunday, at Toano, on Terrace Mountain, where the Sabbath was kept as regularly as in New England—the men went hunting or rested at the gambling hall; the girls had a dance or got drunk. Next at the lively and furiously speculative town of Elko, outfitting point for the rich White Pine region, and consequently a place of importance—while the mines held out. Then at Argenta, Winnemucca and Reno, gray dots upon a white desert, and but slight relief to the landscape. Every-where west of Utah we find California work and ideas, pay in coin, and encounter the Chinese with their chip hats and linen blouses, rice feed, cheap labor, and universal "no sahvey" to any question they don't *want* to understand. They then worked for thirty-one dollars per month, boarding themselves, which amounted to an embargo on white labor wherever they came in competition.

The Humboldt, which is a good sized stream as long as it keeps within the cool shadow of the mountains, decreases with every mile as soon as it enters the desert; at last we see it no more, for what little is left has turned southward, and is lost in the "sink." The worst desert we cross in the night, and wake at daylight to glad relief, for we are climbing the Sierras, among the grand pines and along the crystal waters of the foaming Truckee. To one just from the treeless plains, no sight is so grateful as a dense forest, and like a tourist from the State of Maine, who lately passed that way, I felt to exclaim: "Thank the Lord, I smell pitch once more!"

From this region goes most of the lumber used along the road, as far as Salt Lake City; but over all that interior there is an ever-increasing scarcity of good timber. Woods are found only upon the mountains; the inner plains of the Great Basin are as bare of trees as if blasted by the breath of a volcano. At Verdi Station, 5,000 feet above sea-level, we pass the State line and enter California. Crossing the Truckee, we take an additional locomotive and enter upon the steepest ascent of the Sierras. The first large curve brings us above

Donner Lake, so named in memory of those unfortunate emigrants from Quincy, Illinois, who here starved and froze and suffered away the long cold winter of 1846. Next we look down upon Lake Bigler, and another hour brings us to Summit Station, highest point on the Central Pacific, 7,042 feet above sea-level, 1,669 miles from Omaha, and 105 from Sacramento. We enter now upon the western slope, with its steep descent; and with the breaks "set up" and very little steam, we still rush along at a fearful rate, at one place running twenty-five miles in thirty minutes, without an ounce of steam. Forty miles of

SEVEN THOUSAND FEET ABOVE THE SEA.

snow-sheds have been erected along this part of the line at a cost of a million and a half dollars; to the great assurance of winter passage, but an equal hinderance to enjoyment of the view.

Running out upon a more gentle grade, we pass in rapid succession, Dutch Flat, Little York, You Bet, and Red Dog, all old mining towns, the largest still containing three thousand inhabitants. All along the road we see mile after mile of flumes running in every direction down the ridges, and carrying large streams to be used in hydraulic mining below; and in places pass hundreds of acres of "old dirt," which has been washed out and abandoned. All are alert for the view of Cape Horn, the wonder of this route; but the sight is not good for nervous people. An awful chasm, at first apparently right before us, and then but a little to the left, opens directly across the range; and, standing on the steps of the car, it seems as if the train were rushing headlong into it. The first view allows the sight to pierce a thousand feet, almost straight downward to the green bottom, where the trees shrink to mere shrubs, and the Chinamen working at the lumber seem like pigmies; a little further down the gorge the wagon bridge—hundreds of feet above the bottom—appears like a faint white band, and still further the sight is lost in a blue mist. The railroad track is ex-

CAPE HORN.

cavated along the sides and around the head of this gorge, where, in aboriginal days, the Indians had not even a foot-path, as the first descent from the head of the chasm is six hundred feet, nearly perpendicular. When the road-bed was constructed, the men who made the first excavation were secured by ropes let down from a higher point.

The climate changes with every hour's descent. The red earth, resinous pines, and yellow grass show that we are on the Pacific Coast; but the view is wonderfully relieved by the pines, and the red branches and pale green leaves of the manzanita. Settlements thicken; gardens, fields, and orchards appear. Down at last on the California side of the Sierras, we emerge from the foot-hills upon a rather level plain dotted with live oaks, with occasionally a cultivated field. Crossing this plain and the American River, we leave the cars and walk amid the neat squares and well-watered grass plats of the State capital.

A week in Sacramento taught me one important fact: that California malaria is quite as bad in its way as Wabash malaria, for I had the unmistakable old-fashioned ague. The returning miners who brought East such wonderful accounts of the healthfulness of California, spent most of their time there in the hills or on the higher plateaus; for in the low grounds along the larger streams there is miasma enough. For many miles along their lower course, the Sacramento and San Joaquin (which the absurd natives pronounce *Wahkeen*) are bordered by vast marshes and *tule* lands, which yield slowly to flood plains, all overflowed in the rainy season. The days are hot, the nights are cool, the winter and spring very wet, the summer very dry—why should we not find malaria, if nature's laws are uniform? But a little further away from the streams, the dry air of California, slightly tempered by ocean winds, gives assurance of health.

I next sought the rural districts, crossing the Sacramento into Yolo County, and following the raised track of the California Central Railroad as my best passage through the *tule* lands. *Tule* is the Spanish or Indian name of a coarse reed which covers the entire tract, green during winter and spring, but now dry as tinder, and furnishing fuel for extended fires. Far down among the reeds, which often exceeded ten feet in height, I saw cattle hunting for scattered clumps of grass, which still had a little shade of green in the moisture preserved by the *tules*. Beyond this tract, the road emerges into a vast plain, overflowed for many miles out in winter, but now dry and dusty, and covered with coarse grass of a yellowish brown color, which looks, to the Eastern eye, as if every particle of nutriment were burnt out of it.

At Davisville, fifteen miles from Sacramento, I remained a few days to investigate the fruit farms and silk culture. A large field had been planted in mulberry trees; a factory large enough to employ a hundred hands was being erected, and the experiment is now in active and favorable operation. Sericulture will some day constitute one of the leading interests of California, as capable men are entering upon it at several places, and there can scarcely be a doubt that the climate and soil are well adapted thereto. The want of cheap labor has been the great hinderance; and this is supplied by the Chinese, who will probably become silk manufacturers here as at home. Vineyards extended in all directions. The picking season was over, but there were still grapes enough on the vines to furnish a plentiful repast. Many thousand bunches had dried upon the stem, and tasted more like raisins than grapes, unless of the acid Sonoma variety; these had a strong fiery taste. Every known species, from the extreme north to the tropics, seems to find here a second native country, as it were, where it attains to great size and fineness of flavor.

Every district in California produces its own peculiar wine, but all the lighter kinds go by the general name of "Sonoma White," the manufacture having begun at Sonoma. It has been claimed that the use of light wines lessens the demand for strong liquors. It certainly has not produced that effect in California. While the Eastern tourist is eager for his draught of ice-cooled Sonoma, the old Californian invariably calls for whisky. Perhaps it is because they used whisky so long before wine became plenty. On every road from the larger towns is a series of hotels, with bar attachment, usually known as the One-mile House, the Two-mile House, etc.; and a man's capacity (in other words the length of time he has been in California) is usually guaged by the number he can patronize on his way to and from town. The "pilgrim" often falls before he reaches town. The man who has been here a few years gets in with his team, disposes of his load, and usually has to spend the night at the One- or Two-mile House. But the old Californian drinks at every place on his way in, transacts business with a clear head, reverses the drinking process at every place going out, even to the Ten-mile House, and gets home in good condition to do his evening's work and enjoy himself in the bosom of his family.

Besides figs and grapes there is very little fruit grown in the main valley; but in all the little mountain vales, both in the Coast Range and Sierras, is produced almost every fruit of the temperate and tropical climes. Apples are not so finely flavored as in the East, and pears are large and coarse; but peaches are better, and plums, damsons, and nectarines perfectly delicious. It is in grapes, however, that California particularly excels.

From Davisville I traveled up Putah Creek all day through a rich level country, covered now with the rich haze of autumn, the air seeming full of red dust and smoke; passed occasionally clumps of trees and very inferior looking farm-houses, *seldom* painted or well-finished; traversed mile after mile of continuous wheat fields, with stubble still bright though the crop was harvested four months ago, and found the same dry, dusty, grassless look over the whole landscape. The entire valley is devoted to the growth of wheat and barley, with the exception of occasional stock-ranches which also appear devoid of life at this season, with the same old look, and half-Southern, half-Spanish air of shiftlessness. The road runs unfenced through a constant succession of wheat fields, whence the grain had been cut late in May; and the prevailing impression was of drought. There were fields parched and cracked open, dust in great heaps among the dried vegetation, grass withered and burnt, while the largest creeks were entirely dried up or shrunk to mere rivulets, pursuing their sluggish and doubtful course away down at the bottom of deep gulches, which in winter and spring are filled by immense torrents. At night the horizon was lighted up by fires raging in the stubble on the high lands, or among the *tules* lower down, and by day the sun was obscured, and distant objects hidden by the smoke or light haze, which corresponds to our eastern Indian summer, and is here the immediate precursor of the first rain.

Having since visited California at other seasons, I find it to possess an almost aggravating regularity of climate. To begin with the year, January is the month when the heaviest rains are passed, and the ground is settling for the spring growth. Soon this valley is beautiful indeed. Strawberries and other early fruits are early in market, the plains are of a rich green, plowing is pushed forward with vigor, wheat is sown, and springs quickly into growing life. In March the rainy season appears to come again, though, generally, the "later rain" is light. Thence the showers grow slowly less and less frequent till some time in May. The wheat is about full grown, early potatoes begin to appear, and slight signs of drought are manifest. The grass gets ripe, the Spanish oats (wild) begin to turn yellow, and early in June the wheat is harvested.

It lies or stands in shocks on the ground, to be threshed out at will; for no rain need now be apprehended. The surface begins to show signs of extreme drought; by the middle of July the freshets are all past and the marshes dried up; the ground cracks open in long fissures, into which the grass seeds fall and are preserved to another growing season. As summer advances all the minor vegetation loses its green; the grass, dead ripe, stands cured to a bright yellow, varied in places by a dirty brown; creation assumes a gray and dusty color, and only the purple fig leaves and faint green of of those trees which have a deeper root relieve the general aspect of barrenness. On the slopes of the Sierras, the red dust lies six inches in depth, and the prospect is brightened only by occasional patches of verdure along the mountain streams, and the pale-green oval leaves of the manzanita.

Still the heavens remain clear. Then one may see through the valley of the Sacramento great stacks of wheat in sacks, standing in the open fields till a convenient time arrives for hauling it away, and threshing-machines running in the open air with no fear of rain. The stubble of the old fields retains its brightness, and the long dry autumn of California is fairly inaugurated. The marshes become

CALIFORNIA AGRICULTURAL REPORT.

beds of dust, which is blown up in stifling clouds; the mirage appears upon the plain in deceptive floods of what the Mexicans call "lying waters;" the *tules* become dry as tinder, and at night the Sacramento is lighted for miles by the fires that rage over the same area where, eight months before, a steamboat could ply at ease. The yellow grass is eaten to the ground, and the herds are driven far up the mountains; the dust, which has become insufferable in the roads, seems to blow away and on to the fields; the roads are often bare and dry, hardened like sunburnt brick, and the depressions in the fields knee-deep in dust. The sky becomes obscured; the sun rises red and fiery, and disappears about 4 P. M., in a bank of haze. People prepare for winter by nailing a board here and there on an apology for a barn, and hauling away any wheat that remains in the field. After a few preliminary showers, the "early rain" comes in force; torrents descend upon beds of dust, and the plain becomes a sea of thin mud. Then all the mountain gulches are swollen with muddy red water; the Sacramento spreads for miles over the *tule* lands, and steamers again ply over what was a baked plain three months before. In a few weeks the worst is passed, and the growing season begins again. Moral: To enjoy California, come in the first half of the year. From June till November it is too dry for comfort; from that till the middle of January too muddy.

I have only described the climate of the interior—that series of broad plains bordering the San Joaquin and Sacramento, and extending to the foot-hills of the Coast Range on the west and the Sierras on the east, which includes three-fourths of agricultural California. Taken as a whole, however, the State has three grand divisions of climate. First is the coast climate; in that narrow strip between the Coast Range and the ocean, the fields are watered nightly by the ocean fogs, and are green from January to December. Hence their leading industry—expressed in the local phrase—"the cow counties." Next is the interior climate, above described. The region bordering the bay of San Francisco enjoys a mixture of two climates. The third might be called the mountain-valley climate. From the Sierras some forty little valleys open westward; down each one flows a bright stream, affluent of the San Joaquin or Sacramento, and each has a different climate, from Sonora, where figs ripen, and strawberries grow in February, to Yreka, where snow sometimes lies for three months. Our artist has faithfully depicted the average Californian's description of the products of his State. The reader may discount the picture opposite by a very large per cent.

Next I went to San Francisco, by way of Vallejo, taking steamer thence to the city. The rainy season had set in, and I awoke next morning to a view, from my room far up the hill, of a city half hidden in mist, from which spires and cupolas projected like sharp rocks above a swelling flood. Three days of rain, and then the city put on its "winter" look. The citizens boast of their winters and apologize for their summers; and well they may. August is the coldest (to the feelings) and September the warmest month in the year! One can feel no difference in temperature between January and June; furs are worn from July 1st till late in August, then left off till near Christmas again. The latter part of the winter is singularly mild and equable—about as May in the latitude of Philadelphia. The genesis of these strange contradictions is in the coast winds. In July and August they set hard and full upon the coast, bringing with them a dense fog that lowers the temperature till an overcoat is a necessity. In September comes a calm, while there is still heat enough in the summer sun to warm the air; later comes the softer wind from the south-west. But this south-west wind also drives in the rain clouds upon the interior plains; so while San Francisco has her nicest weather, the interior has its rainy season. The clouds thus driven north from the South Pacific drop but scant moisture on Southern California; the rain-fall at Fort Yuma rarely exceeds two inches per year. Northward they are caught by the higher mountains, and the rain-fall increases; till at last, entangled amid the sub-ranges of Oregon, they shower almost constantly from October till May.

I like San Francisco for its variety. If one don't enjoy staid American society, there are French, Italian, and Spanish quarters, and not far off Kanakas, and ever-present Chinese. Society is in a transition state. This is a land of the beggar and the prince. The oppressive land monopoly which was fixed upon California by Mexican policy, the wonderful fluctuations in mining property, and the daring speculations of its business men, have given over the wealth to a few hands. There seems to be no well defined middle class. Public taste inclines to the showy; for wealth and fashion naturally outran culture in a community which, in twenty years, rose like another Venice, from the salt marsh and sand-hill to unmeasured opulence.

The city is strangely picturesque and interesting. On the west side of the bay and facing the east, the business blocks cover the flat along the water front and extend a little way up the slope; thence the residences and public buildings continue to rise in terraces, to the very summit of the ridge—a spur of Monte Diablo. With this slope and its sandy soil, it is of necessity clean and free from malaria. The ocean fogs are bracing to some constitutions, death to others. No man can reason beforehand as to how they will affect him; they refuse to follow *a priori* rules. The first San Francisco was built almost entirely of wood, and vanished one day in a sweeping fire. The second was built in a rather fragile manner with more solid materials; the frequent fires finally cured the first fault, and the earthquakes frightened them out of the second. In one year the city had eleven "shakes."

The Chinese, seen in every part of California, are never out of sight in the city, of which they constitute one-sixth of the population. Some twenty squares along Dupont Street are given up to them, the locality appropriately known as "Barbary Coast." We found it settled so thickly that it seems scarcely possible human beings could exist so, and could scarcely repress a feeling of fear as we plunged into the dark alleys lined by little cubby-holes, and alive with yellow women. But our guide assures us we are always safe here; "though," he adds, "I can't give you any such promise two squares from here, among the whites." This suggests the "hoodlum," or young rough, which San Francisco has in fearful abundance.

Of course my resident friends took me to the Chinese Theater, where we witnessed part of a play representing some marvelous incidents in the career of Rip Sah, or some other old humbug, whose name and monarchy were great in China about sixty thousand years since. I may not have the date quite correct, as Celestial history consists of the annals of a series of dynasties, evolving civilization and philosophy through successive eras of such magnitude that a variation

"BARBARY COAST," SAN FRANCISCO.

of twenty thousand years, more or less, is regarded as a trifling discrepancy. The musicians sit upon the stage directly behind the actors, who enter and retire always by the wings; and the dying groans of Rip Sah, who expires in a fit just after having beheaded fifty thousand prisoners, are drowned by the monotonous droning of something like a tin drum and two three-stringed instruments, about as musical as a hog with his nose under a gate, but not half as expressive.

The California Chinese (and I include in this class all in the Far West,) seem to me to have the coldest, most gloomy and repellant religion, the most chilling philosophy, of any race in the world. There is but one redeeming feature in the case; they are all in a skeptical state, and do not more than half believe their own faith. I once witnessed in Sacramento their great "devil-drive," which includes nearly all the ceremonies of their religion. At least four thousand Chinese were present; and with the blowing of horns, beating gongs, talking and yelling, by Mongolian courtesy called singing, and open-air theaters and bands, they made the evening lively. Nearly all the Chinese in America are orthodox Buddhists, who reason the matter thus: "If God good, why pray? Tend to the devil." Hence this ceremony of driving out the latter.

We found the devil "out in the cold"—a hideous black figure, easily recognized as the evil one, set upon a pedestal just outside the door. Within were two enormous "Joshes," ten feet high, one in each corner, and over them a shelf filled with little household gods, two feet or so in length; while behind the altar the Buddhist priests and attendant boys were going through a ceremony very similar to High Mass. The Buddhists, like the Mormons, believe in a regular gradation of *gods*, rising one above another to the great head *god*, whom the Mormons call Eloheim, and the Chinese "Top-side Josh."

Outside, booths with open front were erected, in which various plays were being performed in choice Tartar, the view free to the crowd. This continued till midnight, when a general chorus of priests and bands announced the close of the festival (?) and a torch was applied to the devil. The figure, which proved to be full of fire-crackers, "went off" in brilliant style till nothing was left apparently but the hideous head and back-bone; these then shot upward like a huge Roman candle, leaving a trail of blue fire, and exploded high in the air with a loud report, followed by a shower of sparks and insufferable stench. And that was supposed to drive the devil away for a year! Turning away with a feeling of relief that the devil was gone at last, I encountered Ah Ching, our Mongolian laundryman, at the Pacific Hotel, who spoke some English, and had an intellect that was "not to be sneezed at," of whom I sought information, and received it thus:

"Hallo, John, do you believe in him?"

"Oh, velley, Melica man, me believe him."

"All Chinamen believe in him?"

"Oh, China like Melica man. Some believe him, sahvey; some tink him all gosh damn." And I felt that I was answered.

CHAPTER VIII.

TWO YEARS OF CHANGE.

From the Golden Gate I returned to Utah and trouble. I had often dealt theoretically with the Mormon courts. I was now to have practical experience of their beautiful uncertainty.

Corinne, where I had my legal residence, an exclusively Gentile town, had sprung up suddenly in the center of an old Mormon county. The county judge was one Samuel Smith, husband of six wives, two of whom were his own brother's daughters, sealed to him by Brigham Young, with full knowledge of that relationship. As editor of the only Gentile paper in Utah, I had occasionally commented on this fact with considerable severity; nevertheless, when summoned to his court as party to a civil suit, I attended with the innate American confidence that every body is safe in the shadow of a court-house.

The trial was over, and I was just stepping off the court-house portico, when I received a thundering whack in the back of the head which sent me face forward upon the gravel. There was a rush, a sound of curses, and I felt, first a shower of blows upon the head and shoulders, and then one or more persons walking over me with heavy boots. I distinctly heard bones snap *somewhere;* then there was a void, and next my friends were picking me up and taking stock generally of my condition. My left collar-bone was broken in two places, one of my ribs loosened, my temple badly cut, and about two inches of my scalp torn off, besides being badly hurt myself. We were but nine Gentiles in a Mormon town of twelve hundred people, so there was nothing to be done but haul me over to Corinne, where my wounds were dressed. In one week I was walking about town in pretty good condition, and just a month from the attack was discharged cured, and able to travel.

Wonderful as this recovery seems, it is nothing to what I have known to occur in the pure air of the Rocky Mountains. A blacksmith living in Montana, located on the stage-road a hundred miles from the nearest surgeon, had his knee shattered by a pistol-shot. He sharpened two bowie-knives, strapped the leg over a bench, and amputated it half way between the knee and hip-joint, taking up the arteries with his own hands, and searing them with irons heated by himself in the forge. His wound healed by what physicians call "the first intention," and he still lives, to walk pretty well upon a wooden leg, and be known throughout the mountains as "Nervy Bill."

I saw a man in Stockton, California, who had been "bodaciously chawed up," to use his own language, by a grizzly bear. In the

"BODACIOUSLY CHAWED UP."

death-hug he had an arm and leg broken, and all the flesh torn from his forehead and crown, after which he lay two days and nights in the cañon before being found. Yet he lived, in good health, and not badly disfigured. Chief-Justice Brookings, late of the Supreme Court of

Dakota, broke through the ice in the Big Sioux River, and was held fast for twenty-four hours, his legs crushed by the ice and chilled by the cold water. Both limbs were amputated; but he enjoys good health, walks upon corks, and to use the language of an admiring constituent "is able to stump 'round an' do a heap o' devilment." It's the physical condition at the time that does it. Debauchees have died from the scratch of a rusty nail; mountaineers have survived a dozen gaping wounds, any one of which, by sound medical reasoning, should have killed them.

My principal assailant proved to be the son of Judge Smith. He was arrested by the Mormon authorities and *fined five dollars*. It is well known in Utah that, in such cases, the fine is seldom paid. Two years afterwards, W. R. Keithley, a lawyer in Salt Lake City, struck a Mormon editor two blows with a light cane, doing no particular damage. He was taken before the Mormon justice, fined a hundred dollars, and put under bonds of four hundred to keep the peace. That was about the percentage of difference in those days between justice to the Saint and the Gentile. It is different now—thanks to Ulysses Grant and Judge McKean. But as for me, I can safely swear that I have a little more than balanced the account with the Mormons. I can lay my hand on my heart and say that they don't owe me a cent.

After a winter visit to the East, I returned to Utah early in 1870, eager to be fighting the old battles again. There had been great changes. The first reaction, following the completion of the Union Pacific Railroad, was past, and the mountains were lively again. Rich silver veins had been opened in the Wasatch, and miners by hundreds were pouring in. Better than all, U. S. Grant was at the helm, and had sent *men* to represent the government in Utah. His civil career has been fiercely criticised, but his was the first administration that accomplished any good for Utah. No more bowing to Brigham in the Gentile programme. No more of Federal officials dancing with his "wives," and taking an invitation to his house as a high honor. No more asking his gracious permission to remain in Utah; and especially no negligence in looking after Gentile interests.

Every day brought tidings of rich discoveries in the mountains. When I visited the Sevier district in 1869, there was not a mining shaft fifty feet deep, and not more than a thousand non-Mormons in Utah; by the close of 1870, the mining population increased to 4,000, and it was soon established, beyond doubt, that Utah was a rich mining country. In one month the Walker Brothers shipped

4,000 tons of ore. The early history of the Emma Mine now reads like a romance. Mr. J. B. Woodman had never wavered in his faith that the hill north of Little Cottonwood Cañon contained a rich deposit. He had followed a narrow vein till his means were exhausted, without making a "strike." His faith was infectious, and one or two grocers in Salt Lake City furnished him on credit a hundred pounds of flour and some meat, which he and his partners carried up the cañon, wading through the snow. Before that provision was exhausted, they came upon the upper part of the deposit, since known as the Emma Mine. In a month thereafter the most sanguine spoke of it as worth $40,000, whereat the many laughed. Every foot of additional development showed the ore-body to be greater, and the property was successively sold and stocked at higher prices. In September, 1872, after it had been sold in London, a gentleman familiar with the workings of the mine presented the following exhibit:

Depth of workings	230 feet
Breadth of workings	6 to 40 "
Length of workings	475 "
Cubic feet excavated (about)	500,000
Tons of ore extracted	30,000
Tons of waste and third-class ore	15,000
Value of ore	$2,500,000

So small had been the expenses of working, on account of the loose nature of the ore, that $2,200,000 of this had been clear profit. The mine might honestly have been sold for $2,000,000. It was stocked at $5,000,000. The result was a failure to pay dividends on such a capital, a cessation of working, caving in of the mine, a disgraceful lawsuit, and an international scandal. The nation at large has little to ease the smart. In Utah we have one consolation: all the honest work on the mine was done by Gentile residents; all the fraud was perpetrated by men who live outside of Utah, some of them our worst enemies. But we have suffered most of the ill effects. A cloud was thrown upon Utah mines which delayed our progress for two years.

In May I went to Washington City, as agent for the Corinne Gentiles, and remained two months and a half. The next December and January I also spent in Washington on the same mission. We were without representation in any legislative body, and our only recourse was to have an agent at Washington, who, besides being unofficial in character, had the constant hostility of the Mormon delegate in the

House of Representatives. It was then I learned the miseries of a lobbyist. Then I knew what it was to wait wearily on legislative action; to besiege the doors of congressmen and ask favors I could not return, and cool my heels in the ante-chambers of official greatness. It was poison to the soul of a mountaineer. Of all the varied employments I have taken a hand at, I look back with the least satisfaction upon this Washington experience. I do not wonder that lobbyists are suspected of monstrous sins and multitudinous petty crimes. Surely one who should follow the business long would be mean enough for any thing.

In midsummer I attended the remarkable debate in the Tabernacle at Salt Lake City, between Rev. J. P. Newman and Orson Pratt, which ended as might have been expected, each party claiming the victory for its own champion. It did not interest me as it might have done two years before; for I had been long enough in Utah to know that polygamy was far from being the worst evil of Mormonism. To its victims it is doubtless a horrible institution, but to the on-looking Gentile it partakes more of the nature of a comedy. As for instance, when it is gravely announced by some old frog of an elder, that "a man can't git no exaltation in the celestial world 'thout he's gone into plurality." Or when one learns that it is the style among the wealthy to have three wives; while your true saintly epicure, if unable to afford three, has at least "a lean wife for summer and a fat one for winter."

MORMON WIVES FOR SUMMER AND WINTER.

But occasionally comedy and tragedy are united, as in the case of Bishop Smith, married to two of his cousins and two of his nieces; or in that of Elder Allsop, who has a mother and daughter for wives, both mothers of his children, the whole brood living together in a little cabin. In the southern part of Utah may be seen two towns without parallels in America—Taylorsville and Winnville. Two worthy Mormon patriarchs, Elder Taylor and Elder Winn, have each taken numerous "wives," and each of their sons has done the same. The result is two villages, in one of which all the inhabitants are Taylors, and in the other all Winns. The Taylors have been the better Saints, and outnumber the others two to one, which is very disheartening to the Winns. Old man Winn is reported to have said, to an official who visited him not long ago, that life to him was but a weary desert, and at times he felt like fainting by the way-side. At other times he declared that never more would he go through the Endowment House and take another young wife, "for that old Taylor can just naturally raise two children to my one."

After six weeks' travel in the mines, and a winter's work for Gentile interests, the opening months of 1871 found me again a traveler. This time I came eastward, and, after a brief rest, made a tour of the Missouri Valley. I had been three years in the Far West, and before I relate more extensive journeys, perhaps this is as good a place as any to present a general view of our Territories and the adjacent States.

First let it be noted that our maps give no idea of the nature of the country; they do not show the comparative elevation and barrenness. Here and there on the common maps may be seen the words "Great American Desert," the assumption being that all the rest of the region is fertile. The fact is that barrenness is the rule and fertility the exception; though much of the land that is not cultivable still furnishes a coarse grass.

Draw a line on longitude 100° from British America to Texas; then go 800 miles westward, and draw another from British America to Mexico, and all the area between these two lines—800 by 1200 miles in extent; or in round numbers a million square miles—is the "American Desert:" a region of varying mountain, desert, and rock; of prevailing drought or complete sterility, broken rarely by fertile valleys; of dead volcanoes and sandy wastes; of excessive chemicals, rock, gravel, and other inorganic matter. Only the lower valleys, bordering perennial streams, or more rarely some plateau on which water can be brought from the mountains for irrigation, or still more rarely a green plat in some corner of the mountains where there is an unusual amount of rain, or percolation of moisture from above, constitute the cultivable lands; all the rest is rugged mountain, rocky flat, gravel bed, barren ridge scantily clothed with sagebrush, greasewood or bunch-grass, or complete desert—the last covering at least one-third of the entire region.

The reasons for this sterility are many: Elevation and consequent cold; drought caused by the trend of the bordering mountains and direction of the prevailing winds; rock in all forms, and such destructive chemicals as salt and alkali. Wyoming contains 98,000 square miles, and not a foot of land less than 4,000 feet high. Colorado has about the average elevation of Wyoming, Denver being nearly on the level of Cheyenne. Manifestly the high plains of these two Territories can never be of value except for grazing. Utah, as reduced, contains over 60,000 square miles; but, except possibly a few of the sunken deserts of the south, the lowest valley is higher than the average summit of the Alleghany Mountains, the surface of the Salt Lake being 4,250 feet above the sea.

Hundreds of little valleys in the Rocky Mountains, beautiful as the Vale of Rasselas from May till October, rich in grass and game, are yet useless to the farmer; grain can not be made to grow in them by any art of the husbandman. In Parley's Park, Heber C. Kimball tried for seven years to raise wheat; it was invariably "cut off in the flower" by the September frosts. At Soda Springs, Idaho, 6,500 feet above sea-level, the "Morrisite" Mormons tried farming for years; but only succeeded with rye and potatoes, which will mature in a three-months' summer. On all the higher plains of Wyoming, frost may be looked for with certainty every month in the year. At the Navajo farms—in Arizona—I have seen icicles six inches long on the rocks, only 300 feet above the fields, on the 18th of June; and, in 1871, when the Indians had, with great labor, brought forward a crop of corn, and planted orchards, on the night of May 31st a storm of sleet froze every plant and tree solid to the ground. Nor are these such difficulties as can be overcome by industry; we must wait till nature flattens out the country and brings it down into the region of warm air and abundant moisture.

If all the low lands were fertile, there would still be a large area for agriculture; but they are far more barren than the mountains, except those tracts lying immediately at the base of the ranges, or in low valleys along some perennial stream. Every-where in the larger basins the land at a distance from the mountains is a complete desert, generally whitened by alkali. For days of travel the face of nature is a dirty white, and in dry weather an acrid and irritating dust powders the traveler until all races are of one hue. In every Territory are found such tracts, known by suggestive names: The *Jornada del Muerto*, or "Journey of the Dead," in New Mexico; the Salt Desert, west of Great Salt Lake, covering 5,000 square miles; the Great Nevada Desert, 25,000 square miles of utter desolation; the White Desert, Red Desert, Mohave Desert, Skull Valley, Death Valley, the *Mala Pais* of the Spaniard and the *Mauvaises Terres* of the French *royageur*. Where the stage route crosses such a tract, the animals labor through a cloud of dust, and the coach drags heavily; the wheels "cry" as they grind in the sand and soda, and the passengers endure as best they can the irritation to eye and nostril and the slime formed upon the body by dust and sweat. This penetrating alkaline powder sifts in at the smallest crevice, and even the clothing in a valise is often covered by it.

Such are the worst sections of the West. Next above them are the grassy plains, though still unfit for agriculture. Of the million square miles above bounded, at least one-third produces bunch-grass, which chiefly differs from the verdure of the East in that it never forms a continuous sod or green sward; it grows in scattered clumps, six or eight to the square rod, or thicker where the locality is favorable. One can span a bunch at the roots, but above it spreads; sometimes several bunches grow so as to form a clump a foot wide. It is never of a deep green, and for three-quarters of the year is a regular gray-brown; hence an Eastern man might ride all day through rich pastures of it, and think himself in a complete desert. It gets its entire growth in about six weeks, some time between January and July, according to the locality. It then cures upon the ground, and stands through the year looking very much like bunches of broom-sedge. It is as nutritious as ripe oats, the species with a white top, containing a small black seed, being particularly fattening. With it animals make journeys of a thousand miles without an ounce of grain; without it, nine-tenths of America between meridians 100° and 120° would be totally worthless.

Probably the most disappointing feature in Rocky Mountain scenery, to all new-comers, is the absence of a green landscape; for with rare exceptions the traveler's eye does not rest in summer upon an unvarying carpet of green as in the East. The bunch-grass is a pale green, or quite gray or yellow; the small sage-brush is white, and the large variety blue; the greasewood is a dirty white, and the earth and rocks white, yellow or red; the general result is a neutral gray, which seems to shroud all creation in sober tints. One may ride all day through good bunch-grass pasture and his horse be walking in sand all the time; or through a tolerably rich country and never see an acre of that lively emerald which is the charm of an Ohio landscape. A plat of green sward is a rare sight in the Rocky Mountains; but eastward, on the high plains, other grasses appear, changing by slow degrees to the heavy verdure of the Missouri Valley.

Last, and least in extent, are the arable tracts, which are all the more fertile from receiving the wash of the high lands; they are in fact the most fertile in the world. Utah alone contains some fifty valleys, of every width from one mile to fifteen; in them the soil needs only water to produce thirty and sixty and a hundred-fold. But between one such valley and the next, intervene from five to fifty miles of rocky ridges, gravel plains or alkali beds, the first two perhaps yielding bunch grass, the last a waste. In Nevada the proportion of good land is much less; in Wyoming least of all, though that Territory has immense tracts of good grazing land. Up to 5,000 feet above the sea all the fruits and grains of the temperate zones are produced in abundance, above that the products lessen rapidly. In a few places wheat can be grown at or above the 6,000 foot level; rye and oats 2,000 feet higher, and near Central City, Colorado, I have seen heavy crops of potatoes produced at 9,000 feet above the sea. Even the highest parks, where the snow is six feet deep in winter, and does not melt away till the middle of May, often produce heavy crops of grass; but neither fruit nor grain can be grown there.

The want of water hinders settlement in many places where the land is fertile. If every drop in Utah were utilized, it would not irrigate one-tenth of the Territory. If the Ohio River were turned into the north-west corner of the Great Basin, not a drop of it would ever reach the Colorado above ground; the hot sun, dry air, gravel beds and alkali plains would absorb it all. Southward this difficulty steadily increases; the water is scantier while more is needed. In the Rio Grande Valley a given area requires from two to three times as much water as in the Platte Valley. The Mormons in Arizona put five times as much water on an acre as the Mormons in Idaho. The traveler among the mountains of the Great Basin finds in the higher cañons hundreds of streams of which not one survives to reach the valley; scores of "rivers" are marked upon the maps, which do not contain a drop of water after the first of June. South of latitude 37°

or 38°, even the attempt to secure a reservoir for the summer irrigation fails; when the water above the dam has risen two or three feet, it seeks an underground course through the porous soil, and when most needed the *aguada* is dry. In Arizona I found evidences that the old race (Aztec or Toltec?) had tried to remedy this by "puddling" the bottom of the *aguada*, in places even laying it with bricks made of most tenacious clay; but even they were in time compelled to abandon most of the valleys by the ever-increasing drought.

A Western man may be allowed a smile at the suggestion of President Grant, that all the streams issuing eastward from the Rocky Mountains might be utilized by a great National work, so as to irrigate all the plains. Such a work would cost hundreds of millions, while every drop of water in all those streams would not irrigate one-tenth of the vast slope extending three hundred miles eastward from the mountains. Many suggestions are made as to new methods of cultivation to meet the difficulties. Drought might possibly be overcome, but I see not how rocky flats, gravel-beds and plains of sand and alkali can ever be made productive. If there is a total change in the climate, corresponding changes in the land will of course follow in due time; but that does not seem to me imminent. To sum up: At least nine-tenths of America between longitude 100° and 120° seem to me irredeemable (for agriculture) by any art now known to man.

Important political consequences follow. Such a country can never sustain a dense population. The isolated trading town or mining hamlet, with perhaps half a dozen cities of 50,000 people, and detached farming settlements, will occupy a very small portion of the whole area; all the rest will be the range of the nomadic hunter or herdsman. The limit of rapid settlement, (unless from a mining excitement,) is already reached; the phenomena of swiftly growing States like Iowa and Illinois will never be witnessed again in this country. None of the Territories, except possibly Dakota, is increasing in population as fast as are the States. Utah, for instance, has been settled thirty years by a race whose constant boast is their prolificacy; it has barely 100,000 people. This, the most loudly blowed and persistently advertised of the whole sisterhood, has been knocking for admission into the Union since 1849; yet it has but one-tenth the population of New York City, two-fifths that of Cincinnati, and nothing like the wealth or intelligence of a first-class county in Ohio. In the proposed State one Mormon would have a power in the United States Senate equal to that of thirty Christians in Ohio, or fifty in New York. In Nevada the inequality is far worse, though that State has wealth and intelligence to aid us. Wyoming can not sustain a population equal to that of Rhode Island; Idaho is scarcely more fertile; the child is not born that will live to see half a million people resident in the Great Basin. Colorado, has a population nearly equal to that of Utah; New Mexico has a population equal perhaps to that it had three hundred years ago.

It is evident that our form of government must be modified for such communities. Ideal civil systems may furnish amusement for scholars; but a people can only use such a goverment as it has grown to. That "lynch law" should largely prevail all over the West, was as natural, nay, as imperative, as that common and statute law should prevail in New England. Wyoming, for instance, contains 98,000 square miles, and less than 20,000 people; an area more than twice the size of Pennsylvania, with half the population of an average county! Along the Pacific Railway, in the southern part of the Territory, are a few trading towns; all the rest is grassy plains, mountain and desert, traversed only by mining, wooding, hunting or herding parties. A criminal can take a horse from any town and be in the trackless wilderness in two hours. When arrested according to statute a posse must convey him perhaps hundreds of miles, to the nearest jail, and all the witnesses must take the same trip three or four times. Perhaps before final trial there is a mining "stampede," or an Indian war, and all the witnesses leave. It would never do. Justice must be brought home to every little hamlet, and so the Themis of the Rocky Mountains is a wild huntress. The few inhabitants must act promptly before the criminal has time to escape; if it is rape, arson, murder or an aggravated case of horse-stealing, he dies; if a minor offense, a severe cowhiding suffices. Who shall blame them? Justice must be administered, or no man's life is safe an hour. It is charged that they sometimes make mistakes. I have not heard that the regular courts are infallible.

The Territories will soon present an awkward question. It will never do to admit any more "rotten-borough" States; it would demoralize the Senate, and destroy all decent respect for the Federal system. We have already gone dangerously near to that consummation. In certain contingencies one-fifth of the people could elect a President against the united voice of the four-fifths. And yet the territorial condition is anomalous, and to some extent unrepublican. A great reform would be to allow them to choose all their executive officers; the President to appoint only such officials as attend to United States business. Utah might be annexed entire to Nevada; the two would then make a State with population enough for one

Representative in Congress—this to be done after Brigham Young dies, and the Mormon Church ceases to rule. The other Territories might be given more self-government, without the gross injustice of making them States, which is almost as great a wrong to them as to the older States. It is self-evident that an alpine region like Wyoming, needs a totally different government from that of a level State like Illinois. Perhaps the cantonal system might be the best, as far as it gives each little valley local self-government.

The present system is an affliction to the pioneers. Had not Utah stood in the way as a possible danger, it would have been remedied ere this. The demand for good appointees from the President is almost futile. The sad fact is: Government can not *afford* good men in office in most of the Territories; the salaries are so much less than they can make at any legitimate business. And worse still, when they try to do their duty they are almost certain to be removed before they learn how. An Eastern man is worth very little his first year or two in any Territory. The official, if honest, is exposed to a constant pressure from those ruled over, and a constant war on the President to have him removed. If he had no care but doing his duty, he would still have trouble enough; but efficiency and duty are no dependence upon the favor of the administration;* and while the official in the Territory is harassed by complaints, by a salary insufficient for himself and family, by the damning criticisms or equally damning overpraise of the local press, he is more and more disquieted by notes from his friends at Washington, where the fiat of Executive wrath hangs daily over his official head, like the ever-trembling sword of Damocles suspended by a single hair. There are men in every territorial capital who turn uneasily upon their beds from some dark hint in the evening paper, and whose matin slumbers are disquieted by anxiety for the morning paper, to see "the latest from Washington." Let certain members and senators die, or resign, or be defeated, or differ with the President on some pet scheme, and away their heads would go like pins from the alley; and the more they had done their duty the more they might expect decapitation. Hear, then, my conclusion of the whole matter: the system should be completely reorganized, so as to give the Territories self-government, and allow their delegates in the House to vote as well as talk; then they should so remain, to be hunting and roving ground for the rest of the nation till climate and soil change, or some other cause shall have made them rich and populous.

* Written previous to March 4, 1877.

CHAPTER IX.

THE MISSOURI VALLEY.

AT noon of a scorching day, our party landed from a Missouri Pacific train in Kansas City—a modern Rome built on seventeen hills instead of seven. Its citizens have ambitious hopes equal to those of ancient Romans, but for commerce instead of war. Real estate is set on edge in Kansas City; so it logically follows there is twice the profit in it. So the citizens would seem to judge, from the prices they ask for lots. A new-comer, looking for an investment, was pointed to a cone-shaped tract by the owner who was willing to sell.

"But isn't it too steep and rough?" he asked.

"Just what you want," was the reply; "see that lot down there?"—pointing to a funnel-shaped plat some hundreds of feet below—"well, the man that owns that will give you $5,000 for this hill to level up his lot with."

Next day he was approached by the owner of the lower lot. "Isn't it too low and wet?" he asked. "Oh, my goodness, no! D'you see that hill? Well, the owner of that has got to level it, and he'll give you $1,000 for the privilege of dumping it on this lot." The "pilgrim" did not invest.

This is the metropolis of western Missouri and eastern Kansas, and adds immensely to the wealth and population of Jackson County—the "Land of Zion," according to the revelations of Joe Smith. Hither in the spring of 1831, came the Mormon Prophet and followers, located the New Jerusalem at Independence, and prophesied a greater glory than earth had ever known. They notified the citizens that it was idle for them to open farms or build houses; they were standing in the way of the Lord, who would sweep the land with destruction. But the Gentiles saw the matter in a different light; they gathered their forces, and after a sharp fight, in which two were killed and many hurt, drove the Saints across the Missouri into Clay County. Jackson now contains a population equal to that of Utah, and five times as much wealth. It is indeed a goodly land. Prairie and grove alternate in pleasing variety; every commanding knoll is the site of a neat hamlet, every little grove contains a tasteful farm-house, while the open prairie is rich in all the fruits and grains of this clime. The Saints made a good selection for Zion. Could they have held it, they would doubtless have prospered as have the Gentiles; but the Prophet proposed, and the Missourians disposed, and things are as they are.

Thence we crossed the Kaw into Kansas, and in a two hours' ride up the heavily wooded valley of that stream reached Lawrence, the Athens of the Missouri valley, a town rich in historic interest and pleasant to dwell in. In the summer of 1849, a party of gold-hunters camped for the night near the junction of the Kaw and Wakarusa, where the level prairie of the lower valley begins to yield to high ridges and rolling plains. They were enchanted with the beauty of the spot, and on their return from California organized a company in Massachusetts; again sought this spot, and founded Lawrence, a lone settlement of "Free-State men," forty miles from the slave border. The city has already an ancient and a modern history, a mythical and a heroic age. In its first three years it suffered four regular invasions from Missouri. In March, 1855, the "border ruffians" came, and made a population of nine hundred and sixty-two appear to cast a vote of a thousand and thirty-four. In November, 1855, occurred the "Wakarusa War;" the town was regularly besieged, and several men killed. May 21, 1856, Sheriff Jones "executed the writ" of Judge Lecompte, by burning the Free-State Hotel, and pillaging the town. But freedom gained the day in Kansas, and the city grew. The Eldridge House was built on the site of the Free-State Hotel, and Kansas went through the war for the Union "5,000 men ahead of all drafts."

But the worst was to come. At daylight of August 21, 1863, Quantrell and his gang of two hundred murderers dashed into the place; the rising sun saw the city in flames, and a hundred and twenty-five citizens lying dead among the ruins. Eighteen more afterwards died of their wounds. In the horrid annals of Western barbarism, only the Mountain Meadow Massacre can rival it: this, by a community educated under the discipline of slavery; that, by a community educated under the discipline of polygamy. At one house two men were killed, and, in the presence of their shrieking wives, their heads were cut off, and stuck upon the gate-posts! Again the city rose from its ruins, and grew more rapidly than ever. Verily, it took *men* to settle such a place and hold it for freedom. But

"The grain of God springs up
From ashes beneath;
And the crown of His harvest
Is life out of death."

And Lawrence is now beyond question the most moral and intelligent city in the Far West. Ten churches, two daily, two semi-weekly and four weekly papers, all well supported by a population of 15,000, attest this statement. It is one of the very few places I visit in the West at which I always want to stop and pitch my tent for a life-time.

Thence by way of the Leavenworth, Lawrence & Galveston Railroad, we journey up the valley of the Wakarusa, and through a dense grove of elm, walnut, ash, and hackberry. But a few miles bring us out upon the high and rolling prairies, covered with a variety of bright flowers and native grasses, where we find a strange mingling of Northern and Southern scenery. The year 1871, that of our journey, was the wettest Kansas had ever known; but it is never too wet, and farm products of all kinds were abundant. Three years later came drought, with it chintz-bugs and grasshoppers, and after it destitution. Experience has shown that these dry seasons must be looked for at least once in seven years. At Ottawa, in the rich valley of the Marais des Cygnes, we find a more Southern population than that of Lawrence, but no less active in their own interests. A Southern "Yankee" is the most crafty of the class, as witness this little incident: In the early days a popular clergyman of Ottawa sold what he averred to be a "blooded mare" to one of his deacons. Shortly after, the deacon observed some motions in his purchase he did not like, and sought the minister's study with—

"Brother K——, that mare I bought of you seems a little stiff in the shoulders."

Drawing a fine Partaga from between his lips, the reverend pleasantly rejoined,

"Better not mention that, deacon; it might injure the sale of her."

New light broke into the deacon's mind. He "farewelled," and took his leave.

South of the Marais des Cygnes we rise to the Ozark Ridge, "divide" between the waters flowing North and those draining into the Neosho, a high and rocky tract which for ten miles or more in width is of little value except for grazing. The rock lies in thin layers but a few inches below the surface, which is largely dotted with "buffalo stamps." These are said to have been caused by buffaloes crowding together, stamping and licking the ground, led thereto by a saline element in the soil. Our domestic cattle, naturalized in Kansas, sometimes acquire the same habit. Thence we run down a long and beautiful slope, fertility increasing with every mile, into Allen County, the agricultural center of Southern Kansas. Ten days we traveled about in Allen, gathering figures as to climate, crops, and the price of lands—all included in a later chapter. This county already contains a population of twelve or fifteen thousand, an enterprising and intelligent people. Iron bridges span the Neosho; the roads are equal to those in the East; churches and schools abound, and the immigrant finds himself in the center of an organized and progressive commonwealth. There are more intelligent men than new communities can usually boast; music is extensively cultivated, and the common schools are modeled after the plan of those of Massachusetts.

Seeing that we were eager for information (our business was to furnish facts to intending emigrants), the old settlers gave us good measure. In their account there never was so rich, so great, so prosperous a region, never such another chance to make money; the towns were all certain to make great cities; lots were sure to double in price in a year; pure fat might run in the furrows, and corn be made to tassle and silk in greenbacks; one's children would grow fat by mere contact with the soil, and his wife resume the beauty of her youth; roasted shoats, with knife and fork stuck in their backs, would in due time rub against him and beg to be eaten, and such robust health enliven his frame that when he longed for death he must move back East. One resident of Deer Creek, we were assured, had lived so long that life was a burden (to his heirs, probably). Weary of existence, he moved back to Illinois, and there succeeded in giving up the ghost, having first stipulated that he should be buried on his Kansas farm. But such were the life-giving properties of this soil, that, when laid in it, animation returned to his limbs, his heart resumed its pulsations, and the incorrigible centenarian walked forth, to the disgust of his heirs, and the confusion of those who had doubts about Kansas.

Three years after our visit came the notable dry year; seven years of good crops had made them careless, and from 1873 till 1875 some of the people of Southern Kansas actually suffered for the necessaries of life. Will experience make them more provident, or will it continue to be a feast or a famine with them?

Continuing our examination of rural Kansas, by successive stages southward, we passed next into Neosho County, a tract of great fertility, but largely unsettled, much of the land still belonging to the railroads. Thence we bore down into Montgomery County, and traversed the beautiful slopes bordering the Verdigris River: a region of inexhaustible richness, and dotted at irregular intervals by those coneshaped mounds of rock and gravel, which are the delight of the traveler and the despair of science. Some are perfectly circular, rising abruptly from the plain with a rocky wall of from ten to thirty feet in height, upon which stands the cone of loam and clay, often crowned with a pretty clump of trees and bushes. Others rise in long swells, abrupt at one end and sloping gradually to the plain at the other; and still others are mole-shaped, of every length from fifty to ten thousand feet, and from fifty to a hundred feet in height. A few have large tracts of fertile land on top, and farms have been located on their summits. Cherryvale, then terminus of the L. L. & G. R. R., was our last stopping-place—a lively town of great pretensions. As laid off, it is about the size of Cincinnati; but only a half dozen squares are built up yet. Thence, late in July, we turned northward to hunt the cooler sections of the valley.

The Southern Kansian we found to be a good fellow, but somewhat prone to the marvelous and romantic. "Snake stories" were abundant. Those reptiles are common, but seldom dangerous. The most formidable looking is the "bull-snake," so called, an immense thing of four or five feet in length, which gets its name from its blunt head and thick, clumsy body. Strangers often mistake its resonant hiss for the rattle of the real *crotalus horridus*, or rattlesnake. The only dangerous snakes are the little "prairie rattlers," seldom over two feet long; they are dull and sluggish, rarely bite, and their bite, I believe, never proves fatal. But they serve an admirable purpose for local romancers. A settler told us of one which bit his horse: the animal fell dead, and when he examined the wound, the marks of the upper and lower fangs were four inches apart! Discount sixty per cent. when a Kansian talks about snakes. Another told of stirring up an immense rattler while he was hoeing corn. He aggravated it till it struck its fangs into the hoe-handle, then killed it, and was proceeding with his work, when he observed the handle growing larger, perceptibly swelling with the poison. This continued for an hour, when "the eye of the hoe popped out." Of course the *trichinæ spiralis* was peculiarly bad in such a country. We were told of one man in Doniphan County, who read all the accounts of that newspaper epidemic, and in turn felt all the symptoms described. He had the "spirals" bore through his skin; in fact got decidedly "wormy." So he took a powerful emetic, and threw up three or four handfuls of pork worms, three lizards, a section of the worm of the still, two bull-snakes, and a few rods of worm-fence, after which, adds the local chronicle, he began to feel better.

From Ottawa we took the Kansas City branch of the road, passing through the beautiful farming regions of Johnson County; and from Kansas City the Missouri Valley Road to Leavenworth. Railroads have been built for future rather than present demands in Kansas; and the reaction in 1873, as it prevented the rapid growth which was expected, has caused many an investor to wail for his money in railway stocks. Ten years from now Kansas railroads will pay dividends; at present running expenses only are counted on. The first station out is Wyandotte, with perhaps 3,000 people, once a rival, now "merely a feeder of Kansas City." A little farther on is the twice-dead Quindaro, once the great city (to be) of this valley. In 1857 and 1858, it supported a rattling daily paper known as the *Quindaro Chindowan*. The first was the name of the Delaware Indian woman who sold the plat to the whites; the second, in the same tongue, means "a bundle of rods"—the sign of authority. Its bright and saucy editorials excelled all specimens extant of Kansas blowing. Here was to be a second Babylon, a city founded on a rock, while Wyandotte, on the sand, would sink to nothingness; here was to be the *entrepôt* of all travel from the plains; Kansians would certainly patronize their own town rather than cross the Kaw into Missouri, and here would be *the* metropolis of the glorious free and boundless West. But an inscrutable law of nature has determined the location of great cities; Kansas City got all the trade, Wyandotte stood still, and Quindaro disappeared. The site was entirely abandoned for some years, and is now occupied by a few farmers. The original locators had kept even by selling lots; later buyers were ruined.

Leavenworth and Atchison we voted "dull," and passed on to Troy, the neat little capital of Doniphan County, and another "city" which had outlived its first aspirations. So many "cities" were laid off and incorporated in Kansas that a wag in the first Free-State Legislature gravely proposed a law "to reserve every fourth section of land for agricultural purposes." Doniphan County is the oldest part of Kansas; the region is rolling or hilly, but the soil is fertile, and timber and running water abundant. The junction of the Atchison and Nebraska Road with the St. Joseph and Denver City Road, is a mile southwest of Troy, giving the traveler the benefit of an omnibus ride up "Almond Avenue." At the corner of the avenue and Broadway, I noticed a fine herd of cattle grazing, and through this part of the city the stock have kicked down the surveyor's stakes, so it is difficult for one to find his high-priced property. Between Spruce and Elm Streets was a fine field of corn, and just beyond, in the north-east corner of the city plat, we found the village of Troy.

After a week there, and a visit to the Otoe Reservation, just over the line in Nebraska, we again turned northward. From Troy to Elmwood, opposite St. Joseph, we pass rapidly over a down grade. St. Joseph looked beautiful from the western bank of the Missouri, but like most of the towns along that stream, was quiet in 1871. The reaction from the speculative fever of 1864–70, which culminated in the panic of 1873, came on two years earlier in the West than in the East. Men who felt themselves growing weaker, withdrew distant investments and concentrated their strength nearer home. Thence we moved up the Missouri Valley, by way of the Kansas City, St. Joseph and Council Bluffs Road; all the way through grassy meadows or wooded vales, stretching from river to bluffs, where not one acre in ten is fenced or cultivated, and there is always a gentle breeze and freedom from dust. Few trips are so enjoyable. It is strange that so little of that broad, rich valley is occupied; it is in easy reach of market, and the Nebraska side is well settled. It is observable that the eastern margin of all these new States is settled more thickly than the western border of the States next east of them. Cities on the western banks of streams grow faster than those on the eastern, and railroads running east and west seem to have more life

"GREAT EXPECTATIONS."

and energy than those running north and south. Before one State is filled to the western border, another is opened and surveyed, and emigrants seem to prefer the newer one. Another cause, perhaps, is that large grants of Iowa land were made to railroads. There were five such strips granted across the State, besides several smaller ones; on the Nebraska side the grants run westward from the river, and not parallel with it. Within railroad grants the settler can only take eighty acres, for which he must pay $2.50 per acre; outside of them he can take a hundred and sixty at half the price per acre.

Omaha and Council Bluffs we also found dull; clerks had time to read the papers, and the stir which attended the last two years of constructing the Union Pacific was conspicuously lacking. Thence to

Sioux City we traveled by way of the Sioux City and Pacific Railroad. All this distance, one hundred miles, is over the broad, level valley of the Missouri. The lower part of the valley is wet, and largely occupied by sloughs and old bayous. That region is settled only on the bordering highlands and slopes. This improves as we go northward; Onawa and Woodbury are fair villages in fine stretches of land, and near Sioux City the country is higher and better improved. That city had held its own better than most places on the Missouri. At one time it was intended that the Union Pacific should run westward from that point, and up the valley of the Niobrara. But mysterious influences were at work at Washington, and Sioux City lost that advantage. She now has, however, four lines of railroad, including that to Yankton.

From Missouri Valley Junction to Sioux City the passengers were a new set entirely. There were emigrants for North-west Iowa or Dakota, Indian traders or agents, cattle dealers who had army contracts, herders, fur dealers, officers and soldiers for the posts on the Upper Missouri, and a sprinkling of passengers for the Red River of the North, Pembina, and the British Possessions. From Sioux City we took stage for Yankton. The night had been rainy, and the mud was like glue. A tenacious mixture of clay and sand, mingled with prairie grass, would collect on the wheels till they resembled vast revolving cylinders, then fall off in immense wads, each weighing at least a hundred pounds. Through this we toiled for twenty miles, reaching a better country, dotted with fine farms and neat cottages. In the corner between the Big Sioux and Missouri is a French settlement; further on are Scandinavian and Bohemian villages. The settled part of the Territory is largely filled with foreigners—all industrious, and most of fair intelligence. In the valley of the Missouri there is a nearly level flood plain, of inexhaustible richness, and adorned by heavy bodies of timber along the streams. The heavy fields of grain were ripe, and in them were Danes and Norwegians at work, men and women binding wheat together in happy equality. The women were every whit as stout as the men, and seemed to endure the heat equally well. Anthony, Stanton, and Livermore would have preached womans' rights to them in vain. Whatever rights they wanted they took, and thought no more about it. Outsiders have repeatedly petitioned the Dakota Legislature to enfranchise the sex, and have as often been refused. The residents care nothing about it, and evidently have an eye to the utility of woman, rather than her rights.

Fourteen hours staging from Sioux City brought us to Yankton, the ambitious capital of Dakota, where I spent a week with my brother, then Surveyor-General of the Territory. This place has the only first-rate site for a city above the mouth of the Big Sioux, and is the natural discharge depot of all the farming section of Dakota. Not more than one-third of that Territory is fertile land, and that lies almost entirely in the eastern and southern sections. Along the Big Sioux, James River and Red River a fertile strip, nearly one hundred miles wide, extends from the Missouri to the British line, while on the south a narrow arm runs up the Missouri. Thus the good land lies much in the shape of a V, the left arm being much shorter and more narrow. Go northward and westward from these tracts, and you rise by imperceptible stages: first to a strip of second-class land, then to a tract fit only for grazing, and finally to complete desert, the last known as the *couteau* or *mauvaises terres* ("Bad-lands"). Enthusiastic promoters of railroad stocks have told us how easily these barren tracts are to be redeemed, but the author begs leave to dissent.

All the white inhabitants are in the extreme southern or north-eastern sections—the latter so far away from Yankton that Congress has lately listened to their repeated appeals for a separate government. They are in the noted Pembina region, a section older in history than Iowa; a section I visited the next year, and found a delightful country—for Hyperboreans. All the rest of Dakota is occupied by straggling bands of Sioux—the original Romans of the North-west—whose business and amusements were to hunt buffaloes and Pawnees. The former furnished them with food, clothing, lodge-covers, bow-strings, and a dozen other conveniences; the latter with victims for the stake and torture. Of late years, by union with the whites, the Pawnees have turned the tables very handsomely on their old foes. The Sioux at the lower agencies and about Yankton are "civilized;" they dress somewhat like white men, raise some grain, swear, gamble, and drink whisky. At the agency near Yankton they have a flourishing church (Episcopalian), and publish a weekly paper in the Sioux language. It is called *Iapi Oahye*—meaning "Talk carried about"—is Republican in politics, and ardently supports President Grant's "humanitarian policy" toward the Indians.

The spurs of the Black Hills project into Western Dakota, and all the adjacent region consists of a series of lofty plateaus, either totally barren or scantily clothed with grass. With an area of 150,000 square miles, the Territory has a body of fertile land as large as Indiana, as much more good grazing land, and at least twice as much of desert. The fertile sections will some day support an immense population of the North-European races, and, in due time, form a prosperous State.

As I have since visited all sections of the Missouri Valley, a few general notes are in order.

This valley is only the lowest and richest part of that great section known as the "plains"—an inclined plane, from four to six hundred miles wide, between the river and the eastern base of the Rocky

DAKOTAS TORTURING A PAWNEE.

Mountains, and stretching from Texas far into British America. Divide this region into three equal strips north and south, and the eastern strip will comprise nearly all fertile land, the western nearly all barren plains and grazing land, and the middle a mixture of the two.

Let one start where he will on the Missouri, and travel westward on any section line, he will for the first seventy-five miles traverse a region rich in landed wealth; the "bottoms" of inexhaustible fertility, the slopes and upland equal to any wheat lands in the world. Everywhere rich prairie grasses are mingled with bright-hued flowers, with the colors of the tropical and temperate climes. Continuing westward, he will notice a disappearance of the timber along the streams; it shrinks to gnarled and twisted shrubs, contending feebly for life against drought and annually recurring fires. Two hundred miles out, the verdure of the Missouri Valley disappears; gama grass and buffalo grass begin to take its place, and only the lower valleys contain cultivable land. Another hundred miles will take him into a region where farming land is the rare exception, and where even the high plains are dotted by tracts of alkali—the range of the buffalo and antelope. In the strip along the Missouri, with an average width of a hundred and fifty or two hundred miles, will be located all the agricultural population of Kansas and Nebraska; in the same strip continued northward along the Big Sioux and Red River, all that of Dakota, and southward the same in the Indian Territory. All the rest, to the Rocky Mountains, will be the range of the nomadic hunter and herdsmen. But in the fertile strip thus bounded are still a hundred thousand square miles unoccupied, of the best land in America—a domain to support in affluence ten million people. Its development will not probably be as rapid as that of Iowa or Illinois, for reasons already given; but ere another generation has passed, the States of Pembina (Huron?), Dakota, and Oklahoma will take their places beside Kansas and Nebraska.

The middle of August I joined an excursion party at Omaha, and with them made my eleventh trip over the Union Pacific. The broad plains of Nebraska, the rugged mountains of Wyoming, the great desert and the plains of Bridger, the alkaline flats of Bitter Creek, and the wild beauty of Echo and Weber Cañons, had lost none of their interest by a short absence; and I arrived at my old home in Utah more than convinced that Western life was the thing for my health and happiness. A brief rest among the Saints and Gentiles, and our party moved on to San Francisco, where we girded up our loins for the high climbs among the wonders of the Sierras.

CHAPTER X.

THE WONDERS OF CALIFORNIA.

ALL aboard for Yosemite and the Big Trees! How the mind swells as these words are called through the hotel, and the fancy paints what is to come: giant vegetation and wondrous woods; the work of riotous nature in a tropical clime and fertile soil, exceeding all the wonders of romance with growing reality; rocky cañons and happy valleys; glacier-hewn cliffs, reared thousands of feet in the air; waterfalls and mirror lakes; immense flumes, cut by living streams in the solid granite; majestic falls, and crystal cascades, foaming from a hundred hills.

But between us and these wonders intervene many miles of wearisome travel, days of toil and nights of broken rest. Before my visit I wondered that so many excursionists visited California, and never went to Yosemite or the Big Trees. I wonder no longer; for the trip is one which may well make the most hardy hesitate, though truly assured that in the end he shall see wonders that have no equal upon this planet. Two hundred and fifty miles of staging upon the rocky Sierras, beneath an August sun, and half the time enveloped in red dust, are enough to make one seriously ask, Does it pay to visit Yosemite?

We leave chilly "Frisco" at 4 P. M., and spend the night at Stockton, experiencing in that short distance about as great a change of climate as if we should go in April from Chicago to New Orleans. Thence at daylight we take the Stockton and Copperopolis Railroad, which runs to Milton, where the foothills begin. In California, every thing under two thousand feet high is called a hill; if it leads up to a mountain, a foothill. At 8 o'clock, of a sultry morning, we take the stage at Milton and strike north-east, over a dusty road, cheered at rare intervals by a transient breath of wind.

Copperopolis is one of the dead mining towns of the Sierras, built in "the great copper excitement." Its history is like that of other mining towns which did not happen to be located in the right place; all summed up in the Piüte Indian's comment: "Koshbannim! heap money spend; goddam, no ketch 'um."

From noon till 5 P. M., we endure the thumping of a Concord coach over the Sierra spurs, those within frying, those without broiling; in valleys where the thermometer stands in dead air at 100°, or over ridges where the stifling dust is mitigated sometimes by a gentle breeze. This all the way to Murphy's, another old mining town, where we receive the cheering intelligence that the real trouble of the route is about to begin. We change from the coach to a "mountain-wagon"—so-called—a street hack with three seats and no springs—capital thing for a torpid liver. Despite the jolting, our condition is improved. We leave the dust; for there is not soil enough up here to create it. We run beside clear, cold streams. We are in a region of cool airs. The road is shaded by rocky cliffs, or on the levels by tall timber; and the wild ever-varying beauty of gorge, crag, or wooded flat makes us forget fatigue.

THE TWO GUARDSMEN.

The vegetation changes as we gain in elevation. The shrubby manzanita, dwarfish oak, and arrowwood disappear, and we are in a magnificent forest of tall trees without underbrush. Every mile the trees increase in size; the smallest we see for hours are three or four feet in thickness, and nature seems to usher us in through fitting portals to the wonders that are to come. The big trees do not stand alone in grandeur, as I had supposed; but, for twenty miles around, vegetation shades off gradually in forests of immense pines. At last we reach the borders of "The Grove" *par excellence,* while there is still light enough to appreciate its glories.

There they stand, the vegetable wonders of the world: some in clusters, joining their branches like the columns of great gothic arches reaching away to prop the firmament, or now and then one isolated, and stretching out gaunt arms and opening boughs as if it would drink the clouds. The majority appear stumpy and truncated, too thick for their length; but others stretch away in long, graceful columns of arborescent proportions, height, thickness, and branches, all in such perfect correspondence, that half the effect of their size is lost; there is such harmony in adjacent trees, and between different parts of the same tree, that the sense of size is lessened by that of elegant uniformity. Most of the trees of two or three hundred feet in height, have a decidedly stumpy appearance, looking like gigantic stubs rather than trees. At first view it seemed to me the tops must have been broken off. The branches add much to this illusion from the fact that they bend downward, starting even from the body of the tree at an angle of twenty degrees below the horizontal. This is caused by the weight of winter snows, continued annually through all the thousands of years of their growth.

THE FALLEN MONARCH.

The smallest of these adjacent trees in an Ohio forest would create astonishment; yet here they appear trifling, as mere striplings shading off and filling nature's interval between the mammoths and common underbrush. Strangest of all, other things appear much dwarfed. As the coach drives between the "Two Guardsmen," at the entrance of the Grove, the horses appear like mere ponies, shrunk to half their natural size. My companion, as he leans against the monstrous trunk, and extends his arms for me to judge its width by them, appears a mere manikin; the smallest tree, one I had guessed at four feet, spreads a foot or two on either side beyond the natural reach of his fingers, and dwarfs him amazingly by comparison. Here is the place for man to realize his littleness. In the evening shades of these green arches how naturally the mind reverts to thoughts of the vast, the unchangeable, the infinite. Heaven itself seems nearer in our thoughts; riotous mirth is hushed; solemn awe fills the soul, and in low-toned exclamations alone we briefly converse.

But forty miles of staging over bowlders and rocky up-grade, with dust enough in us to start a second Adam, incline our party to think more of supper and bed, than of the biggest trees nature can produce. These comforts, first-class, are found at the Big-Tree Hotel, and for a summer resort one can spend weeks very pleasantly there. Daylight at 4.30 A. M. shone through the green arches with a new and wondrous beauty, and we awoke to the contemplation of a new world, another creation, as it were, where nature seems to have proceeded on a special plan, too Cyclopean for the common world outside.

Of course, the first object for to-day is the great fallen tree and stump, the latter now covered with a handsome summer-house, and fitted up as a pavilion for dancing. The tree as it stood was 302 feet in height, and 96 feet in circumference 3 feet from the ground. But there is a little of the "brag" in this measurement, as most of these trees spread greatly near the ground, and do not assume a symmetrical

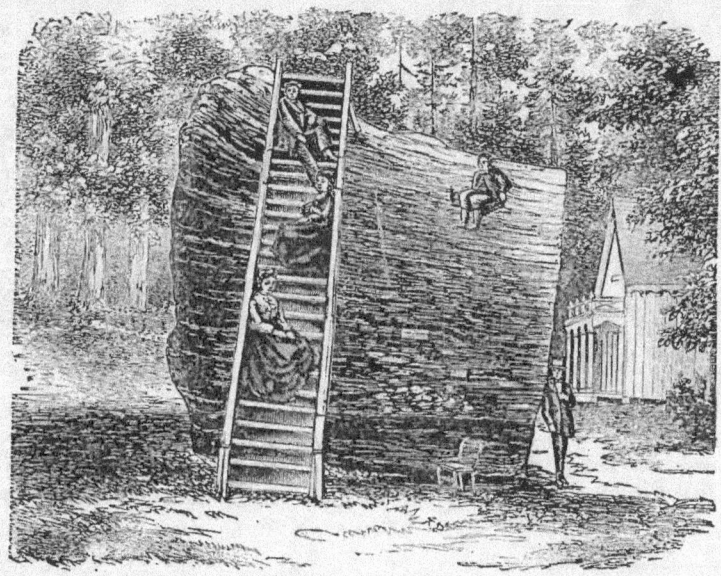

SOMETHING OF A STUMP.

and tree-like shape before reaching the height of ten feet or more. The bark was eighteen inches thick, and the total diameter 28 feet. Five men were twenty days felling it, the object being to have it sawed into cross-sections to be shipped eastward and to Europe. The work was done with long augers, boring it off little by little; but when entirely severed, such was the perfect plumb of trunk and branches, that, to the amazement of spectators, the tree merely settled down and still stood as if refusing, conscious of its majesty, to bow to human endeavors. Vast wedges were then inserted on the northern side, and driven little by little till, heaved beyond the line of gravity, the mighty growth came crashing to the ground. It would seem that nature must have yielded an audible groan at this desecration.

A bowling alley was constructed upon the upper portion of the trunk, but not proving remunerative, has been removed. The "butt cut" of the tree lies as it fell, the top reached by means of a ladder;

then a large portion is gone—sawn out in foot sections and transported Eastward. The "Father of the Forest," largest of all the trees, is also prostrate and slightly buried in the ground, having evidently fallen many years before the grove was discovered (1852). Its circumference at the base is 110 feet; thence it is 200 feet to the first branch, the tree hollow all that distance, and through this tube I can easily walk erect. Unlike the other, it was evidently much decayed, and was broken by its fall, besides breaking down several smaller trees with it. By the stumps of these it is known to have been at least 420 feet in height, and may have been considerably more. Near its base is a never-failing spring of clear, cold water.

"The Mother of the Forest," so named from two round protuberances on one side, is the largest tree now standing. The bark has been removed to the height of 116 feet, but without it the tree is 84 feet in circumferance at the base. Twenty feet from the base it measures round 69 feet, and thus on, decreasing with elegant regularity to the height of 321 feet, making this the most symmetrical of all the larger trees. And for this reason its vastness is seldom appreciated at first view. In such fine harmony, the sense of immensity is lost. It is not until one has gone around the tree many times, and viewed it from different points, that he comprehends its grandeur. The bark was from ten to twenty-four inches thick, bulging outwardly in a succession of ellipsoids around the trunk; it resembles a mass of velvety red fibers, and blocks of it are in use all over the country as memorial pin-cushions. A practical lumberman of our party estimated that this tree contained at least 520,000 feet of sound inch lumber.

Next are the "Husband and Wife," a noble pair of saplings, each 60 feet around the base, and 250 feet in height, growing near and bending lovingly toward each other till their upper branches are mingled in a dense wooden and leafy mass—a canopy sufficient to shade 5,000 persons! Near by is the "Burnt Tree," prostrate and hollow, into which one can ride on horseback for sixty feet. Across the roots it measures 39 feet, and from all indications its height must have been over 300 feet. The "Horseback Ride" is also hollow its entire length; in the narrowest part the interior is twelve feet wide, and can be traversed from end to end. "Uncle Tom's Cabin" is a hollow stump in which twenty-five persons can be comfortably seated; while near by the "Three Sisters" stand side by side in graceful amplitude, each twenty feet thick and 200 feet high, of exact proportions and equidistant from base to crown.

THE WONDERS OF CALIFORNIA.

The trees are mammoth redwoods, assigned by botanists to a class known as *Sequoia gigantea*. In an elaborate description written soon after discovery, a patriotic English scientist christened them the *Wellingtonia gigantea*. This roused the jealous ire of a California *savan*, who, in a ludicrous spasm of national pride, gave them the specific title of *Washingtonia gigantea*. But by common consent they are now known by the name first mentioned. Like all other timber of the *Taxodium* genus, they are but little subject to decay, and the most impaired of the fallen trunks has undoubtedly been prostrate for many hundred years. In this dry air, at an elevation of 3,000 feet above sea-level, with drought in summer and snow in winter, and only the light rains of spring and autumn, decay requires long periods, compared to which a human life seems practically naught.

We have gazed long upon these botanic marvels, and still new beauties appear at each new study; but it is when we come to estimate their age that amazement reaches its climax, and we can truly compare the duration of these monstrous trunks with man's brief period of growth and decay. The trees of this genus require twenty years to increase one inch in diameter; the bark twice as long to gain the thickness of a knife-blade; the timber, in a drying air, will not perceptibly decay within the life-time of man. By these and many other signs, more than all by the number of annular rings, it is demonstrated that the largest of the *Sequoias* must be 3,000 years

A MONSTER.

old. Outlasting ninety average generations of men! And the fallen ones are probably 1,000 years older.

And yet these are not the oldest trees in the world. In Africa there grows a species of mimosa, which, by the same indications, is proved to be 6,000 years old. A sapling when Adam was a stripling! There seems to be no satisfactory theory to account for their growth here. Climate and fertile soil may have done much; but I incline to the belief that they are a sort of relic of the age when all vegetation was gigantic; as one age of geology must have subsided with easy grades to the next, we may have here the last vegetable survivors of the age just before us, and after their fall, no more big trees. Eight miles south of here is another collection, known as the South Grove, and containing 1,380 trees in close order, averaging larger than these, but the largest a foot or two less than the largest here. But we have seen enough for the present to fill the mind with images for years, and weary us in conjecture. Time presses, and with to-morrow's earliest light we are off for Yosemite.

From the Big Trees we take the new or mountain road to Yosemite; instead of going back to the valley, we start directly southward across Table Mountain, the Stanislaus, Tuolumne, and smaller streams. This route takes in the mining and fruit region, and a specimen of all that has made California famous. The Sierras have a general course from north to south, and a height of from ten to fourteen thousand feet; and from them successive rivers put out westward, each in its upper part traversing a mountain gorge or clear-cut cañon, which widens westward to a broad valley bounded by slopes and foothills of genial clime and rare fertility. Our southward route, one-third the way up the slope of the Sierras, involves great variety; we come back on the Big Tree road to Vallecito, and there take a light wagon to cross Table Mountain and the Stanislaus. Parenthetically, the names in this account are either Spanish or Indian, and pronounced thus: *Stan*-is-lowh, Val-le-*cee*-to, Tu-*ol*-un-ny, Mo-*kel*-un-ny, Gar-*ro*-ta, Man-zan-*ee*-ta, Cap-i-*tan*, Mer-*ceed*, Cal-a-*ve*-ras, and Yo-*sem*-i-ta.

From the brow of Table Mountain we look down two thousand feet upon the Stanislaus, a narrow silvery band flowing down a rocky trough. The cañon wall seems to stand at a threatening angle of seventy degrees; but down this slope the stage road goes by a zig-zag, first out upon a projecting shelf, where two feet farther would send us to destruction, and then into a groove in the rocky wall. Down this combination of dips, spurs, angles, and sinuosities, the driver takes us at full trot, with lines taut and foot on brake, ready to check at a moment's notice; for an instant moderating to a walk as we make the outward turn on some rocky flat, then loosing his team to a full run as we shoot into the inward grooves, the coach bounding over bowlders or reacting from the stone bulwarks which line the most dangerous places. We cringe and close our eyes in many places, or cling to the side of the

YOSEMITE FALLS.

coach, half ashamed of the fear our acts betray; but before we can question, or exclaim a dozen times, we are at the bottom, and ready to ferry the Stanislaus. The narrow band, as seen from above, has widened to a considerable river, now quite low; but in winter and spring the melting snow from the notched hills 6,000 feet above swells this stream to a destructive torrent, rising fifty feet above its present level. On the south side another mountain-grooved road leads up 2,500 feet to the divide between the Stanislaus and Tuolumne. No running here, but with slow steps the steaming horses drag us along, and we lounge back over the coach seats, gazing alternately at frowning cliffs above and the river sinking in dim perspective below. No wonder that California is producing a new race of original poets; for, surely, if a man have the poetic instinct, this clime and scenery will bring it out in tropic luxuriance, and cause his genius to put forth wondrous growths of freshness and quaint originality. This society, these scenes and this clime—Italy and Switzerland combined—are the true home of poetry and romance.

Two hours of toil bring us to the summit, and thence down a barren hollow a sudden turn reveals an oval valley of rare beauty, in the midst of which is the pretty town of Columbia, fourteen miles from where we changed coaches. Here we enter the great region of placer and drift mining, once alive with twenty thousand miners, and musical with the hum of an exciting and curious industry. For six miles we run among washed-out-placers, beds of "tailings" and "poor dirt;" wind around sluice-boxes, or cross ditches which lead in the water from a main canal which begins fifty miles up the Stanislaus. At intervals all day we encounter the great ditch of the "Union Water Company," sometimes winding along the mountain side in rocky flumes, sometimes passing beneath us in deep cuts through narrow ridges, and as often far above our heads in mid-air aqueducts—carried on trestlework for hundreds of feet across a rocky hollow—to me a curiosity almost as great as any in the scenery. This ditch, built by an incorporated company at an expense of two million dollars, begins at the very head of the Stanislaus, where that stream is formed by affluents from the melting snows of the Sierras. It is sixty miles in length, winding a devious course to preserve its level, along the mountains and through gorges down to the foothills; furnishes water to a hundred mining camps, and at last, after being used, collected, cleared in reservoirs, and used again half a dozen times, its water, yellow with the refuse of pay dirt, or red with iron dust, spreads in a dozen irrigating streams upon the lower valley. Careful study to select the route, skillful engineering to lay it out, economy of space and material, perseverance and capital—all spurred on by the love of gold—combined to produce the work.

Mining here began with the "rocker," many of which we see even now rotting along the gulches; next came the "long tom," which shares the same fate, and lastly was introduced "piping" and complete hydraulic mining. Little by little this great industry has passed away; the works are fallen to decay; the placers are mostly worked out; three-fourths of the mining camps are abandoned; picks and "long toms" lie among rocks and debris, and California, from an annual production of forty millions in gold, has sunk to half that amount. "Ranching" came next, and all this industry is not lost; the flumes and water are used for irrigation, without which the smaller vegetables and fruits are not a perfect success.

Six miles through old mines bring us to Sonora, where we gladly take a Concord coach for the rest of the trip. Sonora Valley, opening to the south-west, enjoys an Italian clime, and from February to December is glorified by flowers of all hues. Here we see giant oleanders, fifteen feet high, which grow out doors all the year, and gardens excelling the utmost flights of my fancy. Apples, peaches, pears, apricots, figs, damsons, grapes, and quinces we see growing luxuriantly in the same inclosure, many now ripe, and affording most grateful refreshment to our heated excursionists. All along the route to Yosemite fruit is abundant and cheap—all one can eat for ten cents—growing even to within half a day's staging of the valley.

EL CAPITAN.

But this beauty is brief. Right beside these blooming gardens, right up against the walls, are worked-out mines, hundreds of acres of bare boulders in beds, all the soil "piped" away in search of the "pay dirt," which lies below the soil and upon the rocks. A massive brick church stands in the south part of the town, around it lies an acre of ground dotted with tombstones, the city grave-yard, and up to the very walls of the inclosure the dirt is washed away down to an unsightly mass of bare, gray rocks, leaving the church-yard by rare grace perched upon an eminence ten feet above the placer flats. There the rude forefathers of this mountain hamlet—dead miners by scores—lie in "pay dirt"—fit resting place—and their living companions seem to have barely respected their last repose. Over all this region, with rare exceptions, is a peculiar air of abandon and decay; worked-out placers, deserted cabins, dry flumes and sluice-boxes falling to pieces, look as though the site were haunted by the ghost of former prosperity. Fifteen miles of comfortable staging in the valley of the Tuolumne bring us to Chinese Camp, originally settled by Mongolians working "old diggings," but since mining gave place to agriculture, settled by the whites. A few hundred Chinese remain, and as we pass the outskirts of the town, we note a rude frame tent and beside it a dozen China women chattering and howling alternately, and learn that a sick Chinaman has been removed there to die. These people never allow one to die in their cabins, if it can be decently prevented.

Here we change again to the stoutest of mountain wagons; for, we are kindly assured, all the pounding we have suffered is child's play to what is to come. Fifteen miles of stony up-grade bring us to Garrote, which we reach at nine P. M., and gladly sink to sleep. It seems that we have but closed our eyes to half forget in sleep the beauties or toils of the way, when at three A. M. the call comes to take a fresh start. We take the invariable "eye-opener" of ice-cooled California white wine, and after a hasty breakfast are off into a dense forest, the daylight breaking grandly through the green arches and casting great scallops of light and shade to cheer the still sleepy travelers. We are out of the foothills, and upon the spurs of the mountains. The streams are clear as crystal and delightfully cold, for we are far above the mining districts and near their snowy sources.

Vast forests of redwoods and sugar pine, the trees from two to eight feet in thickness, shade the way. At every pause we hear a strange, solemn murmur from far above our heads, a gentle swell as the mountain breeze thrills the tree tops, like the far-off diapason of a monstrous organ, or a gentle tremulo stealing upon the senses with a music all the more subtle that it can not be described. My companion, Mr. J. W. Bookwalter, of Springfield, Ohio, compares the scenery to that of a Florida forest of a winter morning. One by one all who started with us have stopped to rest, but being old travelers, we have held on, and to-day have the coach to ourselves.

Before noon we enter the Tuolumne Grove, where many trees are as large as the average at Calaveras, but none within less than two or three feet of the largest there. Over all this part of the Sierras, probably forty miles each way, the timber is immense. We drive between two trees, each twenty feet in thickness. We find one stump forty feet high and twenty-six feet thick, and hundreds scattered for miles along the way from ten to eighteen feet thick, and from two hundred to two hundred and fifty feet high. If the traveler does not wish to make the diversion by Calaveras Grove, he can still enjoy the sight of tall timber here, on the direct route to Yosemite. Thirty-seven miles from Garrote bring us to Tamarack Flat, the highest point on the road, the end of staging, and no wonder. The remaining five miles down into the valley must be made on horseback.

While transferring baggage—very little is allowed—to pack-mules, the guide and driver amuse us with accounts of former tourists, particularly of Anna Dickinson, who rode astride into the valley, and thereby demonstrated her right to vote, drink "cocktails,' bear arms, and work the roads, without regard to age, sex, or previous condition of servitude. They tell us with great glee of Olive Logan, who, when told she must ride thus into the valley, tried practising on the back of the coach seats, and when laughed at for her pains, took her revenge by savagely abusing every thing on the road. When Mrs. Cady Stanton was here a few weeks before, she found it impossible to fit herself to the saddle, averring she had not been in one for thirty years. Our accomplished guide, Mr. F. A. Brightman, saddled seven different mules for her (she states the fact in her report), and still she would not risk it, and "while the guides laughed behind their horses, and even the mules winked knowingly, and shook their long ears comically, still she stood a spectacle for men and donkeys." In vain the skillful Brightman assured her he had piloted five thousand persons down that fearful incline, and not an accident. She would not be persuaded, and walked the entire distance, equal to twenty miles on level ground.

While we pause, a brief note on the route is in order. From Milton, by way of the Big Trees to Yosemite, is 150 miles; and from Yosemite back by Chinese Camp direct is 109 miles, making a total of staging of 259 miles. Add 100 by rail going to Milton, and twenty by rail and 100 by steamer returning, and we have a total of 220 by rail and steamer, and a grand total of 479 miles in going and return. For all this we pay the moderate price of forty-six dollars per man. To this must be added three dollars per day for necessaries upon the road, and the same for each day in the valley for guide and horse; that is, if you go to see all that is there, and if you do not, you had better not go at all. But hundreds of visitors never go out of the little open flat around the hotel, contenting themselves with a general view of distant wonders. Horace Greeley, when he visited the valley, rode sixty miles on horseback, though he had not been in a saddle for twenty years, reaching the hotel at midnight completely exhausted, and minus at least two square feet of abraded cuticle. He went supperless to bed, and having an engagement to fill, left at noon next day, and the second night thereafter lectured at a town nearly two hundred miles away. When the railroad is completed southward to the Merced, it is estimated that a first-class stage-road could be built from the crossing right up the Merced to the Yosemite, for $100,000, and certainly the State could not make a better investment. The road would have to be blasted out of the foot of the cliffs along the gateway, where the Merced flows out of Yosemite; below, the grade would not be difficult, and it would save two-thirds of the wear at present required. All that man can do has been done on the present route, and still the trip is very exhausting.

BRIDAL VEIL FALL.

With all set and every thing tightly "cinched," we took the start with guide in front, finding the first mile and a half to Prospect Peak not particularly difficult. A sudden turn brings us in view of the valley, but little is to be seen as yet; then we emerge from the timber upon a shelving rock, and the guide stops for us to take our first view at Prospect Peak. We walked out upon the rock, which becomes level as we near the edge, with a feeling of disappointment; but suddenly, when far enough to see below, we paused and trembled. Astonishment and awe kept us silent for a moment. At our feet yawned a chasm bounded on this side by a precipice with sheer descent of near two thousand feet; on the other a mist-enveloped cascade poured from heights so high and dim, that to our eyes it seemed tumbling from the clouds. Far, far below, the Merced foamed through the rocky gateway which forms the outlet of the valley, while the whole wall below us seemed fringed with pines, jutting from every crevice, and growing apparently straight into the air from the solid wall of rock.

We turn again to the left into a sort of stairway in the mountain side, and cautiously tread the stony defile downward; at places over loose boulders, at others around or over the points of shelving rock, where one false step would send horse and rider a mangled mass two thousand feet below, and more rarely over ground covered with bushes and grade moderate enough to afford a brief rest. It is impossible to repress fear. Every nerve is tense; the muscles involuntarily make ready for a spring, and even the bravest lean timorously toward the mountain side and away from the cliff, with foot loose in stirrup and eye alert, ready for a spring in case of peril. The thought is vain: should the horse go, the rider would infallibly go with him. And the poor brutes seem to fully realize their danger and ours, as with wary steps and tremulous ears, emitting almost human sighs, with more than brute caution they deliberately place one foot before the other, calculating seemingly at each step the desperate chances, and intensely conscious of our mutual peril. We learn with surprise that of all the thousands who have made this passage, not one has been injured. Such a route would be impassable to any horse but these mountain-trained mustangs, to whom a broken stone staircase would be as safe as a macadamized road.

At last comes a gentler slope, then a crystal spring, dense grove and grassy plat, and we are down into the valley. Gladly we take the stage, and are whirled along in the gathering twilight. To our right, Bridal Vail Fall, shedding a brilliant sheen in the twilight; further up Inspiration Point, and to the left El Capitan rearing his bare, bald head 3,300 feet above us, beautifully, purely gray, in clear outline against the rosy sky. Darkness shuts out all beauty by the time we reach Hutchings' Hotel, and we gladly sink to rest, with little thought of the wonderland we are in.

We rise to view a new creation, as it seems—a rift in the earth five miles long and nearly two miles wide in the center, walled in by everduring granite. Here is a minor cosmos, where nature seems to have proceeded on a more extensive plan, as if determined to outdo all in the outer world of common-place. A forenoon we give to rest and gazing, for there is enough to be seen for that time from the porch of the hotel. After noon we start out northward, to the foot of Yosemite Falls, one and a half miles from us. The cliffs in front rise nearly 3,000 feet above us, and all along the perpendicular wall we see the marks of ancient glaciers and waves wearing smooth the rocky face; but above, where first the peaks rose from the sea of primal chaos, rough and frowning battlements attest the violence of the rent which divided this from the southern side. About half way up the cliff is a small offset, where grows a beautiful pine, with branch and foliage forming a perfect cone, seeming like the larger growth of ornamental shrubbery. Yet that shrub is a monster tree 160 feet high, and above it the perpendicular cliff is just eleven times its height. Go into the forests of Ohio or Indiana and select the tallest tree, and remember that the upper division merely of Yosemite Fall is at least ten times that height! Or imagine ten Niagaras piled one above another.

A thick forest of pines and firs fills the center of the valley, and through it we follow up the bed, now almost dry, of Yosemite Creek, the bowlders increasing regularly in size as we proceed, until at last the way is blocked by vast masses of granite, hurled, as in Titanic war, from the cliffs above. The immense wall gives back, leaving an inlet into the mountain, the sides of which, like buttresses, approach each other at a sharp angle, and down one side of this inlet pours the Yosemite, now shrunk to a mere rill. But in May and June the congealed floods, on heights 5,000 feet above, are loosed and fill the high flume with a raging torrent. Then great liquid volumes fall from the first height, 1,600 feet, strike and break to a thousand splintered streams, lacing all the second fall for 400 feet with dazzling lines of foam; then gather in another flume, take another plunge, and rebounding from the cliff in a million comminuted streams, roar into the basin below. Large logs from the mountain forests plunge a thousand feet without check and splinter into fragments, but sometimes pass entire, and with many tumblings are drifted far down the plain. The three divisions of the fall are, respectively, sixteen hundred, four hundred and thirty-four, and six hundred and thirty-three feet, making the total fall two thousand six hundred and sixty-seven feet. Climbing for two hours, we reach the highest accessible ledge, inscribe our names, and return.

A cool evening follows, and on the porch at Hutchings' I rest and gaze and think. To the north-west is El Capitan, glorified in the soft moonlight; opposite Yosemite Fall, to the right, the Royal Arches, and all around the monster battlements with shrubby fringe, till we seem walled in far down in the depths of earth, and involuntarily ask: What if ancient order suddenly return, and these cliffs again unite, as science tells us

SENTINEL ROCK.

they were once united? What ages of cosmic process were required to bring about this wondrous combination which I can survey in one quick glance; what infinite forces, working silently in God's laboratory for inconceivable ages, produced all this scene my eye can sweep over in ten seconds? What ages; what unending æons of duration—an immensity clipped out of eternity—were required to perfect this work? Can the mind with utmost stretch revert to a period when all was ethereal, gaseous; when earth was a nebulous mass; when Cosmos first had being—then the time required for it to become a molten mass; the ages thence to solidity—the first crust—the shrinking, the ridging, the upheaval; then the earthquake wave which rent these cliffs asunder; then the convulsions lasting through millions of years, and ending in the mighty subsidence in the bottom of this fissure crevice! Then came the age of erosion, the glaciers successively writing their history on these rocky tablets; the ages of wear required to polish smooth these granite walls, and symmetrize the facings of the cliffs. At last came the age of disintegration, of mold, of soil, of growth, of animals, and last of all man—the last by all reasoning the shortest.

The next day is set for the great excursion to Mirror Lake and Nevada and Vernal Falls; and, after a hasty breakfast, we are off for the most toilsome and yet most enjoyable day to be spent in the valley. Saddles are carefully set, and mules "cinched" with these mountain girths, eight inches wide, until it seems they can scarcely breathe; for we are to have perils of water and mountain—perils by the way. We cross the crystal Merced, of deceitful depth—it looks four feet and is really ten—and lively with mountain trout, in front of the hotel, and take our way eastward up the valley, with the Royal Arches to our left. In some convulsions past, the granite has fallen from the north side in successive sections in such shape as to form the likeness of five great arches, one within the other, half a mile long from west to east, and rising in the center 1,500 feet.

Standing on the northern shore of Mirror Lake, we view, reflected in the lake from right to left, South Dome, Old Man of the Mountains, Cloud's Rest, Mount Watkins, and the Watch Eye, all notable and noble peaks upon the south side, rising from 2,000 to 4,000 feet above the cliffs that bound the valley. Crossing in a skiff to the south side, we see, reflected from the north, Mount Washington, Mount Calhoun, and the far-reaching wall of the lower valley. The lake is a great crystal map of all the adjacent hills and cliffs, beautiful only because of beautiful surroundings, not remarkable in itself, but dazzling by reflection of greater glories.

From Mirror Lake we come back on the same trail a little way, then straight south across the valley till we are directly under the southern cliff, which, instead of being perpendicular, here overhangs, and seems momentarily to threaten destruction; then eastward up what may be called the main branch of the Merced to the head of the valley. The smaller branch comes in from the north-east, under the shadow of the North Dome and the Cap of Liberty—the last a wondrous cone, rising directly from the north cliff, 1,000 feet of beautiful yellow and smooth rock, completely inaccessible. The south-east branch of the Merced plunges down from its source in

NORTH DOME AND ROYAL ARCHES.

the ice-peaks by two magnificent cataracts, Nevada and Vernal Falls, and a series of beautiful rapids and cascades between them. But there is no reaching the foot of the lower fall on horseback; we are to return by it from above, down a perilous stairway, and now must make a wide detour to scale the cliff, or first offset, which frowns 2,000 feet above us.

No possible passage is visible to our unaccustomed eyes; the side seems almost perpendicular, and when the guide tells us we are to "go up there," pointing with his finger at an angle of eighty to a flat projecting peak—seeming to our vision half way to the sky—we shake our heads incredulously. "But I have piloted two thousand people up there," says the confident Brightman, and we are reassured and follow him. I dare not venture on a description; even now I can shut my eyes, see it all, and shudder.

Imagine the route in, with all its difficulties doubled, and going up instead of down, and some faint idea may be formed. Here, we are told, there has been *one* accident. Three weeks before a saddle, not carefully girted, slipped back, and the mule straightway went to "bucking;" the rider jumped off on the upper side, and the mule undertook to run down the mountain, but soon lost his footing and went rolling from rock to rock, till ricocheting one hundred feet from one offset, he fell upon the next flat, with every bone splintered, and his flesh reduced to a jelly. Two hours climbing bring us to the level above the Vernal, and turning a sharp rocky point, we come in sight of Nevada Falls, the largest and highest continuous fall. The approach here is easy, and we are soon at its foot. Rushing down a rocky flume from heights four thousand feet above and miles away; the Merced comes clear as alcohol to the edge, and takes the first plunge, four hundred feet clear; then dashes against the rocks, rebounding in comminuted foam of dazzling white; then collecting again to a hundred tiny streams, it is off at last from the rocky face in filmy slanting lines of cloud and foam, transparent mists so delicately flowing downward that one can scarcely say they move. The silvery sheen, like a hanging crystal-web, is lifted by the wind, swaying now against the rocks, and now far out over the valley; then, in a momentary calm, falls back to break into a thousand transparent fluted sections, gliding downward over the rocks in ever unfolding, ever renewing liquid lawn.

Suddenly the howitzer is fired from the Mountain House across the gulch. The echo breaks sharply upon us from our side, and returns from Cloud's Rest on the north; then seems to die away amid peaks and hollows, but suddenly breaks again upon the startled ear; then repeats in slow declining reports from peak, cliff, and point, again to renew and again die away in a thousand repetitions of splintered sound. The effect of these sights upon different persons is a curious study. The noisy are still, the garrulous silent, and even the least profound are awed to a solemn reverence with something akin to fear.

After a frugal dinner at the Mountain House—every thing has to be carried thither on mules—we come down by the hand-rail beside Vernal Falls, while Brightman returns the mules by the other route as far as Registry Rock, the first point where we can meet him. Piwyack—"cataract of diamonds"—as the Indians call it, well deserves the name; though known by the whites as Vernal Falls, from the beautiful emerald tints it displays. It consists of one clear fall of three hundred and fifty feet, and is accessible at more points than any other fall in the valley. The water starts from the cliff in two great rocky flumes, twenty feet wide, and perhaps a foot in depth; but long before reaching the bottom is utterly broken into minutest fragments, and rolled into one great airy sheet of foam; snow-white and dazzling, bordered apparently by pearl-dust, it seems a column of cloud breaking upon the rocks to light surf and starry crystals. As the foam floats upward the sky clears suddenly, and the sun pours a flood of bright rays into the gorge; the dropping lines of emerald take on a brighter tint, and a rainbow in five concentric rings springs upon the sight. The wind sways back the gauzy column; the penciled rays lose their exact focus; the rainbows break into two, four, eight, an infinite division of iridic tints, and the whole presents a luminous aureole a hundred feet in diameter: another draft of air, and we have a dissolving view; then a lull, and back swings the fleecy foaming column in two bodies, and twice the number of circling rainbows delight the eye. Back comes the wind, and away swings the watery column, bringing again the double breaking lines of iridic tints; the eye is relieved by new prismatic combinations, and the overwrought senses roused to new delight by fresh showers of more brilliant constellations.

NEVADA FALLS, 700 feet high.

The stairways about Vernal Falls are well arranged, and the steps hewn in the rock afford many favorable points to view the entire fall. Gladly would we have lingered here, but the approach of evening called us away while our enjoyment was still at its height.

The hours of rest pass pleasantly at our hotel on the banks of the pellucid Merced. The inhabitants are only second in interest to the valley. In 1862, Mr. J. M. Hutchings walked in, and pre-empted the land where his hotel now stands. Years ago he came in on snow-shoes to see if the valley was habitable in winter, and soon after moved his family in. From May till October all is lively in the valley, then a gloom, born of perfect isolation, settles upon the place; and the few who winter through are as completely cut off as one can imagine.

Once a month or so, an Indian works his way down the south slope on snow shoes, bringing in mail and taking out reports from the imprisoned. With three hotels, saw mill, and two ranches, some fifty persons reside in the valley. There is a saloon, billiard-hall, bathing-rooms, barber shop, and reading-room; and the general arrangements are such that one could spend the summer there very pleasantly.

VERNAL FALLS.

Want of space forbids a fuller account of the sights upon the southern cliffs: of Pohono—"Spirit of the Evil Wind"—called by the whites Bridal Vail, a tiny stream with a fall of over nine hundred and forty feet; of Lung-oo-too-koo-ya—"Long and Slender"—or the Ribbon Fall, amounting in different cascades to 3,300 feet; of Tis-sa-ack—"Goddess of the Valley" —or the South Dome; or of Tu-lool-we-ack—"The Terrible"—the wild, craggy gorge of South Cañon. Nor is my pen equal to the task of doing justice to Tu-toch-ah-nu-la—"Great Chief of the Valley"—or El Capitan, rising at something more than a perpendicular, leaning over the valley, to an elevation of 3,300 feet; nor to Wah-wah-le-na—"The Three Graces"—whose heads shine from a height of 3,750 feet. All that the utmost stretch of fancy can picture of the giant-like, the colossal and Cyclopean, is but a shadowy conception of this immense reality. No description has ever been written. None can be written on this earth. The subject is beyond the province of mere word-painting. A man must die and learn the language of the angels before he can describe Yosemite.

The return route, all the way down hill, was as rough as the going, but took less than half the time. We found four changes of climate. From the cool Sierras to the hot valley was a trial of endurance. Taking the steamer at Stockton, we were soon down among the *tules* on

MIRROR LAKE.

the San Joaquin. At 3 P. M., the thermometer stood at 100°; at dusk, on the river, it was just pleasantly cool; we woke next morning at the San Francisco wharf, where the cold sea-breeze made overcoats a necessity. The seasons are all mixed up in that city. August is the coldest (to one's feelings) and September the warmest month in the year. There is no perceptible difference between January and June. Ladies wear furs in July and August, then lay them off till November. The changes in the ocean-winds account for this paradox.

A day in August is a miniature copy of the seasons, except that no snow falls to represent the hard winter of the East. We rise at 7 A. M., to a balmy early spring morning; if very hardy, even a visitor can go without a summer overcoat; but, to stand around the streets, I find it more pleasant to wear mine. The rising sun scatters the light, fleecy clouds, and shines out with some fervor, and by 10 A. M., I take off my overcoat, for a mild summer has set in. This continues with beautiful steadiness until 2 or 3 P. M.; then the thermometer falls about five degrees very suddenly, as the afternoon fog comes rolling over the city. November continues from 4 till 7 P. M., at which time regular winter sets in. It is, in reality, only eight or ten degrees colder than at noon, but the change makes it seem to me like December. I button tight my overcoat, slap my fingers vigorously, and exercise till I get acclimated; then take a hearty dinner, and two cups of hot coffee, put on my muffler, and go out for an evening view of this most cosmopolitan of cities: first to the Chinese Theater, and then in turn to all the local oddities.

The beauty of Sunday afternoon tempted us to accept the local custom and use that day for an excursion to the Cliff House. It stands on the opposite, that is, the western side, of the peninsula, about four miles from the main part of the city. Whirling along through the sand-hills, on which I noted a plentiful supply of two old Utah acquaintances—sagebrush and greasewood—a sudden turn to the left gave a free outlook towards the West; there I took my first view of the Pacific, and in a few minutes was upon the seaward porch of the Cliff House.

The day was calm and almost cloudless; the sight westward free even to the meeting of sea and sky; the blue vault, and the soft air of the Pacific, were over and around us; to the right the Golden Gate opened into the bay; while below us, and far down the coast, the white surf was breaking upon the shore, with that sublime music which has been the delight and the despair of poets since the *poluphloisboio* of Homer. The house stands upon a projecting rock, some forty feet above the waves, which beat incessantly upon the jagged points below, and at times even dash their light spray into the faces of those upon the seaward porch. Apparently a hundred yards out—really three times as far—stands the cluster of rocks which are the resort of the sea-lions. They were there in numbers, not playing in the waves as sometimes, but lying in groups upon the top of the rocks, their deep, hollow bark mingling with the roar of the surf. A lone rock, a little further out, is covered in the same way with gulls, visitors not being allowed to fire at either.

Below the Cliff House a road, cut into the rock and walled on the side next the ocean, leads down to a sandy beach below, where the hills recede from the shore. A long salt marsh, easily forded, is shut off from the ocean by a sand "spit," on which is a firm and excellent drive, even to the edge of the surf. Taken altogether, this may be called the Long Branch of the West.

As the afternoon drew on, while we were watching the gambols of the sea-lions, which had aroused, to unusual activity, the air suddenly grew dim, the rocks appeared to recede, the view of the ocean was shut off, and a dense bank of fog came rolling inland, while long lines of mist spread over the hills and went creeping through the hollows towards the city. By 4 P. M., the breeze was coming in strong from the ocean; the air, which three hours before was quite warm, grew uncomfortably chilly, and the crowd turned towards town. Reaching Montgomery Street, we found it dark with fog and mist, and a damp cold night set in where the morning had been so bright and warm.

A week was scant time to see and enjoy San Francisco, but the mines of Utah were fast rising into importance, and demanded a historian; my old friends called for me, and I regretfully left the Pacific coast for the very unpacific Territory.

CHAPTER XI.

UTAH ARGENTIFERA.

THE Gentiles were all talking of silver mines; the Mormons of "persecution of the Saints" and "God's wrath at the wicked Gentile government." Chief-Justice McKean had ruled all the Mormon officials out of the District Court, and made the United States Marshal the ministerial officer; the latter had selected non-Mormon grand juries who were ferreting out all the crimes committed by the Saints in the old "blood-atonement era." Lawsuits as to mining titles doubled and redoubled. The District Court at Salt Lake City, which formerly finished the term in two weeks, now sat ten months in the year; one-half its time settling titles to mines, the other half trying Mormon criminals. Five indictments were pending against Brigham Young; a hundred Latter-day Saints were under arrest, or hiding in the mountains. Money by tens of thousands was pouring in to purchase silver lodes; every body swore by the Emma Mine which had given the Territory such a reputation. Every miner expected a fortune; many Gentiles looked forward to the early overthrow of Brigham. There was no little bird to whisper "Schenck—Stewart—Trainor Park—Baron Grant," or hint that before twelve months the Supreme Court would upset the Utah Judiciary. There were visions of wealth beyond the dreams of avarice, of monstrous lodes of silver ore, of a Territory redeemed; the Gentile speculator rode on the crest of a swelling wave, and smiling hope beckoned him on to greater ventures.

Though Judge McKean was then the central figure, the other Federal officials came in for an equal share of Mormon abuse. No matter what they had done or left undone, they were guilty on the main point: they recognized no sovereignty in Brigham Young; they loved republicanism and hated theocracy. Governor Geo. L. Woods especially came in for unstinted abuse. His conduct in suppressing the Mormon militia was painted in frightful colors. History and Scripture were ransacked for precedents. The fruitful annals of Israel furnished the Mormon preachers with abundant similes: He was a Roman governor, oppressing the Holy Land; an Amalekite, hindering the march of Israel; he was Pharaoh, enslaving God's chosen; he was Herod, thirsting for innocent blood; he was Pilate, crucifying the Lord afresh. Daniel and Revelations were reopened: the Government was like haughty Babylon rushing on to destruction; war was soon to scourge America; all our cities were to be desolated, and Washington in particular was to be sown with salt and rooted up by swine! The Gentiles were equally fierce in their zeal to prove Utah's mineral wealth; religious fanaticism and the love of gain were playing a strange drama in the shadow of the Wasatch.

THE MORMON MILITIA.

It was the dryest and sickliest season I ever knew in that Territory. The Great Salt Lake, which had risen year by year till it stood fifteen feet higher than when first surveyed, had suddenly fallen far below the water-marks set up by Captain Stansbury in 1849. On the north and east the bordering marshes were dry, their basins shining with salt. The pleasant babble of the water-seeks along the city streets was not heard; the channels were dry, and full of dust and refuse. What little water City Creek supplied was needed for irrigating the inner lots, and every-where on the streets the shade-trees had a strange, half-dead look, the leaves curled and withering. When I arrived from California, September 1st, fifty-five persons had died in three weeks out of a population of fourteen thousand. Two-thirds of the people complained of the malaria. No such season had been known in Salt Lake since the notable "famine year." So I soon took stage for the hills, and for three months devoted most of my time to inspecting the mines.

Sixteen miles across the valley and over the "bench," brought us to the mouth of Little Cottonwood Cañon; while a storm swept over us and tipped the summits of the Wasatch with snow. In these enclosed basins clouds rise from the lakes and marshes and float away, without shedding their moisture, to the mountains; there they are checked and fall in rain, causing the mountain sides in places to be covered with timber, while the valleys are always bare. A damp, numbing wind swept down the cañon, growing colder as we gained in height, till overcoats and gloves failed to secure warmth; while above and around us every-where the peaks glistened with snow, seeming by imagination to add to the cold, and by the middle of the afternoon we saw the trees on the slopes gray-white with rime, and knew that we had invaded the domain of winter.

For two days the storm continued, and then the late mild autumn of the mountains set in. In summer and autumn the Cottonwood district is the most delightful of cool retreats; in winter a lofty snow-bank, with here and there a gray projection. In the winter sunshine it would, but for the occasional patches of timber, present a painfully dazzling expanse of white; and as it is, serious snow-blindness is not uncommon. When a warm south wind blows for a day or two, there is greater danger of snow-slides. In January, 1875, the snow fell there, without intermission, for eight days, filling the deepest gulches, into which the few stray animals plunged and floundered helplessly. In the circular mountain-hollows, with a good growth of timber, the snow drifted from ten to forty feet deep, leaving the largest trees looking like mere shrubs. Distant settlements were quite isolated, and the narrow passes thereto stopped by snow. However, in the best developed mines work went on under ground, all the side chambers and vacant places being stacked full of ore as fast as it was mined. In a few more days the sun came out bright and clear, and though the thermometer rarely rises above the freezing point during the first two months of the year in the higher camps, yet the warmth seems to have been sufficient to loosen the snow not yet tightly packed; and in every place where the slope was great and the timber not sufficient to bind it, avalanches of from one to a hundred acres came thundering into the cañons, sweeping all before them. One of the largest swept off that part of Alta City, Little Cottonwood, lying on the slope. Six persons were killed outright, either crushed by the timber of their own cabins or smothered in the snow, and many more were buried five or six hours, until relief parties dug them out. One woman was found sitting upright in her cabin with a babe in her arms, both dead. The cabin had withstood the avalanche, but the snow poured in at the doors and windows, and they were frozen or smothered. Thirty-five lives were lost in Utah that winter by snow-slides. Six men were buried in one gulch a thousand feet under packed ice and snow. Search for them was useless. But at length the breath of June dissolved their snowy prison, and the bodies were revealed, fresh and fair, as if they had just ceased to breathe.

Alta City, the metropolis of Little Cottonwood, is at the center of an amphitheater, the ridges rising one or two thousand feet high on all sides, except the narrow opening down the cañon. In this circuit is a mining population of twelve or fifteen hundred people, and most of the old and noted mines of Utah—The Emma, Flagstaff, Davenport, South Star, Titus, and a dozen others. The ore carries from $100 to $200 per ton in silver, and from thirty to sixty per cent. in lead. Thus the base bullion produced from this ore is from ninety-six to ninety-nine per cent. lead, and is shipped eastward for separation. The old question, "Which is the heavier, a pound of wool or a pound of gold?" has its correct application among miners; for gold and silver are estimated by Troy weight, wool (and lead) by Avoirdupois. This distinction is preserved even when lead and silver are in the same ton of base bullion. Hence a pound of wool *is* heavier than a pound of gold or silver, though an ounce of either metal is heavier than an ounce of wool!

North of Little Cottonwood, and also opening westward upon Jordan Valley, is the cañon of Big Cottonwood, with a similar class of mines. Far up the cañon is Big Cottonwood Lake, in the center of a beautiful oval vale, where the Saints usually celebrate Pioneers' Day—the 24th of July, on which date, 1847, Brigham Young and party first entered the valley. From any commanding point above either cañon, one can look out westward over Jordan Valley, over the lower sections of the Oquirrh Range, over Rush Valley west of it, and on a clear day, upon the far summits of Deep Creek Range, glittering like silver points in the dim distance. But the grandest view is from the summit of Bald Peak, highest of the Wasatch Range, and nearly 12,000 feet above the sea. Thither I climbed towards the close of an autumn day, and overlooked one quarter of Utah. Eighty miles South of me Mount Nebo bounded the view, its lowest pass forming the "divide" between the waters which flow into this basin, and those flowing out with the Sevier into the Great Desert. Below me lay Utah Lake and vicinity—a clear mirror bordered by gray slopes; far down the valley, Salt Lake City appeared upon the plain like a green blur, dotted with white; northward the Salt Lake rolled its white-caps, sparkling in the sunshine, while the Wasatch Range, glistening along its pointed summits with freshly-fallen snow, stretched away northward till it faded in dim perspective beyond Ogden. A hundred and fifty miles from North to South, and nearly the same from East to West, were included in one view—twenty thousand square miles of mountain, gorge, and valley.

Eight days sufficed to visit most of the mines of Little Cottonwood. From thirty to fifty tons of ore were leaving the cañon daily, and at least a thousand new locations had been made, every one of which the confident owners expected to develop into an Emma. The last day the air suddenly grew hazy, and, looking northward, we saw the sky of a peculiar ash and copper color. Old miners shook their heads ominously and said: "The fire is sweeping Big Cottonwood." Next morning the peaks were shrouded in smoke, and about 4 P. M., a great white column shot into the sky for thousands of feet, apparently just over the "divide," then, swaying back and forth, settled into the shape of an immense cone, and we knew to a certainty that the wind was "down the cañon," and, consequently, the fire nearing the Big Cottonwood smelting works. It took me all the next day to pass the "divide," for the lowest point on the ridge is 2,000 feet above Central, and the descent still greater on the northern side. When I reached Silver Springs the fire was nearing the town, and after night-fall the sight was indescribably grand. From the summit of Granite Mountain, dividing the heads of Big and Little Cottonwoods, down through the lake region and Mill Cañon, to the tops of Uintah Hills—for eight miles in a semicircle around and above us—the view was bounded by great swaying sheets of flame. The sky to the zenith was a bright blood-red, and down to the West a gleaming waxy yellow; while almost over us Honeycomb Peak, where the timber had burned to a coal, and which was divided from us by a large rocky gorge, stood out detached and glowing red like a volcano outlined against the sky.

Morning came, and with it detachments of miners from neighboring camps, working their way through the lower defiles, to fell timber and "burn against the fire." The town is in a grove of quaking asp, and was in no great danger; but, across Cottonwood Creek, where the Smelting Works stand, the growth is mountain pine, which burns green or dry. The whole cañon was so full of smoke that the sun could barely be discerned, and the pyrotechnics of the night had given place to a death-like gloom. From the creek to the mountain summit south was a roaring mass of flames, when at noon the wind suddenly changed, and for twenty-four hours blew almost a hurricane up the cañon. The timber had been felled for two hundred yards around the works; it was now set on fire, and the great business enterprise of this camp was saved. After the day of wind came rain, then snow, and next morning the latter, four inches deep, was melting slowly into black mud.

South of the Cottonwoods, American Fork Cañon opens upon the Utah Lake Basin; a succession of wild gorges and timbered vales cause it to be known as the Yosemite of Utah. A narrow-guage railroad, built by Howland & Aspinwall, to transport ore, runs down the cañon and out to the Utah Southern; so that the traveler can reach the head of this cañon by rail from Salt Lake City. There a rich gold lode has lately been discovered, and there is a prospect of big developments in that direction. The silver ores are mainly carbonates; transportation is vastly cheapened, and low grade ores can be worked profitably.

East of American Fork, over a very rugged range of peaks, is the Snake Creek District. The creek empties into the Provo River, and most of the mining has been done by the Mormon farmers from the valley below, who go up and mine only in the intervals of farm work. Such workmen develop a camp very slowly, and the Mormons generally, except those from mining regions in Europe, are singularly deficient in ability for the business. The student in social science might find here some curious matter for reflection, in the way the two classes are located in Utah. The Gentiles are on the hills, the Saints in the valleys; and along a single street in the old Mormon towns the ore wagons pass to and fro, and the tide of Gentile travel ebbs and flows, making scarcely any impression upon the slow and sleepy Europeans. Occasionally you will see a Gentile located in one of these places; but he is always keeping a way-side hotel or restaurant, and looks singularly out of place. Without church, school, or society, his sole interest centers in the Gentile travelers. If able, financially, he sends his children to boarding-school in the city; if not, they get an education as they can catch it. His neighbors charge him about a third more for produce than they do each other, and never patronize him in return. The rules of the "Order of Enoch" are that a Saint can sell to a Gentile, but must not buy of him. The city council—for every village is incorporated in Utah—always charges him the largest license they think he will endure, always raising it if the trade increases; and thus some of these little governments are almost supported by the Gentile travelers. Eastern orators and editors frequently ask why we don't feel more kindly towards the Latter-day Saints. It *is* singular, isn't it?

I went next to the Western Districts. Passing the southern point of the lake, where the Oquirrh leaves barely room for a broad wagon-road, we enter upon Tooele Valley, eastern section of Tooele County. This county contains 7,000 square miles, and not more than a hundred sections of cultivable land! Of the rest, one-third or more consists of mountains, rugged and barren, or scantily clothed with timber and grass; and 4000 square miles of the worst desert in the world. But it contains three of the richest mining districts in the West, and a dozen more which promise equal richness when developed. Hence the agricultural (Mormon) population is small, while the Gentile miners have increased rapidly; hence, too, this is the first, and as yet the only, county in the Territory to pass under Gentile control, and is known in our political literature as the "Republic of Tooele." Tooele City, the county seat, and only considerable town, was long inhabited by the most fanatical Mormons in Utah; and when, in 1870, the opening of mines first set the tide of Gentile travel flowing through the place, they resisted change with stubborn tenacity. At length Mr. E. S. Foote, now representative elect from the county, ventured to set up a Gentile hotel; but they led him a merry dance for a year or two. The city council raised his license every quarter, until it took one-fifth or more of his receipts to pay it; and every Gentile who smoked a cigar, ate a dinner, or stayed over night at Foote's, was putting from ten cents to a dollar in the city treasury. Still he pulled through; one after another came, and now the flourishing Gentile colony in Tooele have church, school, and social hall of their own, and the young Mormons welcome the change. When the county offices passed into Gentile hands late in 1874, the old Mormons seemed to expect nothing less than ruin and confiscation, and are yet scarcely recovered from their amazement.

Eight miles beyond Tooele is Stockton, the "lead camp of Utah." Most of its mines yield from $20 to $40 in silver, and from a thousand to fourteen hundred pounds of lead per ton. Hence the ore works almost as easily as metallic lead melts; and though long considered the slowest, as it was the oldest, mining town in Utah, with more capital and cheaper transportation, Stockton is steadily growing in importance. Here we enter Rush Valley, an oval some fifteen by thirty miles in extent, with a water-system of its own, and cut off from the Great Salt Lake by a causeway some 800 feet high. Twenty years ago the center and lowest point of this valley was a rich meadow, and included in a government reservation six miles square; now the center of that meadow is twenty feet under water, and a crystal lake eight by four miles in extent covers most of what *was* the reservation. Such is the change consequent on the aqueous increase of late years in this strange country. Three deep cañons break out westwardly from the Oquirrh. In the southern one, known as East Cañon, "horn-silver," or chloride, was discovered in August, 1870. In three months a thousand men were at work in that district. Bowlders were often found lined with chloride of silver, which yielded from $5,000 to $20,000 per ton. Ophir

City, the metropolis, stands in the bottom of a cañon 2,000 feet deep, which makes a very singular division of the district. On the south side are *bonanzas* of very rich ore, mostly chloride in a limestone matrix, with little or no admixtures of base metal; on the north side are larger bodies of lower-grade ore—a combination of sulphides of iron, lead, arsenic, antimony, and zinc, carrying in silver from $30 to $80 per ton, and from twenty to fifty per cent. of lead. From the series of mines on Lion Hill, south side, known as the Zella, Rockwell, etc., have been taken at least $800,000 in silver, leaving an immense amount in sight.

CHLORIDE CAVE, LION HILL.

Over the sharp ridge which bounds East Cañon on the north is Dry Cañon, which was the leading camp of Utah in 1874. There one mine yielded three-quarters of a million. In this camp carbonates of lead and silver predominate, all the ore smelting freely. Both cañons are included in Ophir District, which has passed through the three periods destined for all new mining camps. The year 1870 was the era of discovery and high hopes; 1871 of wilder speculation, not unmixed with fraud; then came the era of reaction and long drawn-out lawsuits, which were aggravated by the wretchedly unsettled condition of the Utah courts. It was the era of transition from the old Mormon system of juries directed by priestly "counsel," to the Gentile system. The Saints were determined to retain their hold on the courts, or cut off supplies; the Federal District Judges were equally determined the courts should not run unless independently of the Mormons. Courts of Equity in the afternoon enjoined proceedings directed by Courts of

Law in the forenoon; injunctions tied up every thing, and restraining orders confronted every body, and the weary way of contending claimants lay across a desert of fruitless litigation, diversified only by mountains of fee-bills, and strewn with *certioraris*, *nisi priuses*, and writs of error. Capital fled the scene of so much contention. There were more lawsuits impending than the Third District Court could have settled in ten years. At last some of the disputes reached a conclusion in court, twenty times as many were compromised, and in 1874 the district entered on the more satisfactory stage of steady work and development. The deepest mine is now down 1,400 feet, and the great question as to whether these are permanent fissure veins is being solved in the only way it can be—by digging. The district contains some 1,200 working miners, and about half as many women and children.

Language fails me to portray the hardy enterprise, nerve, and perseverance of the miners who are opening the silver lodes of Western Utah. Roads are being laid out across every desert, trails over every range; and on every mountain that lines this Territory and Nevada, hardy prospectors are hunting for "indications" and opening new silver districts. The latest enterprise of note is in Dug-Way District, lying some ninety miles west of Ophir City, across one of the worst deserts in this desert region. Though this chapter begins with the autumn of 1871, I have condensed in it my later observations on Utah mines, and may as well insert here a more complete description of the Western District.

All the interior of the Great Basin, between the Mormon settlement which line the foot of the Wasatch, and the corresponding valleys which open eastward from the Sierras, has one uniform character of rugged grandeur and barrenness. It is divided into many inferior basins by a number of short and abrupt mountain ranges, running north and south, and furnishing scant supplies of water, with here and there a stream large enough to irrigate a few acres. Between these ranges lie almost level deserts—plains where the soil is a compound of sand, salt, alkali, flint rock, and an incoherent red earth, destitute of all vegetation, save rare patches of stunted white sage-brush, resembling pennyroyal more than any plant to be seen in Ohio. At times, however, the entire soil is of an ashy white earth, half of it probably alkali, solid only in winter and wet weather, but in the dry season easily stirred up in blinding white clouds. An area of some 60,000 square miles does not contain a hundred sections of cultivable land; but at the mountain bases are found considerable tracts of the yellow bunch-grass. In the old freighting days, the custom of teamsters was to skirt along these ranges to the narrowest part of the desert, recruit their stock at the last grass and water on this side, then drive night and day until they reached the first grass and water on the other side. Take it for all in all it is about as worthless a region as ever lay out doors; and, on the Hoosier's "Coon-dog principle," ought to be rich in mines, for it is of no account for any thing else.

The only game in most of that region is jack-rabbits and sage-hens; other animals are the sandy or horned-toad, rattlesnake and ground-mice. On many of the hills grows the pinion pine, on the nuts of which, with grass seeds, and roots, and a chance capture of game, the Goshoots (Gosha-Utes) eke out a miserable existence.

GOSHOOT LOVE-FEAST.

The sand-flies live on the greasewood; the horned toad lives on the flies; the snakes live on the toads, and the Goshoots eat all three. From September to December, the Indians fatten up considerably; the rest of the winter they pass in a half comatose state, crouching over a little fire in brush "wickiups," or lying on the sunny side of a rock, sleeping as much as possible, with a meal or two per week of ground-mice or frozen snake, coming out in the spring as lean and lank as fence-rails. There are no deformed or idiotic among them; the winter kills all the old or weakly ones; only the hardy can breed, and the struggle for existence secures the survival of the fittest.

Across that region I went in May, 1875, to visit the new mines in Dugway Range. From Ophir City, forty miles westward through the passes of the Onannoquah Range, brought me to the ranche of "Peg-leg" Davis, the last house this side of the Great Desert. All the miners who had visited Dugway told me to take careful directions from Davis, for that a new trail had been located straight from his ranche to the camp, and only thirty-five miles long—a little slough of water about the middle of the route. But Mr. Davis informed me that every stranger who took that route got lost, as it led among some sand-hills, where the trail would not hold, and only direction could guide one; but the sand-hills shut off the view and left one without direction. My best plan, he thought, was to follow down the old Overland, guided by the telegraph poles where the sand had obliterated the track, nine miles to Simpson Springs, where I would find the last water, thence nine miles to River Bed, and just beyond that a trail led straight across, and only twelve miles long to the foot of Dugway Mountains, and into a rich, green cañon, where I would find water. Thence it was only twelve miles around the foot of the mountains to the mines. But, he added, "if you get lost or don't find the water, start back immediately, for if your horse goes more than a day without water, you're a goner."

I set out gayly on a cool May morning, and took in liquid supplies (a canteen-full) at Simpson Springs. Thence it is fifty-five miles on the stage road to the next water, at Deep Creek, where is an oasis large enough to support twenty Mormon families. Until 1874, they were as completely isolated as if on an island in mid-ocean; but now a new mining district is opened near them. Deep Creek Range is so high that its summits, capped with snow throughout the year, can be seen a hundred miles away. Dugway Range is over thirty miles in length, north and south. At the north end five or ten miles of desert intervene between it and Granite Range, which trends north-west, and is so full of heavy galena mines that they are literally of no account. That is, no locator can sell one of them, for any man who can handle a pick can go there, and find a mine for himself in a week. The mountain is literally full of lead; but it is a new district, and a hundred miles from the railroad, and time and capital are required for development.

Nine miles from Simpson Springs I descended into River Bed, the strangest phenomenon of this strange country. For nearly three hundred miles—all the way from Sevier Lake to the western shore of Great Salt Lake—runs an immense dry river-bed. Once the channel of a stream as large, apparently, as the Ohio, it is now a channel of the purest white sand. It is scarcely possible for the stranger nearing it to resist the illusion that he is approaching an immense stream. There are the bold bluffs, the gentle slope, which looks as though it ought to be clothed with blue-grass, and is scantily clad with cactus and greasewood; the broken bank and the sandy bed from half to three-quarters of a mile wide. If the Ohio ten miles below Cincinnati should suddenly dry up, and every green thing on its banks perish, it would present an exact picture of this channel. Piles of minute shells, long winrows of wash-gravel, and plats of white sand, all indicate that the current was to the northward, and swift and strong. Having crossed it to near the western bank, a smaller channel with minor indications presents itself, all going to show that after a stream the size of the Ohio had flowed on for uncounted thousands of years, there was a shrinkage in volume, after which a stream more like the Little Miami continued for thousands of years more. Here and there along the three hundred miles of this extinct river, sharp mountain spurs put out from main ranges and cut it off, and more frequently there are up-heavals; but the stream impartially continues on its course, up hill and down, and over them all. Our local scientists say that wet and dry cycles follow each other around the world; that Utah once had the rainiest climate on earth, followed by a dry cycle; that the latter has slowly run its course, and that we are once more entering on an era of abundant rain. Very pleasant to hope, "But all may think which way their judgments lean 'em."

Beyond River Bed I struck the trail, and twelve miles across a hard bed of gravel and alkali brought me to the foot of the mountains, and into the richest bunch-grass pastures I have seen in Utah. I entered the cañon, hunted two hours, and found no water; then skirted along the foot of the mountains northward for five miles, but saw no camps and no sign of road or trail. Night came on suddenly, as it always does on these deserts, and the situation looked blue. Expecting to eat supper with the miners, I had taken no provision. My horse had plenty of grass, and I had water enough to last me thirty-six hours. Could we stand it thus another day? I thought we could, concluded to camp till daylight, and hunt again for the road to the mines. Tying the lariat to a sage brush, that my horse might graze its length, I lay down in a gully with only the saddle-blankets and my overcoat for a bed. In twenty minutes the sky was overcast, and in twenty more there came a cold, almost sleety rain, chilling me to the bones. No sleep for that night. I must walk to keep from freezing, and might as well walk toward comfort and safety. Here was a situation! Forty miles from the nearest food and shelter, thirty miles from drinking water, on the mountain side, 10 o'clock at night, and a storm of sleet coming on. Sadly I rigged up again and set out afoot on my return. At intervals the clouds broke away, and by the fitful glimpses of the moon I selected a mountain peak which I had marked by day as due east, and made that my landmark. Hour after hour I toiled on across the desert, warm enough now with exercise and anxiety, and sustaining fatigue by thoughts of how much worse the travel would be in the daytime. Soon after midnight the storm ceased; and at two in the morning, I found myself on the western slope of River Bed, and in another hour the telegraph poles loomed up out of the darkness. Never would I have believed that a man could be so glad to see a telegraph pole. Thence the road was plain; the sky was clear, though the air was very cold, and I thought to sleep till daylight. But it would n't do. I could n't cuddle to sagebrush, and stiff with cold, I got up and toiled on.

Looking back from the rising ground over the desert, I saw the most sublime scene I have witnessed for many a day. There was not a cloud in the sky, the air was in a dead calm, and the gibbous moon was just sinking behind the Dugway Range. Bathed in its mellow light the white plain took on a glory that

LOST ON THE DESERT.

was indescribable. The mountain ranges and isolated red buttes glowed like silver on one side, and on the other cast great pointed shadows for miles upon the white surface. The snow-clad peaks above Deep Creek shone with a dazzling light; the blue peaks of Granite Mountain seemed to be painted against the clear sky, while on its western face the porphyry dykes gleamed like burnished copper. Between the mountains where the view of the plain was unobstructed, it seemed to rise and fade away into the horizon. I forgot cold and hunger in gazing upon the sight. Soon, however, mountain, peak, butte, and plain, seemed to sink down into an abyss, as the moon disappeared; and for an hour I had only the stars to guide me. Then suddenly from the peak I had made my landmark, a purple streamer stretched away to the zenith; then another between that and the southern horizon; then another and another, and soon the whole firmament took on a purple glow, while the rugged top of the Onannoquah Range seemed clearly outlined against the eastern sky. Then the purple hue gave way to a pale rosy color, the rose to crimson, and the crimson again to yellow; one by one the stars faded out, and I saw the snowy tops of Deep Creek Mountain faintly tipped with the yellow rays of the coming sun. The line of telegraph poles seemed to rise out of the ground far ahead; the morning note and flutter of a sage-hen were occasionally heard, and my horse gave a loud neigh, as if to attest his joy that the tiresome night was gone.

His neigh was answered by another, and I soon came upon a camp of Mormons, who had, the previous day and night, made the fifty-five mile drive from the last spring on the other side to Simpson Spring. From them I got a biscuit and cup of coffee, and after watering and resting my horse at Simpson, made the ten miles to Davis's place by 10 A. M. At first I thought myself in good condition, but in an hour or two, my anxiety being over, I felt that ninety miles walking and riding in twenty-seven hours, without food, had produced effects. How my bones ached! But nature does wonders for a man in that dry, bracing air, and in twenty-four hours I was myself again.

I have said that the Salt Lake Basin is the largest and most important of the various subdivisions of the Great Basin; the finest view of it as a whole can be obtained from the deck of a steamer on the lake. This is now the most pleasant excursion in Utah, and our celebration of Independence Day, 1875, on the lake, will long be held in delightful remembrance. The steamer "General Garfield," formerly called the "City of Corinne," made two and three hour trips all day; first to the eastern shore of Stansbury's Island, then to the western shore of Antelope, and again through the deep soundings between. Stansbury's Island lies eighteen miles from the landing, and is about ten miles long from north to south. We went on board at 10.30 A. M., and at fifteen minutes after twelve grazed the shore of the island, having a strong wind to contend with. But nobody cared to land, as the island is nothing but a vast red and yellow rock rising to a height of 2,000 feet above the water. Antelope or Church Island lies some fifteen miles east of the former, and is sixteen miles long, nine miles wide in the center, and rises 3,000 feet above the lake surface, its summit being 7,250 feet above the sea. Remember that the water on which we were sailing is higher than any mountain in Virginia or Pennsylvania.

From the deck of a steamer on the lake, the view eastward includes two hundred miles of the Wasatch Range, its summits every-where glistening with the remains of last winter's snow, not yet yielding to the July sun. Westward the nearer Cedar Mountains obstruct the view, but here and there through the lowest gaps can be seen glistening from afar the white summits of the Goshoot and Deep Creek Ranges. Between the two are Granite and Dugway Ranges, but so much lower than the others that they are invisible. As the day advances the fine haze rising from the lake blots out all the lower portions of the ranges, and the glittering summits stand outlined against the sky like points of burnished silver suspended in mid-air. From three corners of the lake great tongues of open country project back into the mountains, constituting the three great valleys of this basin. To the north-east Bear River Valley lies in the shape of a half open fan, the lower end twenty-five miles wide, the valley running thence to near the Idaho line, where it narrows to a mere cañon. South-east, Salt Lake Valley proper runs southward between the Wasatch and Oquirrh, in shape very like a horse-shoe. Early in the day we can see from the deck of the steamer many buildings in the city, the oval dome of the Tabernacle shining conspicuously; but as the haze deepens the "rising mirage" appears, and the whole city seems to rise slowly and melt away into nothingness. This haze is not visible to the eye. The day is apparently as clear as ever; the sky is blue, the sun shines with his full power, and the sharpest eye can not discern any mist. But distant objects fade out of sight, and fine outlines become blurred and indistinct. The finest time for a view is, of course, in the early morning. Then the mountains fifty miles away seem as distinct as if within a mile, and all the peaks shine through the clear air with great beauty.

It is often said that there is no living thing in Great Salt Lake. There is a minute animalculæ on the bottom, resembling a fine shaving of the skin from one's finger, more than any thing else I can compare it to. As it grows in size it beats in towards the land by the action of the waves, and finally swells up into the likeness of a worm, and floats upon the water. The boatmen think that the flies, which are so numerous around the edge of the lake, breed from this worm, and this idea is strengthened by the fact that the empty hulls of the worm, like abandoned shells of chrysalis, float on the water in large sections extending in long dark lines for hundreds of feet. At first I supposed these collections were merely the bodies of drowned flies, but on examination they proved to be the husks, so to speak, of what had been worms. All sorts of attempts have been made to propagate life in the lake, or mouths of the affluent streams, but one and all have failed. Oysters have been planted at the mouths of the rivers, but when the wind was up stream, the dense brine setting in from the lake killed them. Jordan was stocked with eels a few years ago, but they floated down into the lake and died. One was picked up long afterwards on the eastern shore, completely pickled. The finder cooked and ate it, and found it very palatable. Gulls and pelicans abound in places around the lake, feeding on the flies and worms. Captain Stansbury reports finding a blind pelican which had been fed by its companions and kept fat. At points where grassy marshes border the lake the buffalo gnats are numerous and troublesome. There are indications that buffalo were abundant in this basin a hundred years ago. The Indians say the Great Spirit changed them all to crickets! The latter were very destructive to the first crops of the Mormons, until the gulls came in immense flocks and devoured them. The Mormon historian in pious gratitude says: "There were no *gulls* in the country before the Mormons came." In the slang meaning of that word, this is on a par for facetiousness with that statement in the Book of Mormon: "Great darkness overspread the land: yea, darkness wherein a fire could not be kindled with the dryest wood."

We next try a sail on the yacht. Several sail-boats are now run on the lake by various clubs; ours only held ten persons besides the four sailors. A strong wind from the north-east enabled us to make eight miles an hour, the neat craft riding the waves like a sea-bird. But when we turned towards the point, and had to take the side waves, four of the passengers suddenly turned pale behind the gills. By heroic efforts and frequent recourse to a black bottle, we kept down our dinners, but at the end of two hours "chopping" were glad to get on solid ground again. At 6 P. M. dancing began, and the latest comers put through the night in that amusement. Almost every public occasion in the Far West begins or ends with a dance.

Space fails me to describe in detail the rich mineral districts of southern Utah. Beaver County alone has a dozen districts and several hundred miners. The county contains almost every mineral useful to man—silver, iron, copper, coal, kaolin, and fire-clay of most excellent quality. Withal, the climate is singularly mild and equable. The summers at Beaver City I found a little cooler than at Salt Lake; the winter much like that of middle Tennessee, only dryer. The fertile valleys there would yield provisions for 50,000 people; and with the extension of the railroad to that point it will doubtless be the richest region of the South, the metropolis of southern Utah and northern Arizona. Utah now contains ninety mining districts; the mines and improvements are valued all the way from fifteen to thirty million dollars, and the annual yield of lead, silver, and gold has reached five millions. All this interest has been built up since 1869, by the work of those whom the Saints stigmatize as "d—d Gentiles," and whom apologists for Brigham call "adventurers and carpet-baggers."

Copper is found in vast quantities in Tintic and some other districts, but the reduction thereof has not made much progress. Bismuth ore is found in the southern counties in abundance. Graphite, black-lead, native sulphur, alum, borax, carbonate of soda, and gypsum are widely disseminated. Beds of the latter have been discovered that will richly pay for working. Salt is so plentiful as scarcely to be an article of commerce. Near the lake, and in many other localities, it can be had for shoveling into a wagon and hauling home. Fire-clay and sandstone are abundant, as is building stone of every description, including marble and granite. Kaolin of the finest quality abounds. All the ochres used for polishing, pigments, and lapidary works are in inexhaustible supplies. The Territory will not average one acre in forty fit for agriculture, but nearly all the rest is valuable for some kind of mineral. This growing interest has created a party in favor of annexing Utah to Nevada. The new State would be about as large as Pennsylvania, Ohio, Indiana, and Illinois combined, but it takes something more than area to make a State. The population would be, perhaps, 150,000—just about enough for one member of Congress. The advantages would be immense. It would bring them under the mining laws of Nevada, which are probably the best in the world; it would give the non-Mormons a free ballot, and some chance for representation, and balance the crushing power of the priesthood by a large population of miners and Americans. Perhaps it would be well to annex only the two northern degrees first—containing the most mines—and when Nevada shall have assimulated them, add the rest. With some such consummation as this, I have no doubt the American public would be only too happy to bid farewell to Utah Territory.

To many Americans Utah is even yet a land of mystery—the home of strange rites and unhallowed religion; but to me, in its physical features, it is already as the home of the soul. As more and more I become familiar with it, I see how little Mormonism has to do with its real greatness, how small a space it will occupy in its future history, and what countless other matters there are of wonder and interest. Long residence and frequent travel have made the Territory as an entirety far better known to me than any other part of our country. On the instant a mental picture, colossal in outline and interesting in details, rises to my vision: its snow-clad peaks glowing in the clear air of June, and dazzling white beneath the burning sun of August; its 30,000 square miles of rugged mountains, seamed from side to side with mineral wealth; its cañons and cool retreats; its shadowed trails and dashing mountain streams swarming with trout. Not less romantic, though mingling the useful and waste, and filling the tourist with delight, are its lake of pure brine covering 4,000 square miles, and its 25,000 square miles of white deserts and sand plains; its narrow, fertile valleys with irrigating streams and water tanks, with an orientalized population, half pastoral, half agricultural, and wholly peculiar and heterogeneous; its long, long wastes, crossed only by winding trails; the sand storms on the deserts, and the mild air of the valleys—all combining in one's imagination to invest the picture with a charm which has all the delight of romance, and all the permanence of reality. It does not seem possible that a region of such interest should long remain under the blighting domination of an incestuous priesthood. When the present depression in business is past, and the mining development continues, this Territory must, ere many years, reach an annual yield of twenty-five millions in minerals. The result will be wealth and cultivation, progress and a fixed Gentile population. Every year there are more permanent settlers, and fewer hasten away as soon as they have made a fortune. With its favorable climate, and the physical and intellectual culture to follow this season of moral storms; with a more homogeneous population and a republican government, the result must eventually be a state of society in Utah which will cause Mormonism to be forgotten, or remembered only as the "Stone Age in Art" is remembered by archæologists.

CHAPTER XII.

A CHAPTER OF BETWEENS.

It was a horrid night. I had never known the severe winter weather to come on so early in Utah; for "late fall and late spring" is the weather formula for the mountains. But now the fierce wind from the great desert was sweeping eastward, bringing with it inky snow-clouds, and sending down into the cañons a fierce sleet, which rendered walking on the mountain trails almost impossible. From our cabin on the hill the saloon lights in Ophir City burned bluely, while every hour increased the storm that gathered strength in Rush Valley and drove fiercely up the cañon.

There should have been comfort in shelter and warmth; but that night there was little satisfaction in Teeter's cabin, where a half dozen of us crouched over the fire and grumbled at our luck. We had just come down from a day's picking and blasting on Lion Hill. The Ida Elmore Lode, which one month ago we thought good for a cool million, was now worth about $5 in a flush market; and, as for the Ad Valorem—well, Teeter said the last time he saw any ore the vein was about the thickness of a knife-blade, and pitching into the hill nearly on a level, and as crooked as a worm fence. That meant "no regular vein—no continuation—no depth," and, consequently, no selling value. So, as aforesaid, we bewailed our hard luck.

Suddenly out spoke Joe Allkire: "Behold me; I am the Jonah."

He was given to odd figures of speech, but this did not lessen our surprise; for he was the quietest, steadiest man of the lot—just the partner one would have picked out for luck. But he persisted: "Why the very town I was born in was wiped out—nothing left of it but a tater patch."

"Tell us about it," was the universal request. It was something, any thing to rid us of unwelcome thought. Joe slowly filled his glass, seeing that the quart bottle of valley-tan already looked pretty sick; and

"All were attentive to the warlike man,
When, stretching on his chair, he thus began:"

"Yes, I reckon I started on the worst streak o' luck in the State of Illinoy. I took my first shot at daylight in the town o' Union Flats, and in doin' that I made the big mistake o' my life. The town was settled by a lot from Botetour, Virginia—folks that said 'bin gone done it,' and made their women do the milking; and then come some caow-paling Yanks from C'neticutt, and Quakers from Pennsylvania, and natives from Indiana, and so they named it Union Flats. It's flat enough now, but as to the Union—you'll hear my gentle voice.

"Lemme see; there was first Whig and Democrats—just about an even divide, and stiffer'n a liberty pole on both sides; but when it come to 'lectin' a constable, I reckon the fightinest man stood in with the boys, and as for whisky, wh-e-u-w! It was sod-corn barefooted. The valley-tan these Mormons make ain't nowhere. I mind old Mike Gardner drunk a pint of it, and went home and stole one of his own plows and hid it in the woods, and didn't know where it was when he was sober, and had to git drunk agin to find it.

"These was only the common fellers. The good folks was awful religious. The Old School Baptisses never went nigh the Methodis' meetin' house, and tothers was jist as stiff on thar side; but there was a sprinkle o' Quakers to soften things, and a little blue spot o' Presbytarans, but not enough for a meetin' house, bein' there was no more'n six or seven hundred people in the whole place. So they was only two meetin' houses, and three or four groceries for whisky and such, besides Chew's store, which was the only place that sold bourbon—tothers only 'sod-corn.' Then they was Masons and a lot of Batavy New Yorkers that was agin the Masons, and some agin all secret societies; and along in 1843 come some Millerites, crazier'n loons about the eend of all things on the 11th o' August, and pretty soon after come some Washingtonians and dug in agin Chew and the others that sold whisky, so if a feller wasn't tuck on one side he was on tother. But the boys soon busted them up, and, no matter what the prophecies said, the eend didn't come on the 11th, and things was sort o' dull till these new-fangled notions come in and the Methodis's they set up a choir. But they was nigh half agin it, and that set up another meetin' at tother eend o' town, and split folks all up agin.

DEACON CHEW.

Then come this nigger business, for it was only forty miles to the Ohio, and the new meetin' folks got a real cranky little chap from some'eres East for preacher, and took the abolition shoot, and so all the others preached on Onesimus, and Hagar, and 'Cussed be Canaan,' and things got real lively agin.

"Next thing Misses Chew she split the choir about leadin' in the singin'; and when a fuss gits among a lot o' singin' folks, you jest bet it spreads. She was dognation purty, and slung more style than a speckled show-horse, and I mind more'n one young fellar that felt like he'd like to put a spider in old Chew's biscuit. He was purty well off, and jist doted on her, and brought her shawls and all sorts o' things from New York; but his face was sort o' weazened up, and the top of his head gittin' above the timber line, and not so young and gay as his woman might have wanted him, and that give the other women in the choir a hold. But I sha'n't dwell; you know what *they* said. Then the young fellers that was invited to the Chewses got out with them that wasn't, and all the folks took sides—and there we was agin. You see folks in these little towns is *so* neighborly. They stand by their friends in a fuss — you hear my racket?

"THEY BROKE LOOSE AND LIT OUT DOWN THE STREET."

"Well, one day Joe Tucker, a long, gauntlin' mud-mummy, was slungin' along the street with a long, lean yaller dog that allers follered him every-where, and come by where a farmer was unloadin' some wood, an' quicker'n wink the farmer's big bull-dog pitched into Joe's, and knocked him four rod, and so scared Bob Stevenses', the blacksmith's, wife, that was a takin' her man his dinner, that she yelled for all that was out, and keeled over agin the wagon, and her old sun-bonnet a floppin' off and her a yellin' scared the horses so they broke loose and lit out down the street, like the devil a beatin' tan-bark, and run agin a ladder where was John Baker a paintin' the up front of Abraham Miller's store, and knocked down the ladder, crippled poor John for life, and upset the wood into Burnstein's oyster cellar, killin' one of Burnstein's children stone dead, and so scared Misses Burnstein that she dropped a pan o' hot oysters into the lap of a customer, and set him to swearin' and dancin' like all possessed.

"Well, I reckon if there was any one thing Joe Tucker did love, it was that same long, lean, yaller and spotted dog; they was more like twins than Christians, and folks did say they slept together in that little den back of Joe's gun-shop. So as soon as he conceited what was up, he gathered a dornick, and was just drawin' back to send the strange dog where they's no fleas, when the stranger saw him and went one better. He had a fist like the hand o' Providence, and when it landed behind Joe's ear some folks thought it was a fresh blast down at the quarry; even old Chew heard it, an' folks say Joe doubled on himself twice as he went through Abraham Miller's big winder. Well, Miller run out and first tried to stop the dogs, when the stranger yells out:

"'Let 'em fight! My dog can whip any dog in town, an' I can whip the owner.'

"He'd better not a said that last, for just then Bob Stevens run up, rarin' mad about his wife's scar, and just in time to hear them words, and the next minute he let out that blacksmith's right o' his'n, and cut a calf's nose on that stranger's jaw. So they went at it, fist and skull, and in about four minutes you couldn't a told that stranger's face from a map o' this territory, it was so full of red buttes and black deserts.

"AND THEY CLINCHED."

"'Friend, perhaps thee is *equally* mistaken as to thy dog,' was all that Abraham Miller *said*, for he was a real quiet man, but he did have some pride about his town, so he went into the back-yard and onloosed a regular old English bull that he kept in the store nights, and it was just beautiful to see that dog go to the relief of Tucker's, an' between 'em they soon put the strange dog to his trumps. As Abraham stood over 'em to see fair play, the Methodis' preacher come up, and sez he, 'Fie on you, men, citizens of Union Flats, to get up a dog-fight right in the face of day,' and was raisin' his cane when Abraham gave him a gentle shove, and he yelled out that he was struck—them Boston chaps is so tender.

"'I struck thee not, friend,' said Abraham.

"'You did, sir.'

"'But thee draws wrong conclusions.'

"'Sir, you mistake facts.'

"'Thee utters a mendacious assertion.'

"'You tell an infernal lie,' bawled the preacher, and they clinched. Well, of course a thin Boston bran-bread chap had no show agin one o' our corn-fed men, and Abraham was about to mash him, when most o' the men in town bein' there by this time, the preacher's congregation turned in to help, when Abraham's clerks run in to back their boss, and in less time'n I tell it in they was six or eight on a side, fightin' across toward the Court-house, and leavin' a red trail as they went. It was jist beautiful to see 'em peel; we don't have any such fun in Utah.

"But it happened the stranger with the wood was a Mason, and he had some friends down at Chew's, an' in three minutes after he got away from Bob he had 'em out in line, and along with 'em old Chew—drunk on his own whisky for a wonder—brandishin' a green ax helve, and swearin' by the great horn spoon of the Ancient Scottish Rites that he could whip any Morgan man in Union Flats or sixty miles round. He'd jest got the words outen his mouth when one of the Batavy New Yorkers sez he, 'I don't take that from no Morgan killer,' and fetched ole Chew one that drapped him. Then they did have it beautiful. I reckon they was about twenty-five Masons in town, and they lit on the Yorker and his friends and druv 'em back into Miller's store, when they forted and held their own, and they daresn't an anti-mason show hisself.

"HALF THE TOWN TOOK A SHY AT HIM."

"But 'twant for long. In jist no time they come up heavy, and with 'em the folks that was down on the Chewses, and the women egged on the men, and in fourteen minutes they went through the Chewses and their party like alkali water through a Johnny raw from the States. They might a got it stopped then, but old Colonel Darby galloped into town (his wife was one of the Virginny Mason family), and he yells out, 'It's all on account of the infernal abolishnists; they'd out to be druv outer the town,' and that gave the thing a new turn. The new meetin' folks joined in with their preacher, and all the Darbys yelled to go for the abolishnists, and the last man in town was in it in three minutes. Old 'Squire Hooker, the head abolition man, run outen his house like mad, yellin' for freedom or death, and it looked like half the town took a shy at him. The dornicks and brick flew like distraction, and one as big as my fist went through the winder and into the parlor, where it hit Maria Hooker square in the bosom, and broke two of Bob Carter's fingers, that was payin' his attentions to her. The constable rushed in and was jammed through the jeweler's window, the preacher was knocked clear out o' all likeness, and 'Squire Hooker and a dozen other abolishnists shamefully whipped.

"By this time the Irish at work on the grade got wind of a free fight, and they double-quicked into town and lit in generally, and Miss June Davis's man thought it was a good time to get even with the Wrights, and about forty fellers concluded to pay off old scores; and the grand jury that was in session up stairs in the Court-house come runnin' down, and upset the stove, and in less'n four minutes the old shell was all ablaze, and the fighters set two or three more houses afire, and in an hour all the heart of the town was burned out, an' all the little men badly whipped that hadn't run away; for the fightin' kept up more or less for three hours, and never stopped till every body was satisfied. I mind well the last man out was little Si Duvall, a splintery feller with no legs to speak of, and every body said no account, and that you couldn't make any thing outen him, 'less it was a preacher or a schoolteacher. But they wan't no exemptions in that war, and Si had to go in along with the rest. You see it don't take much to start a fuss when they's blood in the air; and an independent people will have their little differences in the glorious air of the free and boundless West. An' I reckon they was fusses settled there that had been runnin' for twenty years—neighbors that had quarreled about jinin fences, and relatives that had lawed about settlin' estates, and men that got cheated in hoss trades—every man got full satisfaction, and the books was squared."

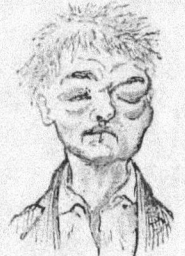

THE SEAT OF WAR.

"Is that all?" I asked, seeing that he made a' long pause.

"It's all the liquor," said Joe, gazing regretfully at the black bottle which had held our last supply; "but of the history they's a few more pints, and at your service."

"Well, the town was half burned up, and its character ruined, and all the whisky spilt, and the constable and sheriff and 'Squire Hooker and about fifty more, badly whipped, and the dog that started it all so chawed up a Chinaman couldn't 'a made him over into chow-chow, and the row only stopped when a big thunder shower separated the forces—and then they was peace. But Misses Chew declared she wouldn't live in no such a heathen country, and they moved back East, and so the neighborhood lost tone; an' the new preacher, what was left of him, had a call to go further north, for he 'lowed a man with one ear chawed off might be ornamental, but couldn't shine in a pulpit in Southern Illinois; and Abraham Miller was so disgusted with himself about breakin' the rules and fightin' that he took to his bed, and his new store went all to shacks; an' all the abolishnists left, too, and the Virginny people swore the place had no style about it anyhow, and they moved, and some o' the houses was hauled off into the country, and the rest was took by a big fresh, and you won't find any thing there now but a corn-crib or two. And all that from one dog-fight.

"But so 'twas nobody from that town ever had any luck, 'cept that same little splintery Si Duvall. He went off to Oregon and got to be a lawyer, and went to the legislater, an' was in the big land commission, and jest coined money; but, after all, the luck o' Union Flats overtook him at last. He up an' married one o' them school-marms sent out from Boston, and when they took their tower down to Frisco, she got sea-sick and throwed up all her teeth, that Si thought was so pretty an' regular; and Si tried for a divorce, and said it was failure o' consideration an' fraud in the contract, an' not the goods he bargained for at all, but the judge differed with him, an' he had to support her. So you see, boys, my luck's bound to foller me, and until I leave the outfit you'll strike no horn silver on this hill."

The whisky being exhausted, the conversation now took a more serious turn. There were accounts of the great "Frazer River Excitement," when the miners rushed off to British Columbia, and most of them came back minus; of the stampede into Sun River Gulch; of the Calaveras frauds, and the mob that hanged the perpetrators—for our miners were men who had tempted fortune in many fields. There were blood-curdling tales of Indian massacres; sad narrations of toil and exposure on the cold mountain-side or the wind-swept desert; and depressing stories of the long, long search for gold which had still evaded the prospector. I was particularly struck by one account, given by a weather-beaten mountaineer of sixty years, whose memory ran back to the time when trappers and hunters constituted the sole white population west of the Missouri. As his style was obscure, I venture to give the story in my own language:

It was the good old time—the grand, good old time—when buffalo by thousands came within two days' ride of the Missouri; when beaver dams adorned every stream in the mountains; when the wild horse ranged from Laramie Plains to the Rio Grande; when the Indians welcomed the trapper and trader, though they still fought the soldier and emigrant; and the nomadic plainsman could ride two thousand miles in a right line without sight of a human habitation. Then Clear Creek, Colorado, was lively with beaver; then the mountain sheep threaded a hundred trails on the eastern slope; the migration of the buffalo was as regular and certain as the return of the May sunshine, and every wooded cañon invited the hunter to rest and a gamy feast. The trapper looked upon two parts of the earth as terrestrial paradises: in the Mexican settlements of California, or the towns on the Rio Grande. When rare good fortune carried him that

"WHERE WARRING TRIBES MET IN PEACE."

way, he could dance, and drink, and make love with the bright-eyed *señoritas;* then, when pleasure palled, be off again for the life-giving air of the mountain, the cañon and the desert.

These towns were neutral ground, where warring tribes met in peace, and white and Mexican danced and drank, and danced the jolly hours away. The white cross of the chapel, without which no Mexican town can be called a *pueblo*, spoke peace to all; the priest joined heartily in all the sports, and stood ready to grant extreme unction if *aguardiente* and gambling resulted in fatal "accidents." On the plaza, every *die de fiesta*, was gathered a motley crowd: the plains Indian exhibited his wild horsemanship; the *señorita* coquettishly flaunted her *rebosa* before the admiring hunter; the Mexican lost his all or won a little fortune at *monte*, and even the boys took their first lesson by pitching for *quartillas*.

St. Louis the trapper must sometimes visit, to sell the proceeds of his hunting and lay in supplies; but it was not his choice to linger there long. How could he contentedly tread the pavements who had trod the green turf of the prairie? how could he rejoice in city air, having breathed the sweet air of the mountains? His gains were often great. More than one trapper has realized two thousand dollars from the proceeds of a single season. These were spent with reckless generosity, and then he was off again to range from Huerfano to the Yellowstone, and from the Black Hills to the Salt Lake. Such a time it was, when Will and Bob McAfee set out from San Luis Park to make a hurried trip to St. Louis.

It was their year of good fortune, and they hurried down the Arkansas to cash their wealth of furs and return before the late mild autumn should give place to the biting winter of the plains. With what joy the returning plainsman hails the first sight of heavy timber! Will and Bob had got far enough down the river to find dense groves, and in one of these, late in October, they prepared to camp for the night. But Will, the older and more experienced, grew strangely nervous at sight of the dead trees standing so thickly among the live ones, and called attention to the fact that the river bluffs came in close to the stream, and rose almost perpendicular; in fact, that this was a cañon rather than a valley.

"Bob, do you see these dead trunks, and the way this gorge opens east and west—and it's the time for storms now—d'ye remember what father once told us about such a place as this?"

"Git out," said Bob, "no old stories now. Don't ketch me campin' out on the perrairie to-night."

Will yielded, but his heart was heavy with forebodings of danger; their evening was dull, despite the jocular style and sprightly sallies of Bob, who recounted the pleasures of a brief stay in St. Louis. The animals were picketed, and the trappers lay down wrapped in their blankets, each upon a pile of dry bark, which served them here instead of their mountain bed of pine boughs. They slept the sound, sweet sleep of tired men whose only nurse was nature; pure air and water their stimulants. Suddenly, said Bob, in the only account he ever gave of it, "We were raised by a roar as if heaven and earth were coming together." He sprang up bewildered. The heavens were lit by the glare of lightning; the next instant inky blackness succeeded, and then thunder, which shook the foundation of the neighboring hills. The autumn storm had come with unusual suddenness and force, and they were in the mouth of a natural tunnel.

For a few minutes the air was comparatively calm, while the electric glare illumined the grove, and thunder rendered conversation impossible. For an instant there was silence, and after it a great moving mountain of air swept down the gorge, and then the wind and rainstorm was upon them in all its fury. Bob felt himself hurled backward, but with the instinct of self-preservation sprang behind an immense green tree, whose spreading roots seemed to bid defiance to the blast. He screamed with all the force of his lungs to Bill, but there was no response. The dead trees snapped like pipe-stems; the rain and wind drowned his loudest cries. He saw that two dead trunks had fallen on either side of the tree that sheltered him; but only noted that this added to his safety, and redoubled his cries for his brother. But no answer.

In two hours the storm ceased almost as suddenly as it had risen, and daylight showed the fearful ruin it had wrought. The forest of yesterday was a tangled, almost impassable jungle. Only a few of the largest trees still stood. Bob gazed around him, marveling at his safety, then shouted with all his strength for Will. There was a faint, mournful response from somewhere near; it seemed almost under his feet. He climbed hurriedly over the logs about him, and shouted again. Again came that feeble response. His heart gave a great bound, and then stood still. That was not the voice of the deep-chested and lusty mountaineer of yesterday; it was rather the moan of a sick woman or fretful child. Again came the faint call, this time in words.

"Bob, for God's sake, come."

In a shallow ravine before him was his brother. But what a sight! Will lay upon his back, alive and conscious; but his legs were crushed beneath an enormous trunk, which pinned him to the earth.

Bob sprang forward and madly tugged at the weight, which would have resisted the united strength of hundreds. The imprisoned hunter smiled, then groaned with a sudden spasm of pain.

"Bring me some water, Bob, and listen to the few words 1 can speak."

Refreshed by the draught, he went on:

"Do you love me, Bob?"

The stalwart, unwounded man sobbed like a child.

"Would you do me the greatest favor man can do another? Would you hurt your own heart for me? Would you save me days and nights of misery? 'Cause, if you would, Bob, there's jist one thing for you to do." And he laid his hand upon the pistol in Bob's belt.

"Oh, don't say that, Bill. For the Lord's own sweet sake, don't say that. Any thing else. I'll start now and bring help."

"Help!" said Will, with the faintest touch of sarcasm in his faltering tones; "help; the nearest white man's three hundred miles away, and where 'd I be by the time ye got back? Don't ye see I can't live?"

"But I will get the ax and chop the log off ye; I'll get ye out."

"No use, Bob, no use. It's only a matter of how and when I'll go under. Can't you see I'm rubbed out? I've pinked my last buff'ler—I've set the last trap in this world. Would you let me lay here days and days and suffer ten thousand deaths? No, Bob, do as I bid ye. Don't be chicken-hearted. Jest one ball from that pistol—and right in the head, Bob, right in the head. Oh, dear boy, why won't you help me?"

The uninjured brother sank trembling on the ground; clasped Will around the neck, and with strong, crying tears begged the sufferer to spare him this.

"Brother," said the wounded man, a strange, tremulous sweetness in his voice, "do you mind the days when we played among the limestone hills in old Kaintuck—and what our grandfather McAfee told us about the Injun troubles when he was young—an' the kind o' blood there was in our family? Do ye mind it, Bob? Ain't the blood there yit? I ain't afeared to die, but think o' layin' here, or anywhere else, an' dyin' by inches! I'm right in the head now—soon I'll be in a fever, an' then—but you'll help me out, Bob, won't you? No one will ever blame ye. I ask it; I, your brother, beg it of ye—the last favor ye can do me." And he struggled to raise the pistol with his own hands, then sank back exhausted, his gaze turned imploringly to his brother.

*   *   *   *   *   *   *   *   *

The awful conference was over, and the deed was done. Will McAfee lay dead with a ball in his brain, sent there by his brother's hand, and Bob fled from the spot, unable to look upon his work. But it was not an act, however justified by mountain ethics, which the doer could blot from his memory. The light-hearted mountaineer returned to his former haunts a morose and gloomy man. His associates, one and all, excused the deed; it was what they would have done in like circumstances. "But woe, woe, unutterable woe, to those who spill life's sacred stream." That instinct is too deeply implanted in the human breast.

Bob grew solitary in his habits, and finally disappeared. Ten years afterwards a party of hunters penetrated one of the many obscure and difficult cañons that open westward from the Saguache Range, and to their astonishment came upon the rude cabin of a hermit. Within they found an occupant who neither moved nor spoke at their approach. Long, snow-white hair and beard nearly concealed an aged face, on which the rugged lines and leathery skin seemed the marks of a century of suffering. His sunken, unwinking eyes gazed into vacancy, his form so still that the astonished hunters could not be certain that he lived till one laid hand upon his arm. Then starting suddenly from his seat, the hermit cried:

"He is dead, he is dead, and I soon shall follow him!" and with all the strength of his rheumatic limbs the unhappy parricide sought to push them from the living tomb.

But contact with men brought health to his mind, and the only remaining week of his life was one of peace and resignation. Cheered by the kind ministrations of the hunters, Bob McAfee sank to rest, and the unfortunate brothers were reunited, let us hope, in a land where motives are judged as well as conduct.

CHAPTER XIII.

OKLAHOMA.

THE year 1872 opened with a revival of interest in the Atlantic and Pacific Railroad, otherwise known as the Thirty-fifth Parallel Route. This road was already completed from St. Louis to Vinita, in the Indian Territory, and was to run thence westward to the Rio Grande, and through a succession of valleys and passes, nearly on the line of the thirty-fifth parallel, to California, terminating at San Francisco. That city and St. Louis had struck hands on the project; thirty-five million dollars had been pledged; it was the era of speculative railroad construction, and we were promised an early completion of the line. I determined to traverse the proposed route—or as much of it as possible—on horseback, and give the world an impartial report.

Bonneville, the early explorer, immortalized by the genius of Irving, had confidently named this as the best route; Kit Carson had been earnest in its favor, and Government early had it surveyed. But Fremont's work made the nation more familiar with the northern route; the war came, and the South lost her chance. With the return of peace both southern lines were aided by grants of land; but Tom Scott's Texas Pacific has again got the start.

Spring was just tinging the prairies with a pale green when I entered the country of the Cherokees, and soon after crossing Grand River passed a heavy wooded strip, and in the next prairie found the terminus town of Vinita. Here the Missouri, Kansas & Texas Railroad crosses the A. & P., and here we should naturally expect to see a place. In Kansas or Nebraska we should see a city with lots selling at from one hundred to two thousand dollars, dwellings and stores going up on every hand, one or two live journals blowing the place as the "future metropolis of the boundless West, the last great chance for profitable investment," etc., and a dozen streets lively with the rattle of commerce. Here, we see nothing. We feel the dead calm of stagnation; we breathe the atmosphere of laziness. There is one tolerable hotel, one stone store, and two frame ones, kept respectively by a Cherokee and a Delaware; and, besides the railroad employés, there is a population of perhaps a hundred—a few good men, more shiftless whites, average Indians, and suspicious-looking half-breeds.

For five weeks I wandered about the Indian Territory, a pleasant sort of half wilderness for a Bohemian to recreate in. Here are pure-blooded Aborigines who are something more than hunters and root-diggers; here are republican governments run on aboriginal principles, with aboriginal official titles, and such a mixture of races as affords a fine field for the ethnologist. One meets with some awkward surprises, with facts that unsettle a great deal we had considered settled. A region half as large as Ohio (excluding the sand-hills and deserts) has some 60,000 inhabitants: a people rich in flocks and herds, enjoying themselves in a simple, pastoral way, content with their mode of life, and indifferent to the rush and struggle of more artificial societies.

"FINE FIELD FOR THE ETHNOLOGIST."

One may travel for hundreds of miles on the public roads and never see a full-blooded Indian; yet such are in the majority, as shown by the census. They usually live off the roads and in the timber along the streams.

The mild warmth of a March Sabbath in that latitude led me to make an excursion down Cabin Creek to a log church and schoolhouse, where I found a congregation of fifty-two persons. There were all shades, from African black to pure white with blue eyes and flaxen hair. There were families of half a dozen each, representing three or four types of the half-breed. One very intelligent gentleman told me he had a family of nine—of just nine different shades—from pure white to almost pure Indian. His first wife was half Shawnee, from Canada, and her first husband a full-blood Cherokee, the three children of that union being rather dark. By this woman he had four children, only quarter blood, but varying greatly in complexion. After her death he married a blonde Irish woman; they had two children, one a clear-skinned, freckled, blue-eyed Celt, the other dark enough to pass for a "White Cherokee."

"It's singular how it will come back in this country," he explained. "I've known 'em to have regular Injun children after two generations of nearly white, and children of pure white people born here are often very dark. I know two White Cherokees, married, that you couldn't tell either of 'em from a regular white person, and they've a whole family of nearly half-bloods. Old Injuns say it comes back on 'em sometimes after people have done forgot they had any Injun blood in 'em." Even so Europeans resident in Asia often have children that look like little Asiatics.

Our preacher was a white man, but a citizen of the Cherokee Nation; and the society was Baptist, as are a majority of Cherokee Christians. The Methodists, Presbyterians, Moravians, and Episcopalians also have churches in the Territory. The Senecas alone, of all the located tribes, retain their aboriginal heathenism. That entire tribe numbered then but ninety persons, including one baby. They occupy a township in the north-eastern part of the Cherokee country, where sacrifices, incantations, and a separate priesthood are still maintained. They stroke their faces to the moon, and once a year burn a certain number of dogs to propitiate the spirit of evil. These, with offerings of fruits, serve them instead of incense and holy water.

Traveling northward through the Cherokee country, I reached the Kansas line at Chetopa, and with amazing suddenness passed from a wilderness to a thickly settled country. From east to west, far as the eye can see, extends a marked line of division between State and "Nation:" on the south an unbroken prairie, on the north farms, orchards, neat dwellings, and thriving villages. If one side of Broadway should utterly vanish, leaving a vacant plain, the other side remaining as it is, the contrast could scarcely be greater. It is a powerful argument, and one in constant use in favor of congressional action to open the Territory to white settlement. Thence, after a short visit, I took the southward train on the Missouri, Kansas & Texas Railroad, having meanwhile been joined by Mr. C. G. De Bruler, of the *Cincinnati Times*. The road was then completed but ninety miles into the Territory, and at midnight we stopped at the new town of Muscogee, in the Muskokee or Creek Nation.

We opened our eyes next morning upon a long, straggling, miserable railroad town, the exact image of a Union Pacific "city," in the last stages of decay. Some two hundred yards from the railroad, a single street extended for nearly a quarter of a mile; the buildings were rude shanties, frame and canvas tents, and log cabins, open to the wind, which blew a hurricane for the thirty-six hours we were there. If Mr. Lo, "the poor Indian," does in fact "see God in the clouds and hear Him in the *wind*," as the poet tells us, he has a simple and benign creed which gives him an audible and ever-present deity in this country, for the wind is constant and of a character to prevent forgetfulness. The weather is mild and pleasant enough, but walking against the wind is very laborious, and the howling so constant as to make conversation difficult inside a tent. I have observed in my travels that windy countries are generally healthful, but a different report is given here. They say bilious diseases of all kinds prevail, and complain particularly of fever, ague, and pneumonia.

We ate in the "Pioneer Boarding Car," and slept in another car attached; five of them being placed on a side track, anchored down, and converted into a pretty good hotel. Here, and about the depot, were the citizens employed on the road. Of the town proper, a majority of the citizens were negroes, formerly slaves to the Indians. Slavery here was never severe, and they are little more their own masters than before. They earn a precarious subsistence, the women by washing and the men by teaming and chopping, and were all sunk deep, deep in poverty and ignorance. All day the wenches were strolling about in groups, bareheaded, barefooted, half naked, stupid-looking, ragged, and destitute. But all around them was nature's wealth, needing only industry to create plenty. Fertile prairies, even now rivaling Ohio meadows in May, rolled away for miles to the north and east; beyond them the heavy line of timber marked the course of the Arkansas.

The records of Muscogee are bloody. During the five weeks the terminus business and stage offices were there and at Gibson, sixteen murders were committed at these two places, and in a very short time five men were killed at the next terminus. One man was shot all to pieces just in front of the dining-car at Muscogee, and another had his throat cut at night, almost in the middle of the town. It is true, strangers, travelers, and outsiders are rarely if ever troubled. These murders are upon their own class, and new-comers who are weak enough to mix in, drink and gamble with them. But a few days before our arrival, a Texan reached Canadian Station with the proceeds of a cattle sale. He met these fellows at night, was seen at 10 o'clock with them, drunk and generous with his money; a few days after his body was washed ashore some miles down the Canadian. And yet I am assured, and believe it, a man with a legitimate business, who will let whisky alone, can travel through this Territory as safely as any other. The visitor can not always feel as certain of this as he would like to. The night "Brick" Pomeroy reached Muscogee three men were shot dead. "Brick" walked from the train to the dining-car, and spent the night; walked thence to the earliest morning train and left the Territory.

After two days at this lively town, we concluded we had better see the Creeks at home, and started afoot for the Agency, traveling over a beautiful, rich prairie, gently rolling, rising from the river into long ridges, which occasionally terminated in sharp bluffs, crowned with pretty groves. The prospect was delightful by nature, and not a little enlivened by the numerous herds of cattle cropping the rich herbage. The tasty groves, the high prairie, and the slow-moving herds, with an occasional group of horses, produced the exact likeness of an old and wealthy estate, with pretty parks and stock grazing about the lawns and meadows. Eight or ten miles west of Muscogee, we entered a region of rude log-cabins and gaunt farm stock, where black faces peered at us through the cracks of "worm fences," and occasional "free nigger" patches showed something like civilization. A colored girl replied, in answer to our queries, "Agency over thar," and a mile further brought us to a beautiful grove, in which was an irregular square of log-cabins, including some three or four acres. We saw no signs of Government buildings, and but one neat, commodious house. There we were directed to a double log building, corresponding to those of the poorest farmers in Indiana, some distance from the square in a field, and that we found to be the Agency.

The place is overrun by freedmen. A continuous line of settlements, with "patches" rather than farms, extends for ten miles along the Arkansas, with a population of perhaps a thousand freedmen and a hundred Creeks. Only the poorest and lowest of the Indians live among the blacks, but there has been more amalgamation in this than in any other tribe. The pure Creeks differ noticeably from the Cherokees. They are shorter, broader, and rather darker; without the high check bones and solemn gravity of the others, and with a more cheerful and kindly expression. The white traders say they are more industrious than the Cherokees, but less intelligent. Their history is an aboriginal romance. They long ago occupied a district far west of the Mississippi, whence they slowly moved eastward and northward—a nation of predatory warriors. Just before them were the Alabamas. The two fought at every encounter, and the latter invariably retreated. Thus they fought through Arkansas and Missouri, then across the Mississippi and Ohio, then through Kentucky and Tennessee, and into Alabama. Here tradition says the old chief and prophet of the foremost tribe, supposing the Creeks would not follow them, struck his standard into the earth and shouted: "Alabah-ma—Ala-bah-ma!"—"Here we rest! Here we rest!"

But the Creeks were soon upon them, and finally conquered and absorbed them, as they did all they conquered, if the vanquished had fought well. In this manner they have also adopted the remnants of the Uchees, Natchees, and Hitchitees; and these, with the Alabamas, still have separate towns and distinct languages in the Creek Nation. They continued eastward, and after a long and bloody war with the Cherokees, in which neither nation could conquer the other, made a peace which has never been broken, and turned southward. In the war of 1812, a portion of the tribe who joined the British were driven into exile, taking the name of Seminoles (Say-me-no-lays), meaning "outcasts." These, joined with fugitive slaves from Georgia and the Carolinas, became a separate nation, and long maintained a desperate war with the whites amid the swamps and glades of Florida. Both nations, after years of trouble and broken treaties, with many transactions which reflect no credit upon the United States officials, were finally sent to this country during the administrations of John Quincy Adams, Andrew Jackson, and Martin Van Buren.

The government of the Creek Nation is republican in form; the entire "constitution" and laws are printed in a small pamphlet of less than twenty pages. The law-making power is vested in a House of Kings and a House of Warriors; the members of each are elected for four years, by general vote of all the male Creeks over eighteen years of age. Each of the forty towns sends one member to the House of Kings; to the House of Warriors one, and an additional member for each two hundred citizens. The Kings elect their own President, the Warriors their own Speaker-in-Council; each house elects its own interpreter, and all speeches made in English are forthwith rendered aloud into Creek, and *vice versa*. The records are kept in English.

The Executive of the Nation is styled the Principal Chief, his Vice the Second Chief; they also are elected for four years each, and thus the entire Government is liable to a complete change at each election. The Judiciary begins with the High Court, which consists of five persons, chosen by the Council for four years. They have original jurisdiction in all cases involving over one hundred dollars, and appellate jurisdiction from lower courts in criminal matters. The Nation is divided into six districts, in each of which a judge is elected by the qualified voters; he has jurisdiction of all cases involving sums under one hundred dollars, and local criminal jurisdiction. Of course, with such a brief and simple criminal code, there is much left to the discretion of the judge, and, as far as a white man can see, he seems to have almost absolute power. The death penalty is often inflicted. Each district elects a "light horse company," consisting of one lieutenant and four privates; these act as sheriff and deputies under orders of the District Courts, and are subject to a general call from the Principal Chief to execute the mandates of the High Court, or suppress extensive disorders. In hundreds of instances these light-horse companies and the District Judge simply make the law as they go, calling court on each particular case, following the statute if there is one, and if not, assigning such penalty as in their judgment fits the case. The laws are singularly plain and unambiguous. No space is wasted in definitions, it being taken for granted, apparently, that every body knows the meaning of such terms as "steal" and "murder."

After a few days at the Agency, where we were handsomely entertained, and assisted in our researches by Major J. G. Voré and his assistant, Mr. A. S. Purinton, who were in charge, we determined to visit the Tallahassee Mission, a sort of high school for the Creeks. Starting afoot, Mr. De Bruler and I soon reached the Arkansas, and, after half an hour's vigorous shouting, the ferryman came over, with two negroes. A sudden storm drove us to the nearest hut. A bright mulatto soon appeared, who informed us that he was a slave to the Creeks "afɔh de wah; run away and went off den, which I larnt Ingliss, sah." So, with him for interpreter, we succeeded in an hour in extracting half a dozen remarks from Charon the Silent, as we named the determinedly reticent Creek. The storm passed, and we were set across the river, for which Charon demanded "*pahly-hok-kohlen hoonunvy, pahly osten*"—rendered by our linguist to mean "twenty cents a man—forty cents all." This we disbursed, and footed it across the bottom over a road rendered very toilsome by the rain. At dark, splashed and weary, we reached the Mission, which is beautifully situated in an open grove, appearing to us a very haven of rest—fitting emblem of the faith and hope which planted it in this wilderness.

There we spent a most delightful Sabbath, entertained by the Superintendent, Rev. W. S. Robertson, and family. This mission has been thirty years in existence, and has educated all the leading men of the Creek Nation. The teachers are selected and paid by the Presbyterian Board of Home Missions; the material interests are looked after by the Nation, which sends a boy and girl from each of the forty towns, a new one being selected for every departure. Supper was called soon after our arrival; we took "visitors' chairs," and watched with much interest the orderly incoming of some seventy young Creeks, of every age from eight to twenty-two. Nearly all were pure bloods, and the whole scene was a revelation to me. I had seen the savage-painted Indian, and the miserable vagabond on the white frontier; but the civilized, scholarly Indian boy and girl presented a new sight. Supper over, a chapter was read, and the school united in prayers and a devotional hymn. Then we were invited to hear classes, who volunteered an evening recitation for our benefit.

Their natural talent is surprising, particularly in drawing and figures. Every Creek boy seems to know the law of outline by instinct. In figures they are very quick; in reading not so apt. Creek and English being the only languages used at the Mission, every Uchee, Natchee, or Alabama pupil has to learn a new language before his education proper begins.

Like the common school system of our own people, this school tends to break down tribal prejudice, and make the people homogeneous. Two Uchee boys, of the reading class, conversed awhile in that language at my request. It is entirely devoid of labials; for five minutes they touched the lips together but once. It also rarely requires the dentals; and thus to a Uchee it is almost impossible to distinguish between *b* and *p*, *d* and *t*, or *a* and *e*. This inability produces most ludicrous results in spelling. Pronouncing the words to be spelled orally, the teacher can not possibly determine in the quick sound whether the spelling is correct or not—that is, with Uchee beginners. But, when they come to write it on the slate, *bat* becomes *p-e-t*, *hat h-e-d*, *bad b-e-t*, etc. The Creeks are lively and affectionate, but their original language does not contain a single term of endearment. Some have been adopted from the English, others formed by combining primitive words in their own tongue. The word for *sweetheart* has eight syllables—a nice jawbreaker to murmur in a

"SLEM-LEM-AN-DAH-MOUCH-WAH-GER."

maiden's ear by moonlight. Love (between the sexes) is *slem-lem-an-dah-mouch-wah-ger*. A girl must be delighted to hear a fellow say he has a good deal of that for her.

Mr. Robertson, with the aid of an interpreter, has adapted our alphabet to the language, and published a series of books with translations of many of our hymns. These we heard at the Mission Sabbath School, which was also a delightful surprise in its way. I felt all the enthusiasm of the occasion when the seventy sweet voices, led by Miss Robertson with an organ, took up the strain of "Shall we gather at the River?" in the Creek. Here is the first verse:

BEAUTIFUL RIVER.

Uerakkon teheecyvr haks
Cesvs em estolke fullan
Cesvs liket a fihnet os
Hoyayvket fihnet os.

CHORUS—Momos mon teheceyvres
Uerakko herusen escherusen
Mekusapvlken etohkv liket
Fulleye munkv tares.

C is pronounced as *ch* in *child*, *e* as *i* in *pin*, *v* as short *u; y* between two vowels unites with the preceding one to form a diphthong, and with the latter is pronounced as *y; a* is pronounced *ah* as in *father*, and all other letters as in English.

Thence we continued our survey of the Creek country by leisurely journeys among the farmers. The soil is generally fertile, while almost every dwelling is the center of a beautiful grove of fruit trees, at that season green with springing leaves, or white and red with blossoms, giving off the sweet scents of advancing spring. The people as a rule are simple, civil and hospitable; the Nation contains several churches aggregating a thousand members. But the natural tendency, as with other Indians, is towards a sort of fatalism. Among all the races in the Territory conjurers are found, and the testimony is universal that they never fail to cure snake-bites. There is not a dissenting statement from white, black or red! If you ask the more intelligent how they explain it, the answer generally is: "I don't explain it; I don't believe in conjuration; I only know the cure is certain." The conjurer uses no medicine but a small leaf of tobacco or other plant, which he holds upon his tongue while pronouncing the charm. He applies it then to the bite, pressing it smartly with the ball of his thumb, and in less than twenty-four hours the patient is entirely well.

At noon of a bright April day we return to the railroad at Muscogee, to find matters worse than ever. As we sit down to dinner in the boarding-car, a half-blood Creek, crazy with smuggled whisky, is galloping up and down the row, brandishing a huge revolver, and threatening death to all opponents. At one moment he rides his horse into a shop, emerges the next, and gallops upon a group of wenches, who scatter with a chorus of screams. A file of soldiers from a detachment on the road appear on the scene, arrest and disarm him, and the town returns to its normal condition of listlessness and idle chatter. Severe penalties are prescribed against selling whisky in the Territory, and that which is smuggled in, is the vilest compound known to the trade, familiarly called "tarantula juice," from the deadliest insect in the country. And this reminds me of the appropriate names for intoxicating liquors, which have been evolved by a riotous Western fancy. Nobody says: "Will you take a drink?" At Chicago they say: "Name your family disturbance." At Omaha: "Nominate your poison." At Cheyenne: "Will you drive a nail in your coffin?" At Salt Lake: "Well, shall we irrigate?" At Virginia City: "Shall we lay the dust?" But in Arizona and the more southern Territories the universal formula is: "Let's nip some tarantula juice." Such are the pleasing metaphors wherewith the frontiersman invites to refreshment.

The railroad was pushing southward as fast as a small army could lay track, to meet the Texas Central, which was in like manner pushing northward toward Red River. From Muscogee we traversed the last section then built, to the main Canadian River. Between the two Canadians was the passenger terminus, near the Old Methodist Mission; and here we pause a few hours. Dusty and travel-worn pilgrims are coming in from all points in Western Texas, and spruce, clean looking people from civilization, starting out on long and toilsome journeys through the sandy plains between here and the Rio Grande. Thence to Main Canadian we traverse a dense forest; all the point between the two rivers is heavily timbered, and choked with underbrush. The main stream is now wide and rapid, apparently thick with red mud and sand; but after standing a few minutes, it is sweet enough to the taste, and close examination shows the stream to be tolerably clear, the red showing through the water from the bottom.

We observed, with some nervousness, that Brad Collins, a "White Cherokee" desperado, with a dozen of his retainers had come down on our train. Soon the smuggled whisky they brought begun to take effect, and half a dozen young half-breeds were galloping about town, firing pistols in the air, and yelling like demons. My companion took a brief look, and suggested: "This is a devilish queer place, let's get out of it." I was glad I had waited for him to speak first, but promptly acquiesced; and we crossed the Canadian into the Choctaw Nation, and spent the day with Tandy Walker, Esq. This gentleman, nephew of Ex-Governor Walker of the Choctaws, is nearly white, and strongly in favor of throwing open the Territory to white settlement. Once a leading man, he is now politically ostracized for his opinions. And here I may as well present a view of the party divisions which have caused so much trouble and some bloodshed in this Territory. It is a "Territory" only in a geographical sense, not being governed under an organic act like Utah or Montana. It was set apart by Act of Congress of May 28, 1830, and each Indian nation has its own government. The proposition, before Congress ever since the war, is to organize it into the "Territory of Oklahoma," (a Cherokee compound signifying the "Red men's State") and throw it open to white settlers. Hence the three parties among the Indians:

First—the Territorial party: in favor of Oklahoma and white immigration, after setting apart, in fee simple, a considerable farm to each Indian.

Second—the Ockmulkee Constitution party: in favor of sectionizing the land, giving each Indian his farm and the two railroads their grant, keeping all the rest in common as it is now, and uniting all the tribes under one government of their own (the Ockmulkee Constitution), with American citizenship and local courts; but no territorial arrangement and no white settlement.

Third—the party in favor of the present condition.

On further examination I found that the first party was very small among all the nations, and that the members of it were regarded as traitors to their race; that the third party had as yet a large majority of the whole people, but that the Ockmulkee Constitution promised most for the Indians, and had the support of their most able men.

The Choctaws number 16,000, the Chickasaws 6,000; the two constitute one nation, the citizens of either tribe having equal rights in all respects. Their country lies between the Main Canadian and Arkansas, and is two hundred miles from east to west: an area equal to two or three New England States, the eastern third very fertile, the center good for timber and pasture, the western part running into the flinty hills and barren plains. The citizens are more advanced in civilization than the Creeks; they enforce their laws much better, particularly in cases where whites or half-breeds are concerned.

With their sporadic population timber increases yearly, game is abundant and cheap, common pasturage is plenty, and cattle are grown at a cost of from three to eight dollars per head. The Choctaws were immensely wealthy before the war. Single herders numbered their cattle by thousands. The average wealth was twice as great as that of any purely agricultural community in the States, and golden ornaments of every sort were profusely displayed on horses, carriages, and the Indians' persons. The amount of fine clothes and jewelry sold by traders here at that time seems incredible. The war swept them clean; literally broke up and ruined them, leaving nothing but the land. Before the war Mr. Walker was accounted a millionaire. He began again, in 1865, with fifty dollars and one saddle-mule. He was ahead of his neighbors only in this: his fifty dollars were in greenbacks, theirs were in Confederate notes. Those who "went South" were even worse ruined than those who "took the Federal side." Some died of grief and despair, on returning home in 1865. But most went resolutely to work, and are once more prospering. But many years will be required for those vast herds of cattle to be renewed. This neighborhood has every sign of a prosperous community of civilized farmers. On the whole, I rather like the Choctaws.

We soon returned to Muscogee, and on the afternoon of a sultry day set out to walk to Fort Gibson. Three miles brought us upon the old cattle trail from Texas to Kansas City, where we were soon overtaken by a grizzled and weather-beaten old Texan, who politely asked us to take a seat in his wagon. Eyeing our valises suspiciously, he asked:

"Got any whisky in them?"

"No," was the answer, with expressed regrets.

"Ef ye had, ye'd walk, you bet; would n't have you get in here with one pint of whisky for five hundred dollars!"

This radical temperance platform in this latitude excited our astonishment, and we called for an explanation. He gave it: "A burnt child dreads the fire. One pint, yes, one dram o' whisky 'd cost me this hull load. These deputy marshals—d—n the thievin' rascals, I say—they 'll search y'r wagon any minit; and if they find one drop, away goes the hull load to Fort Smith, and d—n the haight of it d'y ever see again. One trip a nice lookin' chap enough asked me to ride. He got in, and pretty soon pulled a flask. 'Drink,' says he. 'After you,' says I. Well, in less 'n ten minutes comes the marshals and grabbed us. If they find a drop even on a man as is ridin' with you, they take every thing, and nary dollar do you ever git. Why, that feller was in with 'em, of course. They seize every thing they can git a pretense for, and then divide. There won't any body but a scamp or a rough take such an office as deputy marshal in this country. They're all on the make, and in with these roughs. That's what I say."

Three miles with our slightly rebellious Texan friend brought us to the Arkansas River, and to a steam ferry-boat. At the mouth of Grand River, is the head of navigation on the Arkansas. Steamers run up the Grand River, which has backwater from the Arkansas, three miles or more, and land at Fort Gibson. By a series of dams and locks, like those on Green River, Kentucky, I am convinced the Arkansas could have slack-water navigation a hundred miles or more above this. The waters of Grand River and those of the Arkansas show like two broad bands, one misty blue and the other dirty red and yellow, in the main channel as far as we can see below their junction. The two streams, the clear and the muddy, run side by side for nearly twenty miles, when a series of riffles and sharp turns mingles them freely in a fluid of pale orange tint.

At Fort Gibson we found quarters at the usual double-log-house hotel, kept by a Pennsylvania Dutchman, with a "White Cherokee" wife; and there we met Judge Vann, Hon. A. Rattling Gourd, and other prominent Cherokees. This is a rather handsome town for the border, with several neat brick and frame houses. After a few days' study of local politics, we concluded more was to be learned at the capital, and started afoot for Tahlequah. The distance is twenty-two miles, which we must divide in two journeys. "Better stop at Widow Skrimshee's over night; got a good house and a white son-in-law; 'taint but fifteen miles there," said our new friends. So, valise on shoulder, we started for the widow's, through a beautiful and well-improved country for the first six miles. The log-houses here are superior in style to those in most new countries, being high, neatly squared at the corners, and well shingled. There are few frames. The improvements are much finer than among the Creeks, and about equal to those of the Choctaws. From rolling prairie we descended into a broad valley with heavy timber. From the open and windy plain to this grove was like going from pleasant April to sultry July. Our valises seemed to weigh a hundred each; our clothing dripped with sweat, and we were soon exhausted by fatigue. We turned aside to the residence of a "White Cherokee"—the usual double-log-house with porch between—where we lay prostrate in the passage, smoked a pipe of his "home raisin'," and "interviewed" him as to the situation. He had been a Union Cherokee; took a hundred men out of here by night in the fall of '61; went North and became a captain; came back after the war, to find his house and fences burned, and all his stock run off—some to Kansas, some to Texas. "Was rich afo' the war; derned poor now, but gittin' started again. Hated the loss of my sheep wuss'n any thing else—fine bloods—couldn't get others like 'em."

At dark, fagged and heated, we reached the widow's. She was a bright, half-blood Cherokee, and entertained us till late bed-time with accounts of "the old nation in Geaugey," and their fights and troubles till they were sent here. Thence we traveled on to Tahlequah, the Cherokee capital, a pretty town of perhaps eight hundred people. Our first acquaintance was with William Boudinot, brother of the Elias Boudinot who has been so active at Washington pushing the Oklahoma Bill. William is editor of the *Cherokee Advocate*, official organ of the Nation, published in English and Cherokee, and a handsome, well-conducted sheet. The Choctaws also have a small paper called the *Vindicator*, these being the only papers published in the Territory. Tahlequah was for us rich in historic interest, and we spent three days most delightfully among the curious old records of the Nation, here preserved.

The Cherokees represent the best history and the highest hope of the Indian race. If they are a failure, the race can not be civilized—the aborigine is doomed. They have been an organized nation with constitution and written laws for eighty years; far back of that they were superior to all neighboring tribes. The oldest printed law I can find bears date of Broom's Town (in Georgia), 11th Sept. 1808, and is as follows:

RESOLVED, *by the Chiefs and Warriors in a National Council Assembled:* . . . When any person or persons which may or shall be charged with stealing a horse, and upon conviction by one or two witnesses, he, she, or they, shall be punished with one hundred stripes on the bare back, and the punishment to be in proportion for stealing property of less value; and should the accused person or persons raise up with arms in his or their hands, as guns, axes, spears, and knives, in opposition to the regulating company, or should they kill him or them, the blood of him or them shall not be required of any of the persons belonging to the regulators from the clan the person so killed belonged to.

       Accepted: BLACK FOX, Principal Chief.
               PATHKILLER, Second Chief.
               TOOCHALAR.
CHAS. HICKS, Secretary to Council.

Other acts bear the signatures of *Ehnautaunaueh*, Secretary; and "*Turtle-at-home*, Speaker of Council." The constitution of May 6,

1817, sets forth that fifty-four towns have agreed on "a form for future government." The following act, passed in 1819, hints at a Credit Mobilier Scheme:

Whereas, The Big Rattling Gourd, William Grimit, Betsey Broom, The Dark, Daniel Griffin, and Mrs. Lesley have made certain promises, etc.:

Be it now, therefore, known, ... The above persons are the only legal proprietors and a privileged company to establish a turnpike, leading from Widow Fools', at the forks of Hightower and Oostinallah, to the first creek east of John Field's, known by the name Where-Vann-was-shot, etc.

Some of the dark statesmen retained their aboriginal names, some simply translated them into plain English, and others adopted new names from missionaries or noted Americans. Hence we find among the officials: Young Wolf (perhaps a rising warrior), Okanstotah Logan, Bark Flute (probably a musical orator), Oolayoa, and Soft Shell Turtle! Judge Rattling Gourd is a prominent citizen of the nation at present. John Jolly and Spring Frog—perhaps the Sunset Cox and Ben Butler of their politics—were active in effecting the union.

The Eastern and Western Cherokees reunited in their present country in 1839, and the "Act of Union" is signed by James Brown, Te-ke-chu-las-kee, George Guess (Se-quo-yah), Jesse Bushyhead, Lewis Ross, Tobacco Will, Thomas Candy, Young Wolf, Ah-sto-la-ta, and some others. At the conclusion is this indorsement:

"The foregoing instrument was read, considered, and approved by us, this 23d day of August, 1839: Major Pullum, Young Elders, Deer Track, Young Puppy (!), Turtle Fields, July, The Eagle, The Crying Buffalo, and a great number of respectable old settlers and late emigrants too numerous to be recorded."

Some two hundred years ago the Cherokees, then known as an offshoot from the Waupanuckee (whom the French called Lenni Lenape, and the Americans have since named Delawares), were pushing slowly down from western North Carolina towards the coast. On the Yemassee—celebrated by the genius of Gilmore Simms—they came in contact with the whites; and twenty years before the Revolution occurred a bloody contest, in which they were driven westward. In the Continental forces were two lieutenants, afterwards known to fame as General Francis Marion and Major Peter Horry. The major in his account tells with surprise of the superior dwellings and advancement of the Cherokees. Since that time they have made twenty successive treaties with the United States; and if any faith whatever is to be kept with Indians, their title to the region they now occupy is as good as that of any white man to his land. They abandoned all claims to their lands in Georgia, Alabama, Tennessee, and North Carolina, on condition of receiving a fee simple to this land, witnessed by a patent from the President. This title has been twice pronounced valid by the Supreme Court, and recognized in eight solemn treaties. Could title to land be more perfect?

In 1860, they were, as a community, the wealthiest people in the West. Single herders owned stock to the value of a hundred thousand dollars. In this mild climate and upon these rich prairies cattle multiplied rapidly. There was soon no land "running to waste," for all was utilized as pasture. Many white men sought citizenship or married Cherokee girls, and were adopted, and the advance of the Nation was healthful, natural and rapid.

In 1865 their country was almost a waste; the people in extreme poverty. But they came back from the war and sadly went to work again. Now it is proposed, because part of them joined the Confederates, that all shall lose their present title and take their chances under a new allotment.

The Indian Territory contains about 70,000 square miles—one-third very fertile, a third or more fit only for pasture-lands, and the remainder, the westward portion, comparatively a desert. The four little governments—Cherokee, Creek, Choctaw, and Seminole—are republican in form; over all of them extends a sort of Federal protectorate. At least twenty little remnants of tribes have been adopted into these nations, such as the Quawpaws, Senecas, Wyandottes, and Delawares. Their total is nearly as follows:

CHEROKEE NATION.

Full bloods	8,000
Mixed	4,000
Freedmen	1,500
Whites married in or adopted	500
Delawares	900
Shawnees	700
Wyandottes	400
Quawpaws	200
Senecas	100
Total Cherokee Nation	16,300

To which should be added some 2,000 Cherokees now in North Carolina, who are desirous of settling here, and for whose removal the Nation is making provisions, bringing the whole number up to about 18,000. I do not here include those new tribes west of 96°, not yet formally incorporated.

Full bloods	(CREEK NATION.)		9,000
Whites and mixed bloods			1,000
Freedmen			4,000
Seminoles			2,000
Total Creek citizens			16,000
Pure Choctaws	(CHOCTAW NATION.)		10,000
Mixed			4,000
Whites			1,000
Chickasaws			5,000
Freedmen			2,000
Total Choctaw citizens			22,000
Osages west of 96°	(MINOR TRIBES.)		3,000
Kaws, west of 96°			600
Unassigned, perhaps			3,400
Total minor tribes			7,000
Grand total			63,000

The Choctaws and Cherokees have the greatest number of intelligent men, but the Creeks are just now doing the most for the rising generation. They have three Mission High Schools, under control respectively of the Baptist, Methodist, and Presbyterian churches. In 1872 there were in the whole Territory a hundred and sixty common schools—the high average of one to every four hundred of the population. The number now reaches nearly two hundred.

The present weakness of these people is their imperfect land tenure. The land is held in common by the whole tribe, but whatever area any citizen incloses with a lawful fence is his while he occupies it. He may be said to own the improvements, but not the land. Any thing may be removed at the owner's will; hence there is practically no real estate, no conservative landed interest—the only true foundation for a progressive society and a stable civil structure. The herder, hunter or explorer, from Kansas or Texas, rides through a beautiful tract, and, when he asks who owns it, the only answer is: "The Injuns—it's Injun land;" that is, in his estimation, nobody's land, if he can by force or fraud get a foothold. If he were told that it was the property of John Johnnycake or William Beaverdam, or any other individual, with a patent title on which he could sue and be sued, the case would be very different to him. A strong party, therefore, is rising up, agitating for this reform, which is the distinctive feature of the Ocmulkee Constitution.

There are a score of reasons why a little more time should be given the Indians, and why we should not now throw open this country to general settlement. In the first place, we have solemnly agreed not to do it, which is reason enough for any honorable man. Secondly, there is no present necessity for it. There are countless millions of acres lying idle in every State and Territory north of it, untouched by the cultivator, and even unoccupied by the herdsman. It is too soon by half a century to repeat to these civilized Indians the old order: "Go West." There is room in Nebraska for half a million farmers. There is a tract in Dakota about the size of Indiana, yet unappropriated, with a climate suitable for Northern people, and a most prolific soil.

"GO WEST."

When these are filled, and our population really begins to feel crowded, it will be time enough to trouble the Indians. But with Kansas on one side and Texas on the other offering millions of acres of good land, it seems as if thousands are half crazy to get into the Indian Territory just because it is forbidden.

Our true policy is to secure these people their lands, assist them a little in their progress, and make them our agents to deal with the wild tribes. Half civilized and barbarous races can best be reached through the medium of their more advanced brethren. The nations here are already moving in the matter, and a little assistance only is needed to enable them to reach and negotiate with all the wild tribes of Northern Texas and New Mexico. I am hopeful enough to believe that, with a proper policy, all the tribes in the same latitude, except possibly the Apaches, might eventually be made citizens of this Territory. We have sent the Indians, as a rule, our worst men and most destructive practices, and have systematically broken faith whenever it seemed profitable to do so. Here only has a policy something near sensible and just been pursued, and the results are not discouraging. Let it be improved and extended, and we may reasonably hope the Indians of all the southern Territories will be gathered here; that an aboriginal community of two hundred thousand will grow into a high civilization; and in due time we shall have a real native American State—a progressive and prosperous State of Oklahoma.

CHAPTER XIV.

JOURNEY TO THE RIO GRANDE.

No THOROUGHFARE from Oklahoma westward. The country was safe enough for three hundred miles from the eastern border; but between that and the settlements in New Mexico intervened five hundred miles of marauding Kioways and murderous Comanches. Stage coaches run from Fort Smith out to Fort Sill; beyond that the traveler must take his chances for a government train, which might go in a month or a year. For two men like us, unskilled in wood-craft, such a trip alone was courting death. Another line of coaches traverses Northern Texas to Fort Concho, but we preferred a more northern route at that season, and turned toward the Kansas Pacific Railroad.

Traveling leisurely northward through Kansas, we still gained rapidly on the season. Montgomery County presented a succession of fertile vales and rolling hills, the latter often rising into picturesque mounds crowned with clumps of timber, and over all the rich green of advancing spring. In 1868, Montgomery contained twenty settlers and one post-office; in 1872, it cast a vote of 3,000, indicating a population of at least 10,000. The stream of emigration had filled all the valleys, then rolled on westward, and after covering the best parts of Wilson and Cowley counties, had turned north, and was flowing up the Arkansas Valley. The Kansians thus summed up the changes since we visited them a month before: "Fine chance o' corn planted, an' doin' well; splendid prospect for fruit—peaches sure of a whalin' crop—but wheat don't look well. In fact that crop ain't a certain thing yet in Southern Kansas. Garden spot o' the world, sir; no doubt o' that; but we haven't quite got the land worked down to the right pitch for wheat."

At midnight of May 2d we left the State Line Station for the long ride to Denver; and at daylight of the 3d were at Junction City, last point of connection with any eastern line of rail. Thence the Missouri, Kansas and Texas Road runs south-east, down the valley of the Neosho to Parsons, in Labette County. So far we see no signs of a different country from that on the eastern border; timber is plenty along the streams, the soil is rich, and the road is through a continuous line of settlements. We are in the valley of the Kaw or Kansas, (aboriginal for "blue" or "smoky") till noon; then leave it for the Smoky Hill Valley, after crossing Republican, Big Blue and Solomon's Fork. These three are big streams—*on the map*. Combined they would make a river about the size of the Miami.

We find the valley pretty well settled for fifty miles west of Junction City; then rise rapidly to the high plains where nothing is seen but an occasional stock ranche. We breakfast at Ellsworth, which only five years before was the rival of Cheyenne in all that pertains to rush, crush, business and deviltry. It was then the terminus of the road—also the terminus of at least a hundred lives. When I was there in October, 1867, J. H. Runkle, Esq., Prosecuting Attorney, informed me that for ninety-three days there was a homicide every day in the town or vicinity. Those were the palmy days of your "Wild Bills" (I made the acquaintance of the original, and found him quite a gentleman), and "Long

"WILD BILL."—J. B. HICKOCK.

Steves," your "Dad Smith," "Rake Jake" and "Tom Smith of Bear River." "Shall we have a man for breakfast?" was the ordinary morning salutation; and usually it was found that somebody had answered the question affirmatively during the night. "A short life and a merry one," was the motto of these roysterers. The life was short enough; its merriment will be a matter of doubt. Strange to say, officials who had much to do in thwarting or arresting these men, themselves became careless of life, or moody and inclined to suicide. "Wild Bill" sleeps beneath the green prairies on which he figured in so many tragedies—died by the shot of an assassin. "Dad Smith" was hanged by the vigilantes. "Long Steve" met a like fate at Laramie. "Tom Smith" was brained by an ax in the hands of a drunken companion. And saddest of all, but a few months ago (February, 1877) came a dispatch that J. H. Runkle, U. S. Attorney, committed suicide at Columbia, South Carolina. "Rake Jake" made his exit from a tragedy more dramatic than any ever shown upon the stage. With two companions he took refuge in his cabin on the prairie, and maintained a desperate fight against the vigilantes. The infuriated Kansians set the dry grass on fire; the cabin was soon in flames, and issuing therefrom with a revolver in each hand, scattering leaden death on all sides, the three died as became their lives, brave men to the last. What a pity such nerve should be lost. It was the material for heroes sadly perverted.

"Pity they loved adventurous life's variety;
They were so great a loss to good society."

Ellsworth is quiet enough now. During the season for shipping cattle it is a place of some importance; the rest of the year a quiet country depot. From this on our route is through the Big Pasture. It extends from latitude 52° in British America, to the Rio Grande, with an average width of three hundred miles, sloping steadily eastward from the foot of the Rocky Mountains. Say 1,500 by 300 miles, and we have an area of 450,000 square miles, set apart forever by nature as our national grazing ground. Not one acre in twenty of it can ever be cultivated; while at least half the area produces the sweetest and most nutritious of grasses. Take a board, four times as long as it is wide, lay it north and south, and tilt it a very little toward the east, then score it from east to west with a number of furrows, and you will have a tolerable map or miniature copy of what is called the "plains." The western border, the high plateau near the mountains, has an average elevation of 5,000 feet; thence eastward the general slope is ten feet to the mile; so, by the time we reach the settled portions of Kansas and Nebraska, we are but 1,000 feet or so above sea-level. Going westward you are going up-hill and nearer mountains and deserts; consequently into a dryer and colder country, and finally into a region fit for nothing but pasturage.

"SCATTERING LEADEN DEATH ON ALL SIDES."

We hurry on, and soon after noon enter the buffalo country. We see few live ones, for it is too early for their great move northward, but myriads of the dead. Whole herds died here during the heavy snow in the winter of 1871–'72. Far as the eye can reach, or as a good field-glass can sweep the horizon, they lie at intervals of eight or ten rods, and in every stage of decay. Some appear just as they fell, almost entirely preserved—mummified, as it were, by the dry air. Others have shrunk to small compass with the hide still entire, and others—by far the larger number—are picked and licked to clean white skeletons by the wolves. The sight is sad and sickening. About the stations the skins are piled in great heaps to dry for market—not so bad to the sight as the other, but worse to the smell. This region of dead buffaloes extends from first to last, some eighty miles, traversing which we saw many thousand of their carcasses.

Soon we begin to rout out a few live bisons from their herding places in the hollows. The cry of "buffalo!" causes a general rush to the windows; next come antelope, then prairie dogs, and for hours our palace car company resembles a district school at a menagerie. Ere long we find the buffalo more numerous, but always at a distance, feeding in small groups. The whole appearance of the country has changed; the surface is dry and cracked, and the grass has a cured look. Dark overtakes us, still fifty miles east of the Colorado line.

We wake at Denver, and hasten to the Broadwell House, where we sit down to a good breakfast and a copy of Byers' *Rocky Mountain News*. In its columns we learn that the Democrats have nominated Horace Greeley for President! Thirteen years before he and the lamented Richardson made a journey together by stage over the country we have just traversed; his strong suit then was abuse of Democrats as the proslavery party. Time had brought even greater changes in our politics than in the wild region then vaguely known as the "Pike's Peak country." Three days we rested at Denver, a beautiful city with a happy location. But its merits must wait recital till my next visit; I must cut short my stay, as the weather is fast getting hotter and dryer where I am going. I thought I knew something about high tariffs in the West, but when I go to inquire about the fare to Santa Fe the intelligence nearly takes my breath.

The distance is four hundred and fifteen miles, ninety of which we go by rail, and the rest by stage. Fare by rail, ten cents per mile; by stage, twenty cents; total to Santa Fe, seventy-four dollars, with a dollar a meal on the road. Moral: Don't go to Santa Fe, unless you have important business. From what I hear, the rates are still higher to where I wish to go in Arizona, with the comfort added, however, that, in all probability, I can not get there at all, as three drivers have lately been killed by the Apaches. Parties are organizing with a view of going through the center of Arizona and New Mexico, from Santa Fe to Fort Prescott; but all I consult here shake their heads doubtfully on the subject. However, I have generally observed in traveling that dangers lessen as one draws near them. At Denver, Mr. De Bruler's trip ended, much to my regret, for I was just entering on the region where, most of all, I should need an intimate companion. For the first stage I took the Denver & Rio Grande Railroad—the neatest, queerest little narrow-guage in America, but usually called the "narrow-gouge," in delicate satire on its rates of fare. Ten cents per mile

"DIVIDE HOTEL AND RANCHE."

is high; but, before the road was built, it was twenty cents by stage. The road had no land subsidy, and the travel is light as yet. Most who go that way would be only too glad to pay that rate all the way to Santa Fe.

We journey at a *sobre passo* gait of ten or fifteen miles an hour, southward and up the Platte Valley, which has the appearance of an old, settled, and cultivated country. The farm-houses are in much better style, and the system of irrigation more scientific than in Utah. Farmers are plowing, and the spring crops coming forward finely. About 10 A. M. we leave the Platte and follow up a small stream to the "Divide." Here we are in the lumber region, as shown by the immense stacks of the same about the depots; and the "Divide Hotel and Ranche" is built of massive pine logs, in the style of a primitive "Hoosier" cabin. Behind it, the cool, dark-green woods invite to a halt, and in front, the cold, clear pool, fed by rivulets from snow-banks, is well stocked with mountain trout. Singularly enough, near the "Divide," on both sides are considerable fields cultivated without irrigation, there being sufficient rain when one draws near the summit and the timber! The timber causes the rain, or the rain produces the timber, or the mountains are the cause of both, or some other sufficient cause accounts for all three. The plainsmen don't know, and perhaps the scientists are equally wise.

As soon as we pass the summit, and get on the head-waters of the Fontaine Que Bouille, we see on all the slopes immense herds of cattle and sheep. At Colorado Springs lives one man who has 13,000 sheep in this region, and I am reliably informed there are 250,000 head of stock in the system of valleys opening out on this stream. The country is evidently one of the best in the world for sheep. It is high, dry, cool in summer, and not very cold in winter, with just moisture enough to produce good grass. For about fifty miles we traverse a beautiful grazing region. At the Springs we stop an hour for dinner. Here is one of the coming towns of Colorado, having a fine fertile valley, immense grazing area, and the noted chemical springs—already a great place of fashionable resort. I am most agreeably surprised by Southern Colorado. There is very little desert, and, except the bare mountains, it appears to me a country of great natural richness. The valleys are very fertile, and most of the slopes furnish good pasturage.

At Little Buttes we change to the coach, the only passengers beside myself being Captain Humphreys, of the United States Army, his wife and servant, on their way to Fort Union. At dark we make a brief halt at Pueblo, and are off for the night ride. The first night in a coach is always worse than the second; by that time one's sensibilities are dulled, and he can sleep, unless the pounding is harder than common. We breakfast at Cocharas, an old-style Mexican *hacienda*, in a beautiful circular valley, seventy miles from Little Buttes. I am still fresh as at starting, and make havoc among the wheaten cakes, fried eggs, and chopped and stewed mutton, which, with coffee, constitute our breakfast—called here, however, *tortillas, huevos, carne* and *cafe* respectively. A plump and pretty *señorita* sits by, and gives me my first lesson in Spanish, with a pleasing variety of smiles and graceful gestures. Our driver for to-day is "Fat Jack," who, ten years before, lived in Cincinnati, and might have traveled as the "Original Living Skeleton." Some unnamable and wasting disease had reduced him to less than ninety pounds weight. He started West, began to improve, reached New Mexico, went to driving stage, and now weighs two hundred! He is five feet four inches high, and four feet two inches around the waist, and has a voice like a fog-horn

All day we rolled along, the four horses at a sweeping trot, over the finest natural roads and through a succession of sublime scenery that made us forget fatigue. For a mile in one place we drove through a dog-town, the little creatures scampering in all directions but a few rods from the coach. The road runs just far enough from the base of the mountains to secure a level track; to our right were the red hills rising to blue mountains, and above them the ever-snow-clad peaks; to our left the gently rolling plain fading away till its pale green surface met the blue horizon. Most of the day the Spanish Peaks seemed just above us, westward; in front was Fisher's Peak, of the Raton Mountains, glistening white with snow. For hours the last named looks as if it were about five or ten miles away. It is fifteen miles on an air line—as determined by the U. S. Engineers—from the hotel in Trinidad, at the base of the mountains. We reach that place, the last town in Colorado, at 4 P. M., rest an hour, take supper, and change to a small, stout uncomfortable coach, in which to make the passage of the Raton. We reach the summit just at dark, and have a fearful run down the southern side. Fortunately we can not see the danger, if there is any; and have nothing to do but bounce about in the dark inside the coach, butt each other's heads, shift ballast to suit the pitching, and enjoy ourselves generally. About midnight the jolting ceases, and the gentler motion indicates that we have come out into a smooth valley, and on to a good natural road. We compose ourselves, hang to the straps and get two or three hours tolerable sleep.

Shortly before daylight we are roused by the driver, with notice that an important bridge has been washed away, leaving only a foot-log, on which the passengers must cross while the coach makes a circuit of some miles. Our party of four were soon on the banks of the stream, and, by the light of a lamp, saw a fearful gorge, crossed by one narrow log, while fifteen feet below ran a stream strong enough to wash us out of sight in a moment. In vain the ladies were urged to try the passage; lacking confidence, a fall would have been certain. While we stood shivering on the brink, like a group of sinners ready to cross the River Styx, I noticed that the banks were not too steep for descent, and so climbed down by the aid of rocks and bushes, to the water's edge. The other male passenger soon followed, and we found enough of the ruins to construct a half-floating bridge. An hour's labor, with the driver kneeling on the log above to light us to our work, made a bridge on which the ladies succeeded in being helped across with fewer screams than could have been expected. A short walk brought us to the next station, where the coach overtook us in an hour.

We are now out upon the high plains of north-eastern New Mexico, a region of fierce winds and chilling rains at this season, inhabited only by nomadic herders. We breakfast at Maxwell's Ranche, headquarters of the Maxwell estate, an old Mexican grant containing two or three hundred square miles, including fifty sections of the best land in New Mexico, and one gold mine. Maxwell has lately sold the grant to an English company, who are bringing in machinery to work the mine, and utilize the abundant water-power. A good breakfast, with a pint of hot coffee apiece, restored the intellectual balance, and we entered upon the third day of staging with renewed vigor.

We travel all day in a south-east direction over rolling plains and low mountain spurs, leaving the main range some distance to the west, and cross the Rayado, Ocate, and minor tributaries of the Canadian. At noon a cold rain comes on, changing soon to a light sleet; we are miserable, and long for port. Late in the afternoon we reach Fort Union, when Captain Humphreys and family leave us, and my only companion is a young German thence to Las Vegas. This is a little south of Santa Fe on the headwaters of the Pecos River. It dates back to the early days of Spanish occupation, and is a rather prosperous place of three or four thousand. There our coach took on three U. S. army officers and the Right Reverend John B. Lamy, bishop of the diocese, who exerted himself to cheer up the heavy hours of the night as the coach labored through the mountain passes down to Santa Fe. The cold was intense, and the dawn showed three inches of freshly fallen snow. The open growth of mountain pines relieved the landscape but little; the bare knolls looked inexpressibly dreary, and the dark gorges suggested wild beasts and banditti. The rising sun illumined the ragged peaks to our left, and poured a flood of light through the side cañons, bringing out the red and yellow stripes upon the wind-worn rocks, and producing for a brief space a scene of strange, weird beauty. At one station the occupants were dressing a bear which they had killed the previous night.

This is my fourth day of continuous travel, and I begin to weaken; my head pitches forward and back in involuntary "cat-naps" of a minute each. After four hours riding down hill, by 10 o'clock in the morning the snow had disappeared; once more nature asserted herself, and I was really feeling bright again when we came in sight of Santa Fe. In all my travels I never remember being so disappointed. One might pass within two miles of

"SUGGESTED WILD BEASTS AND BANDITTI."

the city and miss it. It is not in the Rio Grande Valley, as I had supposed, but at least twenty miles from that river, quite in a hollow, and appears a miserable, low, flat collection of mud huts. Some squares are walled in with mud, stones and adobes; then the width of a house roofed around the square on the inside; partition walls are built, passages cut through, and a score of dwellings in one group are complete. As the coach rolls through the narrow, ugly streets, it looks more like driving through a dirt cut in some excavation than the streets of a city. As we near the center of town these squares seems more compact; holes appear to have been cut through, making shut alleys or narrow streets, and other openings show the interior of these mud-walled squares to be a sort of stamping ground in common, for pigs, chickens, jackasses, children, ugly old women and "Greasers."

Reaching the *plaza*, things look a little better. There at least is a patch of green, a tract grown up in *alfalfa*, or Spanish clover. We stop at the Exchange, the only hotel in the city for white men, or rather Americans, the other distinction, though perfectly accurate, not being well relished here. The Exchange is a one-story square, like all the rest; but across the middle of the square is a line of buildings containing the dining-room and kitchen, and dividing the stable-yard and poultry run from the open court for human use. An arched way between the kitchen and dining-room connects the two courts; on the human side women and children take their recreation, and men of quiet or literary tastes can sit and read; while the stable side is sacred to dog-fights, cock-fights, wrestling-matches, pitching Mexican dollars and other exclusively manly pursuits. The people of Santa Fe evidently do not take in their philosophy the statement that " Man was made to mourn."

But I have little time to note these facts, for soon after leaving the coach my head is rolling as in a fit of sea-sickness; and I soon take to bed, where I remain for fourteen hours. Rising refreshed, I see the city in a fairer light. The streets are dreary in themselves, but the wayfarers are picturesque. Here comes a mountaineer with a *caballardo* of donkeys, each bearing his little load of wood or hay— piled high on his back and strapped as only a Mexican can strap it. Next is a well-to-do citizen—always fairer than the common people— with all the pride of the *gente fina;* then a Pueblo Indian with redder complexion than his wild congener, and curiously striped and colored blanket wrapping his stocky form. White soldiers in blue are numerous, for this is military headquarters for a large district; stylish officers with American wives brighten the principal street or saunter in the plaza, while heavily loaded army wagons drag slowly through the dust. The local traders, mostly Jews, add not a little to the comfort of the place; they speak all the languages used here, and are all things to all men to make it pleasant for visitors.

The sun shines from a sky of dazzling purity, but the air is cool; fires are necessary in the hotel parlor except for a few hours of midday, and I wear my overcoat on the streets. The city has a summer climate like that of Quebec, and a winter atmosphere much like that of Tennessee. All this is a surprise, as I had somehow got the idea that Santa Fe was in a hot climate. For incipient pulmonary complaints it is most excellent; those in an advanced stage of consumption die very suddenly here. Just north-east of the city, though thirty miles away, "Old Baldy," the noted mountain peak, rears its white head 12,000 feet high; east of us is the Rocky Range; on both sides of the city abrupt spurs put out westward toward the Rio Grande. The elevation is 7,000 feet, making this one of the highest cities in America; hence to the Rio Grande is all the way down hill, a descent of some twenty-two hundred feet.

Santa Fe de San Francisco, ("Holy Faith of Saint Francis,") as the old Spaniards named this city, has been inhabited by white men for two hundred and fifty years; and long before that by Pueblos, one of their old towns having been partly on the same site. In the narrow valley of Santa Fe Creek, walled in on all sides except the west, by abrupt mountains, it is measurely free from winter storms. On the other hand a suit of summer clothes is seldom seen in the streets; there are not thirty days in the year when they are needed. The place looks a thousand years old; the dwellings are low, flat and uninviting. I don't think there are twenty two-story houses in the city. The residences of some of the officials display a little taste; two or three of the merchants have houses with pretty surroundings, and Bishop Lamy has a place which would almost be considered pretty in Ohio. I saw perhaps a dozen gardens; all the rest of the view is bare, gray and dried-mud color. But here are old withered Mexicans, whose fathers and grandfathers were born, lived and died in this valley; for Santa Fe was an important place long before William Penn laid out Philadelphia. Here are old records and Spanish manuscripts, with which an antiquarian might spend months of enjoyment. Yes, Santa Fe has one great merit—it is rich in historic interest.

The Mexicans are a strangely polite, lazy, hospitable, lascivious, kind, careless and unprogressive race. The town saw its best days many years ago, when the Santa Fe trade from St. Louis and Independence was of great importance. It is now but the shell of former greatness. The population is claimed to be 6,000; I do not see where they put them. The whites, not of Spanish origin, number about five hundred. The Federal officials are Americans, from the States; most of the Territorial officers, Mexicans. It is a wonder there is so little conflict of jurisdiction, with all these differences of race and religion; but New Mexico is politically the quietest of the Territories. Instead of the ever-recurring religious squabbles of Utah, or the internecine political strifes of Dakota, these people seem always satisfied with what the officials do, if it is within a hundred degrees of right. They consider a governor as only one remove below the Deity; or, rather two removes, the Virgin Mary coming next, and the governor being about on the same degree as St. Peter. To one like myself, accustomed to the studied contempt, or lordly indifference, or good-natured and irreverent *bonhommie*, with which Territorial governors are regarded, respectively in Utah, Colorado and Dakota, it was something amusing to witness old, gray-headed men, with hat removed, bowing low to Governor Giddings, and to hear the *señoras* direct their children as he passed, " *No hable uste tanto. El Gobernador!*" Politeness is ingrained in all Spanish-Americans.

As with most mixed races, the standard of morals is not high. The *gente fina*, or upper classes, mingle very little with the common people; socially not at all. Except among the aristocracy, who seldom invite travelers to their houses, there seems to be no distinction at social gatherings on the score of character. The indifference on that subject would astonish most Americans. If the Stantons, Anthonys, etc., are really in earnest in the statement that "woman should have no worse stigma than man for sexual sins," they would certainly be gratified here, for the disgrace is, at least, as great to one sex as the other. Indeed, I think the general judgment for marital unfaithfulness is more severe on a man than a woman. The young Americans bring their mistresses to the *baile* with the same indifference the Mexicans do their sweethearts. These "girls" are scrupulously polite, and so unlike the same class in the States, that it can only be accounted for by the fact that they see no disgrace whatever in their mode of life, and feel no sort of social degradation.

A visitor with any reverence in his composition scarcely knows whether to smile or sigh at that "faith without knowledge," which shows in all their customs, and most of all in their names. Jesus, Maria, Mariano and Jose (Joseph) are favorites, the second and third common to both sexes. A prominent citizen is Don Jesus Vigil. His parents probably intended him for a "watchful Christian." Fortunately for sensitive American ears, it is pronounced *Haysoos Veheel*. Irreverent as it may appear in me to write it, there is a well-known citizen whose name is Jesus A. Christ de Vaca (*Haysoos Antonio Kreest day Bvahca*).

Sometimes among the *gente fina*, the marriage contract specifies that the sons take both names (united by " and "), from some principle of law as to entailed estates. Thus Don Jose Vigil y Alarid is the son of a lady of the Alarid family married to Señor Vigil. In like manner my young friends insisted that my rough Saxon patronymic did not suit the soft Castilian, and I became Señor Juan de Bidello. All Spanish-Americans are brilliant in nomenclature. The full name of a cowherd sounds like the title of a grandee. Americans who settle in the country very often translate their own names, or give them a Castilian termination. By such process Mr. Meadows becomes Señor Las Vegas; John Boggs, Señor Juan de Palos; and Jim Gibbons flowers out as Don Santiago de Gibbonoise. An Irishman from Denver settled near El Paso, married a wealthy Mexican lady, and lives in style; his original name, Tim Murphy, is long since forgotten, and he signs his bank checks as Timotheus Murfando.

Twelve days I wandered about Santa Fe, finding much to interest, and picking up a smattering of the language to serve me in my travels westward. Daily I studied the routes through Arizona, and each day brought fresh tales of disaster. First came a Mexican from El Paso, whose two companions were killed by Indians on the edge of the *Jornada del Muerto*; and next a *ranchero* from the south-western border, whose Mexican herders were killed, and all his stock run off by the Mescalero Apaches. And while he was yet speaking came another messenger, and said that nine prospectors, who left by the northern route, went too far south, fell into an ambuscade, and "their scalps now ornament the lodges of Collyer's pets." Simultaneously a lieutenant and sergeant of cavalry were ambuscaded in the Alamosa and their animals "ruched" with arrows. Drawing their revolvers, they dashed bravely on, firing right and left, knowing that to be their only chance for life, and, by rare good fortune, got through and into the open plain. Sorely wounded, and compelled to abandon their exhausted animals, only the darkness of night prevented their capture.

We next receive Arizona papers with the information that the eastern coach was attacked near Tucson, and the driver and messenger killed; and that the western coach was robbed beyond Fort Yuma by Mexican *ladrones*, and the station-keeper and one messenger murdered. The white population of Arizona was 9,600, and they then averaged a loss of twenty per month by Apaches and Mexicans— about half the ordinary mortality of an army. All things considered, I concluded to try the northern route. A soldier was about to start for Fort Wingate with a wagon-load of provisions; and General Myers, quartermaster, kindly gave me passage with him. From Wingate I thought to catch some kind of an expedition to Prescott.

There were stretches of fifty miles on that line without grass or water, but no hostile Indians, which suited me admirably. By waiting a month I could have gone to the Little Colorado with a party of engineers; but life is too short to stay a whole month in Santa Fe. At noon of May 22d I took my seat on an army wagon, and rolled

"DRAWING THEIR REVOLVERS, THEY DASHED BRAVELY ON."

out of the New Mexican capital. Crossing the Rio de Santa Fe, we left the valley and struck across the *mesa* in a south-west direction, the city behind us appearing to sink slowly into the earth. Looking back upon it, this noted town appeared to my eye exactly like a collection of old brick yards. It is my invariable custom to say something good of a town on departing, if I can possibly think of a good thing to say, but Santa Fe "raises me out." It was an important place in the old days of freighting from the Missouri border, because it was on the first level and fertile piece of ground the trains could reach after getting through the mountain passes. But it can never be a railroad center, though it may some day have a branch road.

My only companion from Santa Fe to Fort Wingate was Frank Hamilton, of the Eighth United States Cavalry, stationed at that post. Frank had been detailed to come to Santa Fe on military business, and had improved the occasion by getting gloriously drunk, in which condition he remained most of the time he was there, and was barely sober enough to know the road. His first move was down a three-foot bank into the Santa Fe. I jumped into the water to avoid a fall on the rocks, which stuck up sharply on the other side; but the wagon careened half over, lodged and righted again, when the mules took a forward surge, so I got off with nothing worse than a drenching. Hamilton, being drunk, and limber as a rag, of course escaped injury. For warmth and dryness' sake I walked most of the afternoon.

We turn south-west, rising by successive "benches" to a vast barren table-land. We pass in the afternoon one Mexican hamlet, looking like a collection of half a dozen "green" brick-yards—dry, hard, dusty and desolate. Crossing the high *mesa*, level as the sea, we approach an irregular line of rocks, rising like turrets ten or twenty feet above the plain, which we find to be a sort of a natural battlement along the edge of the "big hill." Reaching the cliff we see, at an angle of forty-five degrees below us, in a narrow valley, the town of La Bajada. Down the face of this hill the road winds in a series of zigzags, bounded in the worst places by rocky walls, descending fifteen hundred feet in three-quarters of a mile. La Bajada is the stereotyped New Mexican town—a collection of mud-huts, among which one or two whitewashed *domos* indicate the residences of persons of the *gente fina* (hen-ta fee-nah), or, as they themselves style it, of the *sangre azul* (blue blood).

The town has a hotel, consisting of a quadrangle of rooms around an open square, which contains some flowers, two shade-trees, benches, and wash-stands. The rooms have floors of wood, instead of dirt; the walls are whitewashed; two mirrors and a buffalo-skin lounge adorn the sitting-room, and generally the place ranks high. Two bright-eyed, graceful, copper-colored *señoritas* bring me a supper of coffee, side meat, eggs and *tortillas de mais*, and entertain me with a voluminous account, in musical Spanish, of their personal recollections of the place. I have learned enough of the language to be able to say "ah," "yes," and "no" at nearly the right place, and that is the most required to keep a Mexican woman social. My companion, jolly drunk, was barely able to get his team into the *corral*, when he fell back into the wagon asleep, and, as he was the cook of our outfit, I was obliged to stay over night at the hotel. Except the two houses mentioned, the whole town is of a uniform dull clay color, walls of of mud, fences of mud, door and window-casings of mud-colored wood, roofs of slightly sloping poles, covered with earth two or three feet thick, floors of native earth beaten hard, and nowhere a patch of grass to relieve the wearied eye. It is one of the few Mexican towns not named after some saint; La Bajada means "The Descent," the words being pronounced together, *Lavvahadda*.

Thence, in the cool of the morning, we journey at a *sobre passo* gait of two miles an hour, down the valley towards the Rio Grande. The first point of interest is the Pueblo of Santo Domingo, where I visit for an hour. The houses are all in a bunch; a few have doors, but most are still entered from the roof, there being a ladder or rude stairway at the corner. All the men were in the public field at work, and the women and children appeared strangely quiet and undemonstrative. The only man I met accompanied me three miles on the road. He gave his name as Antonio Gomez, and talked fluently of their mode of life and system of government. We were more social, indeed, than could have been expected of men with but a few hundred words in common; but words are like dollars—a few go a long ways when one is pinched. But my main question: "How many years since your people first came here?" he answered, with a laugh: "*Quién sabe? Quisas doce quinientos!*" (Who knows? Perhaps a dozen times five hundred!) They generally reckon by tens; are seldom able to count high numbers, and any thing above two or three hundred is "infinity," vaguely expressed by *quinientos*.

Three miles brought us down into a beautiful *vega*, containing some two miles square of rich, natural meadow, on which the Pueblos had several hundred head of horses and mules. My companion pointed out with some pride his own *manada* of sixty mules and mares, attended by his three boys, and urged me to stop at his *rancheria* and take dinner. But appearances were not inviting, so I plead *no tiempo*, and hurried on after the team, Antonio leaving me with a friendly grasp, and, "*Addio, Señor, pasa buenas dies.*" (May you pass good days.) A little farther on we drove within a quarter of a mile of the river, where some twenty Pueblos were hauling a rude seine. They held up some good-sized fish, shouting the price, but, on my declining, waved me off with, "*Buena jornada, Señor!*" (A good journey, sir.)

We pass the little pueblo of San Felipe, and from this *vega* rise to another desert—for ten miles the same eye-wearying panorama of dry sand, dark-gray rock, and treeless, grassless *mesa*, the whole uninhabited. About 3 P. M. we descend to another oasis of two or three square miles, where we spend the night at the town of Algodones. All that I had previously seen of unsightly Mexican towns is eclipsed by this straggling row of unburnt brick-kilns—walls, fences, houses, fields and corrals of dried mud. My companion had fortunately got sober enough to cook our supper, while I hunted for some additions to our fare, which consisted of army bread, pork, coffee and potatoes. I found three luxuries for sale: *vino de pais* (native wine), eggs and goat's milk. My soldier took the milk by choice, but I confined myself to the eggs and wine, with the regular fare. After supper I ran about town till I found one intelligent citizen, who gave me much information about the country, in a mixture of French and Spanish. "When will the thirty-fifth parallel road be built?" and "Will New Mexico be admitted soon as a State?" were the questions on which he earnestly desired information. He set forth the arguments for a State government at great length. The strongest, in his estimation, seemed to be, "The rich (*los ricos*) are all in favor of it." As they must pay the expense, he thought they should have whatever they wanted.

We were off at six next morning, and a few miles from Algodones entered the great oasis of Albuquerque, the largest body of good land in New Mexico. For nearly a hundred miles, with slight breaks, extends the fertile valley of the Rio Grande, varying from two to eight miles wide. In this portion an *accequia*, taken out of the river above, runs along the bluffs, from which side-ditches, one every furlong or oftener, convey the water among the fields. There we see ridges of dirt thrown up, dividing the field into little squares of some five rods each, to hold the water. The labor of irrigating seems much greater than in Utah. In comparison with the sterile *mesas* we have crossed, this fertile strip seems a very Eden. Wheat, which at Santa Fe was just high enough to give a faint tinge of green, is here a foot high, rank and thrifty. We are twenty-two hundred feet lower than that city, and in a climate at least ten degrees warmer. Not more than one-tenth of the whole area of New Mexico is fit for cultivation. Even of that so fit, not more than half lies in a position to be irrigated, with the present system. But that which is fertile is exceedingly so.

At least five-sixths of the population of New Mexico lives in the Rio Grande Valley, or along its immediate tributaries; there are all the important towns, while one may cross the country from east to west, and travel for days without sight of a dwelling or green spot. In most towns one sees no shade trees, no rills of sparkling water coursing the streets as in Utah or Colorado; even the Rio Grande is often exhausted in dry weather, and the many irrigating ditches it supplies leave its bed dry for miles. Albuquerque appears in the distance like a collection of brick-yards unburnt; but a nearer view shows many vineyards and gardens. Among the little farms near the city, the inhabitants are repairing their fences, as usual just before the summer drought. A box-frame, some two feet square and a foot deep, with no bottom, is placed upon the ground and filled with tough mud mingled with a little grass; then, the frame being lifted, leaves a section of the wall in place to be hardened and whitened (a little) by the sun. Successive blocks are stacked on this, till the mud wall is four or five feet high. Such are the only fences one can see for days of travel along the Rio Grande.

Reaching Albuquerque my soldier decided that he had enough money left for a two days' spree; we would therefore remain till Sunday morning. So I rested, wrote, and rambled in the queer, flat, old city, calling also on the *padre*, who is usually the most intelligent man in a Mexican town. All the acting *padres* are now French or Irish; the native Mexican priests have been *retired*, whether on half-pay or not I did not learn. The *padre* gave me many facts: that the oasis of Albuquerque was some eighty miles long, and averaged four miles wide, and that it was now two hundred and fifty years since the Spanish Duke of Albuquerque encamped on this spot, though the city is not so old. His name in full was Don Alphonso Herrera Ponto Delgado de Albuquerque. I asked the *padre* "what was his *front* name," but he did not seem to know. His descendants now belong to the *gente fina*, that is to say, the first families before mentioned—people who have the *sangre azul* in their veins. The city is some two hundred years old, contains about 2,000 people, and boasts of the finest church in New Mexico—a stately pile of adobes, with two lofty and whitewashed towers. The people generally are poor, pious, and contented. A *palacio* of dried mud, a meal of corn and *pimiento*, and a slip of corn-shuck filled with tobacco and rolled into a cigarette, is the height of a "Greaser's" ambition.

CHAPTER XV.

TOLTECCAN.

ALVAR NUNEZ CABEZA DE VACA was the first European who stood upon the soil of New Mexico. A survivor of the unfortunate Pamphilo de Narvaez's expedition, he wandered for ten years among the aborigines between the Mississippi and Gulf of California; reached the Spanish settlements in Mexico, and lived to write a book as full of marvels as Swift's Gulliver. The miracles, supernatural cures, and other nonsense in the work, have caused many to reject it entire; but as it is proved by other testimony that he went into the wilderness at one time and came out of it at another, and as his descriptions of places are as correct as could be written today, we are justified in regarding the *possible* part of it as true.

PUEBLO MAIDEN.

The private journal of Vaca begins on the 4th of September, 1527, when the few survivors of the Narvaez expedition were making boats to go to Mexico. All these boats were lost except that of Vaca, which was wrecked upon the coast of Texas. With some fifteen others he was captured by the Indians; and of this number but three reached Mexico with him—Dorantes and Castillo, Spaniards, and a Barbary negro named Estevanico. Sometimes slaves, sometimes peddlers, and again treated as guests and acting as physicians, they got as far north as the Canadian River. Then they turned westward, traversed what Vaca called the "cow country," and came to a desert. Crossing this with much suffering, they visited in turn nearly all the strange tribes of New Mexico, and at last reached the vicinity of the Gulf of California. There they came upon the force commanded by Diego de Alcaraz, who was exploring the country under orders of the Viceroy of New Spain

(Mexico). Thence they went to the City of Mexico, being everywhere received with public demonstrations, and ending their journey "on the day before the vespers of Saint James," in 1536. Vaca afterwards married a wealthy Spanish lady, and attained to considerable rank. In Peña Blanca, New Mexico, lives one Don Tomas Cabeza de Vaca (who will probably be Governor if the Territory soon becomes a State), who is the tenth in direct descent from Alvar Nunez.

The next expedition into New Mexico was by Don Francisco Vasquez Coronado, in command of some seven hundred cavaliers, in the years 1540–'46, in search of the "Seven Cities of Cibola." At that time all this region was called by the Spaniards *Cibola*. This word in the Spanish lexicons is translated "A quadruped called the Mexican bull;" but in Mexico it means the buffalo. The cities Coronado went to find were said to be situated in a vast oval valley, the most fertile on earth, and walled in by mountains full of rich mines; they were paved with gold and silver, the houses lighted with precious stones, and the richest metals were in common use for domestic utensils. In short, it was the biggest kind of a *bonanza*. But they never found the cities, though they hunted six or seven years, and, by the right of first occupation, added to the Spanish possessions a region twelve times the size of Ohio. All this but twenty years after the conquest of Cortez, and two hundred and fifty years before the founding of Cincinnati.

Coronado returned to the city of Mexico in disappointment and disgrace; but with him was a gentleman and scholar named Castaneda, who wrote a very fascinating account of the trip, and incited others to turn explorers. He described most of the important mountains, rivers and tribes of Arizona, New Mexico and North-western Texas; and thirty years after him, two friars led in a small missionary company, of whom all were killed by the Indians. Next came Antonio de Espejo, who is credited with having founded Santa Fe in 1580; and after him Don Juan de Onati, who made the first permanent settlements, about 1591. Other colonists followed fast, but seventy years afterwards the Pueblos, native Indians, rebelled and drove out or massacred the Spaniards. Governor Otermin and General Vargas soon came back with a Spanish army, and by a bloody war thoroughly subjugated the Pueblos. The more warlike fled to valleys in the western mountains; the remainder settled into docile subjects of Spain, and in time became devoted Catholics.

For a hundred years after the conquest miscegenation went on rapidly, producing the present Mexican race; then, by the operation of some mysterious law it ceased, and the people now appear fixed in permanent types. It is as rare for one of the upper classes to marry among the common people as for white and colored to marry in the States. In nearly all lands where there are mixed bloods, the ruling caste is the whitest. In the Turkish and the Mexican armies the officers are quite fair; the common soldiers dark as Indians. The *gente fina* of New Mexico are comparatively mild brunettes; but the "greasers" are at least mulatto color. In the States we say "as dark as a Spaniard;" in Mexico they say "as fair as a Spaniard." We take our idea from the mixed races; they take theirs from the pure Castilians they see, who are fair as Scotchmen. Their Creole descendants in Mexico and the South-west are almost equally fair, but often delicate in physique and devoid of energy. I have spoken of their long names. When one inherits several estates his title often includes the names of all of them; and it is reported that the "shoddy" sometimes insist on being addressed by the full title. Hence the following (reported) sad occurrence: A young nobleman, Lopez y Interlopez de las Casas Filatas y Aman de Cor, was walking with his intended, Señorita Inez Pranalada, along the Rio Grande, her mother acting as duenna. While he was at a distance Inez fell into the river, and the mother screamed, "Oh, Señor Lopez y Interlopez de las Casas Filatas"—but by this time the fair Inez had sunk to rise no more.

In New Mexico there are about half a dozen castes, the regular dark Mexicans outnumbering all others. The population is classified thus:

Americans	6,000
Mexicans	86,000
Citizen Indians (Pueblos)	10,000
Wild Indians (perhaps)	20,000
Total,	122,000

The common people are incredibly poor. If a late *peon*, now free, has a dollar, he neither labors nor thinks till it is gone. Twenty-five cents of it buys flour, twenty-five goes for *dulces* for the *señora*, another twenty-five pays for absolution, and the rest buys a lottery ticket. No matter if his ticket draw a blank a hundred times in succession: "maybe some time I win," is to him sufficient answer. A few families own all the wealth of the country. Even they have their wealth mostly in flocks and herds, and immense as it is, it brings them but few of the luxuries of life. If this Territory is admitted now as a State, it ought to be called the State of *Pobritta* ("Little Poverty.") Each of these wealthy families has from a hundred to two thousand dependents, some of whom were their *peons* before that system was abolished, and continue to yield obedience by nature and habit. If a State, this would be a most complete "rotten borough"—the worst "carpet-bag" State in the Union. Fifteen families with ease would rule it—the Chaves, Gallegos, Delgados, Señas, Garcias, Pereas, Oteros, Quintañas, and a few others. These families have three-fourths of the wealth of the Territory, and all the influence. The poor Mexicans do any thing they are told; in fact don't know how to do otherwise than as they are told. These families, in combination with half a dozen priests, and a dozen or more Americans, would divide the home offices between them, and send whomsoever they pleased to Congress. It is usually the aim of speculative Americans to "stand in" with one of the noble families. But many of our people have disdained such sycophancy, and yet won for themselves an honorable place in New Mexican annals. Chief among these was the noted Kit Carson, scout, trapper, and hunter; then guide to Fremont, and afterwards Federal colonel, and last of all Indian Agent for the Utes, in which capacity he died at his home in Taos.

The Pueblos are evidently a decaying race. Anciently they consisted of four nations: the Piros, Teguas, Queres and Tagnos. According to their own account they number only one-tenth what they did before the conquest. A regular pueblo ("village") consists of a large square, with open court in the center; the stories rise in terraces, each giving back a few feet from the one below. There are no doors on the outside, the entrance on the roof being reached by a ladder. But in the long peace they are slowly adopting the style of dwelling used by the Mexicans. They are stout and muscular, with rather pleasant countenances; speak Spanish fluently, but learn English with difficulty, and never teach others their language. They dress in woolen of their own manufacture, and are very industrious, chaste, and honest.

Who are they? is the puzzling question. They did not learn their civilization from the Spaniards, that is certain; but were found by the latter almost as far advanced as to-day. Castaneda says the Pueblos came with a nation from the north-west, and their own tradition is that they are Montezumas Indians. Against this, however, Baron Humboldt contended that the Aztec language differed essentially from that of the Pueblos, and Castaneda further says that they were unknown to the people of Mexico until Cabeza de Vaca and his companions brought account of them. Before 1871, they were not considered citizens; then the question was raised, and the Supreme Court pronounced them legal voters. They still dress in the ancient costume, which is neither Indian nor Spanish, but a sort of mixture, with pantaloons somewhat in the Turkish style, and when in

KIT CARSON.

full dress with a profusion of red and yellow. They inhabit twenty-six villages, principally in the valley of the Rio Grande, the most important of which is San Juan, thirty miles north-west of Santa Fe. They live totally distinct from the surrounding Mexicans, each village having its own government, and no bond of union between them; but all live in the greatest harmony with their neighbors. Each village has a governor, a *cacique* or justice, a *fiscal* or constable, and a "council of wise men." Besides these civil officers there is also a war captain, who attends to military affairs.

The territorial government will average with that of other Territories. "Since the Occupation," meaning since the Americans took possession, is a phrase in constant use like "Since the war" in the South. After the conquest in 1590–'95 comes a list of forty-six Spanish and Mexican captain-generals who governed the country, ending with General Manuel Armijo in 1846, who gathered a large army to meet the Americans, marched out to the pass commanding the country, and then marched back again, abandoning the province without firing a shot. The Americans took possession, set up a feeble government and passed on; the Mexicans rose, treacherously massacred the officials and several other Americans, and were again subdued. They are now apparently as good "Yankees" as any of us.

PUEBLO CACIQUE.

They are very tenacious of all their old customs in the administration of law. They stipulated for this at the American occupation, and General Kearney, by proclamation, continued all their judicial officers with the same code; and as the civil or canon law was in force in all Spanish America, it is the common law of New Mexico to-day. Under it the power of parents is practically almost without limits— no matter what age their offspring may be. A son who lives with his mother is subject to her orders always, and the *alcalde* in rural districts is occasionally called upon by a woman whose "boy" of twenty-five or thirty has rebelled. In such cases the *alcalde* goes with his constable, arrests the "boy," puts a *riata* into the hands of the mother and bids her lay on until the youth roars for mercy. Sometimes a *señorita* living with an American is punished severely by her mother for some slight to her "man;" and though he protest, the mother asserts her right.

Their lack of enterprise produces ludicrous results. I saw but one Mexican wagon in Santa Fe, and that had broken down. Every thing is transported on the backs of *burros*, the native breed of asses.

Occasionally one loaded thus with wood loses his balance or trips and goes over; then he can not rise till unloaded. One morning I noticed a miserable little *burro*, no bigger than a good-sized ram, staggering under an entire bedstead, piled up and strapped together on his back; and another with an immense trunk strapped "cut-angular" from his left hip to his right shoulder. They are the wealth of the poorer class, and when the household donkey dies a Mexican family goes into bankruptcy.

With these notes, set down in a month's travel, and from observation and conversation with all classes, I resume my personal experiences:

On the 26th, we left Albuquerque, just as the Sunday amusements began. They usually have splendid religious services in the morning, a dog-tussle about noon, and a cock-fight later in the day. In the evening, if reflective, the "Greaser" smokes cigarettes and meditates; if sentimental, he goes courting. My soldier was sober again, by chance, and eager to start, while I felt refreshed and ready for the desert.

The "June rise" of the Rio Grande (*El Rio* they call it there— "The River") had come on a week or two earlier than common, and a vast bayou covered two-thirds of the "bottom" between the city and the main channel. In this we encountered dangerous whirls and "chuck-holes," the wagon often plunging in up to the bed, and two or three times the little lead mules were obliged to swim a rod or so. When we reached the narrow strip of high ground near the river, the whole population of the string-town opposite were collected on the bank, on their way to the cathedral and other Sabbath amusements. Half a dozen families were laboring across in their own skiffs, while the main ferry flat was loaded to the guards. The women, in gay robes and black *rebosas*, were laughing and singing, while the men screamed, swore and shouted directions all at once to the four boatmen, and the flat drifted in circles down the swift current. Fortunately, the actual channel is not more than four hundred yards wide, and the flat only descended half a mile in making the passage. A boat load of Mexicans on the way to church can make more noise than two circus shows. Having passed the main current, the ferrymen jumped overboard, and, wading up to their armpits, with tow ropes, hauled the flat to shore. This trifling incident is a beautiful illustration of the Mexican style of doing every thing.

Once landed, the male passengers took to the bayou without a thought for their summer pantaloons; but the women, being gayly dressed for church, dropped upon the grass, snatched off their under clothing, raised their dresses "about so high," and waded to town with the utmost nonchalance, laughing, chattering, and singing hymns to the Virgin! Here and there was seen a youth of unusual filial piety, carrying his mother astride his shoulders; but most of the women encountered the difficulties of the way with a hardihood fully equal to that of the men.

Two hours of Mexican awkwardness set us across, and we left the west bank for the sand hills just as the great bell of the *adobe* cathedral was calling these copper-colored Christians to morning mass. The western hills looked bad enough from the town, and more than kept their promise. One mile across the valley brought us to the first *mesa*, not more than fifty feet above the river, and covered for four or five miles with a tolerable growth of greasewood, cactus and bunchgrass, indicating some fertility. Then we entered upon another gradual ascent for two miles, which brought us fairly upon the desert. The awful, the unutterable desert! Miles on miles of blistering sand or rock glowing in the midday heat.

At 2 P. M. we halted for a brief rest, ungeared the mules, and crawled under the wagon for shade. North, south and west we saw only desolation; eastward a faint line of green marked the course of the Rio Grande. Oh, to be on its green banks once more. To us it appeared "more to be desired than Abana and Pharpar," or all the rivers of Judea and Damascus. The water in our canteens was exhausted before noon, and the soldier, just recovering from a long debauch, was almost frantic with thirst. He tried the usual resource: to scrape a bacon rind and chew it; and allow me to add, it is a splendid substance with which to mitigate thirst. Soldiers tell me they have gone two days without water, and avoided any serious suffering by this simple expedient. A piece of silver, or small splinter of mountain pine, held in the mouth and rolled about with the tongue, is often used for the same purpose.

In an hour the evening wind rose, and we moved on. At 5 P. M., we reached a down grade, and saw on the western horizon a straggling line of dwarf pines, indicating the course of the Puerco. Our mules showed new life, gave a grateful whinny, and broke into a trot. Fortunately we found some water still in the channel, though fast sinking. Three weeks ago the Rio Puerco ("Hog River") was a torrent; one week more, and it will be a *resaca* ("dry channel"). It runs but two months in the year; at other times, travelers must hunt along the dry bed till they find a brackish pool, or dig in the lowest depressions. The water looked exactly like dirty milk, and its temperature was about 70°; but it was grateful enough to us. The driver drank two quart cups of it in ten minutes, and the poor animals crowded down the only accessible place, and shoved each other into the stream in their eagerness to get at the dirty fluid. Fortunately the dirt which gives it color is so fine that one can not feel it grit in his teeth, and aside from the earthy taste, the water is not disagreeable.

The valley of the Puerco, some two miles wide, is very fertile, and the Mexicans had attempted to settle it; but no plan could be devised to secure enough water and their settlement was abandoned. We spread our blankets in one of their vacant houses, and slept sweetly till 2 A. M., then took to the road to pass the next desert before noon. All that was yesterday so drear has a fascinating beauty by moonlight. The turbid Puerco looks like a band of molten silver; the sand glitters with pearls, the red and yellow rocks are glorified in the brilliant light. The stream had fallen two feet during the night, from which the soldier inferred it would be dry in a day or two. Thence we rise again to another desert, and in ten miles reach the ancient border of the Navajoes (or Navahoes, if spelled as pronounced), a series of rugged gulches and narrow cañons, bounded by perpendicular walls of yellow soapstone. They run from north to south, and form a break in the road something near a mile wide, evidently the bed of a long extinct river. Wash gravel and marine shells are heaped in fantastic piles by the wind. The deepest gulch is known as Dead Man's Cañon, where are buried twenty whites massacred many years ago by the Navajoes.

We saw our first specimens of this tribe at Albuquerque: one chief and eleven warriors, who had been into the Comanche country on a fighting and stock-stealing expedition. They got no horses, but had three men wounded, and were making their way homeward with only such provisions as they could get in the Mexican settlements. The sole *ranchero* at the cañon told us they had passed there on Sunday, having made the forty-four miles on foot in a little over one day. Our early start avoided the midday heat upon the desert, but the drying air produced strange effects. My nose, lips, and wrists, which blistered yesterday, peeled to-day, and I started to grow a new cuticle on those members. My nose was coloring like a new meerschaum, forming a very striking feature of my countenance. How convenient if a man could sprout new members in place of the lost, as a lobster does his claw, or a bee his sting. But if the evolution philosophy be sound, we only need to feel the want of such a faculty, and ardently desire it for several hundred generations, and it will spontaneously develop. Beautiful theory!

From Dead Man's Cañon we rise gradually for twelve miles, traverse a wide pass walled in by mountains red with iron-stain, and descend again to a vast baked plain of barren clay, hard as the sun's rays can cook it. On its western border appears a green oasis, bounded by yellow hills scantily clad with timber and bunch-grass; and on the baked plain beside the oasis stands the hamlet of El Rito ("The Little River"). We had made our drive of twenty-six miles by noon. The "Little River" is little indeed; at its best one can jump across it; now it is all used for irrigation. The country is full of dry channels, many of which are located as rivers on the map; but in three-fourths of them one finds only piles of gravel and shifting sands.

El Rito is a strange, old, isolated Mexican town, away out on the edge of the desert, twenty-five miles from the nearest neighbor; and yet it is a century old, and has doubtless contained the same families—perhaps forty in all—during all that time. No church, no school, no papers, no books, or very few, to introduce a new idea; but family concerns, town concerns, the winter's rain and the spring rise; the rare passage of a government train, and the rarer visit of the itinerating *padre* to baptize the children and confess and absolve the elders, make up their little world of incidents. The oasis is plowed with a sharpened log, well seasoned and hewn into the shape of an Irish spade, and the crops tended with hoe and rake; while the goats, sheep and asses are pastured in the mountain hollows, and the hens live upon crickets and earth-worms. If the family *burro* does not die, if the goats do well, if the water is sufficient for enough of *mais* and *chile Colorado*, and the hens lay eggs enough to send off by the weekly peddler, and procure a little tobacco and flowered calico, then *Quien quiere por mas?* (Who cares for more?) In this little community of degenerate Spaniards A's children have married B's children, and *vice versa*, and in the next generation double-cousins married double-cousins, for a hundred years, till the wine of life has run down to the very lees, and flows dull in sluggish veins for want of a vitalizing current of alien blood. Every person in the settlement is akin to most of the others. The same practice has had much to do with the degeneracy of the Pueblos, isolated as each of their settlements is.

While Hamilton attended to his team, I walked about the town. The men and larger boys were at work in the public field, or tending flocks among the hills; the women asleep, or sitting on the dirt floor smoking cigarettes of corn-shuck and tobacco, and the whole juvenile population looked like a miserable batch of rags, sore eyes and sin. There was not a tree, a flower, or a spear of grass in the place. Those persons I spoke to were even too lazy to understand Spanish—as I spoke it, anyhow. They only grunted, "*No sabe*," and, pointing to a rather superior *adobe* on the hill, remarked, "*Alli, un Americano.*"

I found him an "American" indeed. His name was Ryan, and he was "from Tipper-ra-r-ry, be dad!" Years ago he drifted here, liked it, married a Mexican woman, had several Pueblo servants and a flock of sheep, and was general adviser, advocate and scribe for the settlement. A delegation of Pueblos from the next town were at his house to complain of the Navajoes, who had been stealing their stock. He took me to the public *fonda*, where I got a good supper of goat's milk, *tortillas* and eggs, and a clean room, and spent the evening quite pleasantly. The nights there are delightful; a little too cool towards morning, perhaps, for comfortable sleeping in the open air, but with abundant blankets we did well. The entire mountain range southwest is said to be a mass of minerals—coal, iron and copper. It is a region of curiosities. In the next valley south is the largest one of the abandoned cities of—whom? *Quien sabe*, is the universal answer of Mexican and Indian. Most of the houses there are of sawed stone. Three miles ahead, and on our road, is the noted Pueblo de Laguna ("Town of the Lake"), probably the best built of all the Montezumas towns, and so called because in former times the Pueblos built a vast causeway across the upper end of the valley, to retain the winter floods from the mountain for summer irrigation. Now the dam is broken down, the lake is dry, the cultivable land reduced to a few acres, and the pueblo slowly dying.

Starting next morning at the first flush of daylight, and climbing a rocky trail for three miles, while the team made a circuit of seven, I gained two hours for a visit to this place. The sun was just rising as I entered the pueblo, and the inhabitants were mostly on the housetops preparing their implements for the day's work. The town is situated upon the east end of an oval rock or mole, some two miles long, and rising gradually at each end to a height of a hundred feet above the bordering plain. The top is comparatively level, and the sides fall off in a succession of abrupt benches, each a yard or so in width and height, rendering the whole place a splendid natural fortification. On these rocks the Pueblos first built for protection, and are slow to change, though in the present lengthy peace some of them are beginning to build out on the farm. The *cacique* was a man of considerable intelligence, spoke Spanish fluently, and gave me information with unusual courtesy.

Most of the houses have a second story, not more than half or one-third as extensive as the lower one; and some few have a sort of tower or third story on top of the second. To this I several times signified a desire to ascend, but the *cacique* either did not understand me, or did not see fit to comply—probably the latter. Uneducated and semi-barbarous people are generally suspicious on all matters connected with their religion; and the accounts of missionaries, especially their first accounts, among such people, must be received with caution. It is nearly or quite impossible to make an Indian understand why any one should want him to give up his religion and adopt that of another; he can not assign any probable motive for such solicitude, and invariably concludes there must be a swindle in it somewhere. He will readily acknowledge that the white man's religion is true and good—for the white man; and, of course, the Indian's religion is equally true and good—for the Indian.

When the Spanish Jesuits "converted" these people, some two centuries ago, they found it impossible to eradicate entirely the Montezumas faith, and so made a compromise. They gave them the Catholic religion, with its most impressive ceremonies, and permitted them to keep all their Montezumas customs which did not amount to actual idolatry. These consisted mostly of dances and feasts at stated times, which had more of a national than a religious significance.

The houses here are solidly built of stone, cement, and adobes. The joists are large as ordinary house-sills in the States, which I judged to be for the better support of the upper stories, as I noticed the walls of these in some instances not continuous with or resting on the walls below, but built directly across and over the rooms. The interior of the lower rooms was whitewashed and pleasantly neat, but in and about many of the houses was an unpleasant odor of green hides, which were hanging near, this being a general butchering time with them. Their windows are made of a material they call *acquarra*—a kind of mica found in the adjacent mountains, which is translucent but not transparent, and lights a room about as well as oiled paper. All the Pueblos of New Mexico and Arizona build in substantially the same manner; and all accounts, as well as the ruins so numerous in the country, indicate that the fashion has not changed for many centuries. This pueblo has a population of seven hundred, who cultivate in com-men an oasis of some twelve square miles. Closely tended it produces amazingly. Wooden plows were running, breaking up the ground for late crops, and on the adjoining hills I saw large herds of sheep and goats attended by young Pueblos.

Crossing this oasis we entered another broad cañon, which we followed for some ten miles to the town of Cubero, somewhat better than the ordinary Mexican hamlet. It is built on a series of shelving rocks; some of the dwellings are of stone, nearly all have stone floors, and the place seemed literally basking in the fierce rays of a New Mexican sun. There we found another party of Pueblos on a general spree. One able-bodied "buck" was staggering along the street, his wife after him and occasionally thwacking him on the head or back with the butt end of a heavy whip, while the whole Mexican population looked on laughing and cheering.

Thence we crossed another small oasis, traversed another rugged cañon, and came out upon another small green tract, and to McCarty's ranche, where we spent the night. McCarty is an Irishman, married to a Mexican woman, whom I found superior to most of her class. Beyond McCarty's is a fertile valley, through which runs the line of the Thirty-fifth Parallel Road; and beyond that a gorge, not more than two hundred yards wide, opens into another valley. The last three miles of the former valley is mostly marsh, and thither the officers from Wingate often go to hunt ducks. At the west end rise the springs which water the valley.

"WOMAN'S RIGHTS."

They boil out from under the rock, half a dozen streams of cold, clear water. But a few rods from them the lava beds begin. As I walked over the plain, it looked as if the lava had just cooled. I could see all the little waves and ripples in its surface, and near the springs it had evidently overflowed in successive layers, each an inch or so thick, the lower cooling a little before the one above it was deposited. In places these layers had been broken directly across, folded and contorted, leaving singular gaps and fissures, the sides of which appeared coated in places with lime or sulphur, and in others by what looked like red sealing-wax turned to stone. Where contorted or twisted, the lava rock presented precisely the same appearance as if one should lay down successive folds of tarred canvas till the pile was ten or twelve feet thick, and then roll the mass over and over and into long heaps. Some extensions of this twisted mass reached even to the edge of the springs, and I saw indications where it had overflowed into the pools; but most of the way across the valley one could trace the division between the lava and the original rock base on to which it had flowed as easily as with a daub of mud thrown upon the floor of a house.

By a rise of perhaps ten feet we entered upon this *mala pais*, and soon came to where the lava was not in waves, but seemed to have cooled in a mass, presenting a granulated appearance, much like cooling sugar; and a little farther we found it light and frothy looking, as if a hot, foaming current had cooled to stone, porous and spongy, like pumice-stone. A mile westward brought us out into the broader valley, and, looking backward, it seemed to me that the lava flow had been choked in the narrow pass about the time the supply was exhausted. Five miles over the level land brought us to another descent, leading to another oval plain; and, running in a serpentine course across it, I saw a shining line which I judged to be water—the irregular course of some mountain stream. But it soon appeared too dazzlingly bright, and we found it only a narrow, dry gully, bottom and sides crusted with salt and alkali, painful to the eye. A little water runs there in winter—just enough to bring down the alkali from the mountains.

From the plain of the *mala pais* we descend a little into Red Valley, about *Agua Azul*. It is walled in by fearfully abrupt mountains of black and red stone in an irregular circle, and is about five miles by three, containing at least eight sections of land of the utmost fertility. Near the bordering mountains the soil is red, giving name to the valley and the central *butte*, but lower down it is dark. Running water was found only at the south-west corner of the valley, and there M. Provencher first began to cultivate the soil, when he established the ranche four years before. The yield from this soil of volcanic origin was astonishing; wheat produced thirty-six bushels per acre; corn thirty-eight *fanegas* (a *fanega* is 136 pounds), and oats grew to the height of a man's head, yielding bounteously. But only one crop was raised; then the dry season, which lasted for three years in western New Mexico, set in; the water failed, and it is a question whether the place can ever be utilized. Give but a stream of pure water, and this little basin would bloom like a garden, supporting a thousand people in affluence.

About 3 o'clock next morning we were awakened by a terrible racket and barking of dogs, just in time to see that our mules had broken *corral*, and were lighting out towards Wingate with a speed which showed there was no place like home to them. The soldier went in pursuit, and I visited the Red Butte and the old crater. The *butte* is nearly two miles long and a mile wide, rising evenly from the plain on every side, and so abruptly, by a series of "benches" or narrow terraces, that it can only be ascended in two or three places, and the dimensions on top are only one-fourth less than at the bottom. M. Provencher's theory is that the entire valley was the original crater, and, when it had slowly died out, a smaller one formed at the center. The *butte* appears from the plain to be level on top; it is, in fact, a mere shell—a little copy of the walled basin around it. From the narrow rim there is an abrupt fall towards the center, and inside it has the appearance of an old furnace, long since burnt out and abandoned.

At midnight the soldier returned, hitched up at daylight, and, in a steaming state of military wrath, whipped his mules through the forty-three miles to Wingate by sundown. Twenty miles east of that post we passed the dividing summit of the Rocky Mountains (or Sierra Madre; both names are used indifferently there). We reach the western slope through a long pass, in many respects resembling the South Pass of the old California trail. It is simply a high and sandy valley through the mountains, bounded on the north by almost perpendicular sandstone cliffs from five hundred to a thousand feet in height, and on the south by scantily-timbered hills which rise one above another to the highest mountain peak. In the pass and neighboring hills rain is frequent; twenty miles east or west of it none falls for three or four months at a time. The Atlantic and Pacific Railroad line is located through this pass, and the grade is so gentle that no difficulties are met with. For three hundred miles west of the Rio Grande nature seems to have provided a series of valleys especially for a railroad. The real trouble is that the country has so little in it worth building a railroad for. It is a splendid country to travel through; a miserably poor one to stop in to make a "stake."

On the evening of May 31st we drove into Wingate; my soldier "reported," and in precisely twenty minutes was a close prisoner in the guard-house—"held for trial."

"Charge—Unwarranted disposition of stores placed in his care."

"Specification—In this, that the said Frank Hamilton, being intrusted with a team to transport one thousand pounds of potatoes from Santa Fe to this post, did unwarrantably dispose of three hundred pounds of the same on the way, etc., etc."

He was found guilty of this, and more ; and during my stay I was daily pained at sight of him "cleaning quarters," with a most uncomfortable bracelet attachment to his ankle.

Take him for all in all, he was the most unfortunate traveling companion I ever had.

Moral—Don't go for a regular soldier; or, if you do, don't trade government potatoes to Mexican women.

Eight days I remained at Fort Wingate, and enjoyed every moment of the time. Having letters to Lieutenant S. W. Fountain, formerly of Pomeroy, Ohio, he made me comfortable at his quarters, and a full hand at his mess. Captain A. B. Kauffman, commanding the post in the absence of Colonel Wm. Redwood Price; Lieutenant D. R. Burnham, of Company "H," Fifteenth United States Infantry; and Dr. R. S. Vickery, Post Surgeon, were most courteous and pleasant officials. If I had to be exiled to a Far Western fort, I don't know any other command I should prefer to go with. Lieutenant H. R. Brinkerhoff, formerly of Union County, Ohio, also assisted me to much information as to the surrounding country ; and he and his estimable lady made my stay more like a renewal of home-life than one would have thought possible in this wilderness.

Fort Wingate is nearly two hundred miles west of Santa Fe, directly at the head of the Rio Puerco of the West. Along this stream a sloping valley can be followed down to the Colorado Chiquito ("Little,") and down that to the main Colorado—this post being thus on the "Pacific slope." Just south of the fort rises a rugged spur of the Sierra Madre, from which Bear Spring (or Ojo del Oso) sends out a cold, clear stream, sufficient to turn a mill-wheel. Two miles below the channel is dry; the loose red earth has drunk it all. With this stream the soldiers irrigate a few acres of garden, producing most of the vegetables except potatoes. These can not be grown in the greater part of New Mexico; the vines grow night and day, and the result is, in each hill a handful of dwarfed tubers, about the size of chestnuts. The latitude of Wingate is 35° 28'; the elevation 6,600 feet. Hence the summers are short and the nights cool. Corn will not silk; wheat is generally cut off in the flower. Only the short-lived plants come to perfection. The records show that drought has been increasing for forty years. During my stay they enjoyed the only heavy rain for three years.

Gypsum, salt and iron are abundant. A short distance west of the fort is a whole mountain of gypsum, so to speak—enough to bury an eastern county. Neither gold nor silver has been found in paying quantities. Precious stones of various kinds have been found near, particularly garnets and turquoises. Lieutenant H. R. Brinkerhoff has a large collection of curious stones, picked up within a mile or two of the fort. Magnetic stones, the size of one's fist, can be had by the bushel. Some of them, when thrown loosely upon the ground, will roll over towards each other till they gather in a group. All the hills are covered with timber, and in the larger cañons is abundance of pine fit for lumber. The mountains north and east present the appearance of a succession of lofty cones, with here and there an oval hill. In many adjacent valleys are ruins of towns, and *acecquias*, where no water now runs at any season. Thirty miles south-west is a valley strewn with ruins, indicating a large settlement; it is now a desert.

Wingate is the center of a region of curiosities. Among our visitors were some Zuni Indians from the great pueblo forty miles west. This is an enormous building of five terraced stories, containing eight hundred semi-civilized Indians. In this great human hive are carried on all the complicated affairs of a community life: government, manufactures, art, and religious rites. They cultivate their little patches with great skill, producing abundance of corn, wheat, beans, and melons; their mercantile wealth is in sheep, goats, blankets, beads, and pottery. They are severely chaste, any departure from virtue being rigidly punished. They once had the art of writing, and still preserve one book; but the last man who could read it died many years ago, and the priests regard it merely as a holy relic. It consists simply of a mass of finely dressed skins, bound on one side with thongs; the leaves are thickly covered with characters and drawings in red, blue, and green—squares, diamonds, circles, serpents, eagles, plants, flying monsters and hideous human heads. One of their *caciques* says it is the history of their race, and shows that they have moved fourteen times, this being their fifteenth place of settlement. No Spanish priest has ever been permitted to enter their town; their religion appears to be a mixture of Spiritism and Sabianism.

They are quite domestic in their tastes, and fond of pets. Turkeys and tame eagles abound among them, living about the terraces of the pueblo, and even in their dwellings. They are keen traders, and have most perfect command of their features. The few I saw had a uniformly sad, mild expression of the eye, but were quick in motion, well-made, and rather graceful. Unfortunately I was compelled, for company's sake, to take a route north of Zuni; and did not know its value to the explorer till I had passed westward.

A hundred miles north of Wingate are the great ruins on the De Chaco River, supposed to be those of the "Seven Cities of Cibola" (*See-vo-la*); and north of those, on the San Juan in Colorado, the ruins, as supposed, of a fortified city of the Aztecs. One of the walls still stands, five hundred feet in length, with joinings as true and smooth as in any of our buildings. They were constructed of hard sandstone, and probably enclosed a city of several thousand inhabitants. Lieutenant McCormick, who explored all of them, thinks that at least a quarter, possibly half, of a million people devoted to agriculture, once occupied the system of valleys opening upon the San Juan. They are gone long ago, and their places are occupied by the nomadic races: Utes, Navajoes and Apaches. The streams upon which they depended dried up, and cultivators necessarily yielded to hunters and shepherds; just as we find wandering Arabs encamped in the ruins of Baalbec and Palmyra, or barbarous nomads wandering over the once populous and fertile Babylonia.

Here, too, we find the Navajoes at home; a most interesting race of barbarians, friendly in peace but savage in war. These are the first Indians I have met who have not the stereotyped "Indian face"—the face we have heard described so often, either overcast with a stern and melancholy gravity, or lively only with an uncertain mixture of cunning and ferocity. Their countenances are generally pleasing, even mild and benevolent. They have many young fellows whose faces show the born humorist. Wit, merriment, and practical jokes enliven all their gatherings, and, quite contrary to our ideas of Indian character, they laugh loud and heartily at every thing amusing. They are quite inquisitive, too, and seem vastly pleased to either see or hear something new. Both men and women work, and are quite industrious until they have accumulated a fair share of property; then they seem content to take things easy. But here, as elsewhere, only the worst class of Indians spend their time about the fort. Their women come and go in frequent groups, and may be found almost any payday in the adjacent woods; the result being that Dr. Vickery has a very extensive practice among the private soldiers.

On the 6th of June, I set out for Fort Defiance, in company with Wm. Burgess, blacksmith for the Navajo Agency. The distance is forty-five miles, which we traversed in nine hours, finding water at but one point on the road, namely, Stinking Springs, sometimes politely called Sheep Springs. Our mules drank of it, under protest, and with many sniffs and contortions of the lips; and I tasted it from curiosity. It looks like a solution of blue-dye, and tastes like white-oak bark. To some it is a dangerous cathartic, but to most a powerful astringent. Four miles from Wingate the valley makes a great U to the northward, and our road runs over the foot-hills for three miles; then enters the valley again, which there narrows to a mere pass. A vast dyke of hard trap-rock extends across the country from north to south, standing out above the sandstone like an artificial stone battlement, and runs out from each side of the valley in abrupt causeways, leaving a rugged gap only a hundred yards wide. This opens into a broad and fertile valley, across which three miles bring us to the Rio Puerco of the West. The Puerco I crossed on the 26th of May runs south-east into the Rio Grande; this one south-west into the Colorado Chiquito. We cross this Puerco, rise again into the northern foot-hills, and stop for noon in a piñon thicket. Next we reach the "Hay Stacks," a series of cones of yellow sandstone, something over a hundred feet high, and fifty feet wide at the base, running up to a sharp point. They stand upon an almost level plain, but half a mile away is a rocky ledge containing a vast natural bridge, arched gateway, and all the forms of rocky tower and battlement which can be imagined. Eight miles farther brought us to Defiance, situated at the foot of a low rocky range, and almost in the mouth of Cañon Benito.

Approaching the post across a sandy plain we first come to a dry river-bed, with enough of stunted grass to show that water still runs there sometimes. Following up the stream we find first a pool of water, then a flock of sheep, then Indian farms, and occasionally a *hogan*, from which the Navajo squaws and children peep out at us with a sort of hungry curiosity. We cross a common field of a hundred acres or so, which the Navajoes have thrown up into beds two or three rods square for irrigation, and ride into the fort, which was my headquarters for the next ten days.

CHAPTER XVI.

WILD LIFE IN ARIZONA.

It is bright noon in the gorge of Cañon Benito. The red cliffs glow in the hot sunshine, and the dark pool below, the only body of water in an area of hundreds of miles, is now simmering warm. At midnight it will be cold as ice-water. The Navajo boys are plunging and splashing in the tepid bath, their handsome dark bodies shining through the clear fluid like bronze statues *vivants*. Around each boy's waist is the tight "geestring," from which a single strip of cloth runs between the limbs from front to back—these two articles never being removed from the person in the presence of another. Down the steep trail from the south comes a band to the "count and distribution," which is expected in a few days. The speckled ponies cautiously tread the perilous way, bearing the pappooses and household goods; the men stalk in front, carrying their weapons and articles for barter; behind come the squaws, less heavily laden than is usual among the Indians, and consequently far more shapely and graceful.

COMING TO THE "COUNT."

An occasional yelp indicates that some hapless cur, of the little black, fiery-eyed and fierce species kept by the Navajoes, has got under the sharp hoof of a *broncho;* then a loud chorus of not unmusical cries shows that the band have recognized their friends coming from an opposite direction, and soon they unite in the quadrangle inclosed by the Agency buildings.

There the scene is gay. The girls have on their brightest blankets; each neck is encircled by numerous strands of beads, the number indicating the wearer's wealth; the men are fancifully touched up with red and white paint, while even the withered old squaws have tricked out their worn bodies and weather-beaten visages in some remnants of faded finery. Groups are seen here and there gambling with Spanish cards; others are playing a peculiar aboriginal game like pitch and toss, while even the boys are shooting at a mark for wagers of *loot-chsin*. The men are tall and vigorous; the women finer looking than those of any other tribe, the younger ones often very handsome. Garnets, quartz crystals, flakes of mica, chips of aqua-marine, and a dozen kinds of glittering stones are displayed in quantities, and often worn as ornaments. Occasionally a slab of malachite is seen, and more rarely a turquoise; for the whole region abounds in curious stones and petrifactions, with more fossils than Agassiz could classify in a month. All the hillocks made by the desert ants are found to be dotted with garnets, which, both plainsmen and Indians say, the insects have gathered from the adjacent plain and piled there—evidently attracted by their brightness, whether from a sense of beauty or otherwise.

Three hours before one would not have known there was an Indian in the vicinity; now the square is full, and others are still pouring in. But all are doomed to disappointment. Congress has been too busy President-making to pass the appropriation bills, and the agent sadly says: "No provisions yet." It is a time of scarcity with them too. The annuity for the previous year has long been exhausted; their crops for 1870 were very poor; in 1871 there was a total failure. Their miserable, dry, burnt-out and barren country is yearly growing dryer and more barren; the bunch grass is abundant, as it grows without summer rains, but they have not had time to recruit their flocks since the devastating Navajo war, and starvation threatens half the tribe. The last grain in the agency store-house was issued on the 14th of June; the Indians have eaten all their oldest sheep and goats, saving the young, especially the ewes, to the last, and when I visit their *hogans* I sometimes see them gnawing away at what look suspiciously like equine shanks. The Agency employés have not been paid for a year, and have to buy their own provisions from the nearest Mexican settlements. Still the Navajoes are cheerful and lively, in their worst troubles still looking for better times; and I spend many days of enjoyment rambling among them.

My first task is to learn enough of the language for the usages of common life; and a severe task it is. I begin with *ah-tee-chee* (" what is it?") and proceed to the words for bread or meat, fire and water, viz: *chinneahgo, knuh* and *toh*. The language is extremely nasal, equally guttural, and abounds in sibilants and triple consonants, many sounds having no equivalent in English. In every band are some Mexicans, captured young and adopted by the tribe; and a few Spanish words are in common use, but so changed in the pronunciation as to make them new. Thus *Americano* becomes *Melicano; azucar*, ("sugar") *tsucollo; serape*, ("blanket") *selap*, and *ombre* ("man") *ombly;* for no Indian or Chinaman can pronounce the *r*. Their social customs and adornments have a singular resemblance to those of the Japanese. They treat their women as well as most white nations. Men do the out-door work, women that of the household. The latter are very communicative, humorous and mirthful, and nothing seems to amuse them so much as my attempts at their language, at which they listen and laugh by the hour. They say that a woman first taught them how to weave blankets and make water-jars, for which cause it is a point of honor with a Navajo never to strike a woman.

In my visits I frequently heard them speak of *En-now-lo-kyh*, sometimes joined with the word *el-soo-see*, and as I stooped to enter a *hogan*, could sometimes hear the head of the family call to order with "*Huh-koh! El-soo-see En-now-lo-kyh!*" Learning that this was my Navajo name, I sought the interpreter, highly flattered at my noble title, to learn its meaning. A broad grin adorned his features as he informed me that the two words, translated literally, meant "Slim-man-with-a-white-eye." Feeling this to be somewhat personal, and inferentially abusive, I had him explain somewhat of my business to them and construct a name indicative of my profession; and henceforth I hope to become historical among the Navajoes by an unpronounceable word of six syllables, meaning in English "Big Quill." When a communication is twice translated, it triples the ambiguity; and that is the method employed with them: one interpreter speaks English and Spanish, the other Spanish and Navajo. I made my remarks in the plainest, most terse English I could command, which the American translated into the florid Castilian; this, in turn, the Mexican rendered in the hissing, complicated phrases and cumbrous polysyllables of the aboriginal tongue.

It was but seventy miles to the ruins on the De Chaco, and I had arranged to visit them with Navajo guides, when one of the party which had gone to San Juan arrived, completely exhausted, and announced that Agent Miller had been murdered, and all their horses stolen but one; that he had started immediately with that, and the rest of the party were coming afoot. Next day the others arrived, quite worn out, having walked a hundred miles in three days, carrying their baggage. Their account is as follows: The party consisting of Agent Miller, B. M. Thomas, (Agency Farmer,) John Ayers and the Interpreter, Jesus Alviso, left Defiance on the 4th of June, to inspect the San Juan Valley, with a view of locating the Navajo Agency there. The examination was satisfactory, as they found one fertile and beautiful valley near the river, capable of being irrigated by a single *acccquia*, and sufficient to support the whole tribe. At the same time, three others left the settlements on a prospecting tour, reached San Juan one day after the Agent's party, and were camped twelve miles from them on the bluff. Neither party dreamed of danger from the Utes, as that tribe had been at peace many years; and, though they annoyed the Navajoes greatly, had not molested white men. On the morning of the 11th, just at dawn, Miller's companions were awakened by the report of a gun and whistling of an arrow, both evidently fired within a few rods of them. They sprang to their feet, and saw two Utes run into the brush; ten minutes after they saw them emerge from the opposite side of the thicket, and ride up the bluff, driving the company's horses before them. They did not know, at first sight, that the Utes were hostile, or that they had fired at them. John Ayers spoke to Miller, who did not reply; he then shoved him with his foot, still he did not wake. They pulled off his blanket, and found him dead. The Ute's bullet had entered the top of his head and passed down behind his right eye, without disarranging his clothing in the slightest. His feet were crossed, and hands folded exactly as when he went to sleep; his eyes were closed, his lips slightly parted into a faint smile, as if from a pleasant dream—all showed beyond doubt that he had passed from sleep to death without a struggle or a sigh. Thus died James H. Miller, a true Christian, a faithful official and brave man.

Congress did not adjourn without passing the Indian Appropriation Bill, and soon came the welcome news that the agent at Santa Fe had started several thousand bushels of grain for Defiance. Again the employés took heart; there was joy in the *hogans*. Mr. Thomas V. Keams, Agency Clerk, was acting in place of Miller, deceased, and I gladly acknowledge the many courtesies I received at his hands. Indeed, all the employés, like people generally in these out-of-the-way places, vied with each other in making my stay pleasant. I recall particularly Dr. J. Menaul and lady, preacher and teacher for the Agency; Lionel Ayers, post-trader; J. Dunn, wagon-master; A. C. Damon, butcher, and Andy Crothers, in charge of grain-room. Altogether, the whites at the post numbered sixteen men and four women—a little colony far beyond the border of civilization, and the last whites I was to see for some hundreds of miles.

The situation is pleasant and romantic. The Benito Hills, averaging five hundred feet above the plain, run directly north and south. On the west side of them is a vast inclosed basin, from which Cañon Benito breaks directly through the hills—a sharp, abrupt gorge, square across the formation, with perpendicular walls entirely inaccessible. The east end of the cañon broadens into a little valley, at the mouth of which, though out on the plain, the fort is situated. A river once ran through the gorge, of which the successive periods can be traced on the sandstone walls to a height of two hundred feet. There seems to have been the original bottom of the cañon, whence the river steadily cut deeper until it had completely drained the basin above. The river had long been dry when the fort was located, but several springs in the east end of the cañon created a stream sufficient to irrigate a section of the land on the plain. Here the Navajoes had raised corn and melons from time immemorial; they had no other vegetables when found by the whites. The present occupants of Defiance have thrown a dam across this end of the cañon, producing a beautiful artificial lake some three hundred yards long, and rising so high as to leave barely room for a wagon-road. The lake is strongly alkaline, but a few rods below is a spring of the nicest and purest water to be found in these mountains. It is the one important treasure of this post, which, without it, would be almost uninhabitable. In the States, towns are located according to convenience for trade; in the mountains, settlement is determined by the presence of never-failing water.

I had exhausted the sights near Defiance, and was eager to be off. Mr. Keams called in Juerro, the old war-chief of the Navajoes, and together they selected an intelligent young man to be my guide to Moqui. The Navajoes were scattering out on their summer hunt and trading trips, and we were likely soon to have abundant company. My new guide took a stout *burro* for the trip, while I rode a good-sized American horse. I was to provision myself and one man to the Mormon settlements, and one man back, besides his fee. Thus ran the bill: Thirty pounds of flour, ten pounds of bacon, ten pounds of sugar, five pounds of coffee, and six boxes of sardines, the whole costing but twenty dollars. The same sum to my guides, and five dollars for the hire of a *burro*, made the total expense, for a trip of nearly five hundred miles, forty-five dollars—not much more than railroad fare.

My horse, bridle, saddle, lariat, gun (a Spencer), and two Navajo blankets cost me two hundred dollars. My Navajo knew a few words of Spanish, perhaps fifty in all—about equal to my list in his language; but, unfortunately for general conversation, our words covered about the same objects. Such words as the following were in constant use:

Tohh	Water.
Klohh	Grass.
Chizz	Wood.
Knuhh	Fire.
Klee	Horse.
Klitt	Smoke.
Hahkohh.	Come.
Tennehh	Man.

I represent the sharp accent at the end of some words by doubling the final letter, and the prolonged nasal sound by *nh*. The numbers as far as twenty-two run thus: Kli, nahkee, tah, dteen, estlahh, hostonn, susett, seepee, nostyy, niznahh, klitzetta, nahkeetsetta, tahtsetta, dteentsetta, estlahta, hostahta, susetetta, seepetta, nostytsetta, nahta, nahta kli, nahta nahkee, etc. "Thirty" is tahta, "forty" dteenta, and so on, while after each the ten integers run as at first.

We are off before noon of June 18th, the whole white population joining us in a "stirrup cup," and white, brown, and red waving a good-bye. John, as I christened my Navajo, led the way up Cañon Benito, and over a low spur of red hills into a beautiful green valley about a mile square, quite level, and covered with grass a foot high. On every side of it rose bare columns and ridges of sand-rock, but from their base trickled here and there tiny rills of water—enough to keep the valley fertile. Herds of sheep and goats, attended by Navajo girls, and some horses attended by boys, enlivened the scene. Through this, and on to another sand-ridge, then three miles more, brought us to a long narrow valley, winding for miles among the hills, and looking as if it had once been the bed of a river, and been heaved up by some convulsion. For hours we crossed such valleys every two or three miles, none of them more than a hundred yards wide, and separated by barren ridges. The grass in the valleys was rank and thrifty; the ridges had nothing but an occasional sprig of sage-brush or cactus. Every-where along the grass-plats were shepherd girls with considerable flocks, each girl carrying a set of Navajo spools and spindle and a bunch of wool, on which she worked in the intervals of watching. These spools are very similar in shape to those used in our rural districts, but large and clumsy. With a pointed stick, turned in the right hand, the spinner runs the wool on to the larger spool in rolls somewhat smaller than the little finger. Having filled it, and transferred to a smaller stick, she runs it to the smaller spool in the form of a very coarse yarn, when it is ready for the "filling" in a blanket. Herding is the most laborious work the Navajo girls have to do. They have all the advantages of the healthful climate, without the fatigue of long expeditions, and are, as a rule, stronger and healthier than the men. They are the only Indian girls I ever saw who even approximate to the Cooper ideal. Their dress is picturesque, consisting of separate waist and skirt; the former leaves the arms bare, and is made loose above and neat at the waist; the latter is of flowered calico, with a leaning to red and black, and terminates just below the knee in black border or frills. Neat moccasins complete the costume, the limbs being left bare generally in the summer. They are very shapely and graceful, and their strength is prodigious.

This plateau, the ridges being of sandstone and the narrow valleys of mixed sand and black earth, is at least 7,000 feet above the sea. Thence we descended to a wooded hollow, again toiled up to the plateau level, and soon entered the most magnificent forest I have seen outside of California. A cold wind had chilled us on the ridges, but in the forest there was a dead calm, though we could hear the breeze sighing far above us. This splendid park continued for ten miles; then we descended to another valley, where the soil was evidently rich, though perfectly bare for want of water; but around the edges was a bordering meadow of good grass, spangled with red and yellow flowers. This valley is an oval some five miles long, opening northward, and lacks only water to become a little Eden. From this we rose to another forest, also of sugar-pines, but not so large or thrifty as the first. My guide informs me that these forests are as long as they are wide, and, as we traveled twelve or fifteen miles through them, they must cover some two hundred square miles. This will be a great source of wealth to the Navajoes, if they learn how to use it.

The timber continued to the entrance of Bat Cañon, by which we enter the De Chelley. There my guide points to a side gulch, exclaiming, "*Tohh klohh no mas*," and we stop for the night. Hoppling the horse for a night's grazing, we sample our provisions, with satisfactory results, and retire. Navajo blankets will not admit the moisture of the ground, even if there had been any, which there was not; and with two over me, and the saddle-blanket below me, I was comfortable till towards morning, when the cold was intense. We hasten to descend into the cañon before the sun is hot, and go down from the grove upon a sandy plain, dotted with scrubby hemlocks, and sometimes with timber of larger growth. The surroundings all show that we are on the Pacific coast; the dry, gray and yellow grass, straight sugar-pines and scraggy hemlocks, and the soft airs loaded with resinous odors. We enter next upon a vast flat of sandstone, on which the little feet of Navajo *burros* have cut the trail into a groove two inches deep, and cross it to the head of Bat Cañon. The first view is discouraging. We come suddenly to an abrupt break in the sandstone, no more than a rod wide, down which we can look a thousand feet perpendicular to the yellow bottom. A few hundred yards beyond we find a side groove, which lets us down to the first offset, and thence, by a succession of rocky grooves, we work our way with cautious steps to the bottom.

We appear to be at the bottom of a vast funnel, but there is a pass three rods wide, still leading downward. Soon the cliffs above us overhang, and we pass through a gorge where the sun never shines, and thousands of gaunt bats, of a strange species, inhabit the crevices of the cliffs, and flit about in midday twilight. According to my guide, this is the place by way of which cowardly Navajoes must enter the spirit-land after death.

Passing this the narrow walls give back, and we are in a little valley with running water and occasional clumps of grass, and bounded by perpendicular cliffs. As we proceed, the valley gets wider, but the walls appear to overhang rather than maintain a plumb line. Occasionally, an entirely detached rock is seen standing out from some sharp corner where there is a turn in the cañon, a sort of tower several hundred feet high, and no more than a hundred thick, its sides and summit cut into a thousand fanciful shapes by the action of sand and wind. Other pieces of the cliff appear to have been loosened, and to have slipped down; and in many places there were enormous slabs two or three hundred feet high leaning against the wall. Wind and loose sand had cut the face of the cliff into ten thousand fanciful shapes: elephants, hippopotami, alligators, and most ludicrous human heads looked down upon us, and from a peak two thousand feet overhead a gigantic bear appeared just plunging from the summit.

"*Mahloka!*" exclaimed the guide, and following the direction of his finger, I saw the "woman," a shepherd girl, springing down over the rocks in a narrow side gulch. She showed me, through the narrow opening into the gulch, that the latter widened out behind the cliffs into a rocky valley where her herd of goats were feeding. She preferred the common request for *chin-ne-ah-go* (bread), and in return for a small gift, conducted us to a plat of good grass, near the junction of Cañon de Chelley, where we let our animals graze two hours, as I intended remaining in the cañon all day. We had scarcely got our baggage piled, before the whole community of three families were about us. I pacified them with tobacco, preferring, if we got into a strait, to do without that, rather than bread.

Bat Cañon there runs nearly straight west, and is joined by Cañon de Chelley from the north-east; the meeting of the two and the turn below produces three grand peaks, facing to one center, some fifteen hundred feet high, and quite perpendicular. But the most remarkable and unaccountable feature of the locality is where the two cañons meet. There stands out a hundred feet from the point, entirely isolated, a vast leaning rock tower, at least twelve hundred feet high, and not over two hundred thick at the base, as if it had originally been the sharp termination of the cliff, and been broken off and shoved further out. It almost seems that one must be mistaken, that it must have some connection with the cliff, until one goes around it and finds it a hundred feet or more from the former. It leans at an angle from the perpendicular of at least fifteen degrees; and lying down at the base on the under side, by the best "sighting" I could make, it seemed to me that the opposite upper edge was directly over me. That is to say, mechanically speaking, its center of gravity barely falls within the base, and a heave of only a yard or two more would cause it to topple over. Appearances indicate that it was originally connected with the point of the cliff, but the intermediate and softer sand-rock has fallen, been reduced to sand, and wafted away down the cañon. Climbing to some of the curious round holes in the cliff I could see the process of wear going on; the harder particles of the sand blown into the holes, were being whirled about by the wind, slowly and steadily boring into the cliffs, and beginning that carving which is to result in more of the grotesque shapes.

It was but a few miles now, the guide informed me, till we should reach the celebrated "cliff cities" which have made this cañon so famous. While leaning on the pommel of my saddle in an after-dinner rest, I was startled by a shout from my guide of "*Ah-yee! Ah-yee, Melicano, ettah-hoganday!*" ("There, there, sir American; the mountain-houses.") Looking, I saw the first hamlet, a small collection of stone huts some fifteen hundred feet above the cañon bed, and perhaps three hundred feet below the summit. One glance served to disprove many of the theories advanced about rope ladders and the like. It could not have been reached thus, for the cliff overhung considerably both above and below it. Indeed, a rope dropped from the brow of the cliff above would have swung over the cañon a hundred feet farther out than the ledge on which the houses stood. As near as I could judge at the distance, the ledge was fifty feet wide, and the houses some twenty feet square. Evidently the "Aztecs" who boarded there did not go to bed by means of a rope-ladder.

My guide was now all life and animation, shouting and calling my attention to every thing of note on the cliffs as we walked our horses slowly down the sandy stream. He seemed to take as much interest in the *ettah-hoganday* as I did. An hour more brought us to a better object of study: the ruins of a considerable village were on the bottom of the cañon, by the foot of the cliff, and about a hundred feet straight above them, ten or a dozen houses in perfect preservation, standing all together on a ledge a hundred feet wide, and completely inaccessible. Above the village the cliff was perpendicular for a hundred feet or more, then gradually swelled outwardly till it extended considerably over the houses, leaving them thus actually in a great crevice in the rock. Here was a wonder. My Navajo ran about with the activity of a cat, and in several places managed to climb up twenty feet or so, then the smooth wall cut off further progress. Hunting along the rock he found and called my attention to some holes looking like steps cut into the stone, which seemed to lead up to a point where one of the peculiar stone slabs I have described leaned against the cliff. The opposite side of the cañon was accessible, and not more than two hundred yards distant, so we went over there and climbed to a point somewhat higher than the pueblo. I then saw that the ledge or groove in the rock, in which the pueblo was built, ran along the cliff for a quarter of a mile, some distance beyond where we found the stone steps; and thought I saw indications of steps, leading down from it a little way toward the detached slab. Possibly, I thought, this slab may have been fast above when the village had inhabitants, and furnished them a winding stairway. I saw, also, that the houses were of a most admirable construction, built of flat stones laid in mortar, and neatly whitewashed inside; and that the joists were of massive timber, round, nearly a foot thick, and dressed with some care. At the distance of seven or eight hundred feet there was much uncertainty, but I fancied I also saw fragments of iron and leather on the floor of one house—the only one into which the sunshine fell directly. From the situation of the cliffs, I judge that about 10 o'clock in the morning the sun would be shining directly in the front doors.

A remarkable echo is observable here. A sentence of ten words shouted from the south side, is returned clearly and distinctly. Not far below we found the ruins of another house, not more than forty feet high, with shelving rock below. The Navajo found steps to lead half way up. He then walked along a flat offset five or six feet below the house, and held his hands against my feet while I climbed a shelving rock and reached it. It was in ruins, and most of the material lay in a heap in the cañon below. Only the fire-place and chimney, built against the cliff, remained whole; they were of the common Pueblo pattern, and showed dabs of whitewash. I sustained one serious disappointment. Through some blunder of my guide or the interpreter who instructed him at Defiance, I missed the greatest wonder. We ought to have turned up the Cañon de Chelley from where we entered it, and a mile or two would have brought us to the largest pueblo, one capable of containing a thousand people, situated on a cliff fifteen hundred feet high and utterly inaccessible.

And who once inhabited these towns? Well, I am of opinion the people were substantially of the same race as the present Pueblos. The houses are an exact reproduction of those at Pueblo de Laguna, including stone, mortar, towers, *acquarra* windows, and whitewashed interior. From the lower valleys they retreated to these cliffs where their mounted enemies could not pursue them. But the streams on which they depended are dried up, and the little nooks they once cultivated are fast being buried by the drifting sand. The disintegrating cliffs are spreading barrenness over all the valleys; the cañon bed is like a vast river of sand. As we journey down it a feeble stream sometimes shows itself for a few rods, and is then lost; again our animals' hoofs turn up moist sand. Occasionally bright meadows of green grass appear; and again the sand river seems to divide and flow around a fertile island a little higher than the main land, and containing a few acres of dense wheat-grass, as high as a man's head. Again we find the cliffs sinking from a perpendicular to a slope of sixty degrees or so, and bordered by considerable foot-hills; and there we see shrubby hemlock, bunch-grass, a few herds and Navajo *hogans*. Above are their goats clambering up what appears the bare, yellow face of stone; but riding near we observe hundreds of little gullies worn in the rock, each with a slight stain of soil and a few bunches of yellow grass. Looking for camp early, we came upon a green island of some ten acres, containing three Navajo huts; my guide shouted to the first shepherd girl he saw, who pointed to a peak half a mile away, exclaiming, "*Klohh, tohh!*" We rode thither, and to my surprise found that the cliffs gave back and inclosed a level plat of a few acres, a sort of mountain cove, sodded with luxuriant grass, and containing another Navajo settlement. Their goats were kind enough to prefer the high gulches, leaving the green grass of the plat in abundance for our stock. In the center was a dug spring, but no running water. The community had abundance of goats' milk and white roots—nothing else.

While the Navajo prepared our supper, I went to the first *hogan*, finding an old man quite sick, who asked—the only Spanish he knew—if I had any *azucar y cafe*, adding that he had not tasted food for a week. His daughter went back to camp with me, after the sugar and coffee, and all the other women in the settlement having arrived, they waited to see us eat. Opening a tin box, to their great astonishment I took out a sardine and jokingly held it out for them to see, then ate it, when they turned away with such expressions of horror and disgust that I was heartily ashamed of myself. Their feelings were probably about the same as ours would be on seeing a Fejee chewing on the corpse of his grandmother. Fish and turkeys either will be or have been human beings, in their theology; they never touch the former, and the latter only to escape absolute starvation. I had been warned that I would find my Navajo prone to disregard cleanliness; I found him rather neat and careful. But imagine my astonishment when I saw that all his native politeness could not entirely conceal his disgust at eating with me. The sardines had done for my reputation among the Navajoes.

Supper over, I climbed as far as possible up one of the side gulches, lighted my pipe, and sat down to watch the line of sunshine and shadow creep slowly up the sixteen hundred feet of the opposite cliff, while the red sun sank behind the mountains. Sunlight gave place to dusk, and the day's heat to a sharp air which made me draw my blanket close around my shoulders; then came on the brilliant night of this climate, in which every silvery star seems to stand out from a firmament of polished steel. But in a few minutes the moon rose above the eastward peaks, and poured a flood of glory on the barren rocks, transforming the red peaks to shining mountains of gold, and the sand-flat to a flowing, glittering stream of gems. The air held no trace of moisture. I was weary, but the sight was too glorious to admit of sleep. I sat and gazed; tried to reason on the geology of these hills, but soon nature compelled me from the domain of science to that of imagination. It was a time to admire and enjoy, not to philosophize; for, though we go back in scientific fancy from age to age, from cosmic process to cosmic process, we come at last to a mighty void which reason can not pass, and can only think: "IN THE BEGINNING, GOD—"

There, in childhood, we began; there, after ages of scientific conjecture, must we rest. Reason exhausted leans on faith, and learning's last endeavor ends where revelation began.

We were off next day at the first glimmer of dawn, hoping to reach grass and water early in the afternoon, and knowing that at the best we had a long day's ride before us. It is delightful for travel till about 10 o'clock; then the morning breeze dies away, and, as the afternoon breeze does not rise till about three, the intervening heat is terrible. We are already nearly two thousand feet below Defiance, and going a little lower every day, with corresponding change in the climate. The grand scenery continues to the very mouth of the cañon, which we reached in two hours, then breaks down into a brief succession of foot-hills and ridges of loose sand, and brings us to an open plain. Here were two or three sections of land under some sort of cultivation by the Navajoes, but it was the most pitiable prospect for a crop I ever saw. The feeble, yellow blades of corn, three or four inches in height, had struggled along through drought and cold till the heavy frost of June 17th, and now most of them lay flat on the ground. My guide waved his hand over the field, exclaiming, mournfully, "*Muerto, muerto*" (dead); "*no chinneahgo Navajoes.*" A few of the more resolute were out replanting, which they did with a sharpened stick, or rather paddle. They dig a hole some ten inches through the dry surface sand to the moist layer underneath, in the edge of which they deposit the grain. They plant wheat the same way, in little hills a foot or so apart, and weed it carefully till it is grown enough to cultivate. If there is water, they irrigate; otherwise, it has to take its chances; and the guide informed me that the *acecquia* we saw issuing from the cañon had long been dry. Twenty bushels of corn and ten of wheat are extra crops. If any citizen of rural Ohio, who can deliberately sit down three times a day and recklessly eat all his appetite craves, is dissatisfied, he ought to travel awhile in this country.

Crossing the dry *arroyo* we rose on the western side to a vast flood-plain, ten miles wide, and running as far as I could see from north to south. The surface showed that it had been flooded some time within the last few years; there was not a trace of alkali or other noxious mineral, and the soil was of great natural fertility. But there was not a spear of vegetation on it, simply for lack of moisture. Here are at least a hundred square miles, formed of *detritus* and vegetable mold, now utterly worthless for want of water. If artesian wells are possible, the whole tract may be of great value. We rose thence by a succession of white sand hills to a horrible desert, which extended some twenty miles. Our horses suffered from both heat and thirst, and the water in our canteens was soon simmering warm. As we neared a low range of gray and chalky-looking hills, the sage-brush appeared a little more thrifty, and sometimes showed a faint green tinge, indicating there was water somewhere in the vicinity.

A faint track, as if made by sheep or goats, crossed our trail, whereat the guide whirled his horse toward the ridge, ran his eye along the peaks, and selecting one which to my eye in no way differed from the rest, exclaimed, "*Toh!*" and we started for it. At the mouth of the gorge was a sickly little cottonwood in a small depression, at which the guide remarked: "*Toh pasar muchos años*" (water many years ago), and we struck up the nearest gulch. The rock every-where was crumbling away; it was like riding up a mountain of chalk. At the foot of, and partly underneath a large cliff, we found two holes, scooped out by Indian hatchets, and containing a gallon or so of water to each, the one almost cool and the other blood warm. After treating ourselves to a quart or so each, my horse drank the cool one and the *burro* the other, and we struck into the desert again. On the western side, my guide had told me, we should see the last Navajoes; but we soon met most of the colony driving before them their little herds, and to the guide's question they replied that the grass there was gone, the water dried up to one spring, and that was *hohkawah ki wano* (decidedly not good). Though I did not quite understand this, I saw, by its effect on the guide, that it was bad news for us, who had already ridden forty miles.

There was but one family left, and the girl showed us a specimen kettle of the water. It was horrible stuff, but we must have some of it, and climbing an hour we reached the pool. All around it the sandstone had been trodden to powder and was drifting into the water, which was green, slimy, full of vile pollywogs, and looked and smelt as if ten thousand goats had waded through it. The horse and *burro* drank with many sniffs and brute protests, and John and I downed a pint or so each; but it was a signal triumph of catholic stomachs over protesting noses. We had no more than reached the plain till both of us were sick, and in an hour I dismounted, unable to ride further. John ran about in great distress, gathered some dry yellow flowers, and burnt them under my nose, producing a violent sneezing and retching. Placing his hand on my stomach, he indicated, by most expressive signs, that "it must come up." Having lighted my pipe and placed it in my mouth, he moistened some tobacco and placed it under my arms and on the pit of my stomach. The convulsion was terrible, but the vile water did come up.

Two hours more and my thirst, aggravated by the previous sickness, became intolerable. John decided that we must climb the mountain to our right, to another "pocket" which contained good water. We toiled upward for a thousand feet, to a point where a soft limestone reef broke across the sand-mountain. Here he pointed out a black pass between two rocks, and leaving our horses we entered it to find a beautiful pool of cold, clear water, nearly a rod square and completely covered by overhanging rocks. Here we drank, filled the canteens, and rested until the moon was high enough to light us back to the plain. My horse either smelt the water or heard its splash, and uttered a low pleading whinny that went to my heart. It was impossible to get him under the rocky arch into the cave, and I had no vessel but a tin-cup. I tried that, but could not even moisten his tongue; I wet my handkerchief and tried to "swab" his mouth; he chewed it to rags and bit my finger in the operation. About to give up in despair, I thought of my wool hat, and filled that for him. It fitted his mouth admirably, and by eleven trips with it he was satisfied. Half a dozen hatfuls sufficed for the *burro*, and we worked our way down hill again. But this time my Navajo's sense of locality failed him, and on the steepest part he took the wrong chute, pulling up his *burro* just in time to avoid his plunging head first into a ravine, but not in time to save himself, as the saddle girth gave way just at the wrong moment. As he went head first into a pile of bowlders and sand, I looked on in horror, fully satisfied that I was left alone in this terrible place; but he sprang up instantly, and with a silly smile, and "*Vah, vah, Melicano, malo, malo!*" remounted and rode on, only rubbing his crown occasionally.

Getting back to the plain, we continued our former course southwest along the foot of the *mesa*. My eyelids began to droop with weariness, and for fear I should drop off my horse in sleep, I loosed my feet, and raising the stirrup leathers, wrapped them about each arm. The position was not favorable to sleep, nor could I keep entirely awake; and soon I suffered from that queer symptom of dreaming with the eyes wide open, and fixed upon the very object of my dream. The bright moonlight fell upon the projecting peaks of the ridge to our right, and I endeavored to keep awake by contemplating their beauty; but as I gazed I saw suddenly a score of bright, clear streams dashing down as many gulches, and a broad *savanna* on the plain below, rich and green with inviting grass. I shouted to the guide: "*Kloh! Toh!*" (grass, water), and jerking up my horse, pitched forward on his neck and awoke. I braced myself more firmly to keep awake, and in a few moments, looking on a rock a little ahead, I saw a hideous painted Indian bound out from behind it and take position in the sage-brush near the trail. I yelled to the guide and grabbed my gun, and just as the hammer was clicking under my hand, Indian and rock disappeared, and the answering shout of the guide brought me to my waking senses. I knew there was not a hostile Indian in fifty miles, so, for fear I would shoot my own horse, I gave the gun to the Navajo, and again resolved to keep awake. He still pointed ahead for grass, but indicated that it was now "*pokeeto*" (a little way). While gazing on a sand ridge we were crossing, I seemed to see it covered with grass and flowers, and shouting that this was the place, reined up my horse suddenly, and again butted him in the back of the head, at the imminent risk of giving us both the poll-evil.

At last, near midnight, we reached the little oasis I had anticipated in so many fitful dreams. There was abundant bunch-grass but no water, and we made a "dry camp." While the Navajo hoppled the horses, I wrapped my blankets about me, laid my head upon my saddle, and in two minutes was sound asleep. It seemed that I had scarcely closed my eyes when I was awakened by a "*Hah-koh, Melicano!*" and, starting up, saw my Navajo holding the animals ready to mount, and pointing to the east, already rosy with the coming dawn. Moving his hand thence towards a point half way to the zenith, he remarked: "*Kloh, toh! No calor,*" Navajo, Spanish and sign-language, meaning in full: "By starting now we shall reach grass and water the middle of the forenoon, and before the heat of the day." Nevertheless, I decided that a cup of coffee would help things, as there was sage-brush enough for a fire, and a pint of water still in the canteen.

After coffee and bread, we found the morning ride delightful, and through a better country which produced considerable grass. The valley slowly narrowed to a mere pass; beyond the rugged jaws of this red cañon there opened an extensive plain, and in its center rose an oval *mesa*, which the guide designated as Moqui. We made our midday halt at the point of the mountain; but when the guide indicated grass and water up and over a perfectly bare white sand-hill, I shook my head. He only smiled, and led the way. With frequent rests to our horses, we had toiled up and over the rising sand-hills for something like a mile, when a sudden descent brought us into a circular hollow, containing half a dozen shrubs and nearly an acre of densely matted grass. At the foot of the cliff was a slight moisture, and pointing to a black rock which appeared nearly five hundred feet straight above us, the guide intimated there was our spring. Every thing was stripped from the animals except the lariats, but how we ever got them up that hill is a mystery to me; but we did, and found plenty of good water, brought down our supply, and remained in this camp until 3 P. M. We cooked a fresh supply of bread, ate a big dinner, and enjoyed a delightful "laze" in the shadow of a big rock.

We here overhauled our kit, brushed up a little, and put on our best gear for a visit; and, when the afternoon breeze had sprung up, entered upon the sandy plain, and followed a slight trail towards the *mesa*. Occasional depressions were filled with yellow bunch-grass, but most of the plain was of hard, bare white sand, seeming to literally bake in the heat of the sun. Approaching the foot of the *mesa* we found the sand a little more loose and dark. Here I noticed rows of stones a foot or so apart, and was amazed to find, on examination, we were in a Moqui field. By every little hill of corn or beans they had laid a stone, the object being to mark the spot during the long period between planting and the appearance of the shoot above ground.

From the foot-hills I gazed with astonishment upon the perpendicular walls and projecting cliffs of the *mesa*, rising a thousand feet above me. It is little over half a mile long and half as wide, and rises abruptly from the plain on every side; around it run galleries and foot-paths, winding in and out upon the crevices and projecting shelves of rock; and far above my head, as it seemed almost in midair, I saw goat-pens upon the very face of the cliff, opening back into dark cool caves, where the stock is inclosed at night. Here and there was to be seen a Moqui woman toiling wearily up the rocky gallery with a water-jug strapped upon her back.

It was a strange sight. I was thrilled at the thought that I was looking upon the chosen stronghold of the most peculiar race of American Indians: a city about which conjecture and romance had taken the place of knowledge, a country vaguely described by hunters, but never by careful writers, and therefore one the very existence of which is often pronounced fabulous. It is perhaps the strongest natural fortification in the world. Around the entire *mesa* there is but one narrow way that a horse can ascend, and on that, at a score of points, a squad of boys with nothing but stones could defy the cavalry of the world. The springs which supply the community are situated around the base of the highest cliffs, where the foot-hills begin, but so far up that most of them can not be reached by horses from below; and even most of their little fields are hidden among the foot-hills, and only to be found from above. From the general level of the plain to the flat top of the *mesa* I estimate at a thousand feet. Half of this rise is by a succession of rolling sand ridges, and then we come to a perpendicular cliff, only surmountable by these rock-hewn galleries. The community owns neither horses nor cattle; nothing but goats, and equally agile *burros*, can surmount the obstacles of such a situation.

We entered upon the ascent in a hot and narrow pass between two sand ridges, and soon reached the first spring, below which was a succession of walled fields. Each field was about three rods wide and six long, and contained some three hundred hills of corn; they were built up against the sand ridge, a stone wall four or five feet high forming at once the division for one and support for the dirt in the next, the fields rising in a succession of terraces. The feeble stream was exhausted before it passed the second field, and it is only in the night that the lower ones can be irrigated. Farther down, where there is no water, the Moqui digs a hole in the sand eighteen or twenty inches deep, and plants his corn where a slight moisture has percolated from above. We passed the slope, and were about to enter on the gallery road, when a Moqui shouted to us from directly overhead, and in obedience to his directions, though at the imminent risk of our necks, the guide turned down a rocky foot-path to another gallery. A few steps showed us that a vast sand-rock had fallen across the other road, and a new one had been built.

As we turned the last groove in the gallery, and, almost before we were aware of it, the houses looking so much like stone, we were right in the first town, all the men of which seemed to be absent. At Defiance I was told to ask for Chino, the *Capitan* of this *mesa*, before I talked to any one else; so I shouted to call out some one. A woman came on top of the nearest house, and seeing me immediately set up a cry of *jokow! jokow!* Then from every house women and children, with occasionally a man or good-sized boy, came running on to the house-tops and down the ladders to the street, while the cry went ahead from house to house, *jokow! jokow! jokow!* A population of several hundred was soon crowding about me, or gazing in astonishment from the house-tops; the women were chattering and exclaiming, and the children when I rode near a house yelling with fright, and altogether we were creating a decided sensation. Again I called for Chino, and a dozen boys jumped into the road and ran along the cliff, beckoning me to follow. We passed through the first town, the whole population following in a tumultuous mass, and in the second town—a hundred yards on—found and were admitted to the lower part of Chino's house. He was not at home, but they let us into an extension of his dwelling, containing but one story, where we deposited our packs. Twenty boys and women were already on the house-top, jostling each other to look through the square opening at us; as many more were crowding into the room, and about four hundred were outside struggling for a good place.

It is not pleasant to be stared at, even by barbarians, and I was greatly relieved when a tall old fellow, with a merry twinkle in his eye, arrived, addressed me in pretty good Spanish, and intimated that he did the talking for Chino when strangers came. His name, which he had on a card written by some white man, was Misiamtewah; he had visited the Mormon settlements and Santa Fe, and could speak Spanish, Moqui, Tegua and a little English and Navajo, besides being fluent in the sign language. I cultivated his acquaintance at once.

Chino soon arrived, and assured me, per Misiamtewah, that this was my town, my house, my country as long as I wanted to stay, and assigned me quarters in a very comfortable room, one they usually reserve for white visitors. We stored our baggage, sent out our animals to graze with the common herd, opened our provisions and took supper with Chino and his son. I was in pleasant quarters again, and devoted a few days to rest, study of these peculiar people, and jotting down notes on my trip through the two Territories, for all of which see next chapter.

CHAPTER XVII.

AMONG THE AZTECS.

ARIZONA and the western half of New Mexico constitute a vast parallelogram, down the center of which, as dividing water-shed, runs the Sierra Madre range. From its summit, varying from seven to ten thousand feet high, the country falls off each way in a succession of plateaus to the two great rivers. The traveler proceeding westward from the Rio Grande, over an almost level *mesa*, sees rising before him a range of rocky hills from a hundred to a thousand feet high, and naturally looks for a corresponding descent on the western side. Instead, on reaching the summit, he finds again the level, barren *mesa* spreading away before him, till its sandy and glistening surface fades into the blue horizon. Across this succession of terraced plateaus a few valleys put out eastward, and in the lowest portions of these, where some running water is found, are the only cultivable lands. A series of such valleys, connected by singular natural passes, furnish a feasible route for the Thirty-fifth Parallel Road.

Still, there is a sort of regularity on the New Mexican side; but far otherwise west of the summit. There the high plateaus are broken across by awful chasms; gorges with perpendicular sides go winding tortuously through the formation; all the streams run in great cañons from two to five thousand feet in depth, with bottoms from one to four thousand feet above the level of the sea. Here and there the barren plateau appears to drop suddenly to a level plain, and rocky ranges of hills inclose an oval valley, walled in on every side by inaccessible mountains, and with passes out only up or down the beds of ancient streams, long since dry. It is the oldest country on earth, except perhaps the "back-bone" of Central Africa; natural convulsions have slowly heaved it far above the region of abundant rains or dews, and the great Colorado, with its affluents, has for ages been slowly cutting deeper and deeper channels in the sandstone formation, tapping the sources of the springs at lower points, and steadily sucking the life out of its own basin. On the rocky hills are still some fine forests; on the slopes the Indians find abundant bunch-grass and wild sage for their hardy animals; and, at rare intervals, a hidden valley is found, low enough to have a growing season without frost, with water enough for irrigation, its soil the volcanic *detritus* of neighboring hills, and of wonderful fertility. Perhaps one-fortieth of the entire area is fit for agriculture.

ON THE MESA CALABASA.

Three races inhabit this strange region. The white Americans of both Territories number, perhaps, twenty thousand; the Mexicans at least a hundred thousand. The latter are the result of miscegenation between the Spanish conquerors and the aborigines, the blood being about half and half; but the aristocracy have more Spanish, the *peons* more Indian. The pure Indians of all the South-west are divided in two general classes—Pueblos and Nomads. The first are all friendly, including the Zunis, Moquis, Teguas, Oraybes, Papagoes, Pimos and Coco-Maricopas. Of the Nomads, the Navajoes are now friendly, the Apaches and Comanches fiercely hostile, and the Utes a little doubtful, but nominally peaceful. In the southern sections, the San Francisco, White and Magollon Mountains and their spurs break up the country into a thousand hidden valleys, in which the murderous Apaches hide and graze their stock; the few trails go twisting through narrow cañons, in which, at most unexpected places, the savages let fly upon the unwary traveler a shower of poisoned arrows; and dreary intervals of desert separate the scant water-holes on which the way-worn explorer must depend.

On the map Arizona appears to have abundance of water, but it is an optical illusion. Nine-tenths of the so-called "rivers" are dry; in the four hundred miles between Agua Azu and Lee's Ferry, on the Colorado, I crossed eleven considerable river-beds, and saw running water in but one place. The Colorado is barely navigable for part of the year, and not far up, as Brigham Young found to his cost when he built the Callville warehouses. The channel is crooked and changeable below the cañon, rocky and full of cataracts in the cañon, shallow and impassable above it. Practically it is useless above Fort Yuma. For fifteen hundred miles it will float no boats; there is no timber on its banks that can be got at or is worth getting, no gold deposits in its bars, no fish in it worth catching, no quarries along it that can be utilized, and no land that can be cultivated. It is purely an ornamental stream.

Along the Gila (*Heelah*) live the semi-civilized Pimos, Maricopas and Papagoes. They cultivate the earth with some skill, and produce abundance of wheat, corn, pumpkins and melons. Like all the Pueblos the men are scrupulously honest—the women virtuous to a most un-Indian degree. They are well supplied with horses, cattle, sheep and goats, are exposed to Apache raids, and freely join with the whites in fighting the latter. The Papagoes took a very prominent part in the notorious Camp Grant massacre. At first these Indians were delighted at the coming of the whites; now they are sullen and uncommunicative, saying that the agents have defrauded them and tried to debauch their women. Probably correct.

The nomadic tribes, except the Navajoes, are dying off at a very satisfactory rate. The Yavapais have four natural deaths to one birth. One-tenth of the Mohaves have died annually for some years. It is rare to see one of this tribe entirely free from the scrofulous taint. The whole Apache race numbers less than 7,000; 2,000 warriors is the utmost they can raise. Forty years ago they numbered

"CONVERTED ON THE SPOT."

25,000, and could easily collect 4,000 warriors for a grand raid into Mexico. But they are incurably wild, and often hunted like wild beasts. For the most part they attack white men at sight, and many are the fearful tragedies enacted in these wilds. When an Apache is killed, the white settlers, in gleeful sarcasm of Collyer and other "humanitarians," speak of him as "converted," or "civilized on the spot."

Among the Arizona Indians there are no strong tribal organizations, and no men of much influence. The hostile parties are not made up from any one clique or small settlement, nor do the members join at the command of a chief; but some ambitious leader sends word that he will start on a raid, and invites the braves of the vicinity to join. It is therefore impossible to govern the tribes through the chiefs in the manner practiced east of the Rocky Mountains.

To all these remarks the Navajoes constitute an encouraging exception. They are the original Romans of New Mexico. Spanish accounts say that at the Conquest a branch of the ancient Mexican Indians, disdaining to submit, took refuge in the hidden valleys and on the inaccessible plateaus of the Sierra Madre; there they joined a wild tribe of the Athabascan stock, and from the union of the two sprang the present Navajoes. Kindred, on the Athabascan side, of the Shoshonees, Comanches, Apaches and Arapahoes, they have all the bravery and best qualities of the wild tribes, while from the old Aztec or Toltec blood they inherit a peculiar civilization, fair habits of industry and thrift, and something like a spirit of progress. For two hundred years they carried on almost perpetual war with the Spaniards; then a sort of peace was patched up and continued till the Americans got control of the country, and established agencies. Then war followed, of course. It lasted seven years, and did not end till General W. H. Carleton, in 1863-'64, had destroyed all their orchards and corn-fields, killed their sheep and goats, and literally starved them out.

Barboncito, their great chief, a born diplomat, succeeded in 1868 in making a very advantageous treaty with General Sherman; and since then the tribe has slowly built up again. Before the war they numbered 12,000, and it is claimed they owned over a million sheep and goats, and at least 30,000 horses. Even now there are few adults in the tribe who do not own one or more horses each. Ganado Mucho ("Big Herd"), a prominent chief, owns four hundred. In 1870 they began farming under direction of the agent, but so far it has not been much of an improvement on their own system. In 1871 they planted extensively, and had a young orchard growing finely, when, on the night of May 31st, a storm of sleet killed every tree. The seeds furnished by the department were utterly unsuited to this altitude, and they have returned to their old system. The country appears to get dryer year by year. It is a pity they could not be transferred *en masse* to the Indian Territory.

They work in iron, wool and leather; but to no great extent, except in the second. Of this they make blankets, which are the wonder of all who see them. The loom is rude and primitive, consisting only of beams to which two sticks are lashed; on these the warp, or "chain," is stretched very tight, the two sets of strands crossing in the middle. This, with two loose sticks, dividing the "chain," and a curved board, looking like a barrel stave with the edges rounded, constitute the entire loom. The squaw sits before this

NAVAJO LOOM.

with her balls of yarn for "filling" conveniently arranged, works them through the strands, and beats them firmly together with the loose board, running it in between the strands with singular dexterity. The woolen yarn for "filling" is made from their own sheep, generally, and is of three colors—black, white and red, from native coloring. Running these together by turns, with nimble fingers, the squaw brings out on the blanket squares, diamonds, circles and fanciful curves, and flowers of three colors, with a skill which is simply amazing. Two months are required to complete an ordinary blanket, five feet wide and eight long, which sells at from fifteen to fifty dollars, according to the style of materials. At the Fort, officers who wish an unusually fine article, furnish both "chain" and "filling," but those entirely of Navajo make are very fine. One will outlast a life-time; and though rolled in the mud, or daubed with grease for months or years, till every vestige of color seems gone, when washed with the soap-weed (*mole cactus*) the bright native colors come out as beautiful as ever.

They also manufacture, with beads and silk threads obtained from the traders, very beautiful neck-ties, ribbons, garters, cuffs and other ornaments. More interesting to me than any of their handicraft, is the unwearying patience they display in all their work, and their zeal and quickness to learn in every thing which may improve their condition. Officers and agents universally tell me that Navajoes work alongside of any employés they can get, and do full work. They dig ditches and make embankments with great skill, handling the spade as well as any Irishman. Surely such a people are capable of civilization.

Mrs. Charity Menaul, teacher at Defiance, reported considerable progress among the Navajoes under her charge. I found the older people curious to learn about our customs, and very communicative as to their own, though like all barbarians a little reticent as to their theology. Their religion, or superstition, is vague; there is a difference on minor points between the bands, though some ideas are common. *Chinday,* the devil, is a more important personage in their system than *Whylohay,* the *god;* as, like the Mormons and many other white schismatics, they charge all they don't like in other people to the direct personal agency of the devil. About the only use, in fact, of their *god,* is to lay plans to outwit the devil. Their moral code is extremely vague: whatever is good for the tribe is in general right; whatever is not *pro bono publico* is wrong. Cowards after death will become coyotes, while braves will continue men in a better country. Women will change to fish for awhile, and afterwards to something else. But they don't trouble themselves much about the next world. If they had plenty in this, they would consider themselves in luck.

On minor points there are as many sects as in Boston. The general belief is this: there is one Great Spirit; under him each people has its own *god.* The *god* of the Melicanoes is very good to them; they have corn and horses, blankets and much *chinneahgo.* But it is useless for Navajoes to pray to him. Each cares for his own. The coyote will not take up the children of the rattlesnake; the eagle will not give his meat to the young hawks. It is light, it is nature.

Whylohay (a female, by the way) made the Navajoes in the San Juan Valley; they were rich, and had abundance of all things. But one night *Chinday* dammed the San Juan, and drowned them all. Besides the fish, only two creatures escaped; the snake swam ashore and the turkey flew up to a peak in Colorado. The goddess made the turkey into another man, and made a woman from a fish, and from these two are descended all the present Navajoes. However, this may be only an allegorical statement of the general masculine belief that the sex divine are inclined to be slippery and hard to catch.

Women after death change to fish for awhile; after that their destiny seems unsettled. Because of this, Navajoes eat neither fish nor turkeys. The snake is the only animal that knows any thing about what took place in the first creation. Hence, Navajoes seldom or never kill one. From other fish *Whylohay* recreated the animal kingdom. The turkey was made from a fish in a lake covered with foam, which lodged on his tail as he swam ashore; hence, the white feathers in the turkey's tail. White men after death go up into the air; Navajoes go down through Bat Cañon and into the earth. Thence they come out a long way west, on the edge of a great water. The shore is guarded by terrible evil spirits in the form of men, but with great ears reaching from above their heads to the ground. When asleep, they lie on one ear and cover with the other. Whether they ever "walk off on their ear," the old men could not inform me. Only half of them sleep at a time, and the Navajo has to fight his way through them. If he is brave, and has treated his women well, he gets through; then the goddess takes him across the water. There, like the white man, they stop; from *that* country no one has ever come back, to say what is there, or tell us about the climate.

Their women are often quite handsome; but like barbarian races generally, they sell their daughters in marriage. Common to average can be had for property to the value of $25; prime to fine for $50; while young and extra go at $60, the standard price of the Navajo speckled pony. While in Cañon de Chelley, I was offered a beautiful Miss of fifteen for $60, or the horse I was riding. Perhaps I should have closed with the offer—it is so much cheaper than one can get a wife in the States. Two months vigorous courting will cost more than that—particularly in the ice-cream season.

The men do the hardest work, in the fields and on the chase; to the women is left the weaving, household work, tending the herds and grinding. The last is done with the *mitata*—consisting of two flat stones, the lower stationary, the upper rubbed upon it with the hand, the result being a pasty flour. Of this and water they make a mixture no thicker than starch, which they cook on hot stones. The fire is built in a small hole, on which is placed the flat stone, no more than an inch thick; when sufficiently hot, the squaw thrusts her hand into the starchy solution, and rapidly draws a handful, which she spreads upon the stone. In a half-minute it is cooked in the form of a brown wafer, no thicker than card-board. Another and another follows till they have a layer some inches thick, which is rolled up conveniently for carrying.

They are the only wild tribe I know who do not scalp dead enemies. They never had that practice. In fact, they never touch a dead body, even of their own people. Each *hogan* is so constructed that the weight rests mostly on two main beams. When one dies in a *hogan*, they loosen these two outside, and let it drop upon him. If one dies on the plain, they pile enough stones upon him to keep off the coyotes, but never touch the body. This observance is a serious drawback in one respect: it prevents them from building permanent dwellings. It is said to be a part of their religion, but I apprehend it originated during some plague, when contagion resulted from touching the dead.

One surprising fact to me was that an Indian would sunburn by exposure as readily as a white man. But many of our current notions about the Indian are erroneous. For instance, it is a great mistake to suppose they can travel so long without eating. They know the country, and what roots are nourishing or poisonous. In many places over this section between the two Coloradoes grows a species of milky weed, with tough, stringy root, in taste resembling the "sweet hickory" the boys use to pull and chew, along the Wabash. The Navajoes cook this in boiled milk, or with bacon when at home, and on journeys without supplies take it raw. They get poor as snakes on such food; but it does keep soul and body together for awhile, and prevent the deadly faintness resulting from complete fasting. But they endure thirst much better than we, and for obvious reasons. Their food contains no salt, their bread no chemicals; they rarely get intoxicating liquors, and use very little tobacco. With unsalted bread, a scant indulgence in bacon, and coffee night and morning, I soon found I could go half a day without water with no inconvenience whatever. I also tried the practice of riding bareheaded, and found that an easy accomplishment. In short, though it takes forty years to civilize an Indian, I am positive a well-disposed white man could go wild in six months.

The origin of the venereal poison is a subject much discussed by the Indians. Most of them assert that they had none of it till the Melicanoes came, but the old men admitted that cases were introduced, many years ago, from Mexico. The Coyotero, White Mountain and Mogollon Apaches have never had a case of it. If one of their women offend with a white man, her nose and ears are cut off, and she is made a slave. The Moquis appeared quite ignorant of the existence of such a disease. The Tabequache Utes have a woman publicly whipped for infidelity with whites. If she be found diseased, she is forthwith lanced and her body burned. This savage quarantine has effectually preserved the tribe, and I supposed at first it was for that purpose; but the Navajo old men asserted that it was rather as an act of mercy to the woman. The Mohaves are perishing rapidly from this scourge. The Navajoes claim that there is now very little of it among them, and that they treat it successfully. To sum up on my Navajo friends: they are the only Indians in whom I could ever take much interest, and I am confident they can be civilized, and that the "humanitarian policy" will be a success as applied to them.

I stop four days with the Moquis; I should need six months to learn all that is interesting in their mode of life, theology and social organization. They are aboriginal Quakers; live at peace with all men, and have a horror of shedding blood. As a natural consequence they have retreated from the open country, and now occupy this rocky mole, safe from the hostility of mounted Indians. Who are they? Well, this is one of those things no fellow can find out. The conundrum must be referred to that large class relative to the Mound-Builders and other prehistoric races of America; for it is self evident that the semi-civilized Indians of the South-west are but the feeble remnants of a long series of races.

The three towns on this *mesa* contain about a thousand inhabitants; and are known as Moqui, Tegua, and Moquina. (*Mokee, Tawah*, and *Mokeena*.) A little way westward are four other towns of the same race: Hualpec, Shepalawa, Oraybe, and Beowawa. (*Wallpake, Shepalawa, Orybay*, and *Baowahwa*.) The total population is about three thousand. Their houses are of good architectural design, built of flat stones laid in white cement, plastered neatly inside, and whitewashed with a material which gives a hard, smooth polish. The lower story is not as high as a man; but that they occupy only in winter. On this the second story rises ten or twelve feet, seldom more than half as wide as the lower, leaving a broad margin on which they usually sleep. The first story has no doors and very small windows; they ascend to the second by a rude ladder or stone stairway at the corner. The better class have carpets of sheep-skin, and all have them to sit on; the climate is too dry for mold, and I found the residences very agreeable.

The people are exceedingly kind and communicative. When the novelty of my appearance had worn away a little, and I could walk about town without a wondering crowd after me, I rarely turned toward a house without receiving the welcome wave of the hand to the lips and breast, with the words, "*Ilo, Melicano, messay ro;*" or sometimes, as many know a few words of Spanish, "*Entre: Pasar adelante.*" Then a boy or girl would run down the stone staircase, and extend a hand to steady me in ascending. They took me into every room in their houses, and seemed to take a pride in exhibiting their best specimens of pottery, wicker-jugs, and other property. Of their children they were particularly demonstrative; and, indeed, they looked well enough. I did not, in all the towns, see a single birthmark, blotch, or deformity, except albinism. Children of both sexes go entirely naked till about the age of ten years. I noted one curious fact: the little ones seemed almost as white as American children, till the age of six months or a year; then they began to turn darker, and at ten or twelve had attained to a rich mahogany color. They play for hours along these cliffs, chasing each other from rock to rock at that dizzy height, and yet the parents seemed surprised when I asked if accidents did not happen.

Their mode of living is very simple, and I happened upon a time of unusual scarcity. The general drought of the past three years had cut off their crops. As often as Chino, the *Capitan* of this *mesa*, visited me, I had presented him a tin of warm, sweetened coffee, of which they are very fond, and which was the only thing I could spare; and had partaken of parched corn with him the evening of my arrival, when I received a special invitation to dine with him "the day before I left." (People with weak stomachs may skip the next paragraph.)

They breakfast early, and dine between 11 and 12. Besides Misiamtewah, a sort of official interpreter, there is another Moqui, who speaks Spanish tolerably well, having been a year in Tucson and Prescott; and both were at dinner with us. We sat upon sheep-skins on the floor, in a circle around the earthen bowls, in which the food was placed. The staple was a thick corn mush, which to me was rather tasteless for the want of salt. The regular bread of the Moquis is a decided curiosity. The wheat is ground with *mitats*, as by the Navajoes, but much finer, six or seven women grinding together, reducing the flour to the merest dust. It is then mixed as thin as milk; the woman cooking dashes a handful on the hot stone, where it cooks almost instantly, and comes off no thicker than paper, and of a bright blue color. The flakes are about two feet long, and as they are stacked two or three feet deep on the platter, look remarkably like a pile of blue silk. They raise white, blue, and red corn; and by various mixtures produce bread of seven different colors. They are not as clean in their cooking as the Navajoes, and it is hinted that they sometimes mix their meal with chamber-lye for these festive occasions; but I did not know that till I talked with Mormons who had visited them.

The *piece de resistance* was the hinder half of a very fat young dog, well cooked, that animal being the favorite food of the Moquis. It is subject to greater extremes than beef; the meat of an old, lean dog is very tough, and that of a fat, young puppy, very tender. I took from my own store a box of sardines, and Misiamtewah was prevailed upon to eat one; but Chino and the rest rejected them with horror. There's gastronomic prejudice for you! This man is sweet on dog, and rejects a sardine with abhorrence. My Eastern friends take sardines with avidity, but their gorge rises at the thought of dog, while my catholic stomach takes dog and sardine with equal impartiality. Parched corn completed the bill of fare, with beverage of goat's milk. Both the Moquis and Navajoes never use it until heated almost to the boiling point; but after one cup of this, I requested and was served with mine cold. The stove, ingeniously constructed of flat stones, is either on the ground just beside the door, or on the roof of the first story, by the door of the second.

With my Navajo guide and Chino's son, we formed a very pleasant party of six, and had quite a social time. The second interpreter informed me that he went to Prescott with Melicanoes and Meshicanoes, and that they named him—it was probably in sport— Jesus Papa (*Hay-soos Pahpah.*) He was much more communicative than Misiamtewah, and had a very fair idea of the Americans. To these simple people I represented in person all the dignity of that great nation, of whom such wonderful reports had reached them. And here I must own to a little deceit. They were at first very inquisitive as to my business, and could not imagine why a white man should be making such a long trip with only Indians for companions. Savage people can rarely understand that intelligent curiosity which is the product of civilization, and suspect some ulterior purpose when one has nothing to trade, and is not a prospector for mines. So I told them I was collecting information about the friendly Indians for the use of government, which may be passed as in a sense true.

The Moquis have a close struggle for existence. The sand surrounding the *mesa* presents the poorest show for farming I ever saw, yet every-where among these sand-hills are their little walled fields, three or four rods square, and from the measure Papa showed me, I estimated that his field had produced what would amount to twelve or fifteen bushels of corn, and half as much wheat, to the acre. The water from neither of the springs runs more than ten rods before sinking in the sand; but in some places they have constructed little troughs of rock or wood which carry a stream perhaps as big as one's finger to the field, and help the case a little. With a sharp stick they dig a hole about eighteen inches deep through the top sand, which brings them to a moister stratum, in which they lodge the grain. Around the hill they then place a few stones, and after dressing in clean clothes, sit in solemn silence for hours by the fields—supposed to be praying for rain. If no rain comes, which is generally the case, they carry water in their wicker-jugs from the spring, and pour a pint or so on each hill. If the season is favorable, the corn grows about two feet high, and yields ten to fifteen bushels per acre; if unfavorable, they get nothing, and live upon goat's milk and white roots, with a rare dessert of wild fruit, *mescal*, or game.

I said "supposed to be praying," as I could learn of no religious belief among them, though their Mormon visitors credit them with being very pious. I explained at great length our ideas of God and nature, and asked Papa as to theirs, with this result:

Papa—Nothing! (*Nada.*) The grandfathers said nothing of *Dios*—what you say Got—God (making several attempts at the word.)

Myself—But, say to me, who made this *mesa*, these mountains, all that you see here?

P.—Nothing! It is here.

M.—Was it always here?

P.—(With a short laugh)—Yes, certainly, always here. What would make it be away from here?

M.—But where do the dead Moquis go? Where is the child I saw put in the sand yesterday? Where does it go?

P.—Not at all. Nowhere; you saw it put in the sand. How can it go anywhere?

M.—Did you ever hear of Montezuma?

P.—No; Monte—Montzoo—(attempting the word)—Melicano man?

M.—No; one of your people, we think. What are these dances for that you have sometimes?

P.—The grandfathers always had them.

So ended my attempts at Moqui theology. Probably they were too suspicious of a stranger to let me know any thing about it, for an Indian considers his religion *his* even more exclusively than his horse or his wife. But they have one curious custom which seems to have a religious significance. Every morning, at the first break of day, a young man runs the whole length of the *mesa* with several cow-bells tied to his belt; the entire population rise at once, and while the rest proceed to milk their goats, the bell-man and a few others descend to the plain and go a mile or so towards the east. An army officer, who spent some time with them, says they expect a Deliverer to come from that direction, and send an embassy to meet him. Thus the Moquis, like all other races, look for One to usher in the time

> "When useless lances into scythes shall bend,
> And the broad falchion in a plowshare end;
> When wars shall cease, and ancient fraud shall fail;
> Returning Justice lift aloft her scale;
> Peace o'er the world her olive wand extend,
> And white-robed Innocence from heaven descend."

Their traditions say (or in their own phrase "the grandfathers said") that the ruins on the adjacent *mesa* were once the homes of a powerful race of Moquis, and then an immense spring watered all the plain; but an earthquake threw down the pueblo, split the rock, and dried up the spring, and the remnant of that people went far to the South. Telashnimki and Tuba, two Oraybes, husband and wife, once accompanied Jacob Hamlin to Salt Lake City, and were delighted with all they saw. Since their return, a portion of the Oraybes have seceded from the main body, and established a new settlement, to which they invite white men, and propose more friendly relations. The Moquis pointed out Oraybe in the distance; but did not think it safe for me to visit it, as the Apaches are often there. The Mormons are establishing friendly relations with all the tribes of north-western Arizona, and will, it is to be hoped, succeed in peace in their vicinity. One question frequently asked me was, "Are the Mormoneys Americans?" A plain affirmative was near enough to the truth for the views of the Indians; but, in point of fact, the question is open to argument.

The dress of a Moqui man consists of very loose jacket and drawers, made of calico obtained from traders. The first is made close at the neck, and flows loosely to the hips; the second reaches from the waist to a little below the knees. Heavy sandals protect the feet. But this dress is only conventional, and they often appear entirely naked, except the girdle and breech-clout. The women wear a heavy woolen dress, of their own manufacture, consisting of a single skirt and sort of half-waist, which leaves one arm and breast bare. Polygamy prevails to a slight extent. Chino and Misiamtewah each have two wives, but from what little they said on the subject, I conclude they consider it a burden rather than a privilege. The women are rather homely, short and stumpy—I think from carrying loads upon their heads. None of them will compare with the graceful and shapely Navajo girls; nor are they prolific. The town at the south end of the *mesa* is slowly falling to ruins; not half the houses are inhabited, and through the other towns there are many abandoned dwellings, now used for stables and sheep-pens, or for storing hay. The kindly law of nature will not permit increase in a country which can only furnish a bare living. Moqui means "Dead Man," and Moquina may be translated "Little Dead Town." This is the half-abandoned town on the south end of the *mesa*; and I was informed by Jacob Hamlin that some five years before my visit most of the inhabitants there died of small-pox.

The Tegua town, the one we first enter on coming up the cliff, has a language quite distinct from the ordinary Moqui. Those who have examined say the Tegua is the same as that spoken by the Pueblos near the city of Mexico. If true, this is a most important fact, and to my mind goes far to supply the missing link in Baron Humboldt's history of the Aztecs. Governor Arny, of Santa Fe, collected many facts on this subject, but whether they have been published I know not. Among these people are many albinoes, with sickly white skin, red hair and pinky eyes. Many romantic stories have been told as to the origin of these white Indians, the most sensational being that they are descendants of some Scotchmen, carried away by the Spaniards in their war against Queen Elizabeth; that they were sent to work in the mines of Mexico, escaped in a body and joined the Indians.

The un-romantic truth is, they are Indians as much as the others. Their whiteness is simply a disease. If the term be medically correct, I would call it a species of American leprosy. We need not go far to find the causes: a people living in this dry climate, on hard, dry food, in the midst of burning sands, drought, and misery, and shut up in these little isolated communities, where the same families have intermarried in all probability for a dozen generations. The only wonder is that they are not totally extinct, or ring-streaked, speckled, and grizzled. In the "good old time" when the Pueblos were ten times as numerous, intermarriages took place between the various towns, their language was nearly the same, and they were prolific and progressive. Now they constitute but little islands, as it were, in an ocean of Utes, Navajoes, and Apaches; the separated towns have gradually grown apart, and become distinct nations; they have no central priesthood or ecclesiastical connection; their religion and learning steadily decay, and even the tradition of a common origin is fast becoming obscure.

Perhaps a theory as to the origin of the Pueblos may be constructed by a system of comparative ethnology and archæology. Beginning in the Ohio Valley, there is a regular line of ancient works down to the central section of the Andes. The Scioto and Licking valleys are thickly dotted with the works of some race to whom we have given the vague title of Mound-Builders. There is the great circle at Newark, which now incloses the fair-grounds; the square and circular fortification near Chillicothe; the Great Serpent in Adams County, 1,000 feet long; the funereal mound, fort, and intrenched way at Marietta, and hundreds of others in adjacent districts. There is the Pyramid at Seltzertown, Mississippi, six hundred feet long and forty feet high; and two thousand other mounds and fortifications described by Squier and Davis in their work, an authentic document published by the Smithsonian Institution.

But as we go south-west the ruins are larger and nearer their original condition. Had our predecessors built of stone instead of wood, we should doubtless have found such in Ohio. There are the great Casas Grandes on the Gila; the remains of the original or Aztec City of Mexico; the immense pyramids at Xochicalco and Cholula; the City of Tulha, ancient capital of the Toltecs, and a regular line of ancient cities runs down through Central Mexico and into Guatemala, from which, and the inscriptions on them, we learn much of the common life of the Aztecs and their predecessors. Every-where there are *tumuli, acecquias,* and *aguadas,* or artificial ponds. Yucatan is dotted with the ruins of cities, temples, and palaces. The great forests covering a large part of Guatemala and adjacent States, an area the size of Ohio, contains the key to America's ancient history. There is conclusive evidence that it once contained from five to ten million inhabitants. The facts are to be found in the works of Del Rio, who explored part of it in the last century; of Captain Dupaix, who penetrated far enough to get exact measurements of the largest towns; of

Stephens and Catherwood, and of Brasseur de Bourbourg, last and most thorough of explorers. The most important places mentioned are as follows:

Palenque, in the Mexican State of Chiapas, extends for fifteen miles along the river Chacamas; among the ruins are those of fourteen large edifices, handsomely built of hewn stone. "The Palace" has a raised foundation, 40 feet high, 310 long, and 260 wide; on it the building is 288 feet long, 180 wide, and 25 high, with fourteen doorways on each side, and eleven at each end. Copan, in the western part of Honduras, is three miles in length, and contains stone buildings sixty feet high, richly carved with arabesque designs. Quirigua (Keercewah), on the river Motagua, consists of a vast array of broken columns and monoliths, with no building standing. Mitla, in the Mexican State of Oaxaca, was evidently built in splendid style, but only three buildings remain entire. It abounds in carved figures and relievos. In the same region is an astronomical monument; on it the sculptured profile of a man holding to his eye a tube which is directed to the stars.

AZTEC PRIEST AND WARRIORS.

But Peru contains the most striking monuments of the ancient civilization. There once flourished a proud empire extending over twenty degrees of latitude. There was a paved road five hundred miles long, part of it remaining to this day. Beautiful monuments abound, and curious manufactures have lately been unearthed. There are gauzy articles of pure gold, so light that a breath will waft them from one's finger. There are fragments of the *quippus*—a knotted cord with threads of various colors, with which they kept accounts.

The mummies show that trepanning, tooth-drawing, and amputation were practiced. They had timbrels, stringed instruments, drums, flutes and trumpets. Their principal city was supplied with water through lead pipes inlaid with gold, of which one was recovered entire, and now supplies the Convent of Santo Domingo. But the obscurity hanging over their history seems impenetrable. It is proved that this ancient people, both in the Ohio Valley and further south, must have had a tolerably regular government and a good system of agriculture to sustain a dense population; that they were often at war with a more savage people than themselves, and that they left our country at least five hundred—more probably a thousand—years ago.

A score of theories have been projected. This civilization and these ruins have been in turn attributed to the Assyrians, Egyptians, Phœnicians, "Lost Tribes of Israel," Greeks, Romans, Malays, Northmen, and the Tartar expeditions sent out by Kublai Khan; but each theory has in turn been proved untenable. The *Book of Mormon* tells with wearisome details how an Israelite family came to America six hundred years before Christ, gave rise to two nations who alternately built cities and battered them down in war, and finally the white half became extinct and the others turned to Indians; and Orson Pratt has amplified the subject in a number of works which show the plausible absurdities of the astronomer run mad. Hence, in all Mormon literature, the Indians are spoken of as "Lamanites"—whom, for their wickedness, "God cursed with black skins." But the average Gentile mind is not equal to the task of swallowing such a story.

But why should we assume that these people came from the Old World? Is all civilization necessarily exotic? There is nothing in these ruins particularly suggestive of Roman, Greek, or Egyptian architecture. We see in China that a spontaneous civilization arose and ran its peculiar course without any aid from Europe. In Europe we see that civilization began in the south and spread towards the north; that it was overthrown by northern barbarians, again rose in the south and spread to the north. The latest investigators are of opinion that a similar movement took place in America: that civilization originated among the Colhuas in Peru and ancient Mayas in Yucatan; that their successors, the Toltecs, carried it towards the north; that in the latitude of Ohio they met the northern barbarians and were slowly driven south, where civilization revived somewhat, and was again advancing northward when the Spaniards came and destroyed it. In this theory the Toltecs are set down as our Mound-

Builders, and it is concluded that the last of them left the Ohio Valley a thousand years ago. There is a vast mass of evidence confirmatory of this view. And, incidentally it may be remarked, that a Mr. Wiley, of Kinderhook, Illinois, in the year 1843, did discover in an ancient mound six bronze plates, curiously corresponding to the description given by Joe Smith of those from which the Book of Mormon was translated. Many impartial critics have since concluded that, impostor as he was, Smith did obtain from a mound in New York some kind of curious plates. The entire subject has been strangely neglected by American scholars. The finest mound in Marietta was sold by the city to a private citizen, who carted it away to make brick of! In a similar spirit an English merchant in Greece, who needed some marble for the front of his house, tore down a classic pile which had survived the invasions of Thracian, Roman, Goth and Turk for two thousand years. But there is yet in America evidence enough for some determined antiquarian to decide whether the Toltecs were our ancestors in Ohio.

I give this as the latest theory. As for myself, I grew intensely interested in the matter from what I saw in Arizona, and on my return to the States eagerly embraced the first opportunity to investigate. I read Baldwin's "Prehistoric America," and was only half convinced; I consulted Stephens and Catherwood, Squier and Davis, and got facts without conclusions. I then examined all the authorities above quoted, and finally came to the deliberate conclusion that the whole subject is considerably mixed. If the reader don't like this theory, he has my permission to construct one of his own.

CHAPTER XVIII.

FROM MOQUI TO THE COLORADO.

It was still eight hundred miles to the end of the Thirty-fifth Parallel Road. But universal testimony agreed that the desert grew worse all the way, till one should cross the Sierra Nevada and enter settled California. Nor was it possible to go unless one had a large party well armed. It was but three hundred miles to the Mormon settlements, and some four hundred farther to Salt Lake City. That way, then, was my easiest and cheapest route out of the wilderness.

Navajo parties were scattered along the route, and we should doubtless have plenty of company. My guide from Defiance returned there, carrying with him an immense roll of manuscript which I had prepared at odd hours since leaving that post. He left Moqui June 24th; Mr. Keams, agreeably to my written request, sent another Indian on to Wingate with my letters; there they caught the semi-monthly military express to Santa Fe, and thus my communications of June 24th appeared in the *Cincinnati Commercial* f July 13th—a marvel of aboriginal mail service. The last day of my stay at Moqui, came the father and sister of my new guide, the former *en route* to Utah, and the latter merely on a friendly visit to the Moquis. My guide arrived on the 23d, and presented his *nelsoass*, which read as follows:

"*To all whom it may concern :*

"The bearer, a Navajo Indian, with his father, have permission to accompany J. H. Beadle, Esq., to the Mormon settlements. They are good Indians, and I trust any one who meets them will treat them kindly.

THOMAS V. KEAMS,
Clerk Navajo Agency,
June 21, 1872.   Acting Agent."

For convenience sake I christened him John, the universal title for Indians and Chinese.

The loud rattle of the Moqui bellman roused me betimes on the morning of the 25th, and immediately I heard the long resonant cry of Chino on the summit of the highest house, chanting the order of the day's work, according to their custom. In this morning call he also recites any special events expected to occur, and doubtless set forth my intention to depart, for long before the bellman and guard returned from the plain half the population of the *mesa* were around my *domo* waiting to see us off. No "stirrup cup" this time; I divided my tobacco with Chino, and presented him the only linen shirt I had with me, for I had about as much use for it as a Highlander has for a knee-buckle. The Moquis do not use money in any form, that I could see, and the flowered calico I had taken along to pay expenses with was exhausted, as the people had been most kind in furnishing goats' milk and eggs and carrying in blankets full of grass for my horse. Chino presented me in turn with a huge roll of *mescal*, and after a warm embrace—Moqui good-bye—from him and the interpreters, we mounted and were off, the whole population joining in a loud song that died away into a sort of wail as we descended the rock-hewn gallery.

We traveled north-north-west all day, through a somewhat better country than that east of Moqui; good bunch-grass was abundant, and on the ridges were considerable thickets of scrubby pine. In the mountains which border the oval valley about Moqui there are many peach trees; the Moquis dry the fruit, and also pound up the seeds and make a thick paste therefrom. *Mescal*, also one of their luxuries, looks when dried like a mass of soft sole-leather, and tastes much like ripe sugar-cane. It is slightly cathartic, and is a good change from dry bread and bacon.

To our left all day was a considerable ridge, and by expressive pantomime and a few Navajo words John informed me that west of it there was a desert with neither grass nor water, which horses could not cross in a day, but we should go around the north end of it. About 4 P. M., we reached the first pool, and refilled our canteen and wicker-jug, as we must make a "dry camp" to-night. Turning to the left we reached the summit of the ridge in an hour's hard climbing, passed a dense thicket of pines, and came out upon a splendid prospect. The cliff we stand on slopes gently for a hundred yards, then drops suddenly by a rugged precipice, a thousand feet, to a plain which stretches north and west as far as I can see. But to the north a dim, blue range appears, and this side of it a dark depression with overhanging mist, which may be due to the great distance or the presence of water. John indicates that there is a great cliff there, three times as high as the one before us, at the bottom of which there is much water running very fast, and deeper than over my head three times; but it is as far as we could travel from sun-up till the middle of the afternoon, and horses could not get up or down there for many days' travel east and west. This, of course, is the Colorado.

We skirted the precipice before us till we found a crevice and sort of rocky stairway, by which we got down to the plain, and thence traveled nearly straight west till dark, camping on a ridge with abundant grass, but no water. After supper John made a large bonfire to signal the other Navajoes, but we received no answer. We were off by moonlight next morning—John being all impatience to overtake another party, he said was near; and in three hours reached them, but they proved to be part of a band of five families who had moved to a valley there. Here we find the only living spring and running stream on our route. The valley is bounded on the south by an abrupt cliff, not more than six hundred feet high, and on the north by gently sloping hills, rich in grass. This band are the wealthiest Navajoes I have yet seen, the five families having over a thousand sheep and goats, and at least two hundred horses. Men and women have each a good riding horse, rather elegantly caparisoned, with stylish bridles and spurs, and in their camp equipage I notice many handsome vessels and copper kettles. That they are of the aristocracy is further proved by the fact that they did not loaf about our camp, or ask for any thing; but received our advances with civil dignity, and sold us half a gallon of milk for fifty cents, like so many Christians.

Their herds were just coming in to water: their horses galloping down the cliffs, the mounted Indian boys after them on slopes where an American would scarcely venture his horse at a walk, and the sheep and goats filling the vale with their bleatings, presented a scene to delight the heart of a pastoral poet. Two horses excited my particular admiration: a heavy-limbed dark bay mare, and a bright chestnut stallion, light and swift, who galloped around us a few times in provokingly showy style, his sleek coat glistening as if just from the hands of a skillful groom. The pair would have sold for six or seven hundred dollars in the States.

Our horses needed recruiting before taking the desert, and we concluded to stop a day. Buying milk and dried antelope, we had quite a breakfast feast, after which the chief and family came and took a cup of coffee and a smoke with me. He was fluent in signs and Navajo, a born egotist, and as inquisitive as the stage "Yankee." The sign-language proved insufficient for him to tell all he knew; so he went toward the cliff and shouted for *Español*, and soon appeared a bright lad of about twenty, who saluted me in first-rate Spanish, acting thereafter as interpreter. He informed me he was captured in the beginning of the last war, and lived with the Mexicans six years, whence his Indian name, "The Spaniard;" that he had driven teams to Denver, and been on the railroad from there to Cheyenne, and consequently knew all about the Americans and their ways. The chief then struck in: it was three days to the *Mormoney hoganda*, the first one where we would cross the river; his horse could go it in two, but mine could not, for his feet would not stand the stones; his horse was better than my horse, and he could travel better than I; there was sand all the way to Mormoney, no more springs, and only water-holes in the rock. In answer to my questions about the country, he drew a rude map in the sand with a sharp stick, and pointed out that it was nearly a day north for my horse to the big water, and two days south to the little water; that four days west they came together so (joining his fingers in the form of a V), and that three days north-west of that place was a great *Mormoney casa*, and that they were people like me, with plenty to eat and many horses.

This was the last Navajo settlement I visited, though they range down to the junction of the two Coloradoes; and in the evening they made our camp merry with their lively conversation. Those who see the Indian only on the border know nothing of his real character; for it is only the lowest and meanest of the race that hang about the white settlements. And their consciousness of oddity in appearance makes them feel and look meaner. These belonged to a portion of the tribe numbering a thousand or more who do not agree to the treaty, or recognize the Agency party. They are quite friendly with the whites, but have made one raid into Utah since the peace; and at John D. Lee's I learned that the chestnut stallion, which so excited my admiration, had been stolen from him. Two hundred years of war with the Spaniards was surely enough to confuse a people's moral perceptions, and cause them to consider "levying tribute" on the whites as a perfectly legitimate operation.

As we gather up in the evening ready to start early, I find my Navajo whip and knife sheath—among the curiosities I had purchased—missing. I had not supposed that John knew any English, but when I pointed out the loss, his face grew dark and he muttered: "Damn Navajo, shteal mooch," and darted for a boy some fifty yards away, whom he dragged into camp. A violent discussion ensued till the boy, with John's grip tightening on him, pointed to the cliff and muttered "Español." "Damn Español, shteal," said the guide, and ran up the cliff, where I heard another violent altercation, Navajo words mingling amusingly with English and Spanish oaths, and in a few minutes John returned waving the whip and sheath in triumph.

The Navajoes will steal, but if you hire one he will guard your property against all the rest, in which respect they are better than any other Indians. As I made ready for early sleep, Español and other lads came down on a visit, and sat about the fire smoking our tobacco and talking as socially with John as if nothing unusual had happened.

All day, June 27th, we traveled in a succession of zigzags. Two miles down the valley we found it narrowed to a rugged cañon; a little farther the cañon became a fearful gorge, into which sunlight never penetrated. The stream disappeared but a few rods below the spring, but a scant growth of sickly cottonwoods showed there was still a moist stratum below. At length we came to a rift in the side wall, about a rod wide, into which John led the way; there we entered on a steep and dangerous trail, up which we toiled some hundreds of feet to a level sandstone *mesa*. Across this a few miles, and then John, ahead of me, suddenly disappeared, and I hurried up to find him going down another narrow gorge, a mere rift in the rock not twenty-five feet wide. Down this a mile brought us out on a sandy plain; across this some five miles, and we came to a perpendicular cliff at least a thousand feet high. Skirting this westward, a few miles brought us to another gorge, by which we again reached the summit of the *mesa*, and before noon found a depression in the rock which had been filled by a late rain, and around it enough bunch-grass for a noon halt. There we were overtaken by a Navajo lad of about fifteen years, who had reached Moqui the day after we left, and followed our trail. He had several fine blankets, woven by his mother, and expected to trade them for a horse at the *Mormoney casa*. We made a "dry camp" for dinner, took an hour's grazing, and were just off when up galloped Español, also with a few blankets. He had concluded, an hour after we left, to go to the settlements; because, as I suspect, he had noted the size of my provision sacks. We were now four in number, and traveled the rest of the day on a sandstone ridge tending west-north-west. Far as I could see, the country appeared to slope from this ridge northward and southward towards the two Coloradoes.

About 5 P. M., we reached a regular water hole, to find it dry—to the dismay of the Navajoes. After a brief consultation, Español informed me they would hurry on down the slope south-west, and find water on the other side of the next valley; and that I might follow their tracks, *poco-poco-poco*, (moderate walk). They galloped off, and were soon out of sight. I followed, and in an hour had lost their trail on a sandstone flat. Still I maintained the course toward a bright, green valley, which now appeared in the distance. I reached and crossed it, to find that the green was not from grass, as I had supposed, but from thrifty greasewood. There was not a spear of grass nor a drop of water, though the shade of green on the brush showed there was moisture below; and not a horse-track or a Navajo in sight. I began to feel very uncomfortable. The prospect of being lost in that place was decidedly unpleasant. I fired my gun two or three times, and shouted with all my might, but no response. Determined finally to ascend the ridge west and overlook as much country as possible, I struck up a sloping hollow, and in half a mile came upon the three Navajoes sitting round a deep pool of water and grinning in concert. The aborigines had witnessed all my embarrassment, and attempts to trace them below; but, true to the "noble instincts" of the race, preferred to sit and smile at me working out my own salvation.

The horses could not get down in the water hole, so they had taken a blanket full of sand and made a dam across a little depression in the rock; this we rapidly filled with our wicker-jugs, and so enabled our horses to drink. At 6 o'clock we were off again, and at 8 made a "dry camp." I soon went to sleep, but woke in an hour or so to find that the Navajoes had built an immense bonfire on a hill near by. This was soon answered by another, apparently twenty miles to the south. Our party then took torches of pine limbs and waving them as they went, built three more fires in a line a little north of west. The other party responded with three fires in a line apparently due west. Español translated this to mean that a considerable party of Navajoes were half a day's ride south of us; that they would go straight on west, crossing the Little Colorado, and we should not meet them.

Again we were off by moonlight, an hour ahead of the sun, and at 10 A. M. reached the promised water-hole; but it contained only a little mud. Hastily consulting together, the Indians rubbed their fingers in the moist sand and held them up in the air. From this experiment they decided that the late rain had not extended to this region; that this pool had been exhausted but a day or two, and therefore water would be plenty in a hole some fifteen miles north, which always held out a week longer than this. Español told me to follow *poco-poco* as before; that as his horse was fresh, he would hurry on to the pool, and come back with two jugs full to meet me. I was soon alone, and had a weary ride of some twelve miles over a hot sand plain; then met Español with water enough for me and a hatful for my horse. They had decided to dine at this pool, which we found a few miles further on.

In these wastes it is only in a few holes, worn by ancient bowlders, or in the more rare limestone "pockets," that one can find water; and one unacquainted with the country might go within a rod of such a pool and never find it. The boys had only a few pounds of dried antelope and parched corn; but all we had was in common, and we rested and feasted an hour. Thence we bore due west to come upon our former trail, and soon descended into a rich bunch-grass pasture at least ten miles wide. Far southward a mountain peak, its summit dazzling white with snow, rose in the form of a sharp cone; and Español informed me that from the foot of that peak, there was much timber and game to the Little Colorado; also, that when the first snow fell on the lower hills, the antelope and other animals came across into this grassy country by thousands; then the Navajoes went on their fall hunt, and used to meet the Apaches here long ago, and had many fights. But now the Apaches have given up this section. We soon came to where skulls were quite numerous, sometimes with other fragments of human bones. My companions called attention to the difference between those of the two tribes; and when we came upon five skulls in one place, two Navajo and three Apaches, Español said with a grin: "*Todos muertos, pero mas Apaches*" (All killed, but the most Apaches). In the dry climate, on that sandy soil, the skulls may have lain there fifty years.

We passed this and another sandstone ridge, on the west side of which we found a little depression with some five acres of good grass, and made a "dry camp." The dark cavity and blue mist over the Colorado had been visible all the afternoon, and John decided that we should descend the first cliff and go to the nearest spring before breakfast. We were off next morning by daylight, in a sweeping trot, and in an hour I heard from Español, in the lead, the glad cry of "*El monte! Grande agua!*" and hurried up to the cliff; but at the first view recoiled. Before us was an abrupt descent of some 3,000 feet; then a plain some three miles wide, led to an abrupt and narrow gorge, 2,000 feet deep, at the bottom of which rolled, in forbidding whirlpools and rapids, the red and yellow waters of the Colorado. Notwithstanding the great distance, so far did it lie below me that in some of the turns I could see the whole width of the stream. On the opposite side was a similar succession of cliffs, red and yellow sandstone, and seeming even more rugged. How on earth were we ever to get down; or, once down, get out again? John smiled at my look of dismay, and indicated our route down a narrow gulch, breaking into the cliff near us, which it seemed to me certain destruction to enter.

Off horses, girths tightened, and packs carefully examined; then walking behind the animals, with lariats attached to the bridle and trailed over their backs, we ventured on the descent; John in front shouting directions, the boy next repeating them, and Español third translating them to the writer, who cautiously brought up, or rather brought *down*, the rear. I had made up my mind to this at first glance; for if either horse should conclude to go with a *ricochet*, sweeping all below him, I thought two or three Indians could be better spared than one white man.

DOWN THE CLIFF.

The narrow path wound this way and that, to every point of the compass, reducing the main incline of seventy degrees or more to a series with a slope of forty-five or less; at times away into the hill, and again on the outward turn, around the projecting peaks. The danger is less than it seems; as if one fell, he would be caught by the next offset, but a few feet below. Sometimes we found a square offset in the path of two feet or so, when the horses would carefully drop the fore feet, having abundant room to catch, and bring the hind feet down with the caution of an acrobat. Two hours brought us to the plain, when we heard a shout that seemed in mid air above our heads, and, looking up, saw three more Navajoes on the descent. They looked like some species of animal clinging to the cliff.

We reached the promised spring and found no water. The Navajoes insisted there was some in the gulch, so we hunted along it toward the mountain till we found a little moist sand and green, watery grass; there we fell to with our tin-cups and butcher-knives and dug several holes, which soon filled. The water was cool, but tasted like a mild infusion of Epsom salts. It made coffee, but all the sugar it would dissolve did not sweeten it perceptibly. Along the cliff, in a northeast direction, every mile or so a section of the lower cliff seemed to leave it and bend back to join the upper one, and down these "benches" we slowly worked our way. When no more than a thousand feet above the stream we came upon an abrupt ridge, at least two thousand feet high, putting out to the river and completely shutting off the trail in that direction. Over this we must go. But first we climbed to a little cave at the foot of the perpendicular cliff, in which we found a "pocket" of cool, clear water. The path turned south-east, and, walking in front of our horses, we again commenced climbing. It was the worst job we had, and defies description. The Navajoes were an hour ahead of me when I reached the summit; but there was only one trail, and that a plain one. The opposite side of this ridge broke into a dozen pointed spurs. Out one, down a slight slope and into

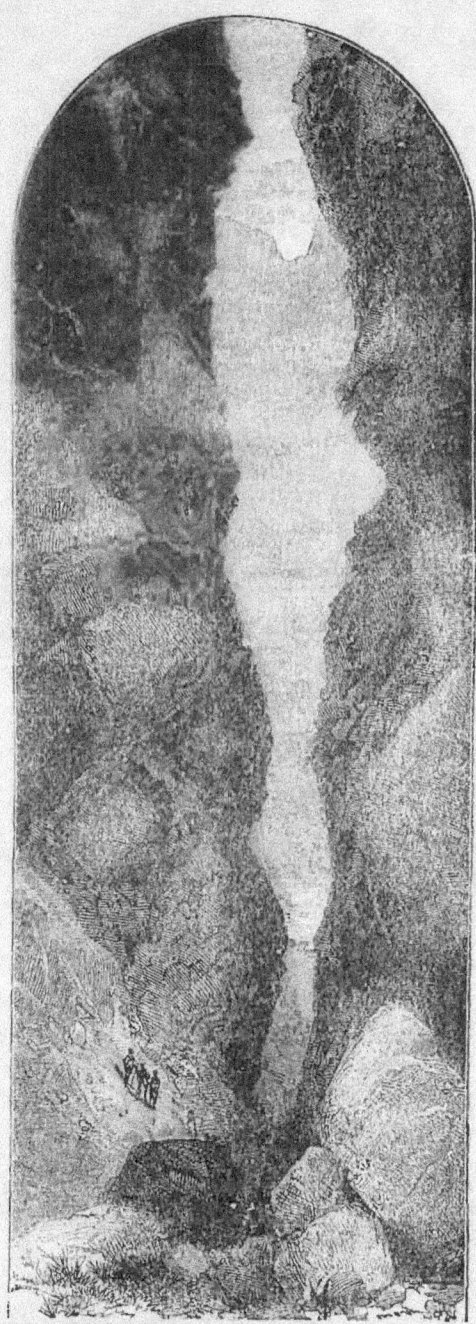

"CLIMBED TO A LITTLE CAVE IN WHICH WE FOUND WATER."

a groove in the rock, I found the trail leading along back into the hollow; then out another ridge and back into the second hollow; then back again around all the windings of the two hollows, and I found myself on the sharp end of the first ridge again, but in a groove five hundred feet below the one where I had left it. Around this peak I followed to the south-west, then back and forward till I was dizzy, and more times than I could count. I came out at length upon a gentle slope, which brought me down to the plain at a point where the river was running nearly straight north. It was 3 P. M., and when I looked back upon the brow of the mountain, which we left at sunrise, it seemed but a mile or two away. But it was at least 5,000 feet above us.

We shouted and fired guns, but in vain. We saw the house on the opposite side, and people moving about, but they failed to take notice of us. John's father and two other Navajoes soon arrived, having killed a young antelope on the way. The meat at this season was very tough and hard, but if we were to stay here long, it must serve as our substitute for bread. We were nearly out of provisions; the sand flat contained nothing for our horses, and we must cross soon. So early next morning we commenced hunting for drift-timber, the boys climbing over the sharp ridge which rose a hundred feet high, just below us. A shout of surprise brought me to that side, and I saw the boys had discovered a boat *cached* against a rock and covered with brush, leaving only the bow visible. They rigged an arrangement to let me down with lariats, where they had climbed, and we all went to work on the boat. In three hours we had it out of the sand and brush and into the river; then the Navajoes were clamorous for me to make an immediate trial of crossing. But we found no oars. The boat was eighteen feet long, with places for four rowers; it had two compartments, and on the stern was the name "Emma Dean." I concluded, correctly, as it proved, that it was one of Major Powell's. But all our search brought to light no oars. They were *cached* so effectually that even Navajoes could not find them. I explained to the boys that only a mile or two below there was a cataract, and, to attempt the passage, we must haul the boat up stream at least a mile. I judged they would never get the boat around the first point, as the rocky headland overhung the river at a height of sixty feet or more, under which the bend threw the full force of the current in dangerous whirls.

But they fell to work at once, and, by a most ingenious arrangement of lariats, brought the boat around. Meanwhile the two old men with their butcher-knives had hacked out rude oars from driftwood, and all were clamorous for me to cross at once. They could not understand why a Melicano, who professed to understand rowing, should hesitate. But I did not like to risk it. The very aspect of the place frightened me: the lofty walls inclosing a cañon six or seven thousand feet deep; the rocky face, red and scarred as if blasted by angry lightnings; the bare sand-plain, and the swift river roaring against projecting rocks, all looked very different from the placid Wabash and Ohio, where I learned rowing. A mile above, the upper and lower cliff appeared to run together, with an offset of but a rod or two, and there the sheer descent from the plateau to the river was at least six thousand feet—almost perpendicular. I fixed my eye on pieces of drift-wood to measure the current; it was a little more than twenty minutes from the time they came in sight above till they entered the rapids below. How could I hope to paddle across in less than twenty minutes?

It was 1 P. M., and we had the boat at our camp and two rude oars. I took my coffee and sardines, chewed *mescal* reflectively for half an hour, and then proposed to the boys that we make our blankets into horse-collars and lariats into gears, and haul the boat across the point. The bend above, I had noticed, would throw it off shore, and with the aid of an eddy put us half way across. They objected decidedly: the horses would kick each other, and forty other evils to their property would result. Ignorant as they were of that element, they much preferred taking it by water. Their own lives and limbs they were ready to risk; but, said Español, their horses were their wealth—did I ask them to go home poor? They had evidently adopted the sound philosophy that life without some property is not worth caring for. So to the river we betook ourselves, though to me the case looked hopeless. The bank was so steep that it could only be descended once in two or three hundred feet, and overgrown thickly nearly all the way with willows and thorny bushes, often twenty feet out into the water. The rope could not be dragged over these; it had to be passed outside of them, taking advantage of a bare point to haul in, rest and make a fresh start. The four young fellows stripped and took to the water. I, in the same condition, sat astride the bow and shoved off shore. They would drag the boat to a convenient point, then take the rope in their mouths and pass themselves around the willows, holding by their hands with bodies in the water. A most ridiculous sight it would have been to one free from our solicitude: the naked barbarians plunging and scrambling in the river, the naked white man, almost barbarous for the occasion, sitting astride the bow shouting in wretched Spanish and mixed Navajo, and sometimes plunging into the shore-mud or swift stream, where a little swimming had to be done. We would toil until steaming with sweat, and then into the river, which felt like ice-water. Nobody ever "catches cold" in this country, or I should have expected a musical case of asthma and catarrh as a result. In the middle of our work a woman came to the opposite bank, but the wind had risen to such a blast that we could not converse, and I could barely make out the words, "old man, to-morrow."

At night the wind fell; the woman reappeared, and shouted that in three days the "old man" would return; if we had provisions it would be safest to wait. Next morning our horses presented fine subjects for the study of anatomy. We must risk it; so, taking John and Español, I shoved off, and, taking advantage of an eddy, reached the opposite side only a mile below. Making our way to the house, I was greeted by the woman with:

"My God, stranger, did you risk your life to swim that river?"

An explanation and request for provisions resulted in the statement: "We are pretty thin ourselves." If we had put up a white signal Saturday, "the old gent would have come down at once, but he thought it was only Injins. Had gone Sunday with his other woman to the ranche near Kanab. These were the other woman's four children here; had five of her own, making a right smart family of nine, 'thout the old gent, but none of 'em big enough to risk the boat; had no meat, and only ten pounds o' flour, but plenty of milk, butter, cheese and eggs—would they do?" I rather thought they would, and requested that about five pounds of each might be served up at once. She got me a splendid breakfast, and gave the Indians a plentiful supply, lending them also a kettle. She gave me the oars with which we could cross at will; but to cross the horses we must wait till "Major Doyle," as she named the "old man," came back.

Two days passed, and our horses were hungry enough to chew sand-burrs and desert weed. The days I spent at the cabin, talking to the Mormon woman; the nights on the other side, sleeping or listening to the old man's stories about his people. They were all of a piece: the Navajoes had been very rich—they were now poor; they were great warriors and good Indians. But the Utes were dogs, and the Apaches wolves and snakes, and the Zunis ground-hogs, and the Melicanoes never would have whipped the Navajoes if they had not got other Indians to help them. In short, his harangue sounded so much like an ordinary Mormon sermon—all self-glorification and disparagement of every body else—that I got tired and dropped to sleep just as he was telling how great a warrior his father was, and how many horses he once took from the *Noch kyh* (Mexican towns).

As Español rendered all this into voluminous Spanish, with many cross-questionings on my part and repetitions on his, to make sure I had the correct meaning, the conversation would have had its charms to the comparative philologist. Sitting in the summer night by our camp-fire on the great river, named by the Spaniard three centuries ago, its current roaring against the rocks below us, part of the romance of the sixteenth century seemed to return—that romance made real by the lingual contest between the Navajo and Spanish languages. It is scarcely possible there should be a greater contrast between any two tongues spoken by man—the one the oldest of living languages, and first heir to the Latin, no one knows how much older; soft, smooth, flowing, musical and rich in expressive inflections; the result of three thousand years of Roman, Moorish and Gothic cultivation; with the wonderful and stately march of the Latin sentence, the soft lisp of the Moor and sonorous gravity of the Goth: the other, youngest born in the family of languages, with roots striking only in the shallow soil of hard and primitive dialects, probably not a thousand years old as a separate tongue; without cultivation, without letters, with no abstract expressions, and names only for the material and tangible, a harsh alliance of the nasal and guttural, the speech of barbarous mountaineers. Yet here they are found on the same soil, struggling for the mastery—the Spanish an enduring monument to the energy and bravery of the Castilians of the sixteenth century, who overran and subdued more than half of the New World. Every time a Navajo says *agua* instead of *toh* he bears unwitting and involuntary tribute to the hardy vigor and bold intellect of that wonderful race, who carried their arms and arts through these remote regions.

On the other side we talked at random, without need of an interpreter. Mrs. Doyle, as the lady called herself, was a thorough frontier woman, and informed me that "Our old gent had had eighteen wives. Two left him, one went to the States, and another to Montana, and when McKean got up such a bobbery he (Doyle) divided his property among them that were living. Old gent had had fifty-two children, most of 'em living; had been through New Mexico, and all that country, with the Mormon battalion, and had been a big man in the Church, but was now here on a mission, tending to this ferry. The Mormons will establish a fine ferry here and a good road, as they intend to settle all the good country on the other side, and are now settling into Arizona as fast as they can. Will settle Potato Valley first, then down in the White and San Francisco Mountains," etc.

Her own history was both sad and interesting. She was born in Brighton, England, and reared in London. Her folks were well-to-do English, and signs of early education and refinement showed plainly through the rough coating of a frontier and Mormon life. She had embraced Mormonism at the age of twenty, and come at once to Utah (sixteen years before) in the first hand-cart company. They got through with little suffering. It was the company after that suffered so. She "had gone in second to Major Doyle," by express request of Brigham Young. They had pioneered all the new towns south. Had a fine place in Harmony, and sold it for $4,000, when ordered here on a mission. She was living here, a hundred miles from the nearest settlement, in the extreme of hardship, and her folks begging her to come to them. And now, at the end of all these sacrifices, a growing skepticism was evident in her talk. It was plain that she doubted seriously whether all this had not been vain—worse than useless. She firmly believed in polygamy, she said, when she came a girl from England, but not now; there was so much evil in it that it could not be from God.

Four days had passed, and still no "old gent." The Indians lost heart, and John came to request a *nelsoass*—my certificate that he had seen me safe across the Colorado. I furnished them all the bread and cheese Mrs. Doyle could spare, and at noon they started to return. I watched them for hours, as they slowly climbed the red cliffs, and with a feeling near akin to sorrow, for the simple aborigines had been more company to me than I could have believed possible. It was my last sight of the Navajoes—a most interesting race of barbarians, and the only Indians for whom I could ever feel any personal friendship. In three hours after their departure "Major Doyle" returned, and we crossed my horse without difficulty. The method pursued is for one to row the skiff, while another holds up the horse's head by the bridle, the animal swimming just behind the boat.

CHAPTER XIX.

A STARTLING INTERVIEW.

THE hot July day drew to a close, and my host and I sat before his log-cabin and gazed upon the red hills, which took on a pleasing softness in the light of the declining sun. The view was one for the poet, the painter, and the novelist. The lofty mountains which wall in the Colorado, here gave back a few rods from the water's edge. From the mountain summits, forty miles northward, Pahreah Creek plunged down by a series of wild cascades into a deep gorge, which, meandering across the plateau, grew into a rugged cañon, and here, at its junction with the Colorado, widened its granite jaws to inclose a small plat of level land. On all sides rose the red and yellow hills, by successive "benches," to a plateau five thousand feet above; on

MOUTH OF PAHREAH CREEK, NEAR JOHN D. LEE'S.

that again red buttes rose thousands of feet higher, their wind-worn and polished summits ever inaccessible to man, and barely brushed by the bald eagle in his loftiest flights.

To this little glen, the only cultivable land to be found for hundreds of miles along the Colorado, there were three entrances: by a hidden and rocky trail up Pahreah Cañon, leading over the summit and down the Sevier River; by the way we came in, and by a narrow track leading up to the Kanab Plateau, and thence south-west around the point of the mountain. A quick eye could command every approach; a quick hand could deal destruction upon all comers if so disposed, or a fugitive in a few minutes reach concealed places where a regiment of soldiers could not find him. It seemed a place by nature fitted for the retreat of the hunted—for an "old man of the mountains" who had nothing to expect from the world but its hostility. And such, in solemn truth, it was.

A surprise of no ordinary kind was in store for me. I had grown well acquainted with "Major Doyle," as his wife called him, and in two days' intercourse we had learned considerable of each other's views and experiences. Like many Mormons with whom I have stopped he had "a word of prayer" after supper; asked fervently for God's blessing on "Thy Servant Brigham," and that "Thou would'st turn away the hearts of the Lamanites from making war on thy people," besides referring warmly to "our making the desert blossom as the rose;" and not long after in conversation referred to the Government's dealings with the Indians as a "d—d shame, that hadn't ought to be allowed." But this sort of incongruity is so common in Utah that I did not notice it. At supper, on the third of July, he grew very animated while telling of some horses he had lost, and how they were recovered from the thieves; and used this sentence: "The sheriff said, 'These are Lee's horses—I know 'em.'" "Lee's!" said I, "Does he live near here?"—for they had told me at Defiance that I ought to go by Lee's Ferry. My host hesitated. I fancied there was a faint flush on his weather-beaten face, as he replied:

"That's what they sometimes call me."

"What!" exclaimed I; "I thought your name was Doyle."

"So it is—John Doyle Lee." I almost jumped out of my chair with astonishment and confusion. Here I was the guest of, and in familiar conversation with, this most notorious of all notorious Mormons—the reputed planner and leader in the Mountain Meadow Massacre! My confusion was too great to be concealed, and I blundered out: "I have often heard of you."

"And heard nothing that was good, I reckon." This, with some bitterness of tone. He then continued, speaking rapidly:

"Yes, I told my wives to call me Doyle to strangers; they've been kicking up such a muss about polygamy, McKean and them, and I'm a man that's had eighteen wives; but now that the Supreme Court has decided that polygamy's part of a man's religion, and the law's got nothin' to do with it; it don't make no difference, I reckon."

Of course this was only a subterfuge, but I could not have ventured to recur to the real reason of his being located in this wild place, if he had not approached the subject himself soon after. Then I hinted as delicately as possible, that if it were not disagreeable to him, I should like to hear "the true account of that affair which had been the cause of his name being so prominent." It had grown dark meanwhile, and this gave him, I thought, more freedom in his talk. (It is to be noted that he did not know my name or business.) Clearing his throat nervously, he began, with many short stops and repetitions:

"Well, I suppose you mean that—well, that Mountain Meadow affair? Well, I'll tell you what is the exact truth of it, as God is my Judge, and the why I am out here like an outlaw—but I'm a goin' to die like a man, and not be choked like a dog—and why my name's published all over as the vilest man in Utah, on account of what others did—but I never will betray my brethren, no, never—which it is told for a sworn fact that I violated two girls as they were kneeling and begging to me for life; but, as God is my Judge, and I expect to stand before Him, it is all an infernal lie."

He ran off this and much more of the sort with great volubility; then seemed to grow more calm, and went on:

"Now, sir, I'll give you the account exactly as it stood, though for years I've rested under the most infamous charges ever cooked up on a man. I've had to move from point to point, and lost my property, when I might have cleared it up any time by just saying who was who. I could have proved that I was not in it, but not without bringing in other men to criminate them. But I wouldn't do it. They had trusted in me, and their motives were good at the start, bad as the thing turned out.

"But about the emigrants. They was the worst set that ever crossed the plains, and they made it so as to get here just when we was at war. Old Buchanan had sent his army to destroy us, and we had made up our minds that they should not find any spoil. We had been making preparations for two years, drying wheat and *caching* it in the mountains; and intended, when worst come to worst, to burn and

HEAD OF THE GRAND CAÑON.

destroy every thing, and take to the mountains and fight it out guerrilla style. And I tell you this people was all hot and enthusiastic, and just at that time these emigrants came.

"Now they acted more like devils than men; and just to give you an idea what a hard set they was: when Dr. Forney gathered up the children two years after—fifteen, I believe, they was—and sent word back to their relatives, they sent word that they did n't want 'em, and would n't have any thing to do with 'em. And that old Dr. Forney treated the children like dogs, hammerin' 'em around with his big cane.

"The company had quarreled and separated east of the mountains, but it was the biggest half that come first. They come south of Salt Lake City just as all the men was going out to the war, and lots of women and children lonely. Their conduct was scandalous. They swore and boasted openly that they helped shoot the guts out of Joe Smith and Hyrum Smith, at Carthage, and that Buchanan's whole army was coming right behind them, and would kill every G—d d—n Mormon in Utah, and make the women and children slaves, and . . . . . They had two bulls, which they called one 'Heber' and the other 'Brigham,' and whipped 'em thro' every town, yelling and singing, blackguarding and blaspheming oaths that would have made your hair stand on end. At Spanish Fork—it can be proved—one of 'em stood on his wagon-tongue, and swung a pistol, and swore that he helped kill old Joe Smith, and was ready for old Brigham Young, and all sung a blackguard song, 'Oh, we've got the ropes and we'll hang old Brigham before the snow flies,' and all such stuff. Well, it was mighty hard to bear, and when they got to where the Pahvant Indians was, they shot one of them dead and crippled another. But the worst is coming.

"At Corn Creek, just this side of Fillmore, they poisoned a spring and the flesh of an ox that died there, and gave that to the Indians, and some Indians died. Then the widow Tomlinson, just this side, had an ox poisoned at the spring, and she thought to save the hide and tallow; and rendering it up, the poison got in her face, and swelled it up, and she died. This roused every body. Well, they came on down the road, and with their big Missouri whips would snap off the heads of chickens and throw 'em into their wagons; and when a widow, Missis Evans, came out and said: 'Do n't kill my chickens, gentlemen, I'm a poor woman,' one of 'em yelled, 'Shut up you G—d d—d Mormon, or I'll shoot you!' Then her sons and all her folks got out with guns, and swore they'd have revenge on the whole outfit.

"By this time the Indians had gathered from all directions, and overtook 'em at Mountain Meadow. They planned it to crawl down a narrow ravine and get in close, and make a rush altogether. But one fool Indian fired too soon and gave the alarm. This spoilt the plan, but all in reach fired, and killed, well, five or six men. Then a sort o' siege began. The men inside did well—the best they could have done. They got the wagons *corraled* and dug rifle-pits. The Indians could not hit any more of the people, but shot nearly all their oxen and some horses. I believe it was after three or four days' siege that I went to the Indians and tried to persuade them away; for our folks had had a council, and while I said, 'Persuade the Indians away, the other brethren said, 'Let the Indians punish them.' I said to the Indians ' You've killed more of them than died of your men, and you've harassed them a good deal, killed their stock, and punished them enough—now let them go.' But they said these white men were all bad, and they would kill all. Jacob Hamlin, the agent, you know, was away from home then, and I had n't much control over the Indians. We was weak then in that section to what we are now, and did not really have the upper hand of the Indians; and maybe, if we interfered with 'em, it would cause trouble with us. I heard women inside begging and praying, and saying that if the Mormons knew how they were situated they would come and help, no matter if some had treated 'em badly. And they begged some of the fellows to break out and go and get help. Then I run a big risk to get inside the *corral*. It was pitch dark, and I could see the line of fire from the guns, and the balls whistled all about me. One cut my shirt in front, and another my sleeve, and I could not get through. But I went back, and was pretty near getting the Indians all right, and would have succeeded fully, but then come the thing that spoiled all.

"Three of the emigrants had broken out of the *corral* and gone back for help; and next day met some of our boys at a spring. Well, I don't excuse our men—they were enthusiastic, you know, but their motives were good. They knew these emigrants at once; one of them was the man that insulted widow Evans, another the one that swung his pistol and talked so at Spanish Fork. The boys fell on them at sight, shot one dead and wounded another. But the two of them got back to the company.

"Then came another council, and all our men said: 'We can't let 'em go now; the boys has killed some, and it won't do to let one get through alive, or here they'll come back on us with big reinforcements.' And, to be sure, why should we risk any thing, and maybe have a fuss with the Indians, to save people who done nothing but abuse us? But I still said, 'Let 'em go; they've been punished enough.'

"I never will mention any names, or betray my brethren. Those men were God-fearing men. Their motives were pure. They knelt down and prayed to be guided in council. But they was full of zeal. Their zeal was greater than their knowledge.

"I went once more to the Indians, and begged them to kill only the men. They said they would kill every one; then I told them I would buy all the children, so all the children was saved. There was not over fifteen white men actually went in with the Indians, and I don't believe a single emigrant was actually killed by a white man.

"An express had been sent to Brigham Young at first to know what to do, and it is a pity it didn't get back; for those enthusiastic men *will* obey counsel. The president sent back orders, and told the man to ride night and day, by all means to let the emigrants go on; to call off the Indians, and for no Mormons to molest them. But the thing was all over before the express got back to Provo. There was about eighty fighting men that was killed. I don't know how many women, though not many. All the children was saved. The little boy that lived with us cried all night when he left us, and said he'd come back to us as soon as he got old enough. Old Forney, when he come for 'em, got all in his tent and would not let 'em visit or say good-bye to any body. One run away and hid under the floor of the house, and Forney dragged him out and beat him like a dog with his cane. They say he murdered the baby on the plains, because it was sickly and troublesome.

"It is told around for a fact that I could tell great confessions, and bring in Brigham Young and the Heads of the Church. But if I was to make forty confessions, I could not bring in Brigham Young. His counsel was: 'Spare them, by all means.' But I am made to bear the blame. Here I am, old, poor, and lonely, away down in this place— carrying the sins of my brethren. But if I endure, great is my reward. Bad as that thing was, I will not be the means of bringing troubles on my people; for, you know yourself, that this people is a misrepresented and cried-down community. Yes, a people scattered and peeled, whose blood was shed in great streams in Missouri, only for worshiping God as he was revealed to them; and if at the last they did rise up and shed blood of their enemies, I won't consent to give 'em up."

Such was the remarkable story told me by Major John Doyle Lee. I will not now anticipate my story by pointing out its truth and errors; for in later chapters I give the facts, and have here set down but a small part of our conversation—only such as I could remember beyond doubt, and jot down at my first halting-place next day. Lee talked over the whole history of his life, before and since the massacre. After that event he continued to reside in Harmony, was a leader in all public affairs there, and often entertained Brigham Young when the latter visited that section. Thence he was ordered "on a mission" to establish new settlements further into the wilderness; and obeyed, as do all good Mormons, without a murmur, selling his fine place in Harmony for four thousand bushels of wheat. From Cedar City to Santa Clara, and thence to Kanab and Mangrum's settlement, he had continued to remove, and was finally sent down here to maintain a ferry and act as interpreter and mediator among the Indians. He spoke the tongues of all adjacent tribes, and had their good will. He dwelt at some length on his liking for the boy whom he had saved from the massacre and taken to live with him; and related with pride the boy's promise to come back as soon as he got old enough. Unfortunately for his own good, that boy, now a man, did return. He became a noted desperado, under the name of Idaho Bill, and is now serving out a long sentence in the Utah penitentiary!

Misfortune followed the poor children to the last. Mormon accounts say that eighteen were saved alive. Of these Jacob Hamlin says that one was captured by, or went off with, the Navajo Indians, and may now be among them; another was killed "because he knew too much," and the youngest, a mere baby, died on the way to the States, after being recovered by Dr. Jacob Forney, Indian Agent in 1859. Of the fifteen who reached St. Louis few could find any relatives, and the remainder were sent to the Orphan Asylum, and in time scattered thence all over the South-west, knowing of their families only by hearsay or vague remembrance. John Calvin Sorrow, the only one who remembered the massacre, lives somewhere in Arkansas; the girl who was supposed to be his sister, is married to a resident of East Tennessee. With no family ties and no parental care, it is not surprising that some of the survivors have done badly.

Midnight had come before we finished our talk, and turned in together upon a straw tick beside the house. Little did I think that three years from that time I was to see Lee a prisoner before the Federal courts; for, like all old residents of Utah, I had long abandoned hope that the Government could be spurred into doing any thing to execute justice in that Territory. Even then I had no doubt of his guilt, though I could, and can now, see extenuating circumstances. John D. Lee was a born fanatic. Of good size and physical frame, with light hair, fiery blue eye, gross composition and warm red blood, he was also a sensualist. His high but narrow forehead, his education—first as an intense sectarian, accustomed to destroy the spirit of Scripture by twisting the letter; then as a Mormon—made him a thorough casuist; so thorough that he deceived himself first of all. The man who deliberately refuses to look at the doubtful points in his religion, from that hour ceases to be intellectually honest. Thence, by successive steps, he often convinces himself that any thing is right which helps his church, and compounds for gross indulgence in one direction by religious zeal in another. Mormonism aggravated all of Lee's faults; it gave free rein to his all-engrossing lust, and spurred his savage temper on to deeds of blood. In Ohio he would have been a sour Puritan, compounding for little tricks in trade or big fits of passion, by austerity in religion and extreme decorum. In Utah he became what I have described. As said by a Mormon elder, later an apostate, who had known him long and well: "John D. Lee is a man who would divide his last biscuit with the traveler upon the desert, and cut that traveler's throat the next hour if Brigham Young said so."

Independence Day, 1872, I celebrated by a ride of thirty-five miles. Bidding the Lees good-bye at an early hour, I slowly ascended the winding trail which leads to the great plateau between the Colorado and the Wasatch. Here this plateau runs to a narrow point, there being but little more than room for a wagon between the cliff on one side and the river gorge on the other. Here, at the head of the long cañon, the Powell party had their rendezvous; they were now in Kanab for a midsummer's rest, but their boats were moored here. From the bridle path I looked straight down the river, which appeared to soon loose itself between red battlements. On both sides rose the water-worn walls, for two thousand feet nearly perpendicular, the lines on every foot of their faces showing the successive points at which the water had stood during all the countless thousands of years in which it slowly fashioned this passage for itself. When it ran in a shallow channel along the present summit, all the Colorado Basin was a region of lakes and marshes, with here and there an island of firm earth, covered by dense forests, and rich in matted grasses and flowers. Then the mist from this inland sea washed the western base of Pike's Peak, and the Colorado descended by a series of cascades, through a fall of four thousand feet, into the head of the Gulf of California.

A little later, and it had cut so deep as to drain the shallower lakes and marshes; then all the interior between the Wasatch and Rocky Mountains was covered by dense forests, lively with game. A little later, and the regions became the abode of strange semi-civilized races. Their remains are found over an area of three hundred thousand square miles. Still the river went on cutting deeper and deeper, draining the last reservoirs, and opening a way for the springs to discharge at lower points; and slowly sucking the life out of its own basin. It cut down through sandstone to limestone, through limestone to granite, and deep into the granite, till the former fertile vales were changed to barren plateaus; the semi-civilized races vanished, leaving few survivors, and the "backbone of the continent" became a desert, with only here and there an oasis.

From the point where I reached the plateau, it slowly widens westward for a hundred miles, the mountains continuing due west, and the river bearing south-west. Fifteen miles south-westward, over a desert and along the foot of the mountains, brought me to the first gulch containing water and grass, where I rested till 2 P. M. Thence over another barren *mesa*, twenty miles brought me to Jacob's Pool, where the pasture lands begin. The pool is a clear, cold spring, at the head of a gulch, sending out a stream the size of one's wrist, which runs two or three hundred yards down the plain before it disappears. The largest mountain streams in this section never run more than a mile or two on to the plain. In some places a channel can be traced nearly to the Colorado. The Wasatch here has an average elevation of five thousand feet above this plateau, and there are but three places in a hundred miles where horses and footmen can get down through side gulches to the river.

John D. Lee had preëmpted the pool, and had his wife Rachel living there in a sort of brush-tent, making butter and cheese from a herd of twenty cows. She and her son and daughter of sixteen and eighteen years were the sole inhabitants, no neighbors within less than forty miles either way. Lee's other wives were scattered about on ranches farther north; four at Mangrum's settlement and two others at Harmony. One left him, and lives at Beaver; another went to Montana with a Gentile, and still another is in the States, "living fancy, I reckon," said the wife at the river, who gave me this information. There was no room in the tent, and Mrs. Lee gave me a straw tick out doors—luxury enough for one who had slept with only a blanket between him and the ground for many weeks; and at this oasis I rested a day and a half.

Thence, on the afternoon of the 6th, I rode eighteen miles nearly straight west to the first water, and encamped for the night in a rich bunch-grass pasture, dotted with scrubby pines. After bread and tea, I hoppled my horse and slept till near daylight, then took a hasty breakfast and canteen of water and was off for Navajo Wells, thirty miles ahead, and the first place where water could be had. I traveled along the original Navajo trail from the Rio Grande to Southern Nevada; and early in the day commenced the ascent of the Buckskin, a low range of partially-wooded hills, putting out across the plateau nearly to the Colorado. All over this I found good blue-grass, which is very rare every-where in the Rocky Mountains. The grass on the plains here consists of two species of bunch-grass—the common yellow and the white-topped varieties. But neither forms a sod or sward, or gives more than a faint tinge of green to the landscape. My general direction for the day was north-west, working toward the Utah line, though the road at times wound about to every point. West of the Buckskin was a singular flood plain some six miles wide, with rich soil, but no moisture, and nearly destitute of grass. I had traveled till 3 P. M., looking closely for Navajo Wells for the last few miles, when I emerged from a rocky ridge scantily clothed with piñons, upon another flood plain, and was at once aware that I had missed the Wells. But soon an Indian overtook me, whom I hailed with "*Toh, agua, water!*" using the three languages spoken in this region; but he understood neither. Then I had recourse to pantomime, when he rejoined, "*Pah to wicki-up*," and directed me to follow. Two miles back and half a mile from the trail was the water-hole, and near by the camp of his tribe, a horribly filthy and repulsive gang of some forty savages. A hole in the sand contained the only water, which was lukewarm, slimy and full of nasty black creatures; but it was that or nothing, and my horse drank it under protest. For his courtesy I divided my stock of meat and cheese with the chief, who became very communicative, preferred a request for tobacco, suggested in pantomime that I camp there for the night, and asked how long since I left the Navajoes. They had at first sight recognized my rig as Navajo, for every tribe in the mountains knows the handiwork of every other. The degraded natives of this region are known as the Pi-Utes, the Pi-Edes and the Lee-Biches, and are the very lowest of the race. In summer they fare sumptuously on piñon nuts, roots, grass-seeds and white sage; but in winter they are reduced to bugs, lizards, grubs and ground-mice, occasionally assisted by donations from the settlements, or the flesh of such Mormon stock as die of disease. They are totally devoid of skill in any respect, and when furnished with boards can not construct a shelter from the rain.

Eight miles farther I camped for the night; was off, by reason of the cold, an hour before daylight, and rode into Kanab just as the first rays of sunshine were streaming over the rugged gaps of the eastern mountains. Kanab sits back in a beautiful cove in the mountains, something like a crescent in shape, the mountain peaks east and west of the town putting out southward to the Arizona line. All the land within the cove appears rich, and the town site is irrigated from a considerable creek running out of a narrow gulch. By direction of the first person met, I went to Jacob Hamlin's house, where I had two days' rest. I was most fortunate in my selection. Three of Major Powell's men were here, waiting for his arrival from Salt Lake City. Here, also, I found Mr. and Mrs. Thomson, of Major Powell's party, so altogether we had a very delightful little Gentile society in this Mormon stronghold. Hamlin, who is a Church Agent of Indian Affairs, struck in on the subject of Mormonism the first meal; but as I was once more in the land of beef and biscuit, hot coffee and other

"THE LITTLE SAVAGES FIXED AN UNWINKING GAZE UPON ME."

luxuries, I could stand up to any amount of argument. We had it hot for two days, but parted friends. Kanab is quite new, and has but two hundred inhabitants. To Mr. and Mrs. Thomson I am under many obligations, not only for writing conveniences, but for many hours of social enjoyment; and as for the Powell party generally, my meeting them here was a rare piece of good fortune.

For the first time in my life I found it convenient to drop my name while making this trip. The Saints might have a prejudice against me, so I introduced myself to Lee by my middle name, "Hanson," and by the same title traveled to Salt Lake City. There was something grotesque in "Mr. Hanson" and "Major Doyle" meeting in the wilderness, when the one was the Mountain Meadow's butcher and the other the Gentile writer who had done his best to make him notorious.

A PI-EDE CERES.

Striking south-west from Kanab, in a few miles I very nearly ran over a group of young Pi-Edes, crouched down in a piñon thicket. The little savages fixed an unwinking gaze upon me, but never stirred or spoke, their Indian nature forbidding expression either of surprise, pleasure or fear at sight of me. It is doubtful if they felt either. A little beyond I saw their mother, or older sister, gathering grass-seeds—the summer work of these squaws—naked as new-created Eve, but hardly so handsome as Milton paints our great mother. By her lay her wicker-basket, which she had dropped at my approach, to retreat behind the bush, whether from fear or modesty was hard to say. At dark I reached Pipe Springs, where is a ranche kept by Bishop Windsor and *one* of his families. I found the Bishop a good landlord, and chatty, agreeable companion. The spring from which the place takes its name sends down a large stream of cold, clear water, which the Bishop leads in stone troughs through his houses, using one of them for a cheese factory. He milks eighty cows, and makes the business a splendid success. All this section is rich in pasture, but has so little arable land that most of the few inhabitants have to import their flour, paying for it in butter and cheese. Even with this large stream the Bishop can cultivate but fifteen acres, the porous, sandy soil requiring five times as much irrigation as the land around Salt Lake City. The place is just outside the rim of the Great Basin, and the country about of the same level as that within. From the foot of the mountain range along which we travel the surface slopes a very little toward the Colorado, but near that river rises again to a height above that along the road.

Thence the next afternoon I traversed a sandy desert for twenty-five miles, reached the first pool and took supper, then rode nine miles further by dark, and made a "dry camp" in a low, grassy valley between two wooded hills. Thence I reached Gould's Ranche (ten miles) in time for a late breakfast and another hot argument on politics. The Church was then straining every nerve to get Utah admitted as a State, the Gentiles fighting the proposition with the bitterness of desperation, and all Southern Utah was hot over the matter.

That day I mistook the road, but did not regret my error when it led me to the beautiful hamlet of Virgin City. The neat, white *adobe* houses were almost hidden in forests of peach, fig, apple, and mulberry trees; the climate rivaled that of Southern California, and damsons, apricots, and pears also abounded. All that part of Mormondom south of the rim of the Great Basin is called Dixie, and produces cotton, wine and figs. And here I first began to be conscious of the oddity of my dress. At Defiance, to avoid being too conspicuous among the Indians, I had dressed in a buckskin suit, with spangled Mexican jacket, stout moccasins handsomely worked, beaded scarf, and flowered calico head-wrap; so, at a distance, I was every-where taken for an Indian. Marriage with Indian women is a strong point in the religion of these Southern Mormons, and the men were delighted with my description of the grace, beauty, and general desirableness of Navajo girls, as they expect to form a close alliance with that tribe. Jacob Hamlin had visited all the tribes in Northern Arizona, making treaties between the Indians and the Church.

My next journey was to Toquerville, where I stopped with Bishop Isaac C. Haight, another leader in the Mountain Meadow Massacre, and a prominent Mormon. Ripe figs, just plucked from the tree, formed part of our dessert. The narrow valley is very fertile; all around are yellow hills and red deserts. A leisurely journey of a day brought me thence to Kanarra, in the rim of the Great Basin. In the south end of town the water flows towards the Colorado; in the north end into the Basin. There I had my first sickness on the trip, as did my horse. We had stood adversity; prosperity ruined us. I indulged too freely in fruit, and he in Lucerne hay. There was no doctor in town, so I worried it through on hot ginger and "Dixie wine;" in three days was able to ride, and proceeded by easy stages to Parowan, in Iron County. But six hundred miles through the Indian country had worn out my horse, and on the 16th instant I "ranched him" twenty miles south of Beaver, and set out for that place in the wagon of a Mormon farmer. Some five miles on the road—when we were on the Beaver "divide"—a cold rain set in and continued for four hours, changing to something very near sleet. The Mormon family and myself suffered greatly with cold. The seasons at Beaver are very late, and wheat harvest does not begin till in August. Little Salt Lake lay a few miles west of our route, on the "divide." Having passed the ridge, I walked down the eight-mile slope to Beaver, which I reached at dark, and was soon warm and happy in the house of a hospitable Gentile.

Beaver had been revolutionized by the development of mines. Gentiles were to be seen every-where, and a military post had been established near town. Thence by stage it was two hundred and fifty miles to "Zion;" and I was pleased to recognize, in the first driver, my old friend Will Kimball, who drove a team across the Plains in the train with me in 1868. Kimball's father was one of the many arrested the previous winter on charges relating to the conduct of the Mormon militia in the rebellion of 1857, but was released with a hundred and twenty others, when the Supreme Court reversed Judge McKean's rulings. In the progress of Utah affairs, nearly all of the family left by old Heber Kimball have become pretty good Gentiles. This seems to be the course of all such delusions which do not end in blood.

I halted for a day's rest at Fillmore, the old Territorial capital, a hundred and seventy-five miles south-west of Salt Lake, and quite a beautiful town. Several wealthy Mormons reside here, in elegant brick and stone houses, and the place is old enough for all the shade trees and shrubbery to have attained a good growth. Some thirty miles west of Fillmore is a remarkable mountain peak, or rather round heap of cinders and lava, five hundred feet high. It is broken square across by a gulch with almost perpendicular sides, at the bottom of which is a spring that is coated with ice around the edges for eleven months in the year. The altitude is no higher than that of Fillmore, but the sun never shines in the gorge, and snow lies on the inner slopes all the year.

Thence two days' slow staging brought me to "Zion," which I reached on the evening of July 21st, exactly four months from the day I left St. Louis for a tour through the Southern Territories. In that time I had traveled fourteen hundred miles by rail, six hundred by stage, three hundred by military wagon, two hundred on foot, and six hundred on horseback—at a total cost of $535. I reached "Zion" in splendid health, but complete disguise, if I am to judge from the conduct of my friends, many of whom passed me on the street without a nod, or with only a slight look of curiosity, as if some old and half-forgotten memory were stirred by sight of a face that "had a sort o' familiar look." However, after a bath in the warm springs, getting off my buckskin pantaloons, spangled Mexican jacket, and Navajo scarf, and donning a new summer suit, my fingers received once more the wonted squeeze, and once more I began to feel very like a Christian.

It was on this journey through Southern Utah, and after my arrival in "Zion," that I heard narrated the personal experiences which are combined in the three succeeding chapters.

CHAPTER XX.

THE FAIR APOSTATE.

MERRILY rang the bells of —— Church, Herefordshire, in the merry month of May, 1847; for Nixy James, the belle of the hamlet, was that day to be married to Elwood Briarly, the sturdiest young yeoman on all the country side. The elder James and Elwood's father had grown from childhood together: intimate companions and fierce rivals for the lead among the village politicians, partners in public sports and at the village tavern, but never, by any possibility, on the same side of any exciting question. Thomas James, cobbler, was often heard to declare that Yeoman Briarly would "contradict for contradiction's sake—he'd argefy wi' t' clock on t' church steeple, rather than go wi'out argefying;" while the yeoman, on his part, insisted that James "was aye runnin' after every dashed new-fangled notion that come along." He couldn't see why simple folk like us couldn't be content wi' t' old church and t' old laws, and not take up wi' every outlanguaged kickshaw from France or 'Merica or other foreign parts." For his part, give him the British Constitution.

Nay, the difference was in the blood; for James' great-grandfather was a hot adherent of the Prince of Orange, while the Briarlys had stood by the "Lord's Anointed," and remained zealous Jacobites even down to the coming in of the House of Brunswick. They held to legitimacy long after Church, Lords, and Commons had forgotten it; but the James' had ever three bogies: a papist king, an Irish rising and a French invasion. Now it so happens that a whole people can not always be scared into submission by Irish risings and French invasions; and so, by and by, new and perplexing questions arose, and certain pestilent fellows began to talk about "more liberty," and "household suffrage," and the "rights of the people." It was an extraordinary proceeding on their part, and Yeoman Briarly stoutly protested no good could come of it; but, in spite of him, he would have told you the James' family and all their adherents went crazy. But it never shook him. Oh, no; he planted himself firmly on the Constitution, and defied the world to move; and, when the others became Chartists, he declared, with great positiveness, over his pipe in the village ale-house, what Parliament ought to do to stop this sort of thing.

But in despite of all this contention, the young people persisted in loving each other almost from the start, and at last the blood of the Old Radical and the Old Conservative were to be united. And all this time, there was growing up in an obscure village across the sea, an ignorant, awkward youth, who talked through his nose, and told plausible fibs as naturally as he breathed, whose career was to strangely affect the blood of the Briarlys and James'. Across the sea an institution was born which was to change the current of all these simple lives in a way the wisest little dreamed of.

The ceremony was ended, the shoe was thrown, the village maidens strung garlands for the bride; there was the feast, the dance, and all the simple pleasantry of the middle class of English farmers. One year Elwood Briarly rejoiced in the society of his young wife—one year of continued courtship. Then came a season of trial, happily ended, said the nurse and doctor; and an infant daughter was laid in the arms of the proud father. A perfect little manikin it was, with the orthodox creases in its perfect little feet, and all the orthodox lines on its perfect little face, by which wise matrons so infallibly fix the resemblance to either parent: a precious little life wrapped up in a perfect little anatomy. But the primal curse still rests, even on the head of the hardy English woman. The weight of the precious fruit broke the parent stem, and the life of the plant exhaled in the sweetness of the opening flower. Nixie Briarly only saw that her babe had started well in this world, then bade her weeping husband good-bye, and fell asleep.

To him it seemed that all which made life worth having was gone. His had been no sudden affection; for long years Nixie had been central to all his plans, and now there seemed nothing worth exertion. His daughter—he could scarcely say at first that he loved her—strange pain! She seemed to him almost as a living reproach. Months passed, and it was remarked that he was "slack;" his hand had lost its cunning, and words of pity were heard. Months again passed, and it was remarked that he went often to the village alehouse, and this time the word of pity was accompanied with an ominous shake of the head. But the current of common life flowed on too fast for others for them to turn aside to cheer him. Old yeomen, on their way home from church, leaned over the fence to look at the little farm he held on lease; and while you might have thought them pondering on the preacher's words, the real thought behind those heavy, unexpressive eyes was, "When will it be to lease?" At the ale-house he sat apart, a moody man; and it was surprising how soon his old companions learned to do without him, and he dropped into the ranks of the half-forgotten. All at once it began to be whispered that Elwood Briarly was drinking a great deal; and then that he was drinking altogether too much, and very soon after, that he was a drunkard, and in an amazingly short space of time that he was an abandoned drunkard, and that his late lease was vacated and the farm to be relet. And so it was that when his little Marian was only three years old, she was taken home to grandfather James, and Elwood Briarly plunged down, down, down along the course of those given over to the national vice of Free (and "Merrie") England.

Counted as already dead by those nearest him, he became a common laborer for the means of gratifying his appetite. His sorrow had yielded to time, but now habit dragged him down. When reason asserted her sway he struggled to his feet for a few days or weeks, then fell again, and each time deeper than before. And now his habits and associates had changed his original nature. At the church or social gathering he was never seen; his only recreation worth the name was at the workingman's club; there he easily learned to criticise every body but himself, and to blame every one for his troubles, the government most of all. The genial young farmer had become first a snarling critic, then a radical, a cynic, a misanthrope.

Again he struggled to his feet, and in one of his sober moods, on a calm Sabbath afternoon, started with his little girl for a stroll upon the village common. His attention was attracted by a small group of people who had gathered around a rude stand, extemporized by piling a few stones together. On this stood a man of peculiar appearance, with what Briarly thought an unpleasant nasal tone, and a complexion that was certainly not English. "It's one o' them new-fangled preachers from America," said a neighbor, as he came up; and for want of some better amusement, he decided to wait and listen. There was a general air of critical indifference in the small audience, idle and seeking only entertainment as they were; but they were respectful. The preacher seemed to fix his eye on Briarly as he pronounced his text:

"If any of you lack wisdom, let him ask of God, that giveth to all men liberally, and upbraideth not; and it shall be given him."—JAMES i: 5. Slowly repeating the text, as if to fix the meaning of each word, the missionary cast a glance over his congregation. In that sweeping inspection he had noted those whom he would most likely reach.

"My friends, brethren and sisters, all; this means *you*. It don't mean the Pope of Rome is to have all wisdom. It don't mean His

Grace the Archbishop. It means that you are to know for yourselves, and not for or by another. It means that you are to receive a witness from God himself, and know of a surety whether this doctrine is true. It is not for the rich alone, or the learned; a burden is laid upon me to open the Gospel to the poor and ignorant, to help those who need it, to cheer the sorrowful, to lift up the lowly, to preach the acceptable year of the Lord," and again his glance fell upon Briarly. The latter was powerfully impressed. He had lost his old friends. He longed for sympathy. If any man could promise him something better, that man was sure of a favorable hearing. The preacher continued: "You have priests who tell you that there is no more revelation, that the volume of God's word is closed. For eighteen hundred years the Christian world has received no message from the Almighty: the heavens have been shut up, the Lord has not spoken, there has been no prophet to inquire of the Lord. Where is their authority to say this? Where is it written in this book that prophecy shall cease? Our fathers did eat manna in the wilderness, and were saved; but the bread my fathers ate is not sufficient for me. I would know God for myself. Go ask your priests for a witness of their mission. They can not show it. Eighteen hundred years ago, they say, God spoke; eighteen hundred years ago He loved His people, and led them by revelation. But now the canon is full; the world is wise enough to do without the daily word of God, and there is no longer a voice from the Most High to guide us! What! Is God dead? Is there less need of a living oracle now than there was eighteen hundred years ago? Or is the world so pure that a prophet has no work to do? Do all men acknowledge God, and worship him, and is there no unbelief that God should refuse us a witness? No, my friends, I'll tell you why it is."

The speaker had warmed into something like eloquence. His audience were impressed, and the nasal tone which at first affected their English ears unpleasantly, seemed to have vanished.

"It is because they rejected God's plan. They would not have a continuous chain of revelation. They have set up churches in which there are no prophets nor apostles; they have not the gifts of the apostolic church, and the Holy Spirit is not with them; they have the form of godliness, but deny the power. Should any one say to them that God had sent a prophet, they would cry out against him. But, my friends, God is *not* dead. The heavens are *not* brass to those who seek the truth. God, who so loved the world that he sent his Son to save it, loves us as much as he did the people who lived eighteen hundred years ago, and has sent us a messenger. As he spoke to the saints of the former days so has he spoken to the Latter-day Saints, and all who will may know for themselves that this message is from God. In America a prophet has been called; the word of God has whispered out of the dust, as foretold by Isaiah, and once more communication is restored between God and man."

The speaker then recited the story of Joseph Smith, his conversion and calling, his mission and martyrdom, as foretold by all the prophets; and supported his doctrine by an array of Scripture texts that astonished and fairly overwhelmed his simple hearers. Their experience had left them unprepared for any thing of this sort. All their lives they had heard the letter of the Scriptures distorted in the petty warfare between the sects; great principles they did not comprehend, and, to come to the point, there *was* no reason why prophets and apostles should not walk the earth now as well as in former times. The missionary's argument on this point was to them unanswerable: if there was wickedness and unbelief in ancient times, so there was now; if men needed a living witness then, much more did they now, when so many claimed to be messengers from God, and all differed as to His nature and government. No text in the Bible said that prophets should cease, while scores of texts implied that He would not leave the earth without an infallible guide.

Elwood Briarly was powerfully impressed. He was in the Slough of Despond, and the missionary brought hope; he was disgusted with all about him, and here was a chance for a new life. Next day he was surprised by a visit from the Mormon preacher. The latter was totally unlike the parish priest. He did not stand off and preach down at the poor outcast; he took a farming tool and worked beside him; aye, did task for task with him, and talked only in the intervals of work. He, too, had known poverty and disgrace; he, too, had been an unfortunate and an outcast; he had not walked in silver slippers, and how mightily did he affect these simple people. From house to house he went, resolving doubts, urging proof texts, preaching and debating; and sitting by their humble firesides of an evening, he sang with unction:

"The Spirit of God like a fire is burning,
  The latter-day glory begins to come forth;
The visions and blessings of old are returning;
  The angels are coming to visit the earth.

We'll sing and we'll shout with the armies of heaven,
  Hosanna, hosanna, to God and the Lamb!
Let glory to them in the highest be given,
  Henceforth and forever, amen and amen!"

What wonder that he prevailed mightily among these simple people. What wonder that the cold, barren, carefully prepared homilies of the parish priest were swept aside! The emotional faith of the speaker went to the hearer's soul. It was no cold, intellectual reasoning; it was warm, robust feeling, and as a natural consequence believers grew and multiplied. In less than one month from that Sunday, Elwood Briarly, his father-in-law James, and a dozen of their neighbors were baptized into the Mormon Church, and eager to set out for "Zion."

But between them and Salt Lake City intervened many months of work for the cause. And now the whole aim of their lives was changed. Preaching and working, at home or abroad, all was for the Church; their talk was of "visions and dreams," "the ministering of angels," "tongues and the interpretation of tongues," "healings and miracles." And so it was, that by the opening months of 1856, this little band of Saints was ready for the long journey to "Zion." Old Man James was beside himself with joy at thought that all his dreams were soon to be realized; that Brotherhood of Man, that freedom he had vainly sought in Chartism, was to be realized in the Rocky Mountains, where God's people were to live under the mild rule of prophets and apostles. Such an idea captivated thousands of young Englishmen. To them, Utah was a land where all legal hardships were to be cured, and all men to be equal; and the spirit of brotherhood among the British saints at this time, to which all observers bear witness, they thought only a foretaste of the perfect oneness in Christ which was to prevail in Utah. In this spirit our friends gathered to Liverpool, where it was announced, through the columns of the *Millennial Star*, that God, by His servant Brigham, had devised a cheaper and better way of reaching Utah; the Saints were to travel from the frontiers on foot, and take their necessary baggage on hand-carts. But what can shake a fervent and fooling faith? Without a murmur of dissent the waiting hundreds crowded on the vessel chartered by the Mormon agents, and, grouped on the deck as the vessel started on their way, they sang with a tone that resounded o'er the waves:

> "Oh, my native land, I love thee;
> All thy scenes I love them well;
> Friends, connections, happy country,
> Can I bid you all farewell?
>   Can I leave thee,
> Far in distant lands to dwell?
>
> "Home, thy joys are passing lovely,
> Joys no stranger heart can tell;

> Happy home, 'tis sure I love thee,
> Can I—can I—say 'Farewell?'
> Can I leave thee,
> Far in distant lands to dwell?
>
> "Yes, I hasten from you gladly,
> From the scenes I love so well;
> Far away, ye billows, bear me;
> Lovely native land, farewell!
> Pleased I leave thee,
> Far in distant lands to dwell.
>
> "Bear me on, thou restless ocean,
> Let the winds my canvas swell;
> Heaves my heart with warm emotion,
> While I go far hence to dwell,
> Glad I bid thee,
> Native land, farewell, farewell."

On ship-board the discipline was perfect. The new converts were distributed in quorums, over each an elder, and over all a trustee or apostle, insuring mutual respect and cleanliness; and in this order the emigrants traveled all the way to Iowa City, their outfitting point for the plains. It was there learned that over two thousand of the poorer and middle class of converts had that year left Europe, all of whom were to continue the journey from this point with hand-carts. But precious time was lost. The Mormon agent had neglected to provide the carts; they were now hastily constructed of imperfectly seasoned wood, and the whole party set out joyfully late in July, and were soon strung along the route thence to the Missouri River. The first five hundred got an early start, and being largely composed of young and strong men, entered Salt Lake Valley just as the first snow of the season was falling. But our friends, with their companions, found themselves the second week in August just prepared to start from the Missouri. Fanatical as they were, some of them shrank from making the attempt so late in the season. The division contained five hundred persons: a hundred and twenty stout men, three hundred women, and children old enough to walk, and seventy babies to be carried by their mothers or hauled upon the carts—this party starting to traverse eleven hundred miles of mountain and desert in the closing months of the season! Totally ignorant of the country and climate, the converts were eager to go on to "Zion," but there were four of the leaders who had been to the valley, and others at Florence attending to the emigration. Incredible as it may appear, all these urged them on but one; Levi Savage used his common sense and knowledge of the country, but was rebuked by the elders, who prophesied, in the name of Israel's

God, that not a flake of snow should fall upon them. "You will hear of storms to the right and to the left, but a way will be opened for you." Each hundred was then put under charge of a captain; to each hundred there were five round tents, twenty persons to a tent; twenty hand-carts, one to five persons, and one "prairie schooner" drawn by three yoke of oxen, to haul the tents and provisions. All the clothing and bedding, seventeen pounds to each person, and all the cooking utensils, were upon the hand-carts, besides a hundred pound sack of flour to each. Thus equipped, rested by the delay and "strong in the promise of the Lord by the mouth of His elder," the second division set out from the Missouri the 18th of August, singing in cheerful concert:

> "A church without a prophet is not the church for me;
> It has no head to lead it, in it I would not be;
>   But I've a church not built by man,
>   Cut from the mountain without hand,
> A church with gifts and blessings, oh, that's the church for me,
> Oh, that's the church for me, oh, that's the church for me.
>
> "The God that others worship is not the God for me;
> He has no parts nor body, and can not hear nor see;
>   But I've a God that lives above,
>   A God of Power and of Love,
> A God of Revelation, oh, that's the God for me.
>
> "A church without apostles is not the church for me;
> It's like a ship dismasted afloat upon the sea;
>   But I've a church that's always led
>   By the twelve stars around its head,
> A church with good foundations, oh, that's the church for me.
>
> "The hope that Gentiles cherish is not the hope for me,
> It has no hope for knowledge, far from it I would be;
>   But I've a hope that will not fail,
>   That reaches safe within the vail,
> Which hope is like an anchor, oh, that's the hope for me."

But neither hope nor faith changed the harsh climate of the high plains and wind-swept plateaus; and seven weeks of travel left our friends still four hundred miles from "Zion," in the heart of the high Rockies, almost out of provisions, worn down, sick, apparently forgotten of God and abandoned by man. It was then the inborn nobleness of the English race shone out. Men toiled on day after day, hauling and even carrying women and children, wading ice-cold streams with the feeble in their arms, in many cases carrying their little children in the morning and themselves dying before night. Fainting fathers took the scant rations from their lips and fed their crying children; mothers carried their babes till they sank exhausted in the snow, and young men nerved themselves to suffer every thing for those they loved. Briarly had never known how much he loved his little Marian till then. Daily the image of her mother grew in her face, and hourly he felt the agony of death lest he should leave her corpse in the wilderness. At times pushing his hand-cart with her weight added to his regular load; at times wading the cold mountain streams with her clasped to his bosom, and yet again assisting others whose husbands or fathers had died on the way, he showed that a false faith had not yet corrupted nature. Day after day the

"WHOSE EXISTENCE FROM DECEMBER TILL MAY IS ORGANIZED FAMINE AND MISERY."

train struggled on in silence and sorrow, and every morning saw from one to ten of their number cold in death. Daily the survivors grew weaker from exposure and insufficient food: old men died as easily as a lamp goes out when the oil is exhausted; women died as a child goes to sleep; young men died sitting by the camp-fire, with their scant rations in their mouths. Still the survivors pressed on, though every day more slowly: by day pierced by the keen winds, or happily sheltered a little by the mountain pines; by night shivering and moaning in a miserable sleep, cheered only by the long drawn and melancholy howl of the coyote.

The regular winter storms struck them at Rocky Ridge, but not until the first relief company from Salt Lake City had reached them. In their worst extremity some had even accepted charity from the wretched Goshoots, whose existence from December till May is organized famine and misery. But help came too late for one of our friends. Old Man James had borne up long and well. The day the first storm of winter came he sank by the wayside with scores of others. John Chislett, commander of this hundred, took off his own blanket and wrapped it around his older and weaker brother; and a few hours later the relief party brought him into camp. They warmed and chafed his cold limbs, and pressed food upon him; but his thoughts were far away. He babbled of green fields, and the hawthorn along the English lanes; of the village ale-house and the Chartist's Club, of his little Nixie, still a child, as he thought. This recalled his later experience, and starting up, he cried: "My curse, my eternal curse on those who brought us from our English home;" then fell back with glazing eye and stiffening jaw.

The Old Radical had found the Brotherhood of Man at last.

But Brigham's kingdom had lost a subject.

*　　　*　　　*　　　*　　　*　　　*　　　*

While fanaticism was corrupting fresh young English hearts, the harsh attrition of rural life in the West was wearing another hero into shape. But who would have chosen Willie Manson for a hero that spring afternoon?—his face covered with dust, through which the tears were washing little tracks; his feet bare, and his head half covered with a dilapidated straw hat. He had but dim recollections of a tall and kindly man who spoke to him as "my boy;" since then his "legal guardians" had made him more familiar with the phrase, "that wretched young one," and the neighbors' children had nicknamed him "Binder," in allusion to the legal tie which relegated him to the authority of his master. How have they wasted their time—those poets who write of "innocent childhood?" Cruelty is bound up in the heart of a child, and is manifested against the helpless of his own age. If you do not believe it, watch a group of school children, when a pauper child, or a "bound boy" or girl is first sent among them.

But to-day Willie Manson had received blows as well as harsh words, and as he came across the fields on his errand, a glance westward showed him a wide expanse of open country; and all at once arose that vague longing which appears to have moved our race ever since the first Aryan turned towards sunset. Obeying a wild impulse—half anger and half a formed desire to run away—the boy fled swiftly across the fields till he reached the high road; then he stopped, and, boy-like, with the reaction came this thought: "Oh, won't I catch it, though, when I get home?" Left to himself, the thirteen-year-old child would, of course, have gone back, taken his punishment, and perhaps sunk into a "white slave," perhaps taken a later occasion to fly. But fate would have it otherwise. As he pondered, there came down the road a high "prairie schooner," drawn by four horses; within the neat white cover sat a cheery looking woman who held the reins, while behind came two men driving loose cattle. They nodded and smiled in a way that warmed the heart of the forlorn orphan; but the next minute turned in haste to head off their cattle, who had broken into a wood lot and were stampeding for wild freedom. With a natural wish to please, and glad of some change, the barefooted boy ran after the cattle, and, by his knowledge of the locality, assisted greatly in getting them past the next open piece of timber. They thanked him heartily, and pressed a silver dime upon him, then bade him good-bye; but, to their surprise, when they camped that evening on the banks of the Wabash, the boy was there. Reluctantly the "movers" consented to his remaining for the night, and in the morning, fearing the consequences to themselves of "harboring a runaway," they sent him back. But to their amazement, when the swing ferry had landed them on the west bank, and they were toiling up the western bluff, the boy climbed out of the rear of the wagon-box and begged to go on with them. His readiness to help had pleased the men, and now something in his pleading face touched the weary but still cheerful woman.

"Isn't he like our Johnnie was? And at the age we lost him"— and she took him into her great motherly heart at once. So, with many misgivings, the head of the family consented to his accompanying them. But it might have been noticed that he made a very long drive that day, and camped at a distance from any dwelling; that he managed to keep Willie very busy if any settler halted to chat with the "movers," and that he pressed upon him a hat very different in appearance from that he had worn. And so it was that in a few days Willie felt as if he had never known other friends than these; that the old life as a "bound boy" was a dream, and that he was to begin a new life away in the West.

By this time they had emerged into what seemed a vast field without a fence, where, for hours, they jogged on over the grand prairie without sight of tree or house. They crossed the Embarras, the Okaw and other streams, threaded their bordering groves, and were out again upon the prairies, then but thinly settled, of central Illinois. Beyond, they descended the gently rolling hills, crossed the great river, and in the early summer entered upon the rolling plains and wooded vales of Iowa—and still on and on. To Willie each new day brought surprise that the world was so big; but still at evening the man replied to his wife's question: "I want to get out where I can have my pick. Reckon a hundred miles or so west of Iowa City 'll suit *me*."

At last the pioneer announced that "this 'ere district looked new enough, and about the right thing," and at noon of a scorching July day they made camp for the last time. Willie had taken the bucket, and was returning from the creek near by with water, when suddenly there came in view the most amazing caravan he had ever looked upon. For a mile along the dim wagon track there straggled in strange array men, women, and children, all panting and sweating under the hot sky of an Iowa July noon. Here and there were heavy wagons drawn by oxen; but most of the vehicles were rude carts with shafts attached, and in those shafts—how could the little American believe his eyes?—were actually women and men, not exactly harnessed like brute beasts, but pushing or pulling at the heavy loads. Dripping with sweat and begrimed with dust, all ages and sexes still seemed eager to press on; little children ran beside the carts, while babies slumbered on the piles of bedding, or hung upon the breasts of bronzed and weary mothers. Behind came the more weary, and with them a man who appeared to be in command, urging them on; and among the last came a man who pushed a cart before him and pulled another from behind, while a little girl walked beside him crying to ride.

"What's the matter, little girl?" said the boy, finding his tongue at last. The child hushed on the instant, but still lingered as if wanting to talk.

"Where are you going, little girl?"

"To Zion—to build up the kingdom of God."

The boy was positively frightened. What *could* this strange little creature mean. But before he could ask, she whimpered: "Oh, I am so tired."

This was something Willie could understand very well; and it was not half so bad to his mind as the other, for, like most children who have been under severe authority, he literally "*feared* God." To him any other prospect was more pleasant than going to the "kingdom," as he understood it. But while he gazed at the little one, and in his boyish way wondered and speculated, the advance of the cavalcade had halted for midday at the creek; and he followed with the weary child, who seemed all at once to have acquired great confidence in him. Meanwhile the pioneer had been down to talk with the party, and Willie had to bid his little acquaintance good-bye and hurry back.

"And who are they, any how?" said the wife.

"Oh, a set of d—d fool Mormons," replied the matter-of-fact Hoosier—"they say they're a goin' to Zion. More likely goin' to the devil, startin' out the way they are."

But Willie had in mind his little friend of an hour, and, after much pondering, concluded that she must be a "bound girl" as he had been a "bound boy," and that some harsh master was taking her away from home; so, with the good woman's permission, he gathered up some delicacies left from their dinner, and ran down to offer them to the little girl. He listened to the talk of the elders, but it was a strange jargon to him; there was so much about "wicked Babylon," and "God's wrath," and "the last days," that he was frightened again, and could hardly say whether he was glad or sorry when the cool of the day came on and the strange party set out again. But the vision remained long in his memory; and months after he astonished his patron by suddenly asking: "Who are Mormons, anyhow? and why don't they use teams just like folks?"

A year passed, and the boy was again moving westward. A year had done wonders in strengthening his body; he was already known as a skillful driver, and when a train set out to haul provisions to the army in the mountains, he was promoted to the management of "one span" and a "light outfit." "Three span outfits," on such a route as that, were reserved for men. Need I recount the incidents of that disastrous autumn and winter of suffering? Our army, marching carelessly and without a thought of resistance, allowed the Mormon troops to run off their stock, and render them helpless on the inhospitable plains of Bridger. There the train to which Willie was attached found them in the dead of winter, and but for this timely arrival they must have suffered for food. The winter dragged on in misery and exposure; but fortune, which had denied our little hero almost every thing else, had at least given him a rugged constitution, and he lived through a season when strong men drooped and died. When spring had dissolved the snow banks from the Wasatch passes, and "King Buchanan had come to his senses," as Mormon history expresses it, peace was made, and the army entered the Territory, traversed Salt Lake City, and was located at Camp Floyd.

And now came the era that was to decide our young hero's future;

for Camp Floyd presented extraordinary facilities for the ruin of character, and Willie was at that period which most often decides one's destiny for time—perhaps for eternity. With the army, or following close after it, came an array of camp-followers outnumbering the soldiers three to one. Government contracts were given out with a lavish hand, and money that was easily got was lavishly spent. Among the superiors, there was high-toned robbery of the Government and the Indians; among the inferiors, gambling and quarreling, and every-where rioting and fatal "accidents." The revolver was in frequent use; renegade young Mormons crowded the camp, and the scum of the mountains made it their rendezvous. For two years our hero was swept along by the tide. He was by turns teamster, commissary clerk, and merchant's clerk; but still preserved enough of nature's nobility to make him, in his quiet moments, loathe the life around him, and long for a purer atmosphere. Gentile merchants had opened stores in the city, and with a sudden impulse he set out one morning to ride there and seek a position. But the life he had lately led had not been

SCENES ON THE COLORADO PLATEAU.

without effects. Exposure and over-exertion when at work, and dissipation instead of relaxation when at leisure, can not long be borne even in the stimulating air of Utah. He felt every hour of his progress a growing lassitude; and had barely entered the outskirts of the city, when he fell from his horse in a paroxysm of that dread disease, mountain fever. When he opened his eyes in his first lucid moment, ten days after, he was amazed at what he thought a familiar face near his pillow. He gazed long and earnestly, and at last, despite all the changes of four years, recognized the little girl he had last seen on the banks of the Boyer, in Iowa.

CHAPTER XXI.

THE FAIR APOSTATE—CONTINUED.

It was in full Tabernacle, in the early autumn of 1856. The reign of lust and fanaticism, known in Utah as the "Reformation," had not ended; and at every meeting fresh schemes were projected to bind the Mormons more thoroughly into a pliable mass, which might be "even as a tallowed rag in the hands of the priesthood." Every Saint had been required to confess the minutest details of his past life; all these were written down, signed by the party, and thousands of them filed away by Brigham Young. The ward teachers had reported every case of real or supposed heresy; the accused had been severely catechised, and the incorrigible driven from the Territory—*or worse*. A grand "experience meeting" was now in progress. Brigham had pronounced one of his fiercely denunciatory and sweeping sermons, and three thousand Saints, wrought up to the highest pitch of fanaticism, were singing the inspiring national hymn of the Mormon theocracy:

> "In thy mountain retreat
> God shall strengthen thy feet,
> On the necks of thy foes shalt thou tread;
> And their silver and gold,
> As the prophets have told,
> Shall be brought to adorn thy fair head.
>
> Oh, Zion, dear Zion, home of the free,
> Soon thy towers will shine with a splendor divine,
> And eternal thy glories shall be.
>
> "Here our voices we'll raise,
> And we'll sing to thy praise,
> Sacred home of the prophets of God!
> Thy deliverance is nigh,
> Thy oppressors shall die,
> And the Gentiles shall bow 'neath thy rod.
>
> "Oh, Zion, dear Zion, home of the free!
> In thy temples we'll bend, all thy rights we'll defend,
> And our homes shall be ever with thee."

Into this assembly came Joseph A. Young, second son of the

Prophet, just returned from a two years' mission in England, and announced that two divisions of the hand-cart emigrants were on the plains, and in danger of starvation. Then Brigham roused himself, and became, in the estimation of his people, indeed "The Lion of the Lord." Without giving his son a day's rest, he started him at once on the return, with authority to press all the wagons and available bedding and provisions in the settlements he passed through. The people contributed gladly, and in all the assemblies of the Saints prayers were continually offered that God would stay the storms of winter; but instead thereof, as though heaven would rebuke the presumptuous, the storms of 1856 (it is the testimony of all mountaineers) came on earlier and with more severity than for many years before or since. The poor emigrants were brought in only when one-fifth of their number had died of cold and starvation, and as many more been maimed in various degrees. Among the fortunate few were Elwood Briarly and his little Marian, and their kinsman, young Thomas James.

The arrival of the sufferers only added to the prevailing madness. "Surely," said fanaticism, "God is angry with His people, or His promise to temper the winds would have held good;" and in an amazingly short space of time most of the new-comers were as insane as the rest—for, indeed, it did seem that at that time all Utah was pervaded by an epidemic madness. Jedediah Grant and Orson Hyde ranged the Territory, breathing out threats against dissenters, and teaching bloody doctrines in figures of speech. The New Testament was laid aside; Hebraic precedents only were cited: Phinehas, who killed his brother and the Midianitish woman; Jael, who slew the heathen; the king who massacred idolaters, and the priest who hewed the transgressor in pieces before the Lord. "The time is nigh at hand," said Grant, "when we will walk up and down these streets with the old broadsword and say, 'Are you for God?'—and whoever is not will be hewn down!" Marrying and giving in marriage went on constantly, as fast as the ordained officials could put the Saints through the Endowment House ceremonies proper to "plural marriage." Every eligible woman in the Territory was appropriated, and girls of twelve and fourteen years were "sealed" to old elders. In one month after he entered the city, in six months after he was an honest citizen of Christian and monogamous England, Elwood Briarly was the "husband" of two girls who came with him in the hand-cart company.

Where now were the lofty ideals with which the English Saints had left home? The old Radical who dared all for greater freedom, was food for the wolves in the Rocky Mountains. The young Radical who sought a land where men were free in Christ, was now the subject of the worst despotism on earth. The maidens who " fled from Babylon because of its corruptions," were prostitutes in the name of high heaven; and the Saxon yeoman, who boasted that "the Briarlys served no man and feared no officer," was now the slave of lust and of Brigham, and a virtual criminal by the laws of his adopted country. That brotherly communion of the Saints, which had so warmed their hearts in old England, they were never to realize again in Utah; the British elders, who had labored long to build up the Church abroad, soon found they had sold themselves for naught, but could not be redeemed even at a great price. Many of them mourned secretly for years, and, when deliverance came, were too much broken in spirit to avail themselves of it. To them Mormonism has proved the loss of all honorable ambition for this world, and only the skeptic's hope for the next.

The madness of the " Reformation" wore itself out, and the plentiful harvest of 1857 made Utah prosperous. On " Pioneers' Day," July 24th, thousands of Saints were joyously celebrating the settlement of the country in Cottonwood Cañon, when suddenly arrived two elders from the States, with the announcement that President Buchanan had removed Brigham from the Governorship, and ordered the army to Utah. Brigham's brow darkened as he said: " When we reached here I said, if the devils would only give me ten years, I'd be ready for them; they've taken me at my word, and I *am* ready." The people were called together, and a defensive war declared. All Utah was soon in a buzz of warlike preparation. Briarly bid his wives good-bye, shook their two right hands and kissed their four lips, and was off for Echo Cañon with two thousand armed Saints, to drive the Gentile army from the borders of Zion. They were wonderfully successful. The little brigade, under command of Colonel Albert Sidney Johnston, was scarcely a match for the wild riders of Utah, who knew every cañon and gorge in the Wasatch. The Mormon boys rode at full speed down hill-sides where a cavalryman dared not venture at a walk; and finding the army wagons parked, and their cattle herded in the *vegas* on Ham's Fork, they set fire to the tall grass, and, when the smoke had obscured the view, dashed across the burning plain and drove off a thousand of Uncle Sam's cattle.

A few such exploits as this filled the Mormons with a vainglorious pride, scarcely yet abated; and many a Saint even now tells with a joyful glow how "the hirelings of King Buchanan gave back before the Mormon boys." Winter found the Gentile army on the bleak plains of Bridger, unable to move, and nearly all the Mormon soldiers went home to enjoy the gayest winter Utah has ever passed. Songs, sermons and dances, varied by glowing prophecies, kept them in

"DASHED ACROSS THE BURNING PLAIN."

splendid humor with themselves. No people in an equal space of time ever produced so much bad poetry as the Mormons; but a few of their *best* songs have a ring in them that then made them popular, especially if they breathed sarcasm and defiance of all the Gentile world. While the elders prayed and prophesied, the boys in the camps sang:

"Old Sam has sent, I understand,
 Du dah!
A Missouri * ass to rule our land;
 Duh dah! Duh dah day!

* Referring to Gov. Alfred Cumming, who was, however, a Georgian, and was greatly enraged when Brigham afterwards spoke of him as "from Missouri."

> But if he comes, we'll have some fun,
>   Du dah!
> To see him and his juries run,
>   Duh dah! Du dah day!
>
> CHORUS: Then let us be on hand
>   By Brigham Young to stand;
>   And if our enemies do appear,
>   We'll sweep them from the land.
>
> "Old squaw-killer Harney is on the way,
>   Duh dah!
> The Mormon people for to slay,
>   Duh dah! Duh dah day!
> Now if he comes, the truth I'll tell,
>   Duh dah!
> Our boys will drive him down to hell!
>   Duh dah! Duh dah day!"

But again were faith and hope vain. When the spring sun had dissolved the snow-packs from the passes of the Wasatch, the army entered the valley, while 30,000 Mormons were on their flight southward. Col. Thomas L. Kane had entered Utah from the south; the Peace Commissioners, Powell and McCulloch, had promised amnesty, and Governor Cumming had entered Salt Lake City. But all in vain. The people continued their mad flight southward, while Gov. Cumming stood by the road-side, tears rolling down his cheeks at sight of their misery, and implored them to remain. It was midsummer before any considerable number returned; with them Briarly and his family. But the mad proceedings of two years had not been without their influence on our friends. Thomas James began to ask himself, in all seriousness, if what he had witnessed could be the result of Divine guidance; and in Utah it is emphatically true, that he who hesitates is lost—to Mormonism. And now began that terrible conflict in the soul of the young man, through which more than one apostate has passed with tears of agony, with doubts and tremblings, with days of painful self-examination, and nights of restless tossing and vain debate. Could it be that all was a delusion? That his father had died on the plains, that he and those near to him were laboring and suffering—and all for a dismal lie? Losses of friends, property, honors, all can be borne, and the strong man rise above them; but who can tell the heart-rending agony of the devotee who has lost his *God!*

He scarcely knew why, but in no long time he found himself in a small circle of those who suffered in the same way. Not that they sought each other, or confessed their secret doubts at once; but little by little they grew to understand each other. They labored to convince themselves that there had only been slight errors; that in the main the faith was correct, and they would receive their reward. But such self-deception was not long possible. Chief among these sorrowing and doubting ones was Elder John Banks. He had early embraced the faith in England. He, too, had been a Chartist leader, and thought he had found true liberty and brotherhood in Mormonism. And now a strange friendship sprang up between the disappointed man and the doubting lad. They walked and talked together; their Sundays and leisure hours they spent in sad but pleasant communion over their troubles, or in renewed study of the "evidences" they had once thought so convincing as to the divine origin of Mormonism. As might be expected, the younger was the first to free himself. Let what might be true, he knew in his heart that Brigham was not sent of God. The Mormon faith he could not reject entirely, but compromised on the idea that a true prophet was yet to arise; that a terrible mistake had in some way been made, and that in due time God would remember His people. But the elder could not then begin a new life; his heart was bound up in Mormonism, for which he had toiled so long, and he urged his young friend to go with him and lay their troubles before President Young. Brigham received them with that paternal kindness he exercises towards all who may yet be saved to the church; he doled out the usual commonplaces about "faithfulness," "obedience," "live your religion," and "pay your tithing." But it brought no healing to these sore minds. Thomas James was already "apostate in spirit," and there was more in the sad heart of John Banks than he could put in words to Brigham Young.

The friends visited the Briarlys, and there saw the young Gentile, now slowly convalescing. The younger looked on him and thought of the great gulf that separated them. Here was a lad but few years younger than himself, but with none of his heart-racking doubts and fears. What was there in the nature of things which made him a prey to conflicting emotions to which this one was a stranger? Sometimes he hoped Mormonism was all a delusion, but dreaded lest it might be true; again he labored to prove to himself that it was true, and still feared that his hope was vain; but whether he hoped or feared, he somehow felt a strange envy of his new acquaintance, who, though now an invalid, was at any rate neither a dupe nor a traitor to his faith. The whole family soon took a strange interest in the young Babylonian, whom fate had brought to their door. He could now sit up and talk, and his talk was such a strange contrast to theirs. Secretly they felt guilty for taking so much enjoyment in it, and yet his lightest utterance seemed fresh and piquant. They did not know it, but they were getting weary of "Tabernacle talk." The strain they had lived under had worn great grooves in their natures, almost without their knowledge. The "wives" were not the fresh and guileless English girls of four years before. Little by little they had learned to shut up their souls, to hide their inmost nature from others, even from themselves. That extreme reticence which polygamy engenders had become a habit; a habit carried into all the concerns of life, even where it was unnecessary. They were transformed, without knowing it, from individuals into parts of a great machine; and though they sometimes felt a strange pain and longing, they scarce knew why, and would have insisted with vehemence that they were happy in their present relations. To them, this pale Gentile, who had seen life from the other side, as it were, and now talked in such a pleasant, grateful way of his past and hope for the future, brought a strange pleasure that had in it a touch of pain. On Manson their kindness had a great effect. Mormonism he knew only from the current talk at Camp Floyd—a view altogether presumed and one-sided; but were not these people humane and gentle? were they not of his own race and color? And could that be entirely bad which produced such good results? And so, though not a word was said on either side about religion, while the light utterances of the Gentile implanted skepticism in the minds of the Saints, the simple kindness of the Saints had almost converted the Gentile.

But none of these things touched Elwood Briarly. Four years in polygamy had seared the delicate tendrils of his English heart; he was, in his fanaticism, a Hebrew of the Hebrews; and to him this stranger was only to be aided in his distress, because he bore the human form, but quietly gotten rid of as soon as possible. And yet there lingered one element of his best days; he loved his little Marian, though he had given her two step-mothers, and brief as had been that meeting in Iowa, he still felt the kindness of the boy, and as far as might be with a Gentile, wished him well. Convalescence in the stimulating air of Utah was rapid, and in due time Willie Manson was able to seek employment with a Gentile merchant in the city, and there he remained two years. His little English friend still retained his friendship, and in that desultory way, in which alone association between the two classes could then take place in Utah, he occasionally visited and kept up his acquaintance with the Briarlys. Thus matters went on till the spring of 1862.

But what strange transformation was this which the little English maiden had undergone! Or was it really the same child he had known, and whose prattle had so greatly amused him during his convalescence? It could not be, he thought, though the change had occurred before his eyes. No, she was no longer English; she had the trim form, the delicate complexion, the arched instep, and the light tripping step of the American girl. She was obeying the climatic laws of sunny Utah, and not of foggy England. And thus have thousands of British parents in that Territory lost their children. For whether it be due more to climate, or to a change of fare, or to exemption from the severe toil and hard life of the poor in Europe, true it is that thousands of foreign-born female Saints, themselves short and stocky, find their daughters growing up in the American likeness; and the young girls "coming on" in Utah are so much more handsome than the young girls just from Europe, that the Saints are bewildered, and the revelation for "celestial marriage" is often set at naught. But what was this other change which annoyed the young man so greatly, and puzzled more than it annoyed him? Was not this his friend, the same girl who had run to welcome him? Why should she now avoid him, or blush and shrink away when he spoke? True, she was older; but what is a woman, he thought, but a girl of larger growth? and why should the woman hate him when the girl had felt so grateful to him? In all his experience he had seen nothing like it. To add to his troubles the poor fellow was lonesome. He had within him the gentle blood of that tall, handsome, and loving man whom he could barely remember, and he could not assimilate with the rude society which was all he could find in the floating Gentile population. The brief period in which he had yielded to dissipation at Camp Floyd, he now looked back upon with disgust. He felt within himself a capacity for better things; he grew shy and uncommunicative, and spent his leisure hours in reading or walking about the pleasant streets of the Mormon capital. Sometimes he wildly resolved on a return to the States, and again that he would outfit with some of the parties going to the "new diggings," away up in the Blackfeet country. Then when another mood seized him, he would venture on another visit to the Briarlys; and though he was sure there was nothing pleasant in the sour looks of the Mormon, or the sad silence of his "wives," and least of all in the shy avoidance of him by Marian, still he would go, because, as he thought, there was nowhere else to go. He pondered, and pondered again, upon the unpleasant change which seemed to have come over every body in whom he felt an interest, and his musings always ended in one unanswerable question: Why should his little friend, who had once liked him, now dislike and shun him?

But if all this was a mystery to Manson, it was clear enough to the Mormon father, who had twenty years more experience in the ways of this wicked world; clearer still to the ward teachers, who visited and catechised every family in their jurisdiction once a week, and clearest of all to the wary bishop of the sixth ward, whose business it was to know every thing that was going on in his bishoprick. They knew, none better, the strange impulses that wake up in the transition period of life; they knew the various motives that influence men to think they are serving the Creator, when they are only moved by the creature. And now look out, young man, for move which way you will, you are almost certain to make a mistake. A few months more, and you will either be a bond-servant of Brigham Young—bound to theocracy by ties you can not sever, and by oaths you dare not break, or an enemy to be harassed and in time expelled.

*   *   *   *   *   *   *   *   *

A new prophet had arisen, and John Banks was wild with joy. Joseph Morris, a simple Welshman, had seen the heavens opened, and through long ranks of shining horsemen the three celestial messengers had come from the throne of Eloheim and bestowed on him the keys of this last ministry. Burning with zeal, he called on Brigham Young to announce his mission, and was dismissed with a short, sharp, and filthy response, which shocked but did not discourage him. Morris at once called upon the people to rally to the true standard, and converts flocked to him from all over the Territory. They were no longer without a living oracle. Brigham had no message to them from the skies; he was a dumb prophet. Joseph Morris abounded in visions and revelations. He was the messenger of God, and the true priestly successor of Joseph Smith. To John Banks this was the fullness of the gospel indeed; he had grieved over the one-man power, and sighed for the Brotherhood of the Saints, and in this mission he saw new hope. For seventeen years there had been no voice from heaven, but now Joseph Morris had revelations so fast that four clerks—two English and two Danish—were required to write them down. The reproach of the Saints, that there had been no revelator since the death of Joseph Smith, was now taken away; and John Banks sought his young friend Thomas James, with the glad tidings. He, too, longed for a living prophet, and in a month was as zealous a "Morrisite" as he had once been a Brighamite, and, with five hundred others, gathered to the camp on the Weber. There revelations, charms, visions, councils, and "speaking in tongues" followed in bewildering profusion. The converts followed the (supposed) example of the early Christians, and had all things in common. Christ was to come and reign in person in a few months, and why trouble themselves about separate property? At length Morris announced to his followers that they need plow and sow no more; they had enough of grain and cattle to last them till Christ came. So all business was suspended except hearkening to instructions, singing hymns, marching in the sacred circle, and listening to revelations. But the millennium failed to arrive, according to promise. Then arose the inevitable quarrel, and secession of a few members. These claimed a larger share of the common property than the orthodox thought them entitled to, and, when refused, levied upon the cattle and wheat of the community. Flour on its way from the mill to the camp was seized by the dissenters; the dissenters were seized in turn and held in close custody by the "Morrisites." The civil law was invoked, and the militia were ordered out. Once more were the old Chartist and the young Radical to be disappointed; once more was fate to give the lie to a prophet, and teach man, by painful experience, what he should have known by the commonest of common sense. The devotees of Morris were soon to learn what the devotees of Brigham are slowly learning—that "who will *not* be ruled by the rudder must be ruled by the rock."

One fine morning in June, 1862, appeared before the camp of the "Morrisites" Robert Burton, sheriff of Salt Lake County and Mormon Bishop, with six hundred armed men and five pieces of artillery; and sent in by the hand of the "Morrisite" cowherd a demand for the surrender of Morris, Banks, and some others. At once the brethren were called together in the bowery—an open shed where they usually worshiped. Morris put on his prophetic robe and crown, took his divining rod, and proceeded to "inquire of the Lord about the matter;" while the whole congregation of five hundred men, women, and children broke into a loud song, an invocation to the God of Israel to descend in a chariot of fire and make known His power upon His enemies. By this time Morris had received the revelation. It promised that God would show His power, and to that end had brought the *posse* upon them; that not a hair of the head of any of His people should be injured; that not one of the faithful should be destroyed. Scarcely had the last words died upon the air, when there was a sharp whizz, followed by the boom of a cannon, then a scream from the upper corner of the bowery. Two women fell dead from their seats, fearfully mangled, and Elsie Nightingale had her under-jaw carried away by the same cannon shot. Never was prediction of a prophet more suddenly and terribly falsified. Ninety-three ablebodied men were all the camp could boast, but they at once flew to arms. The cannon and long-range rifles of the Brighamite militia completely raked the interior of the camp, the people being hid in holes and trenches, while the "Morrisites" had nothing but common guns with which to reply. Nevertheless, they refused to surrender, and for three days, fighting with the desperate energy of religious fanaticism, maintained the unequal battle. The third evening some one raised a white flag. Bishop Burton, after the prisoners were disarmed and under guard, rode in among them and emptied his revolver right and left, killing Morris and two women, and mortally wounding John Banks. Thus ended the "Morrisite" secession.

A second time was Thomas James disappointed; a second time was he the victim of his own fervent and fooling faith. But this time not without recompense. In the "Morrisite" camp he had met one to whom his religious nature instinctively paid reverence. A Danish girl, Christina Jahnsen, alone of her family had been a convert to the new prophet; and through all the troubles of that troublous time the young Briton had been cheered by her companionship and sympathy. Now all was over. The last hope of man for a living prophet was dispelled. He was a captive with the rest, and confessed in his inmost soul that he no longer believed, or could believe, in any man claiming a mission from God. For the rest of his life he was a skeptic. He saw that the woman he loved was safe, at least from personal danger, then determined to escape. While the Brighamite *posse* were busy rifling the houses and tearing down the tents of the captive "Morrisites," he sprang into the bushes and ran swiftly up the Weber. A shot from one of the guards cut a deep flesh-wound along his side, but he escaped. To return to the settlements he knew would be certain capture; there was no chance for him but to continue eastward through the mountains, till he could fall in with some Gentiles upon the Montana trail. Weak from loss of blood, his wound inflamed by exposure, and with nothing but the wheat he could forage from the little patches on the Weber, he still continued his flight. In Echo Cañon, at the house of an old friend, he secretly received some aid and toiled on. Passing the Wasatch, he entered on Bear River Valley, but there his strength deserted him, and he sank helpless upon the ground. He reflected with agony that he was off the main road and upon an obscure trail, and would probably lie there unnoticed till want and fever had done their work. The pain from his wound became unbearable. A strange heat was on his face. As the sun rose higher it seemed that his sight grew dim. The bordering mountains receded, the plain seemed to rise and swallow him up. Strange, distorted images passed before his face, and he fell prone upon the grass, with but a few hours' delirium between him and death.

* * * * * * * * *

It was something of a surprise to Willie Manson, when next he called upon the Briarlys, to be received by the head of the family with smiles of welcome, though he could not but notice that Marian left the room as soon as he entered it. Her father was flanked on all sides by documents: *Orson Pratt's Works*, *The Pearl of Great Price*, *The Key to Theology*, *The Book of Mormon*, and the *Doctrine and Covenants*. There was a long argument, of which he understood but little save the beginning and ending, in these words: "Why don't you accept the truth and become one of God's Saints?" If Briarly had asked him why he didn't fly to heaven without wings, the question would scarcely have seemed to him more absurd. But the elder soon convinced him that he had something to do beside mere pointless objecting, if he would answer the proof texts cited in support of Mormonism. There was first the whole tenor of the Bible, to the effect that prophets and apostles should always lead the true church; there was not a line in the Old or New Testament to imply that miracles and prophecies should cease; and there was, on the other hand, this explicit declaration of Saint Mark: "And these signs shall follow them that believe: in my name shall they cast out devils; they shall speak with new tongues; they shall take up serpents; and if they drink any deadly thing, it shall not hurt them; they shall lay hands on the sick, and they shall recover." To this were added a score of texts promising that God would always be with His people to aid them in doing wonderful works; that they should have ever a witness to confound unbelievers; that they should trust, when sick, not in an arm of flesh, but call in the elders, who should lay hands on them, and that prophecy should not fail, or God leave himself without a witness. Against all this, where was there one text to show that these gifts were to be confined to the apostolic age? For two hours did Elder Briarly continue this argument, heaping up a mountain of facts and texts which no man could meet who had not made theology a study. Poor Manson was utterly confounded. In his trouble, he happened to raise his eyes and glance into an adjoining room. There, hidden from her father's sight, stood Marian, listening intently, her gaze fixed upon Manson with an eager, pleading look that went to his soul. It was but for a second. She was evidently off her guard. But the young man left with a strange pain in his heart that he could not analyze.

Once away from the personal influence of the elder, his mind instinctively revolted against the argument. He could not answer it; but he *felt* that Mormonism was a fraud. He went again and listened to more searching arguments. This went on for weeks. He rarely saw Marian, still more rarely got an opportunity to speak to her; but instead, he listened to all the plausible sophistry of all the Mormon apostles and apologists—a whole library of books devoted to perverting the Scriptures. He could not reply effectively, yet he did not believe. All at once there was a sudden change. There was one visit when no argument was offered, and little courtesy shown. He went away greatly disconcerted; but some influence, he could not have told what, soon took him there again. Elder Briarly received him in silence, then opening one of his works of "authority," read: "If any man, having heard the truth in its fullness by the mouth of an elder, persists in unbelief, he is from that hour an enemy of the faith. From such withdraw yourselves; for it is not possible that such companionship should be profitable." "Young man," said the elder, "that is our faith, and it shall be my practice. For the future—you understand me."

Erelong Manson observed that some strange and evil influence was around him. The old lady with whom he boarded suddenly declined to extend any further accommodations, forcing him to seek a distant and less convenient place. Soon he observed that Mormon customers avoided him, and always waited for some other clerk to attend on them. The young men of his own age quietly dropped his acquaintance, but always without a word of explanation or ill humor. There was no complaint at the store, but his employer could not fail to observe that this clerk lost rather than gained him custom. Strange changes had taken place in Utah. The army was gone, and the new Federal officials seemed completely under the control of Brigham Young. The nation was in a death struggle with rebellion, and every Sunday the Tabernacle rang with fierce denunciations of the Gentile government. This was the consumption decreed, this was the great war foretold by the Prophet Joseph, which was to avenge the Saints on their enemies; this was the beginning of the bloodshed which was to lay waste Babylon, and bring the day when seven women would take hold of one man, and a feeble remnant of the American race come begging the Saints to save them from annihilation. Thus ran

THE FAIR APOSTATE—CONTINUED.

the Tabernacle talk. It was a dark time for the few Gentile residents. Every man must look out for himself, and those under ban were to be avoided. In one month from his last conversation with Elder Briarly, Willie Manson was out of his position in the store, out of his latest lodgings, and in a frame of mind desperate enough for any thing. In this mood he met a returned Californian, who had halted in Salt Lake for a brief space, and instead of going on home, had again been seized with the gold fever, and wanted a companion to the northern diggings. In twenty-four hours they were equipped, mounted and off, taking the route north-east to come upon the Bridger trail, and secure a larger party to pass through the Indian country. Their fourth day of leisurely travel they descended the eastern slope of the main Wasatch, and turning more to the north, aimed for the upper bend of Bear River. Midway upon this plain, Manson was amazed to find lying under a scrubby pine his acquaintance of the previous year, the Mormon apostate and escaped "Morrisite," Thomas James.

Hank Beatty, the Californian, was all impatience to press on to the Montana gold fields. He had spent two years in California, and started back poor as he came, and in a fever to get home; but the older and more persistent fever again seized him, when he heard of the rich discoveries in Montana, and he became again that eager, restless mortal—a gold-seeker. But Manson would not leave the sick and wounded man. He transported him to the nearest place where good water could be procured and a rude shelter erected, and there for a fortnight, while Beatty fumed and fretted, he nursed the unfortunate back to health and strength. As soon as he was able to ride slowly, sharing the two horses between the three, they traveled on to the Bridger and Fort Hall trail, and were soon in company with a jolly party of Missourians, all primed for adventure, and sanguine of getting gold beyond the dreams of avarice. But the adventure came before the gold, for soon the whole country was swarming with Bannocks and Shoshonees.

These warlike savages looked upon the Montana emigration of 1861 and '62 as their legitimate prey. From the eastern foot of the Sierra Nevada, clear to the Laramie Plains, the whole Shoshone nation seemed to concentrate on this trail; with them soon came their kinsmen, the Bannocks, and erelong the way was dotted with the wrecks of captured trains and the bodies of murdered emigrants. From Bear River northward our party had an almost continuous running fight. At last they reached a section where sleep and rest were almost impossible. At night they halted, built fires, and hastily prepared their food; then struck off across the valley, built another fire, as if for camp, then abandoned it, and passed the night on the highest accessible point of some barren rock. By day they grazed their stock only on the most sheltered points, surrounded with scouts; and

"THE BRIGHT WEAPON GLITTERED IN THE AIR—BOW AND ARROW FELL FROM LIFELESS HANDS."

at night again pursued the same devious course, building fires and leaving them, traveling zigzag, taking their water, almost on the run, from the few pools, and never camping near a stream or in a wooded glen, but traveling the direct distance twice or three times over.

Now it was that Thomas James seemed to recover his health of body and mind. Danger made him forget the past, and he soon came to be relied on for every daring work. At the last stream they must cross before entering the mining region, the savages had attained the perfection of ambush; and James and Beatty were sent forward to reconnoiter. From almost beneath their horses' feet, in the worst part of the thicket bordering the stream, rose half a dozen savages. Beatty whirled his horse to the left and spurred him into the timber, but it was too late for James to return, who was in advance. Before him stood a gigantic Bannock, his arrow on the bow and already half drawn. Could he have looked forward a few years, how gladly would he have welcomed the shot which should pierce his heart. But now, life was still sweet, though he had lost so much. His long hunting-knife was in his hand. His spurred animal dashed madly upon the savage. One instant the keen, bright weapon glittered in the air; the next bow and arrow fell from lifeless hands, and the burly Bannock fell back into the pool, which was fast crimsoned with his heart's blood. The momentum carried the horse forward into the opposite thicket; there was a shower of arrows, but the white was out of range. A short, sharp conflict followed; the savages were defeated, and the long harassed emigrants with joy hurried forward into the open plain, and before night were in a region free from Indians.

Common danger and mutual good offices had bound the two young men together as with hooks of steel; for on the plains men long associated must either become warm friends or bitter enemies. Together they mined upon the bar, together they prospected the lonely cañon; they shared in prosperity, and together suffered from the "stampede" and disappointment in Sun River Gulch. They lost property by the "road agents," and acted with the *Vigilantes*. All this time they were growing. Four years amid such scenes had developed them more than ten of common life. But at last they grew weary of wild life. There were those who drew them mightily towards Utah. The common impulse could not be resisted, after they learned that all had changed for the better there. The nation was no longer at war. American soldiers were stationed at Salt Lake City. General Connor had "civilized" the hostile Indians with one hand, and with the other taught Brigham Young to respect the Gentile government. The tide of overland travel again flowed through Utah in a heavy volume. Thousands of miners were going to winter in Salt Lake. The tide was now southward, and the late autumn of 1865 saw our heroes again upon the borders of Zion.

CHAPTER XXII.

THROUGH GREAT TRIBULATION.

THE hot, dry summer of 1866 hastened on. The long trains of the newly converted were strung out from the Missouri to the Laramie, and the deputed Saints from Utah were on their way to meet them. The faint green of the bunch-grass had yielded to its summer brown, and the landscape of Cache Valley already showed that the Utah season was a fruitful one. The July Sabbath saw a gay and happy assemblage in Logan Ward; the harvest had been plentiful, and Bishop Warren was alternately thundering against the ungodly, and thanking the Mormon "Lord," in the ward assembly rooms. The mountain maidens smiled and nodded as they passed into the spacious building; the Mormon lads collected in the back seats, and the bishop changed his strain to a tirade on "the laziness of the young people of the present day." He told of digging ditches, building fences and making dobies, and assured them they must learn it in this world, or they would have a good deal more of it to do in the next. He then branched off to the necessity of improving their stock, paying their tithing, and keeping their covenants; "and, above all," said he, "let no man sell his wheat till we get the word from Brother Brigham, for these Montana men must buy of us, brethren, this year—they must do it, for the Missouri's too low for 'em to run up flour from the States that way. So hold on to your wheat till President Young gives the word." After giving notice where the best bull could be found,* and reading a list of estrays, the worthy bishop announced that certain parties "who had been for awhile out of the Church, would now be received back on profession of repentance, and baptized again," and concluded with: "God bless you all, is my prayer, for Jesus' sake. Amen."

But who is this that comes to be rebaptized and taken back to the fold, "having apostatized from the Saints and been buffeted of Satan?" It is none other than our once true hero, Thomas James! And he is happy as the day is long. The bright sunshine of the bright Utah

* Fact! This was a frequent practice in Utah assemblies when the author first went to the Territory.

summer can add nothing to the sunshine in his heart, for he has found Christina, and she is his promised wife. But she is again a fanatical Mormon. Her brief experience with the "Morrisites" had been enough of independent thinking for her whole life-time, and she was again with her family, and again one of the sister Saints. And she was more beautiful than ever. Her clear complexion had just enough of the Scandinavian tinge, her soft flaxen hair seemed to the ardent youth finer than silk, her mild blue eye told of an affectionate disposition and faithful heart. But all was not pleasant. She was beautiful to others as well as him; and when the apostate youth, after a wearisome winter in Salt Lake City, traced her to Cache Valley, he did so only to find her sought in marriage by the bishop. And was it not more of an honor to be the "bishop's fourth" and his "favorite," as she certainly would be, than the "slavey" of a poor mechanic, to "nigger it on love and starvation?" Such talk she heard daily. But that was only for this world. As for the next—ah, there was the nameless horror she could not shake off. For into the soul of every believing Mormon woman was ground this sentence: "If she will not abide in this law, she shall be damned." And the "Revelation on Celestial Marriage" had too plainly pronounced the future fate of all who marry unbelievers: "They shall be angels only, and not gods; they shall be servants to those worthy of a far more exceeding and eternal weight of glory." If she married a Gentile, there could be no "exaltation" for her in the celestial world; she must remain a servant forever, "blessed with no increase;" go through eternity without a husband, and be a hewer and drawer to other women who had kept the law on earth. It was too terrible.

And so, when her former lover, after long waiting, had an opportunity to speak to her, she told him there was but one thing to do: he must accept the gospel as revealed by Joseph Smith; he must reënter the Church of Jesus Christ of Latter-day Saints, and live his religion, that he might secure "exaltation" for her and himself. "Reënter the Church—be rebaptized? Why, certainly; why not?" thought James. All religions are alike. It is but to pay tithing, and observe the ordinances, to confess the errors of "Morrisite" belief, to be "buried again in baptism," and thenceforward "obey counsel" and run with the current. God knows he had had a hard enough time running against the current; he would let things take their own course now. What mattered it? He could subscribe to one belief as well as another; and so, in sight of all the congregation, he owned his manifold errors, received absolution, went down into the water, was cleansed, and was again "Brother Thomas James, of Logan Ward, assigned to Brother William Sessions' class, and to be fellowshiped accordingly."

How smoothly sped his love-making then! How light appeared his duties on the farm where he had contracted for the season's work! How mild the soft moonlight nights, how grand the calm mountains, how beautiful the crystal Logan River as it dashed down the pebbly rapids near her home! Evening after evening he was with her. The bishop seemed to have given up his suit. Her friends, however, favored the man of position; he was of assured faith; this one might apostatize again. There is an old proverb in Utah, which has something to say about the "danger of being rival to a bishop;" but could any thing be more cordial than the conduct of Bishop Warren to the reconverted man? Almost in spite of himself James was led on to open his heart more freely to Bishop Warren than he would have believed possible a year before. And it must be confessed that he was not as thoroughly versed in some of the minor points of doctrine as a man should be to make a good impression on a bishop. And now James was very much surprised to find that two or three of his acquaintances, young men of his own age, had their doubts also about the truth of Mormonism; and, though he would not have had the bishop know it for the world, he conversed freely with them, and confessed his own motives and mental condition. True, he knew these young men sometimes served as ward teachers, but what of that? Was it not probable that, like himself, the very intensity of their work for Mormonism had set them to thinking? He knew that had been his own case. But there were several things he did not know. He did not know that on the soft, warm moonlight nights, when he lingered in the garden or grove with Christina, there was an eye and ear not far away, trained to the secret service of the Church; and that, as his love-making progressed, and father and mother left them more to themselves, and they spent half the night in the cosy arbor back of the house, there was a mysterious way by which all their familiar secret dalliance became a part of the Church records. No; there were deeper depths in Mormonism than were suspected by the most suspicious English Saint; and even now in Utah not one in ten knows the power that controls him. But human nature, especially male nature, is not changed by the stimulating air of Utah; and so, as the warm nights passed, Christina's soft hair twined in his fingers, her fair cheek resting on his bosom, her young and graceful form clasped in his arms, her heart gently agitated with the half-resisting, half-yielding pliancy of love, it strangely happened that certain lines in the "secret ritual" were forgotten, and the faithful ward teacher, then on duty, had an important account to give the bishop at their next meeting. And the bishop frowned, then smiled, then frowned again, while the faithful teacher waited for his commendation, and really could not tell whether his spiritual superior was pleased or angry.

It was a mild September Sabbath afternoon, and Bishop Warren was thundering against covenant-breakers. He grew furious about "the wolves that would creep into the fold and ravage among the ewe lambs;" he quoted the "blood-atonement" sermons of Jedediah M. Grant and Brigham Young, and called for a "show of hands" as to whether the brethren and sisters sustained these doctrines. All hands were held up, and again he threatened the law-breakers. "There are wolves among the flock, but there are dogs set to guard it, and the dogs have very sharp teeth.* Now, brethren and sisters, keep your own counsels. You all know what was done at San Pete, when Edward Beauvais defiled a daughter of Zion. And I want you to understand that the boys of Logan are as true as the boys of San Pete. Now, keep still and mind your own business. Judgment will be laid to the line in Zion, and righteousness to the plummet in Logan. Ask no questions, and no lies will be told you. If you want information, don't gabble with your neighbors; come to your bishop. He'll tell you what is good for you. And if you hear any thing strange, don't go talking to your women about it; there are those set in authority by the Lord God Almighty to inquire into such things. But you mind your own business. All who say it is all right, hold up your right hands. [All hands up.] May the Lord bless you all, for Jesus' sake. Amen!"

The afternoon meeting ended; the Saints slowly wended their way homeward, smiling and chatting. In the front yards and neat gardens gathered the family groups for a peaceful evening; the red sun sank behind the Promontory Range, and the calm of a Puritan Sabbath settled down upon Cache Valley. How happy these people must be!—at least so many a Gentile visitor has said. How calm, how peaceful, how free from envy, care and strife!

But the dark night drew on. About 10 P. M. three figures appeared in the shadow between the ward meeting-house and the line of box-elders beside it. There was yet no moon; still they kept in the shadow. A fourth softly approached.

---

*See "blood-atonement" sermon by Orson Hyde, in the "Journal of Discourses."

"Are you fixed, brethren?"

"We are, bishop. Which is it to be?"

"You know—the endowment penalty—second grade. The daughters of Zion must be protected."

"But that is not ——"

"No! It is death—so written; but this time the other will be better. You understand? Hist!"

They vanished in the darkness.

Thomas James's cup of earthly happiness seemed full. He felt no consciousness that this was a world of errors, and that he had committed a very serious one. Were not he and Christina to be man and wife in a few weeks, and would it not be all right then? It was midnight before he gave her a good-bye kiss, and took the quiet road down along the banks of the Logan River. The late half-moon was just beginning to peep over the rugged Wasatch, casting great scallops of light and shade across the valley. How musically the river rippled over its clear, pebbly bottom! how pleasantly gurgled the water-seeks along the road-side! And how still was the peaceful Mormon town!—how far superior to the manufacturing cities of the East, where there was riot and strife, and sometimes murder! What a kind and social people was this people! How little crime there was here! He laughed aloud as he thought of the absurd stories he had heard concerning "the danger of being a bishop's rival." And as the bright surface of the crystal stream shone in the moonlight, it seemed to him a fit emblem of the peace over the land; its dancing wavelets represented the joy in his own heart. Yes, this was indeed a land of peace; and if Mormonism was *not* true, these were in a sense "God's people," among whom all honest men were safe.

Ha! What was that?

Nothing, apparently, but some brother's cow moving among the tall weeds. Snapping off the head of a wild sunflower with his light walking-cane, he turned into the dark grove which lay between him and home. Sharp and shrill came a whistle from in front. He started back suddenly. A rope fell about his heels. He instinctively threw up his hands to save himself from falling. A sack was cast over his head. It was drawn tight from behind. He struggled desperately, but his mouth was so bound he could not utter a cry. Stout arms had hold of him; they pinioned every limb. Helpless, voiceless, still desperately struggling, he was borne away, he knew not whither.

If Willie Manson had been astonished at his last visit to Briarly in 1862, how was he amazed by the latter's conduct in 1866! For Briarly had returned from a mission on the Rio Virgen, whither he had been sent in 1863 "to build up the waste places;" and he not only sought Manson at the store where he had found employment, but talked with such graceful fluency that the Gentile was quite confounded. He showered invitations on him to visit them at home; he never alluded to any thing disagreeable that had passed between them; he inquired with almost embarrassing interest of Manson's success in the mines, and talked about the return of peace in the States and the glory of the American nation in a way that would have put the warmest Republican in the shade. Here was a change indeed. Why he did not at once accept these flattering invitations, Willie could not for his life have told. He was sure he retained no malice against Briarly, as indeed why should he? He knew of no harm this Mormon had done him, and he did recall some good. And yet he did not at once accept. He saw that Briarly was now an elder of some rank; that he was in a fair way to become a bishop; that he was loud in "bearing testimony" in all "experience meetings," and at times held forth eloquently in the Tabernacle on the "evidences." But he noticed, too, that Briarly never called on him when other Mormons were in the store, and that his effusive utterances were always in a corner, and when no third party was near.

He pondered the matter until it became really tormenting, and then had recourse to his friend Hank Beatty, who had returned from Montana with a good-sized belt full of "dust," and now lingered in Zion. Beatty heard the account through carefully, cocked his head on one side, closed one eye in profound meditation for a moment, then everted his leathery lips, and, with a regular Missouri "thlurp," ejected a gill or so of ambeer into the water-seek. After it, flavored with nicotine, came this oracular response:

"Keep your eye peeled—somethin's up. This is a queer country."

Manson was painfully aware of the truth conveyed in the last sentence; but now the thought suddenly occurred to him, "What had come over Beatty lately?" The latter lingered unaccountably. He had said that he left home, in New York, in 1860, and went by sea to California; he had, in 1862, and again in 1865, been in a fever to get home, and it ran into Manson's mind that Beatty had once told him something about having a family, but he was not positive about this. And now the man seemed to have abandoned all idea of going home. He was enthusiastic in his praises of Utah and the Mormons; he pointed often to the hills, and said, in his oracular way: "Money there, my boy; don't you run away from it." To add to Manson's perplexities, his dearer friend, Thomas James, had suddenly departed for the northern settlements, and had never sent him word or line. What a horribly selfish passion is love! It makes one forget all the world but two persons—self and the other self.

Manson was almost ready to conclude that human nature itself had changed in this anomalous country. Here were lakes of pure brine with no outlet to the sea; all the streams ran towards the center and none towards the ocean; a river was larger at the head than at the mouth; it had two ends and was biggest in the middle; most of the streams came to an end without joining other streams, and though the lakes were forever fed, they were never full. Why should not man's nature be inverted in such a country? Where there was no consistency in nature it was unreasonable to look for it in man. So he decided to take chances and visit the Briarlys.

There was a change indeed. He saw but one "wife," and heard no allusion whatever to Marian. The elder explained in an awkward way that his "wife Matilda was on the ranche down on the Virgen"—that was all. Manson was strangely distrait and nervous; and was not at all helped by observing every time he looked up, that his host's eyes were fixed upon him with a strange, inquiring look he could not comprehend. But as they sat down to dinner—it was on Sunday—a man appeared at the gate, and the elder broke forth at once, without warning or prefatory remark, into a wordy defense of polygamy. As no previous reference had been made to this subject, Manson could scarcely conceal his astonishment. But his habits of thought were very different from what they had been four years before, and he was prepared for argument, as are nearly all Gentiles who reside long in Utah. The new-comer entered, and made the usual salutations just as Briarly was saying:

"Abraham believed God, and it was accounted unto him for righteousness. He was called the friend of God—the father of God's chosen people. He had no child till he took Hagar to wife, then God blessed him with a son by Sarah also, showing that God approbated his polygamy."

"Yes," said the new-comer, whom Manson soon suspected to be one of the ward teachers; "you pretend to revere Abraham—you might profitably follow his example."

"Which example?" said Manson, "when he married his sister, or when he lied about it? You know he did both."

"Do you revile the patriarchs?" said the teacher, with rising color.

"I only say of the patriarchs what the Bible says of them, that they did many bad things, things which would now be considered crimes."

"But God's word specifies all the sins and crimes. You can not show a text forbidding polygamy."

"Perhaps not in express words, but I *can* show that the general teaching is against it. You can not show a text expressly forbidding gambling or slavery; but we know they are not justified."

"But was not Hagar given Abraham of God?"

"No. The record shows that God had nothing to do with Abraham's polygamy. It resulted from Sarah's want of faith. She had been promised a son, and as the boy did not come along soon enough, she thought she would help the Lord to keep His promise, and so she give her husband to Hagar with the express understanding that the child should be Sarah's. According to my notion, the Lord had nothing to do with it."

"But Abraham *did* practice plurality, and the Lord did *not* condemn him for it—you can't get around that."

"Yes, Abraham's first wife was his half-sister, and his second was a colored woman, and you can't show a line in the Bible to prove that she was married to him. The Lord always speaks of her as a 'bond-woman,' and her son as 'the son of the bond-woman.' She was n't Abraham's wife at all."

"Sir-r," said the teacher—and as he warmed with the debate, his Yorkshire accent came out stronger. "You revile what you do not understand. 'No man knoweth the things of God, save the Spirit of God teach him,' and you have no witness. But we have in us that knowledge which enables us to sense divine truth. I *know* this work is of God. I *know* that plurality is the celestial law." And to this Briarly gave an emphatic assent. He had the *spirit;* there was a witness the Gentile knew not of; he must be baptized for the remission of sins, and receive the Holy Ghost by the laying on of hands of one that held the true priesthood. Then this witness should be given him, and he would know for himself, and not for another, that this work was of God. But among the Gentiles there was no priest or preacher with authority from God; hence they could not have this witness—and much more to the same effect.

But Manson was not to be diverted from the main question. The controversial spirit was aroused in him, and with many interruptions he went on:

"There is not a case of plural marriage reported in the Bible but what it led straight to quarreling, and sometimes to murder. The whole Bible only relates thirteen cases of polygamy among the righteous race, while it tells of hundreds of patriarchs, prophets, and kings who either had but one wife each, or none at all. There was Lamech: the first pluralist mentioned, was the second murderer mentioned. Abraham 'took up' with the hired girl, and she had a baby; his wife abused her, and he sent her and her boy away to die or live in the wilderness. Isaac, the best man of the outfit, never had more than one wife. Jacob was swindled into plurality by his heathen father-in-law; then swindled his father-in-law with the trick of the peeled rods; and after it all his children quarreled, their mothers quarreled, and ten of the boys sold another into slavery.

"BEHOLD OUR LAMANITE BROTHER."

"That was a nice family for us Americans to pattern after, was n't it? Then there was David—married one widow before her husband had been dead a week, and had another man killed so he could get his wife; and after it all, his children quarreled like cats and dogs, and one of them rebelled and drove the old man out of his own house for awhile. And Solomon—he violated their law, which says the 'king must not multiply wives lest his heart turn away.'* He did multiply wives, and his heart did turn away. Now look at the other fellows. When the Lord started man on earth, he created a one-wife man; when he saved the race, he saved a family with one wife each, and drowned all the pluralists; and when Christ came, his earthly parents were one man and his one wife. It looks to me like that's the safest example to follow."

It must not be supposed that our friend was allowed to give this view continuously; that would be a new experience in Utah. The ward teacher had thrown in knotty texts at every pause, and now, wrought up to the "sermon point," he concluded with the usual apostolic curse—"Behold our Lamanite brother!" And to emphasize the matter a Southern Ute entered the yard, tricked out in all the gaudy finery which they affect when annuity goods are plenty. "He is the last of a mighty race that rejected the truth. Look at the cities of the plain. Behold the desolation of the East as foretold in the prophets. The same shall come upon your boasted Union. It's been split in two once, and patched up again; but, mark ye, it's like an old bowl— it'll break again in a little while, and ye can't fix it. Then you'll flee to these mountains for safety; for the Lord 'll come out of his hiding-place and vex the nation in his fury;" and so on for an hour.

As he concluded a light step was heard at the door, and, looking up, Manson saw a face that had vaguely haunted him through all his Montana wanderings. He felt the warm blood rush to his cheeks; and in that instant he recognized the source of his uncertainties four years before. He now knew why he had lost his little girl friend, and why he was so strangely *distrait* in her presence, and she so strangely perverse, apparently unfriendly. He understood it all. She had been in the far South, in "Mormon Dixie," and just returned. A faint flush overspread her face as Manson advanced to meet her; in an instant it passed away, and she accosted him with a manner and words that plainly showed she meant to consider him merely as "some one she had met before." But his frame thrilled as their hands touched. It was all over with him. He was madly, violently in love. He scarcely knew how he got out of the house and got home. There was a messenger waiting—a returned miner from Montana—who bore a note, in a well-remembered hand. But it contained only these words:

Will: For God's sake, come and see me.
Tom James.

* Deuteronomy xvii: 17.

Certainly he would go, only he must make some preparations first. But why was Tom so urgent? and if so urgent, why had he kept silent so long? The Montanian was gone before Manson had thought to ask, and the next minute he was astonished to see Beatty, with a wagon-load of Mormons, driving out the Tooele road. And now it was evening, and he must have some time to think; and when it was morning, he thought he must see Marian once more before he left, for surely if Tom had been sick, or any thing wrong, he would have said so. Now, contrary to the usual rule, bad news does not travel fast in Utah; and when Manson had dispatched a note by the slow mail of those days, a week passed before he could take the first step of preparation; and at the end of that week came another note, and, strange to say, by another returning miner instead of the mail, and it merely said:

"*You need not come; wait for me.*"

And it is almost a shame to relate it, but ten minutes after the note was read, Manson had already dismissed it from his mind, and was pondering on his intended visit to Marian. Ah! love is a terribly selfish passion.

And now the conduct of Elder Briarly was more a puzzle than ever. He came again to the store, but talked very little; and when Manson, after waiting on a customer, happened to glance suddenly at the Elder, he saw the latter watching him with an eager intensity, as if he would read his very thoughts. He could not understand it, and yet he knew that it made him very uncomfortable. Worse still, it made him half afraid; and so, while he was in a fever of impatience to see Marian, he still hung back irresolutely till another Sunday came, and went. He saw her far across the Tabernacle, and was feasting his eyes on her face, when her father was suddenly called upon to "address the brethren." And now, to Manson's astonishment, Elder Briarly rose and delivered a fierce philippic against all Gentiles, from that very uncompromising text: "He that is not for us, is against us." The Mormons, be it noted, have a most unhappy facility of getting hold of all the hard, uncharitable (I say it with reverence) texts in the Bible; and while they preach a thousand sermons a year on this text, not one of them was ever known to quote the rendering given by another Evangelist: "He that is not against us, is on our part."

Manson fairly shuddered while the elder launched metaphorical fire and brimstone on "our enemies, who have followed us to these valleys of the mountains," and denounced every lax saint who favored the ungodly Babylonians. Thence he branched off to the history of the Church, and recounted more persecutions than were suffered by the early Christians. Racks, hatchets, swords and dungeons glimmered through his sermon in mazy confusion, and he galloped recklessly over bloody figures of speech like an oratorical Bashi-Bazouk. Manson was positively frightened, and suffered two weeks more of self-tormenting fancies before he dared venture to see Marian. It was now late autumn, and the evening was cold, but his head felt hot enough as he turned the familiar corner in the sixth ward. To his amazement, as he met the father coming out, the latter bowed low, spoke most graciously, then glanced around and hurried away as if he had been stealing a sheep! What *was* the matter, thought Manson, that people in these peaceful valleys should be so afraid of each other? Surely this was the quietest city on the continent. Every traveler said so, and yet ——.

There was Marian, alone in the large orchard and garden combined, which surrounds these Mormon dwellings. She smiled faintly, extended her hand, and said something about "neglecting old friends." The hot blood rushed over him. His native "Hoosier" impulsiveness had the mastery. He never could have told you how he did it—how then can I? But he had her hand. He was kissing it. He was pouring out passionate words. Now he had her in his arms. He said every thing—and nothing. He left every sentence unfinished. His speech could not have been reported by a lightning phonographer. There were no connected words in it, indeed. But it had the essential element of strength. And at the end of it, they were far back in a thicket; his hat was upon the ground, her head upon his shoulder, and he felt as if he needed a dozen arms and hands. And yet the innocent fellow did not know if his prayer had been granted. Time was needed to make it clear to his mind. But after the storm came a great calm of enjoyment. The cold night was unheeded by the happy lovers, till the step of her father returning from the "experience meeting" aroused them to the painful fact that they were still in a world of difficulties, and that much lay between them and the fruition of their hopes. But Manson went home as if he trod on air. He was too happy to sleep. The first revulsion came when, at the usual hour next day, he saw Elder Briarly enter. But now the peculiarities of the elder seemed tenfold increased. He talked in a loud and aggressive tone with the few Mormon customers. When they had gone, he seemed to fall into a reverie. Manson felt instinctively that the elder had learned all from his daughter, and his heart beat with fearful violence whenever the latter approached him; but every time the elder would again turn away in silence. The suspense became unbearable. At length there came a lull in the morning business. Briarly went to the door as if to leave. He passed into the street, and looked both ways, then suddenly reëntered, and came hurriedly to the rear end, where Manson stood. The latter leaned forward, uncertain whether he was to be denounced or pleasantly entreated, and was about to speak, when the elder hurriedly inclined his mouth to the Gentile's ear, and hissed rather than whispered:

"In God's name, is there any way we can get out of this infernal country?"

The light step of a Mormon woman was heard at the door. The elder turned with a cheery greeting and loud laugh; then passed at once into the street, leaving Manson almost petrified with amazement.

* * * * * * *

It was midwinter, and there was another Gentile panic. The "outsiders" had thought their troubles over; that law was to reign in Utah. But in the spring, S. N. Brassfield was shot dead while walking the streets in the custody of an officer. In October, Dr. Robinson was brutally assassinated. Non-Mormon settlers on the public lands were mobbed, shot, thrown in the Jordan, and driven away. Willie Manson thought he had troubles enough, when one day a pale, spiritless looking man entered the store, and *said* he was Thomas James! Oh, no! It could not be, thought Manson. Not the bold horseman who had cut his way through ranks of brave Bannocks! Not the stout young Briton who had done and dared so much in Montana! Yet it was. But not the same. Never to be the same again. For now Manson listened to a narrative that chilled his blood with horror. Thomas James had suffered at the hands of the priesthood the last terrible indignity that man can suffer—compared with which murder is a light offense. A *creature* walked abroad, called by the same name; but Thomas James, the yeoman, would never again dare death in Indian combat, or rival a bishop in love. Where could he go, and what could he do? asked his pitying friend. He was not alone. Utah in that sad time contained more than one who had suffered like him—*men*, so-called, shrinking along the streets, ashamed to meet their kind. For, let this misfortune come how it may, on innocent or guilty, while reason protests that we ought not to despise such a one, the subtle instinct of manhood commands that we *shall*.

Thomas James went south with a party going to San Bernardino;

and in due time the report reached Salt Lake City that he had died there, *insane*. Bishop Warren extended his possessions, and was a father unto his people. There was peace and order in his bishoprick; the apostle in charge of Cache Valley recommended this good steward for reward; and strangely enough, when Brigham asked his will, the bishop only wanted another wife, as he had but four, and his kingdom was not increasing as fast as he could wish. To Christina Jahnsen, sorrowful and lonely, came the good sisters with a world of good advice. Innuendoes, hints at what had been said and heard, insinuations that her lover had boasted of his conquest, parts of letters said to have been written—all these skillfully woven into an imposing lie—soon did their work. Believing herself doubly betrayed, a sinner against God and a traitor to the Church, she submitted to whatever was required; and before the winter was past the Endowment House witnessed the sacrifice of another victim, and the fatherly bishop went home with his young wife. The laws of Zion had been vindicated. Virtue, according to the Mormon idea, had been protected; the daughters of Zion were warned, and the careful bishop had his reward.

But the married woman soon learns what the ignorant girl could not even have suspected. She learned too soon that she had been cruelly deceived. That calm nature was aroused, and the lovely woman had a devil in her heart. Then began the battle. It was a weak woman against a whole community; an individual against a system. Fierce as a fury she flew upon her "husband," and cursed him with frantic vehemence. She raved and prayed by turns; she could not yet cast off her faith in Mormonism, but she hated it because it was true. Then came the "counsel" of ward teachers; the direction to humble herself, to make her peace with the man who was her "head in Christ." But she raved on. It was now insanity. Then was pronounced the common verdict in such cases: "Possessed of a devil." The elders came with the holy oil and laying on of hands. But the "possession" would not be charmed away. Then she was bound down "till such time as the devil should cease to afflict her."

About her came all the canting sisterhood, the malignant, the stupid, the fanatical, to preach "submission to the will of God." "It is the duty of us all, Sister. Brother Warren is an upright man, a faithful Saint; he will give you a great exaltation in the eternities. With a Gentile you would be a servant, world without end. Just think, dear Sister, how dreadful to be a hewer of wood and drawer of water through all eternity for other women, when you might have been a queen in the celestial heavens." Still she raved, and railed on the Church and all the priesthood. Again was she bound; again the holy oil and laying on of hands. Then "the devil left her." A strange calm followed. The faithful rejoiced over a sister restored. She went about her duties in silence and submission. But there was that in her eye which the dull brethren about her did not note; there was a far away look, that showed a mind set on something the eye could not see. An inward fever scorched her blood, and dried up the sources of her beauty. Her child was born and died, but she heeded it not. Two years passed, and the bishop's "favorite and No. 5" began already to be known as the bishop's "old woman." Another year, and she was away from Logan; now on the bishop's ranche, in Bear River Valley. The bishop now had another "favorite," a No. 6; and few who noticed No. 5 at her wearing tasks, "taking care of things at the ranche," ever stopped to think how fast the bishop's late favorite had become an "old woman," or to wonder that that head, fast turning gray, and that wrinkled face, could belong to a woman over whose head but twenty-five years had passed. At length there came a night when the storm was abroad upon the desert. The fierce wind howled along the Humboldt Range, gathered the red sand in ghastly pillars that rolled over Promontory Range, and swept with blinding force upon the eastern valley. People said: "It is one of our worst dust storms—it will purify the air," and thought of the season, the crops and their several material gains. But the dust storm grew to a tornado; and when it passed, the crazy log-hut on the bishop's ranche was in ruins. A calm and glorious morning followed the storm; the Utah valleys never looked more peaceful than then. But in that storm a greater storm had been stilled. Beneath the pitying stars that shone through the flying clouds that night, a soul had found release; another subject had deserted from Brigham's kingdom, and the sad Danish girl was young again in the heaven of her beloved.

* * * * * * * * *

The mystery of his intended father-in-law was no longer a mystery to Willie Manson. The elder had long been apostate in heart, and secretly mourned his inability to escape from his bondage. But how could he break the ties which bound him in Utah? He now had three wives, but every day he secretly thanked God that the last one was childless. Ten years he had lived in polygamy, and Marian had nine half-brothers and sisters. Could he leave these innocent ones in this country? And could he hope to get them safely away? Could he trust his own wives, whom the ward teachers, in accordance with the "secret ritual," examined separately every week? Could he trust his dearest friend? Was there any one or any thing in this land of intrigue and priestly supervision, who would be true? How often did he gaze upon the snowy summits of the Wasatch, and curse the hour when he made himself a virtual prisoner in these valleys! It was easy to say that the laws of the country protected him in going where he pleased. But there was another law here more powerful than any written law. His property was "consecrated" by deeds which he once thought a mere form, but now knew to be valid. The church owned it all, if the trustee-in-trust but chose to exercise his power. In his days of fanaticism he had bound himself by the "Perfect Oneness in Christ," and now all he had was security for all the other members of his "quorum." Though he had paid his own passage and that of Marian from Liverpool to Salt Lake, yet he had, as requested by the bishop in charge, indorsed the notes for passage money of a dozen of his poorer brethren; and he knew too well that all these notes were ready to be presented at a moment's notice. And the good bishops and apostles who constitute the Utah Legislature had taken excellent care on this point. For a resident there was no end of exemptions; it was scarcely possible to collect a debt by law. But for "one intending to leave the Territory"—it was expressly enacted that there was no exemption. And if one should try to leave before every debt was paid, there was the law against "absconding debtors"—they could be imprisoned "at the discretion of the court." And such a court! The probate judge of each county was the presiding bishop thereof—the sworn servant of Brigham Young. Verily, the "cut-throat laws of Utah" were made by men who have had experience in ecclesiastical tyranny.

For three years Elder Briarly had lived a stupendous lie. Knowing himself to be an apostate, suspecting himself to be the object of suspicion, he thought, as thousands have thought, to make his position more secure by a show of zeal. And then his wives—what was he to do with them? He was but a man, and in his secret soul he confessed that he loved the one, was indifferent to the second, and positively detested the third. What if the detested one should penetrate his designs? He groaned in spirit at the thought. There was nothing for him but determined reticence; and so his home life was a continuing lie—a lie so complex, so gigantic, that it corrupted every element of his nature, and changed him from a man and a Briton to a self-despised *thing*. And so it must be with every man in polygamy, unless, like the Oriental, he regard his women as playthings or slaves, and look with lordly indifference upon them all.

But there came a time when he must choose. He could no longer stand behind the door and grit his teeth when the troubles of polygamy pressed upon him. Brigham was now inaugurating schemes which would make every submissive Mormon a slave. He must escape with whatever he could take, or whoever would go with him, and trust the others to follow. Very secretly he made a few preparations, Manson assisting as far as was safe. Assuredly there was need of caution. The Gentiles were in a condition of panic. The few soldiers at Camp Douglas were of no avail in the city. In one instance a guard had been sent to see that Miss Sarah Carmichael, the poetess, reached the stage coach in safety; but this was an experiment not to be repeated. The President of the United States was now devoting his mighty energies to thwarting the Republican party; and in Utah every Federal official suspected of "radicalism" was removed, and a Mormon put in his place. Burton, the murderer of the Morrisites, held the best office in the Territory. One Federal judge was a Mormon elder. The Governor was expressly instructed "not to irritate the Mormons." Other officials were the subservient tools of Brigham Young. Among the army officers alone could the harassed Gentiles and apostates hope to find friends. At length the general commanding the department announced that an expedition would start for the Missouri River on a certain day, and whoever would might "travel under their protection *through the Indian country.*" The priesthood laughed at this wording, and sneered at the Gentile officer for thus insinuating that any one wanted to leave Utah. The night before the day set, there was not a sign of preparation in the city. Daylight next morning showed a caravan of two hundred people camped about the garrison: men, women and children, miserably equipped indeed, but eager for the journey. Among them were Manson and the Briarlys. They had got away with little indeed,—whatever the elder could convert into ready money, besides his one team and wagon. The rest of his property would go according to the apostolic law of "laying on of hands." But he had all his children, and two "wives." For the one some provision must be made in the States. For the present it was enough to get away.

The snow yet lay deep in the passes, and the winter wind still howled over the high plains; but Manson confessed himself strangely happy in the midst of all the hardships. For now he had a recognized right to care for Marian. The miseries of the journey so early in the season need not be recounted. The open sky, or a rude tent, for women and children in March and April, on the high plains, would seem bad enough; but to Marian and her father they were luxury itself compared with what they remembered of their journey out. They mourned their kinsman, Thomas James, who had gone south a few days before their departure; but for themselves they rejoiced over every mile put between them and Utah. The mountains were passed, and early summer found them on the Missouri, eleven years after they had left it as fanatical Mormons. Eleven years, from the short span of life, in what had been to Elder Briarly a school of degradation.

A new era had set in. The Pacific Railroad was pushing westward, and paper cities were springing up along its way. Leaving his friends in Iowa, Manson again turned his face westward, determined to win a fortune before he should claim Marian for his own. Through all the ups and downs of that strange moving community, from Cheyenne to Promontory, he toiled on, ever keeping in mind the prize that awaited him, and thus guarded against the temptations which prevailed over so many. The autumn of 1869 found him again in Utah, now among the new mines which were every-where being opened. His old friend, Hank Briarly, was exploring the west mountains, and urged Manson to join him. Before determining his course, business called him to Green River. There, as he walked amid the ruins of that railroad "city," he was astonished at being accosted by a lady of pleasant aspect, but with a face on which trouble had left its mark. She had visited in turn every railroad town, and her one inquiry was, "Do you know any man about here by the name of Henry Beatty?"

Startled as Manson was by this inquiry, some instinct made him cautious in his reply. Yes, he did know him, and he *believed* Beatty was now in Utah. The lady overwhelmed him with thanks, and accompanied him on the next train to Ogden. Her joy prevailed over her reserve. She talked to Manson as an old friend. While she gently complained of the long silence of her husband, she yet found a thousand excuses for him.

"He was so high spirited," she said, "and not willing to plod along the common road. I am English born, you know, and had property left me in my own name; and it worried Mr. Beatty that he should not add as much more; and nine years ago—dear me, how long it seems—nine years ago he went to California, and then to Montana."

Manson winced as he remembered some things in that experience, and dreaded something to come, he knew not what; but he held his peace. They had taken the coach at Ogden, and were fast speeding towards Salt Lake, when the lady resumed:

"For a long time he wrote so regularly; then not so often, and now for eight months I have not heard a word. At first I thought it was because he was coming home; and then I got afraid he might be ——." She shuddered and paused. But she was too much pleased with the information Manson had given her to treat him as a stranger, and continued her reminiscences.

They reached the city, and Mrs. Beatty could scarcely rest till she had learned that her husband had gone to Tooele, and had secured a seat in the next coach for that place. Meanwhile she made a few purchases, and again sent for Manson to make some inquiries. As she mechanically unrolled the articles she had bought, talking cheerfully to her new-found friend, her eye fell upon an old copy of the *Salt Lake Telegraph*, in which they were wrapped. Suddenly her cheerful tones ceased. For a minute she held the paper, with her eyes fixed upon it, then a loud scream rang through the hotel, and she sank apparently lifeless upon the parlor floor.

There was a commotion in the hotel. The landlady and chambermaids hurried to help the strange lady. Manson knew that the evil he dreaded had come, whatever it was. When the lady had revived a little, and been taken to her room, he picked up the *Telegraph* and read this:

LEGAL NOTICE.

TERRITORY OF UTAH, }
TOOELE COUNTY, SS: } *In the Probate Court of Tooele County, October Session,* 1868.

HENRY BEATTY *vs.* SARAH ANN BEATTY.

Action for Divorce.

Defendant in the above entitled cause will take notice that plaintiff has filed his complaint in this court, and due publication been made thereof according to law; that plaintiff seeks complete legal separation from said defendant, and exemption from all the liabilities of matrimony. Cause alleged: Abandonment and refusal of said defendant to live with him in marriage. Now, therefore, defendant is notified that unless she appear at the ensuing term of this court, to be holden at the court-house in Tooele City, on the first Monday in December, 1868, and make due answer, said case will be heard and determined in her absence.

JOHN WOODBURY, Judge P. C., Tooele County.

WILSON SNOW, Clerk P. C., Tooele County.

—[*Salt Lake Telegraph.* w-5t.

Five weeks passed, and a pale shadow of the cheery English lady was seated in the Tooele coach. She made no complaints, but rode the long, weary way in silence. Arrived at the Mormon village, she inquired her way, and proceeded to a neat cabin in the outskirts. In answer to her knock, the door was opened by an apple-faced but

"LET ME LOOK TOWARD OLD ENGLAND BEFORE I DIE."

pleasant looking young Mormon woman, with that flush complexion and sort of florid beauty often seen among the young Saints.

"Does Henry Beatty live here?"

"Yes, ma'am; will you walk in?"

"Are you his wife?" asked the strange lady, with rigid countenance, and paying no heed to the polite invitation.

"Yes, ma'am." (This with a slight courtesy.) "I'm his wife Desereta, but he married my sister Nellie the same day. Maybe its her you want to see. But she's with him now, up at the mine."

"No," was the reply. "I only wanted to see who it was that had caused Henry Beatty to forget his family and his God. But if there's two of you, I know enough. Good-day." And she moved silently back to the hotel, and took the return coach for Zion. No one inquired particularly about her; no one asked any questions about the notice of divorce eight months before. The bishop was satisfied with it, and the council had directed that "Brother Beatty be fellowshiped," and that was enough. "Mind your own business," was the rule in Tooele as well as in Logan.

The late autumn found our strange friend lying on a lounge in an eastern city, "only waiting till she should get strong enough to make the voyage." She had disposed of all her property in this blessed land of equal rights and wholesome laws, and was going back to monarchical England, where a man can not marry two wives in a day, or a woman be divorced without knowing it. Her Yankee friends said her head was "turned" by her troubles, or she never would have preferred despotism to liberty. She was but one of ten thousand whom the laws of Utah—tacitly approved by the American Congress—have crucified.

But she had not gained strength as fast as the doctor predicted. She had gazed out of the open window whole hours at the vessels in the bay, but now she seemed to lack energy. Suddenly she spoke: "Let me look toward Old England once more before I die."

The attendant raised her gently. She gazed long and lovingly over the blue ocean, then lay down and, with one brief prayer for Henry, passed away.

* * * * * * * *

"Willie has struck chloride! Willie has struck chloride!" shouted Marian, dancing into her mother's room with an open letter in her hand, greatly astonishing that worthy woman, to whom this language was scarcely more intelligible than Greek. She had not read all that long series of interesting letters, running through the year since Willie Manson and his partner settled down on Lion Hill, to dig for a fortune; and, in her ignorance, was about to ask who "chloride" was, and if he would strike back, when Marian continued:

"Willie has struck chloride! He can sell out for fifty thousand dollars, and he's coming home right away, and—and—" She considerately paused.

Marian had but one "mother" now. In the old Utah days she had addressed her father's wives as "Auntie," according to the safe custom in vogue then; but since the other "Auntie" had found a home somewhere else, and her father's house had but one mistress, she had promoted her to be addressed as "Mother."

Yes, Manson had "struck chloride," and though the vein was not so rich by some millions of dollars as the sanguine partners had expected, they sold it for enough to satisfy Manson; and before the autumn of 1870 had passed, he once more held Marian in his arms. And now I, the writer hereof, am embarrassed; for, if I continue the story, I can not dwell on miners, Mormons and Indians, mountains, mines and adventures. The details of a marriage are beyond my scope. Suffice it, then, to say, that Willie Manson and Marian Briarly were made one, after all their troubles, and contentedly settled down in Iowa, determined there to spend the remainder of their days.

"WILLIE HAS STRUCK CHLORIDE."

And that firm resolution they kept just six months.

For, when the south wind blew softly, in May, 1871, they looked around them and missed something. They did not see the circling peaks, their summits ever glistening with snow; nor the blue waves of the Salt Lake, nor the crystal streams pouring from the hills; and, as they looked into each other's faces, Marian expressed the desire of both, saying: "What a glorious place Salt Lake will be when things get fixed."

Once confessed, her longing increased. She was desperately homesick. The troubles were forgotten, the joys remembered; distance blended her life in Utah into one pleasing whole. What was there in this prairie State to take the place of her beloved mountains? Where was the rocky cañon, with ever-varying beauty of gorge, crag, and wooded slope? where the gray and blue peaks standing out sharply against the rosy evening sky? where the Great Salt Lake, now spread out like a molten mirror in the summer calm, now sparkling in the light breeze, now tossing its white caps in the storm? There was a calm beauty in the rolling prairie; but where was the wild charm of the Utah valley? The calm rivers had their pleasant features—for Iowa people—but what could take the place of crystal streams dashing down rocky cañons, of bright water-seeks gurgling by the road-side, of the sacred Jordan and its mountain affluents? There was no charm in this land for the eye of a mountaineer; and soon Manson also confessed that, for good or ill, he must *some day* live in the shadow of the Wasatch.

After that their progress was rapid. They could not live away from the mountains. And, as I sat in front of their tasteful cottage, overlooking the city from the first "bench," and heard their story, I did not wonder at their conclusion; for surely there are few places in this world which so charm the resident as Salt Lake City. Drink of its waters, walk its streets for one year, and you will ever long to return. Give but good government, and intelligent society, and Utah would be to me even as the home of the soul—Salt Lake City, the particular spot at which I would pitch my tent forever.

CHAPTER XXIII.

SWINGING 'ROUND THE CIRCLE.

Zion was hot in a double sense when I reached it in July, 1872. The season was unusually warm; the Saints and Gentiles were conducting a bitter politico-religious campaign, and the nation was distracted by the spectacle of Horace Greeley running for President on the Democratic ticket. The Mormons all swore by Greeley, and prophecies of his election were abundant. He had visited them in his overland journey of 1858, and out of his letters they had managed to pick many comforting passages; while the "squatter sovereignty" doctrine of Stephen A. Douglas had suited their position so admirably, that they inevitably became zealous Democrats. The contest was not pleasant to a traveler, and, after a ten days' visit, I journeyed on to Soda Springs, then ambitiously styled "The future Saratoga of the West."

Leaving Corinne, Sunday, August 4th, on a narrow-guage mule, I spent the first night with a Mormon rancher in Cache Valley. This beautiful region was long the winter rendezvous of the North-west Fur Company, and many are the legends of grand councils here with Shoshone, Bannock and Uintah; of love-making between swarthy trappers and dusky maidens; of grand revels, often ending in a free fight, in which ordinary hostile divisions were ignored, and every man went in for personal revenge. Now it is the abode of 15,000 Mormons, and the granary of Utah. The valley, or rather basin, is inclosed on all sides by lofty mountains, their summits tipped with snow in mid-summer. Through it Bear River runs in many a winding maze for seventy miles, and from all sides bright crystal affluents join the main stream, each singing of the snowy heights whence it came. The traveler along one side of the valley sees all the Mormon villages on the other side, each set back in a little cove, but those near him are hidden by the projecting mountain spurs.

From the upper part of Cache ("concealed") Valley, the road rises to a rocky plateau. There the Bear River makes a big bend to the north, and the mountains, which have followed close on its eastern bank for a hundred miles, give back, and we find here a broad, green valley some ten miles wide. The floor, so to speak, of this valley is iron; upon it is a heavy stratum of rich earth, and through it, in a hundred places, the subterraneous waters and gases have forced their way. The plain is dotted by soda mounds from five to thirty feet in height, and every-where upon and among them are the soda-fountains. Some boil furiously with a loud, bubbling noise and escape of gas;

SHOSHONEES WITH ANNUITY GOODS.

others show but a faint effervescence; some are always calm, and never overflow, while others send out large and constant streams, and still others sink a foot or two when the air is cool, and rise to an overflow when it is warm. The springs on the soda mounds are mere tanks, but a few inches wide, sending out such faint streams that all the solid contents are precipitated, and the water quite evaporated before reaching the plain.

Some of the mounds have risen so high that the water has broken out elsewhere, and thus new mounds are being slowly built. In some springs the chemical mixture is pure soda, in others pure iron, in still others iron, soda and salt mixed. The best tonic is from the Octagon Spring, containing about equal parts of iron and soda, with slight admixture of other elements. Invalids insist that the first drink does them good, and that they improve every day they use it. On me its chief effect was to create a marvelous appetite. The Ninety-percent Spring, which Gentiles also call the Anti-polygamy Spring, is most heavily charged of all. Of the solid contents, ninety per cent. is pure soda; the rest some mineral or salt which has strange effects on the male human. A few quarts of it will destroy the strongest faith in the necessity for polygamy. This lasts but a few days, however.

Hooper's Spring is the largest and perhaps the greatest curiosity. It is a rod wide, and presents the appearance of an immense caldron boiling furiously; but the water is very cool, and rather pleasant to the taste. The vale near by is covered with heavy grass, which lines the spring and hangs into the water; on all sides rise the majestic mountains, and from the pool a stream six feet wide and a foot deep flows into Soda Creek. The water contains nothing but soda, and all of that it will hold in solution. Mixed with sugar of lemons it makes a drink equal to the best from a patent fountain.

Near by, Wm. H. Hooper, late Mormon delegate in Congress, has a summer residence. The elevation of the valley is some 6,500 feet above sea-level, and the climate in August about like that of October in the States. Farther up the vale may be seen the Formation Springs, where the dripping chemicals have molded a thousand fanciful shapes; and down near the river is Steamboat Spring, from which the water bursts forth at brief intervals with a loud "cough," like the "scape" of a slowly moving distant steam-boat. In a score of places in the bed of the river are springs emitting water loaded with various minerals and gases, from which the bright bubbles play upon the surface. A little way up the river are sulphur springs, and over the mountain eastward is a wooded region abounding in game. The vale itself, some ten miles square, seems set apart by nature as a region of curiosities. The only inhabitants are a few Morrisite Mormons, the remnants of some two hundred taken there by General Connor in 1863; and the few Americans who hold an interest with Mr. Hooper in the location. The only hotel is a rambling log-cabin, and all surroundings are rural and primitive in the extreme. But when the narrow-guage road is completed there from Ogden, I fancy this place will drop the prefix "future," and become at least the Saratoga of Utah and Idaho.

From my Idaho jaunt I returned to the Union Pacific, and late in

August left Ogden for St. Louis in one of those rolling palaces which make travel over this line such a delight. What a change from the back of an ambling American horse, on which I made the tour of Arizona! And I could but ask myself, somewhat doubtfully, too: shall I ever roll along the line of the Thirty-fifth Parallel Road in a Pullman palace, as I now ride where four years ago I toiled with mule teams? The change would be no greater than I have seen here.

As I neared the Missouri I read that twenty persons had died of sunstroke in one day at St. Louis. And I had spent most of the summer where one needed two blankets at night to keep him warm! I concluded to wait a week at the delightful city of Lawrence, till nature should cool things off. The same temperature in the East is much more debilitating to one just from the mountains; it appears more steamy and weakening than in the dry air of Utah and Arizona. But the last night of August a tremendous thunder-storm swept over Kansas and Missouri, and lowered the mercury twenty-five degrees! So I visited St. Louis in comfort, and thence started to make the trip over the Northern Pacific Railroad.

One day I lingered at Nauvoo, for I had long been curious to see this old stronghold of the Mormons. Their elders are never weary of telling the people that it is now a ruin, desolate as Tyre or Babylon. I found it a beautiful town of some 3,000 people. It has the prettiest site in Illinois. The river makes a bend westward nearly in the shape of a U; the point in the lower part is a mile wide, and lies just high enough above the river for commercial convenience; and thence the hill rises by gentle slopes for two miles eastward. At the upper end of the flat on the river is a splendid steam-boat landing, and about half way around the bend the rapids begin, giving a fine front for manufacturing purposes. Here the Mormons had projected a row of cotton mills; they were to bring the cotton up the river, and with their own operatives, converted from the workshops of England, build up a great manufacturing community. Could they have maintained peace with their neighbors, they would have had some fifteen years to perfect this scheme before the railroad era superseded river transportation, and Nauvoo would have had too great a start for the tide to turn. They and their apologists of course maintain that the Gentiles were altogether to blame for the breaking up of these fine schemes; but when a man moves six or seven times, and quarrels with the neighbors every time, as they did, I am inclined to conclude that he takes the worst neighbor along with him every move.

After the Mormons came the Icarians, a curious but harmless set of visionaries. It was the era when communistic experiments were in operation all over the country—the era immediately succeeding "Brook Farm," Communia, and Robert Owen's New Harmony Society. The Icarians, under the lead of M. Cabet, wore a uniform, had all things in common, and worked in detailed squads. But when one man, or an executive board, has to choose what work every other man shall do, it soon appears a most unnatural system as opposed to "natural selection." Here was to be seen a former college professor herding swine; there a Paris goldsmith driving oxen, and a well-known scholar, crack-brained on socialistic theories, was made assistant sawyer at the society's mill. It cured him, however.

The Icarians failed, of course, and were in due time succeeded by a colony of Bavarians and Westphalians, who have made a great success of the wine manufacture. Where the great Mormon temple once stood is now a fine vineyard, and not one of the original stones remains. Three of the neighboring houses are built entirely of the beautiful white rock, and the rest has made walls and foundations all over town. This wonderful structure cost between a half and three-quarters of a million dollars in money and labor, and the Icarians had proposed to fit it up as a social hall and school-room.

BURNING OF THE MORMON TEMPLE.

But at 2 A. M. of November 10, 1848, it was found to be on fire, and before daylight every particle of woodwork was destroyed. It was set on fire in the third story of the steeple, one hundred and forty feet from the ground. The dry pine burned like tinder; there was no mode of reaching the fire, and in twenty minutes the whole wooden interior was a mass of flames. In two hours nothing remained but hot walls, inclosing a bed of embers. At Montrose and Fort Madison, Iowa, they could distinguish every house in Nauvoo, and the light was seen forty miles around.

Joe Agnew, of Pontoosuc, fourteen miles above Nauvoo, afterwards confessed that he set it on fire. He had suffered at the hands of the Mormons, and sworn no trace of them should cumber the soil of Illinois.

The walls long stood in such perfect preservation that the citizens determined again to refit it for an academy. But in November, 1850, a fearful hurricane swept down the river, and threw down most of the structure. From the deck of a Mississippi steamer Nauvoo, which once had fourteen thousand inhabitants, now looks like a suburb of retired country seats, stretching for two or three miles up a handsome slope; and thousands yearly pass on the river admiring the rural beauty of the place, but little thinking that a third of a century since it was the largest city in Illinois, and the most notorious in America, the chosen stronghold of a most peculiar faith and destined capital of a vast religious empire.

Thence by steamer to Burlington, and thence by the Burlington & Missouri River Railroad to Council Bluffs. There I took the northward route, and in due time arrived at Sioux City, which had greatly improved in the year since I last visited it. The "Hawkeyes," (State designation for Iowa people), are a progressive race; but the "lay of the country" is such that their energy must ever tend to build up a great State rather than any one great city. The growth of Iowa in wealth and population is amazing, but she has no metropolis which takes the place Chicago does in Illinois or St. Louis in Missouri. Her development is destined to proceed on a different plan.

We staged it again to Yankton, along the line where the S. C. & Y. Railroad now runs; and found the inhabitants hotly engaged in the great job of saving the country. Dakota Territory has always been noted for the heat and acrimony of her politics; and though the Grant-Greeley campaign was marked for its bitterness, the storm in the rest of the nation was as the balminess of a May morning compared with its fury in Dakota. Now, General McCook, Secretary of the Territory, and one of the "Fighting McCook's," was the central figure of a local quarrel. A year or two later he attacked a delicate little banker named Wintermute, and pounded him almost to a jelly. Wintermute walked out, procured a pistol, and returning, shot McCook dead in the ball-room! I could not join in the cry for vengeance which went over the country, for I knew the slayer to be a naturally inoffensive man, who had been cruelly outraged. Most of the Federal officials made it a personal matter to assist in the prosecution of Wintermute, but western juries are proverbially lenient in such cases. He was sentenced to a few years imprisonment; but his delicate constitution could not survive the beating and the sentence, and consumption soon took him beyond the reach of earthly courts. I shall ever maintain that he was the real victim of the tragedy, and should never have been imprisoned.

Our party had various opinions as to the best way to see the country on the North Pacific line. The first plan was to take a team and go up the eastern side of the Territory, by way of the beautiful valley of James River, then over the divide and northward down Red River. The distance was three hundred miles; there were long stretches of country without a settlement, and the season was getting late. So this was in due time reconsidered. The next was to go up the Missouri to the proposed crossing, and stage it across to the end of the road. But soon came a steam-boat down the river with word that navigation was closed for this year, though it was still early in September; then we decided to return to Sioux City, and go through Minnesota. A man can't travel as he pleases in the new North-west.

KILLING OF SECRETARY M'COOK.

We had enough of staging, and concluded to try it by steamer down to Sioux City. The distance by land is sixty-five miles; by river a hundred and fifty. The time is just as it happens. You must start when the boat is ready, and take your chances on board, sometimes getting through in ten hours, sometimes in thirty. We made splendid time all forenoon, the low clay banks receding so rapidly that their natural ugliness was changed to a swiftly gliding view of something nearly like beauty. The water is a little thicker than cream, but not quite as thick as plaster, and of a dirty yellow color, its solid contents consisting of nearly equal parts of fine clay and silt; but when taken aboard and settled, it is very palatable. Immediately on the river, the timber is small and scrubby, but a mile or so back are fine forests of good-sized trees, for a mile or two, and behind them the richest prairie "bottom" in the world, varying in width from five to twenty miles, and yielding to gentle foot-hills and wooded bluffs. In three or four places the river spreads to a mile or more in width, broken by sand-bars and low islands; there the boat usually stuck fast for awhile, till the hands could "pole off," when she would back out and try other channels till one was found passable.

At such times the captain cheered us with such appropriate remarks as: "D—d channel was on that side when I came up. Thought the river would take a sky-wash round the other way, judgin' from the set ag'in that bluff. But there's nothing impossible under *this* administration. Howsomever, we'll make Sioux City by supper time, if we don't fall down." This last was a facetious reference to the system of sparring off with the "boat's crutches." But we did "fall down" about noon, running hard aground on the head of a sand island, located probably where the channel was deepest a month before. Then oaths, spars, "nigger-engine" and all the other available machinery were set in operation; and after two hours of swearing, bell ringing, and toil, the stern was got far enough into the current to swing around; then all control of it was lost, and that end grounded below. Then the bow was shoved off, swung around and stuck again; then the stern made a half-circle swing, and thus on, in a series of swings and "drags," over half-sunken trees, the boat groaning through all her timbers like a thing possessed, we made a final swing off the lower end of the island, and floated on. When they spar thus at both ends they are said to "grasshopper" over the difficulty.

Reaching Sioux City, we found there had been a fearful murder, two robberies and a street fight in which a dozen engaged, all within twenty-four hours. And still Sioux City was not happy. Thence we traveled north-east by way of the Sioux City & St. Paul Railroad, most of the day over a country with the same general character: a high and gently rolling prairie, without sloughs, with very rich soil and rank grass, but no timber. Having passed the "divide," we soon entered upon the system of streams flowing into the Minnesota River, and left the "Land of the Sleepy" for the "Blue-water Land." This poetic designation of Minnesota (from the Sioux *minne* "water" and *sota* "blue"), is the most fitting name the State could have received. In the year 1859, that State was my residence, and even now my heart thrills at recollection of its summer beauties: green plains, tasteful groves, crystal lakes and clear streams lively with fish. But here I ask the reader's permission to turn back thirteen years. The notes in the next chapter are from observations both during my residence and later visits.

CHAPTER XXIV.

MINNESOTA.

IN July, 1859, I stood on the banks of Rum River and watched the long trains of Bois Brules from Pembina, slowly descending that stream to St. Paul. Their carts were made entirely of wood, from bed and wheel to lynch-pin, and were drawn by oxen, one to each cart in most cases; men, carts and animals splashed and clotted with the black mud of the many sloughs they had crossed. The dry season, neglect and alternate soaking and shrinking during the long journey through the "divide" and lake region, had brought the vehicles to a wretched condition; and the heavily dragging wheels kept up a wailing *creechy, crawchy, creechy, crawchy* that could be heard nearly half a mile—"a cry for grease," which went to the soul.

PEOPLE FROM PEMBINA AND THEIR OX-CARTS.

The custom of these people, then, was to devote the late autumn and early winter to hunting and trapping; the rest of the winter was fairly divided between merry-making and preparing the furs and pelts they had taken; and when the late May sunshine had brought forward grass enough for their animals the trains departed southward. At St. Paul they sold the proceeds of their last hunt, and laid in supplies for the next year. The importance of the trade to St. Paul was great;

for weeks one or more trains arrived daily, each with from ten to two hundred carts, and each cart piled high with furs and skins.

Most of the drivers were of the pure Bois Brules stock, and merely greeted me with the quick, forward jerk of the head, and the sharp "Bon-jour," which is the universal salutation in the North-west; but here and there in the train was a cart of more than ordinary preten-

WINTER IN THE MINNESOTA PINERIES.

sions, generally drawn by two oxen, and sometimes shielded by a rude awning, containing one or two white men, factors of the fur companies, or young Englishmen returning from the posts. Perhaps a score of full-blood Chippeways accompanied the train. These are a tall, well-made race of Indians, with a complexion redder than that of the Sioux or Arapahoes, not so dark and beastly looking; and their half-blood descendants share in all these peculiarities.

The words *Bois Brules* signify "burnt woods," and happily indicate the dark-red complexion of the half breeds. They and the Mexicans constitute, I believe, the only permanent types resulting from the union of Europeans with our Aborigines. As near as I can determine from their appearance and history, they are about half white, half Indian, and have long maintained this blood in a condition of purity. They live both in our Territory and over the line, number thousands, and are a polite, gay and hospitable people, more musical than thoughtful, more lively than intelligent. The neighboring whites have corrupted the name into "Bob Ruly," as their *Bois Blancs* (White Woods), slang for white men, has in turn become "Bob Long;" so the original population of Pembina is made up of the two classes, Bob Rulys and Bob Longs.

These are to be mentioned first, as the original settlers of Minnesota. Save the occasional missionary, Indian trader, hunter or government official, the country contained but few white men before 1845. The Chippeways (Ojibbeways) dominated the northern section, the Sioux the southern; and the "divide," between the drainage of Red River and Minnesota, was their border and battle-ground for ages. At last the whites began to crowd the Sioux, from the south; and the Chippeways, under the lead of the great Pahya Goonsey—red Napoleon of the North-west—drove them beyond Red River, which remains the boundary of the two races. Then French settlements slowly stretched down from the north, and American up from the south; and in 1850–'55 came the great speculative era of Minnesota. Every new country must have such a rise—and, alas! such a fall.

There was for years the humbug and hurrah of the "glorious free and boundless West;" and in 1856 and '57 every thing was selling at three or four times its actual value, and every third man was a millionaire in town lots. The crash came, and the wealthy, who had indorsed for each other, fell like a row of bricks, each knocking down the next. Every man rushed off to his lawyer to sue his neighbor, compromise with his creditors, or put his property out of his hands. The laws of different legislatures were in conflict; judges construed them one way in one court, and in another directly the opposite. The Democratic administration of 1858 burdened the young State with a heavy railroad debt, which the next administration, Republican, repudiated, and on top of all this came the grasshoppers.

The crop of 1856 was half destroyed; the next year every green thing was eaten, the insects leaving the country black behind them. The crop of 1858 did not half pay taxes and debts, and when I arrived, in May, 1859, the mass of the people were living on corn-bread, potatoes and "green truck," with an occasional mess of fish or game. It was a nice country for a delicate young student, just removed from school on account of bad health. I hoed corn, drove teams, chopped wood and cultivated muscle. There was plenty to eat, such as it was, but no luxuries, and before the close of the year I was again in sound health. But I have no desire to repeat the experience. There was too much pure Darwinism in such a country—"natural selection and survival of the fittest." The man who could not accommodate himself rapidly to poverty and hardships, had to die or emigrate.

Better crops came, and the settlers looked forward to the end of their troubles, when the Sioux war of 1862 suddenly cut off their hopes, and many of my friends in Blue-earth County were ruined, a few losing their lives. But the country had natural wealth in abundance, and Yankee energy has triumphed over all difficulties. After thirteen years I entered a rich and prosperous county by rail, where I had tramped, knapsack in hand, through a comparative wilderness. The Winnebago Reservation, unbroken by the plow when I first crossed it, is now a populous farming district; and Mankato, then a straggling village of six or eight hundred, is now a flourishing city of five thousand people. But the effects of the "hard times" of 1857–'59 still remain in many places, in the shape of interminable lawsuits, unsettled titles, broken fortunes, neighborhood feuds, and men whose energy is gone and their temper soured by disappointment. Many a Minnesota woman is prematurely old from the troubles of that period, and even in the faces of those I then knew as children I fancy I can see some pinching lines which ought not to mar the visage of blooming youth, unpleasing reminders of a childhood passed without its natural pleasures, and stinted because of parental poverty.

Thence to St. Paul I noted, with the pleasure of a pioneer, the great improvements of thirteen years. Hamlets have become large towns; unimportant towns have grown to cities. St. Paul I found nearly trebled in size, and lively with twenty thousand visitors attending the State Fair. On the grounds were specimens of vegetation from every spot for seven hundred miles north and west. Notable among these were bunches of wild rice from the northern lakes; monster turnips and beets from the line of the Northern Pacific; native grass from Red River Valley, four feet long, and wheat grown at Fort Garry, Red River Settlement, B. A., which yielded seventy bushels per acre. St. Paul is in the south-eastern corner, and is the natural *entrepôt*, of a wheat-growing region four hundred miles square. Fertile land continues to a point two hundred miles north of our national boundary; there a sandy desert sets in, and continues to the Arctic Circle.

This State and Dakota Territory have many features in common. On the western border of the State, and forming a part of the boundary line between it and Dakota, are two lakes—Big Stone and Traverse. The southern one, lying north-west and south-east is Big Stone, thirty-one miles long and only three-fourths to one and a half miles wide, with bold shores fifty to eighty feet high—beautiful in summer, filled with fish and abounding in water-fowl. On its shores 50,000 people could witness a boat race over a course of ten miles or more. About it linger many curious and wild traditions of the Indians. This lake is simply a deep, wide river channel, resembling points on the Upper Mississippi, where there is no valley or low land along the river. Lake Traverse was originally a part of it—a continuation of it northward—resembling it in all respects. But now they are separated by about four miles of low valley of the same width.

Into and through this valley runs a creek—head of the Minnesota River—which rises in Dakota and flows close by the south end of Lake Traverse and into Big Stone Lake, issuing again from its southeastern end, and joining the Mississippi near St. Paul. Traverse is not so large or long as Big Stone, and as one passes along its western shore, the hills grow lower and recede from it. Its shores become marshy, and it narrows to a lagoon, and finally into a stream or river with scarcely a noticeable current. At Breckinridge, Minnesota, or Wahpeton, Dakota, this stream is joined by the Otter Tail River, a somewhat rapid stream of considerable volume. Where the two unite (the one from Traverse is called the *Bois des Sioux*, or properly the Sioux Wood River) both names cease, and the Red River of the North begins. It is a river at once. From this point it flows three hundred miles, in a right line, to Lake Winnepeg, in British America.

The fertile valley of Red River, is about a hundred and fifty miles wide, half in the State and half in Dakota. Westward it yields to the higher lands and soon to the barren *couteau*, fit for nothing but scant pasturage. In the valley are now some of the largest wheat farms in the world. There a dozen or more teams can be seen in early summer, following each other with successive furrows—plowing on the same "land," which is a township. The furrows are six miles long. They just make two rounds per day, going up and back, taking dinner and then repeating. One mounted man commands the whole, and a cart with a few tools accompanies. If any thing befalls a plow or team the driver turns out and lets the other pass, starting in again when the repair is made. Upon a large wheat field, in 1876, six self-binding reapers worked in like order.

But there are other novel features. The northern boundary is the forty-ninth parallel. Hence the days in summer are noticeably long, and the twilight in proportion, so that at Pembina, June 20, it is not entirely dark much before 10 P. M., and early dawn begins but little later than 2 A. M. People who desire to sleep long retire while it is yet light, and darken the windows, very much as they do in Norway or Iceland. But winter presents a sharp contrast. Daylight delays till half-past nine, and dark comes soon after three. At Pembina one is on the 49th degree north, while the sun in December is 23° south of the equator—total 72°, which from 90° leaves 18°, the height of the sun above the horizon at noon. The sky is often brilliantly clear for weeks at a time, but there is not warmth enough in the sun to loosen an icicle on the south side of the house.

But it is warm enough in summer. The winter before I was there, Wright County enjoyed four months continuous sleighing. The next June a pumpkin-vine I measured grew four and a half inches in twenty-four hours. The snow is usually gone by the 10th of April; the ground dries rapidly, and farmers often plow upon the south slope while the snow still lies on the north slope. The soil has a mixture of black sand, and freezes so hard in winter that it never clods or "bakes" in summer. The local records show that the year should be divided thus: Winter, five months; spring, one month; summer, four months; autumn, two months. The summer heat would be very oppressive but for the breeze which is almost constant from the west and south-west. If it changes to the east, there is apt to be a cold, chilly rain; if it ceases, which is rare, the heat is so great the natives can scarcely work.

A suggestion to tourists is in order. Through the lakes to Duluth, thence by the Northern Pacific Railroad to Fargo, thence down the Red River—on which steamers ply all summer—to Winnipeg and Garry, is a summer excursion yielding more variety in men and manners than any that can be taken in the West. The scenery is often sublime, though not equal to that of the Rocky Mountains, and always beautiful. The lakes are alive with fish; water-fowl are abundant. Here is a highway northward into the heart of the upper country, all the way easy of passage, and much cheaper than the trip to California, or even to Colorado. There are splendid hotels at Duluth, Brainard, Moorehead, Fargo and Glyndon, and tolerably good living all the way from there down. "Barring" the mosquitoes, which you can guard against by "taking the vail," as the residents do, there is no physical inconvenience, and the air is ever pure and bracing. You can enjoy the sensation of a day eighteen or twenty hours long, and see the sun as low at noon in summer as it is in Ohio in winter. With this hint I resume my personal narrative.

From St. Paul we took the cars northward along the left bank of the Mississippi, passing through rich prairies and "oak openings," the latter looking very much like old orchards. We are rarely out of sight of crystal lakes, which add such a charm to the Minnesota landscape. The State contains ten thousand lakes, varying from a few acres to

MINNEHAHA IN WINTER.

many miles in extent. In the angle between the Mississippi and Minnesota Rivers is a region rich in scenery and historic interest. There the Minnehaha plunges down from the prairie level to the Mississippi by the Minnehaha Falls, so well known to the world through the genius of Longfellow. On the prairie level are crystal lakes, sylvan groves and picturesque knolls, among which the tourist may spend weeks of enjoyment. The railroad ended at Sauk Rapids, where we halted for a day. This is to be the great manufacturing city of this region, the rapids of the Mississippi furnishing unlimited water-power, but as yet the citizens have done little beyond the preliminary wind work. In 1859 this was thought to be the head of all navigation, and only two little steamers plied above St. Anthony Falls; now smaller boats run from Sauk Rapids to Brainard, and sometimes farther. The Mississippi parts with its greatness slowly. Away up here it still has the appearance of a big river.

From Sauk we take the stage-coach—a little jerky carrying ten passengers, among them a Sister and Mother Superior of the Order of St. Francis. These were on their way to Belle Prairie, a mission in the "Big Woods," to take charge of a frontier academy, and teach letters, language and religion to little half-breeds and Chippeways. The Mother Superior was a lady of rare intelligence, just from Europe, where she had been nursing the sick and wounded of the Franco-Prussian war. To my remark that I doubted the possibility of converting an Indian, she replied with great feeling: "Oh, perhaps not in my time, but surely soon, the race will know and accept the truth. We work for God, and He will take care of it. If we convert one it will repay us ten thousand fold."

Near midnight we left them at Belle Prairie, a hamlet of a few cabins, with a small school-house, and near by a chapel, its white cross gleaming in the cold moonlight, fit symbol of the Sisters' life and work. How wonderful is this wide extended power of the Church of Rome! Who can travel beyond the reach of her world-embracing arms? Alike on the banks of the St. Lawrence and the Rio Grande, I have seen the white cross of her chapels; and on the wild frontier and in the hut of the savage have met her hardy missionaries, bronzed by every sun and weather-beaten by the storms of every sky from Pembina to Arizona. Is it any wonder, considering her celibate clergy, who make the flock their family and the whole world their home, and her holy orders of devoted women, to whom suffering and self-denial are sweet for the sake of the Church—is it any wonder that a quarter of a billion souls attest her power, and, to the reproach of us Protestants, over half the Christian world still owns allegiance to Rome?

Soon after we reached Crow Wing, and remained till near noon next day. Thence an hour of rapid driving brought us into the Black Pine Forest, in the center of which we found the "city" of Brainard—on the Northern Pacific Railroad at last. The streets were lively with representatives of three great races—for it was Sunday—and all the railroad employés were in town to drink and trade. The principal saloonatic had secured a rare attraction: a band of fifteen Chippeways were performing the "war dance" before his door, to the music of a drum and buckskin tambourine, and drinks were going as fast as two men could serve the crowd. After each dance the only "brave" who could speak English went around with the hat, exclaiming,

"Ten-n-cen-nts a man-n! ten-n-cen-nts a man-n!" the result being money enough to treat the band to white sugar, of which they are passionately fond. Near by a white roué was trying to strike a bargain with a rather pretty Chippeway girl of fourteen years or so, who was in charge of an older sister, a withered hag at least thirty years old, and therefore past all show of comeliness, as is the nature of Indian women. Behind stood a half-breed squaw, about as " pretty " as a wild-cat struck with a club. Ten rods away, afternoon service was in progress at the Episcopal Church, the only one in the place; and across the street a *maison de joie* kept open doors, its inmates at the windows with a lavish display of mammiferous wealth. No work was in progress; most of the men had on clean shirts, and the holy Sabbath was strictly kept—in Far Western fashion.

The "city" had one great advantage over Union Pacific towns: the houses were all of lumber, and the native pines still lined the streets. Here the great Mississippi has at last shrunk to a stream no more than a hundred yards wide and perhaps ten feet deep; a hundred miles north would bring us into that circle of lakes—Itasca, Leech, Cass and Plantagenet—which jointly form its source. Around, mostly to the east, are ten thousand square miles covered with the white and yellow varieties of Norway pine, constituting the great wealth of Upper Minnesota. Next morning a lowering sky gave notice that the first storm of the season was at hand, and as the train moved westward the air hinted of snow. For seventy-five miles the country is nearly worthless for agricultural purposes; then we move down a gentle slope, and enter the fertile valley of Red River. The little lakes are beautiful. In winter they are frozen almost solid, and then is the best time for freighting; the sled routes take a direct line from point to point without regard to lakes or sloughs.

Moorehead, on the eastern bank of Red River, is the end of a passenger division, and the nominal head of navigation; but it is only in the months of June and July that any steamers run to that point. Frog Point, sixty miles below (northward), is the head of navigation for the rest of the summer, though boats rarely ply before the latter part of May. As Red River has a general course due north, the thaw occurs at the head first, and forces a great break up and massing of the ice down at Fort Garry and other ports in Winnepeg. Straw-ticks, beef, bread and potatoes could be had for $2.00 per day in either of the new frame hotels then adorning Moorehead; but there was nothing to be seen requiring more than a night's stay. Omnibuses were not, so we carried our baggage a mile, across the bridge and through

Fargo, Dakota, to the construction train, on which we traversed the last hundred miles of the road. For fifty miles west of Red River the country appears as level as the calm ocean; the rank grass above, and the black soil below, as shown in the cuts, indicate great fertility. The biting wind from the north-west brought a chilling rain, and after it sleet and finally snow, which last was a great improvement on the sleet. We had been assured by Jay Cooke that "the isothermal line takes a great northward deflection west of the Great Lakes," giving this a mild climate; but a snow storm in September did not indicate it.

We crossed the Shyene River twice, and soon after ran through the edge of Salt Lake—so called, though little like the great one in Utah. It appears to be about five miles long, is thickly impregnated with salt and alkali, and has an outlet only in very wet weather. The terminus of the road was then at Jimtown, near the western limit of fertile land. The cold was severe and the wind blowing almost a hurricane. As my blue fingers stiffened around the handle of my valise, and the canvas town clattered in the wind as if it would fly away, the thermometer standing at 28°, and the air full of flying snow, I was inclined to set down most I had heard about this "mild and salubrious climate" as the exuberance of a playful fancy. But in a day or two the storm yielded to sunshine, October came in gloriously, and good weather continued a month longer. The storm prevented our excursion beyond the terminus, but from abundant testimony I am convinced there is little to see but rolling plains scantily clothed with grass, alkali flats and sand-hills. The fertile land lies along the eastern border.

From Jimtown eastward to Duluth developed no new features. First we had a hundred miles of Red River Valley to Fargo and Moorehead; fifty miles of the same on the eastern side; then the rise to Detroit lakes, and then the half-barren strip of marsh and pine, tamarack and scrub-oak flat, till we got within seventy-five miles of Duluth. Thence the country rapidly improved; the soil and timber were fine, and scenery on the St. Louis River approaching the grand. Duluth had become historic—it is more historic than commercial, still, for that matter. "The Zenith City of the unsalted seas," as the local poets modestly styled it, did not appear to advantage just after a September snow-storm; but it was lively with immigrants, colony agents, real estate speculators, travelers and freighters.

Since then the German-Russian Mennonites have been pouring into Southern Dakota by thousands, and it is evident the future population of our new North-west will consist largely of Scandinavians and kindred races. They are wheat-eaters, Bible-readers, and Calvinists; they establish schools and churches, are anchored to the soil, and constitute a conservative and most desirable class of citizens. An old traveler relates that he was toiling over the black sandy prairie, one of the hottest days of their hot but short summer, when to his joy he came upon a dirt-roofed log-house with the word ICE in prominent letters on the right side of the door. Drawing near with thirsty haste he saw on the left side, in smaller, dimmer letters the word

DALLES OF ST. LOUIS RIVER.

POSTOFF. A Russian or Swedish name, he thought, and called for ice-water. The woman, ignorant of English, handed him a bundle of letters with instructions, in pantomime, to pick out what belonged to him! He made out after a lengthy discussion with the woman that the two signs were to be read together, and meant POST-OFFICE.

I have sufficiently described the climate of our new North-west; it is severe but healthful. There has been a deal of miscellaneous lying on this subject. Storms of fifty hours' duration are not uncommon even in Nebraska; and at Cheyenne I have experienced weather cold enough to freeze the most hardy animals if unsheltered. Five hundred miles south of the Northern Pacific I have seen cattle frozen stiff in their tracks, horses left in the spring with only the stump of a tail, birds fallen dead from the air in cold wind storms, Indians without nose enough left to blow after a winter's journey, and buffalo by tens of thousands literally frozen to death on the plains. But settlers can provide against storms and cold; experience shows that man comes to perfection in such climates, and the old resident can truthfully say,

"Man is the noblest growth our realms supply;
And souls are ripened in our Northern sky."

CHAPTER XXV.

THE WAY TO OREGON.

Brown October found me again rolling through Iowa, in the palace cars of the Burlington and Missouri River Railroad, on my way to Oregon, after a brief visit to the States. The four years and a half since I crossed the State on foot had added three hundred thousand to its population, and a thousand miles to its working railroads. And still there is room. The State still has vacant land enough for two million farmers.

Westward from Omaha there had also been great changes. In 1868 we ran out into open prairie soon after leaving Fremont; now there is a nearly continuous line of farms on both sides of the railroad as far as Loup Fork. Beyond, cattle ranches multiply, and but a few years will elapse till all this section of the high plains will be utilized by stock-growers. It is claimed that as ranches increase and farms are opened the climate changes, grows more moist, and thus carries the border of fertile land farther west; but, on this point, I will suspend judgment. My fourteenth trip over the Union Pacific Railroad was more pleasant than any previous one. The brown plains east of the mountains were just as brown, the red hills and alkali deserts of Wyoming quite as monotonous; but the sublime scenery of Echo and Weber Cañons was glorified by the rich hues of autumn, and over all the gray-brown landscape of the plains, hung the soft haze of what would be Indian summer at the East.

In Utah I found Saint and Gentile in their normal condition of attack and defense. First one side got a blow ahead, and then the other, like a pair of badly-matched oxen; or, as we used to say in Indiana: "Like a half-sled on ice." It had grown monotonous, and, after a few days' rest in Salt Lake and Corinne, I took passage in one of the new silver palace cars of the Central Pacific. In them travel is a luxury; one eats, drinks, smokes, sleeps, reads, or writes at the rate of twenty miles an hour; free to look at the scenery where it deserves it, and with abundant enjoyment indoors where it does not. November 1st we found the Nevada Desert very bleak, and the Sierras fast being covered with snow. Between Truckee and Cape Horn the road is protected by forty miles of snow-sheds, the same of which the British traveler complained—"Blarsted long depot; longest I ever saw!" They continue down the western slope to an elevation of only 4,500 feet above the sea, where there is no danger of a blockade; and cost a million and a half. No snow can fall sufficient to block the road, as they are built against the cliffs with such a slope as to shed the snow into the deep valleys.

At an elevation of 3,000 feet, we were out of the region of snow, and soon after among the brilliant leaves and yellow grass which mark the autumn scenery of the Pacific Coast. Only two light showers have fallen; the stimulating air and cloudless sky show that the rainy season has not fairly set in.

BLUE CAÑON—SIERRA NEVADA.

At Sacramento I find great difference of opinion as to the better route to Oregon, by land or water, by the weariness of stage-coach pounding, or the pains and perils of sea-sickness. In order to give an unbiased opinion, I decided to go by land and return by sea. Through tickets from Sacramento to Portland, by land, can be had for forty-five dollars; by sea, for ten dollars less. The railroad terminus was then at Reading, a hundred and seventy-five miles from Sacramento; thence one must stage it two hundred and eighty miles to the southern terminus of the Oregon Railroad. The autumn rains came on in due order, and, as our train moved up the Sacramento River, the summer-dried grass was taking on a velvety brown, with rare patches of faint green. Northward, signs of fertility increased; and, at Chico, the face of nature was so beautiful, that I halted for a day.

Here General John Bidwell has a ranche of some 20,000 acres, one of the finest in California. The plains of the Sacramento have a varying width of from twenty-five to fifty miles, between the foot-hills of the Sierra and Coast Range; and his ranche occupies the richest portion of this strip. He is a pioneer of the pioneers, having come to California in 1846, two years before the discovery of gold. The same year came Governor Boggs and party, from Missouri; Edwin M. Bryant, first American alcalde of San Francisco, and the unfortunate Donner party, whose sufferings and fate have laid the foundation for many a thrilling romance. At least five thousand Americans had crossed the plains and settled in California before the "great rush" of 1849. They all engaged in cattle-raising, the sole business of the native Mexicans; for, even as late as 1850, few people believed that these dry plains would admit of regular farming. A few of them got possession of old Mexican grants, the titles to which were afterwards confirmed by treaty, and have since been sustained by the Supreme Court of the United States. Hence that oppressive land monopoly, which is now the worst hinderance to the development of California.

On General Bidwell's ranche are grown all the roots and grains of the temperate zones; besides fifty varieties of fruit, from the little black grape of the North to the fig of the tropics. He had already made the manufacture of raisins a success, and wine can be produced almost as cheaply as cider in Ohio. I find all the wines of California very agreeable to the taste, and most of them healthful. But the old resident seldom drinks wine. At every hotel the salutation in cool weather is, "Walk right up to the bar—warm you up for four bits, and heat you red hot for a dollar." This is a "survival" of the tastes of early settlers, who worked hard with pick and shovel, lived on bread, beef, pork, and beans, and did not taste milk, wine, or fresh vegetables for years together.

As we walked around the grounds adjacent to the Bidwell mansion, we saw oranges, olives, and pomegranates growing luxuriantly, while the borders were a brilliant maze of white and red, diversified by the branching palm, pampas grass ten feet high, with beautiful white plumes, and the delicate tints of the giant oleander. Workmen were busy covering the young orange trees, which must be shielded from the coldest winds during the first three or four years, but on the full-grown trees the growing oranges were nearly of full size, the green rind beginning to change to a pale yellow. And yet, fifteen hundred miles straight east of this, at my old home, snow is fast covering the fields, and no green-growing plant will delight the eye for months to come.

At Reading, I tarried again, making pleasant excursions among the surrounding hills and valleys, the most pleasant to Shasta City.

This region was the range of the poet Joaquin Miller, during the wild days in which he absorbed poetry from free nature, and found inspiration in the companionship of Shasta squaws. The county records contain papers of strange import as to his reputation. The worst accusation against him is of stealing a horse; but his friends maintain that the owner of the horse owed Miller a debt which the latter could not collect, and therefore levied on the property in a somewhat irregular way. Be that as it may, the grand jury at Shasta found a bill of indictment against him; he was in jail for some time, then broke out and fled to Oregon. Joaquin's native wife was of the Pitt River band of Diggers, and she now lives near there with an old mountaineer named Brock. This man and Miller were crack shots, and supplied themselves and brown families plentifully with game, living in all other respects as the Indians do. The poetry in Joaquin (whose real name, by the way, is John Heiner Miller) worked out in very odd ways for some years. The most charitable opinion in Shasta is, that he was then slightly "cracked," with a crazy affectation to imitate the heroes of Spanish romance. His name was adopted from that of Joaquin Murietta, a noted outlaw, who was long the terror of the Joaquin River region. He was of the "dashing, chivalrous" Claude Duval style of bandits, spending his gains freely among the Mexican *señoritas;* and the character fascinated Miller.

From what I saw of the Shasta and Pitt River squaws, I should say a man must needs be very crazy to live with one of them. The sight or smell of most of them would turn the stomach of any other than a poet. Their chief luxury is dried and tainted salmon. White men not only learn to eat it, but are said to like it even more tainted than do the Indians. Many old mountaineers are scattered through these hills, each living with a squaw; and it is common testimony that after a white man has lived with a squaw some years, he would not leave her for the best white woman in the country. They learn to do housework after a fashion, and on gala days rig out in hoops and waterfalls of most fantastic pattern. But they boil or roast the carcasses of their dead relatives; mix the grease with tar, and mat it on their heads and necks, making a sort of helmet, with only the eyes and mouth free; then for seven weeks they howl on the hill-tops every morning and evening to scare away the evil spirits. I saw one of these "in mourning," and am convinced that if she *don't* scare the devil away, he must be a spirit of some nerve. A white man disposed to Indian life, can adopt all their customs in six months, while an Indian can not adopt ours in fifty years. Arithmetically speaking, it is a hundred times as easy for a white man to go wild as for an Indian to become really civilized. We left Reading by stage at one o'clock in the morning, seven men in a little coach, which carried also seventeen hundred pounds of delayed mail. On top, rear, and "boot," it was piled as long as it could be strapped fast, and half the inside was filled with it. The passes ahead were fast filling with snow, and delayed mail and passengers were scattered at every point along the route. At daylight we crossed Pitt River, where the valley of the Sacramento may be said to end, as the spurs of the Sierras put out westward toward the Coast Range, and, in mining parlance, "pinch in" upon the plain. Pitt River is really the Upper Sacramento, being the largest of the confluent streams, and preserving a general course south-westward, after emerging from the mountains. Along its right bluff, we preserved a general north-east course all day. Again and again we thought we had left it, as the coach turned directly away and labored up mountainous passes, and along frightful "dugways" for miles, to an elevation of hundreds of feet above the stream; then we would turn to the right, and come thundering down a long rocky grade for two or three miles to the water's edge again. And every time we appeared to be coming back to the same place; there were the same timbered hills and rocky bluffs, perpendicular on one side of the stream and sloping on the other; the same immense gray bowlders, rocky islands and towers in the bed of the stream, and the same white foaming rapids.

COTILLION ON THE STUMP OF THE MAMMOTH TREE.

For fifty miles the river is a series of cascades; and though, through our ups and downs, we but kept even with the stream, we must have been gaining rapidly in general elevation. The sun rose clear, and the bright day and sublime scenery made us forget the fatigues of the way. The immense timber through which this road runs is a constant astonishment to the traveler. For two hundred miles, broken only by two or three open spaces, stretches a vast forest of firs and pines of every diameter, from one to ten feet. Southward the big trees grow more numerous, till they culminate in the Calaveras Grove and the thirty-two-feet stump, on which there is room for a dancing party, with musicians and spectators. Here is inexhaustible wealth in lumber. The fir is harder to work than the pine, but more durable. With good facilities for shipping, every acre of this forest would be worth two hundred dollars.

Near night we left the river, and toiled slowly up-hill for two hours to a mountain plateau. To our right was Mount Shasta, 14,400 feet high, a scene of indescribable beauty in the cold, clear moonlight. The lower portion looked like polished marble, shading off by degrees to the bright green of the pine forests on the foot-hills; the summit, covered nearly all the year with snow and ice, shone a monument of dazzling whiteness. But sentiment was soon overpowered by sense, as the drivers had lost time, and now took advantage of the down-grade; the coach bumped over great bowlders, throwing us against the roof and back against the seats till phrenological development went on at both ends with uncomfortable rapidity. Lean men can not endure coaching like plump ones; and if Darwinism be true, in my many years of travel I should have "developed" a series of gristle-pads. Our present anatomy is all very well for home life in a level country; for mountaineering I could suggest an improvement: a cast-iron backbone with a hinge in it, terminating below in a sole-leather copper-lined flap.

At Yreka I had to stop and rest between stages; and, after nine hours' sleep, still felt as if I had been pounded all over with a clapboard. Yreka has the coldest climate of any city in California, and a location of wonderful beauty. From the town a gently undulating valley extends in every direction, rising by a succession of timbered foot-hills to the lofty mountains, whose notched and pointed summits, now dazzling white with snow, seem to join the blue heavens or lose themselves in clouds. But it is only on the points of the mountains that any mist can be seen; above us the sky is cloudless, and the cool air is exhilarating as some ethereal gas. A few miles eastward was the home of the Modocs, and soon after my visit this region became notorious for that tempest-in-a-teapot, the "Modoc War." These are the gentle savages with whom Walk-in Miller claims to have affiliated, at mention of which claim the old pioneers smile meaningly, with a closure of the left optic.

Wyeka was the original Indian name; for no Indian or Chinaman can pronounce the letter *r*. There is a tradition that a Dutch baker painted the present name on his sign by mistake, and it was noted that "YREKA BAKERY" spelt the same both ways, which struck the citizens as such a happy combination that the name was retained by general consent. Similarly, Siskiyou, name of the county first organized, resulted from the attempts of miners to pronounce the French *Six Cailloux* ("six bowlders"), as the district was called, from six immense rocks in the river. As most of the early American settlers learned French and Indian by the aid of "sleeping dictionaries," the pronunciation may not be strictly academic. Like all old mining counties, this is heavily taxed. An unsettled population of twenty thousand often organized a California county, voted magnificent public works, and issued bonds to complete them; in no long time the miners

VIEW IN THE MODOC COUNTRY.

mostly left, and a smaller community of farmers, graziers and vine-growers have to pay the debt and run the county.

Early next morning we took the coach again, and soon after daylight crossed the Klamath River by a "swing-ferry." The valley amounts to but little, as the river runs between rugged hills through most of its course; but on its headwaters is the greatest game district in the West, perhaps in the world. All varieties of game abound, and the cool waters of Klamath Lake are alive with trout. Only its remote and inaccessible position prevents its being a place of great resort. Soon after we enter Oregon, and the first impression is that the State is covered by one immense and gloomy forest. In places the very daylight seemed to vanish into a mild twilight, and in the few "clearings" we passed through, the sunshine was novel and enjoyable. After noon the country began to show signs of improvement; settlers' cabins became numerous, and, after running down a narrow cañon, we came out into the beautiful valley of Rogue River. Here is said to be the finest climate in Oregon, and to wearied passengers just over the mountains the sight was a revelation of beauty. Where we enter, the valley is no more than two miles wide, but as we go down it widens gradually to fifteen or twenty, while on every hand appear fine farms, thrifty orchards, great piles of red and yellow apples of wondrous size, barns full of wheat, and fine stock, and we feel with delight that we are out of the mountains and "in the settlements." Though far retired from the road, the mountains still appear rugged and lofty, sending out a succession of rocky spurs—one every two or three miles—and between these, far back into the hills, extend most beautiful coves. The air was mild, the roads firm and smooth, and the coach rolled along with just enough of motion to give variety—and appetite.

Plows were running in the fields, "breaking summer fallow for spring wheat," said the natives; and the farm work showed that no freeze was to be apprehended for some time. Another night's travel on the mountains, and daylight came slowly upon us in the dense woods lying between Cow Creek and the South Umpqua. The sun's rays did not reach us through the dense and leafy mass above till nearly noon, and soon after we entered on a timbered cañon down which we bumped and thumped for four hours, making but fifteen miles. The coach alone would have been too heavy a load for the four horses, every one of which filled Isaiah's description of the natural man: their whole heads were sick and their whole hearts faint; and from the crown of the head to the sole of the foot they were wounds and bruises and putrefying sores.

At Cañonville we ran out into the Umpqua Valley, at a point where the river comes in from the east and turns due north. After crossing we traveled the rest of the day down the east bank. Many clear and pretty streams dash down from the Cascade Range, cross our road and empty into the Umpqua. The range bends in towards the coast, and hence none of these valleys are as wide as that of the Sacramento. Reaching Roseburgh at dark, we found that the Oregon and California Railroad had just been completed to that point, saving us eighteen miles of the staging we had expected. Next day was Sunday, and I can not recall a more pleasant Sabbath than this, which we spent in a slow ride down to Portland. Roseburgh is south of the "divide" and on the slope towards the Klamath; but the intermediate ridges are not so high as those behind us, and far more pleasant as seen from the inside of a car. Forty miles brought us fairly into the Willamette Valley, the largest body of good land in Oregon, containing nearly six thousand square miles. The soil is wonderful, being in many places from six to thirty feet in depth. The high Cascade Range shuts off all hard winter storms; the lower Coast Range on the west only admits the mildest airs of the Pacific; the summers never get so dry or hot as in California; all the rains are gentle, and destructive storms and freshets are unknown. The surprisingly slow development of such a region can only be accounted for by the method of settlement, the first comers getting title to nearly all the land. The new settlers eagerly seize on every chance for improvement, and are doing considerable; but it is complained that these old fellows "hold on to the land like burrs, and die mighty slow." And from longer experience with the "first families," I am driven to the painful conclusion, that about a hundred first-class funerals would prove of great advantage to Oregon.

In the lower portions of the valley the road traverses what are called "Beaver Lands." The theory of their origin is that the beavers, by damming up the shallow creeks and building their houses in them, caused the beds and adjacent low lands to overflow and fill with accumulations of earthy matter and decayed vegetable deposits. This must have been the work of many centuries, and has left a soil which only grows more fertile by cultivation. But these lands are found nowhere but in the Willamette Valley, and do not altogether exceed twenty thousand acres.

I reached Portland at sunset of a beautiful sabbath evening—not at all suggestive of the fog and rain which are generally attributed to this climate. For two days the weather was delightful, though everybody spoke of it as the coldest they had ever experienced. The wind was from the north-west, very gentle, the sky clear, and ice half an inch thick formed on the gutters—a rare thing in Portland. The third evening the thermometer rose from 28° to 38°, and next morning I wondered why I had waked and was so restless in the night. I turned over suddenly, and an old shot wound in the knee gave me a fearful wrench. Then I felt something like ague along my backbone. I struck a match, looked at my watch, and it was after 8 o'clock.

Such a fog! One could chew it up and spit it out. With a sharp knife it might be cut out in chunks and stored for dry weather. They say the winters here are healthful. It must be for differently constituted lungs from mine. It don't seem to me like breathing; it is rather a sort of pulmonic swallowing. Only the smoke and dust of a great city here is needed to give Portland occasional fogs fully equal to those of London. This fog continued till noon, then broke away, and a gentle drizzle finished the day. Portlanders all agree that they have the finest climate in the world in summer, and part of the spring; but admit that it is rather unpleasant in the winter or rainy season. From November till March every wind brings rain, unless it be from the north-west. In that case the clouds sail away over the Cascade Range, the mercury falls to 35° or below, and the sky is clear for a brief space. But let the mercury rise to 40°, and rain comes again. Sometimes there is a continuous patter for six weeks, the air being chilly and penetrating. The summers are never so hot and dry as in California; the hills are covered with timber, and every thing grows without irrigation.

One week sufficed to conclude my business in Oregon, but before leaving a few general notes are in order. Portland is on the west bank of the Willamette (pro. Wil-*lam*-et), twelve miles above its mouth and near the head of tide-water. But the Columbia often rises so as to cause backwater, giving the Willamette a variation of thirty-two feet. Ocean steamers load at the wharf, and the place has direct water communication with all the ports of the world, the chief exports being wheat, lumber, beef and salmon. All the older portion of the city is very beautifully improved; elegant residences abound, with many evidences of taste and wealth. The location is picturesque. The Cascade Range is only occasionally visible, but Mount Hood rears its snowy summit sixty miles eastward, and looks as if it were just out of town. Mount Saint Helens is sometimes in good view, though eighty miles to the north-east. All the hills around the city are covered with heavy timber, and in town every street is double lined with shade trees.

Of the 25,000 people in Portland, one-sixth are Chinamen. They are porters, washer-men, railroad laborers, cigar makers, and artisans of other sorts, with an occasional member of the higher caste engaged in trade. Sam Poy Lahong has seven stores on the Pacific Coast, his head-quarters being at Portland. I made his acquaintance, and found him a gentleman of great intelligence. The firm of Tung, Duck, Chung & Co., charter vessels and import extensively from China, as do some smaller firms. Other foreigners are scarce; the Jews predominate. Portland is almost exclusively an American city, in fact, a Yankee settlement; though most of the people in the country are from Missouri and other South-western States. The city seems to have all the enterprise which the State at large lacks. The rural "web-foot," as the residents are called, in ironical allusion to the climate, is *sui generis*: there is a distinctively Oregonian look about all the natives and old residents which is hard to describe. Certainly they are not an enterprising people. They drifted in here all along from 1835 to 1855, and some of them at an even earlier period, when many western Americans came to the Pacific Coast to engage in cattle-raising—not considering the country fit for much else. They left Missouri and Illinois—most of them—because those States were even then "too crowded" for them, and they wanted to get away where "they was plenty o' range and plenty o' game," and have a good, easy time. With one team to each family (time being no object to such people) it costs them nothing to move; and the peculiar land laws applied to Oregon gave them every advantage, and have been a serious hinderance to settlement ever since. Each single male settler could acquire title to three hundred and twenty acres, and each married man to six hundred and forty; there were besides some inducements to families, so that the birth of a child was a pecuniary advantage to the parents. The result was that hundreds of girls of eleven, twelve and thirteen years of age were married; with the further result, that all this fine land is owned in vast bodies by these old families, many of whom will neither sell, improve, nor hire any one else to improve. They acknowledge their own laziness, and talk about it so good-humoredly that one is compelled to sympathize with them.

The steamer on which I had engaged passage down the coast was to start at dark, but going on board I was informed that we should delay till next day, " to get high tide over the bar at the mouth of the Columbia." So my friends made an evening of it to see me off properly, and gave me a world of good advice about sea-sickness. Having properly prepared my nerves, and emptied fourteen bottles of " Bass," they saw me aboard, with the parting words: " Good-bye, Jonah; and when you begin to heave, think of us!" An " old salt " then gave me his advice: " Take half a dozen limes in your pocket, eat one whenever you begin to feel giddy, wrap up well and walk about, stick to the deck with me, and I'll insure you." This I did, and found it the best plan.

At daylight, the bang of a six-pounder on the bow aroused me from dreams of shipwreck, and pretty soon the " hoh-he-hoh " of the seamen's chorus, and the rattle of lines and jingle of bells announced that we were off. The easy motion of the vessel lulled me to another nap of an hour, from which I awoke to find that we were dead still—neither tied nor anchored, but swinging with the current, and buried in a fog, so dense that I had to feel my way along the berths to the cabin door. We were near the mouth of the Willamette, and were to stay there any time from one to twenty-four hours. Hour by hour the fog slowly lifted, drizzle and mist taking its place, and chilling one to the very bones. The cabin passengers crowded around the stoves, while the Chinese and other steerage passengers walked the deck, or stood around the smoke-stacks for warmth; the melancholy " Johns," with glazed caps and black pig-tails, looking like a lot of half-drowned crows. About 2 P. M., blue spots began to appear, bright rays broke through the gloom, a light wind was felt from the north-west, and soon the fog was sailing away in fleecy clouds toward the Cascade Range.

We were soon out in the Columbia, and at once surrounded by large flocks of ducks and wild geese, with an occasional gull or walloon. At dark we reached the principal salmon fisheries, stopped for the night, and took on a hundred tons of canned salmon—" No put up at all," the clerk said. The amphibious race who follow the calling of fishermen on the lower Columbia, know all about salmon and next to nothing of any thing else. Three hours persistent questioning among them developed these facts. The salmon vary in weight from five to thirty pounds, twelve being a fair average. When they enter the Columbia from the ocean, their meat is of a bright red color; every mile they go up stream they get poorer, and their meat whiter. In the Willamette it is a pale vermillion, further up almost white; but no Oregonian will eat of salmon taken above the mouth of the Willamette. They continue up stream as far as possible, and have been seen twelve hundred miles from the ocean. On all the rapids they are found "bucking against the stream;" where only the most daring boatmen venture, they glide swiftly up over the rocks; and where man descends at the risk of his life, the graceful salmon is seen shining through the foaming water. Having reached the highest attaina-

RAPIDS ON THE UPPER COLUMBIA.

ble point, on whatever stream they turn into, they spawn among the gravel and on the rocks, where the water is but two or three inches deep. Then they die by thousands, and masses of dead salmon are cast ashore, or found floating in the eddies. It was thought they all died; but the fishermen say it is now known that many of the old ones survive to return to the ocean, though they float sluggishly with the current, keeping very low in the water. Next year the young ones go out to the ocean in vast schools, and occasionally one of them is caught with a hook, but not often. The meat of the salmon is poison to a dog. There is a remarkable difference between various localities. At places on Puget Sound, the salmon is not fit to eat; at others, it is inferior, but still palatable. The Columbia takes precedence of all points on the coast.

We spent three hours at Astoria, a curious old town strung along under the wooded hills, and a party of us walked out to see the first house built in Oregon—the old residence of Astor. The place is now of little importance except for shipping salmon. The call to a late breakfast showed the fifty cabin passengers all on hand, each one speculating humorously as to how many would sit down to the next meal; for we could already see the white foam on the bar, and knew that a "high sea was running outside." The Columbia bar was long the terror of navigators, but it appears to have been such only through ignorance; and, since proper soundings have been made, no more accidents have occurred in the last twenty years than at the mouths of other large rivers. We passed it in an hour, without difficulty, and soon were upon the "heaving ocean," of which we read. It was a rough introduction. The heaviest sea encountered on the voyage was at the start. One minute the bow appeared to be rearing up to square off at the midday sun, and the next to get down and root for something at the bottom of the ocean. Bets were made as to who would be the "first to fall," and a large party of us went to the hurricane deck to stand it out. With songs, shouts, and laughter we danced about on unsteady footing, attempting an "Ethiopian walk-around" on the heaving deck, determined to fight off the sickness to the last moment. Then we practiced balancing against the waves, watching the water in the hollows of the deck, and seizing on the moment when it started one way to throw ourselves to the opposite. While enjoying this pastime, a lad of some fifteen years suddenly sank to the deck, then rose and emptied his stomach at one vast heave. There was a yell of laughter as he started below, but in a minute two more followed suit. Then they fell away rapidly, and in an hour only five of us remained. As I gazed on the bow, admiring the majestic sweep of its rise and fall, it suddenly appeared to stop, then stood dead still, and the whole body of the ocean appeared to rise and fall instead, and in a moment my head seemed to rise and fall with it, leaving the bow between us quite fixed. I had been warned not to look at the bow, but I forgot it. I tried in vain to restore the natural order, but the illusion had become to me a reality: the bow was still, and my head and the ocean alone moved. At every rise my neck seemed to stretch out longer, my head get farther from my body, and my stomach to rise and fall with the ocean. Lunch was called, and I went below. One mouthful of soup I swallowed, but felt it coming back. I clapped my hand upon my mouth and rushed to my berth, badly defeated. Next door to me was a family of four, making their first trip away from Oregon. As I passed, the little girl and boy were lying in the lower berth, with their heads over a basin, moaning with sickness; the young mother lay above, pale as the sheet, and unable even to resist the motion of the vessel, which tossed her from side to side; and the husband sat by trying to cheer them, while the dark bile swelled up in his cheeks, and his eye showed the composure of despair. I could not repress a sickly smile, for he had been the most hilarious of our party on deck. From all sides came a mixed sound of curses, groans, and regurgita-

CAPE MENDOCINO.

tions. My sickness lasted three hours; then came a delightful calm, succeeded by a long, sweet sleep.

I learned a new fact, to me: there are really two kinds of sea-sickness; one begins in the head, and the other in the stomach, and a man may have either or both. The latter, I am convinced, is simply a reversal of the peristaltic motion of the stomach and bowels. In the long swells, as the boat rises, one feels perfectly delightful; the "insides" settle down, down, down, and are at rest. But as the boat sinks all the internal viscera rise—as one passenger expressed it, "You fall away from your grub"—they press even against the throat, producing a fearful and indescribable nausea. And one may have this kind of sea-sickness without being a particle giddy. But the other kind begins in the head: it is the result of the eye having nothing fixed or solid to rest upon. Every thing one looks at is moving—the boat, the lamps, the waves are so many sources of irritation to the brain and optic nerve. Some persons get sick in a swing, or car; but they find one relief: there is the sure and firm set earth to come back to. But on a vessel every thing is in motion. This is the kind of sickness I had; and, hence, when I lay down and shut my eyes, it gradually passed away. But for those whose sickness *begins* at the stomach there is no such remedy. They must suffer it through.

Next morning the sea was calm, the boat running "on an even keel," and the rest of our voyage to San Francisco was delightful. The third day the table was full again; every body protested they "had not been very sick;" good appetite was the rule, and jollity reigned. So I stick to my original advice: Take a day's sea-sickness on the way to Oregon rather than go by stage. The second night, we saw from afar the glowing summit of Point Arena Light-house—a sublime sight from a distance on the ocean; and viewed the glories of Cape Mendecino by the yellow light of the setting sun. Next night we passed the Golden Gate, and anchored at the San Francisco wharf; and, at daylight, I was delighted to find myself once more on *terra firma*.

CHAPTER XXVI.

LAS TEXAS Y LOS TEJANOS.

"G. T. T." Forty years ago these mysterious letters might often be seen chalked or charcoaled on the door of an absconding debtor in the Middle, Southern and Western States. On the tax returns one occasionally saw them, opposite the name of some ne'er-do-well who had defrauded the State and other creditors by departing between two days. "Gone to Texas" was the universal verdict in such cases; and in due time the rural wags cut it down to the initial letters. The State had a hard name. As all who left their country for their country's good were supposed to have gone to Texas, its population was thought to be composed mainly of refugees from debt and justice; and its society, such as is broadly hinted at in General Sam Houston's reported farewell to his young wife: "Madame, you may go to hell, and I'll go to Texas."

The glories of San Jacinto, Goliad and the Alamo, the bravery of Texan troops in the Mexican War, and the able representatives the State sent to Washington, rapidly raised our opinion of the new commonwealth; but its development continued slow till after the war. Then a fresh spirit of emigration was excited in the Old South, which soon spread to the North and West, and within seven years after the peace, Texas was said to be receiving immigrants at the rate of four thousand per week. On this south-westward wave I was again borne along in the early part of 1873, for every body was curious about it, and the State needed a pen-painter.

One may now ride without change of cars from St Louis to Galveston, 1,009 miles; and from all points east to St. Louis. It was proposed to push the western branch of the Texas Central to Camargo, on the Rio Grande, and eventually to the City of Mexico; and grading was in rapid progress when the panic of 1873 suddenly stopped it. Only a few years, however, must elapse till one can ride by rail from New York to the Mexican capital. By the Missouri, Kansas & Texas Road, I passed leisurely through the first two States, and late in a cool April day entered the Indian Territory. Daylight next morning found us in the center of the Choctaw Nation, and still sixty miles north of Red River. In the valleys the soil appeared very rich, on the upland rather thin. About half the country is covered by timber, and very few cultivated farms are seen. Occasionally appears a cattle *corral*, and near it a stylish log-house or rude cabin, from which "White Choctaws" peer out at the train, with an air of lazy admiration. In the heaviest timber, wild turkeys often fly near us, and smaller game are quite abundant, while on the high prairies large herds of horses and cattle show the wealth and employment of the Choctaws.

Crossing the yellow Red River, which is rather narrow at this point, we enter the sovereign State of Texas, and four miles further disembark at the "city" of Denison. A regular "norther" is blowing, and for the first day of my stay an overcoat is not too heavy. This is a cosmopolitan town. About half its citizens are from the North, half from the South; a third or more are foreigners, the rest from every State in the Union. It is curious to observe how often a Northern and a Southern man are in partnership, and that the clerks in large establishments are similarly divided. The wants of commerce demand amnesty. The Alamo Hotel, where I stop, deserves a week's study. It unites the characteristics of the Yankee hotel, the foreign *hostelrie* and the Southern "public house;" among its guests are the swarthy Southron, the darker Mexican, the blonde Englishman, the pale Bostonian, and the omnipresent Jew, whose features are the same from Puget's Sound to Key West. The neighboring region is very fertile, the climate healthful, and if the State develops half as fast as it promises, Denison must make a considerable city.

The "norther" blew all day. At night it suddenly ceased; the air grew warm, and the streets of Denison were thronged by hundreds of loungers. Let us walk, listen to the music from half a dozen concert-saloons, and take notes of the denizens. There is the regular railroad follower, with glazed cap or slouched hat, dark red complexion, red shirt and brawny arm; the "sporting gent" of faultless exterior, whose wide-awake air in the evening, and eye with dark under-stain, indicate wakeful nights and sleep by day; and the Yankee merchant and his Southern clerks, the usual combination here. And there are the rural Texans lounging in groups of four or five, most of them dark, gaunt, and grizzly; a few Mexicans, who have come with cattle herds all the way from San Antonio, and numbers of white "bullwhackers," sunburnt, healthy, and jolly, carrying with them constantly their murderous whips, which look as if one heavy stroke with them would flay a cow's back. All are good-humored and sociable. Their language is the horror of grammarians, and such phrases as "dun gone," "clean clar out," "git shet of it," are elevated to the dignity of good ordinary speech. About ten per cent. of the crowd are negroes, the waiters and barbers usually light-colored, sleek and polite, but the great mass black, ragged, and offensive.

"How's the haalth on Nohth Fohk?" asks one native of another. "Pooty fayh," is the reply; "but the spiral maginnis tuck a good many on Main Trinity this winter." This is Texan for spinal meningitis. Long afterwards I asked a negro in South Carolina how his people stood the winter, and received for reply: "Pooty fayh, but de menin-jeesus tuck lots of 'em." Similarly the motto, *Sic Semper Tyrannis*, best known in the South as the noted exclamation of Wilkes Booth, is freely translated in Texas, "Six serpents and a tarantula."

The farmers adjacent to Denison are of the old Southern type, none very wealthy, but all social, communicative, and glad to see the country improved, no matter by whom. There is no end to the land for sale, at from four to ten dollars per acre. At the hotels one hears of "canned milk" and "sure enough milk," the latter very scarce. All the butter used here comes from New York. There is not a county in this section that sells five hundred pounds of it per year. "Cheaper to sell cattle and buy it," they say; and I suppose they know. There are no dairies, and very few potatoes are grown. Those on the table at the "Alamo" are from Iowa, of picked sizes, and worth from four to eight cents apiece. *Per contra*, good lemons can be bought at "two bits a dozen;" fish very cheap, and first rate Texas beef at the same price as potatoes—six or seven cents per pound. The soil hereabouts is slightly sandy; on the slopes it changes to a rich black loam, and yields large crops of corn, wheat and cotton.

Thence I journeyed leisurely southward, over a soil like that of the Illinois prairies. Not more than one-fifth of this part of Texas is fenced in. Corn was two or three inches high, and wheat rather more advanced; but the air was still cool enough to make a little fire in the evening desirable. Farmers all tell the same story: "Monsus late, cold spring; wust since I've been in Texas. Cawn got up three inches high; then was cut down by a big frost; then we had two weeks o' fine growin' weather, follered by rain an' another frost; now the cawn's doin' well agin, an' we've had the rain, an' the air's a leetle like light frost, but I hope not."

We cross many clear streams, lined with timber; between them are strips of high prairie. In the center of the county we stop at Sherman, a fine old Texan town, and metropolis of this section before Denison was built. Thence our way is down Main Trinity, at an average of five miles from the river. As all the timber lies along the streams, we are much of the time in a forest. It is estimated that one-half of that section of Texas east of the Trinity is still covered with the primeval forest. All the improvements worth noting are on the prairie, but a "free-nigger patch," with demoralized log-hut, occasionally appears in the low wooded bottoms, where that class mostly live. Inquiring of a philosophical native why this was thus, he replied: "Wall, they don't care for the breeze like we. Reckon they want to bleach out. You Northern folks are mistaken about that. 'Tain't the heat that burns dark; it's the wind, a-stoppin' the sweat. Folks that live indoors, or in the timber, an' sweat free, are whiter than up North. Find as fair girls in Galveston as ever you saw." Whether the colored American will, by operation of this principle, eventually become a white man, is another question.

In Collin County we enter the cotton belt proper. Here is a region a hundred and fifty miles square, with this county on its northern boundary, which could be made to yield more cotton than is now grown in all the States east of the Mississippi. Not more than one acre in ten of this area is now inclosed; and, of that inclosed, the smallest part is devoted to cotton; yet the product is already important. In the year 1870 the entire State had only 2,964,836 acres of land under cultivation, yet the cotton crop amounted to 350,628 bales. Thirty thousand square miles, suitable to the production of cotton, still remain in a state of nature.

Peaceful as it looks along this route, a short ride would bring one into a hostile country. Not fifty miles west is the heavily wooded strip known as the Cross Timbers; and, just west of that, the Comanche may occasionally be found in all his savage glory. Tradition tells of a time when these fierce nomads were at peace with the whites; and tells, too, I am sorry to say, that a long truce was broken by the cruel outrage and murder of a Comanche girl by a young Texan. The truth of this matter it would be hard to trace, but since that date the Comanches have waged unending, inexpiable war. Issuing from his hiding-place in the western highlands, the warrior descends with remorseless fury upon the settler; and every man of the tribe has cost State or Nation thousands of dollars.

Thence through Ellis and Navarro counties, the country is of the same general description, as far as Corsicana, where I make a long halt. Navarro and Corsicana—husband and wife—were wealthy and enterprising Mexicans who ruled this region, and owned most of it forty-five years ago. They welcomed American immigrants gladly, but did not relish the revolution and change of sovereignty, especially as it deprived them of many of their rights and privileges. So they sold what land they had left, and retired to Mexico. The county is named for the husband, the town for the wife. Here I find that

COMANCHE WARRIOR.

summer is rapidly coming north to meet me; corn is a foot high, and the midday heat is a little uncomfortable. Here corn, wheat and cotton are produced side by side; but four-fifths of the country is still unfenced, and land can be had in abundance at surprisingly low rates. The planters tell me three-fourths of a bale of cotton to the acre has often been produced; but they seldom estimate that way, not counting the land as an important item. They say "so many bales to the hand," and consider eight or ten bales for each worker a fair average.

The planters are rich in land and cattle, but their style of living is strangely primitive. Farm-houses are of an open, roomy sort, with porches on three sides usually, built against heat rather than cold. Milk and butter are accounted luxuries. There is but one grade of society among whites, all living very much alike; the negroes alone constituting the "lower classes." The latter are lazier than the whites, which is a dreadful thing to say of them. They might, in ten years, own half the land in the country if they would work steadily. Fleas are the curse of the country. In Corsicana the dust seems to breed them, and house-keepers have a regular science of ways and means to get rid of them. Other undesirables are the tarantula and centipede, the former a badly slandered creature at the North; for it is comparatively harmless, and death very rarely results from its bite. The centipede's sting is more venomous; it never strikes unless hurt or disturbed, but its venom causes the flesh to rot from the afflicted part, leaving the muscles bare. But all unite in saying they never knew it to cause death. I am, therefore, inclined to pass as fabulous the statement a "returned volunteer" once gave me of this creature: "An insect, sir, that runs like lightnin', and spits a juice that'll knock your eye out at a rod off; hit's got a diamond eye, a back like a hairy spider, and a belly like a tobacker worm, with a thousand an' forty-four legs; each leg has four stingers, and every stinger carries second death."

From Corsicana the train on the Texas Central Railroad carried me nearly straight south, leaving the valley of the Trinity and bearing across the high country to the Brazos. Not one acre in ten of this region is under fence. All the rest is common pasture, though most of it belongs to private owners, and is for sale at two to six dollars per acre. The region is high and gently undulating, about one-fifth in timber, the rest fertile prairie. My next stopping place was Houston, which I thought, at first view, the most beautiful place in Texas. There had been a twenty-four-hours' rain, and at 9 A. M. the sun shone out clear; the orange groves, magnolias, and shade trees looked their richest green, and Houston presented to the newly arrived Northerner a most enchanting appearance. That city, the original capital of Texas, is at the head of Buffalo Bayou, a long projection of Galveston Bay, but for some days there had been quite a current owing to late and heavy rains. Three steamers were anchored in the narrow channel, and half a dozen or more alligators, about six feet long, were sunning themselves on the drift-wood. The view there was not lovely, but back in the city, and on the level tract in every direction around, it was all the tourist could desire. Attending Baptist Sabbath-school and Presbyterian Church, I found about three dozen persons at each; whence I argued that the Houstonians are not piously inclined, or that a bright Sunday had greater charms outdoors than an orthodox sermon within.

Monday morning I was early awakened by a few shots, and rose to find some of the patriotic citizens celebrating the thirty-seventh anniversary of the battle of San Jacinto. I was evidently in an extreme Southern latitude at last. Pictures of Lee and Stonewall Jackson adorned the places of resort; the boys whistled "Bonnie Blue Flag" and "Dixie;" and two of my neighbors at the breakfast table had an animated conversation about "the doings of them d—d thieves up at Austin," a polite reference to the present legislature. By midday the weather was as hot as it would have been in Ohio; then the weather-wise said: "We'll have a norther," which is recognized as nature's regular plan in Texas for settling the weather. The day invited to repose; and Houston is a "reposeful" place. All the dwellings have a delightfully home-like look, with wide porches around them, and are almost hidden in dark-green groves. If one were rich, and correspondingly lazy, I can't think of a better place for him. But to be poor, in the far South—ah, that is bad! If that's your condition, better stop in upper or central Texas.

Thence to Galveston the "mixed train" consumed four hours in going fifty miles. At every station little darkies invaded the train to sell gorgeous tropical flowers, especially the immense magnolia buds, which expand to the complete flower in a few hours after being gathered. The road slopes to the south-east so gently that the eye can not perceive the decline, and on the whole route one does not see fifty houses. I am curious to see the thickly-settled part of Texas, for I have never found it yet. Herds of Texas cattle are seen in all directions, and grazing appears to be the only use made of the fertile plain extending thirty miles inland from the coast. Nearing the shore we find a few houses, surrounded by little farms devoted to fruit, vegetables, and poultry for the Galveston market, but nothing to indicate the vicinity of a great city. Passing these we enter open country again, and flat, marshy land of little value extends some five miles from the Gulf.

Passing the Confederate earthworks, erected to defend the channel against Yankee gun-boats, we enter on the two-mile trestle-work, which conducts us to the beautiful island and delightful city of Galveston. An island of hard white sand, thirty miles long and from one to four broad, rises evenly on every side from the salt surf; nowhere more than ten or twenty feet above high tide, the location has just slope enough for convenient drainage. The city is on the northeast end of the island. The streets run with the cardinal points, and are lined on both sides with heavy shade-trees. Except in the center of town and the business front, on the north side and known as the Strand, the houses are surrounded by oranges, oleanders and other Southern trees and flowers, the neat white dwellings rising from this dark green and leafy mass. All day the gulf breeze sweeps inland through the broad streets, and after an hour or two of sultry calm the land breeze blows outward all night. In the morning there is another warm calm of an hour or two, then the ocean breeze comes again. One would think it ought to be the healthiest place in America. But there are drawbacks. About once in five years the yellow fever visits the place. The last time the city was almost entirely abandoned. Already the papers and physicians are arguing *pro* and *con* the momentous question, "Will it come this year?" Late arrivals report it as very bad at Rio Janeiro, and slowly advancing along the "Spanish main."

It was a gala day in Galveston, and in the evening I found every resort thronged, while on the streets bands of music discoursed lively airs, and a thousand negroes thronged the streets, "happy as clams at high tide." San Jacinto was being celebrated, and every body and every thing Texan was mightily glorified. Nothing disloyal or unfriendly to the nation was heard, but there was a general agreement that Texas produced the bravest men in the world. I am too good-natured to differ with them. I have run down ten degrees of latitude in less than a month, from late winter to early summer, and begin to feel the effects of such a change. But in the open halls and on the wide porches of the Exchange, with the gulf breeze by day and the outward breeze by night, I soon get my constitution accustomed to a deal of rest, and like the lotus-eaters of Homer's fabled isle, having tasted the delights of an ocean beach in the tropics, nothing but compulsion takes me away.

No man can ride on the beach there without falling in love with Galveston. Between the highest and lowest tide-mark is a firm, white expanse, some two hundred yards wide, extending around the head of the island and down the southern side for thirty miles. The heaviest carriage-wheel barely marks it, the foot of a horse scarcely dents it; sloping gently to the water's edge, washed occasionally by the highest tide, and always swept by a gentle wind, it is certainly the most beautiful drive on our coast. From 4 P. M. till dark there is the place to see the beauty, wealth and fashion of Galveston. Instead of a winter resort, as I had supposed, this is becoming rather a midsummer resort. Old settlers from Virginia and Kentucky tell me they visit those States in the spring or autumn, but make it a point to spend midsummer here, for coolness.

From Galveston to Austin the railroad runs through the very heart of Texas, connecting its most important cities; but less than one-fifth of the country is inclosed, and every county contains immense tracts of fertile, uncultivated land. At Houston more railroads center than at any other point in the State—the Galveston Road, the Brazoria Road southward into the county of that name, the San Antonio Road westward to Colorado County, the Houston & Northern Road into Anderson County, and the Texas Central to Red River, with a branch from Hempstead to Austin. Along this last line the country seems very new. "Too much land in Texas" is the popular explanation. In other Western States one finds settlements thick along the eastern boundary, and a rapid falling off near the western border; in Texas the "border" is all over the State. Settlements and farms are nowhere coterminous; and until one goes some distance up the slope, north-westward, he finds about as many people in one section as another. The pursuits of the original Texans, a minimum of farming to a maximum of hunting and herding, required large open areas between the farms. Now cattle-raising, as an exclusive business, is confined to the far western portion of the State, and all the center and eastern section are calling for immigration.

Soon after crossing the Brazos, from Austin County into Washington, I found an old Arizona acquaintance, the prickly cactus, scattered thickly over the prairie—a pretty sure indication that we were getting into a dryer country. A little further, and we were among the *mezquit* thickets, which look to the stranger very like old peach orchards. They grow in patches on the highest and dryest lands, and are full of thorns as long and sharp as needles.

Soon after we enter Travis County, and descend a beautiful and fertile slope to the city of Austin, which appears from afar like a scattered collection of neat white cottages, embowered in groves and grass-plats. The cityward bluff of the Colorado rises almost perpendicular for thirty feet or more from the water's edge, thence a beautiful plain extends for some two hundred rods northward, and rises by a gentle grade to several picturesque knolls. On the crest of the central one, which slopes evenly toward all the cardinal points, stands the capitol; north of it are other public buildings, all around and for two miles further north are the finest private residences, while the city proper, of trade and crowded streets, extends from the capitol down to the river. Except the main street due south from the capitol, and a few of the nearest cross-streets, the city appears like an extension of retired country seats. At three or four places only is the steep bluff graded down to give a passage to the river; but north of town is a more gentle slope, and a broad sand-bar. On the opposite side is a range of heavily-timbered hills, and all around, far as the eye can see, and twenty miles further, extends a gently rolling country, alternating strips of fertile prairie with pretty little groves. The commissioners who selected this site for the capitol deserved well of their country; but they looked a long way ahead, for it was then (1839) " far up the country," on the Indian border, and even now this may be considered the western limit of connected settlement. But they had faith in the future, and selected the most available spot near the geographical center. In 1841 several men were killed by Indians within the corporate limits of the city, and Castro, a Lepan chief, was regularly hired by the infant government to scout north and west and keep off the Comanches. The growth of the city has been slow and regular.

Here we enter the land of border romance. Hence to the Rio Grande south-west, and to the Rocky Ridge west and north-west, every grove, cañon and valley has been the scene of some romantic and daring incident; but should I attempt to repeat all that are told here, the world itself, to borrow a simile from Scripture, would not contain the books that should be written. Hunters and herders alternately fought and fraternized with both Mexicans and Indians, and many a brave Texan has risked and suffered sudden death by venturing back to the hostile region after a favorite Indian girl or *señorita*. Noted among the wild riders of those days was one Bob Rock, an outcast from Mississippi, who, like thousands of others, had sought Texas as a land where legal requisitions were not valid. His skill with the rifle passed into a proverb. " If Bob Rock draws a bead on him, he's gone," was the general verdict. But the desperado was conquered at last by a little *mestiza*, who, though of mixed blood, affected most the company of her wild kinsmen; and she, by her native coquetry, succeeded in drawing the hunter into the rocky region near the head of

416 WESTERN WILDS.

the Colorado. Attacked most treacherously in the tent, the stout frontiersman succeeded in breaking the cordon and getting into the open plain with his trusty horse and rifle. But he had another range of hills to cross, and every pass was guarded, while the nearest pursuer was now but two hundred yards behind him. "I felt orful streaked," said Bob in his account, "but I knowed 'old blaze' had

"I SPILED HIS AIM."

never failed yet, so I turned, up with the old gal to my eye, and down goes Mister Injun. That brought 'em out all 'round, an' I seed—an' I done some quick thinkin' then—that in one pass thar war but one Injun. He dodged back as I turned agin, to lay for me, but I seed it was my first, last and only, and I sot old Sally at a gallop for that pint, holdin' 'old blaze' to be ready for him. Sure enough, just a minute too soon to take me on-a-wars, Mister Injun riz with his piece ready cocked. But I was too quick for him, and spiled his aim. His bullet cut pretty close, but mine took him center, and 'fore another could get up to the pass I was through an' out, an' I tell you I kept clar of that squaw arter that." Fortunately for the community, Bob's blood cooled as he grew older, and he settled into a very respectable citizen.

My first call in Austin was upon Governor E. J. Davis, last Republican executive of the State, then holding his own against fearful odds. Also his Adjutant General, none other than an old Evansville friend, Captain Frank Britton, formerly of the Twenty-fifth Indiana Volunteers. Between them and other State officials a hot conflict was raging, and the Legislature was devoting all its energies to undoing the work of its predecessors, so as to cut down the Governor's power as much as possible. This body had lately come into power as the result of the revolution of 1872, when the election was carried by the Democrats by an overwhelming majority. It was the first State Legislature I ever saw, and later experience has not changed my first impression, that it was a very able one. In the House the Democrats had three-fourths and in the Senate only lacked three of having two-thirds, all very industrious in repealing the laws of preceding Legislatures. The regular proceeding was to pass a law, send it to the Governor, get it back with a veto message, and then spend a week bringing over enough Republican Senators to pass it over his veto.

I was taking notes from Hon. C. B. Sabin, representative from Brazoria and Matagorda counties, when Hon. "Shack" Roberts, of Harrison County, an immense black man, rose to speak. His address was replete with humor and sarcasm, causing great laughter and applause. He is a Methodist preacher, very black, and uses the broadest "plantation-darkey" English. The six colored members of the House and two in the Senate added a pleasing variety. The members generally would compare quite favorably with those of Indiana or Ohio. (After that comparison, further description would be "risky.")

I was introduced to the Honorable "Shack," and after giving his testimony to the improved condition of affairs generally, he added: "The Methodists have done wonders for our people in edication, and we're a doin' more. Our church at home—the A. M. E.—has just 'stablished the Wiley University at Marshall, Texas—named after Bishop Wiley. We bought two hundred acres in a mile an' a half of the court-house, afore the town started up so with the railroad, an' now we're sellin' it off fast in buildin' lots at from fifty to two hundred dollars a lot, savin' just twenty acres in the middle for the university. We'll soon have it runnin', and it will be free to both sexes, 'thout regard to color or previous condition."

Texas is the most tolerant and liberal of all the reconstructed States. While under Republican rule, very stringent laws had been adopted to repress disorder; for the condition of the State just after the war was deplorable. Before the war, it had not been as bad as reported, though quite bad enough. For instance, in 1860, with a population of 650,000, Texas had a total of 121 homicides; while New York, with 3,000,000 people, had but 37. There was a steady and rapid increase of crime until 1869, the first year of the new *regime*, for which there are full returns, when the State had no less than 1200 homicides! In this state of facts, the leading Republicans brought forward what are sometimes called the "Five Administration Measures:" The militia law, the State police law, the concealed weapon law, and the school and immigration laws. The first authorized the Governor to suspend the *habeas corpus* at his discretion, to order the militia from any part of the State to another part, and to arm any portion of the population in any disturbed neighborhood. The police law organized a small body of mounted men, to be continually under pay of the State, and ready to go to any section. They never numbered more than three hundred.

Many brave Confederate soldiers joined this militia and aided in putting down disorder. The moral effect was tremendous. Eight hundred robbers and desperadoes fled the State in a body. There was a hanging in every county, till in the State, except in the extreme west, life and property were as secure as in New England. Then, unfortunately, these extraordinary powers were perverted. It was the old story over again: a condition of strife and social disorder leads to the placing of immense power in one man's hands; but when the disorder is passed, the ruler has grown too fond of his power to part with it without a struggle, and employs it to crush opposition. The people seek refuge from anarchy in a sort of legal despotism, and are driven by despotism into anarchy. In 1872 the State police were used to break up Democratic and Liberal-Republican meetings. But in another year the revolution was complete, Governor Davis yielded, in an awkward hurry, to a Democratic Governor, and now Texas is the most solid outpost of the "Solid South."

CHAPTER XXVII.

TEXAS—CONTINUED.

ROBERT CAVALIER, Sieur de la Salle, led the first European immigrants to Texas, landing near the entrance to Matagorda Bay, on the 18th of February, 1685. William Penn had founded Philadelphia three years before; the French were stretching their settlements from Canada down the western rivers, and the Spaniards were advancing slowly northward into New Mexico. A hundred and fifty years before, some survivors of the Pamphilo de Narvaez expedition had traversed Texas as captives among the Indians, but no title to the country could result therefrom.

La Salle, as American history calls him, had discovered the mouth of the Mississippi, April 7th, 1682, and soon after took possession of all that region by proclamation and *proces verbal*, in the name of Louis XIV. He was on his return with four ships to make a settlement, when an error in his calculations brought him on the Texan coast. All his people were in ecstasies over the beauty and richness of the country, and a settlement was agreed upon at once. Soon after they moved over on a stream they called Les Vaches, which the Spaniards afterwards translated into La Vaca, both meaning "the cow-s." Hard work and imprudence in such a climate produced sickness; carelessness led to murders by the Indians; Beaujeu, commander of the fleet, sailed away with two of the vessels; one of the other two was soon after wrecked, and the little colony got badly discouraged. By the law of nations this country, thinly occupied by wild Indians, now belonged to France; but in due time Spain took a different view of it, relying on previous Spanish explorations, never proved however, to the satisfaction of diplomats. Near the close of the sixteenth century Philip II., the gloomy tyrant of Spain, issued a royal order forbidding all foreigners to enter this territory under penalty of extermination. Thus began a "border question," which, passing down successively from Spaniard to Mexican, and from French to English and American, lasted two centuries and a half, till settled by the treaty of Guadalupe Hidalgo, on the 2d of February, 1848. In this controversy, reader, find the key to the whole history of Texas as connected with other governments.

Its settlement cost the lives of many thousand good men. The Comanches were then, as now, a race of nomadic thieves; the Lipans and Carankawaes dominated the country between the Rio Grande and Colorado. Other tribes were the Caddoes, Cenis and Nassonites. Texas had neither boundaries nor a name. The origin of the latter nobody knows, but it is supposed to be from an Indian word meaning "good hunting-ground," and was long spelled indifferently Tehas, Tejas, Tekas or Texas, which differ very little in Spanish pronunciation. Even now the residents are known as Tejanos (*pro*. Teh-hah-noes) by the Mexicans.

La Salle started northward with a considerable company, to open communication with Canada; and was murdered by two of his men. The survivors quarreled among themselves; the murderers were in turn assassinated; others were drowned or captured, and of all that colony only five lived to see France again. Those left on the Lavaca were surprised by the Indians, part killed, and the rest carried into captivity, whence in old age they were reclaimed by the missionaries. Thus ended the first settlement in Texas.

Soon after the Spaniards planted missions and military posts in the south-west, but drought and hostile Indians drove them out, and for twenty years the country had not one white inhabitant. In 1712 Louis XIV granted to Anthony Crozat all Louisiana, as far west as the Rio Grande, and sent out an embassy, which was captured by the Spaniards. "The year of Missions" in Texas was 1715, when the Spaniards began again to plant them in the country. Thereafter it was permanently occupied by Spain, and its various sections known as the New Philippines and New Estremadura. For some fifty years now we have the Mission Period, as in all Spanish American countries. Those in Texas were controlled by zealous Franciscan priests, who spent a life-time in toil to convert the savage natives. At each mission was a *presidio*, or commandant's head-quarters, with officers enough for two hundred and fifty men, though the latter rarely numbered so many. The first move was to capture by force or stratagem a hundred or more Indians. On these kindness and persuasion were exhausted, and they were taught all the ceremonies of an exceedingly ceremonial religion. When sufficiently trusty they were sent out to persuade others in; abundance of food was insured them, agriculture was taught, all the feasts and fasts were scrupulously observed, and at some missions the daily exercises in prayer and other services occupied five hours! Those whom this system converted it in due time wore out; those who resisted it were made wilder than ever. Then the fathers began with the women and children, with far better success; and in due time there grew up about each mission a considerable population of domesticated Indians, who cultivated the soil, were painfully pious and as docile as sheep. The fathers called themselves

UN INDIO BRAVO —TEXAS.

gente de razon, or people of reason, in contradistinction to the heathen; but in due time arose a better nomenclature. The wild Indians were known as *Indios bravos*, the converted as *Indios reducidos*. And badly "reduced" they were. Little by little the *reducidos* were merged, largely by intermarriage with discharged soldiers. Hence the *mestizoes*, nearly the same as regular Mexicans of the present day.

Meanwhile great things had happened in Europe, which changed the political map of America. William of Orange, the Champion of Protestantism—if he had not been that, we should have thought him a sullen Dutchman—had fairly worn out Louis XIV, and made peace with him. But soon after, the lunatic King of Spain died, and all the other lunatics fell to cutting each other's throats about the "balance of power," that mysterious abstraction which has caused more wholesale murder in modern Europe than all other causes combined. The English, Dutch and Germans would not allow the crown of Spain to be bestowed on Philip of Anjou, grandson of Louis XIV, as provided by Philip of Spain, in his so-called will. Hence another bloody war, and a general rearrangement at the treaty of Ryswick. But this left open certain questions between France and Spain; so they went to war in 1718.

The Louisiana French attacked and drove out the Spaniards as far west as Bexar. But the latter soon recovered the country. After a deal of reconnoitering, some sharp fighting, and many brave actions and romantic incidents in Texas, a sort of peace was patched up between France and Spain, and the latter determined to colonize Texas regularly. Soon after, the French handed over Louisiana to the Mississippi Company, then controlled by the notorious John Law, the original "greenbacker" and great "soft money" advocate. Other schemes now occupied the two nations, and their respective colonists had time to attend to legitimate business. In 1728, Spain sent to Texas several families from the Canary Isles, then peopled by a race known above all Spaniards for rigid adherence to the Catholic Church, domestic purity, and respect for women. Another colony came, composed of the original Tlascalans, whom Cortez could not conquer; they assisted greatly in capturing *Indios bravos* for conversion. But the country was in bad shape. Many dissolute soldiers had been discharged there. It invited wanderers and adventurers; and had a bad name as early as 1750. Apache and Comanche raids were frequent, and pirates began to hover along the coast. So in 1745, Texas contained no more than 1,500 whites—less than in 1722. *Mestizoes* and "converted Indians" were more numerous.

Thence to 1758 there was a dead calm. That year the Indians captured San Saba Mission, and killed every one there. Thenceforward the missions declined. Meanwhile England and France got to fighting again; there was, therefore, a general rectification of boundaries in America, and a new deal all around the board in Europe. France was so weakened by this contest, that in 1762 she ceded Louisiana to

Spain, to keep England from getting it. Bear in mind that Louisiana then meant all the country drained by the Mississippi, except where the English had obtained prior rights on its eastern affluents. Next year peace was made, by which England got Canada and all the French country east of the Mississippi and above the present Louisiana. One clause in that treaty was afterwards of immense importance to the United States, viz.: "The navigation of the Mississippi to be free to the subjects of both England and France."

This state of affairs continued forty years, and was of immense advantage to Texas; the missions died out, and regular colonists began to take their place. Meanwhile the American Revolution occurred, and there was no end of fighting between England on one side and France and Spain on the other. Spain refused the free navigation of the Mississippi, and the people of the western States swore they would take it by force. Then the French Revolution took place, and for awhile France had to fight all the rest of Europe. By secret treaty in 1800, Louisiana was transferred back from Spain to France, though the United States did not know it till two years after. All this time the boundaries of Texas and Louisiana had remained unsettled; the French had often claimed as far west as the Rio Grande, the Spaniards always as far east as the Sabine. This condition invited revolutionists and adventurous spirits, and there were numerous incursions, battles, skirmishes, and massacres which have no connection with the general history. Meanwhile the French Revolution progressed; Bonaparte got control of that country, and found himself engaged in a life and death struggle with England. He could not hold Louisiana, and needed money; the United States was on hand with the cash, the sale was made, and the transfer completed by imposing ceremonies in New Orleans, in December, 1803.

This brought up the old border question in a new shape. While the diplomats of Spain and the United States used up two years in attempts at a treaty, the provinces were a dozen times on the point of actual war. Governor Claiborne, of Louisiana, called out the militia, and forbade the Spaniards to cross the Sabine. At length it was settled that the strip between the Sabine and Arroyo Hondo should be neutral ground for the present. This was a beautiful arrangement. Of course the neutral strip was soon infested by desperadoes, and countless robberies and outrages were perpetrated. In one instance two desperadoes were captured, and to make them betray their companions were severely whipped. Then live coals were passed over their raw and bleeding backs. But they were gritty rascals, and refused to the last. To this stage of Texan history belong the establishments on the coast by pirates and smugglers, such as that of La Fitte at Barataria.

Early in 1812, Lieutenant A. W. Magee, left his post in the United States territory, and with a mixed force of adventurers from the States, volunteers from the neutral ground, and natives of Texas of Spanish blood, marched westward to redeem that region from the rule of Spain. There had been a sort of civil war in Mexico between the popular party and the aristocrats; the Anglo-Texans had taken the popular side, and Magee came in to assist them. It would have been money in his pocket and in theirs had he stayed away. He was steadily victorious till he reached La Bahia, west of the Guadaloupe. There he was confronted by a large force under Salado, and agreed to retire. This his men refused to accede to, and at once attacked the Spaniards, and gained a bloody victory. Overcome with shame, Magee died by his own hand. After various successes this army fell into an ambuscade, and were nearly all killed or captured. The prisoners were brutally murdered by the Spaniards.

Bonaparte's wars were now stirring up devilment and wholesale murder in every corner of the civilized world. He had invaded Spain, deposed the feeble king, banished the royal family, then at war with itself, and put his brother Joseph on the throne. Two Spanish parties at once arose: for accepting Joseph and for opposing him. Blood flowed on all sides. The divisions extended to all Spanish America. In Mexico the ruling classes favored Joseph Bonaparte; the common people supported the juntas, or revolutionary bodies which resisted him. On all sides the standard of revolt was raised. The Indians burned to avenge the wrongs of three centuries; the common Mexicans were greedy for spoil; the Church labored for aggrandizement. There were murders and riots in every section; towns were sacked and prisoners massacred by thousands, and Mexico entered upon that career of bloody anarchy which has continued with only occasional intermissions to this day. When this condition was at its worst, war broke out between England and the United States. La Fitte and other pirates and smugglers received a general pardon for serving under General Jackson at the battle of New Orleans, and after the peace returned and took possession of Galveston Island. There they set up an independent government—the most ridiculous little sovereignty that ever existed—which flourished greatly until broken up by the American authorities.

Mexico obtained her independence, and established the celebrated

Constitution of 1824, about which there has been so much fighting since. We have seen how the division in Spain excited revolution in Mexico; in exactly the same way civil war in Mexico brought on revolt, and finally independence, in Texas. No sooner was the Constitution of 1824 adopted, than the ruling classes insisted on a strong central government, the reduction of the States to departments, and a president with greater powers. These were called Centralists; their opponents Federalists—a name meaning the exact opposite of what it does in the United States. Santa Anna, by intrigue, treachery, and the support of the Church, obtained control as a Centralist; his great rival Bustamente stirred up numerous revolutions among the Federalists. At first Texas appeared equally divided, but in no long time the Federalists got control, as it was obviously for her interests that there should be separate State governments. Embassies and petitions were sent to Mexico City; the petitions were disregarded, the envoys often imprisoned. Thus, little by little the war spirit was excited in Texas.

Meanwhile Moses Austin had obtained his large grant of land in Texas from the Mexican government, and dying, left its settlement to his son Stephen. Having completed this work, Stephen Austin took an active part in political affairs, and went to Mexico as an envoy from Texas. There he was thrown into prison, where he remained two years and a half. All this time the Mexicans went on pulling down one and setting up another; and, as the result of half a dozen revolutions, Bustamente and the Federalists came into power. But their rule was as bad for Texas as that of the Centralists. They concluded that the Territory contained too many Americans, and forbade the immigration of any more! They passed about all the vexatious laws against free trade they could think of. Whenever it was certified to them that the Anglo-Texans were making money on any article, they straightway proceeded to restrict its sale or production. Among other bright laws, was one that no planter in Texas should sow more than one bushel of tobacco seed! Tobacco growers will see the point. The largest planter in Ohio does not use a gill.

To further aggravate the Texans, their province was attached to Coahuila. The Mexicans of that State furnished two-thirds of the legislature; and the inhabited part of Texas was nearly a thousand miles from the State capital. The Texans agitated and interceded for a separate government; the Mexican authorities responded by a more oppressive tariff law, and by introducing garrisons into the country to overawe the "rebels." Meanwhile there was another revolution in Mexico. Bustamente retired, Santa Anna took the reins, and established the firmest government Mexico ever enjoyed. As soon as he had tranquillized the other States, hanged and shot a few dozen of his opponents, and banished the rest, he collected a large army and marched on Texas, to settle things, as he said, effectually. He did it; but not exactly as he had intended.

The white population of Texas did not exceed 50,000. They had been divided, but the approach of the army united them; and they resolved on independence. Their army easily drove out the feeble garrisons in South-western Texas, but in no long time was overwhelmed by disaster. Early in 1836, Santa Anna entered the Territory with an army of 8,000 men, sending word to the Texans that he intended to "sweep away every thing save the recollection that they once existed." The brave William Barret Travis commanded the Alamo Fort with only a hundred and thirty men. He sent off, with all speed, for reinforcements; announced that he would hold the place till the rest of the country could be put in posture for defense, and concluded with the words: "*God and Texas! Liberty or Death!*" Of that hundred and thirty men, only Moses Rose escaped; and he, ashamed of having abandoned his companions, and slipped out through the Mexicans at the last hour, never gave account of the siege till on his death-bed. For two weeks the Mexicans kept it up, making daily assaults, and being picked off by the Texan rifles. The last evening the enemy withdrew to prepare for a final assault. Travis ranged his few surviving followers, and thus addressed them:

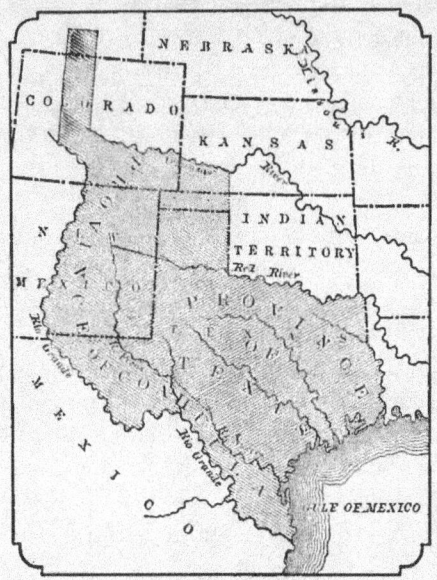

TEXAS AND COAHUILA IN 1830.

"Men, we must die! Our speedy massacre is a fixed fact. Let us choose that mode which can best serve our country. If we surrender, we shall be shot; if we try to cut our way out, we shall be butchered before we can kill twenty of the enemy. We could but lose our lives without benefiting our friends—our fathers and mothers, our brothers and sisters, our wives and little ones. Let us, then, vow to die together. Let us kill as many as possible. Kill them as they scale the wall! Kill them as they leap in! Kill them as they raise their weapons; and continue to kill them as long as one of us shall remain alive. And, be assured, our memory will be gratefully cherished till all history shall be erased and noble deeds be forgotten among men. *God and Texas! Liberty or Death!"*

He then traced a line with his sword, requesting all who would die with him to step over it. Every one complied but Rose. He, disguised as a Mexican, and speaking the language fluently, crawled out down a ravine and escaped. Long before daylight the Mexicans advanced, with discharges of musketry and cannon. The cavalry formed a ring around the infantry, for the double purpose of urging them on and preventing the escape of any of the garrison. Pressed on by those behind, the foremost assailants tumbled inside the walls by hundreds. Every Texan died fighting. Travis was shot, and a Mexican officer rushed forward to dispatch him; he rallied all his strength, pierced his assailant with his sword, and both expired together. Major Evans was shot in the act of attempting to fire the magazine. Bowie, then disabled, was butchered in his bed. When only seven were left they asked for quarter. It was refused; and, drawing their bowie-knives, they rushed to a final assault, and died on the bayonets of their foes. Their remains were savagely mutilated and refused burial.

Among the slain was one, with bowie-knife clinched in his stiffened hand, and surrounded by a heap of the fallen enemy, whose countenance bore even in death the impress of that nobleness which had animated it in life, conjoined with the healthful freshness of the hunter's aspect. It was Colonel David Crockett, of Tennessee—a man whose real life was a romance more thrilling than novelist ever portrayed. He was a product of nature in her most bounteous clime, of active life and free institutions. In childhood the axe and the rifle were his playthings; in early manhood he fought for his country against the British, and in peace his personal qualities earned promotion from his neighbors. Hospitality kept cheerful watch at his door; welcome sat smiling at his table, and social humor gleamed in his bright eye. His career in Congress was not a success, but gave him a keener relish for a free, western life; and he left his native State for Texas, to assist in making her free. Brave Crockett, thou didst deserve a better fate; but in thy death was born a zeal for Texan freedom which did more than a thousand lives. In thy memory the State has a legacy that will glorify her early annals, and animate her sons till the last hour of her existence.

The best accounts place the Mexican loss at twelve hundred. The dead heroes had accomplished their object; Santa Anna was weakened and delayed, and the young State was saved. Shortly after Colonel Fannin, with four hundred men, began his retreat from Goliad to Victoria; but was surrounded, and surrendered his command to General Urrea, as prisoners of war. They were barbarously massacred by order of Santa Anna, only a few medical men being spared, because the Mexican army needed them. On all sides the Anglo-Texan families now fled before the invaders; the latter followed close, burning every thing they could not carry away. Finally General Sam Houston, the Commander-in-Chief, with only eight hundred men, made a stand at San Jacinto, on Buffalo Bayou, where he was attacked by the whole army of Santa Anna. The Texans advanced furiously to

GENERAL SAM HOUSTON.

the charge, a hand-to-hand combat followed, and in one hour the Mexicans fled in confusion, leaving six hundred and thirty dead upon the field, and eight hundred prisoners in the hands of the Texans. This battle, fought April 21st, 1836, settled the question of independence forever. Early next morning a party of Texans found, hidden in a marsh near the bayou, a slender and light complexioned man, wearing a valuable ring on his finger, but awkwardly clad in the dress of a common Mexican soldier. He begged for his life; and when his captors told him he was safe, seized the dirty hand of the nearest and covered it with kisses! It was Santa Anna! Other Mexican officers, similarly disguised, were detected in like manner by their complexion; for the officers are, as a rule, of purer Spanish blood than the privates.

When brought to General Houston, stiff with cold and barely able to speak, the prisoner announced his name and rank, and asked for opium. Having swallowed this, his spirits soon revived, and addressing Houston with lofty dignity, he said: "Sir, you are born to no ordinary destiny; you have conquered the Napoleon of the West!" Modesty never was Santa Anna's strong suit.

While a captive he acknowledged the independence of Texas, but repudiated it when free; and a feeble sort of border war went on for eight years, the Texans making several expeditions against Santa Fe, all of which proved unsuccessful. In these and the Mier expedition many barbarities were committed—some on both sides. Then came the annexation to the United States, the Mexican war, the period of development, and the war of the Rebellion, all of which are within the memory of men yet young. Texas suffered less from the late war than any other Southern State. Her soil was barely touched upon the border by invading Federals. She was smart enough to let Confederate money alone, and stick to gold and silver, which constitute her currency to-day. Soon after the war the spirit of immigration revived, and since 1872 Texas has been receiving settlers at the average rate of two or three thousand per week. And still there is room. Of her 270,000 square miles, or thereabout, one-third or more is as fertile as any part of the West; one-third is less fertile, but of great value for grazing; the remainder, lying far up the slope, is dotted with rocky hills and sandy wastes. The Staked Plain, so called from the stakes with which the Mexicans marked a road across it, is mostly an irreclaimable desert. As in all the border States, fertility decreases as one goes towards the heads of the streams, up the slope and away from the larger bodies of water and timber. Her 100,000 square miles of fertile land now contain at least 1,200,000 inhabitants; and there is land abundant for twice as many more. She can accommodate the surplus population of the Southern and Middle-Western States for fifty years.

Dallas is the center of a region two hundred miles square, which is eminently fitted for occupation by Northern men. In the upper sections corn, wheat and cotton grow side by side; farther down corn and cotton are the staples. It is high, dry and healthful; but Northerners should not settle on the "bottom lands" along the streams. Even Texans incline to surrender them to the freedmen. Southern Texas would not suit the majority of Northern born settlers. Not that it is so hot, but the heat continues longer, and in winter the extremes are painful. Warm, moist weather is generally followed very suddenly by a "blue norther" that pinches one fearfully. The streams are more sluggish, too, and malaria is to be apprehended. Some constitutions stand it very well, however. The grazing region proper is in the south-west and west.

The central portion of Western Texas is regarded as the best sheep country in the State. It is a broken, high, rolling country, supplied with an abundance of rocks and clear rippling streams, and excellent grass. The sheep fatten easily, grow magnificent fleeces; and owing to the mild climate, the herders are very successful in raising the lambs, the percentage of loss being very small.

Except in the southern part, most of Western Texas is too dry for agriculture to be a certain resource without irrigation; but by reports of engineers, a considerable portion of the land can be watered by *accequias* from the numerous rivers. By far the largest portion will remain a grazing ground for all time.

In all the central and upper part of the State water-power is abundant. All kinds of useful minerals can be had in the various sections: iron in Burnet, Llano, Lampasas and Mason counties, of the best qualities; copper in several places, and salt in abundance. Gypsum is found in immense beds up in the desert region. Stretching over ten degrees of latitude, and from the 16° to 30° degree of longitude west from Washington, it is evident the State can not be described as a whole, or in any general terms. Every thing said about Texas, whether good or bad, is true—if applied to the appropriate section. It reaches to within one-half degree of as far south as does Florida; while its northern boundary is nearly continuous with the northern line of Tennessee. But its climate and productions are not determined by latitude alone. The entire State consists of one great slope—or, perhaps more properly, a series of narrow plateaus, each breaking gently to the next lower—from near the foot of the Rocky Mountains to the Gulf of Mexico. On the eastern border the slope is nearly due south, and on the extreme south nearly due east; but in four-fifths of the State it is south-east. From the high, bare plains of the North-west, and from the wind-caves of the Rocky Mountains, the "blue northers" sweep down over the *Llano Estacado* and treeless plains of Young and Bexar Districts, and greatly modify the climate to a much lower latitude. But down the streams the increasing timber lessens their force. The climate is singularly equable for the width of three or four counties, and then the heat increases rapidly till you again get within range of the tempering breezes from the gulf.

The thermometer never ranges quite as high as in latitudes a long way north. In Houston the climate seems nearly perfection. For twenty years the thermometer has never been above ninety-five degrees. At one time, in the coldest weather, it sank to ten degrees above zero, but rarely goes lower than twenty degrees. The average of the "heated term," one day with another, is there recorded at eighty-four degrees. There has never been a case of sunstroke at Houston. Only half a dozen are recorded at Galveston. Necessarily, over such an area as I have outlined, we find every product of the temperate zone, and many of the torrid. In popular language, then, Texas is considered in four grand divisions. Eastern Texas includes the country from the Sabine to the Trinity River; Central Texas, that from the Trinity to the Colorado; Northern Texas means the two or three tiers of counties nearest Red River, and all of Young Territory; and Western Texas the whole region from the Colorado to the Rio Grande, including the grazing district.

The old Texans are not very enterprising. With seven million cattle they import most of their milk and butter; there has been too much sameness of production; the climate invites to ease and repose, and the people are too contented. A man with ten thousand cattle upon the range, is content to live on corn-bread and boiled beef, sit on a hickory "shakeup" chair, sleep on shucks, live in a board or log "shantie," chew "home-made" tobacco, and spit through the cracks.

"An undeveloped empire," hackneyed comparison for the West, is literal truth applied to Texas. In 1850 the population was only 212,592; in 1860 it was 604,215; in 1870 it was returned at 818,579, and at 1,592,574 by the last census. And even now an area nearly three times as large as Ohio, with an equal average of fertility, and climate suitable for corn, cotton, tobacco, and a dozen kinds of fruit, is literally begging for inhabitants.

CHAPTER XXVIII.

KANSAS REVISITED.

IN August, 1873, I took a flying tour through the new counties in Southern Kansas. It was the year of Grangers, land leaguers and war on the railroads. Kansas had been, in the expressive language of the border, "railroaded to death." More lines had been constructed than the business of the country would demand for ten or twenty years to come. Except perhaps the one through line, none of the roads were paying more than running expenses. The managers made out to pay their own salaries by the sale of lands granted the roads by State or Nation. The capital invested in the roads was a dead loss, as far as present dividends were concerned. But stockholders insisted on some returns, and the managers attempted to squeeze out a few dollars by cutting down their employés on one side and raising freights on the other. It took three bushels of corn to send one to the sea-board; hence grain worth sixty cents in New York, sold for fifteen cents in Kansas. The premonitory symptoms of the approaching panic were every-where manifest; but the Grangers, feeling that something was wrong, struck at the nearest object—the railroads.

It was a vain struggle. Where the roads were making nothing, it was obviously impossible for them to divide profits with the producers. On the fertile plains of South-eastern Kansas, one man with a "walking cultivator" could attend to forty acres of corn, which yielded in an average season from forty to eighty bushels per acre. One man, between the middle of April and the middle of August, could produce from fifteen hundred to forty-five hundred bushels of corn; but in the midst of abundance they were poor in all save the bare necessaries of life. "Droughty Kansas" was a standing joke. On the eastern border of that area which the old geographers called the "American Desert," corn was a drug; and flaming agricultural reports were headed with sarcastic pictures of mammoth pumpkins, fat cattle, and forests of corn-stalks to which the farmer ascended by step-ladders to secure his crop. But the seven years of plenty ended with 1873. Eighteen months after, corn in the same localities was worth a dollar a bushel. The dry year of 1874 brought with it grasshoppers, cut-worms and chintz-bugs; and in the period between that and the plentiful crop of 1875, the settlers suffered, as they thought, enough for seven years of want. Is this to be the future of Kansas? Must she have every fifth or seventh year a season of drought and barrenness? Well, yes; and no! On the one hand I am convinced that all the States which border on the dry plains will have occasional seasons of extreme drought; on the other, I am sure settlement will be followed by a modification of the climate, and that as the country grows older the citizens will learn how to guard against famine years.

"DROUGHTY KANSAS."

Their true remedy is not a war on the railroads, but diversification of crops, the establishment of home manufactures, and, above all, improved methods of stock-breeding. Kansas is emphatically a "stock country." I am afraid to say how much margin there is for skillful men; but I personally know stock-growers who have made from thirty to sixty per cent yearly on their capital for many years in succession. Cattle fatten upon the open prairie for seven months in the year, and sheep a month longer. First rate prairie hay, on which stock will keep fat all winter, can be put up for two dollars per ton. The climate is dry in winter, very suitable for cattle and especially so for sheep; and there have never been grasshoppers enough to spoil the pasture. What matters it, then, if the grain crop does fail every fifth year, when the other years are so productive? What is needed is improved stock, and a little care to guard against the occasional winter storms.

Kansas has woman-suffrage on a small scale. Women can vote at all school meetings; and at Geneva, in Allen County, I found the community wrestling with school politics in a new phase. The ambitious little "city" had started off with an academy, which was in due time to grow into a college; but, instead, it grew the other way, and was reduced to a graded school. This called for a reorganization of an adjoining district; local questions entered into the contest, and party feeling ran high. The men and women assembled on the day appointed for a school election; the women got to quarreling, and that, of course, drew in the men. One little man was badly insulted, upon which his large and brawny wife rushed in with an emphatic statement that "her Benny should not be imposed on." It is hinted by local chroniclers that hard names, "cuss words," stove-wood and other missiles flew about with disgusting recklessness. The election was set aside for fraud, and the question at issue went to the courts for settlement. "The ameliorating influence of women at the polls" was not apparent in that township.

Thence southward into Neosho County, we found the fertile vales every-where dark green with dense masses of corn. Soon after crossing the line it was evident we were in a county where the "herd law" prevailed. No fences were seen around the corn-fields; but neither were there any large herds of cattle feeding on the slopes. The Legislature has cantoned out the law-making power; each county has the right to adopt or reject the "herd law" for itself. Many and hot are the resulting contests. In counties where the cattle interest is strongest the law is defeated, and cultivators must fence in their crops; elsewhere the cultivated fields have no fences, but stock are fenced in or herded by the boys. The agriculturists state, with some point, that they are not at all afraid their corn will encroach on the cattle; the latter must be guarded by their owners. Through these counties one often sees the poor calves tied to the fence, while their bovine mammas are driven to distant ridges for the day. And, by the way, it was a calf thus tied, abandoned and dead for want of water, which first showed that the notorious Benders had fled.

Our party of four visited the Bender farm while yet the country was ringing with the story of their crimes. Taking an open hack at Cherryvale, Montgomery County, we drove seven miles north-east over as beautiful a prairie as God ever adorned or man defiled. At that distance out we descended by a gentle slope to Murderer's Vale. On the north and east rose those picturesque mounds which so romantically diversify this region; to the south and west the fertile prairie, now dotted with cultivated fields, or brilliant with rank grass and flowers, spread as far as the eye could reach; between was a slight depression of perhaps two square miles, from which a little run put out north-east, and in the center of this happy valley was the Bender farm. If the spirit of murder was there, it was certainly the loveliest form in which that dread spirit ever stood revealed. No black and blasted heath, no dark wood or lonely gorge, such as romance makes the mute accessories of horrid crime; but the billowy prairie, rising swell on swell, as if the undulating ocean, changed to firm set earth, stood fixed and motionless forever. The house had stood in the center of this vale, two miles from the nearest neighbor, and commanding a view of all approaches for that distance. But a few weeks had passed since the murders were discovered, and yet scarcely a vestige of house or stable was left. Visitors had carried them away by splinters! Even the young trees in the orchard had been dug up and removed.

The excavation beneath the house, in which the murderers had allowed their victims to bleed before burial, still bore the horrid signs. The scant rains of summer had not washed away the blood from its margin; it was half full of purple water. In the garden the graves remained just as left when the bodies were removed. Eight bodies were found there, including that of a girl eight years old, who was murdered and buried with her father. They had been buried in all sorts of positions. One man, in a round hole, lay with his head directly between his feet. A Mr. Longcor, one of the victims, lay with his little daughter between his limbs. Besides these eight, three other missing men were traced to the neighborhood, bringing the whole number of victims up to eleven. Other murders have excited the community, but none with such circumstances of barbarity as these. It appeared, from an examination of the house (the Benders kept a sort of hotel), that the victim, when seated at the table, had his back against a loose curtain which separated the room in two apartments. Behind this curtain stood the murderer, and, at a convenient moment, dealt the unsuspecting guest a deadly blow in the back of the head with a huge hammer. He fell back, the trap-door was raised, his throat was cut, and he was tumbled into the pit to lie till the last drop of gore had ebbed away. Thence he was taken at night and buried in the garden. And these fiends incarnate, after this fearful violation of the rites of hospitality and the laws of God and man, went on with their daily life—ate and drank and slept, and perhaps rejoiced and made merry, with that dreadful pool, fast filling with the blood of their victims, just beneath their feet.

The nearest neighbor was a German, named Brockman, who was roughly treated and narrowly escaped hanging by the mob when the murders were first discovered. His account of the family is curious in the extreme, though many of the details are unfit for publication. The Benders, consisting of John Bender, Sr., his son John and daughter Kate, and their mother, were from the Franco-German portion of Alsace, and spoke both languages fluently, as also the English. They had formerly lived in Illinois, but came to Kansas in 1870, and boarded some time with Brockman; then made entry on this piece of land. They were fanatical spiritualists, and Kate Bender advertised as a clairvoyant and healing medium. The young man, her brother, who distributed her hand-bills around the country, was generally regarded as a simpleton; his mother also seemed very dull, and rarely spoke. But Kate was the genius of the family. She stated, in her moments of "exaltation," that she was a "savior come again, but in female form;" that she *could* raise the dead, but it would be wrong to do so. She had a "familiar spirit" which directed all the movements of the family; and several persons visited and consulted her, either from curiosity or other motive. Before burial they mutilated the victims in an obscene and disgusting manner. So thoroughly was this done that when the body of Longcor was raised it was at first supposed to be that of a woman. The excised portions of none of the bodies were ever found, though the ground was thoroughly searched; and among the few neighbors who knew any thing of the family's blasphemous incantations, there are dark and horrible hints as to the disposition made of these pieces. Should we accept the half that is told by the neighbors, we must conclude that this was a family in whom every natural impulse had been imbruted; that they believed themselves in league with powers to whom they offered infernal sacrifices, and murdered for mere lust of blood. It is known that, with one exception, the victims had very little money, and that their spoils did not altogether exceed $2,500. One man was known to have had but twenty-five cents.

The escape of the Benders was long a great mystery. That a family of four persons could drive to the nearest railroad station, abandon their team there, take the train and escape all the officers and detectives set upon their track, was incredible. Nevertheless, that was the report of the local officials, and the State of Kansas, *apparently*, made great exertions to recapture the fugitives. "Old Man Bender" became a standing joke; every old vagabond in the country was suspected, numbers were arrested, and the Utah authorities actually sent a harmless old lunatic, captured in the mountains, back to Kansas for identification. But it was noticed that Kansas officials were rather indifferent on the subject, and in due time some of the facts leaked out. There have been sensational stories about the *posse* overtaking the fugitives in the groves west of the Verdigris River, where a desperate fight took place, in which both the women were "accidentally killed." Without going into particulars, it is safe to say that the Bender family "ceased to breathe" soon after their flight, and that their carcasses rotted beneath the soil of the State so scandalized by their crimes.

A few miles southward bring us to Coffeyville, terminus of the Leavenworth, Lawrence & Galveston Railroad, which was to have continued on to the gulf, had not the Cherokees objected. By the "Treaty of 1866," which settled the present status of these tribes, they consented that two railroads might traverse the Indian Territory, and Congress enacted that those roads which first reached the border should have that right. A race ensued, and the privilege was won by the Atlantic & Pacific Road, which enters from the east, and the Missouri, Kansas & Texas from the north. Coffeyville is the great cattle depot of this section. For the five months of cold weather the laws of Kansas allow Texas cattle to be driven through the State; thereafter they must stop at the border, or be shipped through by rail. None are sent either way in midsummer, and thus it results that Coffeyville and its neighbor, Parker, have one busy season in the spring and another in the fall. The rest of the year they are dull, for border towns; and, in the language of one of our party, "lie fourteen miles outside of the knowledge of God."

A half-hour's ride from Coffeyville brought us to the border, and thence into a rolling plain dotted as far as the eye could see with vast herds of cattle—herds numbering from a hundred to ten thousand each. It was a grand sight. Some were stretched in long lines, feeding in one direction, or grouped in the shape of a crescent; others had collected in a dense mass, their reddish brown coats harmonizing finely with the hue of the prairie, and their immense horns looking not unlike a thicket of dead underbrush. The cattle men have here rented from the Cherokees a strip fifteen miles wide, and collect their stock there, waiting for the shipping season. These cattle, having run wild upon the plains of western Texas, are collected by a grand "round-up;" from the mass each owner selects those bearing his own mark, and thence they set out on the long drive northward through the Indian Territory, along the famous cattle trails. Utterly unaccustomed to being herded or penned, they are almost as wild as the buffalo; it requires both skill and daring to herd and drive them, and the Texan *vacquero* is necessarily a daring horseman. The same treatment which breaks the wild spirit of the cattle not unfrequently engenders disease; the tramp of from three to eight hundred miles to the border causes "heating of the hoof," and the poisonous matter exuding therefrom is left upon the grass. Hence, say the Kansians, the "Texas cattle fever." The Texan animals themselves do not suffer from it; native cattle alone, who feed after them, are infected by it. In the early days the Kansas Legislature set apart the width of one township, a strip six miles wide, along which Texans might be driven to the Pacific Railroad. But in a little while settlements reached this strip, and another was located, terminating at Ellsworth, which became for awhile the great cattle depot. Again the wave of settlement reached and overflowed this strip, and a third was located, with depot at Wichita, on the Atchison, Topeka & Santa Fe Road. And here is noted a marvel indeed. As the border line of settlements steadily moves westward, as domestic stock overrun the country, as fields are plowed and orchards planted, the settlers say the border line between the soft grass of the Missouri Valley and the buffalo grass of the plains, moves westward at the rate of five miles per year! It is common testimony there that, as the country is settled, the climate grows more moist; that timothy and blue-grass can now be grown where twenty years ago only the hardy bunch-grass found a footing, and wheat on the high plains which were once thought utterly barren. From Cherryvale a branch railway runs out to Independence, the bustling capital of Montgomery County, which claims three thousand inhabitants, and has at least two-thirds as many. Five years before, a mowing machine was run over the ground to clear away the rank grass, and after it came the surveyors, mapping out the experimental town; in two years thereafter it had a thousand inhabitants, and was "the future metropolis of the South-west." I found it just entering on the dull times which have ruined so many bright hopes. The second day of my stay the Republicans had a grand mass meeting, "to devise means of relief from the prevailing depression and the difficulties under which Kansas labored." A foreign visitor would have thought himself in a community of natural orators. The speakers were lawyers, doctors, farmers, cattle-breeders, men of all trades and men of none; all spoke with ability, and no two suggested the same plan. It was a meeting of pleasant diversity—one of the most enjoyable I ever attended. One speaker was red hot for free trade—"all our troubles resulted from our wretched tariff." Another protested against any further contraction of the currency, and still another damned the railroads and Eastern monopolists. The Congressman representing the district was present, and suggested two measures of relief: jetties at the mouth of the Mississippi, so that grain could be shipped that way direct to Europe, and opening the Indian Territory so the railroad could continue on to the gulf and afford an outlet. [Loud and prolonged cheers.] Several were emphatic that we should have "more greenbacks;" for, said one speaker, "we have millions of corn and no hogs to feed it to—we need more money to buy stock!"

This region is part of the Osage Diminished Reserve, so-called; and the unreasonable savages persisted in holding on to it long after the white man wanted it. Unlike all other Kansas Indians the Osages are indigenous, from the Osage River in Missouri to the Arkansas: this is their original seat, and they stubbornly resisted all offers of sale. As soon as it was known that Government was pressing them to sell, the whites poured in, and in four years had taken all the good land in Montgomery County, before the Indian title was extinguished. This cut out the railroad companies, and gave rise to no end of quarrels and lawsuits. The Osages persist in all their aboriginal habits. The example of their civilized kinsmen in Oklahoma, the teaching of Catholic priests at the mission long before the whites settled here, the persuasions of agents and the gifts of the Government were alike unavailing. Now and then a chief wanders through the settlements, half-clad in the grotesque finery received as annuity goods, and with a medal on his breast to show that he has signed a treaty or done some other service to the Government, and perhaps a dirty scrap of paper to back up his assertion that he is "Good Osage—heap good Injun." His errand generally is for old clothes and "cold grub;" and if a little whisky be added, the donor can have a war dance improvised for his special benefit. Occasionally a begging Indian receives a "certificate" from some wag, which is not so favorable. One such, which the bearer proudly presented me, ran thus:

"*To whom it may concern:*

"The name of this noble red man is Hunkydori. He is of poor but pious parents. What he would n't steal a hound pup would n't pull out of a tan-yard. Red-hot stoves are supposed to be safe in his presence. Give him some cold grub, or a three cent drink, if you have any about you.

"Rev. Robert Collyer.
"Gen. O. O. Howard."

From Independence I took horse northward, across the sluggish Elk River, and into Wilson County. This stream looks sluggish enough now, but it often gets up in a destructive fashion. Already eleven persons have been drowned in this vicinity. A few rods below the ford is a deep pool, visible enough now when the water on the ripple is but two inches deep; but the winter before two lovers met their death here. They were to have been married in a week, and were on a visit to friends when a heavy rain came on. Hurrying to return before the stream should rise, they unfortunately went too far down stream; the buggy was swept into the pool, and a little below overturned in the floating brush. The drowned lovers were found next day, two miles below, clasped in each other's arms.

"GOOD OSAGE—HEAP GOOD INJUN!"

Neodesha, capital of Wilson County, was named by a committee of local philologists, appointed by the first settlers. The latter resolved: first, they would have an expressive Indian name; second, they would have a name which no city, man, or country had ever been called by. Thus limited, the committee took the Osage words (pro. Ne-o-de-*shay*) meaning, "meeting of the waters," as the town was upon the point between the Fall and Verdigris rivers. Wilson is another cattle county. The fields are fenced in, the stock fenced out; and the aristocracy of Neodesha are the cattle men. Near here a Mrs. Vickars and her daughters had produced a fair crop of cotton from a small patch; had carded and spun it with their own hands, and were knitting it into various articles. It is safe to say the Vickars family will get through the "hard times" without suffering.

Westward from Neodesha I found the country rising more and more into ridges. The first creek I crossed by a deep ford, though an elegant bridge stood not far above, the way to it being fenced up. It appears that Neodesha had erected this bridge at considerable expense, only to find that the road in common use ran a few rods north of the section line. The mulish owner of the land fenced it in, and obstinately refused the right of way, or to sell at any reasonable price; and so Neodesha had an elegant bridge which she could not use. Continuing my journey south and west, I saw that I was drawing near the great "divide" between the waters flowing into the Neosho and those flowing into the Arkansas. Nearly half the country consists of sharp ridges, on which the land is generally fit only for pasturage. The narrow valleys between are very fertile, but as a rule every quarter section of land takes in some ridge; hence the settler's farm runs into the ridges on at least two corners. By and by I come upon two old acquaintances—prickly cactus and desert weed—sure indications that I am nearing a barren strip. Elk River has a wider valley; the land is again fertile, and the heavy fields of corn show good cultivation. Westward I rise again to flinty hills, and am soon upon The Ridge, so-called, the highest point between the two rivers. Overlooking a section twenty miles square, I see that about one-third of it is taken up by these ridges of rock and gravel, while the intermediate vales are of great fertility. The hollows breaking out of the ridge each way are thick set with dense scrubby timber, in which wild cats, deer, and other game are still abundant.

Down the western slope brings me to the fertile valley of Grouse Creek, and in due time to the village of Lazette, where I find the citizens in impromptu convention in the public square, watching the process of boring for cold water. Through all this section the wells are from forty to a hundred feet deep, bored and piped; and the water is drawn in a metal bucket, half a yard long and some three inches wide, resembling a section of a tin spout. A valve in the bottom opens inward, and allows the vessel to fill; then closes when the drawing up begins. The fluid is so saturated with lime that it fairly rises up and takes a man by the throat. It is such "hard water" that one can scarcely bite it off. Washer-women have great tribulations in such a country.

As I near the Arkansas, I find the flint ridges narrowing, the vales between them widening, and see from afar a green strip of level land, resembling the prairies of Southern Illinois. But a vast amount of this land is already in the hands of speculators. Uncle Sam has done his best to prevent his boys from swindling themselves out of their patrimony, but they will do it. All the old tricks are here repeated on a grander scale, and some new ones added. Loose-footed young men erect a cabin, barely habitable in good weather, preëmpt and remain till they get a title, then sell to a speculator and leave; and these abandoned "dwellings" are seen dotting the vacant prairie in all directions. By this operation the preëmptor has a pleasant time of it for a year, raises a small crop of "sod corn," and gets away with, perhaps, two hundred dollars. But I rejoice in the thought that the speculator will be fooled at last; the land's increase in value will be less than his money would have brought at interest, and the residents will make him "smoke" with high taxes on his land.

At the new "city" of Winfield, situated in the Arkansas Valley, at the center of a rich agricultural region, I passed a few days of pleasant rest. It is a cosmopolitan town. There were buffalo hunters just returned from Harper and Comanche counties, cattle men from Texas, Indian traders, and returned emigrants from the abandoned settlements on Medicine Lodge Creek. These people, trusting to the confident assertions of old citizens, that "there is no desert in Kansas, no land too dry for cultivation," had opened extensive farms on Medicine Lodge, a little tributary of the Arkansas. Every thing they planted grew luxuriantly till the middle of June, then began to wither. They dammed the creek for irrigation, but that went dry, too. "Just appeared as if the bottom dropped out," said one of the settlers— "channel as dry as a bone by the first of July." As yet it would appear that the south-western quarter of Kansas is a little too dry and barren for the farmer.

Winfield is on White Walnut Creek, a few miles above its junction with the Arkansas; but the level, fertile valley is here continuous between the streams. Two years before buffalo could be found in the vicinity of town; now the nearest were fifty miles west of the river, in Harper County. This, and Barbour, Comanche and Clark counties are broken in all directions by deep gullies and wooded cañons, the favorite wintering places of the bison; as long as they could winter there undisturbed, summer found them abundant on the high plains along the Arkansas, Smoky Hill, and Republican. But when, forced from these sheltered valleys by the winter hunters, the animals tried to pass the cold season on the open plains northward, they froze and starved by millions. The buffalo range is now only one-twelfth what it was in 1830, and about one-third what it was in 1870.

Mr. William Payne, a returned surveyor, gave me a most interesting account of that part of Kansas south and west of the Arkansas. Unless the climate changes materially, this section must long remain unsettled; in any event it can not sustain a dense population. It is high, dry, fearfully cut up by flint ridges, and gored by rock-walled cañons. Northward, it is more gently rolling, and along the Arkansas there is good farming land even to the border of Colorado. In company with Mr. Payne, I journeyed leisurely up Walnut Creek, finding the fertile valley well settled and cultivated. To the right, the land rose into ridges and swells, where dwellings were rare indeed; this was herding ground in common for the men of the valley. A furrow, run through the prairie sod, constituted a "lawful fence;" and the herds were kept off the growing crops by boys and women. Here and there was to be seen a horse hitched at the gate, with neat side-saddle tightly strapped; and, when the feeding cattle drew near the corn, a tall and graceful Kansas girl would bounce into the saddle, and go galloping up the slope, cracking a little whip, and calling out to the stock in musical English. We voted it a pretty sight, and rode on.

At Eldorado, in Butler County, we took another rest, in a region where the Kansas winds appear to have done their perfect work on the old settlers. The statement that an old resident "can't talk if the wind stops blowing," is repelled as a slander; but the wind, or something else, is certainly making rapid changes in the general appearance of the people. They are of florid complexion, leathery aspect, and "clipper built" as to limbs. And this sets me to wondering whether the future American, when our country is all settled, and these rapid changes of population cease, will not fall into permanent types, on the principle of "natural selection and survival of the fittest." There will, perhaps, be the Yankee type: the people north and east of Pennsylvania, with clear but ruddy skin, rather lean in figure, somewhat severe in aspect, given to grim and sepulchral humor, and with that traditional "blue stripe on the belly." Westward and southward this race will yield gradually to the blue, bilious type, whose central spot will be Cairo, Illinois. They will tend to the pale olive in complexion; will be somewhat languid in their loves and hates till excited, and then fiercely but spasmodically passionate; they will be darker than their Eastern congeners, and given to stimulating decoctions. West of them will come in the bold florid type, with complexion of a rich mahogany, with wiry frame, outline a little too extended, and eyes and hair of the *intense* hues. This type will come to perfection in Kansas. North of them will be the Western Yankees, with less strictness than their Eastern ancestors, but more acquisitiveness. A little way southward will begin the typical Southerner, with characteristics steadily exaggerated as we near the gulf. But in that section will be three races: pure whites, pure blacks, and the "colored." Miscegenation will pretty nearly cease when the late slaves get used to freedom, and the betwixt-and-between colors of the South will settle into a permanent type, without merging on either side into the pure colors. Why not? That happened in Mexico, after two centuries of miscegenation, and the same causes will doubtless produce the same effects here. In the Far West we shall have the mountaineer, of a type totally different from all the others. Any man can see, with half an eye, that nothing but extensive emigration, and the social mixtures resulting therefrom, prevent climatic laws from separating us into different races. By and by emigration must cease, and nature work her will upon us. What then? How can all these diverse races be held together, under one democratic republican government? Ah! that's the conundrum some future generation must solve.

At Eldorado we leave the valley and journey over the high and unsettled prairies to Florence, in Marion County. The route takes me again over the "divide" between the Neosho and Arkansas; but here it is only a high plain without any very barren ridges as farther south. The high land is comparatively unsettled, and only the lower valleys have many cultivated farms. It is evident we are on the border, and pretty near the dry plains; though the settlers, especially the many real estate agents in the few towns, insist that "there is no such thing as the American Desert—it's a myth—every section of land in Kansas can be cultivated." Though there are a thousand of them, and but one of me, I venture to differ a very little. At Florence I take the eastward train, and am soon down among the old farms on the rich plains of the Kaw. But before I close my last sketch of Kansas, a few general notes are in order:

The State is an immense parallelogram, about twice as long as wide, containing 81,318 square miles: ten times the size of Massachusetts, one-fifth larger than Missouri, a little more than twice the size of Ohio, not quite three times as big as Indiana, and exceeding by one-third the area of England. I divide it into three sections: the eastern third is as fertile as any equal area in the world; the western third has not yet been *proved* to be of much value except for grazing; the middle third consists of both grazing and agricultural land, the latter predominating. Thus we have 25,000 square miles of first-class farming land, as much of mixed grazing and farming lands, and a little more of the region fit for pasturage only. The eastern border of the State has an average elevation of some 800 feet above the sea; the western from 2,500 to 3,000 feet. The eastern third—25,000 square miles or thereabouts—when settled as thickly as rural Ohio, will sustain a population of two millions; at present it contains not quite half a million, "and there's room for millions more."

Of land subject to preëmption and homestead there is very little. Nearly all the land of value belongs to the railroads or private owners. Some people of my acquaintance, who talk very glibly of the immense public domain, would be amazed to learn how little good land is still at the disposal of government. Deducting diminished Indian reserves, railroad grants, and lands long ago preëmpted and sold to speculators, there is not much left this side of the barren plateaus. But the railroad lands in Kansas can now be bought at from $4 to $10 per acre, and are generally located in old counties where church, school and society have made great progress. The railroads, as a rule, sell on seven years' time, with interest at seven per cent. on deferred payments.

All the fruits and grains of the temperate zone can be produced in Kansas, and for some things it seems specially suited. In small fruits, especially grapes, no State east of California can excel Kansas. Wheat has not yet proved a perfect success in southern Kansas, because, as I think, the farmers have not experimented sufficiently. They still sow the same varieties, on the same system, as in Ohio. In oats the product is amazing. Mr. A. Hall, whose farm is at the junction of Deer Creek and Neosho River, in 1870 harvested seventy bushels per acre from a large area; and J. C. Clark, on the upland, near Iola, took four thousand bushels from sixty-five acres. Of ground crops all kinds grown in Ohio flourish exceedingly on this virgin soil, potatoes and turnips especially. Vines of all kinds do well; all sorts of melons attain a size and perfection of flavor unsurpassed in this latitude. Peaches are a sure crop at least three years out of four. Apples, for a new country, are about average. But the most money is made on cattle and sheep. The country is generally well watered; there is still abundant range on the open prairie, and enough of sheltered and wooded hollows. And in this respect the settlers west of the Verdigris think they have a great advantage, as the ridges will not be settled and fenced in for a century; they will remain common herding ground for many years.

West of the Arkansas, and in the north-west part of the State, the hunter and herdsman will have free range for generations. Part of the country is completely barren, but most of it produces the nutritious bunch-grass, gama-grass, and buffalo-grass. The topography is the result of the two geologic processes—erosion and drift. The first great upheaval evidently created mountain heights twice or three times as high as any now on the globe. These have worn down to the present Rocky Mountains; and from that wearing came the material constituting the "plains." Near the center of Eastern Colorado a great spur of the mountains puts out eastward, known as the "Divide," and continues, gradually lessening in height, far down into Kansas. This, and all the adjoining slopes, are composed of rounded stones, pebbles, and sand, the washings of ages; and over and among them there is just soil enough to produce hardy grass, but not enough for good farming land, unless upon the lower slopes and valleys.

Kansas is not paradise; but it presents many advantages. There is no section of the West where—

"——— Grain and flour and fruit
Gush from the earth until the land runs o'er."

But there is abundant room in this State for half a million families, in localities where one has room to grow, where the laws are peculiarly favorable to beginners, where society is well organized, where labor will surely result in a competence, and all who will be virtuous may be happy.

CHAPTER XXIX.

COLORADO.

THE summer of 1874 found me once more engaged in mining operations on a small scale—this time in Colorado. The first of June I set out hastily from Saint Louis for the mountains, anticipating great enjoyment in the journey across the plains. But the change in two years had been wonderful; where we saw buffalo in May, 1872, by uncounted thousands, we now looked in vain. Save the grizzled and miserable looking captives in the station *corrals*, and rarely a worn out old fellow in some hollow, not a buffalo is now to be seen on the Kansas Pacific, where only seven years ago they actually obstructed the track in places.

Within the memory of men still living these animals ranged as far east as the Osage in Missouri; once they inhabited nearly all that part of our country east of the Great Basin. Gov. Thomas L. Young, of Ohio, relates that when his party crossed the plains in 1854, they saw a herd in the Platte Valley fourteen miles long and two or three miles wide; and Horace Greeley vouches for herds almost as extensive, which, he says, could only be estimated by millions. Such immense aggregations are only to be accounted for by the tendency of these animals to mass together while crossing streams in their migration. At the old Platte crossing emigrants were often hindered for days by the buffalo moving northward. As late as 1865 their range was three hundred miles wide, and from the Saskatchewan to the Rio Grande. Now they are limited to two small sections: the first includes northwestern and western Texas and Indian Territory, with adjacent portions of Kansas, New Mexico and Colorado; the latter a small section of western Dakota and the adjacent region. At present rates only twenty more years are needed for their extermination. Millions have been slaughtered for their hides and tongues alone; millions more in cruel wantonness, miscalled "sport." Other millions died in the severe winter of 1871–'72, their range in the sheltered valleys being restricted; and a year after long trains of box-cars were loaded with their bones, which the poverty-stricken Kansians gathered and shipped eastward. So disappears the noblest of our wild game.

The tourist who would see a buffalo in his natural state must not long delay.

Denver had wonderfully improved within two years; but the chronic "hard times" had visited it with fearful severity. There had been a decline in real estate of at least forty per cent., and not long after a still further decline occurred. The excursionists from the East were sixty per cent. less numerous than in 1873. Watering places languished and hotel-keepers looked sick. But if there is trade in Colorado, Denver must take toll therefrom: for it has the location. Take half a wagon-wheel; imagine each of the spokes a pass, leading up south-west or north-west, through the mountains to some mining region, and you will have a tolerable idea of Denver and its tributaries. From this place as a center, railroads or first-class turnpikes lead up to Georgetown, Central City, Blackhawk, Boulder, Leadville, and a dozen mountain towns of less note.

The city is on the slope at the junction of Cherry Creek and the Platte River. Both are mere rivulets usually, but they occasionally get up in a way that's rather frightful. In 1864 a freshet took away nearly all the town as it then stood, and the people afterwards built a little farther up the slope. The city was on first view an agreeable surprise to me. I had heard so often and so long, in Salt Lake City, that *that* was the only really beautiful town in the mountains—that it had become a part of my creed, as a man will sometimes absorb without question what he hears reiterated for years. But many people would prefer Denver, on the score of beauty alone. The advantage of Salt Lake City is that it is twice as old, and its shade trees and shrubbery have had more time to grow. But in Denver we find bright irrigating streams, fine gardens, shade trees, grass plats and many elegant residences. In the last respect this far exceeds Salt Lake. But the noticeable point of difference is in churches, school-houses and daily papers. In the two former Denver will compare favorably with any Eastern city of its size, and in the last exceed most of them. A hundred little matters illustrate, in a marked degree, the difference between this progressive, homogeneous people and that of the Mormon capital. At the Post-office, of an evening, one finds almost the population of an average Western city, and has to take his turn after long waiting. At Salt Lake I never saw a crowd at the delivery large enough to be troublesome. This office gives out three times as much mail as that at Salt Lake. Here are a people who read and write, think and question, deliberate, examine and come to a conclusion: there a people who open their mouths and swal-

COLORADO. 449

AFFLUENT OF CLEAR CREEK.

low what the shepherd gives them; obey their bishop like good children; believe the whole outside world to be doomed, and, therefore unworthy of correspondence except on indispensables.

After a pleasant week in Denver we (I had taken a better half while in the States) departed for Georgetown by way of the Colorado Central and Narrow-Guage. The former runs only to Golden City, at the foot of the mountains, where we transfer to the Narrow-Guage. There Clear Creek, which has been a foaming mountain torrent through all its upper course, emerges from the mountains and supplies irrigation to a fertile valley fifteen miles long. From this on our course is up a steep grade and through the domain of the sublime and beautiful. The narrow train dashes from side to side of the rocky cañon, now rushing along at fifteen miles an hour when there is a short stretch of easy grade, and again toiling slowly up and over the rocks; one minute we are under an overhanging bluff a thousand feet in height, and the next out in an open valley where the widening cañon gives us a broad view of green plats, timbered hills and the deep blue sky beyond. At every pause we hear the continuous roar, a soothing monotone, of Clear Creek dashing down its rocky channel, a limpid stream when unobstructed, but churned to milk-white foam where bowlders choke its bed; now to our right, now to our left, and again directly under us, as the train repeatedly crosses it to gain elevation. At times the cliffs so crowd upon the stream that a way for the iron track has been blasted out of the stone wall; and again the roadway is upon immense table rocks in the very bed of the stream. It was a triumph of engineering. The route was only practicable for a narrow-guage road, on which short curves and abrupt rises present no great obstacle to the little engine and narrow cars. All the slopes are covered with dark green forests, and even the overhanging cliffs fringed with delicate pines, softening the outlines, adding fresh charms, and preventing that gloomy grandeur which so marks the mountain scenery of Arizona. Here and there the solid wall lining the cañon seemed split to its very base, and out of the narrow cleft flowed an affluent of Clear Creek, its waters clear as alcohol.

The main line of this road runs up North Clear Creek to Blackhawk and Central City; the left branch is to run to Georgetown, but now terminates at Floyd Hill, leaving us eighteen miles of staging to reach the metropolis of the richest silver district in the new State.

Most of this stage is through a broader cañon, the timbered hills rising three thousand feet on both sides. Towards the last we enter a narrow gorge, then suddenly the cañon widens again, and Clear Creek is seen flowing placidly down the center of a tolerably level tract, some two miles long and from a quarter to half a mile wide. At the upper end of this plat, on the last considerable piece of level land this side of the mountains, stands Georgetown—an attractive Alpine hamlet, 8,410 feet above the level of the sea. Tourists by the Pacific Railway think themselves away up when at Sherman, but here is a prosperous community of three thousand people, and a handsome town, a hundred feet higher than Sherman. Here the creek and cañon run nearly north. Southward, the town ends abruptly against

Leavenworth Mountain, which rises twelve hundred feet above the Barton House—set on a rocky offset at its foot. But the visible peak is only the end and lowest point of Leavenworth, a spur from the Rocky Mountains, which are here known as "the Range."

The fairer section of our party are startled at the crowds of men in the streets, not a woman being visible; for this is Saturday evening, when fifteen hundred men from the hills get their mail here, besides the resident population; while the whole district probably does not contain three hundred females. After a week's rest at the Barton House, we take for the season a roomy cabin in a little pine grove, at the foot of Griffith Mountain, where we dwell in all comfort and coolness for three months. The first sensation of visitors from the low country is a slight languor, and a wonderful tendency to sleep. The nights are so cool and the air so light. For a fortnight we sleep ten hours every night, and can scarcely get through the day without a nap. But if we rashly attempt to run up-stairs, or even hurry on level ground, the laboring lungs swell the chest, and the heart pounds away on the ribs as if it would give loud warning to "go slow." But the thin air is also invigorating; the cold nights and sharp morning air are wonderful appetizers; while the days are rarely too warm for comfort, and in no long time one feels his vigor redoubled, and fairly rejoices in high climbs.

When it is said that the Rocky Mountains have an average elevation of 12,000 feet above the sea, the Eastern imagination is apt to picture them as rising abruptly two miles or more above the plains; but in fact nearly half this elevation is gained by the traveler before he reaches the mountains. All the way from Kansas City, 800 feet above the sea, to Denver, 5,600 feet high, and still twenty miles from the mountains, one constantly travels up-hill; and at the station on the Kansas Pacific, where one gets his first dim and distant view of Pike's Peak, he is higher than the summit of any mountain in Pennsylvania. Colorado contains no land less than 3,000 feet high. Denver is one mile above New York, and the prosperous cities of Georgetown and Central City 3,000 feet higher still. Manifestly all the conditions of animal and vegetable life are changed, and time only is needed to produce in this Alpine State a new and peculiar variety of the genus American. The miner lives at an average elevation of 3,000 feet above the agriculturist, but in most of the large cañons wheeled carriages can be driven 2,000 feet higher: over grassy meads and through dense pine forests, beside brawling brooks, and again out upon bare rocky flats, to the foot of the summit ridge, which rises, abrupt and rocky, 2,000 feet above the timber line. In summer one may go the foot of Gray's Peak with less inconvenience than to any of the secluded mountain towns of Pennsylvania. But it is the last 2,000 feet that cost.

Let us map out the district about Georgetown, beginning at the quartz mill, a mile below the city. First to our right, and westward, is the lowest of the mining localities, Douglas Mountain. Farther along, and rising just to the west of the lower part of Georgetown, is Democrat Mountain, nearly bald on the summit, not because it is above the timber line, but because of an immense slide some centuries ago. Silver Creek Gulch, a slight depression, separates it from Republican Mountain. Several hundred feet higher than Democrat, and crowned with heavy timber to its summit, this latter rears an awful front two thousand feet above the center of town. The bald front seems nearly perpendicular, and has projections the size of the largest church in New York, and perpendicular faces here and there a hundred feet square—a sight of unwearying sublimity. Seen from directly in front, that is, anywhere in town, it would seem that no living thing but a bird could go up or down that face; and yet there is a winding trail along the rocky offsets by which a few daring men descend rather than make a long circuit; and on the Fourth of July, 1875, a French miner ascended to the summit, planted a flag, and returned to the hotel in one hour and forty-eight minutes. This he did on a bet of ten dollars that he could do it in two hours. It's a pity for him, perhaps, that he could only raise ten dollars, for he could have had takers to any amount. On the summit is a flag three feet long which can only be seen from town by a good eye, and then looks about the size of a pocket-handkerchief. A little beyond, the face of the mountain bends toward the south-west, and continues two miles further, to Cherokee Gulch. Beyond comes Sherman Mountain. At their junction is the great mining center, from which I know not how many millions in silver ore have been taken. Sherman runs on nearly a mile further to Brown Gulch, beyond which is Brown Mountain, the last in that direction which has any relation to this district. All of these gulches are very shallow, and do not really divide the mountain; the formation of veins is continuous across most of them, and some of the richest lodes extend across the deepest gulch.

On the left, or east side of the cañon, all the range is known as Griffith Mountain, while from the south Leavenworth abuts sharply on the town. West of it is Right-hand Gulch, down which comes a good sized stream by way of Devil's Gate and half a dozen more beautiful cascades; to the east is Left-hand Gulch, a rocky trough with great fall, in which the stream is a constant succession of cascades and rapids, all the way up to its origin in the snow-banks on the Range. Only two hundred yards above the Barton House a square reservoir was blasted out of the rocky bottom, and in that short distance fall enough for the water-works is secured to throw water over the spire of the Union School building—the highest in town. This stream is cold as spring-water all summer, and quite as pure and healthful. Just across town, on the face of Republican Mountain, is a beautiful fall of thirty feet or so, and all around tiny streams pour down from ice-cold springs or snow-banks near the summit—a natural water system not to be surpassed. The two main streams unite in the center of town to form Clear Creek; above the mills it is crystal clear and sweet to the taste, below them it is now foul with "tailings" and the wash of poisonous ores, and contains no fish, though once lively with them.

Our party celebrated the Fourth of July, 1874, on the dividing ridge of the Rocky Mountains, at least 13,000 feet above the level of the sea. There we loosed the American eagle, and with polysyllabic speech and patriotic songs moved him to soar and scream. We straddled the backbone of America, sat down on the ridge pole of the continental water-shed, ate sardines from California and crackers from Boston, and drank from two ice-cold rivulets which flowed from the same snow-bank, the one to the Atlantic and the other to the Pacific. The occasion was inspiring. Of course we did and said all those patriotic things which are customary on such occasions; the speeches being the result of a geometrical progression beyond ordinary patriotic remarks in proportion to our elevation, and proving us the greatest, freest, wisest people in the world. Whether the British lion howled and the effete despotisms trembled, is not known; but it is to be presumed they did. The real enjoyment was in the trip to the summit, whereof a few notes are now in order, beginning with our departure from the *rancheria* of Charley Utter, scout, guide, and equine purveyor.

A summer morning in Georgetown combines the perfect in climate and scenery. At 8 A. M., the sun is still behind Griffith Mountain, and the city in a shaded amphitheater walled in by cool mountains. But this promises to be one of the few warm days; and, as we tighten straps upon the mountain bronchos, selected for their skill in going up high and narrow ways, the pack-trains are toiling wearily, by carefully devised and winding dugways, up the neighboring cliffs. Over the north end of Leavenworth, on rocky ways, with an incline sometimes of fifty degrees, our bronchos carried us with ease and safety; for one of these native horses could easily go up and down any stairs in Cincinnati. Reaching the main road again, above the reservoir, we followed a gentle up-grade for three miles to the first climb. There the stream plunges down a series of cascades, while the road winds in and out on the face of the cliff, to reduce the nearly perpendicular wall to a series of passable inclines: at times the frowning granite threatening to close in and cut us off; at times the foaming stream sinking clear out of sight in the gorge itself had fashioned, its presence only proved by the roar and spray that issued from the granite jaws; and again road and stream came together, and our panting animals cooled themselves in fording the torrent. At this level we enter on the heavy forests of mountain pine. On all the trees the limbs slope downward from the trunk, the result of heavy winter snows. New beauties appeared at every step. Cold springs bubbled up near the road, and the streams therefrom often formed little ponds which were lined with lilies. Other flowers, too, became more numerous; and, in the timber, the dark green pines, spruces, firs, and hemlocks grew dense and formed a heavy shade. Occasionally we passed a winter camp of miners, where the stumps standing ten or twelve feet high suggested the work of Anakim; but it seems they were cut off level with the surface when the snow was at its deepest.

Another climb of a thousand feet brought us to the region of mountain flowers. There were myriads, of all colors—white, red, and yellow predominating, all of the brightest hues. Singularly enough, all the open spaces were densely matted with buffalo grass, of the same species as that on the plains, which our horses ate with avidity. As we progressed, new species of flowers continually appeared, all small, and growing smaller every mile. Another climb of some five hundred feet, and there was a sudden change in the timber. The tall, graceful pines disappeared, and in their stead came a scraggy, scrubby growth, with a tendency to "crawl" along the ground, or bunch together. It was evident we were nearing the timber line. It is not cold, as many suppose, which causes this "crawling" (thus the mountaineers, scientists call it "procumbence"); for the timber line is reached at about the same altitude in the tropics, and on latitude 50°. It is the want of oxygen in the air, by reason of which the scant growth can not attain any height, but leans and grows along the ground. A few more steps, and we were out of timber entirely, 11,000 feet high, and still the summit stood out clear and distinct, 2,000 feet above us. We were now almost on level ground, a sort of plateau bordering the highest peaks; and, but for the view to the eastward over the timber, might have fancied ourselves on the plains at the foot of a sharp, rocky range. We were in the midst of mountain meadows, every little slope being rich and green with grass and willow brush; but in every gorge, both above and below us, were the hard accumulations of snow and ice, yielding only scant rivulets to the fervent glances of the sun. And yet all around these snow banks were bright borders of flowers of the same varieties we had seen below, but so tiny that they resembled colored grass rather than flowers.

On this plain stood the ruins of Argentine City, which, ten years before, boasted a thousand inhabitants. With the first discovery of silver on the summit, it seemed to be in such immense lodes that its richness was considered inexhaustible, and a city sprung up like magic at the edge of the timber line. But, when they got their lodes developed, they found that though rich in lead they run only sixty to a hundred ounces in silver to the ton, while no man could do more than half a day's work in that rarified air; the same wages being required, and provisions even more expensive, and so all the mines there were abandoned as unprofitable. Still Argentine stands untenanted, and millions of pounds of lead and silver ore wait for owners. It was a strange and romantic scene: the abandoned town in the midst of a green meadow; banks of flowers all around, dotting the sloping plain in red, blue, and yellow; right among them heavy snow drifts, fifty feet deep in the gulches, from which ran tiny rivulets to water the grass and flowers; rising before us the last and highest range, seamed and scarred in every direction, and shining over all the hot sun of July. To stand in the sunshine one might think it no cooler than in Georgetown; but sitting in the shade it soon appears that the heat is all in the direct rays of the sun; the air is really cool. While the ridge was too abrupt to be scaled in front, a gentle slope led away to the north-east, covered with buffalo grass nearly to the summit. Up this we toiled for an hour, reaching the highest point at 11 A. M., and finding there some ten acres of tolerably level land, and another wonder. While the whole mountain is granite, the surface is covered with sandstone rocks, which show marks of long abrasion. This is a complete contradiction; geologically these stones do not belong there. Local geologists have decided that they were brought from the far North and dropped there by an iceberg, toward the close of the glacial period.

Toward the south-west the Pacific slope begins in an abrupt fall of fifteen hundred feet from the summit, no descent at that point being possible; but the grandest scene is to the north-west. Sloping down at an angle of eighty degrees, but still passable to men and mountain sheep, a cliff sinks twenty-five hundred feet to a beautiful valley. Across this, and seemingly not more than half a mile away, is Torrey's Peak; a little to the left of it, separated by a complete ice-gorge, is Gray's Peak, so near that it seems one might fire a pistol ball across the chasm. It is at least five miles in a direct line from where we stand. Between us the green valley is dotted with snow banks, and the little streams running from them now appear ice-locked. But examination through a field-glass shows that what looks like ice is really white foam; the rivulets are strong streams, fed all summer by the melting snows from the gorge between the great peaks. For an hour we amused ourselves by loosening the movable bowlders and prying them over the cliff. If they escaped the first obstruction, they acquired a velocity that sent them bounding over the rocky points below, then rushed with speed, that almost made the head swim, down the granite troughs, jumping fifty or a hundred feet at a time, till, carried by a rebound clear out of their course, they struck on some flinty peak near the bottom and were ground to powder, the dust flying in the air like the spray dashed up when a cannon-ball glances on the water. Two years before a granite bowlder, loosened by a blast, from the mountain east of Georgetown, estimated at two tons' weight, came down the two thousand feet, and struck on one end of a blacksmith shop, while the owner was, luckily, a few rods away. Every plank and timber was ground to splinters; and, it is perhaps needless to add, that smith rebuilt a little farther out in the valley.

Two months later we visited Gray's Peak, and if we had consulted all the almanacs from "Zadkiel" to "Danbury," we could not have chosen a worse time. December would have been better, as we should then have had cold weather all the way, and suffered no sharp contrasts. As it was, the array of red eyes and peeled noses was discouraging. Our party of ten included three correspondents, four ladies, a college professor, and two indefinitely classed as young men. It is agreed by all old settlers, that no one can decide on the weather up there two hours ahead, unless it has just cleared up with a cold wind; then it will probably be clear for a day or two. Therefore, though the morning was the darkest of the season, and a dense fog settling down on Georgetown, the general judgment was that we should soon drive through and get above the fog, and have clear weather at the Peak. So, well supplied with wraps, we set out with the mercury at 40°, and the fog thickening. Our route lay along Main Clear Creek, by Silver Plume, Brownville, The Terrible Mine, Old Bakerville, and many a scene of gloom and grandeur; now in a forest of dense pines, again in a narrow gorge, and a little later along a rocky dugway, hundreds of feet above the stream. Though wrapped in a fog constantly growing denser, our encouraging driver insisted we should soon get through it; and, though now chilled and discouraged, there was sunshine and a bright day above. We did get above it at last; but, just as we emerged from the fog, the upper moisture fell upon us in a terrific storm of sleet. In ten minutes the road was a glare of ice, our wrappings stiff as armor, and the horses' manes and tails white with hoar frost, while their smoking bodies indicated that they were the only members of the party comfortably warm. Then came delusive signs of clearing off; the sun sent an occasional ray through the rifted clouds, the sleet ceased to fall, patches of blue sky appeared here and there; and, to our delighted eyes, the vast red and yellow range of McClellan Mountain rose suddenly before us, almost over our heads, its snowy and icy summit glittering in the sunlight like an exhalation from the mist. But that which brought hope to us, settled the case with our experienced guide, who marked that the rock rabits (conies?) ran from covert to covert with a peculiar low moaning cry, like that of a bird in pain; that the mountain ground-squirrels (gophers?) did not venture out, and that the loose stock on the range was hurrying into the densest timber in the cañon. Animal instinct was ahead of our science, and all the local probabilities indicated a gale. We reached Kelso's cabin, a mile and a half from the foot of the Peak, at 10 A. M.; but were scarcely housed before the storm came in all its fury. Ten minutes before, the sun was shining, the clouds floating away to the south-east, and all of us expecting a beautiful day. Suddenly a vast bank of black clouds moved down the cañon from the neighborhood of the Peak, seeming to have the weight and momentum of a solid body; a storm of sleet rattled against the windows, and sifted through the branches of the pines; McClellan Peaks, but five minutes before so bright and beautiful, faded away into blackness; a rumbling sound, as of distant surf, was heard, only the trees nearest the windows were visible, and the air was filled with driving snow. It was no use to think of making the trip that day; one and all recognized the fact, and set in to make the time as jolly as possible. We could not have been snowed in with better company, or in a better place, for Kelso's is literally a gem in the mountains. The name, Kelso's, is applied to an irregular collection of log and frame cabins, built years ago by the Sonora Mining Company, and now kept as a hotel by Mrs. Z. M. Lane and Son. There are bedding and accommodation for fifteen persons, including first-class fare, warm rooms, library and material for parlor amusements. The cabin is just below the timber line, in the last grove, though a very gentle slope of mountain meadow, rich with grass and flowers, extends a mile and a half beyond, to the foot of the range. The timber line is every-where at about the same elevation, whether in the tropics or far north; and by this token we know that Kelso's cabin is about 11,000 feet high. Nothing can be grown for the use of man, but the grass on all the slopes is exceedingly rank and nutritious. About four months in the year the climate is delightful; then comes a week or two of severe storms, one of which caught us, and after that a month of Indian summer, whose glories are unsurpassed by any thing in New England. The grass retains its nourishing qualities until the snow is too deep for the cattle to paw it away in feeding; but in May, though the old grass is apparently just the same, the melting snow seems to have taken all the sweetness out of it. Back of the cabin (westward) rises Kelso Mountain, perhaps fifteen hundred feet above the creek, containing several valuable mines; east of it the almost perpendicular McClellan range puts out north-east from the summit. Along its ragged and forbidding sides are the Vesper, Stevens, and several other very rich silver lodes, their value greatly lessened by the difficulty of reaching and working them.

The storm continued five hours; then a council of weather was called, and decided it would be clear by midnight. Captain Lane was to rise at 2 A. M., and, if the sky looked favorable, all were to get up and make the ascent in time to witness sunrise from the Peak. He found the mercury at that hour only five degrees above zero, with a sharp wind and penetrating frost; and decided, in his own mind, that "these tender buds of the valley could never endure such a trip," and let us slumber on till daylight. Every body awoke hungry, and declared the almanac mistaken; it was Christmas instead of September 3d, and we must have a Christmas breakfast. Mrs. Lane did the occasion justice, especially in the item of cream from cattle that only yesterday morning grazed on bunch-grass, now buried under six inches of snow, and raspberries picked from the hill-sides below the cabin. But summer luxuries were nowhere. Hot coffee, hot steaks, doughnuts, and griddle-cakes led the demand.

We started on the ascent at 7, with Captain Lane for a guide. There was not a cloud in the sky, and the bright sunshine was just spreading over the highest peaks, changing their icy glitter to a dazzling variety of white, green, and yellow tints. The storm left us one horse short. So Mr. Merrill, journalist, of Pine Bluff, Arkansas, and the writer, had to "divide time" on a single pony. The walking was comparatively easy to the foot of the Peak, then suddenly the walker's breath gave out and he took "tail hold." Then ensued a scene for a comic almanac. With Merrill on deck and the author towing behind, we would struggle ahead for a hundred yards or so, the horse blowing like a porpoise and the man on foot gasping for breath, unable even to say "whoa;" then the author would mount, and Merrill take the tail. In vain the others, now fast getting ahead of us, shouted: "For shame! Let go." Neither dared to loosen his hold, knowing he could never make it alone. When first on foot one would feel peculiarly vigorous, as if he could run right up the slope without a gasp; but after ten or twelve steps the breath would suddenly give out, and leave him completely exhausted. Only a minute or two was required, however, for a renewal of lung-power. Merrill and I were both asthmatics, and the preceding day had been any thing but favorable for us; even the poor horse might be counted a "pilgrim," as he had not been higher than Georgetown for a month. The air, too, besides being so attenuated, was very cold; mane, tail, and nose-hairs were soon white with frost, as were our beards; and I fancied I could see a look of almost human reproach in the pony's eye as he cast frequent glances at the man who held his tail. It was a mean advantage to take—the hill was too steep for him to kick—but necessity justified it.

The morning sun had shone on the snow but an hour or so when bright fleecy clouds began to rise and obscure the view. Then a strong wind sprang up, and the mist in long, filmy lines swept around and buried us in its chilly depths. For five minutes at a time we could see but a rod or two ahead, and those who had one horse apiece soon left Merrill and myself far behind. Even the lady, whose guide and guard I should have been according to law, left us at the last "hog-back," being on a spirited little pony that was determined to keep up with the rest. All the way we could plainly hear their voices far above us, the shout ringing with a peculiar metallic clink, like the "honk, honk" of wild geese, heard over our heads against a wintry sky. At intervals a strong wind would spring up from the south-west and sweep all the mist far away over McClellan Mountain; then we could look back over the sub-ranges and foot-hills and see the clouds banked far out on the plains, at least five thousand feet below us.

Then back would come the breeze and with it the mist, and we would struggle on invisible to each other.

About two-thirds of the way up, the elements presented a wonderful sight. The wind coming around the peaks in two currents created a vast whirlpool in mid-air, the clouds formed in an immense oval, with an opening in the center, down which we could see the deep blue sky, millions of miles away. The sunlight brightened the inner edges of this oval, about which the clouds were rushing round and round with a swiftness that made the head swim to witness it. From this center outward the clouds grew darker by easy gradations till lost in two immense black columns, one coming around Torrey's Peak from one direction, the other meeting it from Gray's. Just at this time we of the rear-guard were passing along the last "hog-back," which is, perhaps, a rod wide and nearly level; to the right the face of the mountain, now covered with snow and ice, slopes away at an angle of 50° for some two thousand feet, while to the left is an open chasm with perpendicular sides and a depth of seven hundred feet. Fortunately, the trail there is over gravel and loose stones, instead of solid rock, and there is no danger of slipping. But a few weeks since, a lady who went up for a sunrise view, on returning by this point, fainted at sight of what she had passed in the dark. The danger is all in the looks. A horse with any experience can go along a ridge two feet wide just as safely as on a broad turnpike. In 1874, a miner got benighted on McClellan Mountain, and rode a mountain pony down one of those almost perpendicular gorges, where no man dare ride in the daytime and with a sight of the danger. The horse took the nearest cut for home, and only added another instance to the truth that the instinct of a mountain pony is more certain than the reason of a man. Had the rider tried to guide him down by day, it would have been death to both.

Soon after this passage a loud shout from the upper air announced that the party had completed the ascent; and hurrying on as fast as our lungs would allow, in half an hour we were with them. Just then a strong wind swept away the clouds, and for ten minutes we enjoyed all the glory of the view—a free outlook for a hundred miles or more in all directions. East of us McClellan Mountain seemed to run down with perfect regularity till it merged in Leavenworth, and that again in Griffith; but that low the clouds were massed so heavily that all view of the plains and foot-hills was shut off. A heavy storm seemed to be in progress at Denver, and the dark clouds hung above that place, but still eight thousand feet below us. Southward we could catch but fitful glances of Pike's Peak, as it seemed to be wrapped in vast accumulations of cloud which revolved around it as a center of attraction. Northward and toward Long's Peak the view was much the same. The clouds seemed driving with force against the highest part of the range. Across the cañons they would move with surpris-

SOUTH-WEST FROM GRAY'S PEAK.

ing swiftness, the sunlight striking through and giving them a soft and fleecy whiteness; but encountering the peaks those behind apparently shoved on those in front till they heaped up in heavy black masses, too dense for the solar rays to penetrate them. Down the Pacific Slope, south-westward, the view for a long time was uninterrupted. From our standpoint the hill fell off evenly, and too steep for descent, for three thousand feet or more to a beautiful green valley, dotted with dense groves of fir and pine; and beyond that we could see over the sub-ranges and look directly down into a score of narrow valleys, through which as many clear streams coursed like narrow bands of silver—all bearing rapidly downward to Bear Creek and Snake River, and thence out to the Great Colorado. Here and there appeared little mining camps, seemingly set like toy villages on the green plats, in among the heavy pines, or against the red and yellow faces of the cliffs.

But this extended view was brief. First came a dead calm, and then a strong wind from the south-west drove the mist over the scene. To the north-west only was the view clear, and in that direction we saw merely the broken peaks in which head the two Laramies and minor affluents of the North Platte. Beyond them, and a mile and a quarter vertically below us, were Laramie Plains, now hidden from our sight by dense clouds. The cold had meantime grown too intense for the most hardy, and we crouched down behind a stone wind-breaker which successive tourists have erected. The brandy, which no one should ascend without, was produced and a light lunch partaken of; but two of the ladies completely succumbed, and recourse was had to ammonia and chafing the hands and face with snow. No serious suffering followed, though some people are greatly affected at such heights. Those of a hemorrhagic tendency often have bleeding at the nose. The only thing that bothers me is a sort of over-action of the heart and a heavy fluttering in the temples, if I move faster than a slow walk. Most of us suffered only from cold; and the most hardy remained upon the summit but an hour. On the descent there was one slight accident. An unskillfully fastened buckle turned in the girth and so irritated the horse, which a lady was riding, that he took the bit in his teeth and started for home. He descended all that winding way in less than three-quarters of an hour—we were two hours ascending—reaching the cabin an hour before us, while she, to use her own words, "hung on to the pommel and trusted in God." That was, however, the best thing to do, even if the horse had been at his natural gait, for in attempting to guide one is much more apt to disconcert him. I am willing enough to be carried up a mountain, but I prefer to walk down, which I did in this instance, reaching the base in an hour and a quarter.

It was now past noon; the snow was entirely melted from the

mountain meadows, just above the timber line; the late ice-locked rivulets again ran unvexed, and the brawling brooks were musically pouring their increased waters into Clear Creek. From the summit, even in the hottest weather, all these streams appear as if frozen solid; the eye can perceive no motion, and the white foam over the ripples has the exact appearance of ice. Our ride over the grassy slope to the cabin was delightful, the air having moderated to a pleasant warmth. McClellan Mountain, to our right, presented only here and there a patch of snow. Nearly all the west face of it is inaccessible, there being but a few ravines filled with earth slides up which zigzag trails have been with great difficulty constructed. From our road the cabin and ore-house of the Stevens' mine seems as if suspended against the cliff in mid-air, the chains which, anchored into the solid rock, hold it in place being, of course, invisible to us. One could scarcely avoid the conclusion that it maintained position contrary to the law of gravity. A few rods west of it is one of these earth slides mentioned, and up this a man and donkey were slowly working their way along a zigzag which looked to us nearly perpendicular. This trail leads up to a point even with the mine, and thence a way is worked along the face of the rock to the cabin. In addition to all these difficulties, the air is so rare that few men can do a full day's work there, but the ore is so rich that the Stevens pays well for working. Evidently there never can be sudden inflation from an increase of the precious metals, for the difficulty of getting will always make them valuable.

I strained my eye to find the cabin of the Vesper Mine, which we visited on the 4th of July, and finally saw it within a few rods of the summit, looking like a pigeon-house stuck on a rock. Below it was the gulch and earth slide, with a slope of seventy degrees for 2,500 feet, down which we rolled the granite bowlders. After a good warming and a hot feed at the cabin, we gladly took carriage at 3 P. M., and, all the way being down-hill, reached Georgetown at five, delighted, disgusted, frost-touched, tired and sleepy.

Moral—Go to the summit between June 15th and August 15th, or wait till settled cold weather.

The three months I spent among the mines of Colorado were among the most pleasant in my life. In August I came down to Denver and thence, by way of Bowlder City, visited the rich Caribou District, which was just then exciting so much attention. Leaving Denver at 4 A. M., with the Sunday morning express sent out by the *Rocky Mountain News*, we drove north-west over the high plains lying between that city and Bowlder. This region is now dotted with artificial lakes, all stocked with trout. All the irrigating canals, taken out as far as possible up the mountain streams, are carried high up on the ridges, and into every convenient depression an *accequia* leads sufficient water to maintain a crystal lake. This insures, in a few years, an abundant supply of fish; and local scientists affirm that the increase of water surface will eventually give this section more rain-fall, and redeem much of the high land for agriculture. Bowlder has a romantic location. Just above the town, westward, the mountain rises very abruptly nearly two thousand feet, its front split by the narrow Bowlder Cañon, from whose rugged jaws gushes the clear and crystal stream. Once issued from the mountain, the foaming creek subsides to a gentle current, meandering through a fertile valley. Some distance up the cañon a flume is put in, to gain a fall, and thence the water is carried along the cliff in trestled boxes; issuing thence far up on the ridge, it circles all the valley, supplying irrigation to thirty thousand acres of land, with abundant surplus for fish-ponds and fountains. Bowlder Valley now yields from a fourth to a third of all the wheat produced in Colorado.

But if you would enjoy Western Wilds in all their native beauty, take the stage from Bowlder up to Caribou, at the head of the cañon—all the way through pine-clad hills, romantic glens or wild gorges, which excite every emotion of awe and sublimity. To the right of the road, shut in by walls of water-worn granite and shaded by dense forests of overhanging pines, are the Bowlder Falls—a mighty work of nature, which will long remain unmarred by the hand of man, for rocky flume, granite wall and pine-clad summit have transcendent beauty without utility. The stream, which rises almost on the summit, issuing from the snow-banks which send out ice-cold rills from May till October, plunges down a series of offsets, each making a majestic cascade, each cascade differing from all the rest. From the foot of each little fall a winding way leads along the mossy hill-sides to the next above; while the whole way is shaded by the immense pines, which in places lean over and mingle their branches above the foamy rapids. Here a well-equipped excursion party might spend days of calm enjoyment, shaded by the evergreen forests, lulled by the roar of the waters, soothing eye and brain by contemplation of nature's wild beauty.

After a day's slow progress upward, our coach suddenly emerges into the open mountain meadows about Nederland (location of the Holland Company's quartz mills), and a few miles beyond darkness comes upon us at Caribou, a mining town almost on the summit of the mountains. There is a singular air of newness in the whole district. In town I find the streets not yet cleared of native timber; of the thousand or more inhabitants most are living in unfinished frames, and the heavy groves of pine on all the surrounding knolls give the place the pleasing appearance of a camp-meeting ground. And here I put in a few days studying the silver mines.

The main ridge, called by the enthusiastic the "Mountain of Silver," was for a mile or more completely pock-marked with prospect holes, but no more than a dozen locations were developed sufficiently to be called mines. It is notable that in all new mining regions one will find hundreds of claims with shafts down fifty or seventy-five feet, and work suspended. In many instances it is because the original locators are not able to push the development, but sometimes because they are afraid to. The vein, they reason, shows well at present; there are good indications of a true fissure, such indications as will impress buyers favorably that a big lode is below, but if they sink a hundred feet, it may not turn out a true fissure after all. So they will sell on present appearances. Buyers should look out for such cases, and, if the shaft is not down at least a hundred feet, be sure anyhow that it proves the existence of a regular fissure.

Down in the Sherman Mine I found a score of men picking and blasting out the rich rock, of which the poorest grade yields a hundred and thirty ounces of silver per ton, the richest fourteen hundred ounces. This estimate is from the mill-runs—the only honest test of a mine's capacity. Assays, of course, show more. The assayer who does not pay for any thing, but is paid for "sample assay," may not be entirely disinterested, but the mill-owner is not going to pay a dollar an ounce for a single ounce of silver more than he can get out of the rock. Most mill men do not claim to get more than eighty-five per cent. of the silver actually in the rock, but the owners at Nederland, where this ore is worked, now claim to get over ninety per cent. This fact also makes the mill run a better test than the assay, for, obviously, investers in mines care more for what they can get out than what science shows to be there. And herein is seen one of the reasons why it pays to transport many kinds of ore from Colorado to Swansea, Wales, for there they save all the silver, gold, arsenic and other minerals.

In the Sherman and some other mines here was used the new compound known as tri-nitro-glycerine. The workmen objected forcibly at first, but the inventor and manufacturer, Professor C. D. Chase, of St. Louis, maintains that it is safer than any other explosive in use. Its power is wonderful. During my stay the workmen in the lower drift drilled one hole four feet deep, and put in a cartridge eighteen inches long, containing eight inches of the stuff; when "shot" it broke out 25 cubic feet of solid granite. It is entirely too powerful to fool with. So, when invited to go down and see it work, I respectfully declined. It is usually "planted" in a metal cartridge, and exploded with battery and cap, but in cases where the cartridge can not be inserted the liquid is poured in. The common method is to bore four holes in the face of the drift, then fill and explode them all at once, tearing off a yard square and a foot in depth of the rock. This explosive has been found cheaper than dualin, dynamite or giant powder, and now that the workmen are acquainted with it they consider it safe enough. But it would take high wages to keep me in its vicinity very long.

Near the Sherman is the Poor Man's Lode, with vein from two to six feet in thickness, and ore-seam from five inches to two feet. The rest of the vein is filled with quartz and decomposed granite. The existence of narrow ore-seams in large veins, the rest of the vein matter often entirely barren, though sometimes containing threads or pockets of silver ore, is a characteristic of nearly all the mines of Colorado, and a never-failing source of speculation and theorizing. The advocates of the sublimation theory of lode-formation rely upon it very largely to prove their case; and it is the one phenomenon which advocates of the eruption theory can not explain in harmony with their views. For, manifestly, if the contents of the vein all gushed up in a mass from liquid reservoirs below, they could not have thus arranged themselves in neat layers of ore and vein-stone; while, if condensed from successive mineral vapors, we should naturally expect the existing order. The "Poor Man" and "Sherman" preserve their course quite regularly in the deep workings, as indeed do most of the lodes here. One great source of lawsuits is found in the fact that the veins under ground will not follow the course laid down for them on the surface in a United States patent. The patent generally locates the claim along the mountain side as straight as a yard-stick; but at a hundred feet or more in depth the course of the vein resembles rather a crack in ice made by a heavy blow—there are whims, droppers, feeders, cross-courses, dips, spurs, angles, variations and sinuosities. Now, if you locate your patent on a cross-course, and I *afterwards* locate mine on the main vein, and we run together a hundred feet down, the question is whether the older location or the truer one should hold. In new mining camps "first blood" generally holds, regardless of law. One set of judges have held that the title follows the vein, when proved that it is the main vein, no matter whether it agrees with the patent on the surface or not; but another class holds that this contradicts the old principle of common law—that the owner on the surface "owns from zenith to nadir," and that if one's vein runs under another's, the latter holds, regardless of priority. Evidently that old rule must be abrogated as to mining property, and the title follow the main vein wherever it goes, if we are ever to have certainty. In the Sherman and Caribou mines a light can be seen a hundred yards along the vein in the deepest workings.

The great Caribou mine has been so often described that the subject has become stale, but its history has the elements of romance. It was discovered December 23, 1869, and located in the names of W. J. Martin, Samuel Mishler, George Lytle, Hugh McCameron, John H. Pickle and Henry Mishler. By them it was worked till September, 1870, paying almost from the start. But the discoverers were not very well posted, and as a rule the locators make little or nothing out of a mine. They sold out rather cheap, nobody knows for how much, and one-half the mine became the property of Abel D. Breed, Esq., with attorneyship for the other half. Sixty thousand dollars were spent in development, and erecting house and machinery for working; but ore enough was taken out meantime to leave a clear profit of $175,000. This demonstrated its great richness beyond a doubt, and it was put upon the foreign market. A small corps of foreign engineers examined and reported upon it, and as a result it was sold to the mining company Nederland, of Hague, Holland, for $3,000,000. It was then worked according to scientific principles, under the superintendency of Mr. Benjamin Rule. Three eight-hour shifts were employed, and no work was done on Sunday. No man was allowed about the mine in a state of intoxication; one appearance in that character was cause for a discharge. The printed rules, conspicuously posted, to which every employé subscribes, also forbade all profane, obscene or abusive language. It is estimated by the best judges that there are at least twenty-one claims with clearly defined veins, known to be of some value, on the entire hill. Ore from each of these, selected at random and mixed, was sent in bulk to Johnson, Matheny & Co., of Hatton Garden, E. C., London, and yielded a hundred and ninety-two ounces of silver per ton. Of course so many veins known, and more suspected, have stimulated the formation of tunnel companies, and no less than half a dozen tunnels were started into Caribou Hill, which is very favorably situated for that work. The hill has a general course east and west. Towards the north (or rather east of north) it falls away abruptly to a beautiful circular park. In all other directions than towards Caribou the inclosing walls of the park rise in gentle rounded hills, closed with heavy forests of pine. From the various gulches run clear streams to the center of the valley, forming a creek large enough for milling purposes; and far to the northeast stretch extensive pastures in the vales and timber on the ridges. In that part is the best locality for a quartz mill which the vicinity affords, and consequently all the tunnel claims are located on that side. They lie only a thousand feet apart, as the law allows each one that space; and if completed will undermine the entire hill in sections of a thousand feet each, striking the various lodes at a depth of from five hundred to a thousand feet. The law allows a tunnel company five hundred feet on any lode they strike, "not located on the surface at the date the tunnel site was located." But if the owner of any mine opened above proposes to dispute title, the burden of proof is on him to trace connection, which it will obviously take him some time to do, and for this reason and the greater convenience of shipping ore through that channel, the interests generally unite.

From Caribou I took the mountain road across to Central City—site of the far-famed Gregory Gulch Diggings, and thence to Idaho City, and up to Georgetown. The way was over mountain meadows, mingling the rich green with bright-hued flowers; through dark pine forests and down lonely gulches, where the indefatigable prospectors had dotted all the slopes with holes in search of "indications." Sometimes the route lay over levels where one could scarcely believe himself on a mountain, though we were from eight to nine thousand feet above the sea; and sometimes in depressions we saw heavy crops of rye and potatoes, ripening in late August, a mile and a half above the Missouri Valley. Near Central City hundreds of acres of bare gray rocks show where the surface soil has been "piped off" to get at the gold dust; and in a few places gangs of Chinese are still at work on the poorest diggings, long since abandoned by whites. But placer mining in this vicinity has long yielded to quartz mining, and the few Chinese at the time of my visit were even worse regarded than in California. A fire, a few weeks before, had laid a large section of the city in ruins; and, as it originated among the Mongolians, they were for a long time forbidden to come into the upper part of town. But the poor, pathetically patient race, bided its time and held its own.

My summer's work was done, and while September heats still lingered on the plains, we left the cool air of Georgetown for the journey to Salt Lake City. From Denver to Cheyenne the mixed train jogged along all one bright autumn day: to our left the blue mountains, the broad plains to our right; sometimes over flats almost as level as the sea, sometimes through gently rolling valleys, and more rarely along the course of creeks long since dried up. On the level the plains present that uniform gray-brown appearance which is natural to them at this season; but on some of the slopes and in all the little valleys were narrow strips of rich green, and a soil looking as if it might be made productive. As we progressed broad lakes continually appeared, shone for a few moments or for hours, then passed out of sight; sometimes to the eastward but oftener straight ahead, the hills beyond beautifully reflected from their mirror like surfaces. But as the train bore down towards them they shifted again and again; sometimes moving off upon the eastern plain, sometimes keeping the same distance ahead, and yet again rising slowly into the air till lost in the clouds. But of real honest water, there was not a drop, for where there is enough of that to make humid the atmosphere the *mirage* is rarely seen. These were the "lying waters" of which Spanish explorers tell, and which, before they were so well known, lured many a voyageur from his course and to his death. As the country is settled it is remarked that this *mirage* is more and more rare; but the best time and place to see it is on the dry plains of California, of a hot afternoon in August.

An hour we stopped at Greeley, the noted "Yankee Settlement," now the center of a rich and well cultivated tract. The shade trees early planted by the colonists already relieve the monotony of the plains; the dark mountains furnish a splendid background, and in ten years more this town will rival in rural beauty the nicest New England village. Soon after we passed the Wyoming line; but a year after I returned, for further travels in Colorado. The summary in the next chapter is from notes and careful study during both visits.

CHAPTER XXX.

THE CENTENNIAL STATE.

Don Francisco Vasquez Coronado, (the chronicle does not give his *other* name,) was the first Pike's Peaker. In 1541 he set out from the City of Mexico to find and conquer the "Seven Cities of Cibola," where, according to the reports of reliable gentlemen and the common belief of all New Spain, gold was so plentiful that the Cibolans used it for the manufacture of common utensils, while their houses were lighted with precious stones, and silver was not accounted of. His command consisted of some seven hundred cavaliers and gentlemen of the New Spain nobility, who gladly sold all they had to outfit, assuring the reporters of Mexico City that "neither themselves nor their families would ever need more gold than they should bring back from the Seven Cities." They marched and fought, and fought and marched: up the Colorado to the mouth of the Gila, up the Gila to the Casas Grandes and northward across Arizona to the Rio San Juan. They penetrated what is now Colorado, then turned south-east to where Santa Fe now stands, and still their Indian guides assured them the golden Cibola of their hopes was a little further on. After a brief rest, having destroyed a few Pueblo towns and temples, and burnt their idols for the truth's sake, they crossed the mountains and marched down nearly to the center of the present Indian Territory, and still found no Cibola, no gold, and no rich kingdom. Then the inevitable quarrel arose, the expedition broke up, and the cavaliers returned to Mexico, seven years older, considerably poorer, and somewhat wiser than they left it. But they added to Spanish territory, by the apostolical right of discovery, an area twelve times the size of Ohio; the same since added to our free Republic by the slaveholder's right of conquest, and payment of ten million dollars. A fascinating account of Coronado's expedition was written by a Spanish gentleman in the party, a Mr. Castenada, who was born three centuries too soon. He should have lived in our day and been a Washington correspondent; he had the requisite fancy and power of romantic embellishment, and was pious to a fault. He would have consented to the death of all the heathen in the new territory, if they had stood in the way of consecrating the gold to Catholic uses.

Many other expeditions did the Spaniards make, but few of them came north of the Arkansas. Finally, some two hundred years ago, Northern New Mexico was settled, and thereafter by degrees the Spanish outposts extended up to the Raton Mountains and into the rich parks and valleys where head the affluents of the Rio Grande. So those who speak of Colorado as so new a country, would do well to remember that a part of it is older than Ohio. Two hundred years passed away and under the auspices of President Jefferson, Colonel Zebulon Pike explored "that part of Louisiana which lieth along the foot of the Sierra Madre" (Rocky Mountains), and in the summer of 1806, gazed with wonder on the snow-capped summit of Pike's Peak. This he set, with some hesitation, at 17,500 feet high. Later and more accurate explorers have reduced his estimate some 3,000 feet. Proceeding southward he was captured and imprisoned by the suspicious Captain-General of New Mexico; and to this day many are the legends among the Mexicans about the "fair-haired Americano," and the gallantry (in its double sense) of his men.

As early as 1820, Colorado was traversed in all directions by white hunters and trappers, and in 1840 the eastern section contained several trading posts, among which Fort Lancaster, on the Platte, and Bent's Fort, on the Arkansas, were most prominent. In 1842, twelve Americans took unto themselves Mexican wives, and employed their dark relations in erecting a fort, which was the foundation of the present American city of Pueblo; and about the same time twenty families of whites and half-breeds made a settlement on or near the Fontaine Que Bouille. Thus stood the population for many years. From midsummer till Christmas there was hunting, trapping and fighting Indians; then the nomadic inhabitants—they could not by any stretch of language be called settlers—gathered to the trading-posts and spent the proceeds of their season's work. At each post was a medley of traders, trappers and hunters, white, Mexican and Indian; their amusements, racing, gambling, dancing and drinking, varied by frequent bloody fights, whereof the accounts are sometimes amusing, oftener disgusting. These contests were nearly always over disputed property—chiefly horses or women, both of which were very valuable—helped in no small degree by the villainous whisky dispensed by the American Fur Company. Almost every prominent point in Eastern Colorado received its name from some tragic occurrence. Instance the following: Fifteen Mexicans from Taos quarreled with about an equal number of Americans at Fort Lancaster, about a trade of horses and furs. The Americans ambushed them and stampeded all their stock. The Mexicans took arms and advanced on their foes; then, the *commandantes* on each side being leaders and spokesmen, ensued the following:

Mexican—"*Que quiere caballero!*" (What do you want, sir?)

American—"*Yo tengo lo caballardo—porque dicirme esta?*" (I have your horses—why do you ask?)

"*Caraho, Americano!*" shouted the Mexican, bringing his gun to his shoulder; but the American was too quick with his pistol and laid the other prostrate, the ball passing through him just below the heart. The result was "the survival of the fittest," and the "superior race" retired with their booty. An appeal to the trading company at the fort brought an international council, which resulted in an amicable settlement. The wounded man recovered in three months, and the place was thenceforth known as "Greaser's Gulch."

Herring and Beer were mountaineers, companions and friends, who paid court to the same *señorita*. Herring married her, and Beer grossly insulted him, with intent to bring on a quarrel and kill him. A duel was agreed on, and Beer, who was a crack shot, confidently expected to kill Herring, who was considered a poor "off-hand marksman." They met, attended by their friends, who arranged that the shooting was to be at any time the principals chose in the count between the word fire and three. At the word fire, the ball of Beer's rifle buried in a cottonwood just over Herring's head; at the word three, Herring's ball pierced the heart of Beer, who was buried in the gulch where he fell. When I visited it long afterward the gulch was still known as "Beer's Folly."

Sadder, more bloody and more romantic was the episode of Vaughn and La Bontè, life long companions and friends, but destined to exemplify the deadly bitterness of "love to hatred turned." Together they had traversed every trail on the plains and trapped on every stream in the mountains; at the old Arkansas crossing they had fought side by side against the murderous Kioways; they had taken beaver together on Clear Creek, and gnawed the same bone in the extremity of hunger when overtaken too early by the winter storms. Common danger and suffering creates strange friendships. Perhaps it is not the intelligent social comity which unites men of some cultivation; perhaps it is more like an exaggeration of that kinship which makes even dumb animals cling to each other, and in a mysterious way mourn another's death. Be that as it may, a little cloud, no bigger than a man's hand or a woman's face, rose on the horizon of their friendship. Chance expressions were repeated with additions; petulant remarks, which the speaker was sorry for ere they died upon the air, grew from lip to lip and reached the other's ears as vile slanders; for "mutual friends" are as busy and blundering in the wilds as in the city.

Vaughn, the elder, was a grizzled mountaineer, with the dry humor of a "Tennessee Yankee"; his sarcasm was cutting, and he affected an indifference to woman's charms. La Bontè, on the contrary, had all the impetuosity of the Frenchman, which had survived through all the generations since his forefathers settled in Canada. The life of a voyageur and trapper had only heightened his mercurial temperament; he was a backwoods dandy, and adorned his person with the handiwork of squaws. One fine morning in 1843, they rode into the Pueblo fort fast friends, as they persuaded themselves, having settled their little differences; that night they parted rivals, and consequently enemies. This transformation was affected by the smiles of a brown *mestiza*, who had previously pledged her "punic faith" to Vaughn, but to-day, seeing La Bontè for the first time, was charmed by his youthful gallantry and French display. To the older hunter this was blackest treachery on the part of his friend; to the younger it was fair emulation. A week after, they met at a trappers' rendezvous. Hot words ensued and knives were drawn; but there was no liquor on the ground so early in the season, and friends separated them without bloodshed. Then spoke the Tennesseean:

"*Compadre*, seein' what you *have* been, I don't want none o' your blood on my weepins. Go you one way, I'll go another. When this season's over, let the best man win her."

"I'm white on this thing," replied La Bontè; "my hunt this year is up the Cache La Poudre."

"Then," was the answer, "I'll go the Sangre de Christo run with these men. No tricks now—you don't turn back to Pueblo?"

It was settled; but unfortunately for Vaughn's resolution his party lingered, and he was deputed to go to Pueblo for further supplies. There he learned that La Bontè had returned, and, after a brief courtship of two days, taken the *mestiza*—his own, as Vaughn considered her—to one of the northern posts. In all the solitary hours of that season's hunt he brooded over his wrong, till hatred possessed his soul. Meanwhile, as if driven by fate, La Bontè crossed the mountains, having found the season bad on the Cache La Poudre, and turned southward into the very region he had promised his rival to avoid. One day, as Vaughn rested his horse in a piñon thicket, he was suddenly roused by an intruder, and looking up, saw his enemy, the very man who had robbed him, coming up the gulch. "Off!" he shouted, bounding on his horse.

"*Sacre!*" replied the Canadian, construing this as a menace, and setting his horse at a run. His rifle was already at his shoulder; the other, in his haste, had dropped his gun, but drew a pistol from his

"THE ANIMALS DASHED MADLY BREAST TO BREAST; THE WEAPONS CRACKED SIMULTANEOUSLY."

belt. The spurred animals dashed madly breast to breast; the weapons cracked simultaneously, and both men fell heavily to the ground.

When Vaughn came to himself, he saw his late enemy and former friend lying dead near him. In his own breast was a gaping wound, from which his life had nearly ebbed away; and the little stream into which he had rolled in his delirious thirst, was vermilion with his blood. When picked up by his friends he made his first and last allusion to the trouble: "A d—d good man killed for a d—d bad woman—better stuck to my old idees."

Varied only by such incidents as these, the first half of the century rolled away with little of historic interest. But the expeditions of Fremont, the Mexican war, and acquisition of new territory, the gold hunters' invasion of California, the opening of Kansas to settlement, and the Mormon war of 1857, caused the whole region to be thoroughly explored, with a view of finding some shorter and better route to the Pacific. All who came this way were eager for gold. If gold there was, it was only an accident who should find it. Traditions of its presence had been numerous for a hundred years. Many an explorer, white or Mexican, had returned with specimens which good judges pronounced gold, but somehow the clue was always lost. At last, in 1858, came the right men. John H. Gregory, Green Russell, and other Georgians, old miners and familiar with the precious metals, found what was unmistakably gold; but it was not till the 6th of May, 1859, that Gregory struck the gold diggings on North Clear Creek, which soon became world renowned as the Gregory Lode, and settled affirmatively the question as to whether this was a rich mineral region. But the country could not wait for verification; nothing was needed so badly in 1858 as a new excitement. The Kansas troubles had been happily settled, the Mormon war was over, and newspaperdom was dying of *ennui*. So, soon after a few ounces of gold dust reached Leavenworth, the whole country was stirred, and for months "Pike's Peak" glared at us in display type from the head of a thousand news columns. Along with the prospector went the able-bodied correspondent, and beat the old Spanish chroniclers on their own soil. Wonder was piled on wonder, and a patient public accepted all as truth; but at last, extravagance run mad effected its own cure. Here is a specimen from an Iowa paper:

"We learn from a gentleman just returned from the Peak that the gold lies in bands or strata down the slope. The custom of the best miners is to construct a heavy wooden float with iron ribs, similar to a stone boat; this is taken to the top of the Peak, where several men get in and guide it down over the gold strata. The gold curls up on the boat like shavings, and is gathered in as they progress. This is the usual method of collecting it."

Within one year this region received seventy-five thousand Americans. The romance and tragedy of this invasion have often been portrayed. I am here chiefly concerned with the genesis and evolution of civil government. There was no constitutional authority in the country, and neither judge nor officer within five hundred miles. The invaders were remitted to the primal law of nature, with, perhaps, the inherent rights of American citizenship. Every gulch was filling with red-hot treasure hunters; every bar was pock-marked with "prospect holes;" timber, water-rights, and town-lots were soon to be valuable, and government was an imperative necessity. Here was a fine field for theorists to test their views as to the origin of civil law.

Poet and political romancer have described in captivating lines, the descent of civil government as a heaven-born genius, full-grown and perfect from the mind of Deity. But to the historian of events is left a far less pleasing task. He can not but see that government is the most awkward and imperfect of all human inventions. Here, as elsewhere, it was a creature of slow, irregular growth, evolved by reason and experience from the hopes and fears of men, originating in the instinct of self-preservation, and developed by necessity and concession. Four different governments sprang up with concurrent jurisdiction. The favorite theory of Senator Douglas, that local self-government was inherent in American citizenship every-where in our territory, seems to have been adopted by a majority of the first comers; and they straightway proceeded to organize the "Territory of Jefferson." On the 6th of November, 1858, an election was held at Denver, and H. J. Graham chosen without opposition as delegate to Congress. He went to Washington, and had the pleasure of paying his own expenses there all winter; for "Jefferson" was not admitted. Nevertheless, delegates from thirteen precincts assembled the next April, took the preliminary steps, and called an organizing convention to meet in August, 1859. One hundred and sixty-seven delegates came together, tried to construct a State, and failed; but a little later "Jefferson" was regularly organized. An elected legislature assembled in November, listened to an admirable inaugural from Governor R. W. Steele, organized nine counties, granted charters for the new towns, and passed a very good criminal code and body of mining laws. Meanwhile, Kansas had organized this counntry into Arapahoe County, and to make a sure thing of it, a full set of county officers were elected, who exercised a sort of hop-skip-and-jump jurisdiction, bobbing around in the mountains, foot-hills, or in Denver, wherever they could get a foothold. But these might be called governments by ambition, rather than by necessity; the latter kind were meanwhile being organized in the mountains and ranches.

The first comers there were generally in little squads, old friends and neighbors, and each party amicably *divided all the gulch between them*. But the next year came sixty thousand more, who wanted a show; and it is highly creditable to the pioneers that rules were agreed upon with so little trouble. The example was set in Gregory Gulch (Central City). A mass meeting of miners was held June 8, 1859, and a committee appointed to draft a code of laws. This committee laid out boundaries for the district, and their civil code, after some discussion and amendment, was unanimously adopted in mass meeting, July 16, 1859. The example was rapidly followed in other districts, and the whole Territory was soon divided between a score of local sovereignties. But these were only laws as to property; there was so little crime the first year that none others were needed. The Miners' Courts, as they were called, were presided over by justices of the peace, chosen by ballot; these, as a matter of form, usually took out a commission, sometimes from the "Territory of Jefferson," sometimes from Arapahoe County, and often from both.

But now money began to be plenty, and criminals invaded the country. The civil courts promptly assumed criminal jurisdiction, and the year 1860 opened with four governments in full blast. The miners' courts, people's courts, and "provisional government" (a new name for "Jefferson,") divided jurisdiction in the mountains; while Kansas and the provisional government ran concurrent in Denver and the valley. Such as felt friendly to either jurisdiction patronized it with their business. Appeals were taken from one to the other, papers certified up or down and over, and recognized, criminals delivered and judgments accepted from one court by another, with a happy informality which it is pleasant to read of. And here we are confronted by an awkward fact: there was undoubtedly much less crime in the two years this arrangement lasted than in the two which followed the territorial organization and regular government. The miners and ranchers were, as a rule, sober and industrious, and few atrocious cases were brought before the people's courts. In Denver three homicides and two duels had occurred down to April, 1860; but soon after came an invasion of thieves and ruffians, and the conflict there was terrible for a time.

If any of that class ventured into the mountains, the miners made short work of them. The miners' laws were usually drafted by committees and adopted in full mass meeting, the government being a pure democracy. Each law began with "Resolved," though it was sometimes changed, as a matter of form, to "Be it enacted." Lawyers were forbidden to practice in many districts. One law I copy from the records of Union Mining District:

"*Resolved*, That no lawyer be permitted to practice law in this district, under penalty of not more than fifty nor less than twenty lashes, and be forever banished from this district."

Another states that, "whereas Bill Payne, commonly known as Cockeye Payne," has committed certain outrages, among which drawing a revolver in court, and threatening the judge, are made prominent; therefore,

"*Resolved*, That a committee of ten good men be sent to bring in the said Bill or Cockeye Payne, and he be required to show cause why he should not immediately be hung."

It appears that he was able to show cause, and got off with banishment.

All these little governments came to an end on the passage of a Civil and Criminal Code by the first Territorial Legislature, in the winter of 1861–'62; but this code legalized all acts of previous governments, "not plainly contrary to justice or the common law." It was enacted that all the district recorders' books should be filed in the office of the county recorder, and be presumptive proof, the burden of proving the contrary to rest on the challenger; and that all decisions of former courts were to be valid "when both parties made appearance or had notice according to such rules as were then in force, whether by law or accepted custom." The change from local to territorial law appears to have been made without a ripple of disturbance, and all disputed claims of any prominence have risen under the present laws. Thus is seen in miniature the course of civil aggregation: first, the individual man yields to the local organization, then the local is slowly merged in the general. Government is seen to be, not a positive good, but only a choice of the lesser evil. Man yields a portion of his natural rights in order to preserve the rest; he supports the claims of others because he must ask support from them. Thus, too, is manifested the inherent capacity of the Anglo-Saxon for civil organization; and those who maintain that government necessarily had its origin in revelation, might profitably study the many proofs to the contrary in the settlement of the Far West.

Colorado became a Territory in 1861, remained such fifteen years, and after four desperate efforts, at last succeeded in becoming a State, just in time to aid in the election of a centennial president. Denver, political and financial capital of the new State, is also the starting point for most places of interest. Thence by way of the Narrow-guage, fifty miles westward, and all the way up-hill, lands us in the mining region, where we will delay for a more specific description, the reader to look on while the writer climbs and talks.

The lowlander, whom business or a love of novelty and wild scenery leads to climb one of the mountains around Georgetown, finds material for continual astonishment in the changes which unfold along his upward way. The white spots seen from below, enlarge to gray faces on the rocky cliffs, often hundreds of feet perpendicular; the darker shades, which seem from the valley mere breaks on the view, open to immense gorges, down which pour torrents of almost ice-cold water from the snow-fed lakes on the summit, and the green plats which pleased the eye as distant masses of shrubbery or thickets of sage-brush, swell on near approach to magnificent forests of mountain pine. The thin dyke of yellow-gray rock, which seems to cap the summit with rectangular blocks, apparently smooth enough to have been set and polished by human hands, swells out slowly as he climbs, till at last it towers hundreds of feet above the general summit level, a solid battlement of weather-beaten granite or trap rock, sometimes in monstrous cubes, but oftener in broken and serrated pinnacles like saw-teeth, fully justifying the Spanish appellation of *Sierra* (a saw). From the streets of Georgetown the gulches which divide the spurs into separate mining districts are barely visible; the face of the mountain between the more abrupt cliffs is tolerably smooth, and except the slope towards the valley it seems that one might drive a wheeled carriage along its side, or that a stone once started would roll into the city. Once on that slope, however, and the marks are found to be gulches often a hundred feet in depth; and instead of the face of one mountain we appear to have a hundred narrow "hogbacks," in the sides of which are openings into the rock and tunnel workings invisible from below.

Our party of seven sets out early, for our first ascent of Griffith Mountain will occupy half a day, and the first stage is up the face of a bare rock, eight hundred feet high, and barely broken enough to afford a foot-path; thence by a more gentle trail along the foot of a granite cliff, which rises three hundred feet almost perpendicularly. And yet every yard on its front has been tried with the pick or sounded with the hammer, to see if it contained mineral; for in just such places have been found some of the richest mines of the district. A peculiar stain on the rock attracted attention. Men were let down from above to "prospect," a crevice was found with "blossom" rock, and often a platform anchored to the cliff till a more permanent footing could be blasted out. The celebrated Stevens' Mine was reached

"THIS WAY AND THAT, IN ZIGZAGS, WE TOIL UPWARD."

by a rope ladder for months after being opened for work, and even now the workmen cling to a guide rope as they go up the trail, and the ore is sent down by a tramway. Yet its richness pays for the trouble.

A few hundred feet along this rock-hewn path bring us to the half-way gulch and a beautiful spring. Down this rock flume runs one of those brawling brooks which are the delight of poets and artists; and yet the mouth of the gulch, only half a mile below, is but a dry bed. Of all the streams that rise far up in the Rocky Mountains, not one in ten reaches any valley or joins another stream; and all the streams of all this slope combined do not furnish the Platte water enough to last it a hundred miles from the mountains. Here we rest and refresh, tighten straps, and then climb out of the gulch and enter on a series of more gentle slopes, alternating pine groves and grass plats. This way and that, in zigzag paths, we toil upward, often leaning on our staves and resting every hundred yards or so, for at this point our breath begins to come short, and if any way delicate, we feel that fluttering of the heart and beating in the temples which result from an attenuated atmosphere. Here is the original home of the mountain sheep. On these grassy knolls they kept fat from August till January, and when Georgetown was first settled they were slaughtered here by hundreds. This mountain bunch-grass and the finer grass on the higher slopes furnished them abundant feed till covered by the deep snows of January and February, as the snows are light here before that time. When the snow melted in April and May, all the sweetness left the grass, and the big-horn "lived on his fat" till June or July again. Black-tailed deer, too, were plenty, and occasionally a grizzly bear made the solitudes lively; now these animals are rarely seen this side of the summit, though sheep horns can be picked up frequently, and adorn the front of many a miner's cabin.

We toil slowly up over these knolls for an hour, at each turn the summit seeming just before us. The grassy region passed, we enter on the more rocky belt near the summit, and now mines are abundant and miners' cabins appear on every hand, sometimes built on a narrow flat, worked on the face of the slope, and again anchored with iron supports upon some projecting rock. At intervals we encounter pack trains coming down with ore, the little Mexican *burros* (donkeys) carrying immense rawhide panniers filled with the minerals, and near the summit encounter a party, consisting of one gentleman and three ladies, cautiously descending from the Highland Park. We see at a glance that they are Eastern people, as the resident ladies generally ride *burros*, sitting astride a sort of modified pack-saddle, but these have ponies and the Eastern side-saddle. The trail looks terrible, but horsemen sometimes get down this way, by walking in the worst places.

It is three hours since we left the valley, and we stand at last on the edge of the tolerably level summit, but across a sort of meadow is the foot of the last rocky ridge, which still towers from five to fifteen hundred feet above us. But this serrated battlement is not continuous on these sub-ranges, which are mere spurs of the Rocky Mountains; it stands out rather in detached peaks, leaving between them large sections of the summit level, over which a vehicle might be driven without difficulty. Every miner's cabin is the house of a friend, and in the nearest we find some hot coffee to moisten our cold lunch; then climb to the highest point, and with a good field-glass proceed to take views over a circuit of a hundred miles. Gray's and Torrey's peaks glisten through the clear air, seeming no more than two or three miles away. To the north and south of them extends the main dividing range of the Rocky Mountains, now spotted dull gray and dazzling white by alternations of bare rock and gulches filled with snow. But the day, though beautiful and mild, is too hazy for us to see the Holy Cross. This is formed by two enormous rifts in the mountain side near the summit, crossing each other at right angles, and never bare of snow. The two white lines form an exact Greek cross, which glitters in the sunlight of a bright day, being thrown into bold relief by the dark gray face of the mountain.

From our standpoint we look down a thousand feet upon summits, which, from Georgetown, seem so high as almost to be lost in the clouds. But the greatest sight is to the eastward. For a hundred miles out from the base of the mountains the plains seem to rise, and the blue line which marks the visible horizon appears just on a level with our eyes. But the plains there are at least seven thousand feet lower than our location. This phenomenon I have often observed from commanding positions in the mountains, and can understand the statement of aeronauts, that as they rise the region directly under them seems to sink slowly into a basin, while the surrounding country remains on a level with them.

The area we can thus survey with one quick glance now contains at least fifteen thousand miners and twice as many citizens and agriculturists. In the year 1861 the site of central Georgetown was an immense beaver dam, the largest in this part of the Rocky Mountains, and known to trappers and Indians all over the country. Even now, on some of the lowest lots in town, the effects of beaver work can be seen; and the rich, mucky soil on the common shows that it was the bed of their pond for long series of years. The first prospectors who pitched their tent on Clear Creek amused themselves on many a moonlight evening by watching the beavers play. Then the mountain sheep crowded these glades in hundreds, and for months the early settlers had no other meat. The black-tailed deer came in about the season when mutton was scarce. The brown bear, and more rarely the grizzly, lived in the timber below us. Even now traces of these animals are met with frequently among the hills. Then, instead of the miner's cabin, or the mouth of shaft or tunnel, one might have seen the unscarred face of nature; and in place of pack-trains laden with ore, or miners toiling up the steep trails, a band of Utes moving through the mountain passes, and sallying out upon the plains to attack their hereditary enemies, the Sioux and Arapahoes. Surely there was as much beauty in these scenes then as now. And yet how seldom the white men who saw this country, cultivated and intelligent as some of them were, speak of its sublime scenery. Their narratives are full, however, of allusions to scenes of blood and danger, to frowning precipices, where one misstep was destruction, and to lonely gorges where ambushed savages might let fly upon the unwary traveler a shower of arrows. Only security and a touch of civilization enable us to appreciate wild beauty and grandeur. Small is the pleasure one can take in the brawling brook, when, stooping to taste its ice-cold waters, he is liable to get an arrow in his back; in the wondrous cañon walls, where every turn may reveal an enemy; in the sweep of the bald eagle, where the next occupation of that eagle may be in picking the meat from his bones, or in the antics of the "noble red man" when that (supposed) nobility is his only security for life.

The richest mineral region is on the mountains west and south-west of Georgetown. First is the Silver Plume group. There the Pay Rock has an eighteen-inch vein of ore, zinc blende, very rich in silver. Down hill therefrom is the celebrated group including the Dives, Dunkirk and Pelican. These locations are stuck in so thick that the patents overlap each other in all directions, and a completed map of all the claims looks like a picture of a pile of boards thrown at random on the ground, and half covering each other. Out of a little plat, perhaps half a mile long and a quarter wide, has come $10,000,000 worth of ore. The Dives alone shipped $640,000 worth in forty days; and, pending certain legal proceedings, $90,000 worth was shipped between midnight Saturday and midnight Sunday. [An attachment can not be levied in Colorado on Sunday.] Besides paying enormous dividends, several of these mines keep two or three good lawyers in pay, and support expensive lawsuits. I am afraid to say how much actual cash has been paid out on the Dives-Pelican suit. The lowest guess here is $100,000, but it is probable a great deal has changed hands very quietly, and without knowledge of the public.

Two hundred feet below is the Baxter, famous for its wire silver, of which I have seen specimens that looked like a "witch-ball," or mass of tangled hair turned to pure silver. Of course there is not much of that sort of stuff, and where it appears on the face of rich rock it looks as if it had stewed out of the stone and curled from intense heat. Most of it is found in bunches lining the inside of little pockets in the stone, and projecting from a streaked rock we used to call in Utah "polygamy lime rock." To discover a mine in that neigborhood was nothing; the great trouble was to sink a shaft down to where the ore was concentrated, and then put up the machinery necessary to work it. Some of these mines originally sold for a trifle, comparatively; then the buyers had to spend $40,000 in development, since when they have paid for themselves a dozen times over. The Pelican Mine extends directly across Cherokee Gulch and on to Sherman Mountain. A little beyond are the Maine, Coldstream, Phœnix, Scotia and Captain Wells, merely different claims along the same vein, all very rich, and supposed to be a continuation of the same ore-channel as the Pelican-Dives. Half a mile or more along the steep face of Sherman Mountain, barely passable by a foot trail, brings us to Brown Gulch, and beyond it Brown Mountain. Directly across the gulch are several valuable mines. Near the top are the Hercules and Seven-thirty. After innumerable lawsuits and fights, the killing of one man and wounding of two others, the claimants of these two locations compromised interests, and sold both for $180,000. Now, under the name of East Row, it is paying handsomely. Down the hill-side, and also crossing the gulch, is the Brown Mine, which has paid for itself half a dozen times over. Still lower—in fact, only three or four hundred feet above Clear Creek—is the celebrated Terrible, probably the best managed mine in the district, though far from being the richest. It was bought of the locators by a company in Cornwall, England, for $500,000, and yielded $150,000 annually, varying but little from one year to another.

Successful mining in Colorado is of necessity deep mining. Rare, indeed, are the cases in which good pay rock is reached at less than a hundred feet, and in many mines the best is not reached under four or five hundred feet. As a rule, the larger the vein is the farther it is down to where all the ore in it is concentrated into one rich seam; for the force which made the seam of ore seems to have been weakened or dissipated as it drew near the surface, and a seam three feet thick at a depth of three hundred feet will often be scattered in twenty little irregular strings toward the surface. The Dives is by no means a large lode, but they sunk on it two hundred feet before they found the ore concentrated in one seam. The ore body may aptly be compared to a tree, which, as it rises, continually divides and subdivides, running out at last to twigs; so the ore-seam scatters until, at the surface, the prospector finds a hundred little lines or stems of mineral scattered over a wide space. Hence it is that silver mining here requires both nerve and patience, for it takes time to get down to the ore in this hard rock, where "three shifts" make but six or seven feet a week.

The curiosities of mining are almost endless. Here and there on the edge of rich ore-seams little accretions of almost pure silver have run together, like "leaf lard," as it were, and, according to its purity, or the chemicals mixed in it, such "nibs" are known as chloride, horn silver, ruby silver, azurite or tetrahedrite. A change of one-tenth of one per cent. in the chemical will sometimes change entirely the color and texture of the ore. "Black-jack," or zinc blende, is a very troublesome combination. Chunks of it are found, which assay five hundred ounces of silver per ton, but its reduction is very difficult and expensive. Azurite is a combination of silver with blue carbonates of copper, and yields all the way from three hundred to a thousand ounces of silver per ton Every year lower grade ores can be profitably worked, with the improvement in methods and cheapening of transportation. When this district was opened, in 1864, ore must yield a hundred ounces per ton to be worth working; now thirty-ounce ore can be profitably treated. The laws as to title in silver mines are now pretty well settled; but no law that Congress or Territorial Legislature could pass has prevented men who stayed on the ground from getting title to thousands of "feet" in mines. The laws also say something about the preëmptor being of voting age; but by "unwritten law" any able-bodied lad of sixteen and upward, who can do the required work, can preëmpt sufficiently to sell out to an adult, who can perfect the title. A shrewd lawyer, of course, might pick flaws in the inchoate title; but it would be unhealthy to do so if the boy had any friends. Various laws, lately enacted, give title in width also, allowing a hundred and fifty feet on each side of a claim for working purposes. But each county is allowed to limit this by popular vote, and many counties do. Thus it will be seen that original location, preëmption and sale, and each successive transfer, being recorded in the old district records, now legalized as part of the county records, these titles are just as susceptible of proof as those of a farm.

Over the sub-range which bounds Georgetown on the north-west, through a lofty region of forests, parks and mountain meads, and over another more gentle range, brings us to North Clear Creek Cañon, where gold was first discovered. The gold placers have long since yielded in prominence to silver lodes. On the old Gregory claim is now part of Central City, the historic town of Colorado. There sprung up a rattling "city" of logs and rough-sawed plank during the week that Horace Greeley was inspecting the mines in 1859; and there, for a time, was the territorial capital, until the sudden and amazing growth of Denver overshadowed all the mountain towns, and absorbed all the Federal fat things. Mining in the old Gregory district has long since passed out of the era of romantic uncertainty and excitement to that of regular work and legitimate investment. Another day's journey to the northward, over the eastern slope of the mountains, and through a region rich with scenic interest, brings us to Caribou, Nederland, and all that rich region at the head of Bowlder Creek. Caribou, ten thousand feet above the level of the sea, on a gentle slope, and in the midst of a dense pine forest, was the most delightful of new mining towns when I visited it in August, 1874.

Of course that part of Colorado which drains eastward is much the best known and developed, but beyond the main range are many new and promising mining camps, as Leadville and the San Juan District, which seem to lie across the very center of the great upheaval that, perhaps, made the mines. In every district are ten times as many locations as will ever be developed, and ten thousand hopes that will never be realized; for, despite his plain surroundings, the miner is the most romantic and imaginative of men. But his is a singularly unromantic work. It implies cold, dirt and wet, possibility of sudden death, probability of severe injury, soon or late, and certainty of sore trial and frequent disappointments. The history of a silver mine includes these stages: prospecting, locating, opening, developing and working—and at every step in development the chances of final failure are many. Thus it has been well and truly said that mining is a lottery, but it should still be remembered that this applies only to finding and developing mines. Once it has depth sufficient to prove it, and has opened into a regular vein, a mine is as certain as any property in the world. But on the surface, where the prospector makes his location according to the "indications," there is no science that enables him to judge what it will prove on depth. That he must learn by digging, and many are the alternations of hope and fear as he goes down. First a little "pocket" of rich sulphurets raises his hopes to fever heat, then comes a "cap" of barren rock, and down they go to zero; next, perhaps, he finds the vein widening, with here and there a "nib" of chloride, azurite or ruby silver, and straightway his spirits mount as on eagle's wings; again he encounters a "pinch" or "cap," and hope almost dies out ere he gets through it. Sometimes he follows a "pinching vein," scarcely thicker than a knife-blade, for many a week, at an expense of fifteen dollars a foot, hoping that it will lead him to the main vein. At last, at the depth of one hundred feet or more, his varying crevice either opens into the main vein and rewards him a thousand fold for all his toil, or, as it does in nine cases out of ten, it ends in barren rock, beyond which there is no thoroughfare, proving it to be a dip, spur, dropper, gash vein or any one of the thousand things which mislead the miner. Not one location in twenty is ever pushed to the depth of a hundred feet; of those so pushed not more than one in ten proves a valuable mine, and even of tolerably valuable mines not one in twenty proves a Caribou, Pelican, Dives or a Comstock. But if every location were as valuable as the owner thinks it to be when he first starts down on it, silver would soon cease to be a precious metal. We might manufacture it into doorhinges.

As a rule only the developed and proved mines are bought by Eastern companies, but in the great speculative era of 1864-66, Colorado was literally sold out to New York capitalists, who took stock in the future with amazing readiness. Thirty-eight companies were organized, with an aggregate capital of $24,000,000! And this when all the mines in the Territory were not worth the half of that sum. Hundreds of mere "prospect holes" were purchased at high figures, and mills were erected to work the ore before the buyers knew of what kind it was, or whether there was one ton or a million. The era of mad speculation has given place to that of practical mining, and Colorado has advanced to an annual yield in ore and bullion of from $12,000,000 to $15,000,000.

Colorado is divided nearly down the center by the main chain of the Rocky Mountains—or, in miner's phrase, "saddle-backed across the range." West of the summit not one acre in a thousand is fit for any thing but grazing. As depressions in the summit appear the great parks, a curious and attractive feature of Colorado. As summer retreats and grazing grounds, they will ultimately be of great value. The slope eastward from the mountains is the pasture land of the new State. The whole section is being rapidly dotted with ranches, and all kinds of stock thrive on the nutritious grasses. But it is only on the low land along the streams that farming can be carried on.

At the heads of the Fontaine Que Bouille and other tributaries of the Arkansas, bounteous nature seems to have exhausted her powers in the way of scenery and climate. There the sheltered valleys opening to the south are green early in the year; there reluctant summer lingers longest, and glad spring hastens to return. The hot pools, the vast reservoirs and bubbling fountains of soda, the medicinal springs, the wooded parks, the gateway to the mountains and the Garden of the Gods afford unfailing delight. Over all rises Pike's Peak, outlined against a sky of dazzling blue, landmark for a hundred miles in every direction. Around the heads of all the streams that feed the

Arkansas are the finest bunch-grass pastures, on which feed vast herds of sheep and cattle.

The valley of the Arkansas is fertile some distance eastward. But a little south the scene changes suddenly, and the extreme south-eastern part of the Territory lies in that great desert which includes all the neighboring portions of Texas, New Mexico, Kansas and the Indian Territory. There the water-holes are few and far between; the thorny *mezquit* alone can be said to adorn the landscape, and the region can only be crossed at the risk of death from thirst. On the southern edge of this desert my friend, Thad. Buckman, took refuge in a *mezquit* thicket from the Arapahoes, and, though previously noted for his modesty, when he got out of there, with his skin hanging in ribands, he was the worst stuck-up man in the Rocky Mountains. Every bush has a thorn and every insect a sting; all the Indians are hostile, and if one should meet a white man, the chances are even that he is an involuntary exile and a cattle thief. The principal productions are *mezquit*, tarantulas and centipedes.

The Arkansas was formerly the northern boundary of Mexico, and across this desert marched, in 1843, from their rendezvous on that stream, one of the many Texan expeditions against Santa Fe. Its members are now glorified on annual San Jacinto days as noble and devoted patriots to whom dishonor were worse than death; but I am afraid they would not know themselves in that character. They arrived almost dead from starvation at the Mexican settlements, and, having supplied themselves, found that Governor Armijo had warning of their approach; accordingly they marched back and disbanded. After a brief rest a new party was organized, numbering a hundred and eighty, which found a little better route over the desert, and came up with the Mexican forces while in fighting condition. Texan histories, in florid, South-western rhetoric, describe the daring charge and furious onslaught of the little army, the fierce conflict and bloody victory, adding in confirmation that the Texans lost two men—wounded! I heard while in Texas that one of the two cut his fingers accidentally with a bowie-knife. Pity those historians had not taken a lesson from *Cæsar's Commentaries*—that to praise the enemy's bravery is to exalt the victor.

Turning back from the South-eastern desert to the foot of the mountains, fertility increases with every mile, until we are again among the rich pastures and mountain meadows along the heads of the streams. Thus it will be seen that Colorado is naturally divisible into four great sections; twenty thousand square miles of complete barrenness, whether of mountain or desert; fifty thousand square miles of plain and valley, fit only for grazing; an unknown area rich in mines, and perhaps two thousand square miles of agricultural land. On the grazing lands cattle and sheep are multiplying by hundreds of thousands yearly. It is estimated that Eastern Colorado will afford abundant pasturage for two million sheep and cattle. Facilities for manufacturing exist on every mountain stream, and great attention is being paid to the production of fine wools.

Farther up in the mountains the few cultivable plats require no irrigation. From a summer's residence at Georgetown I am convinced that three times as much rain falls there as at Denver. But elevation is a great hindrance to crops. Wheat can be produced at an altitude of 6,000 feet, oats at 7,000, rye at 7,500, and near Central City I have seen potatoes yielding bounteously at 9,000 feet. Colorado flour has attained a world-wide celebrity. Enthusiastic prophets speak of reclaiming all the barren plains, but I respectfully submit that it is impossible, unless the climate changes. All the streams in Eastern Colorado would not supply irrigation for a strip across the Territory ten miles wide. The high plains are irreclaimable by any process which would be remunerative, and must continue for many centuries to be the herd-grounds of the West.

What, then, are the possibilities of Colorado? If the pressure of population is to be no greater than in the Ohio Valley, I estimate it as follows: 200,000 engaged in agriculture and mining, and as many in stock-ranching, manufacturing and commerce. But the floating, or rather visiting, population will always be large. Colorado's beauties are of a kind that art can not mar. No amount of "improvement" can lessen the grandeur of her peaks, the romance of her secluded cañons, the reviving air and inspiring scenery of her wonderful parks; time will only more fully demonstrate the value of her mineral springs, and in her Western Wilds many successive generations of sportsmen will find health and relaxation.

In general intelligence Colorado is not surpassed by any community in the world. Dullards and desperadoes do not build up such a commonwealth as this. A hundred thousand people who have created in eighteen years a wealth of fifty millions, and now add fifteen millions annually to the national treasure; who support a score of daily and weekly papers; who organized civil government out of social chaos, and have grown to Statehood with so little trouble to the nation, may be trusted to govern themselves wisely in the future. Whether in material or moral greatness, we may be justly proud of our Centennial State.

CHAPTER XXXI.

THE MORMON MURDERERS.

IN September, 1874, I resumed my residence in Salt Lake City, and there remained one year—part of the time as Clerk of the Supreme Court of Utah, the remainder as assistant editor of the *Daily Tribune*. The sensation of that autumn was the capture and imprisonment of John D. Lee; of the next summer, his arraignment and trial. In the two years after I left him at his stronghold on the Colorado, he had grown bolder and visited the nearest settlements without disguise, fully persuaded that all the Mormons were as devoted to his safety as they had shown themselves to be fifteen years before. But he was mistaken. While he enjoyed the society of some of his younger wives at Panguitch, on the Sevier River, some one conveyed a hint to the United States Marshal at Beaver, and a scheme was at once concerted for the capture of the murderer.

Marshal Owens, with a *posse* of five men, set out from Beaver just after dark, and by night marches, lying concealed in the timber by day, came upon Panguitch just after daylight. But cautious as he had been, before he got into town word was conveyed to Lee, and the latter had time to hide. Once in the town the Marshal and *posse* found a dense ignorance prevailing. Nobody knew whether John D. Lee had a wife there, or where she lived, or what name she went by. Enraged at this general collusion with the criminal, the *posse* seized a small boy, who afterwards proved to be Lee's son, and threatened him with death unless he directed them to the house. The little Mormon gazed calmly at his captor, then at the pistol in the latter's hand, and said, "Shoot away, d—n ye; I don't know nothin' about it." Had not all the roads been guarded, the murderer could even then have escaped. Meanwhile the sun rose and the citizens went about their daily tasks; but it was evident that a few were all the time within easy reach of the *posse*, and that a word from the bishop or ruling elder of the place would have precipitated a bloody fight. Fortunately the right house was found before there was time for consultation among the criminals. The nest was warm, but the bird had flown. In the cow-yard was an old shed; the under logs had been pulled out, and the roof was now only four or five feet from the ground and covered with straw. It looked like a shapeless heap of straw, but was a hog-pen and chicken-coop. As long as the *posse* searched the house the women were passive enough; but when Marshal Owens commenced examining this straw pile, the older one hastily grabbed a gun. That settled it.

"He's here," said the Marshal, quietly, and the pen was surrounded.

CAPTURE OF JOHN D. LEE

The woman had been disarmed, but Lee's retainers were flocking in from all sides. A cordon of Mormons already surrounded the house and cow-yard. The women seemed to be urging them on, and a few of them came forward to the pen. It was discovered that Lee had thirty sons, sons-in-law and grandsons in Panguitch, besides some wives and more distant relations. The *posse* numbered but five.

Marshal Owens gazed long and earnestly into the little dark hole, the only entrance to the pen; and when his eyes grew accustomed to the darkness, he saw a greenish, glaring pair confronting him from the black corner. Here was his man—but how to get him? Determined not to risk his men's lives, the Marshal directed them to cut into the straw pile at the rear, while he would keep watch, and if the man made a motion, would shoot. At these words the inside man exclaimed:

"Don't shoot, boys. I'll come out." And he did.

Once secured, Lee grew unnaturally social and even merry. He urged the *posse* to come into the house, and ordered his wives to cook breakfast for all parties immediately. But the Gentiles did not feel so merry. The whole town appeared to be concentrating in that vicinity. It was evident the place contained at least seventy-five fighting men, and that they only waited a signal from Lee, or some one else, to begin. Directing his men to keep their weapons in constant readiness, and placing two of them as a special guard over Lee, the Marshal informed that worthy that the first move towards a rescue would be the signal for his instant death. The signal was not given. The *posse* ate breakfast, silently and in haste, and departed for the hills, the whole population waiting and watching. By forced marches the Gentiles reached Beaver next morning, and John D. Lee soon reposed in the strong room at Camp Cameron with fifty pounds of iron on his person.

Before entering on the details of his trial it is necessary to give some particulars of the crime, a thousand times told, for which he finally suffered. It was the result of three motives, prominent in the order named: revenge, lust for plunder and fanaticism. When the Latter-day Saints left Illinois, 20,000 strong, they hurled back apostolic curses at the whole Gentile nation. That nation, they said, had rejected the gospel by the murder of the Prophet and Patriarch, and should perish in its sins. In the Rocky Mountains the Saints would establish a kingdom, and in due time take vengeance on their enemies. In the endowment oaths, every true Mormon was sworn to avenge the death of Joseph Smith. A peculiar system of diplomacy and attempt to establish a theocracy in the States, had brought the Saints into conflict with the Americans, and now that conflict was made the means of uniting them more solidly against the Gentile world. With the doctrine of a temporal kingdom came in the long train of Hebraic similes: the Church was in bondage in Egypt; it was in the wilderness of Zin; it was to overthrow the Amalekites (Missourians), and repeat all the wonderful achievements in the fruitful annals of Israel. And as the Amalekites resisted, and many Mormons grew disaffected, all the bloody devices of the ancient Hebrews were legalized, and thus Mormonism became the terrible thing it was in 1856 and '57.

When they first settled in Utah they determined their government should be a pure theocracy, but it was necessary to have some form which the United States would recognize, to give jurisdiction over Gentiles who might pass through or tarry in Zion. A State government was agreed upon. Its boundaries were declared to be from the summit of the Sierras to that of the Rocky Mountains, and from latitude 42° down to the Mohave Desert and divide of the Colorado plateau; it contained all the present Utah and Nevada, with considerable portions of Idaho, Wyoming, Colorado and Arizona. The proposition carried by a unanimous vote (all propositions do in the Mormon Church), and the heads of the theocracy were in like manner elected chiefs in the "State of Deseret:" Brigham Young, Governor; Daniel H. Wells, Chief Justice and Lieutenant-General; the Twelve Apostles divided the Judgeships and State officers among them; the State Senate was made up of Presiding Bishops, the House of inferior Bishops and Elders, and the local officers in counties were appointed according to priestly rank. This queer institution ran a year. The Legislature immediately assembled and divided the whole adjacent territory into grants; the timber, streams, pasture lands, and valleys were given to the heads of the Church; they in turn parceled them out, each to his laity, and thus color of title was established to all the land in Utah of any value. As Brigham pithily said, "If there's nothing for the d—d Gentiles to settle on, they can't settle." And they didn't.

Congress, in the long and memorable session of 1850, cut up our new possessions into various governments, and, among others, established the Territory of Utah—about two and a half times as large as it is now; of which Territory President Fillmore, with his customary sense of propriety, appointed Brigham Young Governor! Immediately the whole State machinery of Deseret was floated on to the new government. As far as the Organic Act of Utah gave power, all the old officials were chosen in the new system; the Legislature re-assembled, sat six months (its expenses were now paid from Washington), confirmed in bulk most of the legislation of "Deseret," and divided up all the valleys which had since been discovered. Thus began that remarkable interlock of church and state, the most perfect despotism of modern times, which lasted unbroken for twenty years—until Judge McKean and his colleagues made the first breach, in 1870.

The average citizen can have no conception of the empire obtained by this theocracy over the minds and fortunes of its subjects. Three concurrent governments took charge of every detail of common life: the territorial or civil of all affairs concerning Gentiles, or cases between Gentile and Mormon; the ecclesiastical of all religious questions; and the Church civil system of all the industries and commerce of the people. Brigham was Prophet and Seer in the ecclesiastical; First President in the industrial and civil; for seven years Governor in the territorial government, and long afterwards virtual dictator of the policy of his successors. The same man in an outer settlement was Judge under the Territory, Bishop under the Church, and "President of the Stake" in the civil and industrial organization. John D. Lee was Bishop of one settlement, President of a "stake" or commune, Major of the county militia, Representative of the same county in the Legislature, official Indian interpreter, the husband of eighteen wives, and father, from first to last, of sixty-four children. Isaac Haight, his colleague in murder, was likewise a Bishop, a Captain in the militia, member of the council (upper house of the Territorial Legislature), husband of four wives, and father of numerous children. Wm. H. Dame was Colonel of the regiment ordered out to commit the massacre, and Bishop of Parowan, and held numerous minor offices. Higby, probably the most blood-thirsty of the lot, was an inferior Elder, a Captain in the militia, and generally held some executive office under the Territory. Bill Stewart, who boasted for years after the massacre that he "took the d—d Gentile babies by the heels and cracked their skulls over the wagon tires," was only a private in the ranks, but for years before and after the massacre a member of the Church in good standing, as were all the other murderers down to the very day the United States officers chased them into the mountains. And yet there are good souls who maintain that the Mormon Church bears no moral responsibility for this massacre.

Had an inferior officer of our army, when camped before Washington, gone into the country and massacred the people of a Virginia village without regard to age or sex, and had General Grant not only overlooked the offense, but promoted the offender, the world would have resounded with denunciations. Yet the control General Grant had over his army was laxity itself compared with that Brigham Young had over Mormondom. To say that these men, of their own motion, and without a hint from head-quarters, did such a deed, is to say what every old resident of Utah knows to be a transparent falsehood. For fifteen years these men had never once followed their own minds in any matter of importance. One must take "counsel of the priesthood" on all occasions, whether he would go abroad or remain at home, open a farm, or go into trade, buy a cow or take an extra wife. There was no corner of the mountains so remote but some theocratic arm reached it. There were no walls high enough or thick enough to shut out church spies; there was no domestic confidence that was safe, for the ward teachers were expressly instructed to visit weekly every family in their jurisdiction, and "examine the man apart from his wife and the wife apart from the man, to the end that heresy may be rooted out." To say that this was the *first* crime of these men is to say what every lawyer knows to be folly. Criminals are not made in a day. Men do not become utter and conscienceless villains just for one occasion. Whole communities do not suddenly turn to assassins. Starkie and Greenleaf teach a sounder philosophy of crime. The whole previous life-time of the Mormon Church was no more than enough to educate men to such action.

Perhaps all these causes would not have been sufficient, but the year 1856 was full of disaster and incitements to fanaticism. The Church leaders had determined that immigrants from Europe should walk from the Missouri to Salt Lake City, and trundle hand-carts loaded with their baggage; and the first attempt resulted in frightful suffering and three hundred deaths. This dire calamity appeared to excite an epidemic madness in Utah.

The "Reformation" which had already set in, now became a veritable reign of terror. The doctrine of "blood atonement," or killing men to save their souls, was taught by Brigham Young, Orson Hyde, and others. In all the sermons of that period one will not find twenty quotations from the New Testament, but every page is red with the bloody maxims of the Mosaic code.

Meanwhile, Parley P. Pratt, "Isaiah of the Latter-day Church," was killed in Arkansas by Hector McLean, whose wife Pratt had taken away some time before. To the Gentiles this would seem but the rash act of an outraged husband; to the Mormons it appeared the murder of an able apostle, who had obeyed the "celestial laws," in taking another man's wife. The spring of 1857 found the Mormon community in a mixed state of fanatic enthusiasm, grief for the lost, zeal for the cause, and fierce anger against the whole American race. While in this state the news arrived that President Buchanan had removed Brigham Young from the Governorship, and determined to station a part of the army in Utah. The immediate consequences were frightful.

A yell of rage and defiance sounded from one end of the Territory to the other. The few American officials who remained slipped out at once. Dr. Hurt, Indian agent, did not trust the roads, but was piloted through the mountains by the Utes. All the apostates who could do so fled at once. The rest held their peace, or outdid the orthodox in their zeal. Several frightful murders and still more frightful mutilations took place. To deprive a dangerous man of virility was regarded almost as a joke. Dozens of cases are known to have occurred between 1856 and 1863—those being the years in which the "blood atonement" doctrine was preached. All opposition was silenced, and the people were hot for war. Wheat was dried and *cached* in the mountains preparatory to a guerrilla war; and every able-bodied male was under arms. Brigham issued a proclamation warning all emigrants out of the Territory, and announced in a sermon that if they came, he "would turn the Indians loose on them." While things were in this state, the doomed train arrived in Salt Lake City.

It was, perhaps, the richest train that ever crossed the plains. There were half a dozen or more wealthy old gentlemen from Missouri and Arkansas, with their sons, sons-in-law and their several families, including a large number of young ladies; also a few young men from Vermont, a German doctor and man of science, two lads from some Eastern city, and a son of Dr. Aden, of Kentucky. All the Missouri and Arkansas people were related by blood, and when they were killed a whole clan, so to speak, was cut off. The recovered children, in many instances, could find no relations. There were forty wagons, several hundred horses and cattle, a piano, some elegant carriages, several riding horses for the young ladies, and an immense amount of jewelry, clothing, and minor articles. The value of the booty taken has been estimated all the way from $150,000 to $300,000.

Seeing that they were in a hostile country they hastened on; but as they advanced southward from Salt Lake (they were going to Los Angeles), they found the people steadily more hostile. They were denied passage through some of the towns, and had to make a detour on the desert; they could purchase no provisions, and found that in spite of themselves they were constantly violating municipal ordinances, and liable to arrest. At Beaver they were joined by a Missourian who had been in custody among the Mormons; he urged them to hurry on as they valued their lives. Passing through Cedar City it is believed they saw signs of their coming danger and redoubled their exertions to get beyond the Utah limits. At last they reached the glen known as Mountain Meadows, on the "divide" between the waters flowing into the Great Basin and those draining into the Colorado, and paused to recruit their stock before entering on the Ninety-Mile Desert.

Meanwhile some secret work, not yet fully explained, had been going on at Salt Lake City. There is some evidence that a plan was once agreed upon to have the emigrants killed as they crossed the Provo "bench," only forty miles from Salt Lake; but it was finally thought best to let them get beyond the settlements. George A. Smith, Brigham's First Councillor, went south ahead of the party, forbidding the people to sell them any grain; and some lawyers, who have examined the evidence, think he planned the massacre, as he then held military command of all the Territory south of Provo. Down to this point all agree upon the facts; what follows rests upon testimony from many sources:

Philip Klingensmith, Mormon Bishop and participant in the crime, who fled to Nevada, made a full confession, and was the main witness on the trial; Joel White, a private in the militia, also present at the massacre, unwillingly, as he claims; one Hawley, a lad, also present; several boys who assisted in burying the dead; Robert Keyes, who saw the dead soon after, and was familiar with the local accounts; Asahel Bennet, who visited the scene and saw the dead; the confession of Spencer, a school teacher in St. George, who died of grief and remorse for his share in the act; Albert, an Indian boy, who was herding sheep for Jacob Hamlin, in the upper end of the Meadows; several Indian chiefs who assisted at the massacre; Mrs. Ann Eliza Hoge, a French Mormon woman, "plural wife" of one of the leaders, who was present at the "councils" where the death of the emigrants was determined upon; the various confessions of John D. Lee, and a mass of collateral testimony. The evidence is conclusive as to the following facts:

The day after the emigrants passed Harmony, John D. Lee, Bishop and President, called a council and stated that he had received command "to follow and attack the accursed Gentiles, and let the arrows of the Almighty drink their blood." He stated that they were from Missouri, which had expelled God's people, and from Arkansas, which had sanctioned the murder of the apostle; he recited the Hawn's Mill massacre of Mormons, the murder of Joseph and Hyrum Smith, and others, and called for an affirmative vote. All hands were held up, and the expedition was at once fitted out. Lee turned out the Indians under his charge, who surrounded the emigrants and prevented their going on, while a regular call was made on the county militia by Col. W. H. Dame, Major John D. Lee, and Captains Haight and Higby. The siege lasted eight days, during which a few emigrants were killed.

Some men living in the vicinity testify that they were ordered out as militia; others that they went at command of the Bishop, and still others that they were asked to go but managed to avoid it. Two men say that they sat inside the wall of a garden all night, talking and praying while the wagons carrying supplies ran back and forward; that they wept and asked the forgiveness of God if they were about to do wrong, but finally had to go along with their company of militia. When all were collected at the Meadows, on the eighth day of the siege, Lee and some others bore a flag of truce to the emigrants, and arranged for their surrender. They were to give up every thing, including their arms, be taken back to the settlement and taken care of, but held till the war was over. On this agreement they started on their return. There were sixty fighting men, forty women, and forty-eight children. In front were two wagons, driven by Mormons and containing the men wounded in the siege; behind them were the women and children, and lastly the men. Beside the men marched

MOUNTAIN MEADOW MASSACRE.

the Mormon militia in single file. Off on either side were mounted men to intercept any who might break through the lines. A hollow crosses the road there; on each side of the way as it enters the hollow are rocks and bushes where the Indians lay in ambush. As testified to by one witness, the women talked joyfully of their rescue from the Indians, and thanked God that they were under the protection of white men.

All was in readiness. As the wagons passed the gully and the women and children were just entering it, Ike Higbee, standing on the bluff above, waved his hand as a signal. Haight gave command: Halt! fire!! On the instant the Mormon militia turned, and with their guns almost touching their victims, discharged one volley, and almost every man of the emigrants fell dead. With loud screams the women and children turned and ran back toward the men. The Indians and Mormons rushed upon them, shooting, stabbing, braining, and in twenty minutes six score of Americans lay dead upon the ground, the hapless victims of Mormonism. No circumstance of horror was lacking. Indians and Mormons bit and tore the rings from the fingers and ears of the women, and with insulting yells trampled on the faces of the dying.

One girl knelt and begged a son of John D. Lee for life. He hesitated, but the father pushed him aside, and shot her through the head. Several broke through the line, but were killed by the mounted men. Two girls ran down the gully and over the ridge, to the slope where the Indian boy Albert was hid, to watch the massacre. He says that they begged him to save them, and he directed them where to hide in a thicket. The next minute John D. Lee and Bill Stewart came galloping across the hollow, and, with savage curses, ordered him to point out the runaways. He dared not disobey, and soon the girls were dragged out. Kneeling to Lee, they poured out the most passionate prayers for mercy—they would be his slaves, would never betray him, would work for him forever. While one clung to his knees he jerked her suddenly upon her back, and, placing his knee upon her breast, cut her throat from ear to ear! The other had, meanwhile, run away. He overtook her, and, by a savage blow on the back of the head with a ragged stone, crushed in her skull. Both these bodies were missed by the burying party, and, strange to say, lay there ten days untouched by the wolves. When Hamlin returned from Salt Lake City, Albert pointed them out, and they were buried. Hamlin adds that there was not the mark of a tooth on either body, and no sign of decay, so pure was the air. Their fair countenances were like those of persons just dead, and their handsome forms untouched by the beasts and birds of prey. Nature and the wild beasts of the mountain were kinder to them than men of their own race and color.

Mrs. Hamlin, wife of Jacob Hamlin above mentioned, before her death gave this account:

"A Mormon woman, far advanced in pregnancy, was at Hamlin's; her husband was driving one of the wagons containing the wounded, having been ordered on that duty by Bishop Klingensmith. When the massacre began this man took a fit, and soon died of excitement or fright. When the bloody wagon, containing the children and the dead body of her husband, was brought to Hamlin's, this woman went into a spasm, prematurely gave birth to a child, then became insane, and lingered twelve years a raving maniac." The driver of the other wagon says that besides children and wounded men he had in his wagon a venerable old man, with long white beard, richly dressed, and evidently a man of consequence among the emigrants. He insists that this old man jumped out of the front end of the wagon, got into the bushes, and was never captured. None of the burying party could ever find his body. Possibly the poor old man wandered awhile in the mountains, afraid to approach any settlement, and either died of want in some lonely place or was killed by the Indians.

One witness—a lad at the time, and present with the militia—says that when they came to look over the ground he found one woman only stunned and recovering consciousness. Bill Stewart ordered him to kill her at once.

"Never!" was his reply. "I've got none of this blood on my soul, and don't intend to have any."

Stewart cursed him for a coward, then stepped behind the woman who had risen to her feet, and drove a bowie-knife to the hilt in her side.

Three men escaped the general massacre. The night before the closing scene the party first became convinced that white men were besieging them. They then drew up a paper addressed to the Masons, Odd Fellows, Baptists, and Methodists of the States, " and to all good people every-where," in which they stated their condition, and implored help if there was time; if not, justice. To this were attached the signatures of so many members of various lodges and churches in Missouri and Arkansas. With this paper three of their best scouts crept down a ravine and escaped, starting afoot for California. The next day Ira Hatch and a band of Indians were put upon their track. They came upon them asleep on the Santa Clara Mountain, and killed two as they slept. The third escaped, shot through the wrist. He traveled on and was relieved by the Vegas Indians, on the Santa Clara. After a day's rest he started on, but meeting John M. Young and another, they told him it would be madness to attempt the Ninety-Mile Desert in his condition, and promised to try and smuggle him through to Salt Lake City. A few hours after, they met Hatch and his Indians on the hunt for the fugitive. Said Hatch, " Boys, you can pass, we've nothing against you, but this man must die." The doomed man thanked the boys for their trouble, offered a moving prayer, and submitted to his fate. Unwilling to look on his death, Young galloped away. A few rods off some impulse caused him to halt and turn around. The Indians had shot the fugitive full of arrows; he was still upon his knees, and an Indian just drawing a knife across his throat. This brings the whole number murdered up to a hundred and thirty-one. The paper dropped by the fugitives was given by an Indian to Jacob Hamlin, Church Indian Agent, who kept it many years; but one day showing it to Lee, the latter took it from him and destroyed it.

The bloody deed was done—the most cruel, pitiless, massacre white men were ever guilty of. It only remained to divide the spoil and guard against discovery. A tithe of the plunder was turned over to the Church. The Indians received the arms and ammunition and some of the clothing; but long complained that they did not get their share. The finest stock was distributed among the dignitaries in the neighborhood; and in 1872, Bishop Windsor, of Pipe Springs, Arizona, pointed out to me cattle in his own herd descended from stock taken at Mountain Meadows. Forty head of cattle were driven to Salt Lake City, and traded for boots and shoes to Hon. William H. Hooper. Thirteen years afterward this man stood up in his place in the American Congress, and solemnly called God to witness that the Mormons had nothing to do with this massacre—it was all the work of the Indians. The clothing, even that stripped from the corpses, was put in the cellar of the tithing house at Cedar City, and "sold to pay expenses." The carriages, wagons, and jewelry were divided among the leaders. And then, Major John D. Lee, as military commandant, and Philip Klingensmith, as bishop, went to Salt Lake City and laid a full report before Brigham Young—"Governor of Utah and *ex-officio* Superintendent of Indian Affairs," by the grace of His Excellency Franklin Pierce.

And what then? Of course there was a loud outcry for justice; of course there was a legislative committee of inquiry; of course the Governor of Utah promptly moved upon the criminals, and the *ex-officio* Superintendent of Indian Affairs reported it to the department. Nothing of the kind. Brigham sent word to the Bishops, "Let no man talk about this thing—don't mention it even among yourselves— especially let the women keep silent about it. Let it be forgotten as soon as possible." Haight and Lee came up to Salt Lake as senator and representative; sat that winter in the legislature; attended the usual dinner given by Gov. Brigham Young, and each went home with a young wife, sealed to them in the Endowment House by the Prophet, Seer, and Revelator, Brigham Young! Nobody left the neighborhood; nobody lost caste. Lee remained a bishop for fourteen years afterward. Dame is a bishop yet; Higbee is a prominent citizen, and Haight was still a bishop when I last saw him in 1872. The dead were buried; peace was made by Commissioners Powell and McCulloch with King Brigham; a new emigrant road was laid off, lest Gentiles might discover something in passing through the meadows, and no mention of the affair was made in Mormon society or in the Mormon organ, the *Deseret News*.

And so all was done, and the dread secret was safe. The last adult emigrant had fed the wolves; the only child old enough to remember any thing about it had "disappeared," and the rest, distributed in various settlements, soon looked upon the Mormons as their people, and forgot that they ever had Gentile parents. Even the women, obeying Brigham implicitly, "quit talking about it." Lee called a meeting of all who were at the former council, and swore them to eternal secrecy, under penalty of the punishment invoked in their endowment oaths. Brigham preached in the neighborhood, was the guest of Lee, and urged the brethren "to be united and not tale-bearers, one against another." All avenues of discovery were apparently shut up. The job was a complete one. The secret was safe.

"Ah gentlemen!" said Webster, of a similar case; "that was a terrible mistake. Such a secret is safe nowhere. The universe of God has no corner where the guilty can bestow it and say it is safe. The human heart was not made to be the depository of such a secret. There is no refuge from confession but suicide; and suicide *is* confession." Even the banded murderers of Mormondom could not keep it. There were too many concerned. There were men with human blood in their hearts; there were women with mothers' milk in their breasts. They could not carry so oppressive a secret. The madness of 1856 and '57 wore itself out. Dazed and bewildered, men slowly emerged from the state of excitement, and asked themselves what had been done. Strange rumors spread northward from settlement to settlement. Some of the boys from Washington County came north after the peace, and met their friends who had served against Johnston's army; and often muttered over their cups that they did not like "the business they had been engaged in down south." A lad in Beaver began to act very strangely—he drank deep of native whisky, and never staggered under it; but told of very strange things that he saw.

Young Spencer wasted to a skeleton, and wrote imploring letters to his bishop and to Brigham Young, begging for some word to relieve his remorse. All at once several young Mormons ran away from that section, and the next spring an account of the massacre appeared in a California paper. But the young Mormon who brought it never showed himself again, and the editor was laughed at. Pretty soon, however, it was found that a company of emigrants certainly was lost; and then Brigham Young spoke out.

The *Deseret News* officially pronounced it a lie. Privately the leaders said: "It was a necessity—we only regret that they had to kill the women." Still new facts kept coming out, and in 1859 Judge Cradlebaugh, with a military escort, visited the section, collected the available evidence, and published it. Since then the Mormons have fallen back point by point. First they insisted no such thing occurred; then, for a few years, that it was the work of Indians alone. About 1865 they began hesitatingly to admit that "a few reprobate whites were engaged—men of no standing in the community." In 1869 the writer hereof collected and published a mass of newly discovered evidence on the subject; in 1870 the Federal officials made a little inquiry. In 1871 the Mormons nominally cut off John D. Lee from fellowship, and sent him on a mission down to the Colorado. There I visited him in July, 1872; spent three days at his house, and heard his version of the massacre.

Meanwhile public sentiment among the Mormons was growing better. Old Mormons died; young ones grew up infidels; Gentile notions took root, and it began to be whispered that murder was a crime even when done by a priest. In 1874 Congress passed a law which took the organization of juries out of the hands of Brigham Young, and all at once there was abundant evidence forthcoming. Then followed the indictment, the capture of Lee, and flight of the others accused, except Bishop Dame, who was arrested soon after Lee. The law's delay and the awkwardness attendant on getting a new jury system into operation prevented Lee's being tried till midsummer, 1875. Then the Mormon town of Beaver became the scene of a strange drama. Correspondents from the East and West flocked thither, and for the first time a little of the inner life of Mormondom was brought to light in open court, and reported to all the world. The most incredulous were compelled to acknowledge Mormon guilt, and there began the series of trials which will eventually make the world acquainted with Brigham Young as he is.

It required the most persevering exertions to get the witnesses together. When Lee was "cut off" from the Church, in 1871, all the Mormons in one day, as it were, changed their tone and began to denounce him as the bloodiest villain of the age. In fact they were extremely anxious to have him punished—they even wanted him strung up at once. As the day of trial drew near, you might have read in all the Mormon prints savage denunciations of his crime, and pitiful plaints "that innocent and noble men should have been accused of complicity with it." When it was announced that Lee was about to turn State's evidence, the Mormon prints indulged in joyful congratulations that his statement would "completely exonerate President Young and the Heads of the Church." All this looked very strange, to say the least. And, sure enough, when Lee's statement was submitted to the District Attorney it was easily proved to be a tissue of lies from beginning to end, as shown by abundant testimony. All the guilty, he said, were either dead or out of the Territory long ago. Not a line did it contain about any one of those in custody. It is now believed to have been a Church trick from the start. The only guilty man, according to Lee, was Klingensmith, the principal witness against him.

This confession was afterwards repudiated by Lee himself; and, of the four he made, the last one alone contained the truth. The trial was set for July 12, 1875, in the District Court of the Second District of Utah, presided over by Hon. Jacob S. Boreman. This gentleman deserves more than a passing notice. A brother of Senator Boreman, of West Virginia, but long a resident of Western Missouri, he unites the genial qualities of the typical Western man with the earnestness of a thorough lawyer; and is, withal, a devout Christian, and a man of irreproachable morals. When he went to Beaver, it was the center of the most unpromising section of Mormondom; but undeterred by the spirit of disloyalty and hatred to Gentile laws and institutions which animated that community, he has held steadily on his course. As an official, he has maintained the dignity of the judiciary; as a Christian, he has fostered the Church and Sabbath-school; as a citizen, he has been of immense advantage to the place. Even his enemies have learned to respect him; and, as the American population grows in numbers, he enjoys the warm friendship of all who make his acquaintance.

Hon. William C. Carey, United States District Attorney, assisted by R. N. Baskin, Esq., of Salt Lake City, and Judge Wheedon, of Beaver, conducted the prosecution. The prisoner's counsel were Messrs. J. G. Sutherland, G. C. Bates, Judge Hoge (a Mormon), Wells Spicer, and W. W. Bishop, the last named of Pioche. It was evident from the start that there were grave differences between the attorneys for the defense. Messrs. Spicer and Bishop were earnestly laboring for the acquittal of their client; to them the Mormon Church was a secondary affair, and they would willingly have cleared Lee by proving that he had orders from his military and ecclesiastical superiors. Messrs. Sutherland and Bates, on the other hand, were really the attorneys of the Church, employed and paid by Brigham Young. That interest was totally indifferent to the fate of Lee, if only the inquiry could be made to stop with him, and the heads of the Church suffer no stain. This want of harmony produced curious and ludicrous results through the entire trial. The first difficulty was in selecting a jury. The two hundred names from which it was to be drawn, under the terms of the Poland Bill, were half of Mormons and half of Gentiles. Then was shown the difficulty attendant on all judicial proceedings with men who held their duty to a church to absolve them from allegiance to the state. The Saints swore without hesitation that they had formed no opinion; many of the Gentiles admitted they had; so the jury, as finally settled upon, consisted of nine Mormons, three Gentiles, and one "Jack-Mormon." Consider the following cases of jurors sworn upon their *voir dire*, and picture to yourself a scene which certainly could have occurred in no other part of the world than Utah:

Joseph Knight, sworn on his *voir dire*—Was a native; lived three years in same town with Lee, but never heard much about him; had formed no opinion. Accepted.

George F. Jarvis sworn—Had lived in St. George (where most of the perpetrators now live) fourteen years; had heard little or no talk of the "affair;" had formed no opinion. Accepted. This Jarvis looked like a thorough "Danite."

Robert Heyborne sworn—Had lived eighteen years in Cedar City, a neighbor to Lee; had heard nothing more than rumor (!!) about such an occurrence; had no opinion! Challenged by prosecution.

Christopher J. Arthur (a son-in-law of Isaac C. Haight, one of the accused) sworn—Lived in Cedar City at the time of the "reported difficulty;" was a member of the militia, but was entirely ignorant of any facts; might have heard something about it; did not remember; formed no opinion. Challenged by prosecution.

John C. Duncan sworn—Had lived twenty-two years in Utah, but heard nothing about the massacre! Had visited Mountain Meadows and saw the grave and a monument, but never asked what it was for! Never heard any body say any thing about any massacre, and had formed no opinion. Accepted as a "model juror." And so on through the list. What a world of trouble Brooklyn courts might have saved, if they had allowed Plymouth Church to select jurors.

This sort of thing occupied several days. Meanwhile the deputy marshals were scouring the country in search of witnesses, every sort of obstruction being thrown in their way by the people. The secretiveness and cunning of the Mormon laity renders proof of daring crime a work of extreme difficulty. "Keep still and mind your own business," is the standing exhortation to the men. "If you see a dog run by the door with your husband's head in its mouth, say nothing till you have consulted with the bishop," are the exact words in which Brigham counseled the women of this district. Joel White, an important witness, was brought in with great difficulty. Marshal Cross traversed the Great Desert alone, and found Klingensmith in Southern California. On Sunday, July 18th, Lee's "confession" was read by the prosecution, and promptly rejected as unworthy of belief. On Friday, the 23d, the trial at last began. After an able opening address by District Attorney Carey, Robert Keyes was put upon the witness stand, and testified as follows:

"In October, 1857, he passed through Mountain Meadows valley, which is situated south-west of Cedar City. Saw two piles of bodies, one composed of women and children, the other of men; the bodies were entirely nude, and seemed to have been thrown promiscuously together; they appeared to have been massacred. Should judge there were sixty or seventy bodies of women and children; saw one man in that pile; the children were aged from one and two months up to twelve years; the small children were most destroyed by wolves and crows; the throats of some were cut, others stabbed with knives; some had balls through them. All the bodies were more or less torn to pieces, except one, the body of a woman, which lay apart a little south-west of the pile. This showed no signs of decay, and had not been touched by the wild animals. The countenance was placid, and seemed to be asleep. The work was not freshly done—supposed the bodies had been here fifteen or sixteen days. Witness passed the ground October 2d, 1857. There were eleven in the company. Seven went to see the pile of slaughtered men which lay a few rods off. Witness did not go. All the clothing he saw was a stocking on the leg of one of the bodies. The woman lying apart had a bullet hole on the left side, a little below the heart."

Asahel Bennett, of the same party, testified to substantially the same facts. Then Philip Klingensmith was called, and there was a general movement in the audience. Every eye and ear was strained, and the man was thoroughly photographed by every attendant. He was a heavy, rather stolid looking Dutchman, six feet high, well muscled, slow, heavy, and phlegmatic. He had been indicted along with the others, and a *nolle* entered. He began with extreme slowness, amounting almost to stupidity, but as he went along gradually grew more animated; his dull eye lit up, the blue veins stood out on his forehead, and his every feature and muscle seemed to work as in sympathy with the horrors he was reciting. In the most blood-curdling scene, where he told of the shooting of some women who had children in their arms, every eye in the room turned as with one impulse to Lee. His light hair fairly vibrated with emotion; his Hibernian features were mingled red and purple; and, as he literally shook in his chair, the great veins stood out on his neck like cords, and he seemed to grasp at his throat as if choking! In that awful moment he tasted the bitterness of death. I would not have recognized him as the man at whose table I ate, three years before, on the Colorado. Beside him sat two of his wives, and close by, most of the Gentile ladies of Beaver.

The material part of Klingensmith's testimony ran thus:

"We were halted a quarter of a mile from the emigrants, and in full sight. A man went on with a flag of truce. A person came out from the emigrant camp, and Lee went down, and he and the emigrant negotiated. They sat down and had a long talk. Lee then went inside the camp, and the soldiers stood in line three or four hours. Lee was inside the intrenchment most of the time, and finally the emigrants came out.

"Higbee ordered the proceedings. Lee went ahead with the wagons containing the men wounded in the attack made by the Indians. The young children and women were marched behind. The men came out next in double rank. The soldiers marched by their side with their pieces across their arms. We were protecting the emigrants. Some expressed their thankfulness at being delivered from the Indians. We marched from a quarter to half a mile, and command was given to halt. The soldiers had been instructed when they halted to fire on the emigrants; might have been shifted to single rank; think they were. Higbee gave the orders to fire; suppose there were fifty men killed; might have been more; none escaped; saw some attempt; there were mounted men to dispatch the fugitives. Bill Stewart chased one fleeing man; I think I saw him fall; he did not go far. Ira Allen was mounted and placed on the left wing. Witness was with the men in the ranks and fired one time. John M. Higbee cut one man's throat. One large woman came running from the wagons calling for her husband. A man standing near to me shot her in the back, and she fell dead. Being ordered to gather up the children, I went a quarter of a mile to the wagons; the wounded men had been killed before we got there; did not see Lee put the children in the wagon; went to Hamlin's house. The soldiers then dispersed. The company from Washington County went south; the company from Cedar City went to Hamlin's. I had my hands full with the children; seventeen of them, from two to seven or eight years of age; two were wounded, and one died on the way. [The witness then details the gathering and distribution of the property.] The draught animals, wagons, and clothing were taken to Cedar City; fifty head of the emigrants' stock were branded with the church brand (a cross). [He also describes the meeting of Lee in Salt Lake, where he had been sent to report the massacre to Brigham Young.] Witness and Charley Hopkins called upon Brigham; he directed witness to turn over the property to Lee. Brigham turned to witness and said: 'What do you know about this affair? Keep it secret and don't talk about it among yourselves.' Lee was present at this interview. Fifty head of cattle were driven to Salt Lake, and sold to Hooper, formerly delegate to Congress, for boots and shoes." [Witness then tells how he was sent to the old lead mines at Vegas, Arizona, with two others to get lead, and when he returned, the property at Cedar City had been auctioned off.]

Judge Sutherland subjected the witness to a long and searching cross-examination, but failed to shake his testimony in the slightest. Joel White testified at great length as to the orders issued for calling out the militia, which he understood to come from Col. Dame; of the massacre and distribution of the property; of the seventeen little children saved, and of afterwards seeing the Indian, deputed for that purpose, cut the throat of the boy who was "big enough to remember and talk about it." He insisted that he took no part in the massacre, and only went with the militia because he feared death if he refused. Klingensmith had admitted actual participation in the killing.

Mrs. Ann Eliza Hoge testified to what was done at both councils, where the massacre was determined and where Lee made his report. Also to hearing the boy say of an Indian: "He killed my pa—he's got on my pa's clothes," and that this boy was taken away by John D. Lee, and never seen again. Witness was a French Mormon; at the time of the massacre the wife of an elder at Harmony. I afterwards talked at great length with her, in Salt Lake City, and gained many important particulars.

Thomas D. Willis told of a council Haight had with him and his father as to the best way to kill the emigrants, and confirmed other witnesses as to the goods distributed. John H. Willis, brother of Thomas, told of driving the team which conveyed the children; and confirmed many other points. William Matthews described the richness of the train; the orders to sell no corn to the emigrants; of the circulation of the story that the emigrants had poisoned a spring, and other matters. William Young gave more in detail the facts of the massacre, where he was present, and confirmed previous testimony on other points. Samuel Pollock told substantially the same story. John Sherratt testified to the storing of the goods, including clothing from the dead bodies, in the cellar of the tithing house at Cedar City, and seeing it sold by Lee at auction. William Bradshaw told of sermons preached to excite the people against the emigrants, and threats of death to all who did not aid the Church in whatever was commanded. Robert Kershaw told the same story; also as to the orders not to trade with the emigrants. He wanted to sell them some vegetables and was forbidden. The bishops had employed Samuel Dodge as special policeman to watch the train and see that no Mormon sold them any thing. John Morgan traded them a small cheese for a bed-quilt, and was "cut off" for it. This man's testimony was of more interest as showing the rigid discipline maintained in the Church, and the danger of disobedience, than as to the massacre. Many other witnesses confirmed the foregoing, and testified to facts I have set forth in the previous summary. All were severely cross-examined, but their testimony remained unshaken.

Five days had passed when the defense began. They first attempted to prove the old slander, invented in 1859, to deceive Judge Cradlebaugh, that the emigrants had poisoned a spring near Corn Creek, and then that they had poisoned the flesh of an ox and given it to the Indians to eat; but broke down completely on both charges. On this point Elisha Hoops testified:

"Lived in Beaver in 1857, and knew George A. Smith and Jesse N. Smith, ex-Bishop Farnsworth, and other shining lights of the Mormon Church. On September 27th of that year he accompanied the Smith party as guard as far north as Fillmore; camped at Corn Creek, and found the Arkansas emigrants encamped there, about 150 paces distant. Some members of the company came and talked to the Smith party; they inquired of George A. Smith where they could get grass and water to recuperate their animals, who referred them to Jacob Hamlin, and he designated Mountain Meadows as the best grazing ground.

An ox lay dead between the two camps, and just as witness' party was about to start, he saw a little German doctor, who belonged to the emigrant company, draw a two-edged dagger with a silver guard—such as gentlemen carry—and make three thrusts into the ox. Next he produced a small, half-ounce vial, filled with a light colored liquid, which he poured into the knife-holes. The question had previously been asked by these men whether the Indians would be likely to eat the carcass, and some thought they would. Witness did not see the train again. Ten or fifteen minutes after the German had poisoned the ox, some Indians came up and dickered with him for it. They finally gave him some buckskins, and then began skinning the ox. Witness supposed the Indians wanted the hide to cut up into soles for their moccasins. Don't know how long they were flaying the animal, as witness' party was driving away at the time."

During noon recess, as it appears, some one suggested to this witness that he had missed his mark in saying that the ox was poisoned just as they started away, and that *fifteen minutes afterwards* the Indians came and *bought* the ox (which they could have for nothing as soon as the emigrants left), and then flayed it! Afternoon he tried to piece out his testimony by saying that the hame-strap broke and they were delayed to fix it. Mr. Baskin pressed him so closely on the cross-examination that he was completely tangled. The other witnesses for the defense produced very little of consequence.

Meanwhile the country had been heard from. A roar of execration had sounded from Maine to California, and Brigham felt the necessity of being exonerated. He filed a deposition, and Judge Sutherland attempted to get it admitted on the trial, on the plea (sworn to in the deposition) that Brigham's health forbade his making the journey. Only a short time before he had gone to St. George, a hundred and fifty miles further south than Beaver. It was not age and ill health, but the dread of Mr. Baskin's cross-examination that kept him out of the court-room. But his deposition was published in the papers, and proved an extraordinary document. Here is the material part of it:

Q. When did you first hear of the attack and destruction of this Arkansas company at Mountain Meadows, in September, 1857?

A. I did not learn any thing of the attack or destruction of the Arkansas company until some time after it had occurred, then only by floating rumors.

Q. Did John D. Lee report to you at any time after this massacre what had been done at that massacre; and if so, what did you reply to him in reference thereto?

A. Within some two or three months after the massacre he called at my office and had much to say with regard to the Indians, their being stirred up to anger and threatening the settlements of the whites, and then commenced giving an account of the massacre. I told him to stop, as, from what I had already learned by rumor, I did not wish my feelings harrowed up with a recital of details.

Q. Did Philip Klingensmith call at your office with John D. Lee, at the time of Lee's making his report; and did you at that time order him to turn over the stock to Lee, and order them not to talk about the massacre?

A. No. He did not call with John D. Lee, and I have no recollection of his ever speaking to me, nor I to him, concerning the massacre or any thing pertaining to the property.

Q. Did you ever give any directions concerning the property taken from the emigrants at the Mountain Meadows massacre, or know any thing as to its disposition?

A. No. I never gave any directions concerning the property taken from the emigrants at the Mountain Meadows massacre; nor did I know any thing of that property or its disposal, and I do not to this day, except from public rumor.

Q. Why did you not, as Governor, institute proceedings forthwith to investigate the massacre and bring the guilty authors to justice?

A. Because another Governor had been appointed by the President of the United States, and was then on the way here to take my place, and I did not know how soon he might arrive; and because the United States Judges were not in the Territory. Soon after Governor Cumming arrived, I asked him to take Judge Cradlebaugh, who belonged to the Southern District, with him, and I would accompany them with sufficient aid to investigate the matter and bring the offenders to justice.

Q. Did you, about the 10th of September, 1857, receive a communication from Isaac C. Haight, or any other person of Cedar City, concerning a company of emigrants, called the Arkansas company?

A. I did receive a communication from Isaac C. Haight or John D. Lee, who was then a farmer for the Indians.

Q. Have you that communication?

A. I have not. I have made a diligent search for it, but can not find it.

Q. Did you answer this communication?

A. I did, to Isaac C. Haight, who was then the acting President at Cedar City.

Q. Will you state the substance of your letter to him?

A. Yes. It was to let this company of emigrants and all companies of emigrants pass through the country unmolested, and to allay the angry feelings of the Indians as much as possible.

(Signed) BRIGHAM YOUNG.

Here was a Governor, Prophet, Indian Superintendent, and absolute head of a theocracy, who only heard of a massacre "some two or three months after it occurred," by "floating rumors," and refused to listen to an account of it lest he might have his "feelings harrowed up!!" Too tender-hearted to do his sworn duty! And so ignorant of what was going on that he heard "only rumors." Verily, the world has been sadly mistaken about Brigham Young.

CHAPTER XXXII.

GUILTY OR NOT GUILTY?

THE case went to the jury, and all Utah waited in deep suspense for the verdict. Among Gentiles the general voice was: "Brigham can't afford to let him be convicted—the Church *must* stand by Lee." The evidence was conclusive of guilt, but we all knew that Church policy alone would dictate the verdict; and it was evident the jury had been "counseled." Agreeable to Western instincts, there was much betting on the result, the odds largely against conviction. But Hon. George C. Bates, the Church attorney, soon arrived at Salt Lake City, and telegraphed to John W. Young, Brigham's "apostate son," as he was then called, that conviction was agreed upon; and John W. took all the bets offered. He was in the Board of Trade rooms at Chicago, while Johnnie Young, Brigham's nephew, went about Salt Lake City doing the same. Then it was known that the Church had taken the least of two evils, and resolved to convict.

But all parties were mistaken. And this from a miscalculation on the part of the Church. It appears that just before the trial the Mormon leaders concluded that they could keep away the most important witnesses; that the prosecution would therefore break down, and it would be safe to acquit. So the Mormon jurymen were "counseled" to that effect. But Baskin and Carey completely outgeneraled the Church and its attorneys; the vigor and daring of the United States marshals insured the attendance of the proper witnesses, and a far worse case was proved than even the bitterest anti-Mormon had looked for. It was then decided by the Church to convict; but it was too late. Seven deputy marshals had been sworn in to watch the jury; and of the three Gentiles on the panel, each constituted himself a special detective to see that no hint from outside reached his Mormon colleagues. Even their correspondence was withheld unless they would consent to have it first read by the judge. Signals were made to them in open court, but they failed to understand what was wanted. They were in blissful ignorance of the storm of rage sweeping over the country, and its effect on their priestly masters, and so obeyed their first instructions. They had all sworn they knew nothing of the case; but on reaching the jury room, they proceeded to controvert the testimony for the prosecution by facts within their own knowledge. The vote stood from first to last, nine for acquittal and three for conviction. The majority first installed the Jack-Mormon, J. C. Heister, in the chair, and then one by one delivered elaborate Mormon sermons: against the prosecuting attorneys, against the court and all Federal officials, against the emigrants, against the United States, against all who were not of the Mormon Church or its most subservient tools. It was perhaps the most curious and irregular jury proceeding ever had in any civilized country. The three Gentiles on the panel held their ground for two days, smiling grimly on their foes, and willing to see the latter commit themselves;

SALT LAKE CITY--1857.

then consented to a disagreement. Promptly, as if pulled by one string, all the Mormon papers appeared with articles having a wonderful family resemblance, and claiming that the verdict was a complete vindication of the Church, and a "pointed rebuke to the prosecution!" And to cap the climax of absurdity, Captain John Codman, their Eastern apologist, rushed into the New York prints with an effusive statement that "Gentile slanderers were at last silenced, and President Brigham Young fully exonerated!"

One can scarcely say whether the Americans in Utah were pleased or chagrined at the result of this trial. They knew that justice would some day be done, and meanwhile the action of the Church would rouse the indignation of the whole country. But even they had underrated this effect. There was a storm of rage in the Rocky

Mountains; the Pacific Coast papers bristled with denunciations of Brigham and the leading Mormons. The staidest journals seemed to grow wild. One advocated a reign of martial law till every murderer in Utah was executed. Another called for the immediate arrest of Brigham, on a bench warrant, before he could fly the country. And still another complained that the civil law was too slow: "The streets of Salt Lake should be ornamented with the heads of the Mormon leaders." Then came answering echoes from the East. Nearly every influential paper in the country called for prompt justice. Utah was excited as I never saw it before. The six Mormon papers literally bowed before the blast, and appeared afraid to say any thing, or had nothing to say. Beyond a few commonplaces about "waiting for the facts," and deprecating "the mob spirit," they attempted no defense. In the States were two journals which can always be depended on to espouse the cause of the Mormons in every emergency—the Omaha *Herald* and the Washington *Capital*. But both remained silent over this affair, virtually admitting that the worst was proved against the Mormons. Captain Codman, with a faithful friendship that did him honor, came to the rescue of Brigham in the columns of the New York *Post;* and the editor of that paper mildly hinted that the Mountain Meadow massacre was "a feature of the Mormon rebellion of 1857," and had perhaps been condoned by Buchanan's proclamation of amnesty, made in 1858. Beyond these no word of palliation was heard; the press and the country were unanimous in the opinion that the Mormon theocracy was morally responsible for this great crime, and that a solemn duty devolved upon the government to see that full justice was done.

But of all the Mormons in Utah, the case of none excited such horror and regret among the Gentiles as that of Hon. W. H. Hooper. It is proved that he received forty head of the murdered emigrants' cattle; and it is scarcely possible that he, a Mormon high in the confidence of the Church, could have been ignorant of the matter. And yet he, through all his congressional career, again and again, and that most bitterly, laid the whole affair on the Indians; and more than once, in company with senators, he solemnly swore that no Mormon had any thing to do with it. He even employed journalists to write up the Mormon view of the case. And can it be possible that all that time he knew it was a cruel lie? Can it be that he has taken the money of the Government even while employing fraud and perjury to defeat justice, and shield those who had murdered its citizens? If so, this earth has no damnation deep enough for him. But among his

Gentile friends there is still some hope. It is barely possible that he may have been deceived; that while all other leading Mormons knew the facts, he was kept in ignorance. From every part of Utah came implorings for some explanation in his favor; and if it shall appear that he acted innocently and ignorantly, ten thousand Gentiles will be gratified.

A calm followed the storm, and Utah took a rest till the next term of court. It was proposed by a few Mormons that Lee should be brought to Salt Lake City and tried; but the proposition was so readily favored by the prosecution that it was promptly withdrawn. Fourteen months passed, and Lee came to his second trial in September, 1876. It excited far less attention in the East, for the nation was then busy with national concerns. But it was evident, almost from the start, that the Church had at last decided to sacrifice Lee. The evidence, as on the former trial, was overwhelming, and Daniel H. Wells, Brigham's right-hand man, was present all the time to see that every thing went right. The witnesses for the defense had forgotten all they ever knew; Mormons, for the prosecution, testified with amazing fluency. Lee was doomed. The Church was present in spirit, and by her representative, consenting unto his death. W. W. Bishop, Esq., the prisoner's counsel, was completely taken by surprise when he saw that the Church was actually aiding the prosecution. It was so totally unlike what he had a right to expect. His theory now is that the prosecuting attorney, or some one in authority, had a secret understanding with Brigham Young to the effect that if Lee were convicted and executed, the matter would stop there, and the main obstacle to the admission of Utah as a State be removed. Mr. Bishop has a great deal to learn about the duplicity and treachery of the Mormon leaders. Five years residence in Utah would clear his vision considerably.

And now occurred one of those strange transformations for which Utah is notorious. On the former trial the prosecution had sought to show that Lee acted *as* a Mormon, inspired by some orders or hints from the heads of the Church. Now Sumner Howard, Esq., U. S. District Attorney, emphatically disclaimed all intention to implicate the Church, and hinted that the conviction of Lee would be the exoneration of Brigham. Mr. Bishop, for the defense, on the other hand, made a fierce assault on the heads of the Church, for their evident intention to sacrifice Lee. He said:

"I see a State government looming up in the distance. I see a future prospect for individuals, political and financial. I see a shifting of the responsibility for this crime upon John D. Lee, and I see the Gentiles, who aid the shifting, riding into the United States Senate." Mr. Howard disclaimed any such bargain, but stated his satisfaction at the fact that the jury was composed entirely of Mormons. He told them that Mormon juries were now on trial, and their verdict must decide whether their church was to stand before the world convicted of shielding assassins. Despite his disclaimer, it is generally believed in Utah that the Mormon authorities were led to believe the death of Lee would strengthen them before Congress. As strategy, this was a great success for the prosecution; whether it was "professional," lawyers must decide. One thing, however, is certain: it did not produce the effect desired by Brigham; the world is more than ever convinced of his connivance at crime or concealment of crime.

My sometime friend, Jacob Hamlin, figured extensively on this trial. Without a blush he succeeded in remembering a score of things he had forgotten on former occasions; and gave, at great length, Lee's statement to him, made soon after the tragedy. Lee told him in detail of the murder of the two girls who escaped the general massacre; and the manner in which Hamlin recited Lee's account convinced some who heard it that another crime was committed before the girls were killed.

Hamlin testified that he had never before repeated Lee's words except to George A. Smith and Brigham Young, and that Brigham told him "to keep still about these things till the proper time came to tell it all!" I ask the Eastern reader to pause at this point, and ponder this startling fact. Here was Jacob Hamlin, a most reputable citizen of southern Utah, a man whom I know to be in many respects high-toned and honorable, receiving the confession of a double-dyed murderer, carrying it in his mind all these nineteen years, and never going near a court or grand jury, never breathing it to an officer, just because Brigham Young so commanded! And in the spring of 1859, when Brigham made a great show of wanting the matter investigated, Hamlin was with General W. H. Carleton and other U. S. officials—gave them a circumstantial account of "this Indian massacre," assisted them to gather up the children, and could not remember any thing whatever tending to criminate a white man. At the mere request of Brigham Young this most excellent citizen, whom I *know* by personal intercourse to be a pleasant gentleman, a patriarch in his town, told lie on top of lie, and covered himself fathoms deep with perjury to screen his brother Mormon. And "when the proper time came," with sublime coolness he came into court and told it all, still at the command of Brigham Young! And yet there are lawyers in the East, and statesmen in Congress, who will maintain that Brigham had no control in southern Utah in 1857; that the massacre was done against his wish; that he did not know of it, in fact!

"Oh, judgment! thou art fled to brutish beasts,
And men have lost their reason."

Samuel Knight and Samuel McMurdy testified to seeing Lee kill several persons; that he blew a woman's brains out, beat one man to death with a gun, and shot others; then came to the wagons and shot all the wounded men with a pistol. At this point in the testimony Lee broke down, and when remanded to his cell walked the floor a long time, cursing the Mormon leaders who, he said, had betrayed him. He knew, even before his attorney did, that the Church had decided to give him up; he had suspected this at the start, and urged his attorney to secure a few Gentiles on the jury, in the hope that they might revolt against this conspiracy. But this had proved impossible. All the Gentiles called had heard or read of the case; the Mormons called "had never heard of it, and had formed no opinion." For "model jurors" they could beat New York City. When the argument of counsel began, the defense had no recourse but to abuse the witnesses. Mr. Bishop took the broad ground that all those present at the massacre were equally guilty and not to be believed.

At noon of September 20th, Judge Boreman delivered his charge to the jury; they retired, and at 3:30 P. M. returned into court with this verdict:

BEAVER CITY, Sept. 20, 1876.
We, the jurors, duly sworn and impaneled to try the case wherein John D. Lee is indicted for murder, do find the said John D. Lee guilty of murder in the first degree.
A. M. FARNSWORTH, Foreman.

By order of the Court, the Marshal brought Lee to the bar. The Court asked:

"John D. Lee, have you any thing to say why the sentence of death should not be pronounced against you in accordance with the verdict of the jury?"

Lee: "I have not."

Court: "You, John D. Lee, prisoner at the bar, have, by the verdict of a jury, been found guilty of murder in the first degree. The proof was clear and positive. At the trial last year the evidences of guilt were plain, but three-fourths of the jury, from some cause, were then for your acquittal. The testimony on the present trial is mainly from witnesses who could not then be obtained. From some cause this evidence is now unsealed, and the witnesses are found ready in your case to tell what part you played in the great crime. They will hereafter have opportunity of telling what others did to aid in planning and executing it. The fact that the evidence was not brought out on this trial to criminate some other leaders, does not show that such evidence does not exist. * * * According to the evidence on the former trial, the massacre seems to have been the result of a vast conspiracy extending from Salt Lake City to the bloody field. The emigrants were hounded all along the line of travel, and nowhere were the citizens permitted to give or sell them any thing to sustain life in man or animal, though they were in great need thereof.

"The men who actually participated in the deed are not the only guilty parties. Although the evidence shows plainly that you were a willing participant in the massacre; yet both trials taken together show that others, and some high in authority, inaugurated and decided upon the wholesale slaughter of the emigrants. That slaughter took place nineteen years ago. From that time to the present term of court there has been throughout the Territory a persistent and determined opposition to any investigation of the massacre. * * * But their efforts to smother and crush out investigation were found to avail them no longer. It was impossible to longer delay when the inside facts of the conspiracy should be brought out; and they have suddenly changed their policy, and seem now to be consenting to your death. * * * The unoffending victims, though their mouths are closed in this world, will meet you at the bar of Almighty God, where the secrets of all hearts shall be made known. And the guilty can not avoid that tribunal. * * * In accordance with the verdict of the jury, and the law, it becomes my duty to pass the sentence of death upon you; and in doing this the statute requires that you may have a choice, if you desire, of three different modes of execution, to-wit: by hanging, by shooting, or by beheading. If you have any choice or desire in this respect, you can now express it."

Lee: "I prefer to be shot."

Court: "As you have made choice, and expressed it, that you be executed by being shot, it follows that such shall be the judgment of the Court. The judgment of the Court, therefore, is, that you be taken hence to a place of confinement within this Territory; that you there be safely kept in confinement until Friday, the 26th day of January, 1877; that between the hours of 10 o'clock A. M. and 3 o'clock P. M. of that day, you be taken from your place of confinement and in this district publicly shot until you are dead; and may Almighty God have mercy on your soul!"

But an appeal was taken, and the Supreme Court of Utah suspended the execution. The case was heard in that court, and an able opinion delivered by Justice Philip H. Emerson, fully sustaining the court below, and concurred in by all the justices. The mandate directed the Second District Court to fix a new date for execution, and Judge Boreman named Friday, March 23, 1877. There was much talk of an appeal to the Supreme Court of the United States, but none was taken, though Congress has granted this privilege in murder cases to Utah alone of all the Territories. Still Lee did not give up all hope. There are mysterious hints of a secret understanding between him and the district attorney, by which the latter was to secure a pardon or commutation in return for evidence that would convict all the others guilty of complicity in the massacre. Lee's wife, Rachel, shared his confinement to the last, and Lee worked steadily on his confession. But if there was any such agreement, it was set aside, and the convicted man at last resigned all hope. He then wrote out a full confession, and gave it to the district attorney; but the latter has only published such portions as would in no way interfere with his plans for convicting others. A previous confession written by Lee, and delivered to his attorney, W. W. Bishop, Esq., has also been published—the lawyer having agreed with Lee to sell the paper to the press, take his fee therefrom, and pay over the remainder to Rachel. In these confessions Lee at last tells nearly all the truth, still shielding himself, however, and denying any actual killing. I append the most important sections:

My name is John Doyle Lee. I was born September 6, 1812, at Kaskaskia, Randolph County, Illinois. My mother belonged to the Catholic Church, and I was christened in the faith. My parents died while I was still a child, and my boyhood was one of trial and hardship. I married Agatha Ann Woolsey in 1833, and moved to Fayette County, Illinois, on Sucker Creek. There I became wealthy. In 1836 I became acquainted with some traveling Mormon preachers. I bought, read, and believed the Book of Mormon. I sold my property in Illinois, and moved to Far West, in Missouri, in 1837, where I joined the Mormon Church, and became intimately acquainted with Joseph Smith, Brigham Young, and other leaders of the Church of Jesus Christ of Latter-day Saints. I was subsequently initiated into the order of Danites at its first formation. The members of this order were solemnly sworn to obey all the orders of the priesthood of the Mormon Church, to do any and all things as commanded. The "destroying angels" of the Mormon Church were selected from this organization. I took an active part as a Mormon soldier, as it was the recurring conflicts between the people and the Mormons which made Jackson County, Missouri, historic ground. When the Mormons were expelled from Missouri, I was one of the first to settle at Nauvoo, Illinois, where I took an active part in all that was done by the Church or city. I had charge of the construction of many public buildings there, and was the policeman and body-guard of Joseph Smith at Nauvoo. After his death I held the same position to Brigham Young, who succeeded Joseph Smith as Prophet, Priest, and Revelator in the Church. I was Recorder for the Quorum of Seventy, head clerk of the Church, and organized the priesthood in the Order of Seventy. I took all the degrees of the Endowment House, and stood high in the priesthood. I traveled extensively throughout the United States as a Mormon missionary, and acted as trader and financial agent of the Church. From the death of Joseph Smith until the settlement at Salt Lake City, I was one of the locating committee that selected sites for various towns and cities in Utah Territory. I held many offices in the Territory, and was a member of the Mormon legislature, and was probate judge of Washington County, Utah. Immediately after Joseph Smith received the revelation concerning polygamy, I was informed of its doctrines by said Joseph Smith and the Apostles. I believe in the doctrine, and have been sealed to eighteen women, three of whom are sisters, and one was the mother of three of my wives. I was sealed to this old woman for her soul's salvation. I was an honored man in the Church, flattered and regarded by Brigham Young and the Apostles, until 1868, when I was cut off from the Church and selected as a scapegoat to suffer for and bear the sins of my people. As a duty to myself and mankind I now confess all that I did at the Mountain Meadow Massacre, without animosity to any one, shielding none, and giving the facts as they existed. Those with me at that time were acting under orders from the Church of Jesus Christ of Latter-day Saints. The horrid deeds then committed were done as a duty which we believed we owed to God and our Church. We were all sworn to secrecy before and after the massacre. The penalty for giving information concerning it was death. As I am to suffer death for what I then did, and have been betrayed both by those who gave orders to act and those who were the most active of my assistants, I now give the world the true facts as they exist, and tell why the massacre was committed, and who were the active participants.

In the month of September, 1857, the company of emigrants, known as the "Arkansas Company," arrived in Parowan, Iron County, Utah, on their way to California. At Parowan young Aden, one of the company, saw and recognized one William Laney, a Mormon resident of Parowan. Aden and his father had rescued Laney from an anti-Mormon mob in Tennessee several years before, and saved his life. He (Laney), at the time he was attacked by the mob, was a Mormon missionary in Tennessee. Laney was glad to see his friend and benefactor, and invited him to his house, and gave him some garden sauce to take back to the camp with him.

The same evening it was reported to Bishop (Colonel) Dame that Laney had given potatoes and onions to the man Aden, one of the emigrants. When the report was made to Bishop Dame he raised his hand and crooked his little finger in a significant manner to one Barney Carter, his brother-in-law, and one of the "Angels of Death." Carter, without another word, walked out, went to Laney's house with a long picket in his hand, called Laney out, and struck him a heavy blow on the head, fracturing his skull, and left him on the ground for dead. C. Y. Webb and Isaac Newman, President of the "High Council," both told me that they saw Dame's maneuvers. James McGuffee, then a resident of Parowan—but through oppression has been forced to leave there, and is now a merchant in Pahranagat valley, near Pioche, Nevada—knows these facts.

About the last of August, 1857, some ten days before the Mountain Meadow Massacre, the company of emigrants passed through Cedar City. George A. Smith—then First Councilor in the Church and Brigham Young's right-hand man—came down from Salt Lake City, preaching to the different settlements. I, at that time, was in Washington County, near where St. George now stands. He sent for me. I went to him, and he asked me to take him to Cedar City by way of Fort Clara and Pinto settlements, as he was on business, and must visit all the settlements. We started on our way up through the cañon. We saw bands of Indians, and he (George A. Smith) remarked to me that these Indians, with the advantage they had of the rocks, could use up a large company of emigrants, or make it very hot for them. After pausing for a short time he said to me, "Brother Lee, what do you think the brethren would do if a company of emigrants should come down through here making threats? Don't you think they would pitch into them?" I replied that "they certainly would." This seemed to please him, and he again said to me, "And you really think the brethren would pitch into them?" "I certainly do," was my reply; "and you had better instruct Colonel Dame and Haight to attend to it that the emigrants are permitted to pass, if you want them to pass unmolested." He continued: "I asked Isaac (meaning Haight) the same question, and he answered me just as you do, and I expect the boys would pitch into them." I again said to him that he had better say to Governor Young, that if he wants emigrant companies to pass without molestation, that he must instruct Colonel Dame or Major Haight to that effect; for if they are not ordered otherwise, they will use them up by the help of the Indians.

The confession then tells of the councils in which the destruction of the emigrants was decreed; the gathering of the Mormon militia, and the siege down to the time treachery was decided upon, and continues as follows:

The plan agreed upon there was to meet them with a flag of truce, tell them that the Indians were determined on their destruction; that we dare not oppose the Indians, for we were at their mercy; that the best we could do for them (the emigrants) was to get them and what few traps we could take in the wagons, to lay their arms in the bottom of the wagon, and cover them up with bed-clothes, and start for the settlement as soon as possible, and to trust themselves in our hands. The small children and wounded were to go with the two wagons, the women to follow the wagons and the men next, the troops to stand in readiness on the east side of the road ready to receive them. Shirtz and Nephi Johnson were to conceal the Indians in the brush and rocks till the company was strung out on the road to a certain point, and at the watchword "Halt! do your duty!" each man was to cover his victim and fire. Johnson and Shirtz were to rally the Indians, and rush upon and dispatch the women and larger children.

It was further told the men that President Haight said that if we were united in carrying out the instructions, we would receive a "celestial reward." I said I was willing to put up with a less reward, if I could be excused. "How can you do this without shedding innocent blood?" Here I got another lampooning for my stubbornness and disobedience to the priesthood. I was told that there was not a drop of innocent blood to the whole company of emigrants, and was also referred to the Gentile nation who refused the children of Israel passage through their country when Moses led them out of Egypt— that the Lord held that crime against them; and that when Israel was strong the Lord commanded Joshua to slay the whole nation, men, women, and children. "Have not these people done worse than that to us? Have they not threatened to murder our leaders and Prophet? and have they not boasted of murdering our patriarchs and prophets, Joseph and Hyrum? Now talk about shedding innocent blood!" They said I was a good, liberal, free-hearted man, but too much of this sympathy would be always in the way; that every man now had to show his colors; that it was not safe to have a Judas in camp. Then it was proposed that every man express himself; that if there was a man who would not keep a close mouth, they wanted to know it then. This gave me to understand what I might expect if I continued to oppose. Major Higbee said: "Brother Lee is right. Let him take an expression of the people." I knew I dare not refuse, so I had every man speak and express himself. All said they were willing to carry out the counsel of their leaders; that the leaders had the Spirit of God, and knew better what was right than they did.

The massacre is then related in detail down to the time when the wounded men in the wagons were killed, after which the confession continues:

At this moment I heard the scream of a child. I looked up and saw an Indian have a little boy by the hair of his head, dragging him out of the hind end of the wagon, with a knife in his hand, getting ready to cut his throat. I sprang for the Indian, with my revolver in hand, and shouted to the top of my voice: "*Arick, oomat, cot too sooet*," (stop, you fool.) The child was terror-stricken. His chin was bleeding. I supposed it was the cut of a knife, but afterward learned that it was done on the wagon-box as the Indian yanked the boy down by the hair of the head. I had no sooner rescued this child, than another Indian seized a little girl by the hair. I rescued her as soon as I could speak; I told the Indians that they must not hurt the children—that I would die before they should be hurt; that we would buy the children of them. Before this time the Indians had rushed up around the wagon in quest of blood, and dispatched the two runaway wounded men.

* * * * * * * *

I got up, saw the children, and among the others the boy who was pulled by the hair of his head out of the wagon by the Indian—and saved by me. That boy I took home and kept home until Dr. Forney, Government Agent, came to gather up the children and take them East. He took the boy with the others. The boy's name was Fancher. His father was captain of the train. He was taken East, and adopted by a man in Nebraska, named Richard Sloan. He remained East several years, and then returned to Utah, and is now a convict in the Utah penitentiary, having been convicted the past year for the crime of highway robbery. He is well known by the name of "Idaho Bill," but his true name is William Fancher. His little sister was also taken East, and is now the wife of a man working for the Union Pacific Railroad Company, near Green River.

* * * * * * * *

Some two weeks after the deed was done, Isaac C. Haight sent me to report to Governor Young in person. I asked him why he did not send a written report. He replied that I could tell him more satisfactorily than he could write, and if I would stand up and shoulder as much of the responsibility as I could conveniently, that it would be a feather in my cap some day, and that I would get a celestial salvation, but the man that shrunk from it now would go to hell. I went and did as I was commanded. Brigham asked me if Isaac C. Haight had written a letter to him. I replied, not by me; but he wished me to report in person. "All right," said Brigham. "Were you an eye-witness?" "To the most of it," was my reply. Then I proceeded and gave him a full history of all, except that of my opposition. That I left out entirely. I told him of the killing of the women and children, and the betraying of the company; that, I told him, I was opposed to; but I did not say to him to what extent I was opposed to it, only that I was opposed to shedding innocent blood. "Why," said he, "you differ from

Isaac (Haight), for he said there was not a drop of innocent blood in the whole company."

When I was through he said it was awful; that he cared nothing about the men, but the women and children was what troubled him. I said: "President Young, you should either release them from their obligation, or sustain them when they do what they have entered into the most sacred obligations to do." He replied: "I will think over the matter, and make it a subject of prayer, and you may come back in the morning and see me." I did so. He said: "John, I feel first-rate. I asked the Lord, if it was all right for the deed to be done, to take away the vision of the deed from my mind, and the Lord did so, and I feel first-rate. It is all right. The only fear I have is of traitors." He told me never to lisp it to any mortal being, not even to Brother Heber. President Young has always treated me with the friendship of a father since, and has sealed several women to me since, and has made my home his home when in that part of the Territory—until danger has threatened him. This is a true statement, according to my best recollection.

This statement I have made for publication after my death, and have agreed with a friend to have the same published, with many facts pertaining to other matters connected with the crimes of the Mormon people under the leadership of the priesthood, from a period before the butchery of Nauvoo, to the present time, for the benefit of my family, and that the world might know the black deeds that have marked the way of the Saints from the organization of the Church of Jesus Christ of Latter-day Saints, to the period when a weak and too pliable tool lays down his pen to face the executioner's guns for deeds which he is not more guilty than others, who to-day are wearing the garments of the priesthood, and living upon the "tithing" of a deluded and priest-ridden people. My autobiography, if published, will open the eyes of the world to the monstrous deeds of the leaders of the Mormon people, and will also place in the hands of the attorney for the Government, the particulars of some of the most blood-curdling crimes that have been committed in Utah, which, if properly followed up, will bring many down from their high places in the Church to face offended justice upon the gallows. So mote it be.

(Signed)   JOHN D. LEE.

The autobiography, of which Lee speaks, is for the present withheld, for obvious reasons. But when the confession was forwarded to the New York *Herald* for publication, the proprietor telegraphed Brigham, asking if he had any statement to make in connection with the publication. Brigham replied as follows:

ST. GEORGE, UTAH, March 22.

James Gordon Bennett, New York:—Yours just received. If Lee has made a statement in his confession implicating me, as charged in your telegraph of the 21st inst., it is utterly false. My course of life is too well known by thousands of honorable men for them to believe for one moment such accusations.

(Signed)   BRIGHAM YOUNG.

Only that and nothing more. And straightway all the Mormon papers of Utah, and all of Brigham's apologists in the East, cried out that the Prophet was completely exonerated; that no one would take the word of a murderer like Lee against so good a man as Brigham. How easily are people deceived, if they ardently wish to be.

The last day drew near, and United States Marshal, William Nelson, with an eye to poetical justice, selected Mountain Meadows as the scene of execution. Judge Boreman did not approve of this, thinking it savored of revenge and spectacular display; he would have preferred the execution should take place at Beaver, where the court was held. But few officials and press representatives knew of this selection till after the escort had left Beaver. Several reporters were present. As his last hour drew near, Lee became very cheerful and communicative. The execution ground was about a hundred yards east of the monument, which is now but a mass of rocks. Lee was attended by Rev. Mr. Stokes, to whom he finally confessed that he killed five of the emigrants with his own hands. This was his first and last confession of actual murder. The shooting squad of five men was detailed from the guard of soldiers who had escorted the party from Camp Cameron. They were armed with needle-guns, and stood no more than forty feet from the coffin, on which sat the condemned. At 10:30 A. M., Marshal Nelson read the death-warrant, and asked Lee if he had any thing to say. Mr. Fennemore, an artist, had meanwhile arranged his material for taking a photograph of the scene. Lee said:

"I want to speak to that man."

Fennemore replied: "In a second, Mr. Lee."

Lee: "I want to ask you a favor. I want you to furnish my three wives each a copy of my photograph—a copy of the same to Rachel A., Sarah C., and Emma B."

Fennemore (in a low tone): "I will."

Marshal Nelson (aloud): "He says he will do it, Mr. Lee."

Lee (in a somewhat pleading tone): "Please forward them—*you will?*"

Lee then stood up and said in calm and measured tones:

I have but little to say this morning. Of course I feel that I am upon the brink of eternity, and the solemnities of eternity should rest upon my mind at the present. I have made out, or endeavored to do so, a manuscript and an abridged history of my life. This is to be published, sir. I have given my views and feelings with regard to all these things. I feel resigned to my fate. I feel as calm as a summer morning. I have done nothing designedly wrong. My conscience is clear before God and man, and I am ready to meet my Redeemer. This it is that places me on this field. I am not an infidel. I have not denied God or His mercy. I am a strong believer in these things. The most I regret is parting with my family. Many of them are unprotected, and will be left fatherless. When I speak of those little ones, they touch a tender chord within me. (Here Lee's voice faltered perceptibly.) I have done nothing designedly wrong in this affair. I used my utmost endeavors to save this people. I would have given worlds, were it at my command, to have avoided that calamity. But I could not. I am sacrificed to satisfy feelings, and I am used to gratify parties, but I am ready to die. I have no fear. Death has no terror. No particle of mercy have I asked of the court or officials to spare my life. I do not fear death. I shall never go to a worse place than the one I am now in. I have said it to my family, and I will say it to-day, that the Government of the United States sacrifices its best friend, and that is saying a great deal, but it is true. I am a true believer in the gospel of Jesus Christ. I do not believe every thing that is now practiced and taught by Brigham Young. I do not agree with him. I believe he is leading the people astray; but I believe in the gospel as it was taught in its purity by Joseph Smith in former days. I have my reasons for saying this. I used to make this man's will my pleasure, and did so for thirty years. See how and what I have come to this day. I have been sacrificed in a cowardly and dastardly manner.

There are thousands of people in the Church, honorable, good-hearted, that I cherish in my heart. I regret to leave my family. They are near and dear to me. These are things to rouse my sympathy. I declare I did nothing wrong designedly in this unfortunate affair. I did every thing in my power to save all the emigrants, but I am the one that must suffer. Having said this, I feel resigned. I ask the Lord my God to extend his mercy to me, and receive my spirit. My labors are done.

EXECUTION OF JOHN D. LEE.

Having thus spoken he sat down on his coffin.

The minister offered a fervent prayer. The spectators were ordered to fall back. Marshal Nelson gave command:

"Make ready! Aim! Fire!"

The five rifles cracked simultaneously, and Lee fell back dead, without a struggle. Five balls had passed through him in the immediate vicinity of the heart. Either alone would have caused instant death. His countenance was perfectly placid; his lips parted to something very near a smile.

Thus died John Doyle Lee, a fanatic and a sensualist, a devotee and a murderer, a kind father, a pleasant host, a hospitable gentleman and a remorseless bigot. The same qualities which, with proper education and surroundings, would have made him an energetic, active and valuable citizen of a Christian community, in Mormonism made him a polygamist and a murderer. Doubtless there was a time in his early life when the weight of a hair either way would have determined the course of his career—as the drop falling on one side of a Minnesota roof may flow down to the sunny gulf, on the other side to the frozen ocean. The accident of an hour turned his life into the channels of Mormonism; thence his way was steadily downward, and the perversion of those forces which would have made him honored in Illinois, consigned him to infamous remembrance in Utah. So may all who are conscious of unregulated passion look upon him as the pious bishop did upon the hardened convict, "There go I, but for the grace of God."

It only remains to inquire into the probable, or possible, fate of his companions in crime, and the proof of Brigham Young's complicity. Of those indicted, only George Adair and Elliott Wilden are in custody, both minor characters in the tragedy, though other participants testified on the trial. But the really guilty, such as Isaac Haight, John M. Higbee and William C. Stewart—the men who planned and carried the matter through exultingly—are in hiding in the Indian country. For a long time they lived in a mountain fastness of southeastern Utah, and Hon. G. C. Bates, their attorney, visited and conversed with them in their chosen stronghold. He gave me a dramatic account of his experience there; of his going in at night and returning the next night, by a way so devious that none but Indians or the most accomplished scouts could find it. But even that place did not make them feel safe; and since the Mormons extended their southern settlements into New Mexico and Arizona, the murderers have retreated there. The community still shields them, but, as time passes, there is a growing number of Mormons who would like to see justice done. The United States Government now has one duty to perform: to offer a moderate reward for their capture, or guarantee the expense. Let this be done, and Marshal William Stokes will pick his assistants and have those assassins in the Beaver jail within two months.

Marshal Stokes, to whom Utah and the cause of justice are so greatly indebted, deserves more than a passing notice. A native of New York, but reared in Wisconsin, he was then thirty-three years of age, in the very prime of mental and physical vigor. He served four years in Company "D," of the Eighth Wisconsin, and was in twenty-five battles and skirmishes, including the battle of Corinth and assault on Vicksburg. With a *posse* of but five men he executed the skillful movement ending in the capture of Lee; and if our somewhat too cautious Congress will but vote to pay the expense, he will capture the others.

Was Brigham Young guilty? To me the evidence seems overwhelming that he was accessory *after* the fact—not quite conclusive that he ordered the massacre. But there is a fearful array of evidence, and steadily accumulating, to that effect, though much of it is moral and inferential rather than direct. Its nature may be judged from one fact: the longer a Gentile lives in Utah the more he is convinced of Brigham's guilt, for he sees more and more that no such action would have been taken by those southern Mormons unless they had been certain of Brigham's approval. The empire that man had obtained over Utah in 1857 and succeeding years, has never been exceeded on earth; it is something Americans can never hope to understand until they have lived years in Utah. As Prophet, he held the "keys of the kingdom," and all Mormons believed that none could enter there without his voucher. As Priest, he alone had authority to "seal" and divorce, whether for time or eternity. As Seer, he literally directed every movement of the community. As Revelator, they regarded his words as the very oracles of God. As First President, he was official head of all orders of the priesthood. He was then officially styled "Prophet, Priest, Seer and Revelator, First President and Trustee-in-Trust of the Church of Jesus Christ of Latter-day Saints." In the last capacity he had control of all the property concerns of Utah. Every thing was done and every body directed by priestly "counsel." No move of any importance was entered upon without his consent; no lay member of his own motion ever ventured upon any new enterprise. Brigham must be consulted if he would change his town or residence, his associations or his business, go abroad or remain at home, buy a farm or take another wife. Nor is this all. Besides being their spiritual head and guide, he was military commander over Dame, Haight and Lee. If there is any power possible on this earth which he did not have, many years search have failed to show it. Is it credible that, under such circumstances, such a momentous affair could take place without his consent? Scores of times have I heard Brigham speak of the power he exercised over "this people." It had been his boast for thirty years that the Saints would do nothing against his wish. We must judge him by his own utterances and those of his nearest friends.

But there are direct evidences. First: His sermon that if emigrants tried to cross the Territory he would "turn the Indians loose on them." Second: His admitted knowledge of the affair soon after it occurred, and failure to denounce or seek to have the guilty punished. Third: His complete silence thereon in his next report as Indian Agent. Fourth: His persistent falsehood for fifteen years afterwards in denying that the whites had any thing to do with it. Fifth: His continued attempts to deceive all who made inquiry into the matter, and a score of other facts already mentioned. Collateral to the main issue, there are other crimes of which Brigham was undoubtedly guilty. The public files show that the year after the massacre he wrote to Indian Commissioner Denver charging the crime upon the Indians—this in accordance with the arrangement made with the murderers, of which Lee speaks—and that he actually charged the Government for the material taken from the murdered emigrants and given to the Indians! Here is a clear case of perjury, proved by documentary evidence. And for this also, had an honest jury been found in Utah, he would have been indicted. Nor is this all. In 1864 a member of the Indian Committee visited Utah, and to him Brigham made complaint that the Mormons had not been paid for their expenses in the late Indian wars. The official gave as a reason that charges against them were on file in connection with Mountain Meadows. Then Brigham called high heaven to witness that the Saints had nothing to do with that massacre—"it was all the work of Indians." As late as 1869, the *Deseret News*, Brigham Young's official organ, contained an article, written by Apostle George Q. Cannon, later a Delegate in Congress from Utah, bitterly denying that any Mormon was engaged. Thus the Mormon authorities went on year after year swearing to lies and publishing lies about Mountain Meadows, when, according to all the evidence on the trial, they knew the facts then as well as we know them now! What rational explanation can be given of such crookedness, except that they had some sort of guilty connection with the actual participants?

I have but touched upon the mass of evidence. Brigham Young has many apologists in the East, but among them all I have heard no attempt at explanation of these things. There is one man to whose life-long friendship the Mormons are more indebted for the immunity they enjoy than to any other one agency. Colonel (since General) Thomas L. Kane, a gentleman of high character, accompanied them in their journey from Council Bluffs to Salt Lake; was the guest of Brigham Young; acted as their mediator in 1858, and has been their apologist to the Government ever since. He first saw them in their extreme misery, after their expulsion from Nauvoo, and his sympathies were powerfully excited in their behalf. He gave his views of them in a fascinating lecture, delivered before the Historical Society of Pennsylvania, March 26, 1850, and that lecture has probably covered more crimes and done more harm than any ever delivered in America. Assuredly, Colonel Kane was benevolent and sympathetic; but it is equally certain that his sympathy overbalanced his judgment. The value of his testimony may be judged from a few facts. He gave his solemn assurance that the Saints were a law-abiding people; that they were rigid moralists in all that pertained to the relations of the sexes; that all the charges made against them, including polygamy, were false and scandalous, and made with a view of getting their property. At the very time these words were written, and when Colonel Kane was a guest in his tent, Brigham was *the husband of four wives!* I am personally acquainted with dozens of men and women who were born in polygamy at the very time Colonel Kane was with the Saints, proving that polygamy had no existence! The Saints were denying the practice then; they now avow its existence since 1843, and laugh at the Gentiles for having been deceived. Between 1843 and 1852 they put on record fourteen sworn or printed denials of the existence of polygamy; since 1852 they have denied their own denials, and now claim that polygamy was an established institution among them three years before they left Illinois. Colonel Kane speaks as if it were little short of blasphemy to doubt the high character of Mormon women; and in the postscript to the second edition he insists that the Mormons, as he knew them, had "a general correctness of deportment and purity of character above the average of ordinary communities." And yet in that same camp were men having mother and daughters as "wives;" one woman who had left her husband in Boston to follow Brigham, and another who had got a divorce from Dr. Seely, of Nauvoo, to become Brigham's "second!" Oscar Young, oldest son of Brigham's third or fourth "wife," was born near the Missouri River about the time Colonel Kane was reporting to the President that no polygamy existed among the Saints; and the perpetrator now acknowledges four murders committed near there, while the Colonel was indorsing the law-abiding Mormons! A little further on the Colonel recites with amazement that gulls were unknown in Utah, till the Mormons needed them to eat the crickets which were devouring their crops! And this, when every explorer for a century past had told of the Salt Lake gulls, which are certainly as much indigenous to the Great Basin as the blackbird is to Ohio! There remains but one question in my mind: Could a man of Colonel Kane's acumen be so grossly deceived, or was there some other reason?

But a little later Colonel Kane *accidentally* states a very important fact. Having endeavored to show that the Mormons in Illinois were sadly belied by their neighbors, who wanted to drive them away and get their property, he adds: "When they left Nauvoo all their fair-weather friends forsook them. Priests and elders, scribes and preachers, deserted by whole councils at a time; each talented knave, of whose craft they had been victims, finding his own pretext for abandoning them, without surrendering the money-bag of which he was the holder." So it appears there were "talented knaves" in the Church while it was at Nauvoo; there were thieves who ran off with "money-bags," and "fair-weather friends" who used the Mormons. And yet while these people were *in* the Church, stealing from Gentiles and laying it to Saints, and stealing from Saints and laying it to Gentiles, Colonel Kane can find no reason for outside hostility to Nauvoo, except that the Gentiles wanted their property. He proves that nearly half the Nauvoo community was composed of adventurers from all parts of the country, "talented knaves" who proved to be thieves, and then maintains that the Illinois Gentiles were responsible for all the troubles there! Verily, benevolence is a grand sentiment; but it *may* be overdone.

CHAPTER XXXIII.

THE NOBLE RED MAN.

On a bright Sunday in June, 1876, while the nation was on the top wave of the Centennial enthusiasm and opening of the Presidential campaign, the news went flashing over the wires that General George A. Custer and all his command lay dead in a Montana valley, the victims of a Sioux massacre. With him had died his two brothers, his brother-in-law and a nephew; and of all that entered that battle not one white man survived. For a brief space there was hope that it might be a false report, but soon followed official papers which confirmed every ghastly detail of the first dispatches. For a few days the public sorrow overcame all other considerations; then, by natural revulsion, sorrow

THE NOBLE RED MAN.

gave place to indignation, and that in turn to a fierce demand for investigation and a victim. The public must have a victim when there has been a misfortune. Then ensued a performance which was no credit to us as a nation. His opponents attacked President Grant as the real cause of Custer's death; his friends foolishly defended the President by criticising Custer; the latter's friends in the army savagely attacked Major Reno and Captain Benteen as being the cause of the General's misfortunes, and thus the many-sided fight went on. Before stating any facts bearing on this issue, a brief sketch of General Custer's previous experience on the plains is in order.

George Armstrong Custer was born at New Rumley, Ohio, December 5, 1839, and was consequently but thirty-seven years old at the time of his death. At ten years of age he went to live with an older sister in Monroe, Michigan, and ever after considered that place his home. There, on the ninth of February, 1864, he married Elizabeth, only daughter of Judge Daniel S. Bacon. He entered West Point as a cadet in 1857, and graduated four years after—away down in the list. Worse still, he was court-martialed for some minor breach of etiquette, and, badly as officers were needed just then, had some trouble in getting located in the army. But we long ago learned that rank at West Point by no means settles the officer's later standing in the army. Soon after graduating he was made Second Lieutenant, and assigned to Company "G," Second United States Cavalry, and arrived just in time to take a little part in the Bull Run battle and stampede. A little later he served on the staff of General Phil. Kearney, and early in the summer of 1862 was made full captain and aid-de-camp of General McClellan. And this contributed not a little to some of his troubles in after years, as he was an enthusiastic "McClellan man," and by no means reticent in his views. Animosities were excited during that controversy which were not settled till long afterwards.

Little by little Custer fought his way up, and the last year of the war the country was charmed and excited by the brilliant movements of Brigadier-General George A. Custer, of the United States Cavalry. After the war we almost lost sight of him. Except that President Johnson took him, along with a few others, as one of the attractions of that starring tour, "swinging 'round the circle," we hear no more of Custer till the army was reorganized in 1866, and he was once more a captain in the United States Cavalry, this time on the plains. But it was a different sort of army to that with which he had won his early honors. Language fails to portray the utter demoralization of our regular army from 1865 to 1869 or '70. All the really valuable survivors of the volunteer army had returned to civil life; only the malingerers, the bounty-jumpers, the draft-sneaks and worthless remained. These, with the scum of the cities and frontier settlements, constituted more than half of the rank and file on the plains. The officers, too, had been somewhat affected by the great revolution. The old West Pointers were dead, or retired on half pay, or had grown to such rank in the volunteer army that they could not bear to drop back to their old position in the regular service. The officers consisted of new men from West Point; of men who had been appointed from civil life or from the volunteer army, in most instances to oblige some politician; and a few men like Custer, to whom military life was both a pleasure and a legitimate business. Desertion was so common among the private soldiers that it entailed no disgrace anywhere in the West. Hundreds enlisted simply to get transportation to the Rocky Mountains, and then deserted. When our wagon-train was on its way to Salt Lake in 1868 a deserter traveled with us two days, dressed in his military clothing, and without the slightest attempt at concealment. In this wretched state of the service in the West, Custer was promoted to the rank of Lieutenant-Colonel, and put in command of the Seventh United States Cavalry.

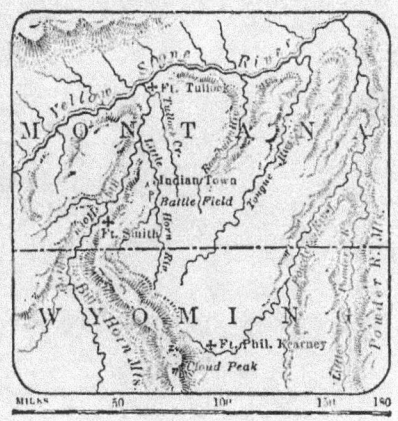

SCENE OF SIOUX WAR OF 1876.

It was but nominally a cavalry regiment. The men were there, and the horses, with guns, equipments, an organization and a name; but as a *cavalry* regiment he had to make it, and he did it so well that it soon became the reliable regiment of the frontier. The new Colonel's career, for some time to come, was among the hostile Indians of Western and South-western Kansas—then the worst section of the Far West for Indian troubles. The tourist who glides rapidly and with such keen enjoyment through this region, by way of the Kansas Pacific or Atchison, Topeka & Santa Fe Road, can scarcely conceive that but a few years have elapsed since it contained thousands of murderous savages; for it is a noteworthy fact that nothing so soon moderates the danger of Indian attacks as a railroad. It seems that, even if no fighting is done, the mere presence of the road, with daily passage of trains, either drives the Indians away or renders them harmless. But in the early days the routes to the Colorado mines were raided at regular intervals. One year there would be almost perfect peace, the next a bloody Indian war. It seems to have been the policy of the Indians to behave well long enough to throw emigrants off their guard, then swoop down and mur der and plunder with impunity. The region between the Smoky Hill and the Republican was particularly noted for bloody encounters. It was raided in turn by Sioux, Cheyennes and Arapahoes, and often by all three in concert. Every ravine and knoll on the route has its own local legend—the details, a blending of the ludicrous and horrible.

"BUSTED."

Tradition relates that two bold settlers started for the mines in a time of profound peace, just after the Indians had concluded a most solemn treaty and shaken hands over their promise to live in eternal peace with the whites; the settlers, in Western mirthfulness, painting on their white wagon-cover the words, "Pike's Peak or Bust." A scouting party sent out from some post came upon them on the Upper Republican just in time to see the savages vanishing in the distance. The oxen lay dead in the yoke. Beside the wagon were the corpses of the two settlers, transfixed with arrows. They had "busted."

In 1864 the savages broke out worse than ever, carrying off several women captive from the settlements in Kansas. In 1865 there was a precarious peace; but in 1866 and '67 the Indians raided every part of the stage road. Meanwhile the noted "Chivington massacre" had occurred, and General P. E. Connor had, by extraordinary exertions, killed some Montana Indians; both events were seized upon by Eastern "humanitarians," and for awhile they succeeded in completely paralyzing all portions of our army. And here it may be observed that our peculiar, tortuous, uneconomical and most unsatisfactory Indian policy, is the result of a certain conflict of forces highly liable to occur in a free republic. There is, first, a small but eminently respectable and powerful party which is opposed to fighting the Indian at all, and think he might be fed and soothed into keeping the peace; and that, at any rate, it would be cheaper to feed all the Indians to repletion than to fight them. And as to this last point they are emphatically correct. There is, next, a considerably larger number, mostly on the frontiers, who believe in a war of extermination, but they have little or no political influence. There are also the traders and agents, some honest and some otherwise, whose interests are involved; and the sensible middle class, who believe in keeping treaties with the Indians, and thrashing them if they break treaties. Of course it sometimes happens that one of these parties is ahead, and then another. As a result our policy is strangely crooked, inconsistent and expensive. The Indian no sooner gets accustomed to one policy than another is adopted; he has scarcely learned to trust one officer till another is in his place, who takes a malicious pleasure, apparently, in undoing all that the former has done. This uncertainty entails frightful expense both in treasure and life. But it is a difficulty inseparable, apparently, from our form of government.

It is unnecessary to trace the causes which led to Hancock's campaign against the Indians in 1867. It was a formidable affair on paper, but accomplished nothing. Our whole force consisted of eight troops of cavalry, seven companies of infantry and one battery of artillery, the whole numbering 1,400 men. General Hancock, with seven companies of infantry, four of the Seventh Cavalry, and all the artillery, marched from Fort Riley to Fort Harper, and there was joined by two more troops of cavalry. Thence they marched southwest to Fort Larned, near the Arkansas. The hostile Indians, consisting of Cheyennes and Sioux, had appointed a council near by; but all sorts of difficulties seemed to arise to prevent their coming up to time. First, there was a heavy snow, although it was the second week in April; and the runners reported that the bands could not come. Then word came that they had started, but found it necessary to halt and kill some buffalo; and again that they had once come in sight, but were afraid on account of so many soldiers being present. Then General Hancock proceeded up the stream to hunt the Indian camp, and was met by an imposing band of warriors. Another parley ensued: midway between the hostile forces Generals Hancock, A. J. Smith and others met Roman Nose, Bull Bear, White Horse, Gray Beard and Medicine Wolf, on the part of the Cheyennes, and Pawnee Killer, Bad Wound, Tall-Bear-that-walks-under-Ground, Left Hand, Little Bull and Little Bear, on the part of the Sioux. There was no fighting, but after a few days more of excuses, the mounted Indians suddenly departed. Then it was discovered that the whole proceeding was but a well-played ruse to enable the Indians to get their women and children to a place of safety, and leave the warriors free for contingencies. The accomplished commanders of the American army had been tricked by a lot of dirty savages. Custer in the lead, pushed on with all possible speed after the Indians, but in vain. They had struck the stage stations on the Smoky Hill route, and murdered several persons; and the war was begun. It ended decidedly to the advantage of the Indians.

CUSTER'S FIRST INDIAN FIGHT.

Custer's first experience in actual Indian fighting was while escorting a wagon-train loaded with supplies from Fort Ellis. The Indians had selected for the fight a piece of ground well cut up with gullies—an admirable system of "covered ways"—by which they hoped to get close up to the wagons without being discovered, and then make a charge. But the watchful eye of a scout discovered their plan, and brought on the conflict on ground more favorable to the whites. The train was simultaneously attacked on all sides by six or seven hundred well-mounted Indians, outnumbering Custer's party twelve to one. The savages attacked in the manner known as "circling"—that is, riding round and round the whites, hanging on the opposite side of their horses so as to be shielded, and firing over the animal's back and under his breast. The scout Comstock had predicted a long and obstinate battle: "Six hundred red devils ain't a goin' to let fifty men stop them from getting the sugar and coffee that's in these wagons." And they did not yield the prize as long as there was hope. The soldiers were located around the wagons in skirmish order. The

Indians encircled them in a much larger ring; but though the firing continued for hours, only a few Indians were hit, so difficult was it to take aim at the swiftly flying horse or rider. All this time the train moved slowly on over the comparatively level prairie, the teamsters shivering with terror, and scarcely needing the command to "keep closed up—one team's head right against the next wagon." This fight lasted three hours, and had the Indians maintained it much longer, the soldiers must have run out of ammunition. But the savage scouts, posted all around on the highest points, gave warning that something was wrong; and soon the whole band ceased firing and galloped off. Five of them had been killed and several wounded. The cause of their sudden retreat proved to be Colonel West's cavalry command, which soon arrived.

Custer's next anxiety was for Lieutenant Kidder and his party of eleven men, who were known to be moving across from the Republican to Fort Wallace, through a country now swarming with hostile Indians. Soon after getting the supply train into camp, Comstock, the scout, was appealed to for his opinion as to Kidder's chances. It was far from encouraging. But Comstock's reply to the officers contains some hints worth recording. Said he: "Well, gentlemen, there's several things a man must know to give an opinion. No man need tell me any pints about Injuns. If I know any thing, it's Injuns. I know jest how they'll do any thing, and when they'll take to do it; but that don't settle the question. Ef I knowed this young lootenint, if I knowed what sort of a man he is, I could tell you mighty nigh to a sartainty all you want to know; for, you see, Injun huntin' and Injun fightin' is a trade all by itself; and like any other bizness, a man has to know what he's about, or ef he don't, he can't make a livin' at it. I have lots o' confidence in the fightin' sense o' Red Bead, the Sioux chief, who is guidin' the lootenint, and ef that Injun can have his own way, there is a fair show for his guidin' 'em through all right; but there lays the difficulty. Is this lootenint the kind of a man that is willin' to take advice, even if it does come from an Injun? My experience with you army folks has allays been that the youngsters among ye think they know the most; and this is 'specially true ef they've jist come from West Pint. Ef one o' 'em young fellers knowed half as much as they bleeve they do, you couldn't tell 'em nothin'. As to rale book larnin', why I spose they've got it all, but the fact of the matter is they couldn't tell the difference 'twixt the trail of a war party and one made by a huntin' party to save their necks. Half uv 'em when they first cum here can't tell a squaw from a buck, because they both ride straddle; but they soon larn. But that's neither here nor thar. I'm told that this lootenint we're talkin' about is a new-comer, and that this is his first scout. Ef that be the case, it puts a mighty unsartain look on the whole thing; and 'twixt you and me, gentle*men*, he'll be mighty lucky ef he gets through all right. To-morrow we'll strike the Wallace trail, and I can mighty soon tell whether he's gone that way."

Next day the relief party, led by Custer, came on Lieutenant Kidder's trail, and after a brief examination Comstock pronounced: "The trail shows that twelve American horses, shod all around, have passed at a walk; and when they went by this pint they war all right, because their horses are a movin' along easy, and no pony tracks behind 'em, as would be ef the Injuns had an eye on 'em. It would be astonishin' for that lootenint and his layout to git into the fort without a skrimmage. He *may*, but ef he does, it'll be a scratch ef ever there was one; and I'll lose my con*fidence* in Injuns."

Custer ordered the command to hurry up, and, following the trail, they came, in a few hours, upon two dead horses with the cavalry brand, but stripped of all accouterments. A little farther, and they saw that the American horses had been going at full speed, while all around Comstock pointed out the minute but abundant evidences that the Indians had fought them from all sides, the pony tracks being numerous. A little farther, and they entered the tall grass and thickets along Beaver Creek, and there saw several buzzards floating lazily in the air, while the trail was sprinkled with exploded cartridges and other debris. That told the tale. Nor were they long in finding the dead. The sight made the blood even of these brave men curdle. Lieutenant Kidder and his companions lay near together, stripped of every article of clothing, and so brutally hacked and mangled that all separate recognition was impossible. Every skull had been broken, every head scalped; the bodies were mutilated in an obscene and indescribable manner, and some lay amid ashes, indicating that they had been roasted to death. The scalp of Red Bead, the friendly Sioux, lay by his body, as it is contrary to their rules to carry away the scalp of one of their own tribe; nor is it permitted among most Indians to keep such a scalp or exhibit it. The exact manner of their death can not be known, but all the surroundings showed that they fought long and well. Custer's command buried them on the spot where found, whence the father of Lieutenant Kidder removed his remains the next winter.

Custer marched on to Fort Wallace with all possible speed, but troubles multiplied. The soldiers had begun to desert. Forty men took "French leave" in one night! The next day thirteen men deserted in broad day, in full view of the command, seven mounted and six on foot. After a desperate run the latter were captured, two slightly and one mortally wounded. It is to be noted that they were then in a region where the deserters apprehended no danger from Indians. Two men were killed by the Indians after all danger was thought to be past. From Fort Wallace the command marched eastward to Fort Hayes. The war was over, and Custer applied for and obtained leave to visit, by rail, Fort Riley, where his family was then located; and for this, and other matters connected with that campaign, Custer was court-martialed! This proceeding appears to have been purely malicious, prompted by the dislike of some inferior officers over whom Custer had exercised pretty severe discipline. The charges were drawn by one whom he had severely reprimanded for drunkenness. He *had* left Fort Wallace without orders, because, under the circumstances, he thought proper to report to his commander in person. To this they added the fact that he went on to Riley to visit his family, and thus constructed a charge that he had abandoned his post for his private convenience! Mean as this attack was, it was successful. Custer was suspended from rank and pay for one year!

Meanwhile another summer campaign was undertaken against the hostile Indians, with equally barren results. General Sully marched, in 1868, against the combined Cheyennes, Kioways, and Arapahoes, whom he struck near the present Camp Supply. If this was a "drawn battle," that is the best that can be said of it. Sully retired, badly crippled, and made no further attempts. At the same time General "Sandy" Forsythe, with a company of scouts and plainsmen enlisted for the purpose, was hunting for the hostile Sioux on the northern affluents of the Republican. He found them. They also found him. Of his total force of fifty-one men, six were killed and twenty wounded; all their horses were captured, and the command was only saved from annihilation by the arrival of reinforcements. The Noble Red Man evidently understood his business better than the Generals opposed to him. The people of Colorado grew sarcastic. Western people often do when mail and supplies are cut off for weeks at a time. It appeared that the mountain territories were in a fair way to be isolated from the rest of the country. California Joe, a scout who had been with several of the commanders, thus gave in his experience:

"I've been with 'em when they started out after the Injuns on wheels—in an ambulance—as if they war goin' to a town funeral in the States, and they stood about as much chance o' ketchin' the Injuns as a six-mule train would of ketchin' a pack o' coyotes. That sort o' work is only fun for the Injuns; they don't want any thing better. Ye ought to seen how they peppered it to us, and we doin' nothing all the time. Some war afraid the mules war a goin' to stampede and run off with all our grub, but that war onpossible; for, besides the big loads of corn and bacon, thar war from eight to a dozen infantry men piled into every wagon. Ye'd ought to heard the quartermaster in charge o' the train tryin' to drive the men outen the wagons and git them into the fight. He was an Irishman, and he sez to 'em: 'Git out of thim waggins. Yez 'ill hev me tried for disobadience ov orders for marchin' tin men in a waggin whin I've orders but for eight.'"

But the rude common sense of General Sheridan, soon after his arrival on the plains, put an end to summer campaigning. He and Sherman united in asking for the restoration of Custer; and, on the 12th of November, 1868, that officer, at the head of his command again, started out on his famous Washita campaign. Soon after the departure from Fort Dodge, on the Arkansas, the command was overtaken by a violent snow-storm; but this the commander thought all the more favorable to his plans. General Sheridan could only point out to Custer the neighborhood of the hostiles' camp, and leave all details to his judgment. With four hundred wagons and a guard of infantry for them, and the Seventh Cavalry in fighting order, he pressed rapidly southward to the edge of the Indian conntry, where a camp was established for the wagons, as a base of supplies, and the cavalry pressed on. California Joe and other scouts accompanied the expedition, besides a small detachment of Osage Indians, headed by Little Beaver and Hard Rope, who did excellent service. After a terrible winter march, the command, 800 strong, arrived at the bluff of the Washita at midnight, and saw below them, in the moonlight, the hostile camp. It was evident, at a glance, that the Indians trusted implicitly in the old army habit of fighting them only in summer. They had no scouts out, and were buried in repose. The command was divided into four nearly equal detachments; and, by making wide detours, the Indian camp was completely surrounded before daylight. The night was terribly cold, but no fire could be lighted, and the suffering was intense. As Custer stood upon the brow of the hill, and peered through the darkness into the camp, he distinctly heard the cry of an Indian baby, borne through the cold, still air, and reflected with pain that, under the circumstances, there was so much probability that the troopers' bullets would make no distinction of age or sex. Soon after daylight the attack was made. Although taken by surprise, the Indians fought desperately, but were utterly routed. It practically annihilated Black Kettle's band of Cheyennes. A hundred and three warriors were killed, fifty-three squaws and children captured, eight hundred and seventy-five ponies taken, and a vast amount of other property. Of the force, two officers and nineteen men were killed, three officers and eleven men wounded. In the very

RUDE SURGERY OF THE PLAINS.

hour of victory Custer discovered that this was but one of a long line of villages extending down the Washita; but he had struck such terror that the others did not gather force sufficient to attack, and he returned to camp in safety.

And here it may be noted that in plains' travel and fighting, there is no difficulty so great as dealing with the wounded. With all the appliances furnished our army surgeons, there must still be many deficiencies; and, with the ordinary plainsman, a bad wound is either certain death or a long and terrible struggle, in which nothing saves the man but an iron constitution. In the old days a regular backwoods' science grew up among trappers and *voyageurs;* they treated gunshot wounds and broken bones, extracted bullets and arrows, or amputated shattered limbs in a way that would have amazed the faculty, but was singularly successful. The camp-saw and a well sharpened bowie-knife were their surgical instruments; their cauteries, hot irons; and their tourniquets, a handkerchief twisted upon the limb with a stick run through the knot and turned to press upon the artery. Arrows were often drawn through the limb, the feathers having been cut off; and bullets flirted out of an incision quickly made with a sharp razor. In winter the wounded limb was almost frozen by snow or ice applied before the amputation; in summer there was nothing for it but to suffer it through. An old *voyageur*, with but one arm, gave me an account of his losing the other, which made my "each particular hair to stand on end." The arm was completely shattered below the elbow; it was amputation or death, and the party was a thousand miles from any surgeon. But with knife, saw, and red-hot iron the job was skillfully done; he survived such rude surgery without a shock to his fine constitution.

After a brief rest Custer was again sent to the Washita, where he alternately negotiated with and threatened the savages until he had recovered some captives they held, and located the Indians near the forts. And here originated the difficulty between him and General W. B. Hazen, then in charge of the southern Indians—Custer maintaining that Satanta and Lone Wolf's bands of Kioways had been in the fight against him, Hazen denying it. It was six years before the matter was settled, Hazen producing unquestionable evidence that he was right. We find evidences, from time to time, that Custer was somewhat hasty in his judgments, and very impulsive in giving utterance to them—in short, that he had some of the faults as well as all the virtues of a dashing, impetuous man.

For two years there was peace on the plains; but in the spring of 1873 the first Yellowstone expedition went out. From Yankton the Seventh Cavalry, with Custer in command, marched all the way to Fort Rice, six hundred miles, Mrs. Custer and other ladies accompanying the column on horseback. There the ladies halted, but it was not till July that the entire expedition started—cavalry, infantry, artillery and scouts, numbering seventeen hundred men—all under command of Major-General D. S. Stanley. The main object was to explore the country, and open a way for the surveyors of the Northern

Pacific Railroad. Custer, as usual, was put in the lead, and soon after reaching the Yellowstone had several skirmishes with the Indians, who were desperately resolved against the passage of a railroad through the country. If they could only have looked forward over the next year of the financial world, they might have been spared all anxiety on that point. During this march the sutler and veterinary surgeon of the Seventh Cavalry were murdered by a Sioux called Rain-in-the-Face; and out of that matter grew the latter's hostility to Custer, and perhaps the latter's tragic death three years after.

Early in 1874 began the memorable Black Hills expedition, an undertaking that began in the grossest injustice and ended in wholesale murder. From the first discovery in California, rumors had constantly prevailed of great gold placers in the Black Hills, but the region was a mystery. The Warren Expedition, in 1857, had gone around the whole district, but the Sioux emphatically prohibited them from entering it, stating that it was sacred ground. Other expeditions proved that the region was a great oval, about a hundred by sixty miles in extent, cut up by numerous low mountain ranges covered with timber; that it possessed, as do all such mountainous regions, a more rainy climate than the plains, and scores of little valleys of great fertility. It is obvious, from the lay of the country, that the region can not contain any great area of agricultural land, but quite probable that it abounds in good mountain pastures and timbered hills. The tenacity with which the Sioux clung to it only the more convinced the Westerners that it contained gold by millions, and many were the exciting stories told. The treaty of 1868 confirmed it to Red Cloud and other chiefs in person in Washington, and the Black Hills were declared inviolable—a section of the Indian reservation never to be trespassed upon by white men. The Custer expedition of 1874 was undertaken in direct violation of that treaty, and upon the half-avowed principle that treaties were not to be kept with Indians if whites needed the country in question. Consistent with this ill-faith the expedition was made the occasion of ridiculous exaggeration, not to say downright falsehood. Correspondents were sent along with descriptive powers suited to an earthly Eden, and they described one; explorers went to find gold by millions, and they found it. The country needed a sensation, and the Government took the contract of supplying it. When the expedition had returned, and the brilliant correspondents had made their report, General Hazen undertook to moderate popular enthusiasm by portraying the high plains as they generally are; but the public rejected him, and found in his testimony only another evidence of his animosity to General Custer. The general result was, settlement of the Black Hills before the Indian title was extinguished, and another expensive and fruitless Indian war.

The next year Rain-in-the-Face, a noted brave of the Unepapa Sioux, was arrested for the murder of Dr. Honzinger and Mr. Baliran, of the Yellowstone Expedition of 1873. He was brought before Custer, thoroughly examined, and sentenced to death, but managed to escape, joined the hostile band of Sitting Bull, and sent word that he was prepared to take revenge for his imprisonment. There is evidence, though not quite conclusive, that this Indian gave Custer the death-blow. Here it is necessary to point out an important distinction in the organization of different bands. The ordinary Indian government is patriarchal, and in many bands a majority of the families are in some way related to the chief; but though the chieftainship is nominally hereditary, its continuance in any line finally depends on the prowess of the claimant. If he fails in any particular, another chief at once supplants him. Hence the absurdity of the plan generally adopted by our Government of trying to choose chiefs for the Indians, or to recognize one rather than another. If the young men can not have the leader they want, they generally join the "hostiles." These bands are made up on an entirely different plan—by convenience rather than relationship. Sitting Bull, Crazy Horse, or some other active fighter, gets a reputation as war chief, and all the discontented braves join him; as a rule there are few women in such a band, and the number of men is, therefore, apt to be underrated on distant view. Still more distinct is a third class, commonly known as "dog soldiers." These are outcasts or runaways from all the tribes, who get together in squads of from five to five hundred; sometimes they dissolve and melt into the original tribes, sometimes are merged into some one big tribe, or simply wear out. Their communication at first is entirely by the "sign language;" if together long enough, a new Indian dialect arises from the jargon of so many tongues. It has occasionally happened that a large band of "dog soldiers" would capture women enough for their wants, conquer a territory for themselves, and in time grow into an entirely new tribe. Thus the Comanches, Arapahoes and Apaches are said to have descended from the original Shoshonees; while the Navajoes resulted from the union of part of the old Aztecs with an offshoot of the Shoshonees—or of the original Athabascan stock, from which the latter sprang.

In 1876, Sitting Bull and Crazy Horse led the hostile Sioux, and to them rapidly gathered all the discontented young braves from the agencies. As near as can be determined the latter chief began the season with eight hundred braves—the former with nearly twice as many. Their position was the best that military art could have selected. From it the affluents of the Yellowstone ran northward; the lower affluents of the Missouri eastward; on the east and north it was doubly protected by the "bad lands;" north-west and west were rugged mountains, and southward the high plains stretched for many hundred miles. Around the extreme outer edge of the hostile country, from north-west and north to north-east and east, ran the Missouri; on that stream were located all the agencies, and from them, through "friendly" Indians, went a constant stream of supplies to the warriors. By careful examination of the books (after the damage had been done), it was proved that these bands received in five months 56 cases of arms, containing 1,120 Winchester and Remington rifles, and 413,000 rounds of patent ammunition, besides considerable quantities of loose powder, lead and primers. It takes many such lessons as this to convince the American people that this machine we call government is the most awkward, expensive and inefficient of all human inventions; and yet the lesson is not learned, for, in spite of daily multiplying evidences of its inherent inefficiency, new parties start up every year urging that government should run our schools and churches, our mills, mines and workshops, our social, moral and industrial institutions. Daily is the lesson thrust upon us, that whatever government does is done wrong; and daily we hear fresh demands that government should do things which it was never organized to do. The plain English of the foregoing figures is, that government first armed the savages with repeating rifles, then sent an inferior force to attack them on ground of their own choosing.

Three columns were to proceed from three points and converge on the hostile region: Gibbon eastward from Fort Ellis, Montana; Crook northward from Fort Fetterman; and Terry westward from Fort Abe Lincoln, just across the Missouri from Bismarck, Dakota. Of course they could not start at the same time. General Crook, with seven hundred men and forty days' supplies, started the 1st of March and reached and destroyed the village of Crazy Horse, on Powder River, the 17th of March. But the Indians got away with most of their animals and supplies. The Gibbon column did not figure greatly till the junction with Terry on the Yellowstone. Meanwhile the Terry column, in which General Custer was the leading spirit, was delayed in a score of ways. It *could* not start as early as that of Crook anyhow, as it was to move through a colder latitude, and, while waiting, Custer was summoned to Washington. The Belknap investigation was in progress, and Hon. Heister Clymer, Chairman of the House Committee, got it into his head that Custer could give important information. In vain did Custer dispatch that he really knew nothing about the case, and Terry urge that his call to Washington would delay and imperil the expedition. Clymer was all the more certain Custer had important information, and should be brought before the committee and rigidly interrogated. On the 6th of March, Custer telegraphed a request that he might be examined at Fort Lincoln. This Clymer flatly refused. Custer had to go to Washington, and there it was found that he really knew nothing about the case, and had only, as was natural to one of his impulsive nature, talked freely about what he had heard. But Heister Clymer had the satisfaction of compelling a General to come before his committee, and delaying Custer's march after Sitting Bull a whole month. Then President Grant took hold. The grim, impassive, hard-to-change General Grant took it into his head that Custer's talk about the case had been an intentional affront to him—*why*, no one ever knew. He refused to see Custer, though the latter repeatedly called at the White House, and once sent in a card asking in plain terms for a reconciliation.

Custer then called at the office of General Sherman, only to learn that the latter was in New York, and might not return for some time; then, on the night of May 1, took the train for Chicago. Next day Sherman returned, and telegraphed to General Sheridan at Chicago, that Custer "was not justified in leaving here without seeing me (Sherman) or the President," and ordered that Custer remain at Saint Paul till further orders. *Somebody* was evidently playing sad havoc with Custer's character and plans. He had, *perhaps*, talked too much—that was his fault, if any thing—but it is impossible for the non-military mind to see any other harm he had done. He was in genuine distress. He telegraphed at length to General Sherman, and then to President Grant; and the final result was that, after a deal of red tape all around, he received permission to go with the expedition, in command of his regiment, the Seventh U. S. Cavalry. The Terry column consisted of the Seventh Cavalry entire, three companies of the Sixth and Seventeenth Infantry, with four Gatling guns and a small detachment of Indian scouts, about eight hundred men in all. Gibbon was coming in from the west with four hundred men, and Crook had made another start from the south with fifteen hundred men. Thus there were twenty-seven hundred armed men, distributed on the circumference of a circle about three hundred miles wide, to concentrate near the center where the hostiles were supposed to be.

Crook first found the enemy. On the 8th of June, his force had a skirmish with the Sioux, and repulsed them. A week later his Indian scouts reported that they had seen Gibbon's command on the other side of the hostile Sioux, on the Tongue River. On the 16th Crook pushed rapidly forward towards the hostiles. Next morning Sitting Bull attacked his camp in great force and with astonishing vigor. It was not exactly a surprise, but all must agree that Crook gained no advantage, and that Sitting Bull handled his forces admirably. Twice during the action he succeeded in getting his warriors into positions where they poured an enfilading fire into Crook's command. Meanwhile Generals Terry and Gibbon had communicated, and the latter had shown, by thorough scouting, that the hostiles were as yet all south of the Yellowstone. A glance at the map will show that the Powder, Tongue, Rosebud, and Big Horn run north into the Yellowstone, and the Little Horn into the Big Horn; and that, after these various scouts, it was certain the hostiles were somewhere on those streams. Accordingly Terry commenced scouting for them in that direction. So far the general plan had worked well; its defect now appeared to be that Gibbon and Terry were separated from Crook by at least a hundred miles of mountainous country, and that in that region somewhere were the hostiles, in good position to move either way. The whole object of this plan was to prevent the Indians getting away without a fight, and as to that it was a perfect success. The contingency of the Indians being well prepared for a fight had apparently not been considered.

Careful scouting narrowed the field, and finally it was decided that the Indians were either on the head of the Rosebud or on the Little Horn, a ridge about fifteen miles wide separating the two streams. Terry and Gibbon, on the Yellowstone, near the mouth of Tongue River, then held a council, and decided that Custer's column should be pushed forward to strike the first blow. Crook was too far south to be considered in this arrangement at all. The general plan is briefly stated in Terry's dispatch to General Sheridan, from the former's camp at the mouth of Rosebud, just before the final movement, as follows:

> Traces of a large and recent camp of Indians have been discovered twenty or thirty miles up the Rosebud. Gibbon's column will move this morning on the north side of the Yellowstone (see map), where it will be ferried across by the supply steamer, and whence it will proceed to the mouth of the Little Horn, and so on. Custer will go up

the Rosebud to-morrow with his whole regiment, and thence to the head-waters of the Little Horn, thence down the Little Horn.

The object, of course, was for Custer to head off the escape of the Indians towards the east, while Gibbon would move up the Big Horn and intercept them in that direction. It has been absurdly said that Custer disobeyed or exceeded the general orders he received from Terry; but, in fact, those orders were so very "general," that, aside from the instructions as to route and sending scouts to seek Gibbon, they might have been condensed to, "Go ahead, do your best; I trust all to you." Similar orders directed the march of Gibbon up the Big Horn. Should both columns march equally, all else being equal, it would result that they would come together on the Big Horn, some distance above (south) the junction of the Little Horn. There appears to have been no special order given as to rates of marching; and so far the witnesses do not agree very well as to what either commander was to do if he struck the Indians first. The reasonable supposition is, that it was understood beforehand they were to fight on sight. It was hardly to be supposed that Sitting Bull would accommodate them by slowly retiring before either, until the other could come up in his rear. Custer's command received rations for fifteen days. Thus supplied, and thus directed with only general orders and plenary powers under them, Custer and his cavalry set out up the Rosebud on the afternoon of June 22, 1876, which is the last account we have from him in person. Thereafter his movements are known only by the report of Major Reno, who succeeded to the command of that section of the regiment which survived; the statements of various officers in the same command; the evidence of Curly, an Upsaroka scout, who alone survived the massacre, and some unsatisfactory accounts from the enemy. From all these sources, and a careful examination of the trails and battle-ground, the following facts are proved:

On the 22d, Custer marched his command about twelve miles up the Rosebud, and encamped. On the 23d they continued up the Rosebud for about thirty-five miles, perhaps a little less. On the 24th they advanced rapidly twenty-eight miles, and finding a fresh Indian trail, halted for reports from scouts. By night they had received full reports, and about 9:30 P. M., Custer called the officers together and informed them that the Indians were in the valley of the Little Horn, and that to surprise them they must cross over from one stream to the other in the night. Accordingly they moved off at 11 P. M.; but about 2 A. M. of the 25th, the scouts gave notice that the command could not get across the divide before daylight; so a halt was made, provisions prepared, and breakfast eaten. Right here, apparently, Custer's original plan failed. It would seem to have been his intention to repeat the Washita battle, and attack at sunrise. By 8 A. M., the command was nearing the Little Horn. Here the regiment was divided. Major Reno took command of companies M, A and G; Captain Benteen of H, D, and K; Custer retained companies C, E, F, I and L, and Captain McDougall, with company B, was placed as rear-guard with the pack-train. As they moved down the creek towards the Little Horn, Custer was on the right bank, Major Reno on the left bank, and Captain Benteen some distance to the left of Reno, and entirely out of sight. As near as can be determined the command had marched some ninety miles since leaving Terry; but it is claimed by some that this last night and forenoon march was much longer than reported.

About noon they came in sight of the Indian camp, on the opposite side of the river, which at that point runs a little west of north, with a considerable bend to the north-east. Enclosed within this bend, on the left (west) side of the stream, began the Indian camps, which continued thence a long way down the Little Horn. As the command now enters the battle in three divisions, we must consider them separately. As far as Custer's plan can be known, it was for Reno to cross, attack the upper end of the Indian camp, and drive them down stream if possible; at any rate, to employ the warriors fully, while Custer himself, to be reinforced by Benteen, should gallop around the bend of the Little Horn and down some distance, then cross, and attack from that side. It was evident that the time for a complete surprise was past. The last order Reno had from Custer was: "Move forward at as rapid a gait as you think prudent, charge afterwards, and the whole outfit will support you." Pursuant thereto, Reno with his command took a sharp trot for two miles down the stream to a convenient ford; then crossed, deployed with the Ree scouts on his left, and opened the battle, the Indians retiring before him for about two and a half miles. And here comes in the first doubtful proceeding. Reno says: "I saw that I was being drawn into some trap. * * * I could not see Custer or any other support, and at the same time the ground seemed to grow Indians. They were running towards me in swarms, and from all directions." He retired a little to a piece of woods, dismounted, had his men fight on foot, and advanced again. He says that the odds were five to one, and he saw that he must regain high ground or be surrounded. Accordingly he remounted his men, charged across the stream, some distance below where he had crossed before, and hurried to the top of the bluff, losing three officers and twenty-nine men killed, and seven men wounded in this operation. In fact, nearly his entire loss occurred in this retreat, men and horses being shot from behind. It would *seem* to a civilian, who has, perhaps, no right to criticise an Indian fight, that it would have been far cheaper, and more nearly in accordance with his orders, to stick to the woods on the west side and fight it out for a few hours. The surgeon present says there was *only one man wounded before Reno abandoned the timber*.

We turn now to Benteen. That officer, having been ordered to the extreme left while marching down the affluent towards the Little Horn, was necessarily several miles off when the rest of the command turned to the right and *down* the Little Horn. Finding no Indians, he recrossed the affluent and marched down the trail left by Custer. About three miles, as he says, from where Reno first crossed, he met a sergeant carrying orders to Captain McDougall to hurry up the pack-train; a little further on he met Trumpeter Martin with an order from Custer, written by Adjutant McCook, and the last he ever penned, which read, "Benteen, come on; big village; be quick; bring packs." About a mile further on he came in sight of the Little Horn, and saw Reno retreating up the bluffs. He also saw "twelve or fifteen dismounted men fighting on the plain, the Indians there numbering about 900!" About 2:30 P. M., he came up to where Reno had gathered his forces on the right bluff. The division of the regiment into three battalions was made at 10:30 A. M.; Benteen says that his scout and return to the main trail occupied about one hour and a half, bringing it to noon. How he consumed the time from then till 2:30 P. M., none of the reports inform us. The distance traversed could not have been over five miles, if we can trust any thing to the military map. It also appears from the report that Boston Custer, brother of the General, had time to come to the rear and pack-train, get a fresh horse, and go back to Custer, passing Benteen, and be killed in the final slaughter. The reports by various survivors seem to leave us in ignorance of much that we should like to know.

It was now near 3 P. M., and as senior Major Reno had in command his own and Benteen's battalions, and the company guarding the pack-train: Companies A, B, D, G, H, K and M, numbering 380 men, commanded by Captains Benteen, Weir, French and McDougall, and Lieutenants Godfrey, Mathey, Gibson, Edgerly, Wallace, Varnum and Hare. With them was Surgeon Porter. These officers are restrained, to a great extent, by military courtesy, but as far as their statements have been made public they indicate that there was no very determined effort made to aid Custer. Major Reno waited on the bluff awhile (length of time not settled yet), then moved slowly down the stream, and sent Captain Weir with his command to open communication with Custer. Weir soon returned with the information that the Indians were coming *en masse;* and, in a little while after, Reno's force was furiously attacked. We learn at this stage of the report that it was now 6 P. M. It seems impossible to stretch any action of which mention is made so as to cover the time between three and six. And yet it appears from an examination of the ground that Custer could not, at three, have been more than three miles away. And, in the interim, the little squad of dismounted men whom Benteen saw across the river, had beaten off the Indians opposed to them and *succeeded in reaching Reno without loss!* But Reno's command was attacked, as aforesaid, about 6 P. M.; held its ground with the loss of 18 killed and 46 wounded, and had the enemy beaten off by 9 P. M. There is every evidence that Reno behaved with coolness and bravery, and Benteen with proper activity, during *this* battle; and still the report does not inform us as to the exercise of those qualities earlier in the afternoon.

And where all this time was Custer? The trail, the heaps of dead and the few accounts from eye-witnesses tell a plain story. He came at high speed to a ford of the Little Horn which would have brought him about the middle of the Indian camps. But in this short space of time the Indians had vanquished Reno, and their whole force were there to oppose him. He gave back from the ford, and the Indians followed in overwhelming numbers. They were now on the way he had come, and he continued his retreat along the bluffs down the river. He had in his command but four hundred and twenty men, and the Indians must have numbered nearly two thousand. Who can tell the agony of that terrible retreat and last desperate struggle? When the command had reached a point nearly a mile from the ford, Custer evidently saw that a sacrifice was necessary to save, if possible, a remnant of his command. To this end he chose his brother-in-law, Lieutenant James Calhoun; with him was Lieutenant Crittenden, their company having been selected to cover the retreat. They were found in line all dead together, the officers in their proper places in the rear, the company having died fighting to the last man.

A little further on another desperate stand was made. Then a mile from the scene of Calhoun's death, on the ridge parallel to the stream, Captain Keogh's company made a stand to cover the retreat. Keogh had evidently nerved himself for death. He was an old and able soldier. He was an officer in the Papal service when Garibaldi made war upon the Pope, and had served in the army of the Potomac during the war. Down went he and his company, slaughtered in position, every man maintaining his place and fighting desperately to the last.

Custer, with the remnant of his command, had taken up his position on the next hill. Curly, the Upsaroka scout, tells us that he ran to Custer when he saw that the command was doomed, and offered to show him a way of escape. General Custer dropped his head, as if in thought, for one moment, then suddenly jerking it up again he stamped his foot and waving Curly away with his sword, turned to rejoin his men. In that brief interval of thought he had decided to die with his men rather than attempt to escape. There had been a short lull in the fight, while the Sioux were maneuvering for a better position. The firing now recommenced with more fury than ever. Curly dashed into a ravine, let down his hair so as to resemble a Sioux as much as possible, mounted a horse, and joined in the next charge; but watched his opportunity to put on a Sioux blanket, and in the heat of the battle slipped away.

Custer had now made his last stand. It was on the most commanding point of the ridge; and there with Captain Yates, Colonel Cook, Captain Custer, Lieutenant Riley and thirty-two men of Yates' command, he fought desperately to the last. One by one his companions fell around him. Nearer and nearer came the Sioux, like hounds baying a lion, dashing around and firing into the command from all sides. Finally the whites made a sort of barricade of their dead horses, and again for a few minutes held the savages at bay. Then Rain-in-the-Face, bravest Indian in the North-west, gathered his most trusty followers for a hand to hand charge. Custer fought like a tiger. With blood streaming from half a dozen gaping wounds, he killed or disabled three of the enemy with his saber, and when his last support was gone, as he lunged desperately at his nearest enemy, Rain-in-the-Face kept his oath and shot the heroic commander dead.

But the battle was not over. Captain Custer and Captain Smith tried to cut their way back to the river, and in the ravine leading that way twenty-six men were found dead. The heroic remnant made their last stand near the river, and there every man was found dead in position, every officer in his place, every wound in front. The awful tragedy ended with the day. General Custer lay dead on the hill. Beside him lay Colonel Tom Custer, who enlisted as a private at sixteen, was an officer at nineteen, and had been twice decorated for bravery in action. In the same slaughter died two more of the family. Boston Custer, forage-master to the Seventh Cavalry, had sought the open air life of the plains to ward off a tendency to consumption which early manifested itself. He avoided a lingering death by a heroic exit, fit subject for epic poem or thrilling romance. And there was young "Autie" Reed, a mere boy, named after General Custer himself, his nephew, son of the older sister, who had, in fact, reared the General. It was cruel that he, too, should die in this fearful massacre. Autie was just out of school and was eager to go on the plains "with Uncle Autie." To please the lad Custer had him and a class-mate appointed herders, to drive the cattle accompanying the column. He had come with his uncle on this last scout, and here met with his death, equally brave with the bravest. Lieutenant James Calhoun, the remaining member of this relationship, had married Maggie E. Custer, the General's only sister, in 1872; and in every emergency showed himself worthy of adoption into this brave family. Cheered on by his voice, every man of his company died in place. With him was Lieutenant Crittenden of the Twelfth Infantry, a mere boy, just appointed, but cool as a veteran through all the terrible scene. A whole brotherhood of brave officers were cut off; for Custer had gathered around him a circle of choice spirits, who admired his dash, and emulated his bravery. There was the Adjutant, Col. Wm. W. Cook, a Canadian by birth, who had enlisted in the Twenty-fourth New York Cavalry at the beginning of the war, and risen to be its Colonel. And Captain Yates, who enlisted as a private at sixteen and worked his way up. They used to call his company the "band-box troop," they were so neat in their dress and equipments; but every man of them died at his post. The last commander of all was Captain Algernon E. Smith, who won renown at the storming of Fort Fisher; was wounded, and for his bravery made brevet Major. But, perhaps, the saddest loss of all was that of Lieutenant William Van W. Reily. He was of heroic stock. His father, an officer in the navy, went down with his ship in the Indian Ocean a short time before William was born. He left his widowed mother for this expedition, and died in company with all the brave men who then made their last fight. The night fell upon all these brave officers and three hundred men, lying dead upon the field.

The full history of the battle is not yet known. This I say, despite the fact that military reports have been made by the commanders, and published by authority. But they leave much unknown. In a quiet way there has been much crimination and recrimination; one party has accused Reno and Benteen of cowardice or disobedience; the other, including General Grant, has charged that Custer exceeded his orders and sacrificed his command. Without adopting the extreme view of either side, this would seem to a civilian about the correct state of the case: The regiment attacked a force of Indians outnumbering the soldiers two or three to one, and well armed, ready for fight, well posted, in broad day, when men and animals were fatigued, and so insured defeat; then Reno and Benteen, seeing that retreat was a certainty, thought best to keep out of the fight, perhaps supposing that Custer would, in like manner, retreat after a brief skirmish. I can not see that victory would have been possible in any event—no matter if the whole force had attacked at once, as originally intended.

This disaster, of course, spoiled the original plan. General Gibbon came up with reinforcements, and the Indians moved. Successive minor battles and skirmishes followed, by which, though no one great victory was gained, the hostiles were slowly worn out and scattered. Many of the braves made their way back to the agencies, others retreated to less accessible positions in the mountains, and Sitting Bull, with a remnant, retreated into British America, whence he has since, with much pow-wow and flourish, returned. The war in that section soon died out, but a few words additional may be appropriate of the Indians in general. A glance at the map of Aborginal America will show that very few of the Indian nations have retained their original locations; but it must not be judged therefrom that numerous tribes have become extinct. The Indian population of this country at the landing of Columbus has been greatly exaggerated. It is demonstrable that all that part of the United States east of the Mississippi never contained half a million Indians; some authorities say a quarter of a million. It is apparent at a glance that a country like Ohio will sustain four hundred times as many people in the civilized as in the savage state. When men live upon game and the spontaneous products of the earth, it must be a fertile land indeed which will sustain an average of one person to the square mile. When we pass to the Indian of the plains the original population was sparser still. But there we find some of the races on the soil where first discovered. The Sioux have steadily contracted their eastern border, while maintaining their western border intact. But if, leaving history we take tradition, we find that the Indian tribes have been engaged for centuries in a series of migrations, the northern ones as a rule slowly pushing southward. As all our mountain chains run north and south, it follows that the people of this country can not grow into distinct races as in Europe, where different climates and soils are partitioned off by natural barriers. Hence the Indian, from Manitoba to the Gulf of Mexico is *one;* hence, too, half a million men of the West rose in arms to prevent the mouth of the Mississippi being "held by an alien government." Of the Indian migrations, the best authenticated are those of the Shoshonees and Sioux, which are referred to in the following legend, as related to the interpreter by Susuccicha, a Sioux chief:

"Ages past the Lacotas (or Dakotas, *i. e.*, Sioux) lived in a land far above the sun of winter.

"Here then the Shoshonee had all, but these basins were yet full of water, and the buffalo ranged even to the Salt Land (Utah).

"Ages passed. The Shoshonees gave place to the Scarred Arms (Cheyennes). The Lacotas came toward the sun and fought long with the Scarred Arms. A great party came far into the inner plain (Laramie) and fell into a snare; all were killed by the Scarred Arms but six; these hid in a hole in the mountain.

"They built a fire and dressed their wounds; they hoped to stay many days till the Scarred Arms left the plain. But a form rose from the dark corner of the cave; it was a woman—old as the red mountain that was scarred by Waukan. Her hair was like wool; she was feeble and wrinkled. She spoke:

"'Children, you have been against the Scarred Arms. You alone live. I know it all. But your fire has waked me, and the full time of my dream has come. Listen:

"'Long ago the Shoshonees visited the Lacotas; the prairie took in the blood of many Lacota braves, and I was made captive. The Shoshonees brought me here, but I was not happy. I fled. I was weak. I took refuge in this cave.

"'But look! Where are the Shoshonees? The Lacotas will soon know them, and bring from their lodges many scalps and medicine dogs. They have fled before the Scarred Arms. One-half crossed the snow hills toward sunset; the other went toward the sun, and now hunt the buffalo east of the Ispanola's earth lodges. But my eyes were sealed for ages till my people should come. The Scarred Arms have long thought this land their own, but it is not. Waukantunga gives it to the Lacotas; they shall possess the land of their daughter's captivity. But why wait ye? Go gather your warriors and attack the Scarred Arms. Fear not, their scalps are yours.'

"The warriors did return. They found the Scarred Arms at the foot of the mountain, and drove them to the South. Our grateful braves then sought the mountain to reverence the medicine woman, who told them so many good things. But woman and cave were gone. There was only a cleft in the mountain side from which came a cold stream of water. Then the Lacotas made peace with the Scarred Arms. Each year our warriors visit the Shoshonees for scalps and medicine dogs, and each of our braves, as he passes the old woman's spring, stops to quench his thirst and yield a tribute of veneration."

The Shoshonees not only have a legend answering to this, but name the various times when the Comanches, Arapahoes, and Apaches seceded from the main body. Thus this great colony of the Athabascan race, slowly moving southward, has sent off branches right and left, from the Saskatchewan to the Rio Grande and Gulf of California.

It would surprise some people who have been indignant over the death of Custer and his companions to learn how small, comparatively, is the number of hostile Indians. A strip of 500 miles wide, from the Missouri to the Pacific, is rarely visited by hostiles; and at no time for the past ten years have more than one-fifth of the race been in arms or even threatening. All the border States except Texas are free from hostiles. Of the nine Territories only three have been seriously troubled since 1867, and the three Pacific States have had even a longer exemption. Within that time Indian hostilities have been confined to three districts. First, and greatest, is that strip of mountain, forest, and desert including all Northern Wyoming, South-eastern and Eastern Montana, and a small portion of Western Dakota. Next are the highlands of Western Texas, raided by the Comanches and their allies; and lastly that part of New Mexico and Arizona dominated by the Apaches. To judge how contemptible a performance an Indian war is, how small the glory in proportion to the aggravation, be it noted that the whole Apache race numbers less than 8,000, and can not possibly mount 2,000 warriors.

If it be decided that the 300,000 Indians in the United States (or rather the 200,000 wild ones) are to "die off," then by all means let a "feeding policy" be pursued; it is so much cheaper to kill them by kindness than by war. Since 1860 the average cost of killing Indians has been about $500,000 each. One-tenth that amount would stuff one to death. If, I say, the theory of final extermination be adopted, the most Christian and, by all odds, the cheapest plan would be this: Let central depots be established along the Pacific Railway and at other accessible points, and give general notice that every Indian who will come there and live shall have all the bread, meat, coffee, sugar, whisky and tobacco he can consume. The last man of them would be dead in ten years, and at a cost not exceeding twenty per cent. of the killing price. Since the Mormons began the feeding policy with their nearest Indian neighbors the latter have died off much faster than when at war. They can't stand petting any more than a rabbit.

CHAPTER XXXIV.

PROSPECTING AND MINING.

LET us "prospect," courteous reader, and find, locate, develop, prove up, and get a patent for a silver mine. We will start from Cincinnati; the reader may do the hard work, and the author will contribute experience and a free talk for his share of the capital. *Imprimis*, then, we need not look for a silver mine in this part of the country; but we can hear of many. For silver and gold, once brought near the surface by cosmic upheaval, are subject to wash and removal the same as other minerals; and as "drift," the loose material of the earth's surface, is made up of the wear and tear of all kinds of rocks, it often contains enough gold or silver to mislead. Sometimes a rocky hollow furnishes a natural trough to concentrate this washed mineral, and then you have a wonderful story—we will hear half a dozen of them in our trip across Southern Indiana. If you can find an Indian tradition to match it, your "hoodoo" is complete; for nothing sets a thing of that sort off so beautifully as an Indian tradition. If you can add to it that some poor consumptive, years ago wandered into the wilderness, and was miraculously cured by an "Injun doctor," who lived in a wigwam back of a rock, and told him about the mine, you will then have the average legend about all the silver mines reported in Ohio and Indiana.

Of course there can be no such thing as a real gold or silver mine in the comparatively level strata of these States; we must find a region where the strata have been heaved up and split across—where the backbone of the continent is laid open. For illustration take a jelly-cake of many layers to represent any part of the earth where the rock strata are in place and undisturbed; then bend it to a sharp ridge and let the ragged edges wear away; the crevices between what were the bottom layers will be exposed on top. Precisely this has happened in mining regions; and after these contact veins were formed, the mountain has often been split directly across its regular formation, thus forming true fissure veins. But uniformity is no part of nature's design, and for every perfect specimen of any kind she produces hundreds of abortions, imitations, and half-made specimens. We shall see how these mislead us when we reach the mines. Going on westward, then, we find various rocks coming to the surface in this order: In Eastern Indiana the Silurian, next the Devonian, and then the Carboniferous, which extend to the Mississippi. After a short strip of older rock we again cross some carboniferous, in Missouri, and after getting into Kansas every day's travel for six hundred miles brings us over newer rock. First is a narrow strip of that limestone which, if all rocks are in place, lies just above the Coal Measures; then we pass rapidly over rocks of successively later eras, and near Wichita, enter on the "Chalk-stones" (Cretaceous). All this was made at so late a day that we need not look for true coal even—much less for gold or silver—but salt and alkali soon become disgustingly plenty. Still further on we find newer rock, and near the foot of the mountains are the fossil remains of huge creatures which lived just before man came on earth. And out of this very recent formation suddenly rises the Pike's Peak range, consisting largely of the oldest known rocks. So science has decided that long after Pike's Peak rose to mountain height its bases were washed by inland seas, and that the eastern one was among the last sections of America to become dry land.

We enter the mountains and observe that we are now where the lower strata have been heaved up and split across, and therefore minerals *may* abound. We examine all the streams carefully for "float"—fragments broken off the croppings of some mineral vein and washed down. If the float shows silver or lead, *good;* if iron or copper, it is not to be despised; but quartz crystals, iron pyrites, and glittering flakes of mica will certainly attract *your* eye, my gentle pilgrim. Even a mineral stain on the rocks is not to be passed without examination, though we don't think much of it down here among the foot-hills. If we find good float, or even specimens of rock or ores usually associated with silver, we are encouraged and toil upward; for we do not hope to locate in the foot-hills or even near the base of the higher range. If there is a mine there, the chances are thousands to one that the outcrop is covered hundreds of feet deep by drift. Obviously the higher we get the less drift there is on the bed rock, till we reach a point where the real mountain protrudes its bare rocky points. Nevertheless we examine the lower slopes carefully, for we may find a "stream of float" which will lead us directly to the vicinity of a mine. It often happens that such a stream leads the prospector to a point half way up the mountain, then suddenly ceases. Where, then, is the mine? The lode from which that stream was derived may be hundreds or thousands of feet further up, and it may be near by and buried beneath the drift. When search above failed to find it, I have known miners to turn a stream of water from the highest practicable mountain torrent and wash a gully to the bed rock, down the mountain side, searching the bottom carefully all the way for evidences of the lode. It may be, however, that the lode is right under us, but shows no evidence at the surface; it is then known as a "blind lode," and is either discovered by mere accident or by tracing from an adjacent gulch.

Right here the "pilgrim" is an unfailing source of amusement to the old miner. One day he goes wild over a piece of iron pyrites ("fool's gold"), the next he locates a mine on the strength of a slab of yellow mica; now his spirits mount on eagle's wings at some trifling outcrop of galena or iron, and again the mercury goes down to the bottom of his boots because he can find nothing that glitters. But the old prospector knows too well that silver in its native matrix is the most modest of all the metals. In nature it is like the native diamond—without luster. It is only the low-grade galena ores, the many-hued sulphur, or the "peacock," which dazzle the eye. Horace has well expressed it: *Nullus argento color est avaris abditæ terris*—"There is no luster to silver hidden in the grasping earth." The richer an ore is, the less like a rich ore it looks to the unpracticed eye.

As we hunt up the mountain side we encounter some "blossom rock," which is merely float of such size, richness, and generally ragged contour as to show that it has not rolled far. The trail is now getting hot. We are certainly near the outcrop from which the "blossom" was broken, and if an assay shows the ore attached to it to be rich, we feel all the enthusiasm of the true prospector; our bacon and beans have a new relish, and over the evening pipe, around the camp-fire, we speculate as to how we will spend all the money we are sure to make. If this is at a point where the bed rock is not covered by drift, we redouble our scrutiny; we tap the rock at every point and search diligently for any indications of mineral. Stains on the rock are now of much more importance than they were among the foot-hills. If the snow is just going off we notice very carefully what sort of a stain the drip leaves on the rock. Iron stains are red; copper stains, a reddish yellow; but lead and silver stains are gray, the brightness varying with the proportion of other minerals. One of the richest mines in American Fork Cañon, Utah, was discovered by following up a stain left by melting snow. But while we speculate on these things we happen at last on a point where there is an unmistakable outcrop of *something* different from the country rock.

We dig and blast and assay, and find that here a mineral-bearing ore actually projects from the surface; and now we *are* in luck.

Are we though? Well, that depends. There is about one chance in twenty that this little outcrop is the end of a large continuous crevice, and about one chance in ten that such a crevice when found will prove a valuable mine. For the reason of this disgusting fact we must go back to the origin of things, and consider how the mountain came to have crevices in it at all. Suppose a mountain of massive rock, or of massive rock below, and capped by sedimentary (stratified) rock above—the whole mass broken across by a force acting from below—obviously this would result: the force would split the mountain in a tolerably direct course until it neared the surface; then it would shatter the cap of the mountain, there being less resistance, and the fracturing force would find outlet in a score or a hundred minor crevices. This, if the mountain were all massive rock; but if it were stratified rock, whether limestone, slate, porphyry, or what not, with lines of cleavage already present, the fracturing force would of course follow these lines, and thus you would find scores of crevices at the surface for the one main crevice far below. Indeed, what miners call a "mother lode" is often like a tree in its upward development: below is the main trunk, above the branches diverge, and sometimes one immense branch strikes off at right angles and reaches the surface hundreds or thousands of feet away. The outcrops which led to the noted Comstock Lode spread over a width of twelve hundred feet. From these originate most of the lawsuits as to mining titles; and if the lucky prospector develops a true vein, or big *bonanza*, he may reasonably expect to find a dozen or more fellows located on the neighboring outcrops, each indulging a hope that the court will decide his to be the true location, or that the owners will buy him off.

But this is only one way in which mines are found, though it is the most common way. Sometimes a blind lode is traced by a faint outcrop in a neighboring gulch; sometimes it is found while running a tunnel for some other purpose or opening another mine; and occasionally a bold outcrop is struck without any indications below it in the way of float. It is the theory of geology that our mountains were once much higher than at present, their tops having been worn away. So, if the crevice extended to the surface of the original mountain—as it often did, no doubt—it, too, has worn away, and its contents are scattered in the drift. But where such a crevice was filled with hard volcanic rock, the softer rock around it wore away and left a dike—a serrated ridge like the Devil's Slide on the Weber. This could seldom, if ever, happen with a mineral-bearing vein. As a rule, not only is the outcrop of such a vein hidden, but the top ore is swept out, and nothing of great value is found until we attain some depth. There is but one way, then, of finding out whether our location amounts to anything: we must dig. When we have scooped out a few cubic yards of rock and earth we then have a "prospect hole," and for a few days—in some districts, according to local law—we can hold title to it by merely leaving our tools in it when absent. If we find good signs, however, we would better post a

NOTICE.

We, the undersigned, of the town of Fair Hope, State of Colorado, this tenth day of April, 1882, claim, by right of discovery, one thousand five hundred (1500) feet along the course of this ledge or vein of mineral-bearing rock, with all its dips, spurs, angles, and variations, as allowed by law; also one hundred and fifty (150) feet of surface ground on each side of the central line of said lode.

Made April 10th, 1882. JOSEPH HOPEFUL,
  LYNN C. D'OYLE.

Ten years ago we should have claimed and located two hundred feet along the lode for each person, and "two hundred for discovery;" so we two could have held but six hundred feet. This was a sort of limit, but every district had many local regulations, and in most of the territories prospectors could "locate" as many friends in their claim as they pleased—two hundred feet for each—by doing work in proportion. Little by little a system grew up out of the original chaos (see pp. 476–478); the territories first passed general laws, and in 1872 Congress reduced the whole thing to a very clear and able code of mining laws. This granted six hundred feet in width and fifteen hundred in length, but allowed territories to limit the width; and in 1874 Colorado cut it down to three hundred feet. Local laws still determine the amount of work required to hold a claim, and in this matter each district is a law unto itself. For the present our "Notice" gives sufficient title, as we want to dig deeper and see what we have.

The first excitement is soon passed, and day after day we pick and blast, inward and downward. If we find a crevice, though ever so small and irregular, we dig on, carefully watching the "indications." We may follow a "pinching vein" for rods through the solid rock: sometimes it shrinks to the thinness of a knife blade; sometimes we see nothing more of it than a mere mineral stain on the wall of our shaft or incline; again it may widen to a few inches, and yet again it may "pocket" suddenly in a chamber the size of a keg, barrel, or hogshead. Many a prospector finds his vein at an end for good and all in such a pocket. But we do not, of course, expect much near the surface: all we look for now is good indications. If our seam gains in width on the whole, if it slowly changes towards the perpendicular, if defined walls show themselves with patches of "slickensides," or even if there is a well marked line of division between the vein matter and the enclosing wall-rock, we are encouraged. Many are the alternations of hope and fear: to-day she widens, with a defined seam of so-so ore; to-morrow we are in the "cap" or pinch, and our hopes are crushed. We may be in the main vein; we may be in a mere "gash" or overflow; perhaps we have located on a side outcrop, with the main vein hundreds of feet away; and, worst of all, we may have fallen on a true fissure and well defined vein, but full of such low-grade ore that the more we have of it the poorer we are.

By this time romance has given place to philosophy, and we are cool enough to consider some ugly facts. The first is that not one location in ten is ever sunk to a depth of sixty feet; that of those so far sunk not one in ten proves a valuable mine; and that of actual mines not one in ten is rich enough to get excited about. The most curious fact, however, is this: the marvelously small proportion which the precious metal bears to the whole mass of the ore, the almost infinite number of chances which determine its presence or absence, and the utter lack of ratio between its *chemical*, or mechanical, and its *commercial* value. For instance, if gold ore yields $40.00 per ton, it is very rich. But what *is* $40.00 per ton? Only two ounces out of 32,000! That is, if the one sixteen-thousandth part of what you hoist out is gold, your mine is very rich. But scores of gold mines are worked with big profits, yielding but $10.00 per ton—one sixty-four-thousandth part of the mass. Yet a mine in the same place, yielding but $8.00 per ton, would not probably pay for working, the $2.00 per ton on the output making all the difference between profit and loss. So this formula,

$$\tfrac{1}{64000} \text{ minus } \tfrac{1}{80000} \text{ equals } \tfrac{1}{320000},$$

shows all the difference between a mine of some value and one of little or none. In silver the disproportion is not so great, but still rather startling. Thus, in Colorado, fifty ounces per ton makes a valuable mine; twenty-five ounces, in most localities, is not worth mining for. So you have $\tfrac{1}{1280}$ of the mass as the real difference between rich and poor ore. Consider how very small this difference is in nature—how many chances in her vast laboratory may lessen the proportion a little; then add the fact that silver will combine with scores of minerals, and you will plainly see that its presence in paying quantities is the accident of an accident, and that one crevice may be full of rich ore, and another but a few rods away too poor to work. You will see, too, that a man is not necessarily rich because he owns a silver mine, and understand why it is that so many mines, undoubtedly true fissures, are not worked. I believe I can go to the western part of Utah and buy a known true-fissure vein, two or three feet wide and full of ore, for a hundred dollars. But the ore is low-grade galena, wood and water are scarce in the vicinity, and there is no railroad. Thus it often happens that a mine of no value becomes valuable by improved transportation or the discovery of coal near by.

At the depth of fifty feet we find ourselves in a crevice with defined walls, containing *some* mineral; we go twenty-five feet further, and the crevice is perceptibly wider, with an occasional "selvage" between the vein matter and the wall, and sometimes "slickensides"—patches smooth as polished glass, supposed to have been caused by the friction of moving walls in the period of fracture. At a hundred feet in depth we are satisfied we have a good mine, and begin to take out ore enough nearly to pay expenses. The enterprise has cost us some $1500, and we think enough of it to want our title perfected. We recorded the location in the District Recorder's books soon after we put up the notice, and have done more than the amount of work the district law requires; so our next step is to apply for a United States patent, and from this on we must comply strictly with the Law of Congress, approved May 10, 1872.

We first apply to the Surveyor-General of the State or Territory, paying a fee of twenty-five dollars. We must, if the question is raised, prove our citizenship or that we have filed a declaration of intention to become citizens. The proof, however, is not made very onerous, our own affidavits generally being sufficient. A corporation need only file its certificate as in other cases. We also file proof from the District Recorder that we located and recorded as claimed, and satisfy the official that we have done work on our claim to the value of $500.

The Surveyor-General then, in person or by deputy, surveys and maps out for us fifteen hundred feet along the lode, and one hundred and fifty feet on each side of it, unless our claim be in Boulder, Gilpin, Clear Creek, or Park counties, Colorado. In these four old counties the locator is limited to seventy-five feet on each side; so a claim there covers but half as much surface as elsewhere. The law strictly provides that the end boundaries must be parallel to each other and at right angles to the central line; so a full claim, outside of the above counties, is a perfect parallelogram—three hundred by fifteen hundred feet, or ten acres and about a fifth; and for this the Government charges five dollars per acre. The Surveyor-General must then make a complete plat of the claim.

We go next to the Register of the Land Office of our State or Territory. We post one copy of the surveyor's plat on a post or rock, conspicuously, on the ground we claim; another copy we file with the Register, with the field-notes, and the affidavits of two competent persons that we have posted notice on the claim. The Register then enters the case for record, and publishes notice of the application as often as once a week for at least sixty days, in the newspaper nearest to such claim. He must also post notice of our application in his office; and, by the way, we must also pay him some fees, and pay for the advertising. If no adverse claimant appears in response to this advertising, all such are barred; it is assumed that our claim is first class, and we go higher.

But if there is one chance in ten, some fellow will be certain to claim that our mine belongs to him. He may file his claim under oath, and, within thirty days after so doing, begin suit in any court with real estate jurisdiction. If he fails to do so within the time, he is forever barred; if he acts promptly, the case goes to trial the same as any other. If we gain it, we file a copy of the judgment with the Register of the Land Office, and proceed as before. But all this time we retain possession of the mine, and take out pay ore—if there is any.

Having gotten rid of the man who tried to "jump" our mine, we pay some more fees, you observe, and the Register certifies all the papers to the Commissioner-General of the Land Office, at Washington, who thereupon issues to us a patent, and we are owners in fee simple of the claim therein described. We, or our assigns, can then hold it for all time, no matter whether we work it or let it lie idle. A patent costs from $125 to $175, all the fees in mining districts being very heavy. The holder can follow his vein downward wherever it goes, but he must not go outside of his end lines. The following general principles of mining law, either as laid down in the statutes of Congress and the Territories or decided by the Land Office Department and courts, are worth noting:

All lands of the United States containing gold, silver, lead, tin, copper, or cinnabar, in workable quantities, are mineral lands, and not open to homestead or preëmption entry. Nor can they be sold in quantities as other lands, nor does a land grant convey them to a railroad or other grantee. Nor is any distinction made by Government between its surveyed and unsurveyed mineral lands.

In cases of doubt or dispute the law leans to the side of the prospector. The decisions of the Department bear strongly against other than miners' titles to lands supposed to be mineral, it being the declared policy of the United States to encourage mining development in all proper ways. (See decision of the Commissioner-General in regard to the town site of Deadwood, Dakota.)

Land once surveyed and thrown open to settlement will be withdrawn from market at any time before vested rights accrue, upon proof that it is mineral-bearing.

That land is within a known mineral region, is held presumptive proof that it is mineral land; the burden of proof is on those who seek to show that it is not.

The miners of each district may make local laws not inconsistent with those of the United States, or of the State or Territory; and these local laws will be enforced by the courts. Similarly a State or Territory may make any laws not inconsistent with the ownership of mineral lands by the United States.

When a patent has been granted, a mine is real estate in fee simple, and subject to local tax, lien, mortgage, and execution, the same as other real estate. Before a patent is granted, the title is still in the United States; the miner has but a possessory right, and, in strictness of law, only his improvements could be taxed.

Where a tunnel is run for the development of a lode or for prospecting, the owners thereof have the right to all veins or lodes cut by it, and all within three thousand feet from the starting-point of the tunnel and lying on its line, not previously known to exist; and locations within such limit by other parties, after the tunnel has been commenced, are invalid. But to secure such rights the tunnel must be driven with reasonable diligence; and a cessation of work thereon for six months forfeits the right to undiscovered veins on its line.

If applicants for patents complain that fees and publication charges are exorbitant, the Commissioner-General has power to limit such charges, or to designate another paper than the one first selected by the Register.

Where two or more veins, separate at the surface, run together below, the oldest title holds the property. Where two veins cross, the older title takes the ore at the intersection; but the other has the right of way across the space for the purpose of working.

The State or Territory may make all needful rules for safe and healthful working of mines, easement, drainage, etc.

All parties along a stream have equal original rights to use of the water; but priority of use or possession becomes a vested right, of which the party can not be deprived even by those who locate above him.

The status of all mineral lands taken up before May 10th, 1872, is in nowise changed by the statute; they remain as rights therein accrued under local or territorial law.

Prospectors can not exercise too much care in defining their locations at the outset, that the same may be distinctly traced on the ground and its boundaries easily marked. The United States statute is also specific in requiring that all records of locations shall contain the names of the locators, the date of the location, and such description of the claim by reference to natural objects or permanent monuments as will identify it. One should also particularly set forth the distance of his claim each way from his center stake, and bound it if possible by a gulch, stream, or prominent rock, and specify carefully its bearing from or towards, and distance from, any adjacent lode.

Work to the value of at least $100 per year must be done on a claim to hold it by mere possessory right.

Now that we have our mine, let us decide what kind of a one it is, and then how we would better work it.

CHAPTER XXXV.

MINING FORTUNES AND MISFORTUNES.

In the closing months of 1878 the white nomads of the West were greatly excited by reports of a new Eldorado and a great mining city modestly called *Lead*-ville. Soon all the journals were spotted with stirring accounts of the Magic City. All old similes were exhausted and a hundred new ones invented: it was the future metropolis astride the Mother Lode of the world; it had sprung up as if from the touch of Aladdin's lamp; it seemed as if built by genii in a night; it was Ophir and Lydia and Potosi, Tyre and San Francisco, all in one. All around it the rock-ribbed hills were said to be thick-set with bottomless lodes of argentiferous ore. All this and much more. Of course the old campaigner knew that at least half of this was the natural gush of the editor whose bright home is in the setting sun, etc.; nevertheless a great longing grew upon me to mingle once more in such stirring scenes. But, alas! business and domestic cares forbade; so I confided my interest in the sight-seeing to my friend and relative, C. K. Bright, Esq., and the purely narrative portion of this chapter is from his diary.

February 10th, 1879, says the diary, I bought of the Indianapolis, Bloomington and Western Railroad a ticket from Covington, Indiana, to Denver *via* Pueblo, for the low price of $44.10. Including all expenses for food and rest, the total cost is less than $60.00: this for a journey which once occupied at least two months, and required an outfit of two or three hundred dollars. Steel and steam have brought the Far West almost to our doors. At 10 o'clock that evening we crossed the Mississippi at Quincy, and at 9:15, next morning landed in Kansas City. Thence we departed at 11 A. M., on the Atchison, Topeka and Santa Fe line, stopping for dinner at Topeka, sixty-six miles out. All the way, and for seventy-five miles beyond Topeka, the country teems with every variety of agricultural products; pleasant homes and thriving villages cheer the traveler's eye, and, except the general air of freshness and smartness, one sees no signs of a new West. It is, rather, a transplanted New England.

Darkness found us at Osage City, and to us the line between Kansas and Colorado is even less than an idea: we went to sleep in one and woke in the other. But the scene had greatly changed: out of a settled and cultivated valley, into an apparently boundless waste where

> "The dewy ground was dark and cold;
> Behind all gloomy to behold;
> And stepping westward seemed to be
> A kind of heavenly destiny.
> I liked the greeting; 't was a sound
> Of something without place or bound,
> And seemed to give me spiritual right
> To seek beyond for regions bright."

In summer the scene is much more animated, for the entire valley is then occupied by stockmen, who drive their cattle farther east in the winter. Fresh beef is now eaten in London which was grown and fattened in this valley, while much of the corn and wheat produced in the Kansas half of it finds a market in the mines and cities of Colorado. We follow up the gently winding valley of the Arkansas, finding no perceptible change, as eastern Colorado climate and scenery extend far down into Kansas.

At La Junta, five hundred and fifty-five miles from Kansas City, a branch road strikes south-west to Trinidad, and thence on to Otero—the first railroad station ever established in New Mexico—and beyond that is stretching towards the Pacific. At late dinner-time we reach Pueblo, six hundred and eighteen miles from the Missouri; and still we are forty miles from Cañon City, the end of railroading for the present.

Pueblo is close down to the river, in the Arkansas Valley, only four thousand seven hundred and three feet above the sea, and, like every other Colorado town in the valleys, is "highly recommended for pulmonary diseases." Here we rested a day, to get our "second wind," then took the afternoon train and ran rapidly up the valley to Cañon City, five thousand two hundred and sixty feet above the sea. And now I begin to feel the altitude—just a little—and various symptoms warn me that I had better wait here a few days before entering on the trying stage-coach ride to Leadville.

Cañon City is situated on both sides of the Arkansas, which is here a noticeably larger stream than it is a hundred miles farther down—though a mere creek compared with its volume in Arkansas. There are mountains north, south, and west of the town, but to the east the view is open. To the eastern eye the valley seems narrow, though there is considerable good land near by and between here and Pueblo. There is, however, hardly any such thing as agriculture in Colorado; it is horticulture rather, farming on a small scale, except where there is meadow land. Hence to Rosita, county seat of Custer City, it is thirty miles south; and a little beyond that is the wonderful Silver Cliff, where the first house was erected the first week in September, 1878, and before Christmas there were hundreds, and the population is now at least five thousand! Such is the suddenness of things in a mining country.

As Cañon City is shut in by the hills from the rudest wintry blasts, nestling close in to the base of the Rocky Mountains, it is regarded as the best winter resort in the State for invalids. To this add the iron and soda springs, the hot mineral baths, and the wonderful scenery of the Royal Gorge and Grape Creek Cañon, and no more need be said.

We spent a day of delight in Grape Creek Cañon, which is the first stage on the road to Silver Cliff. As we wound around the curves of the road it seemed at every turn we were shut in; but following up the stream we found the walls opening on new scenes of grandeur. The rocks are basaltic, and reared in columns, reminding one greatly of the pictures of the Giant's Causeway. They rise in grape-colored pillars to a height of three or four hundred feet, and are often capped with a sort of cornice which gives an odd resemblance to architectural designs. In many places the cañon is so narrow that road and stream occupy its entire width; and since the railway to Silver Cliff is completed, it gives a rare opportunity for a romantic ride. Temple Cañon opens from Grape Creek, through an archway of rock wonderfully like that of the Natural Bridge in Virginia.

The McClure House, our head-quarters, is full of excited humanity. All the restless spirits of the world seem crowding on to Leadville, Gunnison, Silver Cliff, or San Juan. Sanguine "pilgrims" assure us that all the "science, falsely so called," has been upset by the new discoveries at Silver Cliff; for there is just as rich ore there in one kind of rock as another. "You don't even have to find a lode or crevice to get ore, and the biggest greenhorn this side of New Jersey is just as apt to strike a *bonanza* as the oldest professor of mineralogy." And verily, late developments there have about proved this boast true. The bordering mountain is appropriately called Greenhorn Range, as if in compliment to that class of prospectors. And, after finding rich ore almost everywhere except where the old heads told them to look for it, the lucky ones jocosely proposed to install a spectacled *burro* over their budding school of mining science. But of this remarkable place, more anon.

We devoted the whole day, February 7th, to seeing the wonders of the Grand Canon and the Royal Gorge; and surely whole weeks would be scant time to enjoy fully the awful grandeur, the almost frightful sublimity of this place. In ages past the Arkansas has cut a narrow way nearly twenty-five hundred feet deep, directly through the mountain; and far down in the depths, for many a rod where sunlight never penetrates, the foaming water frets its way among the fallen rocks which choke its bed. Many prefer to go around by the old route, thirteen miles over the high levels, to get an opportunity to see the gorge from above; but we chose the walk directly up the cañon, as the way had been opened and made *tolerably* safe by the pioneer parties of the Atchison, Topeka, and Santa Fe Road.

NIGHT SCENE IN THE CANON.

This rock-bound river channel was known to Spanish missionaries in 1642; but it is claimed that no human being passed through it before 1870. The distant hills encroach very gradually on the river as we go up, till at last they shut it in between jagged and almost perpendicular cliffs two thousand feet in height. One can not see the top above him for the overhanging walls; but glancing up on the other side, the sight is sufficient to give some people the vertigo. At last we reach the Royal Gorge, which is over a mile in length, and is, indeed, only an enormous tunnel two thousand feet under the solid rock, with a slight crack opened to the sky and sunlight above. The canon walls above the stream recede from each other for one thousand feet, then slowly approach to within thirty-five feet, making an enormous curve like the two sides of a ().

Since the above was written the railroad has forced its way through this chasm. The original surveys were made while the stream was frozen over; then workmen were lowered from above and a foothold blasted out of the cliff, and then rock masses of hundreds of tons were blown out with dynamite and tumbled into the river bed. May 7th, 1879, the first passenger train passed through the gorge, and then came—a lawsuit! The merits of the case need not be discussed, but the company whose energy opened the way was not permitted to enjoy it. After a tedious suit, and riots and seizures which amounted to civil war, the courts, early in 1880, gave judgment for the Denver and Rio Grande Railway Company; and in April of that year, on payment of construction costs, that company took possession of the line. It at once hurried on the work and completed the road to Leadville that summer. And now the traveler may reach Leadville or Silver Cliff in the most comfortable of passenger cars.

But we had to stage it, and, in the early morning of February 18th, took seat in one of Barlow and Sanderson's coaches, paying $14.00 fare, or about eleven cents a mile, for the one hundred and twenty-six miles to Leadville. The morning was stinging cold, and the ice and snow forbade all enjoyment of scenery. All we note is a bewildering succession of mountain, valley, and timbered slope; the coach laboring away from the Arkansas and uphill for hours, and then coming thundering down to it again wherever the valley was broad enough for a road, till we reached Bayles's Ranche, where we concluded to stop for the night.

At Cleora, a station on our line, coaches start on branch lines for Ouray and Saguache. N. B.—They spell this name right, but pronounce it *Sowahchay!* But it's all the same in Spanish. By the same diabolical process of lingual gymnastics they write the name of the junction where the New Mexican branch of the railway starts, La Junta, and call it *Lah Hoontay.* So, too, they call San Juan, *San Wahn;* Juanita, *Wahneeta;* Albuquerque, *Albookairkay;* and San Luis, *San Looeee.* They will even laugh at a pilgrim who pronounces them as they are spelled. But it's a way they have out here; and if you don't like it, there is no law against your staying in Indiana.

As soon as light was sufficient we departed from Bayles's Ranche, and soon were in the midst of scenery so grand that we lost all sense of danger, though the abrupt turns, sharp precipices, and yawning chasms along the way were enough to shake the firmest nerves. Many a time it seemed to me the coach horses were taking us at full run over a precipice, into a chasm of unknown depth; but just at the right moment the driver dropped his weight upon the brake, the vehicle "slowed," a turn opened to right or left, and we glided gracefully around a jutting corner of rock, into a broad gallery, and then down, down, down along the winding dug-way to the stream which we had left, it might be hours before, to toil up the mountain. At last, at 9 P. M., we reached Leadville to find the whole city illuminated. It was not in honor of anybody, however, but to thaw the ground for digging to lay water-pipes. We then learned that the ground in this remarkable city freezes *almost* every night in the year. They had piled long winrows of wood in the street, set it on fire, and dug a ditch for the water-pipes under the bed of hot embers! And this they would have had to do in any month in the year, except possibly July and August. With this startling information we tumbled into Blanket Bay and for ten hours slept the sleep of the just and weary. Enjoyed it none the less though the small room contained fourteen beds filled with other weary pilgrims.

February 20th, awoke with strange sensations: giddiness, head too big entirely, and limbs rather slow in obeying the motions of the will. First attempt to run about town proved a total failure, for a painful fluttering in the temple and tremor about the heart warned me to go slow. Nor did those symptoms leave me entirely for a week. Leadville is ten thousand two hundred feet above the sea, and the pilgrim should be in no hurry about exercise. Fortunately the tendency to rest is generally too strong to be resisted; laziness becomes a virtue, and one can sleep half the time and lounge the other half. But when I got my mountain legs on the days were too short to view the novelties. My first climb was to the Little Pittsburg Mine, of which one-fourth had just been sold for $262,500. The lucky seller was a poor man a year before, but on receipt of his cash he proceeded immediately to Silver Cliff and reinvested it—so he *may* be a poor man again in due time. The Little Pittsburg was said to be producing $10,000 a day when in full work.

Day after day I gained in lung power, and climbed to higher mines;

and night after night enjoyed seeing the motley crowd on the streets. Nothing surprised me so much as the enormous quantities of mail received and the crowd at the post-office, especially on Sundays. Then one often has to wait in line an hour or two for his chance. It would seem that miners spend all their spare time in reading or answering letters. But there is a good sized theater crowded nightly, and scores of popular resorts, all of which seem well patronized Day after day the town is excited by new reports of rich discoveries in the mountains, "a little further on." And after a month's experience of this sort of thing, and diligent study of the formation, it seems fair to drop the narrative style and give the reader some condensed facts.

Come with us *now*, in the opening of 1882, to Leadville. You need not stage it as we did, for you can lie back in a Horton reclining-chair and view the scenery as you come, on either of two railroads. The Denver and Rio Grande comes directly up the Arkansas from Pueblo, the Denver and South Park in a general south-west direction from Denver; and whichever one you come by, you will think the scenery the finest in the world—till you return by the other. You will land in a city of fifteen thousand or twenty thousand people, with large hotels, immense wholesale and retail stores, an elegant opera-house, with good society, an odd compound of that of Chicago and San Francisco, and some of the worst society in the world—if you look for it.

Leadville lies on the east side of, and about three miles from the Arkansas River, on a gently sloping plain, or plateau, cut through on the south by the famous California Gulch, walled in on the east by the world-renowned Freyer and Carbonate Hills, which are in turn overshadowed by the frowning peaks of the Mosquito Range. On the north the main portion of the city is flanked by an elevation known as Capital Hill, upon which some of the finest residences in the city are located. Looking west, the valley of the Arkansas is seen, beyond which towers the majestic Mount Massive, whose snowy head is often veiled with clouds. Surely no city could be more beautiful for situation.

Near the city—indeed, throughout the district this side of the divide—the geological formation is very irregular. The basis is granite, which crops out frequently. All along the valley of the Arkansas indications of extensive Silurian formations are quite abundant. However, the strata have been so broken up by volcanic action and so extensively converted into metamorphic rock, that it is impossible to determine the extent of the original formations. So far as the mines have developed, there seems to be no regularity or system whatever, but all is in a confused mass. Mines that are but a few hundred feet apart strike very different rock deposits. There is no uniformity in the thickness of the "wash," or of the deposits of limestone, porphyry, and carbonates. One mine will strike valuable carbonates a few feet from the surface, while the mine next to it may go down hundreds of feet and find little or no paying ore. In some mines limestone is found in abundance; others encounter extensive deposits of porphyry. As a rule, the carbonates are found below the porphyry. These carbonate deposits are not at all uniform in extent. Sometimes they contain only a ton or two; and, again, there will be a hundred tons or more in one deposit. The silver-bearing ores also vary greatly in kind. Some are soft or pulverized, called sand carbonates; some are hard, and carry a large per cent. of iron; while others are almost wholly composed of galena, with a small per cent. of silver; still others are rich in chlorides and sulphurets.

Nothing like a true fissure vein has been found in Freyer or Carbonate Hills; but in the gulches over the divide, many rich veins have been discovered. These veins vary from one foot to six feet in thickness, and are often rich in galena. Little of horn or wire silver has been discovered in the deposit mines, though some has been found in fissure veins. During the past season some very valuable gold-bearing veins have been discovered near Leadville. It is believed that there are many rich gold-bearing lodes yet undiscovered in the immediate vicinity of Leadville. Several millions of dollars in gold dust have been washed from the gravel beds of California Gulch—paying dirt having been found there twenty years ago, and it is very probable that the gold dust has been washed down from veins of gold-bearing rock in the sides of the neighboring mountains.

Some suppose that there is a deposit of carbonates underlying all the country about here, which may be struck if the shaft is sunk deep enough. But the more probable opinion is that these deposits lie here and there with no regularity. It will be seen, therefore, that the search for carbonates in the foot-hills about Leadville is one of luck or haphazard entirely. The miner has no indications to guide him, but digs a hole hoping to strike it. Not more than one in one hundred of the holes thus dug has yielded well. So mining about Leadville, at the start at least, is simply prospecting on a large and very expensive scale. But when they do strike it, it is marvelous how the wealth rolls out.

The following table is carefully compiled from the furnace returns and shipments, and shows within a very few dollars the yield of Leadville mines for 1880:

MONTHS.	Pounds of Bullion.	Ounces of Silver.	Ounces of Gold.	Tons of Ore shipped.	Value of Silver.	Value of Gold.	Value of Lead.	Val. of Ore shipped	Total for Month.
January	5,167,429	1,045,356	154	570	$1,194,500	$3,080	$269,546	$148,909	$1,616,035
February	5,092,713	808,758	169	610	916,282	3,380	292,742	173,181	1,385,605
March	5,040,238	741,403	91	1,275	841,916	2,120	261,925	106,152	1,204,083
April	4,953,073	636,716	4	925	724,320	86	246,932	109,394	1,080,726
May	6,177,660	864,388	4	873	986,164	80	282,737	109,683	1,378,664
June	4,227,828	619,489		887	720,281		193,065	126,997	1,040,343
July	4,598,738	676,227	300	664	750,367	6,000	206,932	77,885	1,041,184
August	6,986,039	769,218	350	1,162	878,989	7,000	349,799	128,391	1,364,179
September	7,524,747	848,715	254	2,937	959,027	5,060	375,365	217,147	1,556,599
October	6,443,950	757,366	196	1,696	858,365	3,824	298,721	127,453	1,288,464
November	5,691,982	625,854	12	817	708,186	240	263,431	68,200	1,040,027
December	5,866,851	583,880	157	60	656,783	3,140	262,372	7,000	929,295
Total	67,691,854	8,979,399	1,688	12,470	$10,195,169	$34,014	$3,335,507	$1,460,363	$15,025,153

An aggregate of over fifteen million dollars in one year is truly astonishing. The proved returns and work done in particular mines are even more remarkable. In the Chrysolite Mine alone over twelve thousand linear feet of drifts, raises, and winzes, were made during the year, and in eight of the Freyer Hill mines over seventy-five thousand linear feet of drifts, levels, winzes, and raises, were made, representing about two million cubic feet. Still larger sections of promising territory remain to be opened, and not one-tenth of the hill has even been explored. Less than eight acres are stoped, and about twenty acres are opened, and thousands of tons of rich mineral are exposed to view in nearly every mine on the hill. On Carbonate Hill a very large amount of development work has also been done during the year, but less ore has been taken out. The mines located on the carbonate break show from the Catalpa northward an almost inexhaustible supply of medium grade lead ores that promises to supply the smelters of the camp for years to come.

Large bodies of fine smelting ores have been discovered in the Florence, Brian Boru, and Columbia mines, on the south side of California Gulch; in the Big Chief, St. Mary's, Henriette, and Yankee Doodle mines, on Carbonate Hill; in the mines of Little Ellen Hill, and the Uncle Sam, Little Johnnie, A. Y., and other mines on Breece and Iron hills. Yankee Hill has disclosed ore bodies recently, that, in the opinion of many prominent mining men, will soon make it a formidable rival of Freyer Hill. Recent developments have shown some of the richest chloride bodies ever discovered in the vicinity of Leadville to exist in this hill, and its future possibilities are beyond estimation. In addition to these discoveries of smelting ores, a score of rich strikes of free milling silver-bearing and gold-bearing ores and quartz were made. Some of these are located on Ball Mountain and Breece Hill, and give magnificent returns in gold, while other rich silver-bearing quartz ledges have been opened on Yankee Hill and in Colorado Gulch.

The history of Leadville is a Rocky Mountain romance in real life. When the first invasion struck the territory, the eager gold hunters prospected every gulch on the eastern slope; and in the spring of 1860, parties of Gilpin County miners crossed South Park and discovered rich placers on the head-waters of the Arkansas. These were so much like the old placers of California that they named the locality California Gulch, and in a few months a continuous line of claims and cabins stretched along the Gulch thirty-three thousand feet. One claim for awhile yielded $1,000 per day, and a single firm took out $60,000. They named the principal settlement Oro, and a few of its cabins still stand. Before Christmas, 1860, the camp contained some five thousand men, with all the accompaniments of saloon, store, dance house, and gambling hall, in which the lucky miner too often parted with his *bonanza*. Gold dust was the usual medium of exchange, by weight at $18 per ounce.

In one year the gulch yielded about a million dollars; then one by one the placers were worked out, and the slow decline began. In 1865 but few miners remained, and the total yield to that time was estimated at three millions. In 1869 it was but $60,000; in 1876 but $20,000; and then for a short time there was no town of Oro. But some observing men had noticed a few things which they kept to themselves till they had secured Government title to their claims. Messrs. Stevens and Wood remarked the extraordinary weight of the boulders displaced in placer mining, analyzed the metal, and found silver. They quietly secured titles to nine claims, and began to develop. Maurice Hayes and brother, the Gallagher brothers, and a Mr. Durham also made similar discoveries. Meanwhile the Printer's Boy and some other *gold* lodes had been opened and worked. At length, in the autumn of 1876, the Gallaghers struck a big deposit of rich carbonates, and in a few weeks several others "struck it rich"; then California Gulch awoke from its long sleep and the era of modern Leadville began. For fifteen years miners had taken out one kind of ore directly over fabulous wealth of another kind, without even suspecting it. In how many old camps are they doing the same thing even now?

Early in 1877 two smelters were running, but rich discoveries followed each other so fast that ore was piled up hundreds of tons ahead of their capacity to reduce it. In June, 1877, Charles Mater erected the first house in the present Leadville, and opened a stock of goods therein. Before Christmas the place contained one thousand inhabitants; by spring it had a weekly paper, a school, and two churches. A. B. Wood made the first big sale, disposing of his half interest in the nine claims above mentioned for $40,000. In March, 1878, the

A NEW MINING TOWN.

St. Louis Smelting Company bought the Camp Bird and adjoining property for $225,000. By the first of June half a dozen rich mines were known; then the flood began. First came miners and investors by twos and tens from adjacent camps, then by scores from distant parts of Colorado, and soon by hundreds from every part of the world. Winter brought a slight cessation, but the summer of 1878 increased the arrivals. The next winter made no cessation, and early in 1879 the arrivals averaged a hundred per day. Meanwhile the wonderful deposits on Freyer Hill were opened—deposits so rich and easily mined that they exceeded any thing previously known in Colorado; and were only exceeded, if at all, by the Big Bonanza of Nevada.

In May, 1879, this was the situation: Three stage lines were discharging their daily loads there, and two railroads were pushing forward to Leadville; five smelters and sampling works were taking in ore and shipping ore or bullion; a dozen saw-mills ran day and night, and were a month behind on orders for lumber; six thousand people had a regular residence *in* the place, and unknown thousands more were scattered over the adjacent country; five hundred houses were in process of building, and the sound of the hammer and saw was heard day and night. The luxuries of life followed fast. Dance houses and saloons multiplied, and "dizzy doves" gave an air of abandon to the streets. Enormous sales followed each other rapidly. Men who rarely had an extra dollar in their lives, found themselves rich beyond their dreams, and spent money with lavish hand. It was difficult to make one's way along the streets after night, when sight-seers and roysterers crowded the pavement. A dozen bands were drumming up audiences for as many variety shows and concert halls, and from scores of open doors were heard the click of billiard balls and the crash of ten-pins. Those who make money suddenly, generally spend it carelessly, and life in a thriving mining camp is a continuous invitation to prodigality.

In December, 1879, the official report showed that Leadville contained four banks, with over $2,000,000 in deposits; that $569,070 had been sent east in postal money-orders, and mail received at the rate of one or two tons per day; that corner lots sold at from $3,000 to $8,000; and that the city had that year done a business aggregating over $18,000,000!

Since the opening of 1881, authentic figures are scarce. The population is estimated all the way from fifteen to forty thousand: take your choice. But the town is far more solid than it was. The Tabor Opera House is the finest in the State; and the churches, school buildings, and public halls are equal to those in eastern cities. The city is illuminated with gas; has first-class water-works, police and fire departments; is now a well-ordered place; has three first-class daily and several weekly papers. The post-office is a wonder in itself. Twelve clerks are constantly on the move, and thousands of letters are received daily and delivered here or sent on to distant camps. The hotel business is enormous. The Clarendon took in $260,000 in nine months. Almost every Christian denomination is represented by a fine church; and even the heathen Chinese have a little room which they use on occasion as a Buddhist temple. One dry-goods house sold $350,000 worth in twelve months, and a grocery firm over $400,000 worth in the same time. There are two planing mills and four foundries and machine shops. The smelters ship over $1,000,000 in bullion every month. And as this is *the* test of a mining region, let us finish our chapter on Leadville by a visit to the Grant Smelter, which is among the largest in the world.

The first objects of interest, after you pass through the yard gate, are the great piles of dirt and stone, as you would call them, but which are really piles of valuable ore from the mines. Every load is driven on the scales and weighed as it comes in, and then assigned a place according to its value, which has been carefully ascertained by an assay made by the experts in the employ of the smelting company. Passing into the building, you observe long rows of large bins full of ore, each properly numbered—the number indicating the quality of the ore. Passing these bins, you encounter an army of men wheeling ore, limestone, coal, coke, and slag (which is the cooled refuse of the smelted ore), in all directions, without any seeming order or plan. Further on you observe men shoveling the ore into a sort of hopper, and on the other side of the hopper wheeling away fine dirt, or ore that looks like sand. These hoppers, with huge iron rollers underneath, are called crushers, and the ore is passed through these crushers to pulverize it so it will smelt more easily. There are three of these crushers.

We now see that the men who were wheeling various materials about the buildings, leave their loaded wheelbarrows in front of these furnaces. They are just now charging or filling this one, and we will watch the process. On the first is charcoal; on the second, limestone; on the third, ore; on the fourth, coke; and on the fifth, slag. Observe he dumps the coal in first, then the limestone, and so on. Other wheelbarrow loads are brought and dumped into the furnace until it is full; then the door is shut, and the whole mass begins to melt. You ask why all these different materials are used? Well, the coal and coke are of course put in to furnish the heat required; the limestone and slag are put in to act as a flux. (This word literally means a *flow*.) These substances assist in the fusion or melting, and also in separating the different metallic substances that are combined in the ore. The silica or sand in the ore unites with the lime, and thus frees the silver and lead which are contained in the ore. Other mineral substances also unite with the flux, leaving the silver and lead free from the baser metals. At the bottom of the furnace you see several tubes or pipes inserted. These are called "blowers," and through them the air is forced into the furnace to increase the process of combustion. By the aid of the blowers the furnace is made hot enough to melt the ore, etc. Now you observe men opening a spout near the bottom of the furnace, and draining off a red-hot liquid substance, which looks like melted iron, into cast-iron molds shaped like an inverted cone. This is the slag or waste, and is composed of the sand, iron, lime, and all other base metals which the ore contained. The silver and lead, which are heavier than the slag, go to the bottom of the melted mass, and are taken out at the side of the furnace, from a round opening called the well. Near the well you see a long row of cast-iron molds, each capable of holding about one hundred pounds of bullion, or silver and lead combined. Into these molds the melted bullion is poured, and when cold it is ready to ship. The silver and lead are not separated at the smelter, but are sent as bullion to St. Louis, Philadelphia, New York, and other places, to be separated and sold. Some of the ore is very rich in silver, and contains but little lead, while other grades have a large per cent. of lead and but little silver. Some of the bullion averages as high as twenty-five per cent. in silver.

When all the furnaces about Leadville are in operation they can reduce two hundred and twenty-five tons of ore every twenty-four hours, which will make about five tons of bullion, and will contain a ton of pure silver, and perhaps more. Three hundred men are employed when all the furnaces are running to their fullest capacity. Great care must be taken by the workmen not to get "leaded;" that is, not to inhale the fumes from the melted lead, which are very poisonous, and, if inhaled to any great extent, will bring on a very painful sickness, and perhaps result in death.

I have said that the pilgrim would seldom if ever recognize the richest ore; that his eye would be caught by the glitter of the cheap galena; and this is as good a place as any to give some of the reasons why. First, it is to be noted that though the simple elements in rock and mineral are few, their combinations are almost endless; and the merest trace of some element like sulphur will entirely change the appearance of an ore. In gold mining there is little chance for technicalities, for gold is "free"—that is, in its native matrix of quartz it does not combine with other minerals, and the separation is simple. But silver is the metal with which true science comes in play; for of the sixty or more simple elements of which all creation is composed, he would be a bold miner who would put his finger on one and say,

"*That* is never found with silver." The enclosing rocks, known in reference to the vein as "wall rock," and when spoken of generally as the "country rock," are somewhat more simple in construction.

Of the elements in rock and mineral, the first is—

Oxygen.—This constitutes nearly one-half of the earth's crust; it enters into *all* rocks and nearly all minerals. Next to it is

Silicon.—This makes up about one-fourth of the earth's crust. So oxygen and silicon alone constitute about three-fourths of all the materials the miner has to deal with. Combined in some way they make

Quartz.—This is, in general terms, the matrix of the precious metals—that is, the atom of silver or gold is inclosed by atoms of quartz, so that the metal, as such, is rarely visible, and its presence is known to the experienced miner only by various signs. But if there is much galena present with the silver, that metal nearly always shows brightly with its cubical crystals, looking like marvelously rich ore. If, on the other hand, the silver is a chloride or sulphuret, there is no luster. Thus the richest ore always looks worthless to the pilgrim, and the cheapest looks the richest—the quartz in either case merely aiding to obscure the true ore. Next in rank, probably, is

Feldspar.—A general name given to a class containing several varieties. Next is

Mica.—Which is too well known to need description. Quartz, feldspar, and mica, combine to make granite, in which the shining specks, or flakes, of mica may often be distinguished. The last I need mention is

Lime.—A word used by the miner in a very general sense indeed, and without reference to the many distinctions made by science. The practical miner lumps it all together under the general name of limestone. Limestone is the country rock of all the Cottonwood, American Fork, and Ophir Districts in Utah; of the immediate vicinity of Leadville; of some of the richest mines in Mexico, and of many other districts. In eastern Colorado we usually find granite, or some massive rock; and in other districts the varieties are many. With these definitions you may form some idea of what the miner means by his first question about a new district: "What is the country rock?" That answered, he at once has some idea as to the value of the mines, for in some mysterious way the inclosing rock has determined the ease with which the ore can be worked, and to some extent its richness. For instance, carbonic acid being present in limestone, the reader will easily see why mines yielding carbonate ores must have one wall of that rock. The carbonic acid has been absorbed by, and has changed the character of the ore, solid galena having been changed to carbonates; and mines are occasionally found in which this process is not quite completed.

And here we may appropriately indulge in a little popular science. The miner has his own name for each variety of ore known to him, while the chemist, or metallurgist, has his; but for the commoner varieties these names are the same, and are formed on a curiously convenient system. If the term ends in *yde*, *ide*, or *id*, it means a combination of oxygen or some gas with the metal. Thus we have *oxide* of silver, etc., and *chloride* of silver, a chemical union of chlorine and silver, very rich and easily reduced, it being already in favorable combination with salt. If the termination is *uret*, it means a union of the actual substance with the silver, as *sulphuret*, a combination of sulphur and silver; *sulphuret of zinc*, zinc and sulphur, etc. If it is *ate*, it means the acid combined with the mineral, making an entirely new compound; and of all these, *carbonates* of lead and silver are most familiar to the miner, and generally most welcome, being so easily reduced. Of the carbonates of the Ophir District, it is said that they "run through a smelter like molasses," and those of Leadville are reported even more tractable, where there is lead enough in the combination. Many mines there have an additional element of iron, which is said to add to the ease of treatment. *Galena*, in miners' language, simply means lead in the ore; *galeniferous*, carrying lead, and *argentiferous* carrying silver. The bulk of ore from the large orebodies in Utah is simply argentiferous galena, and Gentile Utah is often spoken of poetically as *Utah Argentifera*.

As aforesaid, the received opinion is that all carbonates were once galena, or some other solid ore; and not very long ago, as nature counts time. In the Emma Mine, Utah, while shoveling up carbonates as loose as sand, one often comes upon a solid chunk of galena; but in the Ophir District, the carbonates are bright and free from other ores. A pile of ore just from some of the mines there looks very like a mixture of sand and lime—the chemical union is complete. Galena is among the heaviest ores, and can nearly always be reduced by ordinary smelting, the lead and silver in combination sinking to the bottom, while the melted *gangue*, being lighter, rises and is drawn off as slag. Of course the bullion so obtained is nearly all lead, and the silver and lead must be separated by refining. Galena, when sufficiently pure, crystallizes in beautiful cubes; these, when crushed, break again into cubes, and so on indefinitely. In all the vast work-house of nature I know of nothing more marvelous than the crystallization of minerals. One forms a cube, another a hexagon, another a tetrahedron, and still another a dodecahedron; some combine with faces at certain angles, and lines of cleavage parallel therewith; others at just half that angle, and still others in multiform figures for which geometry has no name, but all symmetrical beyond the power of art to surpass. And no matter how broken, each crystal follows the law of its cleavage; the cube breaks into cubes, the hexagon into hexagons, etc.

Sulphuret is the general name of all silver ores in combination with sulphur. They are generally rich, mostly in hard rock, and always more or less rebellious. Nearly all the rich ores of eastern Colorado are of this class. The combinations are almost endless, and the presence of zinc, iron, or copper pyrites, antimony, arsenic, etc., presents a perplexing series of problems to the mill men. Sulphurets yield from $200 to $10,000 per ton, one mine sometimes yielding several different grades. Here and there on the face of an ore-seam are sometimes found little accretions of pure silver, which miners speak of as "the fat of the vein." It is supposed that there was more silver than the other materials could hold in chemical union, so it overflowed in these nibs, which hang on the face of the seam like leaf-lard. According to their purity, or the minerals mixed with them, such nibs are known as wire silver, horn silver, ruby silver, silver glance, azurite or tetrahedrite. A change of less than one per cent. in the accompanying chemical will often change entirely the color of such ore. Azurite is a combination of silver with blue carbonate of copper, and yields anywhere from $500 to $10,000 per ton. Tetrahedrite is so named from its crystallizing in tetrahedrons. Sulphurets of other metals are constantly met with, and greatly increase the difficulty of reduction. "Black-jack," or zinc-blend, a sulphuret of zinc and copper, is a very troublesome combination. Chunks of it have been found assaying $500 per ton, but no man is anxious to find it in his mine for all that. It looks like a lump of black wax turned to vitreous stone, and is spoken of as "horribly rebellious." I have seen a lump of stuff from a sulphuret mine, no larger than my fist, which was shown by assay to contain twenty different minerals. Iron pyrites is a sulphuret of iron, protean in appearance, jocularly known as fool's gold. Most of the reported discoveries in the eastern states are due to this cheating mineral.

In conclusion it may be said that from the differences herein described some important political consequences follow. First, that placer mines are almost a curse to a country, while lodes requiring deep mining are a permanent blessing. For the placers attract a swarm of eager adventurers who hasten to exhaust the supply, often to demoralize the country, and then abandon it, while lodes require a vast outlay of capital and years of honest industry. The plant requires from $20,000 to $100,000 in capital and labor, and no good silver district is really developed in less than ten years, while for generations thereafter work goes on with improved methods. Thus, permanent towns and cities are built up, a good market is created, and the adjacent lands are brought under high cultivation; trade is very active, and local manufactures are brought into existence. A thousand miners buy three times as much as a thousand farmers, for they produce nothing they can use. Thus the old placer-mining counties of California are bankrupt and almost deserted, while the mineral development of Utah has more than doubled the value of real estate, and the mines of Colorado have made that State rich in farming and grazing. This distinction is worth considering if the reader thinks of making a settlement in some of the mining territories.

CHAPTER XXXVI.

MINING IN 1882.

May, 1869, was rendered memorable by the opening of the first through railway line across the Continent; the spring of 1881 witnessed the opening of the second; but it passed almost unnoticed, while that of 1869 was the occasion of a national jubilee. In a former chapter the reader will find some account of the projected 35th parallel road and my journey over a portion of its line. The Northern Pacific is of national fame. The Texas Pacific, or 32d parallel, road was to run near the boundary between us and Mexico. But all these were outdone by the Southern Pacific of California, which was started to give San Francisco direct railroad connection with Arizona and New Mexico, and once fairly started was pushed forward towards Texas with amazing vigor. Meanwhile, the Atchison, Topeka, and Santa Fe line was pushed on from La Junta, Colorado, its objective point being Guayamas, on the Pacific Coast of Mexico. Thus its line crossed that of the California road, at an acute angle, in the Florida Pass, New Mexico; and at that meeting they decided to make it one line for through business. So the first train, from ocean to river, on the new trans-continental, reached Kansas City almost unheralded and unnoticed. It is but a question of a few years when both roads will be completed to their original destinations, and the Northern Pacific will be pushed through; then four lines will connect us with the Pacific, and nearly one-half of the Wild West be abolished.

Scarcely had the two roads touched their boundaries when the mineral wealth of New Mexico and Arizona was shown to be great; but other matters are of more immediate interest. First to be noted beyond La Junta is Trinidad, and sixteen miles beyond it a tunnel 2,000 feet long, through which the railroad penetrates the Raton, over which I staged with such difficulty in 1872. Here the formation is carboniferous, and from immense mines coal is loaded on the cars at eighty cents a ton. Thence straight southward to Las Vegas, near the old stage line, the road running conveniently near to the great Hot Springs, which have already acquired fame as a sanitarium. From Galisteo a branch road runs up a canon to Santa Fe; and so the queer old city has a railroad at last, though I was positive, in 1872, from its position, that it never would have. From Albuquerque a branch runs along the old Atlantic and Pacific line to a point nearly a hundred miles west; so all that long dry way I journeyed with United States mules, is now traversed by rail, and the sad-eyed Zunis and strange old Pueblos are brought within four days ride of Cincinnati! Whither shall the enterprising traveler now go for wild adventure? From Albuquerque the road continues down the Rio Grande over 100 miles and bears off to Florida Pass, where, as aforesaid, it now connects with the California Pacific. Thence southward it *will* continue—so the sanguine projectors assure us—down to Mexico City, sending off branches eastwardly to El Paso, and westwardly to Guayamas. Already the work is being pushed rapidly from the Mexican ends of these lines, and the long criticized unenterprising Spanish-Americans seem stirred into wonderful activity by the Yankee railroad builders. These wonderful schemes, so near completion, almost force us into rhapsody; our most eloquent praise is a plain statement of what they have done and are doing. The coffee lands of Mexico are brought within a week's run of Boston; the Orient is at our back door; Australasia is our near neighbor.

From the San Francisco end of the Southern Pacific we run rapidly southward, and soon emerge on the awfully barren sand plains and red deserts of southeastern California. By common consent the Mohave and Yuma Desert, running away up into Utah and Nevada, is considered the most uniformly barren of any large tract in the Far West. Making all possible deductions for oases and green *vegas*, it contains at least 80,000 square miles of irreclaimable desert. A narrow line of faint green relieves the eye at Fort Yuma, where we cross the Colorado, to Yuma City on the east side, and soon after enter on the Gila Valley. This has an occasional oasis, but the Pueblos unite in testifying that from the date of their oldest traditions moisture has been decreasing and barrenness growing; and the local evidences prove it, the country being thick-set with the ruins of abandoned towns. First is the noted Casas Grandes, a vast pile of ruins with form enough to show that it is the remains of many immense adobe buildings—all terraced and run together like those I described at Moqui. Smaller ruins are found by hundreds; by digging in them one can always find the floor of an old Aztec house, and under the hearth one will almost always find human bones, showing that they buried their dead there. In the Salt River valley are the remains of a canal nearly a hundred miles long, which once brought water from the Verde River to irrigate a large tract. Now the miners and prospectors are rapidly developing a new civilization on the tombs of the old, and in a score of districts new mines are opened. That part of Pinal county north of the Gila is almost covered by mining districts, among which the Globe and the Pioneer districts lead. In the

CAPE HORN AND RAILROAD, SIERRA NEVADA.

former is the noted Silver King, which is in many respects the most remarkable mine in America.

Years ago, when the murderous Apaches held this region, an escaping Mexican brought into Tucson a large piece of pure native silver, which he said he broke from an immense outcrop as he toiled on his devious way through the mountain passes. Great was the fever thereat, and many loose-footed men wanted him to guide them back; but dread of the Apaches prevented. At length came a truce; a rush was made, the mine was found, and the Mexican's description proved literally true. The ore was so rich that immense profits were made, before machinery could be brought in, by simply picking it by hand, sacking the best, and shipping it to San Francisco by mule-back and freight-wagon. The ore is peculiar, and the formation a puzzle to one who sees it for the first time. An expert sent from San Francisco to report thereon, condemned the mine as a flyer—that is, a mere freak of nature, without sign of permanence; but it has since that time yielded $1,200,000, and is still doing well. Globe City is new, but the district has forty mines within six miles of a common center. The town supports a newspaper and a branch telegraph down to the main line; and already a branch railroad is projected to connect this group of mines, or rather this series of mining districts, with Tombstone and other more southern districts, crossing the Southern Pacific and traversing some good belts of timber.

The Southern Pacific follows the general course of the Gila for a hundred miles or so to Maricopa, thence strikes straight southeast nearly a hundred more to Tucson, thence eastward to the rocky San Pedro, which it crosses in the midst of savage grandeur and sandy desolation. Here we will leave the railroad for awhile and stage it, southward, up the San Pedro, to the really marvelous district of Tombstone. There is enough even in the town to make a week's visit pass pleasantly if not profitably. In fact, the disagreeable feature will be found in the stage ride coming from the railroad station of Benson, about twenty-six miles distant. Large numbers of heavy freight teams are constantly coming and going, and every new road that the stage company makes to avoid the dust and chuck holes is almost immediately appropriated by the freighters. The jolting is almost severe enough to dislodge a man's eyes from their sockets, while the dust is simply frightful. A passenger alights from the coach with eyes, ears, and mouth almost obliterated, while his hair and whiskers are turned to a creamy white by the villainous powder known as alkali dust. He would not be recognized by his own wife. There is an opposition stage, both lines running a double daily, in addition to cages carrying baggage and treasure. The fare is four dollars for the trip, and all the coaches appear to run full. Eighteen passengers is not considered by any means a *large* load.

The road follows up the San Pedro River bottom and bluffs on an easy and imperceptible grade the entire distance. In places where the road crosses the creek, the scene is pleasant and agreeable, as this stream is the only living water the traveler will notice after leaving Yuma, a distance of about three hundred miles. Arriving at night the first impressions of the town are very favorable. The two long lines of streets, including the cross streets, are brilliantly illuminated, saloons particularly. They and the hotels run all night, while most of the stores are open up to a very late hour. As in all new mining camps, everybody is in a hurry to get rich, and the merchants form no exception to the rule. They think it necessary to take down their shutters at day-light in the morning and do not put them up again until from nine to eleven P. M.

The town is located on a kind of "hog's back," with the principal streets running parallel along the center on an almost even grade, while on either side there is a gentle slope, making a system of sewerage easy of accomplishment. The majority of the buildings in the center of the business portion, are all two-story, and quite a number of new business houses are being erected, the material used being adobe, with brick fronts and finishing. Although lumber is comparatively cheap, there being an abundance of timber in the mountains, about thirty miles distant, where a sawmill is located, very little is used to construct frame buildings, for, owing to the limited supply of water now brought in from the river, about eight miles distant, it is important to have fire-proof buildings. The mines on the ridge overlooking the town have struck pure water, which will be brought into reservoirs, giving an unlimited supply for all purposes. At present the supply is barely sufficient for drinking purposes, and we doubt if it would go around but for the innumerable saloons which furnish beer and whisky at a bit (12½ cents) a drink, the two bit (25 cents) places being the exception.

The banking houses, merchandise and general business establishments, are in a more prosperous condition. One bad feature of California is omitted here entirely, and that is the stock-gambling board. Nearly all the mining property is in the hands of corporations, and if you want to buy stock you can see the property and get just what you pay for. Money is more evenly distributed, there being none of that terrible gathering up of all the loose change the community has for the benefit of the wealthy mining stock manipulators.

One may safely say that the merchandise business of the town is in the hands of old San Diego people, and the judiciary likewise. The mines are owned in Boston, and the miners and prospectors come from Nevada. So the place is pleasantly composite. At the time the town site was located, no one supposed there was ore beneath. Now miners work continuously under the street, and in the still hours of the night you hear the constant exploding of giant powder blasts, which is a trifle jarring to the nerves of the property owners on the surface, whose claim to the ground is disputed by the mining locator. There are half a dozen claimants to the ground. These conflicting claims do not seem to seriously trouble the business men, who get the best title they can and go ahead with their improvements. Possession is the most valid claim. It was so in the case of a shoemaker here, who, after paying three months rent to the supposed owner, on the fourth collection day declined to make any further payments, stating that he had possession of the building and lot, also a shot-gun receipt, and would not stand any annoyance from collectors or lawyers.

The town is strictly American; there is none of the Spanish element. In fact, one seems to have passed entirely out of Arizona when he reaches here. The streets are wide, nicely graded, and laid out at right angles, with sidewalks in good repair. The hotels are good, although small, and the attention and table are equal to any in Los Angeles. Table vegetables are raised also in the neighborhood, and do much to make the fare tempting as compared with other Arizona towns, where everything is brought from Los Angeles. On the river at Charleston, nine miles distant, is an ice machine, and every morning the ice wagon goes its rounds, distributing a generous supply of cooling solid. The price is seven cents per pound, but these people have money and patronize the industry liberally. Two companies are on hand wanting a city franchise for lighting the streets with gas and electricity, and also one for a telephone system. When the matter of the franchise is settled, the town will be lighted and telephoned more in proportion to its population than any city on the coast. The business men located here are ambitious and enterprising, and are willing to pay for all the latest and most advanced improvements of modern civilization. Concerning the mines which have made this town what it is in two short years, and mapped out a great future, they are claimed to be among the most extensive yet discovered. As yet this ore body is only prospected enough to know that it will pay, but mining men concede that in the few mines being worked they have probably six years' ore in sight, and beyond that no one can tell the extent of it. Years ago prospectors knew of rich deposits somewhere in this neighborhood, and made desperate attempts to secure the prize, as can be seen by the wreck of the old adobe building which is on the road to Charleston, and which the miners built sixteen years ago as a common rendezvous and fort of protection against the Apaches. It is here that eleven of them perished so miserably by the hands of the redskins. The present locations do not appear to have been the objective point of these early prospectors, and the supposition is that other and richer deposits are yet to be found to the south and west.

The bullion output for May, 1881, was set down at $482,106, but had the whole amount of custom work at the mills been cleaned up and added in, as the returns show, the amount would have reached $502,000. This result is enormous when one considers the limited facilities, there being only six small mills on the river. All the ore had to be hauled by team from nine to eleven miles. The hoisting works and machinery are of a very primitive nature, mostly hand windlasses or a whim and horse power. Only from a very rich quality of ore could any such result be obtained. True, it is not like the Comstock bonanza. The very rich streaks are small in extent, but the ore averages well and there is little or no waste. When a ton of ore is hoisted to the surface it can all be put into the wagon and sent to the mill, when it will yield from $95 to $150. It is easily mined. One man, with the proper facilities, in one day of eight hours, will hoist to the surface one ton of ore ready for the mill. This is speaking in a general way of the average ore and what can be done when a mine is being worked fair and square. There are about a thousand miners employed, and the mines, for wages and milling expenses, disburse about $125,000 per month. There is also quite an army of freighters, blacksmiths, wheelwrights, and other laborers who follow on the heels of the freight teams.

The surrounding country is both a farming and grazing district. Beef cattle and farm produce are in demand. Prospectors are going out daily. Capital is coming in and being invested. A destructive fire occurred at Tombstone, June 22, 1881, causing a loss of $250,000. Hundreds were rendered homeless. The fire department and officials worked hard, buildings being pulled down by mule teams and men, and the fire was checked. Much to the credit of Tombstone no panic ensued, as is generally the case in such disasters.

So much for Tombstone; and we have detailed its common life fully because it is just now the objective point of thousands. Let us return down the wild valley of the San Pedro, go on to the Gila, and thence northeastward to scenes we visited in 1872. The first fact to attract attention is the amazing difference in climate and vegetation between this region and that north of the divide, in which we wandered ten years ago. We are away down on latitude 32° and 34°, and the strange tropical and desert flora give us the idea of a new creation. There are over one hundred varieties of the cactus, which is *the* plant of all the far southwest. There is the *cereus giganteus*, which has attained a height of sixty feet and a diameter of three; the *maguey*, with a bulbous root as large as a half bushel; the hedge cactus, with which Mexicans fence their fields; the *amole*, used for soap, and many others. All bear fearful thorns and some a most exquisite fruit. From the *maguey* a very strong liquor is distilled, containing fourteen fights to the gallon. A good table syrup is also made from this plant. There is a great variety of flowers, and in the growing season the landscape often presents a gorgeous sight. About two-thirds of Arizona is covered by mountains, fit only for grazing, timber, or mines; half the other third is a complete desert, and still there are at least 2,500,000 acres of good land lying in position to be reclaimed by irrigation. But as most of this would require canals on a large scale, such as only government would undertake, there is probably less cultivated land in Arizona to-day than in any one county in Ohio.

Coming back through New Mexico we find that old, old territory also waked up on the subject of her mineral wealth; development of many new and some old districts is in rapid progress, but statistics are not so easily obtainable. Let us get back into Colorado and take another start from Canon City, visiting Rosita and Silver Cliff. To reach them we take the Grape Creek line, nearly straight south, some thirty miles. The whole country abounds with wild scenery and startling curiosities. Local geologists have a theory that West Mountain Valley was once the bed and valley of the Arkansas river, as the same formation extends along both. On the east of it is the Greenhorn Range, and west of it the Sangre de Christo mountains; and on the west side of the first, in a beautiful glade, is Rosita, with some 2,000 inhabitants. Eight miles away is the noted Silver Cliff, three years ago unknown and unnamed, to-day a city of 10,000 people, with miles of busy streets and all the bustle of a growing mining town. The valley northward from Rosita is very fertile, now taken up by ranches and meadows, which gives these two places an immense advantage in the matter of cheap food and fresh vegetables.

The whole formation about Silver Cliff and Rosita is so remarkable that it would require a technical education in geology and mineralogy for the reader to understand it. Suffice it to say that around and partly over an original granite ridge was poured, at a very late geological era, an enormous flow of porphyry, or trachyte; that after the trachyte had become solid rock there were terrible convulsions which split and cracked it, and through the cracks gushed streams of obsidian, or volcanic glass. All these appear as they hardened into shape; so there is little wonder that the district was at first a great puzzle, seemingly destined to overthrow many old theories. Of course, too, there was great waste at first in working this peculiar ore, but with experience the total cost per ton for mining and milling has been reduced to about seven dollars. This makes it possible to work ten ounce ore at a profit, and as the supply of ore of that grade is practically inexhaustible, it looks as if this magic district would be as long-lived as it was noted for sudden growth. But time and space fail me to detail each of the rich districts of Colorado. The following table, showing the increase in the population of the state by counties, will give the reader a very fair idea of the localities in

GIANTESS, BIG GEYSER OF THE YELLOWSTONE.

which the richest mines have been developed, since the crowd invariably flocks to those places in which the rich metal is found:

Counties.	Population 1870.	Population 1880.
Arapahoe	6,829	38,607
Bent	592	1,654
Boulder	1,939	10,055
Chaffee	New	6,503
Clear Creek	1,596	7,857
Conejos	2,504	5,616
Costilla	1,779	2,885
Custer	New	7,968
Douglas	1,388	2,486
Elbert	510	1,710
El Paso	987	7,903
Fremont	1,064	4,730
Gilpin	5,490	6,493
Grand	New	417
Gunnison	New	8,764
Hinsdale	New	1,508
Huerfano	2,250	4,149
Jefferson	2,390	6,811
Lake	522	23,787
La Plata	New	1,110
Larimer	838	4,862
Las Animas	4,276	8,909
Ouray	New	2,677
Park	447	3,956
Pueblo	2,265	7,617
Rio Grande	New	1,946
Routt	New	140
Saguache	304	1,972
San Juan	New	1,087
Summit	258	5,449
Weld	1,636	5,603
Total	39,864	195,231

An increase of 155,370 for the decade just gone is a showing of which the Centennial state should feel proud. It is safe to predict a still greater increase for the ten years to come.

Almost any railroad office can supply you a table of distances and fares from Denver to all points in Colorado; and from eastern cities to Denver rates have been so materially reduced that the cost of a summer in the Switzerland of America is brought within the reach of nearly all enfeebled professional men.

Of other mining regions but brief mention is necessary. In the Black Hills a prosperous community has suddenly grown up which already challenges the attention of the world; Nevada continues to pour out her treasures, and generally throughout the Rocky Mountains the business of mining grows with pleasing regularity. The following table, from the Mining Commissioner of the United States, shows it better at a glance than would many pages of comment:

ANNUAL PRODUCT OF LEAD, SILVER, AND GOLD.

1870	$52,150,000
1871	55,784,000
1872	60,351,824
1873	70,139,860
1874	71,965,610
1875	76,703,433
1876	87,219,859
1877	95,811,582
1878	78,276,167
1879	72,688,888
1880	77,232,512
Total	$798,323,735

Adding the growth of 1881, and omitting the lead, we find that the United States now produces annually at least $78,000,000 in silver and gold. Thus, in the language of Commissioner Raymond, "The western states and territories bear witness of our great inheritance of natural wealth. Every period of geological change has been laid under contribution to endow with rich legacies some portion of our land. Our territory epitomizes the processes of all time, and their useful results to man. Divided, yet in a stronger sense united, by mountain chains and mighty rivers, our diversified mineral resources may figuratively represent and literally help to secure and maintain our characteristic national life—a vast community of communities, incapable alike of dissolution and of centralization; one, by mutual needs and affections, as the continent is one; many, by multiform industries and forms of life, as the members of the continent are many."

CHAPTER XXXVII.

THE DEAD PROPHET.

WHILE the first edition of this work was going through the press, the telegraph announced the death of Brigham Young. To Americans generally this was simply a bit of interesting news, for this man was, in the language of Elijah Pogram, "one of the most remarkable men of our country." But what Gentile can realize the awful import of that message to the 75,000 orthodox Mormons of Utah; to the 4,000 Saints in Great Britain; to the converts in Scandinavia, and the "stakes of Zion" in Arizona, Idaho and the Sandwich Islands In 1870 there were, among European races, but three persons who were at once heads of Church and State: the Pope, Queen Victoria and Brigham Young. The British Church is *not yet* "disestablished," but the Pope has lost his temporal power and Brigham Young is dead. It was said, a few years since, anent the Beecher and Clendenning trials and similar cases, "This is a hard year for parsons." Similarly: This is certainly a bad period for theocrats. We may yet live to see the Church of England divorced from the civil power.

I am no believer in that evasive maxim: *De mortuis nil nisi bonum.* Certainly not, when the dead are public characters. The dead were once alive, and moral responsibility is not evaded by the mere physical incident of death; and living rulers must learn to act with the assured conviction that they will be judged *after* death. Of all, therefore, which the foregoing pages contain regarding Brigham Young I have nothing to recant; it was my candid conviction when I wrote it—it is my assured belief now. That it will be the unanimous verdict of posterity, I have not a shadow of doubt. It was not written without overwhelming evidence to support it; revelations yet to be made in Utah, and hastened by Brigham's death, will only add to that evidence. I merely ask that the reader will, in previous chapters, substitute the past tense for the present where Brigham is mentioned. It only remains to add a few incidents in the life of this remarkable adventurer; his person and character have been sufficiently described in Chapter VI.

Brigham Young was born June 1, 1801, in Whittingham, Windham County, Vermont. His father was an old Revolutionary soldier, of Massachusetts, the parent of six sons and five daughters. This whole family embraced Mormonism soon after Brigham did. The father died in one of the early migrations of the Mormons in Missouri; the sons and daughters lived to go into polygamy in Utah, and become the parents of large families. None of Brigham's brothers ever evinced any special talent for any thing. Phinehas and Lorenzo Dow Young were barely mediocre; "Uncle John" Young for many years was Patriarch of the Church, but was a mere puppet as pulled by Brigham; Joseph sometimes preached, but with no particular force, and the fifth brother was of so little consequence that his name is scarcely known in Utah. Nor did any of them acquire property to any great extent; at least two were so poor they had to accept assistance—it might be called charity—from Brigham. The sisters are equally obscure. Whatever Brigham's talent was, he alone of the family possessed it. I have repeatedly talked with his nephews and grandchildren concerning him; but his career was as much a mystery to them as to the Gentile world. Oscar Young, Brigham's oldest child in polygamy, is now a thorough-going Gentile, and a frank, outspoken gentleman; but to him, as to strangers, his father's real nature was a sealed book.

Early in life Brigham married, and was early left a widower with two daughters, both now living in polygamy in Utah. Mormonism first took form as a religion in 1830, and among the first preachers sent out was Samuel H. Smith, youngest brother of the Prophet Joseph. He met and exhorted Brigham, and almost "converted" him. A little later, in 1832, he gave in his adhesion to the new faith, and was baptized by Elder Eleazar Miller. He at once set out for Kirtland, whither the young church was gathering; came upon Joe Smith while the latter was chopping in the woods, and, according to their mutual account, was at once blessed exceedingly. Joseph pronounced him a man of wonderful powers, gifted of God for the furtherance of the faith, and added that he would "one day lead the Church." The anti-Brighamite Mormon sects add that Joseph also said: "And he will lead it to hell." He should have said so if he did not, for it has proved very near the truth.

Brigham had previously quit farm life to become a painter and glazier, and he now exercised his trade upon the Temple at Kirtland, glazing the windows with his own hands. It was soon discovered by Joseph that Brigham was the most practical of all his converts; and, as that sort of a man was badly needed, he advanced rapidly in rank. The new church was now on the high tide of furious fanaticism. The accounts given by a score of eye-witnesses would be utterly incredible, did we not know from undoubted history, what such religious mania tends to. Visions, dreams, miracles, speaking in tongues and the interpretation of tongues followed in constant succession. In their "experience meetings" the rule was for each brother to rise and "utter whatsoever sounds came in his mind," the speaker being assured that "God will make it a language." Some men professed to see the Saviour and various holy persons; others ran through the woods shouting and praying; some fell into trances, and many recited rhapsodies or delivered prophecies. Through all this madness, Brigham, it is generally agreed, carried a level head. It was then supposed that every Saint had the gift of prophecy, but Joe Smith soon returned from a preaching tour in Canada and the Eastern States and rectified that matter. It was announced that he alone held the true prophetic gift. The general madness subsided; several converts apostatized, and by their statements, published broadcast, brought great scandal on the Church.

The Saints now established a coöperative mill, store and bank; for, as some wealthy men had joined, they were able to collect some $20,000 in cash. Meanwhile the neighboring people held a meeting and deputized one of their number to go back to Joe Smith's old home in New York, and collect evidence as to his character. Sixty-six of his old neighbors joined in an affidavit that they "would not believe Joseph Smith or any of his gang under oath." It was also abundantly proved that the Book of Mormon was a weak rehash of a weak "historical novel," written by one Solomon Spaulding. But such evidence has no effect on the class of minds caught by Mormonism. Troubles increased between the Saints and their neighbors; finally mill, store and bank failed, and Smith and Rigdon ran away to Missouri to escape the sheriff. All this time Brigham labored in his steady way, and was known among the brethren as " hard-working Brigham Young."

The Saints had made their first settlement in Missouri, at Independence, in the spring of 1831, but were driven across to Clay County in the fall of 1833. The people of the latter county "requested" them to move again; so they settled in Ray and Caldwell, built the town of Far West, and eventually got political control of that section. Then trouble arose, of course. When the Mormons elected the officials there was no justice for Gentiles, and the latter commenced fighting. Brigham had meanwhile been advanced to the rank of an apostle, and was credited with having added many hundred converts to the Church. In the late autumn of 1838 open war broke out. Enraged at some of their neighbors the Mormons drove them from their homes, and eventually burned the town of Gallatin. They had previously driven all dissenters away from Far West. In the first regular battle that ensued Edward Patton, an apostle, was killed; and, on the trials following, Orson Hyde, President of the Twelve, turned State's evidence. This left Brigham the senior apostle, and therefore President. But the battle went against the Saints. Joseph and Hyrum, and nearly all the leaders, were captured and imprisoned; Brigham and others escaped to Illinois, and in the winter of 1838-39 all the lay members followed them. Joseph and the others escaped early in 1839, and the Church was once more organized, with Quincy, Illinois, as head-quarters.

Dr. Isaac Galland at that time owned a large tract of land at the head of Des Moines Rapids, on the Mississippi, part of which he deeded to Joe Smith, on condition that he would settle his people there, and build a city. Forthwith Joe had a revelation that that was to be the great "Stake of Zion" for the present; sold city lots at high prices, and grew very wealthy, while the magic city of Nauvoo sprang up. Brigham went to England; reorganized the British mission; established the *Millennial Star*, which has ever since been the foreign organ of the Saints; did wonders as a missionary, and came home in a year with seven hundred and sixty-nine converts. Thereafter he stood very close to the Prophet. But among those converts was a pretty English girl, named Martha Brotherton, whom Brigham wanted for a spiritual wife; she rebelled, apostatized, revealed the inner workings of the Church, and thus set up a popular outcry against the Saints. Polygamy was regularly established—so says the revelation—in 1843; and early in 1844 a paper was started in Nauvoo by some opponents of the system, called the *Expositor*. It was "abated as a nuisance" by the Saints, for which Smith and his brother Hyrum were arrested; and while in jail they were murdered by a mob, June 27, 1844.

The Church was now without a head. Brigham, as President of the Twelve Apostles, claimed that they should govern till God raised up a leader. Sidney Rigdon claimed the right of succession, because he stood next in rank to the dead Prophet; William Smith claimed it as the only surviving member of the Smith family; and Strang, Brewster, Hedrick, Cutler, and others put in their claims. But Brigham circumvented them all. Rigdon had a revelation that the wealthy members led by him were to found a new "stake" for the others to gather to; then the Church would grow till able to conquer all the kingdoms of the earth; he would lead a party to rebuild Jerusalem, "and stop at London on the way home to pull the nose of Little Vic!" He was brought to trial as an impostor and disturber, Brigham acting as principal accuser; was "cut off, condemned, and delivered to the buffetings of Satan for a thousand years." About a hundred voted " not guilty." These were at once brought to trial and "cut off." It was then moved, and unanimously carried, that all who should hereafter adhere to Rigdon should be "cut off." The church led off by Rigdon has long since gone to pieces, and he died not long ago near Pittsburgh. All the other factions have broken up, and the remnants reorganized as "Josephites," under the lead of young Joe Smith; except that a small branch exists at Independence, Mo., and in that vicinity. The main body who followed the Twelve—Brigham being then merely President of the Twelve—were called "Twelveites;" but are now considered the Mormon Church proper.

It was not long till Brigham was exercising all the power of the apostolic quorum, the other eleven soon sinking into mere lieutenants. He finished the Temple, hurried the people through their "endowments," in which they were bound to the Church by the most terrible oaths, and hastened the preparations for departure. In January, 1846, he and eight of the apostles started westward, and with them 2,000 of the people. Others went as fast as they could; by May, 16,000 Mormons had left, and not more than 2,000 remained in Nauvoo. But an irregular war with their neighbors went on; and in September, 1846, a body of 1,000 or 1,500 militia besieged the city for three days, and finally expelled the remaining Mormons at the point of the bayonet. The Saints spent the fall of 1846 and ensuing winter and spring in a line of camps in western Iowa and eastern Nebraska; and as soon as possible Brigham started with one hundred and forty-three men to hunt a location "in some valley in the Rocky Mountains." Before leaving Illinois he had received a copy of Fremont's Report from Governor Thomas L. Ford, who suggested one of the large valleys of the Wasatch as their best location. The pioneer party entered Salt Lake Valley the 23d of July, but Brigham had remained in the cañon and did not come in till the next day. Reaching the present site of the city he exclaimed: "This is the place," and ordered a halt at once. Prayer was offered, a plow was lifted from the wagon, and a considerable garden-spot plowed before night. A heavy thundershower came on that day—a very rare occurrence at that time in the Great Basin in summer, and a good omen to the Saints. They put in a crop, from which those who stayed gathered potatoes about the size of chestnuts, and other things in proportion. Brigham returned that autumn to Council Bluffs, and at a conference held soon after, was chosen to all the honors and titles of the dead Prophet Joseph. Thenceforward Brigham was Prophet, Priest, Seer and Revelator, first President and Trustee-in-trust of the Church of Jesus Christ of Latter-day Saints. The Mormons were hurried forward to the valley as fast as possible; there a pure theocracy, of the most absolute character, was established, and Brigham ruled as Lord temporal and spiritual, till late in 1850, when Congress organized the Territory of Utah.

Meanwhile the Mormons had filled the country with written, printed, and sworn denials of the existence of polygamy, and Col. Thomas L. Kane had indorsed their denials; so President Fillmore appointed Brigham Young Governor of the new Territory, an office he held till 1857. The President appointed one Mormon U. S. District-Judge, the other two being Gentiles; a Mormon District-Attorney, and a Gentile Secretary, dividing the offices very fairly. Of course there was trouble. Brigham kept the people in such an excited state that the two Gentile judges soon left—not to put too fine a point upon it, ran away, to the great delight of the Saints. And soon after, at the annual festival, the following toast was rapturously applauded: "Our runaway judges; may they go on to where they belong—to hell!" And to further demonstrate his loyalty Brigham preached a sermon on the "earthly reign of the Saints," in which he said: "In that day the chief men of the earth will come to us begging for a place; I expect the President of the United States to black my boots!" Polite reference to the gentleman who had made him Governor. But this sort of thing greatly delighted the foreign-born serfs—natural snobs—who constituted a majority of the Church laity. Unfortunately for them, Secretary Harris concluded to go with the judges; and in spite of threats and injunctions, carried with him the $24,000 Congress had appropriated to pay the legislature of the new Territory, and the Mormons never got a cent of it. This hurt Brigham—right where he lived. He did not get reconciled to it, till long after he had become a millionaire.

In 1854, President Pierce decided to appoint another governor, but could find no suitable person to take the place. More judges were appointed, and things ran along pretty smoothly till 1856, when the climax of Mormon fanaticism was reached; murder by wholesale was inaugurated, the judges were driven out, and the Mormon war began. As a result of that war, Brigham ceased to be Governor; and a somewhat better state of things was established. We have now done with

Brigham as a Federal official, backed by the authority of the United States; it is time to consider him as a marrying man, a husband and a father, in which capacity he is most popularly known. Brigham had two reasons for being a marrying man: ambition and a vigorous, sensual physique. He had a peculiar magnetic power over some people. The way it affected some women may be guessed from the fact that one of the handsomest ladies in Nauvoo got divorced from a good man, in order to be Brigham's concubine, and a refined, rather intelligent Boston lady literally followed him off, taking along her two children to be reared in Mormonism. Brigham was rather kind to this one: called her "Augusta," and honored her with his supreme affections for three whole years.

Brigham's physique was the very best that cool, hardy Vermont could furnish. His youngest child, daughter of Margaret Van Cott Young, was born in 1870; his oldest, now the wife of Edmund Ellsworth, must have been born as early as 1825, for Brigham was a widower with two daughters when he joined the Mormons; and his grandchildren in this line are now well advanced men and women. So his active parental life covered a period of forty-five years, and (though I have no late returns) his children, grandchildren, and great-grandchildren number at least one hundred and fifty. Not bad for an alkali country! Add widows and sons-in-law, and grandsons-in-law, and the number interested in the estate amounted to some two hundred.

The old man outlasted three generations of wives, and had made a pretty good start on the fourth; for he married Amelia Folsom in 1865, and the last time I saw her she was beginning to look like an old woman. Brigham lost his first wife quite young. Her daughters are both in polygamy—that is, their husbands have other "women" than them, and have large families. Their daughters also have many children, and, counting his first and second wives, it is said by some, who ought to know, that Brigham's legitimate offspring are, after all, nearly as numerous as his illegitimate. About the time he was "converted," he married Mary Ann Angell. She was his only legal widow and lived for many years in the "white cottage on the bench"— that is, on the hill just back of Brigham's. She was of the same age as Brigham, and about 1843, he began on his second lot of wives. Joe Smith got his "Revelation on Celestial Marriage," July 12, 1843, and as soon thereafter as Brigham could get authority, he married the Decker sisters. One of them, Lucy, had been for some time married to Dr. Seely, a reputable physician of Nauvoo, but the High Council unceremoniously set that marriage aside; Brigham took her, and the doctor went to "grass."

His fourth wife was Harriet Cook, whom he took soon after the exodus from Nauvoo; but she was a "rebellious spirit," and at Winter Quarters (now Florence, Nebraska), "the devil entered into and did possess her." (For "possession," and the plan of relief adopted, see Captain Dan Jones' account in the 11th volume of the *Millennial Star;* also, Pratt's *Key to Theology*, and other Mormon works.) As a result she railed on Brigham, and denounced polygamy, and ended by trying to strangle her baby, Oscar Young. Brigham managed to prevent that, and in due time "the devil left her;" but he swore she should never become a mother the second time. And she did not. He married a few more wives while establishing the settlement in Utah; but all of this lot retired from business as early as 1855 or 1860.

His great favorite then, and the one who retained his affections the longest, was Emmeline Free, from Portsmouth, New Hampshire. And she was truly a lovely woman. Her children are, I think, the handsomest of Brigham's offspring, and she bore him ten. He was proud of her beauty and accomplishments, and for at least twelve years she was beyond question the queen of his heart. But youth and beauty can't last always, and about 1865, Brigham began to hanker for a new deal. Then Emmeline became desperate. She applied to Mary Ann Angell, the first wife, for help to prevent another marriage, but the latter was long past taking any interest in such things. After two or three trials with rather common wives, who did not please him more than a few months, Brigham's affections twined around Amelia Folsom; and there they clung till his death, save for a few side disturbances, most noted of which was the alimonious Ann Eliza. Emmeline was literally heart-broken, and, to add to her troubles, she had to bear the reproaches and taunts of those she had once displaced. She took to opium for consolation, and died in the summer of 1875, a perfect wreck—a confirmed "morphine drunkard!"

I think it was about a week after the burial of Emmeline (she was buried with surprising indifference to details and appearances) that we had a large party of excursionists from the East. They all called on Brigham, and paid their most profound respects, and were positively indignant at some of us resident Gentiles for the war we made on the hierarchy. One lady took me to task very severely, and afterward sent me a clipping from an Eastern paper, with her able defense of Brigham therein. I like to hear Eastern people apologize for polygamy—especially ladies. They go about it so logically, and it sounds so natural.

Well, Amelia became the recognized Queen of the Harem in 1866, and ruled the old fellow ever after. It was hinted that she knew too much, and that he would have liked to "shake" her, but did not dare. All the style of all the other wives put together would not equal hers. She occupied an elegant palace built for her sole self,

THE MORMON TABERNACLE.

across the street from the main hennery, and generally lives more like the wife of a millionaire and great leader, than did any of her predecessors. Brigham enjoyed four or five flirtations after 1866, and married a time or two, but none of them amounted to any thing. It would appear that Ann Eliza rather thought she could supersede Amelia, and did hold her own well for a few months, but the other soon knocked her clear out of the ring. Hence these tears. Margaret Van Cott, one of the latest, is a good woman, and a mother, too; and it is said this last circumstance irritates Amelia more than any thing else. She has not been at all reticent in her insinuations about "*that* woman's baby," but nobody believes such charges; the character of Margaret is too well established. Saint and Gentile are willing to swear that her little girl is honestly entitled to the two hundredth part of that big estate.

But there was one woman, Selina Ursenbach, who, could Brigham have won her, would have made it lively for Amelia. She was the sister of Octave Ursenbach, famous in Utah as the architect who designed the big organ in the Mormon Tabernacle. Brigham was in love for the thirtieth time, and his love was warm—warmer than his youthful passion in a geometrical progression. Selina was a young, beautiful Swiss lady. She played on all musical instruments, and spoke the purest French. Brigham made himself a perfect dandy for her sake. She smiled on a young fellow, and Brigham sent him away on a mission. Then Selina got disgusted, apostatized from the Church, and went back to Switzerland. But if Brigham could have lived out his days, as nature intended, he might in turn have set aside Amelia, and gone on with the fifth generation of "wives" in the old style, as when in his prime his affection was a flowering annual, or semi-annual, blooming anew every spring and fall, and clinging to new supports each time.

To conclude, those best informed sum up thus: Brigham had from first to last been actually married twenty-nine times; the largest number of wives he ever had at one time was twenty-three, of whom fifteen survive him. But he had been "sealed," on the "spiritual wife" system, to quite a number of pious old ladies, with whom he had nothing to do in this world, but who are to be his in eternity; and of his actual wives four belong to Joe Smith, having been the latter's at Nauvoo, and being destined for him in eternity. And do the women believe this sort of thing? asks an amazed reader. Well, some of them do, and the rest fall in with the prevailing tendency of the society they move in, just as the majority of women do every-where. Take women as a mass, and that which is *established* is right. And right here I would protest against that arrant stupidity, so common in the East, that men alone are responsible for polygamy; that the "poor women are the victims," and that women would, under certain circumstances, put a stop to it. It is akin to that spurious and sickly sensibility of the French school (see Victor Hugo and Wilkie Collins), which makes a prostitute the heroine of the drama; and has maudlin sentiment for "Mercy Merrick" and "Fantine," but sarcasm for the honest woman. It certainly requires no great amount of robust common sense to see that sexual sin requires *two sinners;*

and that in such a matter the woman knows right from wrong as well as the man. The young woman who joins herself to a man who already has a wife, does so in the confident belief that she will always be his favorite; and when she is in turn discarded, she has none but herself to blame.

Well, Brigham was buried with great pomp—though his grave is now sadly neglected and unadorned—and two questions at once pressed for solution: who was to succeed, and who to get his property? There was no law and no well established precedent in either case. Utah had no marriage act, no dower law, and no statute strictly providing for descent and distribution of property. When a polygamist died, the church took charge of and divided the estate according to their notions of equity. When the United States courts were established, a few first wives came in and claimed their legal rights, excluding polygamous wives and children entirely. It would seem, then, that if Brigham's legitimate children had chosen to do so, they could have taken the whole estate, which was roughly appraised at $1,200,000. But the church had an enormous claim against Brigham, amounting, as some asserted, to $1,500,000. Some of the children protested and threatened legal proceedings; one actually commenced a suit; but cooler counsels prevailed; and as all the illegitimates were on the same terms, they finally settled in a way not known to the world, and very disgusting to the lawyers. It was simply impossible to make a legal decision as to what property was actually his and what that of the church, for the title of all was vested in him. So, as supposed, the family got a third or more, the church at least half, and it is safe to suppose that a large per cent. stuck to the fingers of those apostles who managed the settlement.

And then came the surprise. It had long been supposed by Gentiles, and secretly dreaded by Mormons, that Brigham's death would be the beginning of the end—of a dispute about the succession, ending in apostasy and schism. On the contrary matters were managed as easily as when Arthur succeeded Garfield. The Twelve Apostles took charge, just as the same body did after Joe Smith's death, and in due time John Taylor, President of the Twelve, just as Brigham had climbed to the seat of Joseph, succeeded to all the honors and titles of the deceased Brigham. Orson Hyde, former President of the Twelve, had been deposed and invited to a lower seat in the quorum; and it was well for the Saints that it was so, for he was a constitutional blunderer, given to indulgence in red hot prophecies which were generally falsified before they were a year old. Orson Pratt was the best, indeed the only, scholar among the twelve, but a dreaming astronomer whose head was among the stars. In his prime he was quite a man, and his noted debate with Dr. J. P. Newman showed some talent, but he was even then falling into rapid decay, and has since died very poor, much broken in mind and wretchedly neglected. George Q. Cannon, then delegate in Congress, had long schemed for the succession and would have filled Brigham's place quite fairly; but Taylor had a warmer place in the Mormon heart, and for the few years he has to live he will enjoy, with Queen Victoria, the distinction of being a joint spiritual and temporal sovereign—these two the *only* ones in the civilized world since Victor Emanuel took his states from the Pope.

There is something ludicrous and suggestive in the total collapse of all the great plans Brigham, and Joseph Smith before him, had made for their sons. Joseph had ordained his son Joseph, who is now acknowledged by the Josephites, and Brigham had relied on his son Brigham to succeed him. The latter is familiarly known as the Fat Boy, and his father tried long and earnestly to make him a ruler, but it was a hopeless case. The people laughed at it even before the senior's death. For awhile the father placed his hopes on his son Joseph A., who was a decidedly pleasant and liberal minded gentleman; but, alas, he looked upon the Valley Tan when it was red, and died suddenly, in 1875, of whisky cramp. Then the father's heart turned to John W., then called his apostate son, who had left the church and married a lady in Philadelphia. Excited with an ambition to succeed his father, he repudiated his Gentile (and truly gentle) wife, was rebaptized into the church, took some more wives, and was made First Councilor—only one remove from head. His criminal compliance was in vain. He believed in Mormonism no more than you or I, and the Mormon people knew it. He was not even mentioned for the place.

But a few years more and all the original Mormons will be gone, Taylor among them. Soon or late I fancy those who hold out faithful will find themselves adhering to one of the sons of Joe Smith, for they alone have prophecy in their favor. Nobody need hope that Mormondom will suddenly dissolve. I lack space to show why the mass of the people *must* hold together; but for years to come they dare not dissolve. Two or three thousand men and four times as many women are in polygamy; they must stick to an institution which confers a sort of respectability on their condition. Twenty thousand young people are of polygamous birth. As long as possible they will sustain laws and social customs which make them legitimate. Two hundred Mormons have committed murder. Once break the solid alignment that now exists, divide them into sects fighting each other, and the Gentile courts would have these men on the scaffold in two years. Of those not in polygamy, two-thirds have near relatives in it. They can not easily cut loose and stigmatize these. In property matters they are inextricably entangled. By the "Order of Enoch," the "consecration of property," and the "perfect oneness in Christ," their homesteads have been deeded back and forward, tied over and under and criss-crossed, so there is no getting out till all are willing to go and settle things on a basis of pure equity. The apostates must have a clear majority of three to one before they can do any thing, for the elders hold the strings.

Through every part of the social organism runs a complex set of stringers, which will bind it together till all the old Mormons die. The process of disintegration may be rapid enough to end it in ten years, but I doubt it. And at least half of them still believe the faith; the women being twice as fanatical as the men. It may interest some people to know that the *mens conscia recti*, of which some religionists boast, is but a trifle to the women's *conscia recti;* and both are always the strongest in the lower religious types. Or, in plain English, the bigger fool a man is the more positive is he that he knows the design of God; and, other things being equal, the woman is more positive than the man.

Nothing used to vex us more when I lived in Utah, than the amiable folly of certain Eastern people who imagined that this, or that, or the other trifling agency would put an end to theocratic tyranny. But above all others were we annoyed and hindered by the nonsense of those who fancied the Mormon women would effect a revolution by their votes! Who does not know that if the women were opposed to polygamy, it could not exist anyhow?

The growing society follows pretty closely the analogy of the human body. Introduce a foreign substance, and an effort is made to expel it; if unsuccessful, the organism at once begins to accommodate itself thereto, and does it or dies. Similarly, whatever custom or social anomaly you introduce into a society, that society immediately begins to adapt itself thereto, and in a surprisingly short space of time all the petty observances and habits of thought are adjusted to the custom. Take the most pronounced monogamist to Utah and let him live on intimate terms with the Mormons for awhile, and all the novelty vanishes; he hears people talk of first, second, and third wives with scarcely a thought. It is the control the church exercises over business and government that perpetually irritates him—theocracy, not polygamy, is the object of his hate.

And this, too, aids in giving us the proper estimate of the inexcusable folly of learned ministers who go to Utah to argue the question on Old Testament grounds. Just as if polygamy, slavery, incest, and exterminating wars were right *now*, because wandering patriarchs in the childhood of the world were excused in the practice of them. Even if Hebrew polygamy could be proved right, Mormon polygamy would be all the more wrong, because it permits the marriage of close blood relatives. Incest, as allowed in Utah, would be just as much under the ban of law if the Bible had never been written; for its criminality depends not on a command, but on a law of nature, and the more civilized a people become the more deadly and destructive is the crime. Savages have no hereditary diseases: their mode of life kills all sickly stocks, and only the fittest survive. But in civilized life one half the families have *some* tendency to scrofula, insanity, or consumption. The chances are even that two cousins have inherited a common tendency from the common ancestor; if they marry, that tendency is doubled or quadrupled in their offspring. If one marries an alien with a different temperament, they may justly hope to have inherited diverse tendencies which may neutralize each other and let the offspring escape both. It is the marriage of near relatives which has been the curse of Spain, and is the special curse of Utah polygamy; if the custom continues, the pure Mormon stock must die out or retrograde, in physiological self-defense, to barbarism.

But my own opinion is that Mormonism is on the decline. Old Mormons die, young ones grow up infidels; the boys take to Gentile ways, and the girls, wherever practicable, get into the Gentile towns, sometimes to marry Gentiles, quite as often to practice polygamy without the troublesome intervention of the priest. Thus, in the future as for the past ten years, the system will slowly wear out, with some misery and much corruption. The young people will abandon the old folks' religion and have no education to take its place. The social fabric will for awhile fall into chaos, and Utah will pass through a season of moral storm before the better day comes.

CHAPTER XXXVIII.

WHERE SHALL WE SETTLE?

FIVE million Americans are asking this question. They will take Greeley's advice and go West; but are as yet undecided as to locality. Let us therefore briefly note the good and bad features of various sections. *Imprimis*, then, there is no paradise in the West; no region where one will not find serious drawbacks in climate, soil or society.

If you like a middle northern clime, there is no better place than southern Minnesota and the adjacent parts of Dakota. These have one great advantage over northern Iowa: the vacant land is still in the market at government prices; in Iowa it has been granted too extensively, and railroads and speculators own too much of it in large bodies. In the long run they lose money by holding it in this way; they would do well to sell and invest elsewhere; but they have not found that out yet. By and by the residents will learn how to make non-resident land pay all the taxes, as it now pays quite half, and then the speculators will sell cheap; but at present it would be advisable to locate where there is not so much non-resident land. The arguments now so common against these grants apply only to the border States; all the land given to the railroads west of longitude 100, was not worth one day's debate in Congress. The income from it will never pay interest at a dollar an acre. The climate of Minnesota may be divided thus; summer, four months; winter, five months; spring and autumn, six weeks each. In fact it is less than six weeks from the end of the snowy season to the coming of early fruits; but they call it spring the first of April, though the snow be six inches deep.

The quickness of vegetation is amazing. In August, along the Blue-Earth River, one can scarcely believe he is not in a tropical country; the heavy forests of lynn and walnut, the groves of sugar maple supporting a dense leafy mass, the dark green vistas and rich natural parks, with the rank grass on the prairies seem out of place so far north. By November this gives way to snow, which remains till April first or tenth. It then seems to disappear all at once. The black sandy soil dries out thoroughly in a week; but the air is still cool enough to justify an overcoat, and for a fortnight there are only brown plains and gray woods, with no hint of dawning life. A few days of warmth, and there is a swelling and fluttering perceptible on the bosom of nature; then grass, bush, branch and vine spring quickly into living green, and in one month tropic luxuriance succeeds wintry death. But September clothes this region in its most attractive dress. The frost turns one thicket purple, another bright red or golden yellow, while the large timber is still green; through the glades blows the cool and stimulating air, and over all is the soft blue sky of the Garden State.

The advantages of this country are: abundant timber and running water, regular and exceedingly healthful climate, fertile soil, freedom from droughts and freshets, and land of excellent quality still to be had at reasonable rates. Its disadvantages: a long cold winter and occasional liability to grasshoppers—the latter, however, very rare. The vegetable productions are remarkable, though report sometimes exaggerates. Tradition tells of one Minnesota Granger who happened to be examining a cucumber just as the season of rapid growth set in. As he backed out to give it room, the growing vine followed him so rapidly that he took to his heels, but was soon overtaken. It grew all around him, tangled up his legs, and threw him down. Reaching in great haste for his knife to cut himself loose, he found that a cucumber had gone to seed in his breeches pocket.

The adjoining part of Dakota has similar climate and soil, but two disadvantages: there is less timber and more wind. But land is much cheaper. Hundreds of sections in every county can still be had at Government rates; and in the older settlements improved farms can even now be bought very cheap. Timber grows rapidly, and all the old settlers assure me they soon grow accustomed to the wind. I have noticed in all my western wanderings that the regions of abundant wind are those most free from malaria. The only exception, if it is one, is in the Indian Territory, where there is wind enough, and yet much complaint on the score of fever and ague. Despite my experience with the high winds of Dakota, I am inclined to set down as fabulous the statement sometimes made by the envious, that an old Dakotian can not talk if the wind suddenly stops blowing. So used to it, you know.

Iowa I have already described at some length. I can not get rid of the impression that the northern part of it is colder than the neighboring part of Minnesota. There is less timber, and the wind has a fairer fling at a man. Artificial groves grow rapidly, and the soil is of great fertility. And if you find there is too much non-resident land in your vicinity, you can help your good neighbors stick the taxes on it till the owner is willing to sell for whatever he can get. I have a friend who has paid $620 taxes in ten years, on a quarter section of Iowa land, and is now ready to sell to some man who owns a gold mine or a spouting oil-well. We have all heard of the man who ate so much it made him poor to carry it. Similarly, some people own so much western land that it will break them up to keep it. The settlers do not intend that non-residents shall get the benefit of their hard pioneering—and who shall blame them?

Let us go a little further south. Northern Nebraska I know but little about, but in the southern part of that State is a region which seems to me peculiarly inviting to men from the Middle Northern States. "South Platte," as this division is called, contains at least 25,000 square miles of fertile land, of which one-half or more is for sale quite cheap. The climate is perceptibly milder than that of "North Platte," and all the fruits and grains of the temperate zone are produced on a generous soil. Along the line of the Burlington and Missouri River Railroad land is held at high rates, but in the rest of the country it can be bought at from five to eight dollars per acre. There is no government land in this section worth naming. The climate is about like that of central Ohio, with dryer winters and more wind. This last you may retain as a general statement as to all the border States. Society is most excellent. The population is intelligent and progressive, and nowhere does a man find himself out of reach of the church and school-house. Going westward on any line one will find the winters growing dryer, also more "airish." So the doubting emigrant may ask himself "whether 'tis nobler in a man to suffer" cold healthful winds, to have dry roads and freedom from mud; or take refuge in the wooded regions of Indiana or Missouri, avoid the winds and suffer the other evils.

We now turn to a region more affected by men from the middle latitudes. In many weeks travel between the Des Moines and the Arkansas, one-fifth or more of those I met were from Ohio, and nearly all of them had sought this region since the war. Kansas, like Nebraska, is divided into northern and southern—this by the Kaw, that by the Platte. North-eastern Kansas is already an old country; Doniphan County was pretty well settled twenty years ago. A hundred miles west of the Missouri land can still be had at reasonable rates, but I have never visited that section. When we come to southern Kansas an inviting field indeed is open to us. Good land is cheaper to-day than it was five years ago. This I happen to know from painful personal experience. But it don't follow that it will be cheaper still five years from now. Surely "the bottom" is reached by this time. In the second tier of counties, including Anderson, Allen, Neosho and Labette, the Leavenworth, Lawrence and Galveston Railroad Company have large tracts of good land for sale; and private owners a still larger amount.

This region boasts of many advantages: a mild climate, soil of rare fertility, timber sufficient for all ordinary purposes, rock in abundance, and easy communication with the rest of the world. Society is unsurpassed by that of any section, east or west. Churches and schoolhouses are within convenient reach of every section of land, and a man can not settle in so wild a spot that the mail will not bring him late papers at least twice a week. For seven years this region was blessed with good crops; then came the "bad year" of 1874, when drought, chintz-bugs and grasshoppers in succession desolated the land. In Allen County large streams dried to beds of dust, the fish literally parching on the rocks; and pools and springs disappeared which the oldest inhabitant had considered perennial. In 1875 nature resumed her wonted courses; but the people had been too poor to sow wheat, and the country remained in a condition of general poverty. But such a crop otherwise I had never seen. There were miles on miles of corn-fields, yielding from forty to eighty bushels per acre, and for sale at twenty cents per bushel; tens of thousands of tons of hay, worth two dollars per ton in the stack; potatoes by millions, and more feed than the stock could eat. And there was the trouble. The people had not a sufficiently diversified industry. They had relied almost entirely on the sale of grain, and this year there was no sale, and they remained poor despite their immense crops. I came down from the mountains on a visit just after the last grasshoppers had left, and a rural wag gave me this dialect picture of his experience with them:

"You see I bought early in '72—give $2,200 for 240 acres. Could a bought the same for half that two years after; can buy good land right alongside o' mine now for a V an acre. Been a deal o' cramp in real estate in this country. Well, nobody ever makes a crop the first year in a prairie country—think themselves in luck to get fences built and sod broke. I bought a hundred sheep—two blooded rams and the rest common ewes—and put all the rest of my money in improvements. Raised a little corn and oats in 1873, and put thirty acres of the new land, sod broke in 1872, into wheat, and went to work with a hurrah in 1874 to make a God-awful crop. Every thing come a booming, and I thought I had the world in a sling. Corn, oats, potatoes and wheat just got up and laughed, they grew so fine. Thought I never saw such a country for things to grow. Worked all the week, and used to set on the fence Sunday and calculate how rich I'd be. Went out one fine sunny morning about the first of June, and thought, by jiminy, the whole ground was a moving. Ten million hoppers to the square yard—all chawin' away as if the country belonged to 'em. Saturday morning they come into my farm from a ridge just south o' me—Sunday noon there wasn't a green thing where the corn, cane and potatoes had been. Job's luck wasn't a circumstance. My corn lot looked as if forty bands o' wild Arabs had fell onto it. Not a smidgeon left—just bodaciously chawed up and spit out.

"Well, of course I had the dumps. But I rallied. 'All right,' says I; 'got wheat and tobacco left anyhow.' Professor P—— said they wouldn't eat tobacco; but he's a fraud, sir—a barefaced fraud. The hoppers just went up on a ridge north of me and shed their second coats, and then come back on the tobacco. They eat every leaf clean to the ground, then dug up the roots and set on the fence and cussed every man that come along, for a chaw. About that time they got wings, and sudden as could be rose in the air and went off north a whirlin', like a shower o' white and yellow paper bits. 'All right,' says I; 'they've left my wheat anyhow.' Singular enough they didn't touch it; it was on t'other side the place, and out o' their track. Well, I rallied again, and counted on six hundred bushels o' wheat—and wheat's the money crop in this country. About June the middle I noticed all at once that my wheat looked kind o' sick. Come to examine, sir, it was completely lined with a little, miserable, black and yellow, nasty, smelling bug. I took some to a man 'at had been here ten years. 'Neighbor,' says he, 'you're a goner; thems chintz-bugs, and every head o' that wheat that an't cut, 'll be et up in forty-eight hours.' Well, it was Sunday morning, and the wheat nothing like ripe; but it was a chance, and I got onto my reaper and banged down every hoot of it before Monday night. It cured in the sun and the bugs left it, and out o' the lot I got just a hundred and forty bushels o' shrunk-up stuff. It was a hundred and forty bushels more than any o' my neighbors got. You bet there was improved farms for sale in that neighborhood. My sheep had done well, and that was all I was ahead. Taking it by and large, the only sure crop is sheep."

He touched the right point in the last sentence; this is the country for stock-growing. Corn and hay can be produced so cheaply that the cost of bringing a full-grown ox into market is less than half what it would be in Ohio. The best of unimproved land, near the railroad, sometimes sells as high as twelve dollars per acre; from that it ranges down to four. In 1875 the surplus crop of the State was worth twelve million dollars. The report for that year showed that the corn raised in the State, if shelled and put in box-cars, would have loaded a train sixteen hundred miles long!

The Indian Territory is much talked of, but I would not advise any one to go there with a view to permanent settlement. Government can not open the land to immigration without a shameful breach of good faith, and for one, as an humble citizen, I protest against it. There is such an abundance of good land elsewhere that we can afford to leave this to the civilized Indians for the next fifty years. Then their progress will have been such that they will themselves throw it open and invite white settlers. Texas, just south of it, offers a far better field. Dallas is the center of a region two hundred miles square, which offers great inducements to Northern men. The winters are sharp enough to insure health and energy; and the summers are not, as far as I could observe, any hotter than in Minnesota. Land through all this section can be had at from four to eight dollars per acre. There are no Congressional lands in Texas; it is all State land. This comes of the State having been an independent republic when it came into the Union. It reserved the ownership of all lands within its borders, though there are not wanting lawyers who assert that the general government might have rightfully taken those lands from the State after the latter had seceded.

Look out for those beautifully colored maps which divide Texas into various agricultural sections, and locate the "wheat lands" away up on the heads of the Brazos, Colorado and Red River. One can put in his eye all the wheat they will raise up there without an expansive and expensive system of irrigation, and it will puzzle them to find water to irrigate with. If half that region is fit for grazing land it is the best we can expect. Southern Texas is not very suitable for Northern men. Along the gulf are immense areas of fine sugar and cotton lands, but the climate is not favorable. Not that the heat is so great; but the summers are long, the autumns dry, and the winters first warm, moist and debilitating, and then very chilly. Central and northern Texas are free from these disadvantages. The immigrant from the North must learn a new system of agriculture, but that he can easily do.

Society? Well, I found it very agreeable. If there is any special hostility to Northern men, or Republicans, I never noticed it. The latter maintain their organization, sometimes elect their candidate, and always give him a hearty support, though the State has been Democratic since 1872. Texas may fairly claim to be one of the best governed States in the Union. Except on the south-western border the ratio of crimes is very small. In 1873 the law against carrying concealed weapons was strictly enforced in the railroad towns—a good deal more than can be said of any town on the Union or Kansas Pacific Railroads. It is in the "cow counties," in the extreme west and south-west, that some lawlessness still prevails. The law as to concealed weapons excepts those counties, it being considered a necessity that the *vacqueros* should go prepared for "enterprising Mexicans" and other cattle thieves. If you like a wild country, that's the place for you, and if that is not wild enough try the Comanche border. There the mountainous spurs put out towards the lower country and cut it up into numerous little valleys. Down these spurs come the savages, often lying in ambush for days together in the scrubby timber, watching the ranches below. And all this time the settlers go about their usual work in assured safety, for there is not the slightest danger till after the "strike." One might walk within a rod of the hidden enemy and never be molested. The settlers see signs of Indians about, but feel no uneasiness; but once the raid is made, and the robbers on the run for cover, they kill all they encounter, and even slaughter stock they can not take away. They can get five or ten miles more running out of a horse than can a white man; and five minutes after they leave him he is so near dead that he can not be forced to walk. When hard pressed they draw a knife, hastily make a few incisions in the animal's hide and rub in salt and powder. As the cow-boys express it, "it puts new life in a hoss."

But when long immunity has made the settlers careless, there sometimes occur tragedies which thrill the country with horror, and are told for years by the pioneers' hearth-stone, or around the camp-fire, where rude borderers teach their younger companions eternal hatred of all the Indian race. In the year 1850, a Mississippian, named Lockhardt, settled a little farther up the Colorado than was then usual with families, but still in a region thought to be safe from Comanche raids; and, in a few years, was surrounded with most of the comforts of his more eastern home. Wealth and good taste united to improve the wild beauty of nature; his house, elegant indeed for the border, was a temple of hospitality; his flocks and herds ranged over the area of a dukedom; his colored servants scarce knew they had a master, so light was his patriarchal sway; and far and near the name of 'Squire Lockhardt was known as that of a natural nobleman and Texas gentleman. The friendly Indians that passed that way also partook of his hospitality, and he made the too common mistake of supposing that this would shield him against the incursions of their wilder congeners. But, of all his possessions, none was so widely celebrated as his daughter Minnie. The rude *vacqueros* were charmed into unusual courtesy at sight of her; and, from far and near, young Texans of more pretensions sought her society. On the border, a young woman of beauty and accomplishments often acquires a wide-spread fame that would seem impossible to Eastern people; her graces are recounted in such fervid rhetoric that the cold critic of an older community would think of her as a fabulous being. Even so the charms of Minnie Lockhardt were sung in a hundred camps, from the Trinity to the Colorado.

Many other settlers, generally single men, and skillful frontiersmen, had located between Lockhardt and the staked plain, and he had long ceased to think of an Indian raid as even remotely possible, when, suddenly as lightning from a clear sky, the Indian war of 1854-'5 broke out; and, from the settlements on the upper Rio Grande, clear around to the Canadian, the border was in a blaze. The Utes and Apaches on the west pressed the Mexicans and whites, while the Comanches, from their fastnesses, carried destruction far down into Texas. The storm broke while Lockhardt was absent from home. Every settler near him was killed; his servants fled for their lives, and his daughter, then but twenty years of age, was carried into captivity. The frenzied father sent an appeal to his fellow-citizens, and it seemed that the whole Texan border was moved by one common impulse. Every young Texan who could supply himself with horse and gun was eager to assist in the rescue of Minnie Lockhardt; and, as soon as a force of two hundred had assembled, the father led them towards the high country, leaving word for the others to follow. Striking the trail of the Comanches, the Texans followed as fast as the strength of their horses would allow, their furious zeal continually aroused anew by the sights along the way, where worn out captives had been ruthlessly murdered. Suddenly, at daylight, the pursuers came upon the murderers in one of those numerous cañons of upper Texas, where the savages had thought themselves safe.

Then ensued one of the most desperately contested battles of the Texan border. The Indian camp was set far back in a grove of scrubby timber, on all sides of which rose sandy hillocks and detached rocks, furnishing admirable lines of defense, as well as retreat.

Again and again did the Texans, led by Lockhardt, penetrate almost to the camp, only to be driven back; and, on each advance, they distinctly heard the voice of Minnie calling on them for help, and dreaded lest their attack should be the signal for her death. But it appears the savages were bent on preserving their captive if possible. A double line of warriors surrounded the tent in which she was bound; and at last the wretched father, bleeding from a dozen wounds, was forced away by his men, who saw that the attack was hopeless. Having received reinforcements, they renewed the fight the second day after, but the Indians had also collected their force and taken a still stronger position; and to the father, lying helpless with his wounds, the men at last reported that the attack was hopeless, unless with a force large enough to surround the Comanche stronghold and reduce it by a regular siege.

Successive bands of Texans arrived, and in a few days the father again urged them to the attack; but the Indians had managed to retreat, carrying Miss Lockhardt with them. With the devilishness inherent in the Comanche nature, they were all the more determined to keep her when they saw the general anxiety of the whites for her recovery. But she proved a troublesome prize. The fact of her captivity nerved every Texan to desperate measures, and in a short time the Indians were attacked at all points, and forced back towards the Pecos. Then, as afterwards appeared, the band having possession of Miss Lockhardt, sent her northward, and disposed of her to the Arapahoes. Convinced that she was the daughter of a great chief, by the exertions made to recapture her, this tribe opened negotiations with the commandants at Fort Union and Lancaster. But before any thing could be accomplished, the Utes and Apaches were raiding the entire New Mexican border, and the captive girl in some way was transferred to the former tribe. Despite the awful hardships of a winter among the savages she survived, and in some way managed to make known her existence to the American commandant at Fort Massachusetts, New Mexico. About this time the Territorial Governor called out five hundred New Mexican volunteers, who were put under command of Colonel Ceran St. Vrain; and, joined by the First Regiment of United States Dragoons, under Colonel T. T. Fauntleroy, the whole force marched into the Indian country early in 1855. They defeated the Indians in one general battle and several minor skirmishes, but no trace of Miss Lockhardt could be found. The noted Kit Carson was then intrusted with the task of settling with the Utes and recovering all captives; but other means were at work.

Worn down by his wounds and mental suffering, Lockhardt returned home in despair; but another party of determined men set out to find the captive who had, as it appears, been taken by the Arapahoes and Cheyennes from the Utes, with whom they were at war. Again and again were the whites almost successful, and as often was

FORT MASSACHUSETTS, NEW MEXICO, 1855.

the unfortunate girl hurried away to some more hidden fastness, almost before their eyes. The general Indian war ended, and a nominal peace was made; negotiation was again attempted, but the third year of her captivity came, and still nothing was done. At length a company of the Texan Rangers, having penetrated almost to the heart of the Guadaloupe Range, came suddenly upon a village of Comanches, and despite the hurried flight of the savages, who had their own women and children with them, the Rangers saw among them a captive white woman. They charged desperately upon the savages, who fled in all directions, but not till one of them had buried his knife in the body of the girl, who was still breathing when the Rangers came up. It was Minnie Lockhardt. She was but just able to smile, as if to welcome the Rangers, then peacefully breathed her last. "And," said the weather-beaten frontiersman who gave me these facts, as he choked down his emotions, "it was a God's blessin' she was dead, an' her father never seen her." For she had suffered the last terrible indignity savage malice could invent. As is common when a captive woman is not taken by one Indian, she had became the common property of the band; and loathsome disease had worn her to a skeleton. Heart-broken and disfigured, death was to her an unmixed gain. Her afflicted father soon followed her to the grave. The Lockhardt place is now desolate; its dwellings burned, its tenants gone. But the chivalry and hospitality of the father are still the theme of local story, while the beauty and sorrowful fate of the daughter are still told around the camp-fires and hearth-stones of Texas, and warm anew the hearts of its sons to undying vengeance against the Comanches.

Texas ends the list of the border States proper. Observe that in all these States as one goes west he rises slowly to a higher, dryer and more barren country, till at last, about longitude 100° or 101° he enters on "the area of corrugation," as geologists call it, where barrenness is the rule; and this area includes all the western border of Dakota, Nebraska, Kansas, Ocklahoma and Texas, of eastern Washington, Oregon and California, and all of Montana, Idaho, Wyoming, Utah, Colorado, New Mexico and Arizona. Let us skip this region of mountain and desert, and pass at once to the fertile section of the Pacific coast, lying west of the Sierra Nevadas.

California? Well, I should not be in a hurry to recommend it to any man of moderate means. The worst objection is the oppressive land monopoly. "A little ranche of twenty thousand acres" is a common expression. A dozen men each own a dukedom—all but the inhabitants. They will own them after awhile, unless this thing is remedied. The beginning of this system was in the Mexican grants. The old Spanish custom was to grant a county of land to an *impresario*, on condition that he should settle a certain number of families on it. The Mexicans continued the system with some modifications, and in due time the inferiors became *peons* to the lord. These titles were all confirmed by treaty when the United States took possession, and have been sustained by the Supreme Court. Again, when the miners took the country they supposed the land to be worth but little except for grazing, and many of them took up claims and sold them for a trifle to speculators, and thus the best land in California is now held in immense tracts by an aristocracy. Of course these men are in favor of "Chinese cheap labor," and equally of course the poorer whites are unanimously opposed to it. Some have thought that, as our country grew older, all the lands would be held in the same way; but it is somewhat reassuring to note that there is less land monopoly in Massachusetts than in Ohio, and far less in Ohio than in California. In some of the oldest States the land is most equally distributed, thanks to our wise laws of descent and distribution of estates; and in the course of fifty or a hundred years the attrition of a free society will wear out this evil in California.

It is now very difficult for one to get a small piece of land in that State; and it would be better for intending emigrants to organize in some way, and buy out a grant, of which there are always a few for sale. There are a few places—very few I am afraid—where the best land is not in the hands of monopolists, and it is already noticeable that such communities improve faster than others. But for many years to come California will continue to be a land of the beggar and the prince.

In Oregon this evil is not so great, but still great enough. Land in the Willamette Valley is not much cheaper than in Ohio and Indiana, and I can not think that enough is gained to make it worth while to go so far. I do not see how a man, wife and five children—average Western family—can get to Oregon comfortably for less than five or six hundred dollars, which amount would buy eighty acres of first-class land in Kansas or Nebraska, or a hundred acres in Texas; and, having got to Oregon, you must pay more for land than in the other States named, with a moral certainty that the country will develop more slowly. Oregon began to be settled by white men as early as 1830; before 1848 it contained 10,000 Americans; its population now is about 100,000. Kansas was thrown open to settlement only twenty-three years ago; it now contains a population of at least 600,000. It strikes me that's the sort of a country to go to, if you want your future to hurry up. But if you like a romantic border country—one that is likely to stay border for a long time—go to Oregon. Oregon climate? Well, some people like it. I don't. True, it is mild—and moist; but I am just Yankee enough to prefer the cold, dry winter to the warm, wet, muggy, and muddy. No five months' rain for me, if you please. I'd rather freeze than smother. In California it's different. There is no more rain there during the so-called "rainy season" than in Ohio, and half the time not as much. In fact, there never is too much rain in California, though there is sometimes too little. The summers in Oregon are delightful enough—more pleasant than in California; but, as at present advised, I would not recommend either State to the class of emigrants just now going West.

Let us now turn to the great interior, and see if we can pick out any oases inviting to settlement between longitude 100 and the Sierra Nevadas. Nevada is not an agricultural State at all; and, for aught we can now see, never will be. It contains 98,000 square miles, and less good land than three average counties in Ohio. It has population enough for one-third of a member of Congress; but our "paternal" government has granted the State one Representative and two Senators. Nobody need think of going there to engage in farming. In the far distant future, when land is in much greater demand than now, some way will perhaps be found to redeem those arid tracts. Trees will be planted wherever they will grow; the Australian eucalyptus may flourish even on the desert, and thus in a few centuries a moister atmosphere be created. But for the present the population must consist of capitalists and laboring miners, and their congeners. And here I might indulge in wearying words on the romance and hardship of a miner's life, had I not given him a chapter to himself. Strange it is that he should be the most imaginative of men, with a life of such prosaic toil; but it is, doubtless, because his ways are in a path, as Job says, "which no fowl knoweth, and which the vulture's eye hath not seen: the lion's whelps have not trodden it, nor the fierce lion passed by it" (Job xxviii). And no finer, more poetical description of the silver miner's strange life under-ground was ever written than in that chapter, taking Louth's version: "He putteth forth his hand upon the rocks, he swings above the depths. He cutteth out water-courses through the rocks; and his eye searcheth for precious things. He makes a new way for the floods; he goes in the very stones of darkness, in the shadow of death." The perils of the prospector above ground are equally great, but the life has its charms for all that.

In Utah are still a few unoccupied plateaus which could be redeemed by canals taken out from some large stream. Bear River Valley contains some sixty thousand acres of fertile land, which might be redeemed at moderate cost by a canal from Bear River. The climate is mild, not very hot in summer, and decidedly pleasant in winter. The Central Pacific runs through the valley, and the location is excellent for a thriving colony. On the Sevier is a smaller valley of the same character. East of the Wasatch Range are several beautiful valleys. That of Ashley's Fork contains land enough for three thousand farms, all of most excellent quality; and it can be had for the taking. Late in 1873 a dozen stock ranchers settled there, and have raised splendid crops every year since. Be it noted that in no part of the temperate zone is fruit a more certain crop than in Utah. Peaches never fail. The Ashley Valley slopes gently to the southeast; snow rarely lies on more than one night, and all the slopes are rich in bunch-grass. Game is abundant in the neighboring hills, and a good road can easily be constructed to the Union Pacific at Bridger Station. The Valley of Brush Creek, east of Ashley, is about half as large and equally inviting. In these a colony of ten thousand Americans might make for themselves delightful homes.

THE PROSPECTOR'S PERIL.

Farther south are several fine valleys, none quite so large as the foregoing, but very fertile; and small settlements have been made in some of them. It is to be noted that these valleys which open eastward from the Wasatch are free from Mormon domination, and will remain so if settled by Gentile colonies. It has always seemed to me that life would be exceedingly pleasant in one of these alpine valleys. The elevation is about five thousand feet above sea-level; the winters are mild; the summer air dry and stimulating. There is game on the hills, and trout in the streams; land enough to produce grain for a sparse population, and almost unlimited grazing ground. But these districts will never sustain a large population. Between each settled valley and the next there will be a day's ride over barren mountain or grassy hill. All that part of Utah east of the Wasatch will never sustain a hundred thousand people.

Wyoming contains so little farming land that it is not worth while to discuss it; but it is rich in grazing tracts. Of the 98,000 square miles in this Territory, one-half is complete desert; the rest good grazing ground, with perhaps 500 sections of farming land, though I never saw the latter and do not know where it is located. Of course no one pre-empts his grazing land; he merely takes up meadow land when he can get it convenient; and perhaps enough farming land for a garden, if there is so much in the neighborhood. One year with another the herder puts up hay enough for three months' feeding. Sometimes none of it is used, and then it is on hand for the next winter. About half the time the common stock can go through the winter without hay, living on the bunch-grass; but blooded stock should be fed at least two months every winter. By the first of May stock can live well on the range. From that on, the grass appears to get more nourishing every day till December. If the winter comes on with snow, grass remains good till the snow melts; but rain takes the sweetness out of it. It will then sustain life, but stock lose flesh rapidly while living on it. It requires a much larger area for the same number of stock than in a blue-grass country, as the grass makes but one growth per year, not renewing itself after being eaten off. From all these facts it will be apparent that Wyoming never can sustain a very large population.

New Mexico? Well, I must as candidly as may be admit that I was rather disgusted with it—that is, for any thing else than mountains and scenery. Bear in mind that the central portions of New Mexico are really older country than Ohio. Santa Fe was founded a hundred and fifty years before Cincinnati. All the good land in the valleys of the Rio Grande and its tributaries was long ago occupied, and the grazing lands of the central section are taken up. West of the Rio Grande the country is practically worthless to a man used to the system of living in Ohio. The Territory has all the faults of an old country, and few of its virtues. As a stock-rancher you have but two chances of success. The one adopted by most live Americans is to go in partnership with one of the nobility. If you have business ability and a partner who can furnish the blue blood, respectability, local prestige and land, you may in time become a capitalist, and marry ten or twenty thousand sheep, with an incumbrance in the shape of a lady whose priest will rule her, and her father insist on an ante-nuptial contract that the children shall be reared in the "Holy Catholic faith." The other plan is to go with money enough to buy a thousand sheep and a herd-right—that is to say, be a capitalist yourself. But do n't think of going to New Mexico to build up a fortune by hard work. The common fellows there can work for fifty cents a day, and live on jerked mutton and flour.

If you want to lead a wild harum-scarum sort of life for awhile, free from social restraints, where chastity is not a requisite for good society, and morals in general are somewhat relaxed, New Mexico is a splendid place to sow your wild oats. As to the crop to be reaped, I refer you to a very ancient authority. But if you think much of yourself, better set up your sheep ranche in Colorado or Wyoming, where there is not such an oppressive atmosphere of *gente fina*, and where the owner of two sheep is still one of the boys, and can dance with the daughter of the man who owns a thousand. In south-western Arizona a progressive community has been built up of late years, and though the fertile area is small, there is still room for thousands more. Colorado I have described at some length in a previous chapter. It is, in my opinion, the most enlightened and progressive of all the far western communities; though I doubt if it can ever have the population that Dakota will some day contain. Idaho I know very little about, and of Montana practically still less. But it is universally agreed that they are not agricultural Territories. There are valleys in both which contain considerable good land, and large grazing tracts; but mining will be the leading interest of both for some time. Taken as a whole, and allowing for every possible improvement in methods of farming and reclamation of desert lands, the whole vast interior, between longitude 100 and the Sierra Nevadas, can never average one acre in ten fit for the farmer; and not more than half the rest is of any value for timber or grazing.

And can such a region ever be filled by prosperous States, which shall rival those of the Mississippi valley? Never. All calculations as to the shifting of political power, made on the basis of new States, rich and populous, are sure to miscarry. That section has an area greater than that of all the States east of the Mississippi; but its population fifty years hence will not be greater than that of Massachusetts. Only in the Senate will the relative power of the East and West be changed in the future; and probably very little there. Colorado was only admitted after a ten years' struggle. Nevada ought to be set back to a Territorial condition to-day, if there were any constitutional way of doing justice. The child is not born that will live to see her with population enough for one Congressional district. Here is a liberal estimate of the maximum population these divisions are likely to have in the year 1900:

Colorado,	250,000
Wyoming,	100,000
Dakota,	300,000
Idaho,	100,000
Washington,	125,000
Utah,	250,000
New Mexico,	150,000
Montana,	100,000
Nevada,	75,000
Arizona,	50,000
Total,	1,500,000

Extraordinary discoveries may enable some one of the mining regions to get ahead of the others, but the grand total can not be greater than here set down; and only the most favorable contingencies can make it so great. The influence which this may have upon our social and national life opens a wide field for discussion. The good land at the disposal of our Government is nearly exhausted. But a few more years and there will be no more virgin soil awaiting the immigrant. Then the half desert lands must be won with great toil, or we must turn back and fill up the corners which have been overrun in our rush for the best spots. Our surplus population will then have no rich heritage to look to, where a homestead can be had for the taking. The paternal farm in the East must be divided again and again, if all the boys are to have a share. What will be the effect on our discontented classes? Will it add a new strain to republican government, and will the troubles which menace the old world monarchies then come upon us and find us unprepared to treat them rightly? or is there yet room in the Eastern States for us to grow harmoniously for another century? These be momentous questions.

Certain theorists have further troubled themselves about the silver supply; and timid editors and politicians have suggested that if more *bonanzas* are discovered, silver will soon be "cheap enough to manufacture into door-hinges." To such I guarantee comforting proofs. Let them invest heavily in undeveloped silver mines, and before they get their money back they will be convinced that silver is still precious metal—hard to get at and correspondingly valuable when got. One Ohio editor says: "Suppose they should discover a mountain of silver!" Suppose they should discover a mountain of ice cream in August! The one supposition is just as reasonable as the other. In fact the latter phenomenon would violate fewer of the laws of nature than the former. Unchanging law decrees that, even in the richest mineral region, there must be many million times as much dead rock—"attle," "rubble," and "country rock"—as silver-bearing rock. Let silver permanently cheapen but 5 per cent., and two-thirds of the mines in the world would cease to be profitable.

For another class there is comfort. Poet and romancer, as well as hunter and tourist, have lamented that in so short a time the wild West would be a thing of the past; that soon all would be tame, dull and common-place. Let them be reassured. The wild West will continue wild for centuries. There will be a million square miles of mountain, desert, rock and sand, of lonely gorge and hidden glen, of walled basin, wind-swept cañon and timbered hills, to invite the tourist, the sportsman and the lover of solitude. The mountain Territories will long remain the abode of romance; and "Western Wilds" will be celebrated in song and story, while generation succeeds generation of "the men who redeem them."

THE END.